THE TWENTIETH-CENTURY WORLD AND BEYOND

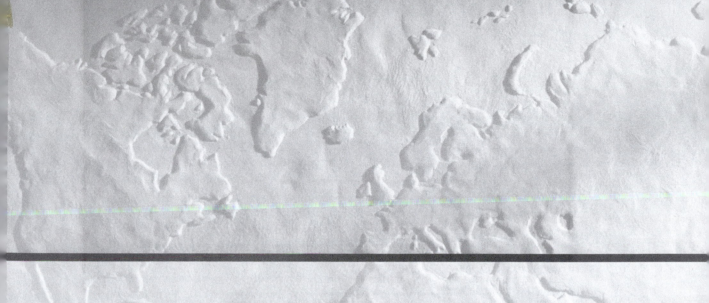

THE TWENTIETH-CENTURY WORLD AND BEYOND

An International History Since 1900

FIFTH EDITION

William R. Keylor

Boston University

New York   Oxford
OXFORD UNIVERSITY PRESS
2006

Oxford University Press, Inc., publishes works that further Oxford University's
objective of excellence in research, scholarship, and education.

Oxford New York
Auckland   Cape Town   Dar es Salaam   Hong Kong   Karachi
Kuala Lumpur   Madrid   Melbourne   Mexico City   Nairobi
New Delhi   Shanghai   Taipei   Toronto

With offices in
Argentina   Austria   Brazil   Chile   Czech Republic   France   Greece
Guatemala   Hungary   Italy   Japan   Poland   Portugal   Singapore
South Korea   Switzerland   Thailand   Turkey   Ukraine   Vietnam

Published by Oxford University Press, Inc.
198 Madison Avenue, New York, New York 10016
http://www.oup.com

Library of Congress Cataloging-in-Publication Data

Keylor, William R., 1944-
  The twentieth century world and beyond : an international history since 1900 / by William R. Keylor.
     p. cm.
  Includes bibliographical references and index.
  ISBN-13: 978-0-19-516842-6—ISBN-13: 978-0-19-516843-3 (pbk.)
  ISBN 0-19-516842-9 (alk. paper) — ISBN 0-19-516843-7 (pbk. : alk. paper)
  1. History, Modern—20th century. 2. History, Modern—21st century. I. Title.

D421.K46 2006
909.82—dc22

                                                                                          2005047286

Printing number: 9   8   7   6   5   4   3   2   1

Printed in the United States of America
on acid-free paper

To Daniel and Justine
From a Loving Father

CONTENTS

MAPS

PREFACE

I composed the first edition of this book in 1984 to meet a need that I had acutely felt throughout a decade of teaching college-level courses dealing with the history of international relations in the modern period. There was no dearth of serviceable textbooks treating the foreign relations of a particular nation or region since the beginning of the twentieth century. But an increasing number of historians of international relations had begun to express dissatisfaction with the limitations inherent in an exclusively national or regional approach to their subject. They insisted that the sovereign political units or regional subsystems of the modern world were all so closely linked, so profoundly interdependent, as to require a global or international perspective on the part of those who study the external relations of states. This new orientation yielded a vast and growing body of specialized scholarship that transcended the narrowly national or regional approach to the study of the relations between and among states over time. Profiting from the declassification of previously inaccessible government archives in a number of countries, the authors of these monographs and partial syntheses profoundly affected our understanding of the international developments of the twentieth century, overturning or revising judgments of earlier works once deemed definitive. Yet there was no college-level textbook that incorporated the findings of these recent specialized studies in a format that was genuinely global or international in scope. This I attempted to do, signaling the persistence of sharp scholarly controversies where appropriate and offering personal assessments when confidence in my own firsthand knowledge of the subject seemed to warrant them.

In the course of the last twenty years, international history has come into its own as a thriving academic discipline. Courses on the subject have proliferated in undergraduate curricula, attracting strong student interest; professional organizations have sprouted to promote research in the history of international relations from this broader perspective; several fine textbooks with a genuinely global approach have appeared in print. In the United States, it has become increasingly unacceptable for historians of foreign relations to approach their subject in the old-fashioned way, focusing exclusively on what one critic has called "the view from Washington."

Yet it is worth pausing to note that the development of a genuinely international perspective poses a daunting challenge, as I discovered during the preparation of successive editions of this book. The writer so presumptuous as to undertake a survey of the entire world since the beginning of the twentieth century promptly acquires the virtue of humility as one confronts the immense corpus of secondary literature on specialized topics far removed from his own particular field of expertise. One learns how utterly dependent one is on the original research of others who have devoted entire careers to the explication of historical developments of which one was either wholly ignorant or only dimly aware. As one patiently excavates this largely unfamiliar terrain, one must keep in mind an organizational principle under which to subsume the disparate facts and interpretations gleaned from the secondary sources in order to supply the coherence and intelligibility that a textbook in higher education ought to have.

Simply put, my purpose has been to provide a narrative account within an analytical framework of the struggle among the nations of the world for power, prosperity, and prestige in this period. The major advantage of such a guiding principle is its exclusivity. It permits the author to pass over several categories of topics that often occupy prominent places in history textbooks in order to concentrate on those events and processes that relate to the underlying theme. Thus, for example, little attention is devoted to the internal social, political, or cultural history of individual states. Such domestic developments are addressed only when they acquire significance for the interplay of forces in the international arena. On the other hand, topics that usually pass unnoticed or receive only cursory mention in most "diplomatic history" texts are dealt with at length herein. For instance, I have given substantial coverage to international economic relations, with particular emphasis on trade patterns, capital flows, and competition for raw materials, as well as on the larger connection between these economic forces and the international contest for political and strategic advantage.

An explanation is due the reader with respect to my spelling of Chinese names. When the People's Republic of China adopted the Pinyin system of romanized spelling for transliterating the Chinese language in 1979, scrupulous writers dutifully modified familiar proper names to reflect the new policy. Thus in this text Mao Tse-tung became Mao Zedong, Chou Enlai became Zhou Enlai, Peking became Beijing, Sinkiang became Xinjiang, and so on. I have decided to resist the conversion to Pinyin in those few cases, such as Chiang Kai-shek into Jiang Jieshi, where it seemed likely to hinder recognition by those accustomed to the old spelling.

The earlier editions of this book reflect the advice and criticism of several friends and colleagues. Norman Naimark gave the manuscript of the first edition a careful reading and rescued it from factual errors and untenable interpretations, especially with respect to the Soviet Union and Eastern Europe. Hermann Frederick Eilts also read the entire piece and drew upon his extensive practical as well as scholarly knowledge of the Middle East to enhance my own understanding of that complex region. Dietrich Orlow reviewed the sections dealing with Europe in the interwar period and offered particularly helpful suggestions for improving the treatment of German foreign policy. John G. Gagliardo and Arnold A. Offner left their mark on this work in two important ways: first, by serving as models of serious scholarship and dedicated teaching, and second, by engaging me in a long and fruitful dialogue about many of the issues treated in the following pages. For the second edition my friend and colleague James McCann earned my gratitude by agreeing to read and provide helpful comments on the chapter on Africa's role in international politics after independence.

A number of friends and colleagues who have used this book in their classes kindly shared with me their (and their students') reactions to it and offered useful suggestions for improvement that were incorporated in the third edition. I would particularly like to express my gratitude to Lancelot Farrar, Carole Fink, Diane Kunz, David Mayers, Cathal Nolan, and Stephen A. Schuker.

My affiliation with organizations outside my own institution has long enabled me to keep in touch with the work of other scholars of international relations in its formative stages. The late Professor Jean-Baptiste Duroselle kindly invited me to attend his graduate seminar on the history of international relations at the University of Paris, where I learned a great deal from the presentations of several of his students on a variety of topics. I also benefited from ongoing access to the Center for European Studies at Harvard University, which has long been an indispensable forum for the presentation of work in progress by advanced graduate students and established scholars alike.

After the appearance of the third edition in 1996, I became the privileged beneficiary of intense intellectual interchanges with two groups of scholars and advanced graduate students working on a wide range of topics in international history. Paul Kennedy kindly invited me to attend the annual conferences at Yale University sponsored by the International Security Studies Group entitled "Recent Work in International History." While there I learned about the research findings of advanced graduate students and junior faculty from several universities.

In the meantime, I had conspired with a small coterie of confreres—Igor Lukes, David Mayers, and especially Cathal Nolan—to establish an International History Institute at Boston University. Erik Goldstein, who had arrived at the university to assume his duties as Chair of the Department of International Relations, became an eager co-conspirator. Ever since, the fledgling organization has sponsored a number of conferences, public lectures, and presentations by faculty and graduate students of work-in-progress. The Institute has collaborated on a number of scholarly projects with the Center for International Relations, whose director, my friend and colleague Andrew Bacevich, has been a constant source of intellectual stimulation for me as I ponder the issues addressed in this work. Another Boston University friend and colleague, David Fromkin, has kindly invited me to participate in several stimulating conferences sponsored by his Pardee Center for the Study of the Longer-Range Future, an organization that, despite its title and appropriate to its director, promotes historical understanding as well as prognostication. Finally, Professor Akira Iriye of Harvard University gave the fourth edition a very close reading and, drawing on his extraordinary knowledge of the history of international relations, offered a number of suggestions for improvement that I took to heart. Most important, his pointed yet judicious comments persuaded me to pay more attention to the role of nongovernmental organizations in the modern world, a subject that I had largely neglected in earlier editions. While revising *The Twentieth-Century World,* I found myself frequently consulting my extensive notes from these stimulating presentations and provocative discussions in New Haven and Boston.

While I was preparing the fourth edition, my longtime editor at Oxford University Press, Nancy Lane, retired after a distinguished career in academic publishing. I am indebted to Nancy for her unfailing support throughout the years. Gioia Stevens and then

Lisa Grzan proved worthy successors by shepherding the manuscript through its various stages with skill, efficiency, and forbearance. My current editor, Peter Coveney, displayed enormous wisdom and sensitivity in recommending what turned out to be radical revisions of the text. Whatever merits this fifth edition contains are due in large part to his patient prodding. After he left the press while this fifth edition was being prepared for publication, June Kim grasped the editorial reins with great skill and efficiency.

My wife, Rheta, has been an essential source of sustenance and forbearance when various deadlines related to the successive editions of this book—both internally and externally imposed—upset carefully established schedules of parenting and housework. She has also been my most treasured conversation partner ever since we met as graduate students at Columbia University in the spring of 1968. My son Daniel and my daughter Justine, to whom this book is dedicated, have given a much deeper meaning to my life ever since they arrived on the scene.

PROLOGUE

THE GLOBAL CONTEXT
OF INTERNATIONAL RELATIONS
AT THE BEGINNING OF THE
TWENTIETH CENTURY

THE EUROPEANIZATION OF THE WORLD

The most salient feature of international relations at the beginning of this century was the extent to which most of the world had come under the direct or indirect domination of a handful of states all located in the same geographical region: that western extension of the Eurasian land mass bounded by the Atlantic Ocean and the Ural Mountains that we call Europe. The expansion of European power and influence in the world had begun in the sixteenth century, when improvements in the technology of oceanic transportation enabled seafaring adventurers from Portugal, Spain, Holland, England, and France to establish contact with and lay claim to territory on distant continents recently discovered or rediscovered—North and South America, Africa, and Asia. European settlements were subsequently established on the coasts of these exotic lands to facilitate the exploitation of their valuable economic resources, such as the precious metals, sugar, and animal furs of the Americas, the spices of the Far East, and the slave labor of Africa.

By the middle of the nineteenth century, the European settler populations in the American hemisphere, their numbers greatly increased by the temptations of a temperate climate and an abundance of arable land, had obtained political independence from their transatlantic colonial masters and were busily engaged in promoting the national unification and economic development of the territory they had inherited or to which they laid claim. The American successor states remained thoroughly Europeanized in the sense that their political institutions, economic practices, religious beliefs, and cultural traditions had been transplanted by the immigrants from Europe who constituted the ruling

1

elites of this region. During the same period, the Slavic peoples of European Russia migrated eastward by land into Asiatic Siberia to Europeanize that desolate domain. Finally, during the second half of the nineteenth century and the first decade of the twentieth, the power of the principal states of Western Europe was projected into the Afro-Asian portion of the southern hemisphere that had previously remained beyond the reach of European power. The consequence of this long process of expansion in all directions was the creation, for the first time in history, of a genuinely interlinked and interdependent world with Europe as its focal point. It was at the beginning of the last century that statesmen, diplomats, and military leaders began for the first time to speak of international relations in the global sense to which we have been accustomed ever since.

The explanation for the sudden resurgence of imperial expansion during the second half of the nineteenth century has been hotly debated by historians of the subject. Some have emphasized the role of Western* economic interests in seeking overseas markets for industrial production and investment capital as well as raw materials that were in short supply at home. Others have focused on the activities of Christian missionaries who penetrated the interior of the colonial world in search of souls to save, only to require military protection from their home governments when the indigenous nonbelievers violently resisted conversion. Others have seen the prospect of strategic advantage—in the form both of military manpower recruitable from the native population and of bases of operation abroad—as the principal motivating factor for this expansion abroad. Still others stress the role of national pride and the search for national prestige. But whatever the source of the imperialist impulse, its consequence was unmistakable: the extension of European power and influence throughout the southern half of the globe.

The first two nations to achieve in this way the position of "world power" were Great Britain and France. Both had established coastal footholds along the non-European land masses of the world during the first wave of European imperial expansion: Britain had disposed of its surplus population during its industrial revolution in the eighteenth and nineteenth centuries by sending large numbers of its nationals to the inhabitable coastlands of North America, Australia, New Zealand, and southern Africa. To the motley collection of islands and coastal enclaves in Latin America, Africa, and the Pacific that had been acquired by Britain during this earlier era was added the subcontinent of India, which had come under effective British control by the middle of the nineteenth century. By that time, France had added the north African territory of Algeria to the remnants of its seventeenth century empire.

But it was only after the opening of the Suez Canal (built by the French between 1859 and 1869, brought under joint Anglo-French financial control in 1875) that authorities in London and Paris began in earnest to promote the cause of imperial expansion. Henceforth, the sea route running through the Mediterranean, the Suez Canal, and the Red Sea into the Indian Ocean—a much safer and more economical route than the passage around the Cape of Good Hope on the southern tip of Africa—came to be regarded by Britain's governing class as a "lifeline" to its possessions in Asia. It was indeed a lifeline in a very real sense: Since its transformation from an agricultural to an industrial economy at the beginning of the nineteenth century, Great Britain customarily produced no more than 30

---

*The term "Western" shall be employed in this study to designate that portion of the northern hemisphere inhabited primarily by Europeans or immigrants of European stock.

percent of the food consumed by its population and an even smaller proportion of the raw materials required by its industries. A considerable portion of its imported foodstuffs and industrial raw materials came from its Asian and Pacific possessions (India, Australia, and New Zealand), and the island nation's very survival seemed to depend on its ability to keep open the sea-lanes over which these vital supplies were transported. Moreover, in order to pay for these enormous imports of food and raw materials, Britain's manufactured products had to be assured unimpeded access to their export markets overseas. For both these reasons, it was deemed essential by the ruling elite of Victorian England that control of the sea-lanes to the Far East be firmly in British hands. This implied the preservation of naval domination of the Mediterranean– Suez–Red Sea–Indian Ocean route as well as the establishment of strategically located bases and refueling stations along the way.

By the end of the nineteenth century, this national obsession with protecting the passage to India, East Asia, and Australia had resulted in the acquisition of a long string of islands, coastal enclaves, and their hinterlands along the southern rim of Asia and the east coast of Africa as well as control of the Egyptian land bridge connecting the two continents and its canal linking the seas. These strategically situated outposts of British imperialism—Gibraltar, Malta, Cyprus, and Suez in the Mediterranean; Aden and Somaliland on opposite shores of the Red Sea; Kenya, India, Burma, Malaya, and Singapore along the Indian Ocean basin—enabled this small island nation to obtain and preserve effective control of the largest empire in the history of the world.

A third motivating factor for British imperialism—in addition to the quest for foodstuffs, raw materials, naval bases, and refueling stations—was the search for undeveloped areas for investment that could absorb the huge amounts of capital that had accumulated in Britain in the form of profits from industrial enterprise. The regions of Africa and Asia that had recently been opened to European penetration were in dire need of investment capital to build the transportation and communication systems that were a prerequisite of economic modernization. In short order the major financial institutions of London began to invest heavily in railroad and road construction, the improvement of ports and harbors, and other ventures undertaken by British firms as part of the preliminary process of colonial development. In this way thousands of British investors were led to believe that their financial well-being depended on guaranteed markets for capital investment in the empire.

All manner of ideological justifications for the spectacular expansion of British power were advanced by the morally upright Victorians. There was much talk of the solemn responsibility to provide the uncivilized, backward peoples of the colonial world with the fruits of Britain's superior culture, in particular the spiritual inspiration of Christianity and the political benefits of enlightened administration. Altruistic missionaries and idealistic civil servants seem genuinely to have conceived of their role as that of rescuing the indigenous populations of the non-European world from the superstitions of their primitive religions and the barbarity of their native customs. But the self-justifying invocations of the "white man's burden" barely concealed the underlying motivation for British colonial expansion, which was primarily economic in nature. Despite the rhetoric of religious conversion and political reform, British colonial policy was designed to leave the preexisting social and cultural arrangements untouched and intact. All that mattered to the government in London was that that imperial system contribute to the efficient operation of the worldwide network of trade and investment upon which (it was thought) Great Britain depended for its economic prosperity if not its national survival.

The reasons for France's acquisition of a colonial empire in the latter part of the nineteenth century are less evident. Self-sufficient in food and far behind Great Britain in industrial development, France was much less dependent on foreign trade for its economic well-being. It had no demonstrable commercial incentive to seek guaranteed markets overseas for manufactured goods it could not produce in sufficient quantity or sources of foodstuffs it did not require. Nor did the French financial community seek colonial outlets for accumulated capital in the manner of the large London banking houses. By and large, that portion of French domestic savings that was invested abroad between 1871 and 1914 went not to distant regions of the southern hemisphere, but rather to the state treasuries of Southern and Eastern Europe. This was so for two reasons: First, these established governments were presumed, wrongly as it turned out, to afford greater security for investment than more speculative ventures in far-off lands in various stages of political disorganization. More important, the flow of private capital to the developing regions of Eastern Europe was actively promoted by the French government, which to a far greater degree than its British counterpart, regarded foreign investment as an instrument of diplomacy. If there was no good economic reason for France to covet a colonial empire in the closing decades of the nineteenth century, there was a persuasive diplomatic reason to direct its financial resources eastward. France's vulnerable position in a Europe dominated by the powerful German Empire that had been formed at its own expense after the Franco-Prussian War (1870–71) dictated a perpetual preoccupation with continental affairs. By encouraging private investment in the Russian, Austro-Hungarian, and Turkish empires, as well as in the fledgling states of the Balkan peninsula, the French government endeavored to surround its only antagonist in Europe, Germany, with a ring of states dependent on France's financial support and therefore amenable to its diplomatic influence.

Yet in spite of this preoccupation with the German menace in Europe, France simultaneously embarked on a campaign of colonial expansion that left it in possession of the world's second largest empire by the beginning of the twentieth century. Historians of French imperialism have sought to explain this paradox by emphasizing a motivating factor that does not lend itself to statistical confirmation in the manner of trade patterns or capital flows. This is the intangible phenomenon of the search for prestige. Abruptly displaced by Germany in 1871 as the dominant power on the European continent, France (according to this analysis) sought the psychological compensation of territorial conquest in distant regions of the non-European world where local authorities lacked the political organization and military power to offer effective resistance. By "France," in this instance, is meant not the government in Paris (which appears to have endorsed this colonial policy belatedly and somewhat reluctantly), but rather the military commanders and merchants on the spot who pursued their own particular interests. One observer went so far as to describe the French empire as having been built by "bored army officers looking for excitement"; he might have added: "and by railroad builders and traders in search of quick profits."

In any event, by the turn of the twentieth century approximately a third of the continent of Africa, a large section of Southeast Asia (consolidated politically as "French Indochina"), and a few island chains in the South Pacific had been brought under French control. While imperial Germany was busy consolidating its dominant position on the continent of Europe, France had joined Great Britain in a scramble for control of much of the rest of the non-European world. It is not surprising that French imperialism had received the amiable encouragement of German Chancellor Otto von Bismarck, the

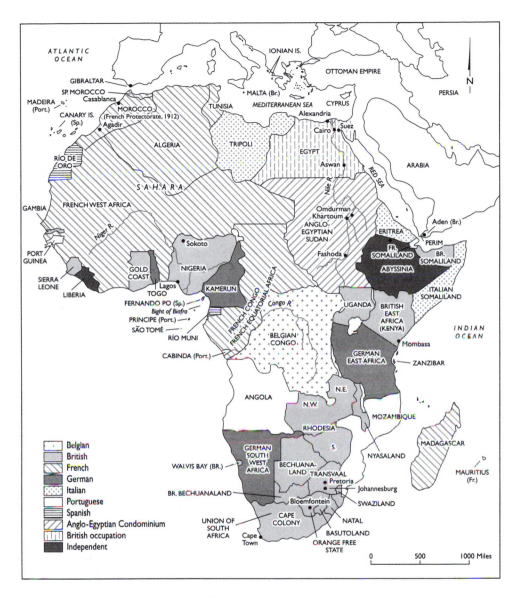

European Penetration of Africa to 1914

architect of his country's continental hegemony. It served to divert French attention from European concerns, particularly the unhealed wound to French national pride represented by the loss of the provinces of Alsace and Lorraine to Germany after the Franco-Prussian War. It also increased the likelihood of tension between France and England in regard to overlapping colonial claims and therefore reduced the possibility of those two nations joining forces to oppose Germany in Europe.

Toward the end of the nineteenth century, however, Britain and France had been joined in this massive land grab by two other European states that sought to carve out for themselves a share of the remaining unclaimed territory of the non-Western world. The first of these was Germany itself. In the years following Bismarck's retirement in 1890, the impetuous young German emperor, William II, grew increasingly dissatisfied with his erstwhile chancellor's "continental policy." The strategy that had effectively preserved German dominance in Europe began to appear outdated in the age of imperialism. Britain and France were rapidly bringing under their control vast colonial domains containing millions of people and unknown quantities of valuable resources. In 1897 the German kaiser caused a sensation by announcing that his nation would no longer be content with its exclusively European role. Henceforth it would conduct a *Weltpolitik*, a "world policy," that was designed to project Germany's military, economic, and political power into the worldwide competition for empire. In response to London publicists' boastful characterization of Britain's colonial domain as "the empire on which the sun never sets," William II asserted imperial Germany's claim to "a place in the sun." Within a few months this bold declaration of Germany's new global policy was translated into action. Plans were drawn up for the construction of a German navy that would contest British domination of the high seas. The Chinese port of Kiao-Chow on the Yellow Sea was seized as a potential refueling station for a future German Far Eastern fleet. The German Empire, which since its inception in 1871 had operated as the arbiter of European affairs, abruptly put the other great powers on notice that it intended to play an active role on the world stage.

Each subsequent reassertion of Germany's international ambitions increased the sense of insecurity in London and Paris. In 1898 the kaiser took the occasion of a much-publicized visit to the Ottoman Empire to declare himself "protector" of the 300 million Muslim inhabitants of the earth. This benevolent announcement represented a direct challenge to British and French positions in North Africa and the Middle East. A year later a German firm acquired from the Ottoman sultan a concession for the construction of a railroad extending from European Turkey to the Persian Gulf. German economic penetration of the Turkish Empire was interpreted by the British and the French as a first step toward German expansion southward into the Mediterranean and that portion of the non-European world that they had reserved for themselves.

The prospect of the dominant land power in Europe challenging Anglo-French imperial interests in Africa and Asia had precisely the effect that Bismarck had feared it would. The kaiser's *Weltpolitik* prompted the leaders of the two imperial nations to resolve their own conflicting claims to colonial territory in the interests of opposing Germany's bid for a global role. France was above all else interested in securing British cooperation in resisting the expansion of German power on the continent. Britain sought French support against Germany's newly acquired naval and colonial ambitions. All that stood in the way of such a mutually beneficial understanding was Anglo-French antagonism along the southern shore of the Mediterranean that had developed during the period of imperial expansion. British control of the two approaches to that body of water (by means of naval bases at Gibraltar at the western end and Alexandria at the eastern) conflicted with France's new imperial interests in Morocco and old ones in Egypt dating from the Napoleonic era. The two powers finally reached an amicable resolution of their North African rivalry in April 1904. France recognized the British occupation of Egypt (with guarantees of French access to the Suez Canal) in exchange for Britain's endorsement of French designs on Morocco (with guarantees of French disinterest in a buffer zone adjacent to Gibraltar that was eventually transferred to innocuous Spain). In March 1906, at a conference of the great powers that had been convened to adjudicate Germany's challenge to France's claim of priority in Morocco, the British government solidly supported the French, and the Germans were forced to back down. Two months earlier the British foreign secretary, Sir Edward Grey, took the extraordinary step of authorizing conversations between the British and French general staffs for the purpose of coordinating strategic plans in preparation for a possible war on the continent. Though London was careful to remind Paris that the Anglo-French entente was not an alliance implying any obligation on Britain's part to defend France, the two nations began to cooperate closely in an effort to check the expansion of German power in Europe as well as in the colonial world.

The other great power of Europe to conduct a policy of imperial expansion during the second half of the nineteenth century was Russia. While the seafaring nations of Western Europe projected their power across the oceans of the world, the Slavs of Russia had expanded from their home base west of the Ural Mountains into the great empty spaces of Asia. This territorial aggrandizement brought under the control of the European Russians a vast collection of foreign peoples with different religions, languages, and traditions who submitted to Russian rule because they lacked the military power to resist it, just as the indigenous inhabitants of North America proved incapable of blocking the relentless expansion of the American frontier from the Atlantic seaboard to the shores of the Pacific. But as the Russian Empire's expanding frontier began to approach the open seas that lay beyond the Eurasian land mass—the Mediterranean, the Persian Gulf, the Indian Ocean, the Pacific—it began to press against the competing interests of other expansionist states. Great Britain in particular was intent on protecting the sea communications to its empire in Asia and therefore strove to prevent Russia from securing a position of power along that route. The result of this British policy, often pursued in partnership with France, was that Russia was condemned to endure one of the most debilitating geographical handicaps imaginable for a state with ambitions of becoming a world power: During the winter months, when ice froze most of her major ports on the Baltic Sea, the North Pacific, and the Arctic Ocean, Russia lacked sufficient harbors to accommodate its navy and merchant marine.

The principal year-round ice-free ports that Russia did possess were located on the Black Sea. But the narrow body of water connecting these ports to the Mediterranean—the Bosporus, the Sea of Marmara, and the Dardanelles, collectively designated in diplomatic parlance as "the Straits"—could be closed at will by whatever power occupied its two shores. For centuries, that had been the empire of Ottoman Turkey. Turkish sovereignty over the Straits and the adjacent Balkan peninsula in Southern Europe thus deprived Russia of a secure outlet for its foreign trade and naval power in the Mediterranean. It was in order to break out of this geographical straitjacket that the Russian tsars pursued during the second half of the nineteenth century an active policy in the southwestern corner of their empire, striving to extend Russian influence in the Balkans and to compel the Turkish government to open the Straits to Russian warships and close them to those of other powers.

The geographical attraction that the Balkan peninsula and the Turkish Straits had for Russia was reinforced by an ideological attraction as well: The largest nationality group inhabiting the European possessions of the Ottoman Empire was of Slavic stock and felt a sense of ethnic identity with the politically dominant Slavic population of Russia. This somewhat vague sentiment of ethnic kinship between the Balkan and Russian Slavs had gradually developed in the course of the nineteenth century into a program for political unification. Dating from the first conference of Slavic peoples held in Moscow in 1867, Russian proponents of the ideology of Pan-Slavism envisioned the creation of a vast Slavic empire united under the scepter of the Russian tsar. The tsars themselves cared little about the tribulations of the Slavic peoples beyond their borders and were scarcely sympathetic to the romantic reveries of the Pan-Slavist movement at home. But they promoted and patronized its campaign, partly to divert attention from domestic difficulties, partly to undermine Ottoman authority in the Slavic regions of Southern Europe. Turkish maltreatment of the Balkan Slavs periodically elicited harshly worded protests from Saint Petersburg together with fervent appeals from Pan-Slavist ideologues and ambitious individuals at the Russian court for their liberation from Ottoman oppression. Added to this ethnic resentment—and the Russian court's willingness to exploit it—was an ancient religious grievance harbored by the Russian clergy against the Turkish regime: For four centuries the city of (Istanbul/Constantinople), spiritual capital of Eastern Orthodoxy (the official faith of the Russian Empire) had remained under the control of the hated Turk. The liberation of the holy city from the clutches of the Muslim infidel had long been a popular cause in Russian clerical circles. Each new report of Turkish misbehavior helped to revive this long-dormant issue. The tsar, though considerably more insulated from popular pressures than leaders of the other great powers, could ill afford to ignore these ethnic and religious sentiments, particularly when they coincidentally reinforced Russia's strategic and economic interest in challenging Turkey's position in Southern Europe.

The result of these internal pressures and external temptations was a Russian drive toward the Mediterranean that produced what was called in the diplomatic lexicon of the day "the eastern question." Twice in the second half of the nineteenth century, Russia attempted to expand southward at Turkey's expense. Twice she was prevented from doing so by the intervention of the great powers, militarily in the Crimean War (1854–56) and diplomatically at the Congress of Berlin (1878) following the Russo-Turkish War. In the course of the following two decades, the Ottoman Empire lived up to its reputation as the "sick man of Europe" by relinquishing political authority over the Slavic peoples of the Balkans. The independence of Serbia, Romania, Bulgaria, and Montenegro was confirmed, while the remainder of the peninsula seethed with insurrectionary sentiment against Turkish rule.

Into this political vacuum moved the Germanic empire of Austria-Hungary from the north. Though beset by the same kind of nationality problems that confronted the Ottoman state whose disintegrating European domains it coveted, the Habsburg Empire enjoyed the decisive advantage of almost unconditional support from the most powerful nation on the continent. By virtue of the Dual Alliance of 1879 (which was extended to a Triple Alliance including Italy three years later), imperial Germany had committed itself to the preservation of Habsburg power in Southern Europe. In the face of this joint Germanic opposition to Russian expansion toward the Mediterranean, the Russian government was eventually obliged to postpone its Balkan ambitions. In May 1897 an agreement was struck between Vienna and Saint Petersburg (with the benevolent approval of the other great powers) to preserve the political status quo in the Balkans. The "eastern question" was put on ice, at least for a time.

Frustrated in its ambition to obtain predominance in the Balkan peninsula and control of the Turkish Straits, the Russian regime redirected its expansionist drive further to the east. Claims to disputed territory in southern Asia that had lain dormant for decades were revived at the turn of the century. The nominally independent but politically weak state of Persia blocked Russian access to the Persian Gulf just as Ottoman Turkey guarded the entrance to the Mediterranean. Russian economic penetration of Persia in the early years of the twentieth century, which included the issuance of loans secured by Persian customs revenues, plans to construct a railroad from the Russian frontier to the Persian Gulf, and the acquisition of favorable tariff treatment for Russian exports, resulted in an acute rivalry with Great Britain. London viewed the prospect of Russian economic hegemony in Persia as a prelude to political predominance there and therefore a grave menace to the security of the British sea lanes to the Far East. Even more threatening to British interests were the progressive Russian commercial encroachments in Afghanistan, the traditional buffer between Russia and British India. As a consequence, Russian expansionism in southern Asia met with British opposition at every turn. British diplomatic pressure in Teheran counteracted Russian efforts to gain financial and commercial ascendency there. In 1901 a New Zealander named William K. d'Arcy secured a sixty-year concession to explore for oil throughout Persia, a privilege that was to give the Anglo-Iranian Oil Company exclusive control of the rich oil fields discovered there in 1908. The increasing British financial presence in Persia, supported by British naval squadrons patrolling the Persian Gulf and military garrisons in India, effectively frustrated the ambitions of the "Persian group" at the Russian court.

A far more promising outlet for Russian expansionist energies lay in the Far East. Just as American pioneers moved westward toward the Pacific Ocean at the expense of the indigenous Amerinds and the weak government of Mexico, Rus-sian settlers drove eastward across the sparsely populated wasteland of Siberia toward the opposite shore of that same ocean, subduing the native tribes and wresting territory from the impotent Manchu empire of China. In 1860 Russia acquired from China the Ussuri region on the Sea of Japan and founded the port city of Vladivostok. But this new acquisition did not afford Russia its coveted outlet to the open seas, for Vladivostok's harbor was icebound for most of the winter. Advocates of Russian expansion again turned their attention southward. As with Turkey and Persia, Russian entrée to a year-round harbor was blocked by a politically unstable, economically backward, militarily impotent state. But unlike the situation at the Turkish Straits and Persian Gulf, no European power possessed the capability of propping up the Chinese "sick man of Asia." Great Britain, which had traditionally served as the patron of the Manchu dynasty (in order to dominate it economically by controlling its principal seaports), was helpless to prevent the penetration of China by land. In 1891 the Russian government began the construction of a Trans-Siberian railroad with the assistance of French loans that had begun to flow into the tsar's treasury as part of France's campaign to woo Russia into an alliance directed against Germany. Upon completion of that railway, military forces could be transported from the heart of European Russia to a frontier that no other great power (and certainly not the Chinese) could defend.

The territories in East Asia that appeared most attractive and most susceptible to Russian exploitation were the two peninsulas that extend from the northeastern Chinese province of Manchuria into the Yellow Sea and afford access to the Pacific. The first of these, the Liaotung Peninsula, included at its furthest extremity the coveted prize of Port Arthur (Lüshun), the year-round ice-free Pacific port of Russian dreams. The second, the peninsula of Korea, represented the key to Russia's control of the Yellow Sea and therefore command of the approaches to its prospective East Asian port. Fortified with these acquisitions, Russia would be well positioned to participate in the China trade that had begun to exert a strong attraction on the maritime states of the world.

In anticipation of the arrival of Russian military power on the northern frontier of China to fill the vacuum produced by the collapse of Manchu authority, the great powers of Europe moved in to partition the decaying Asian empire into spheres of interest. The German seizure of the port of Kiao-Chow in 1897 set in motion a scramble for economic concessions that rapidly revealed the fictitious nature of Chinese sovereignty. Profiting from China's internal disarray, the Russian government extracted from Beijing in 1898 a long-term lease on the southern portion of the Liaotung Peninsula (including Port Arthur) together with the right to construct a railroad linking the port to the railway network then under construction in Siberia. The territory in between, the province of Manchuria, also became the object of Russian ambition: Control of it would provide a secure land route to Port Arthur and the warm water sea together with privileged access to the vast mineral deposits it was believed to contain. In 1900, following the Rus-sian army's participation in the multinational military force that had suppressed the antiforeign Boxer Rebellion in Beijing, a Russian contingent of a hundred thousand men remained on occupation duty in Manchuria to protect Russian interests there. Demands for far-reaching commercial concessions and the economic penetration of northern Korea soon followed. By the turn of the century Russian domination of the Chinese Empire appeared imminent, pending the completion of the Trans-Siberian Railroad, because the great powers of far-off Europe were incapable of projecting sufficient military force into the region in order to prevent it.

But as Russia pursued its campaign of expansion in East Asia, it was soon to discover that the world beyond the outer reaches of European power did not present the boundless opportunity for exploitation that had been supposed. This was particularly true along the western shore of the Pacific basin, where a non-European power that had adopted European techniques of economic, political, and military organization brusquely asserted its right to participate in the division of the Chinese spoils in its own geographical sphere. Whereas the continent of Africa and the southern rim of Asia lay within range of British, French, and German power, the western shore of the Pacific became, at the turn of the century, the object of the imperial ambitions of Japan.

THE RISE OF JAPANESE POWER IN EAST ASIA

Japan is a collection of four main islands and several smaller ones off the coast of China. For centuries it had been ruled by a decentralized feudal oligarchy consisting of territorial lords (daimyō) and an aristocratic caste of warriors (samurai). Hampered by the absence of natural resources and a mountainous terrain that left only 20 percent of its land suitable for cultivation, Japan lacked all of the customary prerequisites for economic development.

Isolated from the rest of the world by a complex language with no close relatives and an intense consciousness of cultural uniqueness, the Japanese people remained inward looking and resistant to foreign influences well into the second half of the nineteenth century. For all of these reasons, Japan seemed destined to remain politically immature, economically backward, and militarily impotent. Yet in spite of these handicaps, this isolated nation was to become the first non-Western state to achieve the position of a modern industrial and imperial power by the beginning of the twentieth century.

Japan's rapid rise to world power began in January 1868 when a political revolution swept aside the authority of the feudal oligarchy and created the so-called Meiji Restoration, with the emperor as the symbol of national unity and centralized authority. Real political power lay in the hands of a dynamic new ruling elite that was committed to the transformation of Japan from a primitive feudal society into a modern world power. The phenomenal success of the so-called restoration was due to the willingness of the new leadership to abandon the isolationist prejudices of the past in favor of Western methods of political, economic, and military organization. The Meiji political class recognized that since the global power of the European nations was the result of their economic modernization, political centralization, and military organization, the best hope of resisting European domination lay in adopting the very practices that had made it possible elsewhere in the world.

The result of this willingness to innovate by imitation was the rapid Westernization of Japan during the closing decades of the nineteenth century. Samurai were required to remove the knot of hair worn on the head and to wear their hair in the Western style; European clothing was given official sanction; the Gregorian calendar was adopted in 1873, changing holidays and festivals. Japanese observers were dispatched to England to study financial, commercial, and naval affairs; to Germany to learn the principles of military organization, strategy, and tactics; and to France for training in law and government. The entire structure of Japanese society was thenceforth reorganized on the basis of these European models. The political and economic power of the daimyō aristocracy was transferred to the central government organized as a European-style cabinet system with a prime minister and a bicameral parliament. The military authority that had previously been the jealously guarded privilege of the samurai warrior class was assumed by the Japanese Imperial Army, which adopted the Prussian institution of universal military service. The development of a nationwide system of banking and currency, transportation, and communication set the stage for Japan's spectacular economic growth during this period. The modernization of the Japanese economy began, as it had in England a century before, in the production of textiles. The country's silk industry captured a large share of the world market; Japan's silk exports surpassed those of China in 1910, a remarkable feat in view of the relative size of the two countries. In the meantime, the mechanization of cotton spinning and weaving in Japan proceeded at a fast pace. By the end of the century, a Japanese shipbuilding and munitions industry had been established. The value of Japanese foreign trade increased from virtually nothing in 1850 to roughly $200 million by 1900.

But the prospects for continued Japanese economic growth were limited by several constraints imposed by the accidents of geography. In addition to the shortage of industrial raw materials and agricultural resources cited earlier, Japan found herself in the midst of a demographic crisis of major proportions as she entered the period of her economic "take-off." With a land area smaller than the state of Texas and a rapidly expanding population

The Russo-Japanese War, 1904–1905

(which at the turn of the century was almost half that of the United States), the pressure of excess population on land and food supply had become a considerable handicap. In the last decade of the nineteenth century, the Japanese ruling class concluded that the only hope for surmounting these geographical and demographic impediments to economic growth lay in colonial expansion. Once again, the European experience furnished the instructive precedent. Just as Great Britain had relieved its population pressures and enhanced its economic productivity by acquiring overseas lands for settlement, investment, and trade, Japan could obtain much needed sources of industrial and agricultural raw materials, markets for its manufactured products, and areas of colonization for its excess population in the hitherto unclaimed territory in the adjacent regions of East Asia.

Less than a hundred miles to the west of the Japanese islands, on the mainland of Asia, the Korean peninsula and its Manchurian hinterland presented an irresistible temptation to Japanese imperialist sentiment. In 1894–95 Japanese forces swept across Korea into Manchuria, defeated the Chinese military forces, and laid the groundwork for imperial expansion on the mainland by securing the independence (under Japanese economic domination) of Korea and annexing the offshore island of Taiwan (Formosa). It was this expansion to the mainland that first brought the parvenu power of Asia into conflict with Russia, whose economic penetration of Manchuria and northern Korea (as we have seen) had begun in the same period. The inevitable collision came in 1904–05, in the first war between great powers since 1870. The Japanese navy quickly bottled up the small Russian fleet based at Port Arthur, while the Japanese army defeated the Russian army stationed in Manchuria. When the thirty-two vessels of the Russian Baltic Fleet arrived at the Tsushima Strait between Japan and Korea after a nine-month voyage from Europe they were engaged by the Japanese fleet and annihilated. As a reward for its spectacular victory, Japan obtained the Russian lease of Port Arthur and the Liaotung Peninsula, a privileged position in Manchuria, and a protectorate over Korea (which it annexed outright in 1910).

The Russo-Japanese War was a watershed in modern history for a number of reasons. It was the first instance in the modern era of a major* non-Western nation defeating a great power of Europe. As such it provided much encouragement to the emerging leaders of the nonwhite peoples of the world that were intent on liberating themselves from European domination. The Japanese had demonstrated that such resistance was possible provided that it was backed by Western-type technology and military organization. Inspired to a certain extent by the Japanese example, nationalist revolutions erupted in Persia (1905), Turkey (1908), and China (1911). The leaders of these insurrections advocated the introduction of economic, political, and military reforms of the Western type in order to strengthen their peoples in the struggle against Western domination. In a very real sense, the Japanese victory of 1905 marked the beginning of Asia's half-century-long war of liberation against European colonial control. The humiliation of the great Russian Empire by tiny Japan also had the effect of undermining the political authority of the Romanov dynasty. A political revolution that swept Russia in the aftermath of the military defeat of 1905 compelled the tsar to grant a constitution, convoke a representative parliament, and guarantee fundamental civil liberties for the first time. Though these concessions were diluted by all manner of restrictions on popular sovereignty and democratic rights, the social unrest that had prompted them set in motion a wave of clandestine revolutionary activity that was to culminate in the overthrow of the imperial regime twelve years later.

From the perspective of the shifting balance of power in the world, the most important consequence of Russia's defeat in the Far East was the gradual rapprochement between the tsarist regime and its other traditional rival, Great Britain. Its expansionist ambitions in East

---

*Afghanistan had defeated British forces in 1842, and Ethiopia had repelled an Italian military invasion in 1896.

Sunken Russian warships at Port Arthur during the Russo–Japanese War: During the Russo-Japanese War of 1904–05, the Japanese navy defeated the Russian Far East fleet and captured its base at Port Arthur on China's Liaotung Peninsula. Later, in the Battle of Tsushima, the Japanese navy annihilated the Russian fleet that had traveled all the way from its base in the Baltic Sea in Europe. These two naval engagements confirmed the arrival of Japan as a power to be reckoned with in Asia. *(Courtesy of the Library of Congress)*

Asia blocked by Japan, the Russian government began to contemplate reviving its long dormant claims to territory and influence at the other end of its empire on the Balkan peninsula of Southern Europe. But before renewing its forward policy in the Balkans, Russia took the precautionary step of seeking a resolution of its long-standing disputes with Great Britain in southern Asia; the focal points of this antagonism were Persia and Afghanistan, the two buffer states between Russian and British power in that region. As it happened, the British government was also anxious to reach an accord with Russia in southern Asia in order to ensure the security of India at a time when Britain felt increasingly menaced by the expansion of German military and naval power in Europe. The destruction of Russian seapower in the Far East had removed one of the principal sources of British anxiety about Russia and left Germany as the only potential threat to Britain's mastery of the seas. In short, these two historic rivals in Asia had both come to regard German power in Europe as the foremost obstacle to the pursuit of their respective national interests as they were redefined in the context of the changing international balance of power.

The reconciliation between Russia and Britain after 1905 was actively promoted by the one power that enjoyed cordial relations with both and that had the most to gain from an Anglo-Russian rapprochement: France. After more than a year of intensive negotiations, an Anglo-Russian agreement was concluded on August 31, 1907, which settled all of the important disputes between these two imperial powers in southern Asia. Russia recognized Afghanistan as a British sphere of influence, thereby according India the security on her northeast frontier that London had long sought. Persia, which had been a flashpoint of Anglo-Rus-sian rivalry for over a decade, was partitioned into three zones: the northern zone, adjacent to the Caucasus and including the capital, Teheran, was to be Russia's sphere; the southern zone, adjacent to India and guarding the entrance to the Persian Gulf, became the British sphere; and the territory in between, including the Gulf itself, was neutralized as a buffer zone. Both nations agreed to cooperate in blocking German efforts to obtain a foothold in Persia. Though the Anglo-Russian agreement of 1907 applied only to those two powers' bilateral rivalries in southern Asia, it paved the way for increasingly intimate diplomatic cooperation among Britain, Russia, and France. Observers began to speak of a "Triple Entente" that had emerged as a diplomatic counterpart to the Triple Alliance of Germany, Austria-Hungary, and Italy. Fortified by its amicable settlement with Great Britain in southern Asia, emboldened by the diplomatic support and financial assistance from its ally France, Russia "returned to Europe" after its disastrous adventure in the Far East. The revival of Russian aspirations in the Balkans, undertaken partly to divert public attention from the domestic troubles sketched above, partly in pursuit of long-standing interests in the region, was destined to bring the tsarist empire into conflict with Austria-Hungary and its powerful protector in Berlin.

While Japan was emerging as the dominant power in East Asia, across the Pacific another non-European state that had adopted European ways began to assert its claim to imperial status in the new global order. The geographical condition of the Japanese empire and the American republic could hardly have been more dissimilar. Japan suffered from a shortage of arable land and natural resources and lacked a large internal market for its industrial output. The United States possessed all three in unparalleled abundance as a consequence of its westward territorial expansion in the course of the nineteenth century. Whereas Japan's curse of overpopulation impelled it to seek external outlets for emigration, the United States' opposite problem of underpopulation required the importation of millions of immigrants from Europe to operate its farms and factories. But the striking similarities amid the contrasts between these two nations explain why they simultaneously joined the ranks of the imperial powers at the beginning of the twentieth century. Both were relatively free from the menace of foreign invasion because of the great distances separating them from the centers of military power in Europe. Both were located in the vicinity of politically disorganized and militarily impotent states whose abundant natural resources made them tempting targets for economic exploitation and military domination. This propitious combination of isolation from great power interference and proximity to economically valuable, strategically vulnerable regions propelled the United States into a policy of imperial expansion in its own region during the very period that Japan began its expansion on the mainland of Asia.

The simultaneous emergence of these two powers on the opposite shores of the Pacific inevitably raised the possibility that their aggressive ambitions would overlap in that ocean. Indeed, both societies contained advocates of transpacific expansion. In Japan there was much talk of relieving the pressure of overpopulation by mass immigration to the sparsely settled Pacific islands and the west coast of the United States. Toward the end of the century, eastward migration had produced a Japanese majority in the Hawaiian Islands. In the meantime, increasing numbers of Japanese nationals had begun to settle in the American coastal state of California, engendering friction with the resident population of European stock that gave rise to demands for exclusionary legislation. During the same period, various constituencies in the United States pressed for expansion across the Pacific in the opposite direction. Commercial interests eagerly eyed the "China market" for American agricultural surpluses and industrial products. Christian missionary societies dreamed of converting the heathens on the Chinese mainland to the true faith. American banking houses sought participation in the financial reorganization of the Chinese railroad network in Manchuria that was being prepared by a consortium of European banks. Naval leaders coveted the natural harbors in Samoa, Hawaii, and the Philippines as potential bases for a powerful American Pacific fleet. The subsequent acquisition of these three island groups by the United States at the end of the nineteenth century posed a potential challenge to Japan's imperial aspirations in the western Pacific.

As it turned out, however, the Pacific ambitions of Japan and the United States were prudently postponed by the governments of both countries and subordinated to expansionist activities in regions closer to home. In spite of Washington's determined efforts to establish the principle of the "Open Door" to China through a series of declarations by Secretary of State John Hay at the turn of the century, the two parvenu Pacific powers worked out a vague *modus vivendi* that removed the principal sources of conflict between them: The United States tacitly tolerated Japanese economic penetration of Korea and Manchuria, while the Tokyo government swallowed its pride and accepted stringent American restrictions on Japanese immigration to United States territory. While Japanese imperial energies were thus diverted from the Pacific to the Asian mainland, American ambitions were similarly diverted from the Pacific to the Caribbean.

THE RISE OF AMERICAN POWER IN THE WESTERN HEMISPHERE AND THE PACIFIC

The central characteristic of the western hemisphere that has decisively influenced the economic and political relations of its constituent states is the enormous disparity in national power between the United States of North America and the disunited states of Latin America.* This "imbalance of power," as one historian has labeled it, was a direct result of the divergent historical experience of the settler populations that inhabited the

---

*By "Latin America" I mean the politically independent states of Central America (including Mexico), South America, and the West Indies where Spanish, Portuguese, and French are the official languages.

successor states of the British and Iberian empires in the new world after they achieved their political independence from Europe.

By the middle of the 1860s the English-speaking heirs to the British Empire of North America had definitively partitioned that vast, resource-rich continent into two sovereign political units, which rapidly underwent a process of economic modernization based on the model of the industrial revolution of the metropole. The United States had extended its political frontier westward from the Atlantic seaboard to the Pacific between 1783 and the mid-1850s by the alternate means of military conquest and diplomacy, expropriating the tribal lands of the indigenous inhabitants or annexing territory previously claimed by Spain, France, England, and the newly independent state of Mexico. By copying European methods of economic organization and political integration, the American pioneers who pushed westward with the active encouragement of the federal government and the protection of its military forces welded that continental territory into a single political and economic unit. After the failure of the southern states' bid for secession between 1861 and 1865, this politically unified, economically integrated system combined its extraordinary God-given advantages—an abundant supply of natural resources, fertile, well-watered soil, and an excellent system of navigable rivers and lakes that afforded access to both land and markets—with the influx of skilled labor and capital investment from Europe to become the world's most prosperous nation by the end of the century. To the north, the unconnected provinces of Canada, long the object of American annexationist ambition, united as a self-governing federation in 1867.* The withdrawal of British authority over Canadian affairs removed the major obstacle to Canadian-American cooperation. Thereafter the two sovereign political entities of North America developed intimate economic and political relations that complemented their close linguistic and cultural ties. By the end of the century, Canada had become the principal market for American industrial exports and a major supplier of raw materials and mineral resources to the United States. The Canadian-American border became, and remains to this day, the longest undefended frontier in the world.

South of the Rio Grande, on the other hand, the collapse of Spanish and Portuguese authority between 1808 and 1822 resulted in the political disintegration of the Latin American mainland into what eventually became twenty independent republics.† Despite the dreams of revolutionary leaders such as Simon Bolívar of creating a political federation of Latin America, the new nations tenaciously clung to their newly achieved national identities. Even economic integration, traditionally the preliminary step to political unification, proved an unattainable goal. As a result of tariffs, import quotas, and other impediments to regional economic interchange established by the nationalistically inclined ruling elites, only a small proportion of the foreign trade of each individual state was conducted within the region. Moreover, instead of following the North American path of economic modernization (which emphasized industrialization and the development of an internal market for domestically produced manufactured goods), the Latin

---

*The four original provinces of Canada united under the British North America Act of 1867 (Quebec, Ontario, Nova Scotia, and New Brunswick) were subsequently joined by six others to form the present federation.

†Excluding British, French, and Dutch Guiana (which remained European colonies) and British Honduras (which became a British colony in 1862).

republics preserved and intensified the neocolonial nature of their economic systems. That is, they produced raw materials and tropical foodstuffs for export and served as markets for finished manufactured products and capital investment from the already developed industrial economies of Western Europe. To make matters worse, whereas feudal practices had been abolished early in England and therefore were not transplanted to British North America (except for the slave system in the southern agricultural societies of the United States that was abolished in 1865), the new Latin American states inherited from Spain and Portugal a feudal land tenure system and a rigidly stratified social structure that remained largely intact after independence.

The failure of the Iberian successor states in Latin America to achieve political and economic integration as a prelude to economic modernization is paradoxical in light of the existence of several conditions that ought to have been conducive to such a development. The Latin republics had won their political independence early in the nineteenth century. Many of them possessed an ample resource base for economic development in the form of extensive deposits of subsoil minerals and fertile agricultural land. Collectively they possessed a common religion, cultural heritage, and (with the exception of Brazil) language, advantages that had traditionally facilitated regional communication and cooperation. Instead, the perpetuation of the political division and economic backwardness of Latin America for the remainder of the nineteenth century produced an enormous power vacuum in the southern portion of the western hemisphere that was destined to be filled by the newly developed economic and military power of the United States.

It has long been fashionable, but entirely incorrect, to believe that the establishment of United States hegemony in Latin America at the expense of the great powers of Europe was a consequence of the Monroe Doctrine. President James Monroe's message to Congress on December 2, 1823, had originally been intended as a warning to the European powers (especially France, which was then suspected of harboring designs on the newly independent republics of Latin America) that any attempt to reestablish European colonial power in the new world would be unacceptable to the United States. In fact the Monroe Doctrine was a dead letter from its promulgation to the end of the nineteenth century, for the United States during that period had developed neither the naval power nor the diplomatic influence to enforce such a presumptuous admonition. It was only by the sufferance of Great Britain that the Latin American republics were permitted to enjoy immunity from political interference and military intimidation by the great powers of the old world. By extracting from France a promise of nonintervention, and by maintaining undisputed naval supremacy in the Atlantic and Caribbean, Britain ensured that no European nation would increase its power position on the continent of Europe by acquiring territory in the western hemisphere. But the doctrine of nonintervention was scarcely absolute. It was violated with impunity whenever London saw fit for whatever reason to suspend its application. Britain itself intervened militarily in Latin America on four separate occasions after the declaration of the Monroe Doctrine: She conducted joint naval operations with France against the Rio de la Plata (the future state of Argentina) in 1845 and with France and Spain against Mexico in 1861, and she occupied the Falkland (Malvinas) Islands off Argentina in 1833 and British Honduras in Central America in 1862. France, in addition to her naval collaboration with England and Spain, overthrew the Mexican government and installed a French client state in 1863, which remained in power for four years. Even Spain was able to reannex the Dominican Republic for a four-year period beginning in 1861. Apart from these overt military operations in direct violation of the Monroe Doctrine, British, French, and German economic penetration of Latin America in the last half of the nineteenth century subordinated the economies of the region to the commercial and financial interests of Europe.

It was not until the decade of the 1890s that the United States, having become an industrial power of the first rank and consolidated political control of the territory on its own continent, acquired the economic and military capability to project its power to the southern half of its hemisphere. The pursuit of American strategic and economic interests in the Caribbean region in particular and in Latin America in general was justified, as has so often been the case in American foreign policy, by a high-sounding moral principle. Just as the westward continental expansion of the nineteenth century was touted as the "manifest destiny" of a chosen people on the march, the subsequent extension of American hegemony over Latin America at the expense of European powers was couched in two moralistic phrases: "hemispheric solidarity" and the more commonly used "Pan-Americanism."

The ideology of Pan-Americanism was rooted in two myths about the geographical and political conditions of the western hemisphere. The first was the widespread misconception that the two continents of the new world formed a single geographic unit that stood apart from the other continents of the earth. In reality the continents of North and South America, though connected by a narrow strip of land, achieved their normal communication by sea in the nineteenth century and by air later in the twentieth. By sea, Rio de Janiero is considerably closer to the west coast of Africa than to any port in the United States. By air, Washington is closer to Moscow than to Buenos Aires. The myth of political affinity derived from the use of the term "republic" as a label for the governmental systems of the Latin American nations. As "sister republics," the United States and the countries to the south came to be regarded as joint custodians of a common legacy of democratic government that distinguished them from the monarchical tradition of the old world. The perpetual tendency of the reputed "republics" of Latin America to lapse into various forms of dictatorship while the nations of Western Europe moved toward democratic rule belied such sentimental invocations of a hemispheric partnership of republicanism.

Nevertheless, beginning with the first International Conference of American States in 1889, the ideology of Pan-Americanism persisted as the moral justification for what rapidly developed into a neocolonial relationship between the North American giant and the weak states to its south. The Commercial Bureau of the International Union of the American Republics, headquartered in Washington under the supervision of the American secretary of state, promoted inter-American economic and political cooperation. Subsequently renamed the Pan-American Union, this organization of free and independent states in the hemisphere became the vehicle for the exercise of American diplomatic influence over the member governments. Though the hopes entertained by some United States officials of establishing a customs union integrating the economies of the sovereign nations of the western hemisphere foundered on the shoals of Latin American opposition at the conference, the groundwork was laid for a hemispheric political system dominated by the United States and emancipated from the overbearing influence of the European powers.

But the projection of American power into Latin America required a direct challenge to Great Britain's hitherto uncontested authority in the region. Such a challenge was effectively mounted in the last decade of the nineteenth century, at a time when Britain's imperial energies were engaged elsewhere by disputes that affected her vital national interests much more directly. The precipitating episode in this transformation of the balance of power in the western hemisphere was a seemingly trivial boundary dispute between Venezuela and British Guiana. Within the disputed zone lay the mouth of the Orinoco River, the key trade route in the northern portion of the South American continent. Venezuelan appeals to the United States for support, combined with American anxiety about the possible extension of British economic influence along the southern shore of the Caribbean, prompted a spectacular diplomatic initiative from Washington. On July 20, 1895, Secretary of State Richard Olney demanded that Britain agree to submit the issue to arbitration, threatened American intervention on the basis of the Monroe Doctrine if it refused to do so, and issued the following historic declaration: "Today the United States is practically sovereign on this continent, and its fiat is law upon the subjects to which it confines its interposition." He proceeded to observe that America's "infinite resources combined with its isolated position render it master of the situation and practically invulnerable against any or all other powers." The boundary dispute rapidly receded in significance—the arbitration award given four years later actually supported the British position on most points—amid the broad international implications of the Olney Declaration. The United States had unilaterally arrogated to itself the right and responsibility to protect the interests of its neighbors to the south by virtue of its position of superiority within its hemisphere. Great Britain, on account of its preoccupation with the deteriorating political situation in southern Africa and the German government's willingness to exploit it at Britain's expense, prudently chose not to become embroiled in a dispute with the United States and therefore acquiesced in this unilateral declaration of American hegemony in Latin America.

In the year 1898 British imperial authority in the eastern hemisphere appeared endangered at every turn by the actions of the other European powers. In March the passage of Germany's first naval law and Russia's acquisition of a naval base at Port Arthur in Manchuria heralded the entry of two new contestants in the scramble for colonies and concessions in Asia. In the autumn Britain and France edged to the brink of war over conflicting territorial claims along the Nile, while tension continued to mount between Britain and the Boer republics in southern Africa. With the great powers of Europe embroiled in distant conflicts in Africa and Asia, the United States embarked on a military and naval campaign in the Caribbean and the Pacific that transformed it from a continental to a global power. In 1895 the harsh rule imposed by Spain on the island of Cuba incited a popular rebellion that won widespread sympathy in the United States, particularly after lurid reports of the Spanish colonial government's many atrocities appeared in the sensationalist newspapers of Joseph Pulitzer and William Randolph Hearst. When the U.S.S. *Maine* was sunk by an explosion in Havana harbor on February 15, 1898, killing 260 sailors, public outrage in the United States compelled Congress to pass a joint resolution proclaiming Cuba "free and independent." The following April Congress issued a declaration of war when Spain refused to relinquish control of the island. A squadron of six American naval vessels under the command of Commodore George Dewey that was docked in the British crown colony of Hong Kong steamed to the Spanish-controlled Philippine islands and destroyed the Spanish Pacific squadron in Manila Bay in May. The Spanish fleet that had crossed the Atlantic to protect the European country's Caribbean possessions was destroyed by American warships in Santiago Bay. Soon thereafter, U.S. ground troops forced the Spanish army to surrender on July 17 and then moved on to capture Spain's last remaining possession in the Caribbean, the island of Puerto Rico. In the meantime, U.S. military forces dispatched to the Philippines defeated the Spanish garrison there on August 14.

The peace treaty signed in Paris on December 10, 1898, brought the war to an end after six months of hostilities. The United States acquired control of the former Spanish Pacific islands of the Philippines and Guam and the former Spanish Caribbean island of Puerto Rico. Cuba was granted its independence but was later compelled to accept the Platt Amendment of 1901, which accorded the United States the unconditional right to intervene in the island's affairs to preserve its independence and social order as well as the right to establish a naval coaling station in the country. The population of the Philippines initially welcomed the Americans for liberating it from Spanish oppression. But the refusal of the McKinley administration to grant the archipelago independence sparked an indigenous insurgency, led by the Filipino political leader Emilio Aguinaldo, which resulted in some 200,000 Filipino and 4,000 American deaths before it was crushed in 1901. While American military and naval forces were evicting Spain from the remnants of its Pacific and Caribbean empire in the summer of 1898, the United States annexed the Hawaiian Islands in the mid-Pacific (a valuable source for sugarcane production and the site of an excellent natural harbor for an American Pacific fleet), whose indigenous monarchical government had been overthrown by a group of American sugar planters five years earlier. By the beginning of the new century the United States had belatedly acquired an overseas empire, which, though much smaller than those of Great Britain and France, qualified it for inclusion in the ranks of the world powers.

The new global power promptly embarked on a naval construction program worthy of its newly acquired status. The advantages enjoyed by the United States over Britain in naval power in the western hemisphere became readily apparent. The replacement of the wind-powered warship by the steam-propelled warship, while increasing the fighting strength of the world's battle fleets, had reduced their radius of action by imposing the requirement of an assured source of fuel (coal for Britain until 1912 when the fleet changed over to oil) on naval task forces operating far from home waters. In 1902 Britain began to transfer the bulk of its Caribbean naval squadron to the North Atlantic in order to offset the growth of German naval power there, in effect conceding American domination of its own hemisphere and recognizing Latin America as an American sphere of interest. In the same year Britain had concluded an alliance with Japan in recognition of that nation's value as a counterweight to Russian power in the Far East, thereby liberating more British battleships for redeployment in home waters. By these two gestures the former "mistress of the seas" accorded the United States and Japan the right to control the sea approaches to their own imperial domains in order to concentrate on protecting the security of the British Isles from the prospective menace of German sea power.

The United States rapidly developed extensive strategic and economic interests in the former Spanish islands in the Caribbean and the independent mainland nations on its shores. Naval strategists, concerned about the growth of Japanese sea power across the Pacific, considered the Isthmus of Panama an ideal site for a canal linking the Atlantic and the Pacific that would permit the concentration of naval forces in either ocean on short notice. American domination of the Caribbean region came to be regarded in American naval circles as necessary for the security of the two coasts of the country as well as

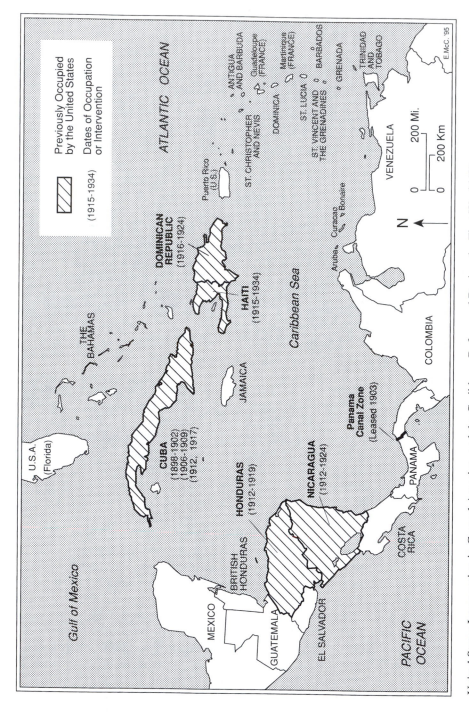

United States Intervention in Central America and the Caribbean Before and During the First World War

for the protection of the eastern approaches of the projected Panamanian canal, just as Britain's control of the North Sea and Japan's control of the China Sea were considered essential by the naval strategists of those two powers.

As "big navy" enthusiasts pressed for the transformation of the Caribbean into an "American lake," American economic interests began to compete with European firms for control of the natural resources of Latin America in general and the Caribbean basin in particular. American penetration of the economies of Latin America characteristically took the form of direct acquisition by United States firms of the agricultural and subsoil mineral resources of the region. Sugar-producing interests obtained a virtual monopoly on the Cuban sugar cane crop. The United Fruit Company of Boston established a huge "banana empire" in Central America, purchasing enormous tracts of land and constructing roads, railroads, and ports to convey the products of its plantations to foreign markets. The petroleum resources of Mexico and Venezuela, Chilean copper, Bolivian tin, and several other industrial raw materials came under the direct control of American firms.

By 1901 the last remaining obstacle to American mastery of the Caribbean region was removed. By means of the Hay-Pauncefort Treaty, Great Britain renounced an earlier agreement stipulating joint Anglo-American construction and operation of a Central American canal. Two years later a revolution in Colombia's northwestern province on the Isthmus of Panama received the active support of the American government, which promptly recognized Panama as an independent republic. In February 1904 the new nation signed a treaty authorizing the United States to construct a fifty-mile-long canal across the isthmus in a zone leased and fortified by the government in Washington. In the meantime, steps had been taken to ensure the right of the United States to protect its strategic and economic interests in the Caribbean. The newly created client states of Cuba and Panama were forced to include clauses in their constitutions stipulating the right of the United States to intervene to protect their independence and preserve social order, and both were induced to authorize the construction of American bases on their territory. In 1904 President Theodore Roosevelt imperiously extended the prerogative of intervention to embrace the entire hemisphere: "Chronic wrongdoing, or an impotence which results in a general loosening of the ties of civilized societies," he announced, "may in America, as elsewhere, ultimately require intervention by some civilized nation, and in the Western Hemisphere the adherence of the United States to the Monroe Doctrine may force the United States, however reluctantly, in flagrant cases of such wrongdoing or impotence, to the exercise of an international police power." With his famous corollary to the Monroe Doctrine, Roosevelt in effect redefined the original prohibition against European interference in Latin America as a unilateral assertion of the United States' prerogative to police the region.

America's self-proclaimed right to manage the internal affairs of the Caribbean nations was frequently exercised in the years following the promulgation of the Roosevelt Corollary. In 1905 the United States assumed control of customs collection in the insolvent Dominican Republic and established a system of financial supervision that was to remain in force for thirty-six years. In 1909 American agents fomented a successful insurrection against the nationalistically inclined government of Nicaragua. Three years later American marines were landed to protect the compliant successor regime, whose transfer of authority over its customs service to the United States had produced widespread internal discontent. Though nominally independent, Nicaragua remained under American financial supervision from 1911 to 1924.

Teddy Roosevelt (1858–1919) wields the "Big Stick": With his famous "Corollary" to the Monroe Doctrine promulgated in December 1905, "T. R." boldly asserted the prerogative of the United States to exercise an international police power to ensure that other nations in the western hemisphere paid their debts to international creditors and maintained social order. On the basis of this new doctrine, Roosevelt and his successors in the White House would use military force to impose financial solvency and political stability on several countries in the Caribbean and Central America. *(Courtesy of the Library of Congress)*

But it was the adjacent state of Mexico that became the major victim of American economic penetration. During the last two decades of the nineteenth century and the first decade of the twentieth, Mexican dictator Porfirio Diaz had welcomed American investment in his country's petroleum industry, transportation system, and agricultural resources. By the time of his overthrow during the Mexican Revolution of 1911, American companies had acquired control of 50 percent of the Mexican oil industry and American citizens held title to over 40 percent of Mexican land. Subsequent outbursts of anti-American sentiment in postrevolutionary Mexico, as we shall see, prompted punitive American naval and military interventions that further inflamed patriotic opinion south of the Rio Grande.

By the advent of the First World War, the United States had established its undisputed mastery of the Caribbean region, a circumstance dramatically symbolized by the opening of the Panama Canal in August 1914, the very month that the armies of Europe hurled themselves against one another on that distant continent. The subsequent construction of American naval bases at Roosevelt Roads in Puerto Rico and Guantánamo Bay in Cuba was to afford the United States command of the eastern approaches to the canal and therefore a position of strategic invulnerability in its hemisphere. In the meantime, the economy of the Caribbean region had been tightly linked to the superior economic system of what resentful Latin Americans had begun to call "the Colossus of the North." Direct American investment in electric utilities, railways, sugar, oil, bananas, and extractive industries generated substantial profits, which were repatriated to fuel the phenomenal economic expansion in the United States. American control of the banking system and customs administration of many Caribbean nations served the dual function of ensuring the repayment of debts to American investors and precluding European interventions on behalf of aggrieved debtors. The prerogative of American military intervention to restore social order or protect foreign economic interests remained in the background as an inducement to good behavior and was exercised as needed. Apart from British, French, and Dutch Guiana on the mainland of South America, British Honduras in Central America, and a few European-controlled islands in the Caribbean, the colonial presence of the Old World powers had been removed from the New World. Though European economic mastery of the South American continent below the American-dominated Caribbean basin persisted well into the twentieth century, that last remnant of European power in the western hemisphere was soon to disappear as well, a casualty of the Great War and its aftermath.

A SHRINKING EARTH AND THE GEOPOLITICAL WORLDVIEW

The projection of Western power all around the world in the closing decades of the nineteenth century was facilitated by two technological innovations that revolutionized the way people and materials were moved across space. The first of these was the application of steam power to oceanic transport. Though the first steamship was constructed in 1802, it was not until the 1850s that the sailing ship disappeared from the merchant fleets and navies of the sea powers. Liberated from dependence on the vagaries of the wind and capable of previously unimaginable velocities, the steamship powered by coal enabled the industrial nations of Europe to extend their economic activity and project their military power to the previously inaccessible regions of the earth. The initial beneficiary of this technological revolution in oceanic transport was Great Britain, which by midcentury still possessed the most highly organized machine industry and the best supplies of anthracite coal. The problem of keeping the fleets supplied with fuel, which represented a potential constraint on Britain's ability to preserve its mastery of the seas, was solved by the acquisition of coaling stations across the globe. As will be presently seen, the search for refueling stations to accommodate battle fleets and merchant marines played its part in prompting the imperialist expansion of the late nineteenth century, when other aspirants to world power joined the naval race. The result was the transformation of previously formidable oceanic barriers into pathways for intercontinental relations. Warships steamed from base to base displaying the flag as a warning to recalcitrant natives or potential enemies, giving rise to the slogan of the age: gunboat diplomacy. Merchant vessels arrived at far-off ports laden with manufactured products and departed with tropical foodstuffs or raw materials for the return voyage.

The second such revolutionary innovation was the application of steam power to transportation on land. The invention of the railroad locomotive enabled the two gigantic continental nations, the United States and, later, the Russian Empire, to acquire effective political and economic control of the vast wildernesses to which they laid claim. It eventually permitted the previously unified nations of Western Europe, especially Britain and France, to penetrate the interior of Africa from the coastal enclaves they had obtained in earlier centuries. The subjugation of the indigenous populations, the projection of political authority into interior regions, and the exploitation and extraction of economic resources therein, were all facilitated by the establishment of railway communication inland from the coasts.

Accompanying these innovations that revolutionized the manner in which people carried themselves, the products of their labor, and the fruits of the earth across land and sea was the invention of a device to permit the rapid transmission of human messages across the airwaves above. With the telegraph and, later, the radio, came the ability to convey instructions and requests for information to and from the far-flung outposts of empire throughout the world. Foreign offices and their embassies, general staffs and their overseas commands, and private firms and their foreign branches acquired the capacity to maintain continuous communication with one another. This revolution in communications technology permitted a degree of centralized direction unheard of in the days when envoys, military commanders, and merchants on the spot were required to make extemporaneous policy decisions that often determined the outcome of diplomatic negotiations, wars, or contests for economic advantage.

The consequences of this technological "shrinkage of the earth" became dramatically apparent during the military operations conducted at the turn of the century. The railroad and the steamship rendered military forces more massive and more mobile. Gone were the long marches and risky sea voyages that depleted the strength of fighting men long before they reached the field of battle. Between 1899 and 1902, in an unprecedented projection of military power across the ocean, Great Britain maintained a quarter of a million soldiers at a distance of six thousand miles on the southern tip of Africa to subdue the army of the Boer republics. In 1904, though with a less happy outcome, Russia conveyed an army of comparable size four thousand miles across the forbidding wastes of Siberia by rail to engage the Japanese forces in Manchuria. Such prodigious feats of strategic transport erased the traditional barriers of space and time that had preserved the isolation of the world's land masses from one another. The entire globe at the beginning of the twentieth century had become a single theater of strategic and economic interaction, knit together by the network of transportation and communication represented by the railroad, the steamship, and the telegraph.

In an effort to advance mankind's comprehension of this new global context of international relations, a new branch of the social sciences called "geopolitics" was established in the centers of higher learning in the Western world. To the extent that it represented a "scientific" (that is, objective) intellectual enterprise, the discipline of geopolitics combined the principles of geography and political science for the purpose of studying the distribution of political power across the surface of the globe. But, as has been the case with many social sciences, geopolitics forfeited its claim to scientific objectivity as its most reputable practitioners employed its teachings to form an ideological apologia for their own nations' right to expand and subjugate. To the geopoliticians, the entire earth represented an arena of acute rivalry in which the great powers struggled for control of economically valuable resources, territory, and populations. No square inch of land, no tiny island in the sea, no river, lake, or ocean was exempt from the operation of the iron law of geopolitics; given the uneven distribution of fertility, natural resources, and strategic advantage in the world, the handful of nation-states capable of projecting their power beyond their own frontiers were locked in a worldwide contest for control of the unclaimed or indefensible regions of the earth.

It is no surprise that the German Empire produced the most detailed and comprehensive doctrine of geopolitics at the turn of the century, when that country's emerging interest in sea power combined with the traditional Prussian preoccupation with land power. In the writings of the German geopoliticians, the entire land mass of Eurasia from Spain to Siberia, from the northern Arctic wastes to the tip of the Indian subcontinent, constituted a vast terrain of land, raw materials, and population, the control of which would determine the outcome of what they saw as the forthcoming contest for domination of the world. In light of Germany's superiority in industrial organization and military power, and of Russia's advantage in territory, population, and natural resources, it was understandable that these scholars confidently expected this approaching contest for world domination to take the form of an epic struggle between "Teuton" and "Slav" in the borderlands of Central and Eastern Europe, where Germanic and Slavic populations had intermingled over the centuries. To the underlying principle of German geopolitics—the definition of Eurasia as a geographical space to be filled by the political authority and military power of the strongest nation—was added the Malthusian doctrine of population pressure against food supply and the Social Darwinist concept of the competition of nationality groups for survival in the uncongenial natural environment.

This witches' brew of geopolitics, demography, and pseudobiological determinism supplied the requisite intellectual justification for the expansion of German power eastward at the expense of Russia. The theorists and their popularizers portrayed Germany as an industrialized nation with a rapidly expanding population cursed with an inadequate supply of foodstuffs and natural resources within its political frontiers. It therefore required additional space for internal migration as well as agricultural land and raw materials for the comfort, nourishment, and prosperity of its people. This space and this soil was ripe for the taking in the fertile plains to the east, thought to be populated by inferior peoples, mainly Slavs, who were deemed incapable of exploiting the potentially productive territory they occupied or of defending it from foreign invasion. Had such perverse theories been confined to the lecture halls and scholarly journals of German universities, they might have represented little more than academic curiosities. But the fact that influential members of the political, economic, and military elite of imperial Germany began to study them with interest after the turn of the century transformed them into prescriptions for a German drive for the domination of Eurasia.

The most formidable obstacle to this German geopolitical design was Great Britain, with its string of colonial holdings along the southern rim of Eurasia and its naval domination of the adjacent seas. It was therefore appropriate that the seafaring people of this island produced the other great geopolitical tradition of the period. Halford Mackinder, in a seminal paper presented to the Royal Geographical Society in 1904, reflected the influence of German geopolitical thinkers such as Friedrich Rätzel while adding a few novel conceptions of his own. Entitled "The Geographical Pivot of History," this presentation extended the scope of geopolitical analysis to encompass the entire globe. The earth, according to Mackinder, was divisible into two regions: The "world island," comprising the interlinked continents of Europe, Asia, and Africa, was the largest, most populous, and richest of all possible land combinations. Arrayed along its periphery were the large insular groups—the Americas, Australia, Japan, and the British Isles. At the center of the world island lay what Mackinder designated as the "heartland," stretching from the Volga to the Yangtze and from the Himalayas to the Arctic. Protected from the menace of sea power by ice floes to the north and rugged mountains and arid deserts to the south, this vast land surface was vulnerable to foreign invasion only on its western periphery, along the lengthy stretch of lowland connecting Western Europe to Russia. Effective political domination of this space by a single power had been precluded in times past because of the limitations of transportation: The periodic invasions from east to west and vice versa by horse-riding marauders, from the ferocious forays of Attila the Hun to Bonaparte's ill-fated march on Moscow, had failed to establish permanent control of this European gateway to the heartland because of the inability to assure a continual supply of men and matériel.

But the invulnerability of the heartland of Eurasia to domination by a single power had been abolished, Mackinder believed, by the revolution in transportation cited earlier in this chapter. Now that Eurasia was about to be covered by a network of railways, he declared, a powerful continental nation stood an excellent chance of extending its political control over the Eastern European gateway as a prelude to its bid for mastery first of the Eurasian land mass and then of the entire globe: "Who rules east Europe commands the Heartland; who rules the Heartland commands the world-island; who rules the world-island commands the world." With this pithy dictum, Mackinder identified the geopolitical nightmare that was to haunt the world's two major sea powers during the first half of the new century—Great Britain and, subsequently, the United States. This nightmare was the prospect that the conquest of Eastern Europe by Germany or Russia would lead to the domination of the Eurasian land mass by one of those great powers as a prelude to its mastery of the world.

At the heart of Mackinder's doctrine were two axioms that underwent extensive criticism in subsequent years in light of later developments. The first of these was the assumption that, by virtue of the railroad, land power had definitively replaced sea power as the primary mechanism of world domination. The second was the assumption of the preeminent strategic importance of the eastern hemisphere (the world island) in the calculations of global power. Both assumptions discounted the potential role of the United States as a participant in the global struggle for empire that he envisioned. Mackinder had formulated his doctrine at a time when America was just beginning to emerge as a world power of the first rank after its victory in the Spanish-American War and its acquistion of the Spanish spoils in the Caribbean and the Pacific. For the first hundred years of its history as an independent nation, the United States was able to abstain from active involvement in the power struggles that transpired across the Atlantic. The advantages of geographical isolation from Europe, Great Britain's policy of employing its naval superiority in the Atlantic to prevent the extension of great power rivalry to the western hemisphere, and the presence of weak states on its northern and southern frontiers enabled the American nation to direct its expansionist energies westward toward the Pacific. It is hardly surprising that this expansionist urge did not dissipate once the West was won. As we have seen, the hunger for land and resources that had inspired the conquest of a continent developed naturally toward the end of the century into an aspiration for empire in the Pacific and the Caribbean. In part this imperialist sentiment of the turn of the century was defensive in nature. The shrinkage of the world by the transportation revolution removed the geographical basis for isolation from world affairs just as the protective shield of British naval predominance began to disappear. As distant nations achieved the capability of projecting military power across the oceans in the form of heavily armed, coal-fired battle fleets, they were able to pose a grave menace to the United States, with its long, vulnerable coastlines. The necessity to divide its second-rank naval forces between two oceans and the difficulty of concentrating the two fleets in times of national emergency engendered a sense of vulnerability to attack by sea that stood in glaring contrast to the invincible power of the American nation on its own continent.

This sense of vulnerability to invasion by sea, along with the growing belief in the economic benefits of empire, indicated the need for a powerful American navy and a network of overseas bases and refueling stations to accommodate it. During the great age of imperialism, when Great Britain, France, and Germany acquired possessions abroad, the United States had seemed paralyzed in the posture of a passive observer while the great powers of Europe divided up the unclaimed spaces of the world and competed for control of its waterways.

The consequences of American inactivity during the age of imperialism were first drawn by the American naval strategist Alfred Thayer Mahan, whose book *The Influence of Sea Power Upon History*, published in 1890, supplied the inspiration for America's rise to world power. Writing before the advent of German, Japanese, and American naval power, when Britannia still ruled the waves, Mahan predicted that the new century would usher in developments that would revolutionize the world balance of power. Huge naval armadas, supported by global networks of bases and refueling stations, would enable the industrialized nations to wage a pitiless struggle for world domination. Any nation caught without sufficient naval power and the capacity to project and sustain it across the seas would at best be consigned to second-rank status and at worst be exposed to foreign invasion. Mahan warned that his own nation was in just such a position and faced just such a risk. The American navy throughout the nineteenth century had been designed for defense of the American coasts. The American navy of the future must represent, as the royal navy had for Great Britain, an instrument of policy to enhance the nation's power and prestige in the world.

The influence of Mahan's writings on his own country, either directly or through the mediation of his friends Theodore Roosevelt and Henry Cabot Lodge, is confirmed by the policies that signaled America's rise to the front rank of world powers: the acquisition of naval bases in the Pacific and the Caribbean, the construction of the Panama Canal, and the decision to build a battle fleet capable of operating on the high seas. But as important as Mahan's teachings may have been in promoting American imperialism and navalism at the turn of the century, they had an equally profound impact abroad, particularly in Germany. The kaiser and his chief naval strategist, Admiral Alfred von Tirpitz, learned from Mahan not only the general truth that sea power was a prerequisite to national security and prosperity in the modern world, but also that Great Britain's undisputed naval primacy was about to vanish. The rise of Japanese and American naval power in the 1890s confirmed this prediction by challenging British naval dominance in the Far East and the western hemisphere. Only by strengthening its overseas squadrons could Britain reverse this trend and regain its preeminent position abroad. But it was precisely at this moment that the advent of the German naval construction program threatened Britain's security in its home

Alfred Thayer Mahan
(1840–1914), prophet of
navalism: In his lectures at
the Naval War College and
in his writings, Mahan
called for the construction
of a large American navy
composed of giant steam-
driven, armor-plated battleships and the establishment
of foreign bases and refueling stations to accommo-
date it. His influence was
profound, not only in his
own country but also in
Germany, Great Britain,
and Japan and contributed
to the naval arms race
among these powers at the
turn of the twentieth century. *(Courtesy of the
Library of Congress)*

waters. This forced the Admiralty to deplete rather than augment its overseas naval strength in order to preserve control of the sea approaches to the British Isles.

From the subsequent testimony of its architects, we learn that Germany's turn toward navalism was intended to frighten Great Britain into entering into an alliance with Germany that would nullify the threat posed by the alliance concluded between France and Russia in 1894. Instead, it drove the British into the waiting arms of the French, who, as we have seen, renounced their old claims to Egypt in return for British cooperation against Germany in Europe. Thus the new navalism at the turn of the century had the unintended effect of restoring, at least for the short term, the centrality of the European balance of power to the forefront of British strategic concerns. The simultaneous naval challenge of the United States and Japan was accepted with equanimity in London and resulted in the relatively painless depletion of British naval strength overseas. But the combination of Germany's existing military power on the continent and its potential naval power in European waters reminded British policymakers that the greatest menace to the security of their island lay across the North Sea.

The geopolitical conception of international relations, to which the governing elites of all the major nations subscribed by the beginning of the twentieth century, presupposed a global struggle for power that inevitably ran the risk of degenerating into a general war. The great powers were thus confronted with the challenge of devising a political mechanism for the peaceful resolution of the conflicts that were bound to arise in such an unstable international environment. The avoidance of a world war until the collapse of the international order in 1914 was to a large degree attributable to the universal desire to manage international conflict by diplomatic negotiation. The Berlin Conference of 1884–85 represented an instructive precedent for the channeling of expansionist pressures in directions that would reduce the chances of great power confrontation. This gathering of representatives of the principal colonial powers succeeded in devising mutually acceptable ground rules for the European conquest of Africa that permitted each power to obtain its share so as to prevent the development of competing claims that might provoke war. Subsequently, as we have seen, bilateral arrangements were reached between France and England regarding territorial disputes in North Africa, and between England and Russia in southern Asia.

When diplomacy failed, multilateral intervention by third parties succeeded in limiting the geopolitical consequences of armed conflict. The Russo-Turkish War of 1877–78, the Sino-Japanese War of 1894–95, and the Russo-Japanese War of 1904–05 were all terminated before the victor could achieve its major objectives because of the diplomatic intervention of uninvolved powers. The traditional policy of international cooperation to preserve the balance of power in Europe was extended to the entire world in the era of imperial expansion. It reflected the powerful conviction among the ruling groups of the great powers that the prevention or at least the containment of war was essential to the preservation of the domestic and international order from which they derived their positions of power. This tacit agreement to avoid recourse to violence in the pursuit of national objectives in Europe remained in force, as we shall see, until the summer of 1914.

THE DEVELOPMENT OF AN INTERNATIONAL ECONOMY

As the great powers sought to reduce the frictions caused by unorganized imperial expansion, a related challenge was posed by the growth of an international economic system that also demanded a high degree of cooperation among the major trading nations of the world. Throughout the first half of the nineteenth century, almost all economic activity was conducted either at the local level or (in those few countries such as Great Britain and France that had succeeded in abolishing internal impediments to economic exchange) on a nationwide scale. Where international trade did exist, it was largely confined to distinct commercial regions defined by physical proximity (such as Western and Central Europe, Russia and the Baltic, and the North Atlantic) in which complementary economic systems permitted the direct exchange of products on a bilateral basis. Economic activity could not expand beyond this limited regional context until two of the principal productive factors of economic development, labor and capital, were free to migrate to regions of the earth blessed with abundant natural resources and until the goods produced by this combination of productive factors were afforded easy access to the markets of the world.

The end of the Napoleonic Wars in 1815 enabled Great Britain to concentrate its national energies on resuming the phenomenal industrial expansion that had begun in the last quarter of the eighteenth century. The restoration of peacetime conditions also promoted the growth of industrialization on the European continent as the governing elites of various states recognized the advantages of economic modernization and sought to emulate the successful British example. During the second half of the nineteenth century, the industrializing countries of Europe had begun to produce a surplus of labor and capital. In the meantime, certain undeveloped regions abroad, notably the continents of North and South America, the Pacific islands of Australia and New Zealand, and the temperate zone of southern Africa, combined the advantages of a rich endowment of natural resources with the disadvantages of an insufficient supply of labor and investment capital to exploit them. The elementary economic law of supply and demand dictated that European workers unable to obtain employment on their overpopulated continent should migrate to those underpopulated spaces with plentiful resources, cheap land, and high wages caused by domestic labor shortages. Similarly, European banks and private individuals whose accumulated savings could no longer command high interest rates at home because of the oversupply of domestic capital should have been enticed to invest abroad to obtain higher returns from the resource-rich, capital-poor areas cited above.

But attempts to expand commercial and financial activities in this economically rational way were frustrated by a combination of politically imposed constraints and technological deficiencies in transportation inherited from the preindustrial era. Tariffs, import quotas, subsidies for domestic industries, and restrictive shipping regulations inhibited the free exchange of products across national frontiers. The absence of a smoothly functioning international monetary system discouraged short-term financing of trade and long-term investment in productive enterprises abroad. The unavailability of cheap, reliable methods of transportation limited international migration of labor in search of employment.

These impediments to the free movement of labor seeking jobs, savings seeking high returns, and exports seeking markets gradually disappeared during the second half of the century. The advent of steamship and railway transportation around midcentury inaugurated a mass intercontinental and transcontinental migration unequaled before or since. More than 40 million Asians, mostly Chinese and Indians, left their homelands to go abroad as laborers. Between 1860 and 1920 over 45 million people left the grinding poverty of overpopulated Europe for the sparsely settled spaces across the seas. The United States received over half of this number, with the remainder going to other underpopulated areas of abundant natural resources and temperate climate such as Canada, Argentina, Brazil, Australia, New Zealand, and South Africa. Joining earlier emigrants who had migrated to these sparsely settled lands, successive generations of white Europeans transplanted the economic practices, social customs, and political traditions of the old world to the new. The indigenous inhabitants—the Indians and Eskimos of the western hemisphere, the aborigines of Australia, the Maori of New Zealand, the Bushmen of South Africa—were geographically segregated and reduced to economic insignificance and political impotence by their new white masters.

Accompanying this migration of skilled and semiskilled European labor to resource-rich, underpopulated areas abroad during the second half of the nineteenth century was the infusion of European capital to the undercapitalized economies of these lands of recent European settlement. France joined Great Britain as a major source of foreign investment in the 1860s. The newly unified state of Germany entered the ranks of international creditors in the 1880s as its rapidly expanding economy began to generate profits in excess of domestic demand. On the whole, these long-term foreign investments in productive enterprises were concentrated either in the industrializing nations of Southern and Eastern Europe or in the overseas regions of abundant resources and European settlement enumerated above. The United States, originally the primary recipient of European capital investment during the early phase of its industrial revolution, began itself to export capital in the 1890s to developing economies within its own region. By 1914 roughly 40 percent of total American foreign investment was in Mexico and almost 30 percent in Canada, with most of the remainder distributed among Latin American countries along the shores of the Caribbean. Though the major proportion of these investments took the form of purchases of foreign government securities to finance the budget deficits of the recipient states, an increasing proportion supplied capital to construct what economists call the "infrastructure." By this is meant public facilities that developing economies require before modern industrial and agricultural systems can function effectively: roads, railroads, ports, power plants, telegraph and telephone systems, and the like. In this way European (and, later, American) investors furnished the capital and European immigrants supplied the skilled or semiskilled labor for the productive development of overseas regions with abundant but previously untapped natural resources.

As the obstacles to immigration and foreign investment began to disappear, so too did the politically inspired impediments to international trade. Here, as in all other areas of economic development in the nineteenth century, Great Britain led the way. The drastic reduction of protective duties on agricultural imports to England (the so-called Corn Laws) in 1846 was followed in 1860 by even more substantial tariff reform that eventually opened the British market to imports without restriction. In short order France, Belgium, the Netherlands, and, later, Germany, reciprocally moderated their duties on imports. The result of this evolution toward free trade was twofold. First of all, it produced an extraordinary increase in the total volume of international commerce that far exceeded the record of any comparable period in history. Second, it stimulated the development of product specialization, which in turn promoted the growth of world trade. The case of Great Britain provides a striking example of the increasing importance of specialization and the free international exchange of products. Britain first learned the lesson that a nation could benefit from specializing in the production of those goods that were best suited to its domestic factor endowment, that is, by conserving its scarce (hence expensive) factors and drawing heavily on its abundant (hence cheap) ones. Instead of employing its surplus population and savings to grow high-cost wheat on its insufficient arable land, Britain took advantage of its abundant supply of labor and capital to produce manufactured goods, which it sold to other countries with sufficient farmland in exchange for the food it required. Britain's exports and imports tripled in value during the second half of the nineteenth century. It began (after the introduction of refrigeration in the 1870s) to receive beef from Argentina, mutton and wool from Australia, dairy products from New Zealand, as well as a host of other raw materials—iron ore, tin, copper, lead, nickel, cotton, and the like—from abroad. In return, it shipped finished manufactured products, principally textiles, which accounted for half of its total exports in the year 1880. Though the performance of other industrialized nations was less spectacular, their increasing dependence on foreign trade for their prosperity became the central fact of economic life in the modern world.

The explosive growth of world trade and foreign investment in the second half of the nineteenth century was facilitated by the perfection of a mechanism of international financial exchange centered in London. Importers and exporters found it difficult to conduct their operations in the new environment of rapidly expanding international commerce on the basis of cash on delivery. In order to finance their worldwide commercial activities, they increasingly resorted to the convenience of short-term borrowing from an emerging network of commercial banks, discount houses, and dealers in bills of exchange. This procedure permitted the exchange of products to transpire without large amounts of gold or currency having to move in either direction since most transactions could simply be cleared against one another on the books of these London financial institutions. Meanwhile, the accumulation of huge reserves of capital in the major British banks soon impelled them, as we have seen, to branch out into the business of long-term lending to foreign governments and firms. The sale of treasury bonds, railroad stocks, and other foreign securities on the London money market effectively channeled the savings of the British and other European middle classes into the developing economies of the rest of the world.

But the greatest contribution of Great Britain to the smooth functioning of the international network of trade and investment was its effective solution to the problem of foreign exchange. Since each sovereign nation of the world printed its own currency, exporters who sold products abroad accumulated foreign money reserves that obviously were of no use in discharging debts incurred at home. These exporters therefore required means whereby they could exchange the foreign currencies thus accumulated for an equivalent amount of their own. Conversely, importers had to find a way of paying for the products they purchased in the currency of the exporting country.

Throughout history, up to our own day, the major trading nations of the world have been frustrated in their attempts to establish an orderly relationship among their respective currencies in order to permit the easy exchange of goods across national frontiers. This persistent problem was effectively solved toward the end of the nineteenth century when the British pound sterling became a sort of world currency, which all of the major trading nations used to settle their international accounts. Britain's preeminent position in world trade and finance inspired universal confidence in the strength and stability of sterling. It became in the eyes of importers and exporters of goods and capital as "good as gold." Furthermore, it was as "good as gold" in a very real sense. Between 1821 and 1914 the British government faithfully kept its promise to exchange quantities of that precious metal for its national currency at a fixed price. The convenience of dealing in a paper currency that was fully convertible into gold on demand at a predetermined price enticed exporters and importers of all nations to conduct their foreign transactions in sterling. By the early 1870s all of the major nations of Europe, the United States, and several Latin American countries had in turn adopted the gold standard by linking their own currencies to gold at a fixed price. The central banks of these nations were ready to sell all the gold demanded at that price and to buy up all the gold offered at that price. The result was a system among the major world currencies of fixed exchange rates that could not fluctuate because of their relationship to a metal in limited supply whose intrinsic value was universally recognized. Never before or since has the world enjoyed such an effective mechanism for the adjustment of international accounts. The twin evils of exchange instability and inflation, which were later to plague the modern world after the collapse of the gold standard, were nonexistent in this benign era.

Thus, toward the end of the nineteenth century, the international economic system had been tightly integrated by means of a complex network of foreign trade and investment centered in London. The universal adoption of the gold standard permitted the adjustment of temporary disturbances in the international balance of payments. British banks financed international trade and supplied investment capital to developing regions. The British merchant fleet transported more than three-quarters of the total volume of world trade. British insurance companies such as Lloyds of London removed the risk of oceanic transport. The consequent expansion of world trade and investment and the effective functioning of the international monetary system was destined to continue so long as Great Britain was able to retain its preeminent commercial and financial position in world markets. But once that virtual monopoly by a single power was contested, cracks in this seemingly perfect system began to appear. Though they did not fundamentally disturb the effective functioning of the system, they foreshadowed its demise. The first of these ominous developments was the simultaneous emergence of Germany and the United States as productive economic powers of the first rank.

In the middle of the nineteenth century Great Britain was the only industrial power of any importance. By 1914 Germany had surpassed Britain in the production of pig iron and approached her output of coal. The United States, which counted for little before the 1880s, experienced the most spectacular growth of all in the ensuing thirty years. By 1914 it was the world's leading producer of coal, and its pig iron production surpassed that of Great Britain and Germany combined. The destructive effects on Britain's loss of industrial preeminence were not immediately apparent for a number of reasons. First of all, America's enormous internal market absorbed most of its domestically produced manufactured goods. Moreover, that country's impressive agricultural productivity relieved it of the necessity to export finished products to pay for imports of food. As a consequence, America's export trade represented a paltry 8 percent of its gross national product in 1913. Those American goods that were produced in excess of domestic demand came largely from the fertile farmland of the Midwest that was afforded access to foreign markets by the railroad construction of the decade after the Civil War. In 1910 fully 75 percent of American exports fell under the category of agricultural produce or semifinished manufactures, and therefore were complementary to rather than competitive with British exports.

Germany, on the other hand, lacked both the huge internal free trade zone and the advantageous condition of self-sufficiency in foodstuffs enjoyed by the United States. It therefore was driven to seek foreign outlets for trade that threatened to produce an acute commercial rivalry with Great Britain. Moreover, by concentrating on the production of finished steel products, cotton textiles, coal, and chemicals, it competed directly with the products of British industrialism. But that competition was mitigated by a mutually beneficial division of world markets. Germany directed the bulk of its export trade to Eastern and Southern Europe, a region of minimal interest to British merchants, who were content to continue profiting from their lucrative commercial relationships with the empire and with Latin America.

Even when Britain's exports of finished manufactured products failed to keep pace with its enormous imports of foodstuffs and raw materials, the resulting deficit in the balance of trade was easily covered by its "invisible exports." By this is meant income derived from investments overseas as well as from various services performed for foreign governments, corporations, or individuals such as banking, insurance, and shipping. In short, Britain's virtual monopoly on the financial and service sectors of the modern world economy afforded it sufficient annual income to balance its international accounts and even reexport a surplus in the form of additional investment in foreign enterprises. But this dependence on invisible exports to preserve its balance-of-payments surplus concealed the ominous threat to Britain's preeminence in world trade posed by the burgeoning industrial systems of Germany and the United States. A nation whose share of the world's industrial production had dropped from 25 percent in 1860 to less than 10 percent in 1913 was unmistakably on the decline in relative terms. It was clearly only a matter of time before the internal market of the United States would become saturated with the products and profits of American industrialism and before aggressive German exporters of merchandise and capital would seek overseas markets in regions previously dominated by British commercial and financial interests. German and American commercial expansion was already in evidence by the turn of the century in Latin America, a traditional British preserve. To make matters worse, Russia and Japan had entered their industrial "takeoff" period in the 1890s and were expected to enter the world market in the not-so-distant future.

These threats to Britain's commercial supremacy were accompanied by the reappearance of political obstacles to international trade throughout the world. Germany had ended its brief experiment with free trade in 1879 by imposing duties on a variety of industrial and agricultural products. France followed suit in 1892. The United States raised its tariff in 1890 and again in 1897. Other European nations quickly fell in line, so that by the turn of the century only Great Britain and the Netherlands remained committed to free trade amid this rising tide of protectionism. The resurgence of economic nationalism was a result of pressure exerted on their respective governments by domestic producers anxious to insulate their own economies from foreign competition in what was widely anticipated to be a forthcoming global contest for markets by the half dozen nations that had undergone the process of industrialization. It marked the first significant departure from the system of free exchange of productive factors upon which the new international economy of the nineteenth century depended for its survival. It foreshadowed the total collapse of the interlocked network of free trade, international finance, and intercontinental immigration, a collapse caused by the First World War.

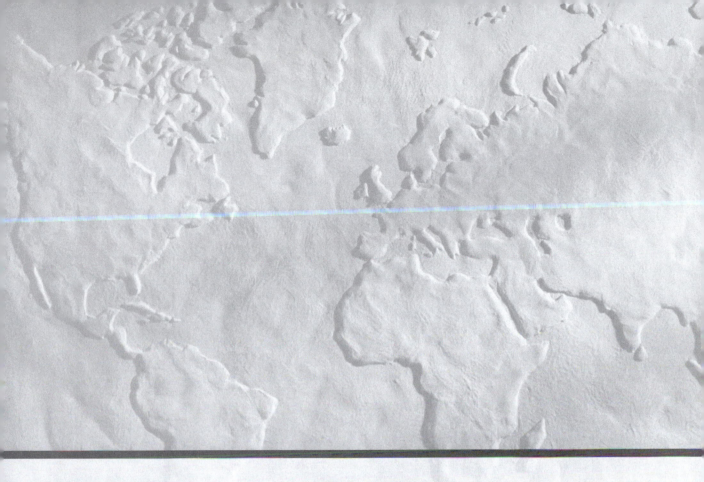

Part One   THE THIRTY YEARS' WAR (1914–1945)

1

GERMANY'S BID FOR EUROPEAN DOMINANCE (1914–1918)

THE ROAD TO ARMAGEDDON

The period from 1914 to 1945 may legitimately be designated as the Thirty Years' War of the twentieth century. No other period of comparable duration has seen so many people killed, so much property destroyed, and so much national wealth squandered. Though the land combat in the two world wars of this era was confined to the eastern hemisphere (principally on the land mass of Eurasia, but also on a reduced scale in Africa), most of the nations of the western hemisphere were at some point drawn into the contest for mastery of the eastern half of the world. The so-called interwar period of the twenties and thirties can scarcely be regarded as an era of peace. It was instead, as the French military commander Ferdinand Foch presciently predicted at the end of the First World War, a "twenty-year truce" that was punctuated by explosions of national animosities, sporadic outbreaks of violence, and great power rivalries that paved the way for the Second World War. The central participant in this thirty-year struggle was the economically advanced, militarily powerful state of Germany. The two world wars were to a large extent the result of that nation's aspiration to achieve domination of the geographical region in which it was located and the determination of other great powers in coalition to prevent it from succeeding, by diplomatic pressure during peacetime and by military force in time of war.

In the course of the 1920s it became fashionable in certain intellectual circles to deny that the German Empire bore any responsibility for the outbreak of what at the time was universally known as the "Great War." Evidence from recently published diplomatic records was marshalled by scholars and publicists to demonstrate that French vindictiveness, or Russian imperialism, or British duplicity, or a combination of all three, had been responsible for dragging Germany into the contest for European hegemony that began in the summer of 1914. The image of the bloodthirsty Hun in spiked helmet and jackboots rampaging across a prostrate continent, so graphically portrayed by the wartime propaganda agencies of the Allied governments, gradually disappeared from the scene after the

39

end of the war and the advent of the German republic in November 1918. In its place arose the contrary image of an Imperial Germany that had sought nothing more than the defense of its legitimate national interests in the face of predatory powers from east and west.

It was not until the post–World War II period that this revisionist conception of imperial Germany as victim was directly challenged by a school of historians that focused attention on the grandiose and expansionist war aims of the imperial German government and its domestic supporters. The leader of this school was a distinguished German historian, Professor Fritz Fischer, who was able to demonstrate by exhaustive research and elegant argument that the political, military, and economic elite of the Second Reich had deliberately planned and relentlessly pursued an ambitious scheme to acquire direct or indirect control of the European continent as well as parts of the Middle East and central Africa. That the other principal belligerents, France, Great Britain, Russia, and Italy, also developed imperial ambitions of their own in the course of the war Fischer did not dispute. But what emerged from his study was a massive body of evidence of an aggressive program of economic expansion and territorial acquisition meticulously planned and actively promoted by influential members of the German ruling class from the late 1890s through the final year of the First World War. Fischer's work has undergone extensive criticism in recent years. Some historians have even argued that a German military victory in 1914 would have resulted in a stable, prosperous Europe (under German domination, to be sure, but economically integrated and at peace, much like the European Union today). But Fischer's overall assessment of Germany's expansionist ambitions has (at least in the eyes of this historian) stood the test of time. Since the sources of this aggressive foreign policy are to be found in the interplay of domestic forces, a brief review of the political, economic, and military context of imperial Germany's power position in the prewar years is in order.

The political structure of the German Reich, as defined by the federal constitution of 1871, may best be described as a facade of a parliamentary monarchy superimposed upon the edifice of an authoritarian state dominated by the reactionary, militarist, landowning aristocracy of Prussia. The hereditary position of German emperor was vested in the king of Prussia, who enjoyed the exclusive power to appoint and dismiss the head of government (the chancellor), to conduct foreign relations, to command the armed forces in time of war, to convoke and adjourn the bicameral parliament, and through the chancellor, to initiate all domestic legislation. Prussian control of the upper house of the parliament (the Bundesrat) was preserved through a complex system of indirect and weighted representation together with the constitutional stipulation of a Prussian veto on legislation concerning military affairs. Even the lower house of the imperial legislature (the Reichstag), though elected by direct representation on the basis of universal male suffrage, was prevented from exercising the type of legislative authority associated with genuine parliamentary systems such as those of Great Britain and France. The chancellor was responsible to the emperor, while his cabinet ministers were responsible only to him. This meant that a government was free to remain in office without a legislative majority so long as it retained the confidence of the hereditary ruler.

The only significant power enjoyed by the democratically elected lower house was a negative one: It could deny the chancellor the funds required for the operation of the state. The periodic debates over requests for military appropriations, an issue dear to the heart of the Prussian landed elite, which monopolized the senior positions in the armed forces, afforded the Reichstag its only opportunity to circumvent the elaborate constitutional limitations on the free expressions of the popular will. But the legislative record in the years before the First World War shows that the policies of successive German governments received the active or tacit support of the principal political parties of the nation. This was true not only of the Conservative party, political mouthpiece of the Prussian landowning class (the Junkers) on which the regime was based, but also of parties representing constituencies whose interests and ideology clashed with those of the Protestant, agrarian, military caste. The Center party, vigilant defender of the rights of the Catholic minority located principally in the southern part of the country, had good reason to mount a campaign of resistance against the Protestant-dominated political apparatus in Berlin. So did the National Liberal party, which represented the industrial and commercial bourgeoisie concentrated in the western part of the nation, whose commitment to political liberalism and economic modernization seemed antithetical to the reactionary, agrarian ideology of the Junkers. The Social Democratic party, spearhead of social revolution on behalf of the industrial working class and opponent of militarism, constituted a potential source of violent opposition to the Prussian-dominated state. Yet none of these political parties mounted a sustained campaign against the authoritarian domestic structure and aggressive foreign policy of the empire. The Center party became a compliant servant of the imperial system once assured that the anticlerical campaign launched by Bismarck in the 1870s would not be revived and that the Catholics of the south would be free to practice their faith unhindered. The National Liberals sacrificed their democratic principles on the altar of class interest, accepting the undemocratic political institutions of the imperial state and supporting its expansionist foreign policy for economic reasons to be sketched below. The Social Democratic party, which by 1912 had become the largest political faction in the Reichstag, represented the most numerous and best organized industrial working class in Europe. But the German workers had been transformed into loyal subjects of the empire as a result of the progressive system of social insurance inaugurated by Bismarck in the 1880s. Its unprecedented provisions for medical insurance and old age pensions, followed in the 1890s by health and safety regulations in factories, afforded the German proletariat more economic benefits and better working conditions than those enjoyed by its counterparts in other industrial nations. It is therefore no surprise that the German Social Democratic party ceased to take seriously the rhetoric of class conflict and evolved into a party of the loyal opposition, signaling its tacit acceptance of the undemocratic political system from which its working-class constituency derived such extensive economic advantages.

The authoritarian political structure of imperial Germany was reinforced by two striking features of the German economic system that sharply distinguished it from the economic systems of other industrialized nations. The first was the remarkable degree of cooperation between the agricultural interests centered in East Prussia and the industrial, commercial, and financial interests in the west. Whereas industrialization had been achieved in other countries (such as England) at the expense of the landowning class, the German industrial revolution was marked by a marriage of convenience between large-scale agriculture and heavy industry that promoted the expansion of the latter without threatening the socioeconomic position of the former. Both sectors of the German economic system campaigned for and benefited from the protectionist commercial policies inaugurated by the government in 1879. The agricultural estates of East Prussia were shielded from competition from Russian and American grain, while the heavy industry centered in the Rhineland-Westphalia region of the west secured the privilege of dominating the domestic market for manufactured products. This alliance of "rye and steel" saved the Prussian Junkers from the fate of the landed gentry in England, which had earlier been faced with the alternative of socioeconomic decline or accession to the industrial class through intermarriage or business partnership.

The second striking feature of the German economy at the turn of the century was the extent of its concentration and centralization. The key sectors of heavy industry (iron, steel, coal, armaments, chemicals, and electrical products) were dominated by a handful of gigantic firms that had acquired a degree of control over production and distribution unmatched in the industrial world of that time. The cartelization of heavy industry was actively promoted by the imperial government through a wide range of public subsidies and protective legislation. At the same time, the German financial system was undergoing a similar process of concentration. By 1913 the four largest banking houses controlled 65 percent of the capital reserves of the nation and were closely linked to the oligopolistic industrial firms of the Rhineland-Westphalia complex through a system of interlocking directorates.

This formidable concentration of economic power, which united heavy industry, big agriculture, and high finance in a close partnership with the government, produced a spectacular spurt of economic growth in the quarter century before the First World War. A comparison with other industrial nations reveals that Germany had far outdistanced its continental rivals and had overtaken Great Britain as the most productive economic power in Europe. But the future of this economic dynamism seemed threatened by an ominous statistic: Between 1887 and 1912, while the value of German exports increased 185.4 percent per year, the value of German imports rose 243.8 percent. This dramatic surge in imports, which far surpassed that of any other industrial country, signified to the industrial magnates and their government patrons that German prosperity was becoming critically dependent on foreign sources of industrial raw materials and foodstuffs. Equally as disconcerting was the shift in the direction of Germany's foreign trade away from Europe and toward distant markets and sources of supply in the southern hemisphere.

These circumstances were not in themselves sufficient cause for alarm. After all, Great Britain had managed to prosper amid an even more pronounced dependence on imports from far-off lands by exporting its manufactured surpluses in exchange. Theoretically, Germany needed only to expand its exports of finished industrial products to cover its mounting trade deficit. But therein lay what many German industrialists feared was the insuperable limit to future economic growth. The markets of the world were being penetrated, dominated, and increasingly monopolized by the three global economic powers: the United States in Latin America, Great Britain in East and South Africa and in South Asia, and (to a lesser extent) France in West Africa, the Balkans, and Russia. Soon the Russian and Japanese empires could be expected to enter the competition for economic advantage in the Far East. Where could Germany turn for new sources of raw materials and foodstuffs as well as the markets for its manufactured products with which to pay for them?

Virtually every attempt to expand Germany's economic power beyond its traditional sphere of activity met with disappointment after the turn of the century. Efforts to penetrate the economies of North Africa, the Balkan states, and the Ottoman Empire encountered stiff competition from British and French firms that had previously obtained footholds there. In the two decades before 1914, France had become the principal source of capital investment for the fledgling nations of the Balkan peninsula as well as for the Russian Empire as it entered the first stage of industrialization. These financial relationships began to incite German fears of economic encirclement by Slavic states to the east and south bankrolled by the traditional Gallic enemy to the west. Even the Ottoman Empire, a prime object of German economic ambition since the turn of the century, had begun to receive massive infusions of British and French capital. The fear of economic encirclement in Europe and the Middle East was heightened by ominous indications that the remainder of the world was being informally partitioned into spheres of economic interest by Great Britain, France, the United States, and Japan.

This concern about the limits to German economic growth coincided with the mounting apprehension in military circles about the undeniable fact that the German Empire was losing its margin of strategic superiority in Europe over the combined armed forces of France and Russia. The Franco-Russian Alliance of 1894 had imposed upon German strategic planners the heavy burden that Bismarck's diplomacy had successfully avoided, namely, that of having to contemplate the possibility of a war on two fronts. With France and Russia committed to defend each other against a German military attack, the necessity to divide Germany's forces between east and west seemed to preclude the type of rapid breakthrough that had been achieved against France in 1870, when France had no ally in the east. Count Alfred von Schlieffen, chief of the imperial general staff from 1892 to 1906, had devised a war plan that purported to overcome the strategic disadvantage caused by the Franco-Russian Alliance. It envisioned the concentration of German military power in the west in the expectation that the numerically inferior French army could be defeated within a six-week period, after which the bulk of the German forces could be transferred to the eastern front to meet the Russian army before it could penetrate Germany's denuded eastern defenses. The Schlieffen Plan rested on two critical assumptions. The first was the preservation of overwhelming German numerical superiority against France. The second was the inability of the Russian Empire, with its primitive system of land transportation, to project its numerically superior army into German territory before the knockout blow in the west. To the consternation of German military strategists, both of these assumptions were undermined by developments in the years before 1914. In 1913 France extended the period of national military service from two to three years. This meant that, despite its stationary population, France would be able to field a frontline army equal to the size of the German army by 1915 or 1916. In the meantime, the Russian government had launched, with French financial assistance, an ambitious program of strategic railway construction linking central Russia with the western frontier. Since the peacetime size of the Russian army exceeded that of the German and Austro-Hungarian armies combined, the possibility that at some future date this mass military force could be rapidly transported to the German border undermined the strategic assumptions of the Schlieffen Plan and caused considerable anxiety among military circles in Berlin.

It was but a short step from this apprehension of economic encirclement and military inferiority to the advocacy of preventive war. The temptation of a quick, surgical strike against France in the manner of 1870 was reinforced by the conviction that a delay of two or three years might prove fatal to Germany's preeminent position in Europe. With

France and Russia removed as counterweights to Germany on the continent, Germany could proceed to rearrange the balance of power to suit its military and economic requirements. The cause of economic expansion and preventive war received strong support from numerous pressure groups in German society that represented a wide range of socioeconomic and professional interests. The officers' corps of the army, in conjunction with expansionist-minded civilians in the Pan-German League, pressed for territorial annexations that would simultaneously remove the strategic menace of France and Russia. The upper echelons of the navy, supported by the propagandistic activities of the Navy League, advocated the construction of a fleet equal to Great Britain's and the acquisition of bases and coaling stations abroad. The interlocked interests of heavy industry and high finance encouraged the government to obtain, by diplomatic pressure if possible or military means if necessary, privileged access to the resources and markets of the continent that the German economy required to sustain its dynamic growth.

Amid this atmosphere of fear mingled with ambition, the long-simmering dispute between Germany's ally Austria-Hungary and the independent Balkan kingdom of Serbia boiled over in the summer of 1914 in such a way as to furnish the Reich with its most promising opportunity for a preventive war against France and Russia. On June 28 the heir to the Habsburg throne, Archduke Franz Ferdinand, was assassinated while attending military maneuvers in the city of Sarajevo, the capital of Bosnia, one of the two former Turkish provinces in the Balkans that had been occupied militarily by Austria-Hungary in 1878 and then annexed outright in 1908. The absorption of this region by the Germanic empire to the north had incited the violent opposition not only of its Slavic inhabitants, but also of their ethnic kin across the frontier who dreamed of a Greater Serbia that would include the two annexed provinces. The precise details of the conspiracy that led to the death of the archduke and his wife, including the complicity of the chief of Serbian military intelligence, were not revealed until long after the event and therefore had no bearing on the decisions that were promptly taken by the Austro-Hungarian government in response to it. All that was known for certain at the time was that the assassins were ethnic Serbs and that they had committed their crime in the hotbed of Pan-Slavist sentiment within the Habsburg Empire. The immediate significance of the episode was that it afforded the authorities in Vienna a convenient pretext for suppressing once and for all this menace to the cohesion of that empire by striking at the adjacent state that assisted and promoted it.

It was well-known to the German government that an Austro-Hungarian military operation against Serbia was almost certain to provoke the intervention of Russia on behalf of its Slavic protégé in Southern Europe. Russia had already suffered a major blow to its power and prestige in the Balkans by acquiescing in the Austrian annexation in 1908 of the two former Turkish provinces that had been earmarked by Pan-Serb enthusiasts for inclusion in a large south Slav state ruled from Belgrade. No one expected a repetition of such inaction on Russia's part while the Habsburg Empire consolidated its control of the Balkans by annihilating the only pro-Russian Slavic state in the region. It was likewise probable that a war between Austria-Hungary and Russia would set in motion the provisions of the competing alliance systems to which those two empires belonged and therefore bring the entire continent to the brink of armed conflict. With full appreciation of these likely consequences, Berlin deliberately encouraged Vienna to issue a humiliating ultimatum to Belgrade on July 23 concerning the investigation of the assassination that the Serbian government could not accept in its entirety without sacrificing its sovereign status. Moreover, the German government assured the Austrian government of its unqualified support in the event of hostilities, and then proceeded to sabotage the efforts of the British government to mediate this bilateral, regional dispute. The expiration of the ultimatum led to an Austrian declaration of war against Serbia on July 28, which in turn provoked the expected decision in Saint Petersburg for a partial Russian mobilization against Austria the following day. But the tsar and his political entourage soon learned that the Russian general staff had no operational plan for a limited mobilization against Austria alone, believing as it did that a war with one of the Germanic empires would inevitably involve the other. Hence, the tsar was induced to authorize a full mobilization on July 30 as a precautionary step to protect Russia's frontier with Germany during the forthcoming showdown with Austria. Here was the first instance of military planning and preparation constraining the decision-making authority of the civilian leadership during the crisis. The second was to come when the German high command reminded the government in Berlin that a war against Russia alone was precluded by the German war plan, which dictated an offensive against France to remove it from the war prior to the concentration of German forces in the east against Russia. Hence, an ultimatum was issued from Berlin to Paris which, like the earlier one from Vienna to Belgrade, was designed by its blatantly unacceptable provisions to serve as the pretext for war: France was required to affirm its absolute neutrality in the forthcoming Russo-German war and to transfer to Germany's temporary custody the border fortresses of Toul and Verdun as proof of good faith. In short, as the Balkan dispute degenerated into a war involving most of Europe at the end of July 1914, officials in Berlin did what they could to ensure that this opportunity for a preventive showdown with France and Russia would not be lost. Germany stood an excellent chance of defeating the combined forces of its two adversaries at the opposite ends of Europe in its present state of military superiority. In two or three years, that advantage might very well be lost.

The possibility of British intervention on the side of France and Russia in the impending war on the continent was discounted in Berlin. Some German officials entertained the naive hope that if the tsar could be induced to mobilize his army first (as indeed he did), British public opinion would refuse to assist what could be made to appear as a Russian war of aggression. More realistic observers knew that the German war plan in the west, which presupposed the invasion of France through the rolling hills of Belgium, would precipitate Britain's entry in the war. This assessment was not based on Britain's commitment to the preservation of Belgian neutrality codified in a treaty of 1839. Such obligations could be conveniently renounced in the name of national interest, as Germany, also a guarantor of Belgian neutrality, promptly proved. Britain's intervention was foreordained because of its long-standing policy of refusing to permit any hostile power to obtain control of the opposite coast of the English Channel as a potential springboard for an invasion of the British Isles. The likelihood of British intervention was accepted with equanimity by Germany because of the universal expectation of a war of brief duration, as in 1870. Britain's naval superiority was useless to prevent the German military conquest of France in the six-week campaign projected by the updated version of the Schlieffen Plan. The small British professional army of 150,000 counted for nothing against the

Europe in the First World War

1.5 million German conscripts that were to be hurled against France. After the lightning victory against France and the removal of the small British military contingent from the continent, Germany would be free to concentrate on destroying Russian military power in Eastern Europe. Britain, with whom Germany had no serious quarrel, could then be offered a separate peace that would confirm German dominance of the continent.

As all of the great powers of Europe except Italy* entered the war in the first few days of August, the governments of the belligerent states began to develop and articulate their respective war aims. The first government to define in considerable detail the concrete objectives it expected to achieve by military victory was that of Germany. Chancellor Theobold von Bethmann-Hollweg strove to mobilize a broadly based domestic consensus in support of the war effort by establishing a persuasive justification for his government's decision to resort to force. This was particularly necessary in the context of the German political situation in 1914. As noted earlier, the Social Democratic party, led by persistent critics of military expenditures and advocates of international cooperation, had become the strongest party in the Reichstag by 1912; the Socialist trade unions constituted the largest mass political organization in imperial Germany. In order to forestall left-wing parliamentary opposition to military appropriations and labor agitation against the mobilization decrees, the government was confronted with the necessity of converting the Social Democrats and the union organizations they represented to the cause of war. It was widely known that the German Left was prepared to oppose any attempt to transform the forthcoming conflict into a war of conquest. Thus the Socialist leaders were persuaded to support the war effort as a "defensive" operation against the imperialist aggression of tsarist Russia. On August 4 the Social Democrats joined the other political parties in declaring a "party truce" in the Reichstag. Unity on the home front was thus ensured at the very beginning of the war.

Once the support of all political parties for the German war effort was secured, the government's public references to a "defensive war" to prevent "encirclement" receded into the background; in their place appeared talk about the necessity to obtain "guarantees" against future military aggression and economic competition on the continent. In this way the defensive rhetoric, intended to allay the suspicions of the German Left and neutralize domestic opposition, rapidly evolved into an ambitious project for continental domination. The German government's war aims were first specified in a statement by Chancellor Bethmann-Hollweg on September 9, 1914. In spite of several temporary deviations and modifications in the course of the war, this "September Program" remained the basis of German military objectives until the Bolshevik Revolution and the subsequent withdrawal of Russia from the war. Thenceforth it was extended to embrace an even more grandiose scheme of German military and economic expansion that had been devised by German economic interests at the beginning of the war.

The September Program of the German government sketched the nation's military and economic war aims during the period of great optimism, as the German army seemed on the verge of overwhelming the Anglo-French defenses in the west. The military plan called for the permanent destruction of French military power through the annexation of the territory containing France's principal fortresses along the German frontier, the occupation of France's major ports on the English Channel, and imposition of a crushing financial indemnity that would prevent the reconstruction of France's armed forces in the foreseeable future. Belgium would be compelled to cede her strategic fortresses and permit the establishment of German bases on the Flanders coast (which, in conjunction with the French Channel ports, would constitute a formidable barrier to the reintroduction of

*Italy renounced her treaty obligations to Germany and Austria-Hungary under the Triple Alliance on the grounds that the two Germanic empires had become engaged in an offensive rather than a defensive war.

British military power on the continent). Once such a punitive peace was imposed upon France and Belgium, Russia was to be systematically "thrust back as far as possible from Germany's eastern frontier and her domination over the non-Russian peoples broken." The removal of France from the ranks of the great powers, the exclusion of Great Britain from continental affairs, and the expulsion of Russian power from Europe would definitively establish imperial Germany as the hegemonic power on the continent. France was then to be offered a pact of mutual cooperation; Great Britain would be given the choice of withdrawing from the war or enduring air attacks launched from ports on the French and Belgian coast.

Closely linked to this military plan for German hegemony in Europe was a project for continental economic domination developed by a group of German bankers and industrialists headed by Walter Rathenau (a leading figure in the electrical industry cartel) and Arthur von Gwinner (director of the Deutsche Bank). These spokesmen for German heavy industry and high finance were motivated by the fear that their country was destined to suffer economic decline unless it obtained control of the resources and markets of the entire continent of Europe to match the gigantic economic blocs of the United States (with Latin America), the British Empire, and the Russian colossus to the east. The recommended method for forging a German-controlled continental bloc was the establishment of "Mitteleuropa." This loosely defined term denoted a total customs union between Germany and the Austro-Hungarian Empire, the annexation of the French iron fields of Lorraine, the economic absorption of Belgium and Luxemburg, and the eventual establishment of a European common market through customs treaties linking the German–Austro-Hungarian bloc to France, Italy, Belgium, the Netherlands, Denmark, and such other independent European states as would wish to adhere.

The principal objective of these spokesmen for German heavy industry was the rectification of the potentially serious economic problem of insufficient supplies of industrial raw materials, particularly those required for the production of steel. Though blessed with sufficient quantities of high-grade coking coal located in the Ruhr Valley and Upper Silesia, Germany's prewar steel industry had become heavily dependent on the iron ore of French Lorraine directly across the border. In 1914 German iron ore reserves totaled 2.3 billion tons compared to France's 8.2 billion tons (of which 2.755 billion were located to the adjacent sector of French Lorraine). Thus, the annexation of the French ore fields would have more than doubled Germany's iron reserves, according it self-sufficiency while severely weakening the French iron and steel industry as a potential competitor in the postwar period.

Other regions offered tempting targets as well. The representatives of German heavy industry advocated the acquisition of the ore fields of Belgium and control of the coal, iron, manganese, oil, and grain of Poland and southern Russia. The economic value of Belgium and a reconstituted Poland coincided with their strategic value as barriers to Anglo-French military power in the west and Russian military power in the east. Plans for the disposition of Belgium varied from outright annexation to military occupation of strategic fortresses and ports, control of the transportation system, customs and currency union with Germany, and administrative partition into Dutch-speaking Flanders and French-speaking Wallonia. The plan to resurrect Poland as a German client state in the east was complicated, however, by the existence of a substantial Polish population in the German territories of Posen and West Prussia that would be potentially susceptible to the attraction of a reconstituted Polish state. In the eyes of some planners, that problem could best be resolved by deporting the Poles from the German to the Russian sector and replacing them with German colonists, who would establish a "frontier strip" to secure Germany's eastern barrier against the Slavs.

With the failure of the German war plan in the autumn of 1914 came the realization that these ambitious military and economic objectives were unlikely to be achieved by force of arms alone in the foreseeable future. The intervention of Britain and the successful defense of Paris, together with the unexpectedly rapid mobilization of the Russian army in the east, produced a stationary front and the prospect of a drawn-out war of attrition. The unprecedented firepower supplied by the machine gun and the heavy artillery piece totally transformed the nature of warfare. The belligerents were compelled to forsake whatever expectations of speedy victory that they had entertained. The infantry forces were issued the only mechanism with which they could escape the murderous barrage of firepower, the trenching spade, and ordered to dig into the earth. By Christmas 1914, the wasteland of northern France and Belgium was honeycombed with an interlocking network of underground trenches stretching from the Swiss border to the English Channel. Though the war in the east was marked by greater mobility and more frequent exchanges of territory, it too bogged down into a stalemate by the onset of the winter snows.

THE DOMESTIC CONSEQUENCES OF TOTAL WAR

The truism that "generals tend to fight the last war" applies equally to their civilian superiors and should come as no surprise in the case of those in authority during the Great War. The generation of military and political leaders who supervised their respective nations' war effort in 1914 had reached maturity during a half-century of European peace. The wars of recent memory were those fought in conjunction with the political unification of Italy and Germany between 1859 and 1871. These had been brief, mobile engagements with limited political objectives whose outcome had been determined by such short-term, technical factors as tactical finesse and the efficiency of mobilization and troop transport. These conflicts had lasted for no more than a few months and required only minimal disruption of civilian life behind the lines. Under the sway of this historical experience, none of the leadership groups of the belligerent states in the First World War had thought it necessary to devise plans for sustaining a conflict of long duration. But the establishment of stationary fronts in the autumn of 1914 had produced an entirely novel type of warfare. The clash of armies in the field was rapidly overshadowed by an epic confrontation of whole peoples. It became the first total war in history, when events at the battlefront were directly experienced by the civilian population, giving rise to the term "home front." The challenge of mobilizing the human and material resources of entire societies caused a revolutionary transformation in the domestic institutions of the belligerent nations.

The most fundamental domestic transformation wrought by the advent of total war was the centralization and regimentation of economic activity. It had rapidly dawned on the ruling elites of Europe that the successful prosecution of a war of indefinite duration would require the production and distribution of war-related materials on an unprecedented scale. All of the combatant nations experienced a severe shortage of munitions and the inability to produce sufficient quantities of artillery shells to meet the demand. The conscription of farmers and agricultural laborers caused a serious decline in food production. The imposition of the British naval blockade disrupted the Central Powers' access to foreign sources of foodstuffs and raw materials. The German occupation of France's most productive industrial region in the northeast deprived that nation of vital resources and factories. The closing of the Baltic Sea by Germany and of the Dardanelles by Germany's ally, Turkey, curtailed Russia's ability to import essential materials from foreign suppliers during the winter months, when the Arctic and Pacific ports were frozen over. When the private sector of the economy proved incapable of resolving the impending supply crisis, governments proceeded to acquire extensive control over all branches of production and distribution related to the war effort. Requisitioning of vital resources and transport facilities, the passage of laws forbidding the production of luxury items, the promotion of substitutes and synthetics, the rationing of food and fuel, and the control of foreign trade all constituted unprecedented intrusions of state power in industrial, agricultural, and commercial affairs. The prospect of labor shortages and social unrest prompted the passage of legislation severely restricting labor union activity and authorizing longer working hours and the employment of women and unskilled workers in the war plants.

With the mobilization of domestic production and labor came the mobilization of capital. Stringent controls of foreign exchange transactions were imposed to stem the flow of domestic capital abroad. Increased taxation and the domestic sale of treasury securities failed to meet the ever-expanding capital requirements of the wartime economies. The growing dependence on foreign sources of raw materials and foodstuffs impelled the governments of France and Britain to borrow the securities of foreign governments and private corporations held by their citizens. They then resold these securities on the open market and used the proceeds to purchase essential products in neutral countries such as the United States, Switzerland, and Scandinavian and Latin American nations.

Such regimentation abruptly removed the relatively liberal conditions of economic intercourse that had governed the prewar era. No longer did individual citizens enjoy the freedom to sell their labor and services to the highest bidder or to invest their savings how and where they pleased. No longer could businesses import or export products according to their commercial requirements. The wartime needs of the state replaced the free market as the mechanism for the allocation of scarce resources, labor, and capital. The prospect of a seemingly interminable war fought by mechanized forces placed a premium on economic organization: Ultimate victory would come to those nations capable of mobilizing and deploying the greatest amount of human and material resources in the most efficient manner.

STALEMATE, SLAUGHTER, AND THE WAR OF WORDS

The periodic attempts to achieve a decisive breakthrough in the land war merely confirmed the futility of hurling unarmored human flesh against the devastating firepower of the machine gun and heavy artillery. The casualty figures of the abortive offensives reached almost suicidal proportions: In the battle of the Somme from July 1 to November 18, 1916, the Germans and British lost 400,000 each and the French 200,000. The reward for the combined Anglo-French casualties of over 600,000 was a maximum advance of about

Three British soldiers in trench, under fire, during World War I: The horrendous casualties caused by the machine gun and heavy artillery during the early offensives of the war led to the "stalemate of the trenches." Protected from firepower by their underground shelters, the soldiers would be periodically ordered "over the top" in desperate attempts to achieve a breakthrough that resulted only in greater and greater casualties. *(Courtesy of the Library of Congress)*

seven miles. In the same year, the Germans conducted a ten-month siege of the French fortress at Verdun at a cost of 336,000 men while the French army's successful defense was paid for with 350,000 lives. At Passchendaele in 1917 over 370,000 British soldiers perished in order to gain forty-five square miles of mud and shell holes.

To meet the challenge to offensive warfare posed by the machine gun, both sides sought technological breakthroughs to restore mobility to firepower. The airplane, successfully tested in the United States in 1903 and first employed in warfare by the Italians against the Turks in 1911, was originally limited to observation use. Neither side interfered with the reconnaissance flights of the other until it became evident that the information thus obtained was of considerable use to the armies facing each other below. Thereafter machine guns were mounted in the observer's cockpit to enable each side to destroy the planes used by the other. When the Dutch aerial engineer Anthony Fokker designed for the Germans an interrupter gear, which synchronized machine gun fire with the propeller so that bullets could avoid the blades, airplanes became deadly gun platforms and the fighter plane was born. But aside from adding a dash of heroism and glamour to the dreary, slogging land war, the aerial duels had no effect on the outcome of the struggle. Even the German bombing raids of Great Britain, which resulted in 1,300 deaths and 3,000 injuries as well as considerable material damage, paled in comparison to the damage wrought to men and property by the guns on land. The smallness of the planes and the inaccuracy of the bombs prevented aerial warfare from breaking the stalemate.

The technological instrument that finally restored the advantage to the offensive by challenging the supremacy of the stationary machine gun was masterminded by a British colonel named Ernest Swinton. His idea for ensuring the mobility of the machine gun in difficult terrain and the protection of its operator against enemy fire consisted of mounting it on Caterpillar tractors that had been used to tow heavy artillery behind the lines and armoring them for offensive action. Once adopted and put into use by the British army, the tank (as the strange-looking contraption was called) revolutionized land warfare and gave the Western allies the wherewithal to penetrate the stationary lines of the enemy. But in spite of great success in the first major use of tanks by the British during the Battle of Cambrai in November 1917, lack of imagination kept the allies from fully exploiting their new weapon to the fullest extent possible. It was only at the time of the dying gasp of the final German offensive in August 1918 that the efficacy of the tank was demonstrated beyond all doubt, as the British Fourth Army used 450 of the new machines to pierce the German defenses near Amiens as part of the Allied counteroffensive that brought the war to an end.

The senseless carnage on the battlefield, together with the economic hardship endured by the civilian populations, severely tested the morale of the belligerent nations. With the prospect of victory fading further into the future, the wartime governments were obliged to devise means of persuading their own citizens that the sacrifice was worthwhile and those in the enemy camp that it was not. The maintenance of morale at home necessitated the suppression of domestic political criticism of the war effort. Accordingly, the Russian tsar suspended the Duma for the duration of the war in September 1915. In Germany the Political Bureau of the General Staff established a virtual military dictatorship. By 1917 Prime Minister David Lloyd George in England and Premier Georges Clemenceau in France had acquired emergency powers unprecedented in parliamentary regimes, governing through war cabinets in utmost secrecy. The limitation on legislative checks on executive authority was accompanied by measures to forestall opposition from press and people. Censorship of newspapers and periodicals prevented the expression of antiwar sentiment and the publication of accurate casualty figures. People suspected of being enemy sympathizers as well as those refusing military conscription on conscientious grounds were interned or otherwise subjected to limitations on their civil liberties.

The conduct of political warfare behind enemy lines began early in the war as a deliberate policy of the German government. The presence of large numbers of discontented ethnic, religious, and social groups within the British, French, and Russian empires seemed to offer a tempting target for German propaganda. The principal objects of this strategy were the Islamic populations of North Africa, Egypt, India, and southern Russia. The German emperor's Damascus speech in 1898 had established his credentials as the "protector" of the 300 million Muslims of the earth. The military alliance between Germany and Turkey signed on August 2, 1914, resulted in the proclamation by the Ottoman sultan (in his capacity of caliph, or Muslim religious leader) of a jihad, or holy war, which enjoined the followers of Mohammed to rise up in rebellion against their Christian European masters. German financial subsidies flowed into the coffers of Islamic nationalist movements opposed to the rule of London, Paris, and Saint Petersburg. Similar campaigns were mounted by the German government to foment insurrection among the non-Russian Christian peoples of the tsarist empire. Emigrés from Russian Poland, Finland, Ukraine, Georgia, and Armenia received subsidies and encouragement from German officials for their movements of "national liberation" against Russian oppression. At the same time, the

German government established contact with and supplied funds to various revolutionary Russian emigré groups in Switzerland and Scandinavia. Foremost among these was the Russian Social Democratic (more commonly known as Bolshevik) party, which alone among the major working-class parties of Europe had actively opposed its government's war effort from the start and continued to press for social revolution at home.

The object of the German government's multifaceted propaganda campaign was twofold: to pin down British, French, and Russian military forces in counterinsurgency operations behind the lines and to acquire a reputation (both in neutral countries such as the United States and among progressive forces in the enemy camp) as the protector of "oppressed peoples" and the champion of the right of national and political self-determination. Throughout the first three years of the war, these German efforts to incite domestic insurrection in the empires of the Entente powers were uniformly unsuccessful. The abortive "Easter Rebellion" in Ireland of 1916, which received the active support of Berlin in the form of rifles, machine guns, ammunition, and explosives, is a notable example of such lost opportunities.

Germany's dual strategy of forming a continental economic-military bloc controlled from Berlin while promoting the disintegration of the British, French, and Russian empires provoked a series of similar countermeasures from the governments of the Triple Entente. Indeed, it is important to note, as many critics of the Fischer thesis concerning Germany's war aims cited at the beginning of this chapter have reminded us, that the member states of the anti-German coalition promptly developed war aims of their own that equaled Germany's in their grandiosity and aggressiveness. In the realm of foreign economic policy, the Allied governments formulated plans for the continuation of inter-Allied economic cooperation after the war in order to shatter the economic foundations of the Central Powers. Just as this economic strategy represented a competitive response to the German Mitteleuropa project, the political strategy of the Entente constituted the reverse side of the German campaign on behalf of revolution behind enemy lines. Great Britain concentrated on inciting an Arab-Muslim revolution within the Turkish Empire; France directed its political warfare campaign at the national groups languishing under Austro-Hungarian rule (principally the Czechs, the Poles, and the southern Slavs of the Balkan peninsula); even Russia paid lip service to the cause of national self-determination by offering independence to Poland under Russian protection in an effort to win the sympathy of the Polish populations of Austrian Galicia and German Posen and West Prussia.

The Entente project for economic warfare against the Central Powers was broached at the Paris Economic Conference held in June 1916. Representatives of Britain, France, Italy, Russia, Belgium, Portugal, and Japan met to discuss ways of giving permanent form to the measures of inter-Allied economic cooperation that had been adopted during the war. The French and British delegations pressed for the creation of an inter-Allied economic bloc linked by preferential tariffs, the pooling of raw materials and shipping, and joint management of financial and currency affairs. Though the resolutions adopted at the Paris Conference fell considerably short of Anglo-French expectations on account of the hesitations of Italy and Russia, they elicited sharp reactions in enemy and neutral countries. The Paris Accords seemed to signify the definitive end of the era of free trade and the beginning of an effort by the anti-German coalition to subdivide most of the world into politically organized regional markets and zones of raw materials. An economic bloc linking the British, French, Russian, Italian, Belgian, Portuguese, and Japanese empires would have sealed off virtually the entirety of Africa and Asia as well as most of Europe from economic competition from the Central Powers and neutral countries such as the United States. Germany would thereupon encounter a form of economic strangulation far worse than the "encirclement" that had allegedly threatened her before 1914.

Linked to this Entente objective of economic warfare against the Central Powers and their allies was the political strategy of inciting nationalist revolution within the states of the German coalition. The first victim of this policy was the Ottoman Empire, which had entered the war on the side of the Central Powers in October 1914 and whose contribution to the German war effort had been much more valuable than anticipated: The closing of the Turkish Straits had sealed off Russia from her European allies; the Anglo-French effort to force Turkey out of the war in the Dardenelles expedition of 1915 was a costly failure. Turkish pressure on Egypt diverted British forces that might have been deployed elsewhere. But the sultan's appeal for an Islamic holy war against the European nations had failed to rouse his Arab subjects, for whom hatred of Turkish overlordship surpassed in intensity the historic grievance against the Christian West. The Arabs' reluctance to join their Turkish coreligionists afforded the British a promising opportunity to solicit their support for the Allied cause. Negotiations were opened with Hussein, Grand Sharif of Mecca, the most obvious candidate to contest the Ottoman sultan's authority in the Arab world. The results of these discussions were incorporated in correspondence between the Sharif Hussein and the British High Commissioner in Egypt, Sir Henry McMahon, between July 1915 and February 1916. The British government pledged its support for the independence of most of the Arab provinces of the Ottoman Empire in exchange for the declaration of an Arab revolt against Turkish rule. On June 10, 1916, Hussein raised the Arabs in rebellion and was soon joined by various chieftains on the Arabian peninsula. The Arab insurrection pinned down some thirty-thousand Turkish troops and helped to keep the Red Sea open to Allied shipping. The British military advance from Egypt to Palestine and Syria in 1917–18 was greatly assisted by guerrilla operations against the Turks mounted by Arab contingents in contact with British officers such as the legendary T. E. Lawrence. As will be seen, British support of Arab nationalism was compromised by agreements concluded with rival claimants to Turkish territory. But for the remainder of the war the strategy was effective in curtailing the Ottoman Empire's capacity to fulfill its obligations to its Germanic allies.

In the meantime the Western powers also used their weapons of political warfare to promote nationalist rebellion within the Austro-Hungarian Empire. This policy was initially developed in response to the invitation of the American president, Woodrow Wilson, on December 20, 1916, for the belligerents to specify their war aims. The Germans refused, but the Entente replied on January 10, 1917, with the first public enunciation of the goals that its member states were ostensibly fighting to attain. In addition to the obvious demand for the evacuation of Belgian, French, Russian, Serbian, and Romanian territory under German military occupation, the Allied governments explicitly formulated for the first time their commitment to the "principle of national self-determination." This referred to the liberation of the Italian, Romanian, southern Slav, Czechoslovak, and Polish subject nationalities of the Habsburg Empire, which unmistakably meant the disintegration of that multinational state into its constituent ethnic regions. Such a pronouncement had the dual advantage of arousing American sympathy for the Entente's war effort while appealing to the subject nationalities of Germany's principal ally to cast off the yoke of their German-speaking masters in Vienna. Instances of mutiny and desertion in the Austro-Hungarian army had already occurred before the Entente's call to arms. They increased thereafter, particularly as exile groups representing the various ethnic factions established headquarters in Paris and fanned the flames of nationalist rebellion behind the enemy lines.

These Allied expressions of sympathy for the cause of national liberation within the two multinational empires in the enemy camp were no less fraudulent than Germany's hypocritical pose as the champion of the Muslims and other subject nationalities of the British, French, and Russian empires. The British government's promise of support for the independence of Turkey's Arab provinces was flatly contradicted by a series of agreements concluded with its allies in the course of the war, which provided for the partition of the non-Turkish portion of the Ottoman Empire into "spheres of interest" among England, France, Italy, and Russia. To complicate further the postwar situation in the Ottoman domains, an official declaration by Britain's foreign secretary, Arthur Balfour, in November 1917 endorsed the proposal advanced by the European devotees of Zionism* for the establishment of a Jewish homeland in Palestine, a Turkish-controlled territory on the eastern Mediterranean, which at the time contained roughly 60,000 Jewish inhabitants out of a total population of 750,000 who were mainly Arabs.

In a similar way the commitment to the subject peoples of the Austro-Hungarian Empire was critically compromised in February–March 1917, when France authorized Russia "to fix her western frontiers as she wished" (a euphemistic phrase that had the effect of sacrificing the independence of Poland). This concession was tendered in return for Russian support for France's acquisition of Alsace-Lorraine and the coal mines of the Saar basin as well as the establishment of an independent state in the Rhineland under French military protection. In April 1915 Italy had been promised territory along the Adriatic coast in direct violation of the principle of national self-determination as it pertained to the southern Slavs who inhabited the region. These instances of great power maneuvering did not prove embarrassing to the Allied cause because they were concluded in utmost secrecy. But there was embarrassment enough in the political institutions and practices of the Russian autocracy, whose very presence in the anti-German coalition mocked the democratic principles that it was ostensibly fighting to defend.

THE SIGNIFICANCE OF THE RUSSIAN WITHDRAWAL

The Russian Revolution of March 1917, which replaced the Romanov dynasty with a parliamentary provisional government dominated by the parties of the moderate left, together with the intervention of the United States in the war against Germany a month later, supplied the ideological consistency that the Entente coalition had previously

---

*Zionism was a political movement founded in the 1890s by the Austrian journalist Theodore Herzl that advocated the establishment of a Jewish national state as a haven for the Jewish populations of Europe and Russia that confronted a resurgence of anti-Semitism toward the end of the century.

lacked. The new progressive government in Petrograd was promptly recognized by the Entente powers and announced its intention to honor the military and diplomatic engagements of the old regime. In the meantime, the Wilson administration's ideological crusade against the autocracy of the Central Powers had acquired a momentum of its own. Even before the United States could contribute significant numbers of fighting men to the Entente war effort, which, owing to America's lack of military preparedness, did not take place until the summer of 1918, the American president had furnished the war-weary peoples of Western Europe with the one thing that they had never had—a moral justification for the seemingly pointless slaughter at the front. "The war to make the world safe for democracy," and the struggle for "the right of national self-determination" no longer sounded like hollow slogans. Progressive Russia and Young America, allied with the democratic powers of Western Europe, were now fighting arm in arm for the extinction of tyranny and the liberation of oppressed peoples.

But the euphoria induced by the American intervention was tempered by the overthrow of the Russian provisional government by the Bolshevik movement on November 7, 1917. This event was widely viewed in Allied countries as the first successful application of the German policy of instigating insurrection behind the lines of the Entente. The evidence of a putative German-Bolshevik conspiracy gathered by Allied intelligence agencies was persuasive, though entirely circumstantial in nature. German government funds had subsidized Russian revolutionary groups in exile. The Bolshevik leader V. I. Lenin had been granted safe transit by railway across German territory from his haven in neutral Switzerland to the Russian capital. Lenin's publicly announced program included the immediate cessation of the war, if necessary by a separate peace with the Central Powers. Allied suspicions seemed to receive further confirmation after the Bolshevik victory. The new Russian government repudiated the tsarist regime's debts to foreign lenders, thereby wiping out roughly a quarter of France's foreign investment portfolio. It published the secret agreements concluded among the Entente powers concerning the postwar redistribution of enemy territory, causing considerable embarrassment to Britain, France, and Italy. Most serious of all, the new Russian government, after inviting all belligerents to make peace on the basis of no annexations and no indemnities and receiving no reply from the Allies, opened separate peace negotiations with the Central Powers in the city of Brest-Litovsk on December 3, 1917.

The decisive causes of the Bolshevik Revolution in Russia, were traceable to the deteriorating economic conditions of the country. The fine points of Marxist economic theory had little resonance among a barely literate, destitute population. But the severe food shortages, the maldistribution of arable land, and the mounting casualty rate at the front collectively represented a sufficient incentive for large sections of the Russian population to respond favorably to Lenin's enticing slogan of "bread, land, and peace." If the causes of the Bolshevik Revolution were largely internal in nature, its consequences were felt throughout all of wartime Europe. After exactly three months of contentious wrangling (December 3, 1917–March 3, 1918), the Russian and German emissaries at Brest-Litovsk signed a peace treaty that removed Russia from the war. In line with the new German government policy, adopted after the intervention of the United States, the treaty of Brest-Litovsk did not result in the direct annexation of Russian territory. Instead, it represented the new policy of "association." According to the treaty (and supplementary agreements concluded subsequently) the Bolshevik regime was forced to cede virtually the entirety of its non-Russian territories in Europe: Poland, Lithuania, Latvia, Estonia, and Finland in the north, Ukraine and the provinces of Transcaucasia (Georgia, Armenia, and Azerbaijan) in the south. In all of these regions independence movements had sprouted after the collapse of the tsarist regime, and many of them appealed to Germany for economic and military support. The German government was only too happy to oblige. By supplying "military protection" to these fledgling nations that had been carved out of the decaying carcass of the Russian Empire, the German Reich hoped to achieve by indirect means two of the principal goals of its original war aims program, namely, the removal of Russian power from Europe and the extension of German economic domination to the non-Russian border zone.

As German troops advanced into the power vacuum created by the unilateral Russian withdrawal from the war, the balance of power in Eastern Europe was radically transformed. Russia was virtually cut off from the Baltic by the establishment of the independent states of Finland, Latvia, Lithuania, and Estonia under German military protection. The creation of German client states in Ukraine, the Crimea, Georgia, and Armenia, coupled with Turkish control of the Muslim state of Azerbaijan, blocked Russian access to the Black Sea and the mineral-rich region of the Caucasus. In the center of Europe, a Polish state was resurrected to serve as a transit zone for the extension of German hegemony in the former Russian territory along the Black and Baltic seas. Russia's retreat from Eastern Europe was further confirmed by the peace treaty between Romania and the Central Powers on May 7, whereby the Romanian annexation of the former imperial Russian province of Bessarabia was recognized by Germany and Austria.

Notwithstanding the long-term strategic implications of Russia's withdrawal from its European borderlands before the onslaught of German power, the immediate military consequences of the Russian collapse were less than spectacular. The much-discussed redeployment of German military forces from the eastern to the western front in preparation for the great offensive planned for the spring of 1918 did not take place on the scale anticipated. In fact, large numbers of German troops were retained in the eastern theater to preserve Germany's hold on the enormous territory ceded by Russia. The immediate goal of the German government was economic in nature: the application of the program, developed early in the war, to obtain control of the foodstuffs and vital minerals in Eastern Europe and the Russian borderlands. The overall objective was the acquisition of self-sufficiency in food and industrial raw materials, not only on a short-term basis to replace resources denied to the Central Powers by the British naval blockade, but also for the postwar period, when overseas sources of supply were expected to fall within the control of the United States and the British Empire regardless of the outcome of the contest for hegemony on the continent.

The territory under German military domination by the spring of 1918 contained virtually all of the resources required by Germany to terminate its dependence on foreign sources of supply and forge the autarkic economic system first envisioned in the September Program. The oil fields of Romania, the Caucasus, and Turkish-controlled Mesopotamia (Iraq) would assure the Germans self-sufficiency in that vital source of energy. The coal fields of the Don basin in Russia would supplement the rich deposits of the Ruhr, the Saar, Silesia and occupied Belgium in the west. The iron resources of Ukraine would be added to those of French Lorraine. The manganese of the Caucasus and Ukraine (which accounted for 50 percent of the world production in 1914 and supplied Germany with three-quarters of its prewar requirements) would now be open to direct

German exploitation. The cotton and wool of the Caucasus region offered essential raw materials to the German textile industry. And, most important, the fertile grain-producing plains of Ukraine, combined with those of the German vassal states in the Balkans, would enable the Reich to break Britain's "hunger blockade" and end its prewar dependence on the United States and Latin America for its food requirements.

Thus, by the spring of 1918 the original objectives of the German war plan had been attained in the east. The establishment of German strategic predominance in the Russian borderlands had tipped the continental balance in favor of the Central Powers. Groundwork had been laid for German economic domination of the region that had been evacuated by the Russian armies. The Austro-Hungarian and Turkish empires, junior partners in the continental coalition ruled from Berlin, opened the path for German expansion overland toward the Arabian peninsula and the Persian Gulf. This land route to the Middle East and southern Asia, which was to be improved by the construction of a railway system financed by German capital, potentially represented a much more secure line of communications to this economically valuable region than did Britain's vulnerable lifeline on the sea. Here was the beginning of the dream come true of the German industrial and financial oligarchy: a vast Mitteleuropa bounded by compliant satellites and subservient allies chained to Germany by military and economic agreements. To complete this grandiose scheme for German control of Mitteleuropa and the Middle East, the expansionists in Berlin added the project of Mittelafrika: a central African empire, enlarged by the attachment of Belgian, French, and British colonial territory to Germany's existing possessions in Africa and protected by German naval bases on the eastern and western coasts of that continent.

All that stood in the way of the full realization of this plan for German domination of the three interconnected continents of Europe, Asia, and Africa was the Allied military force on the western front. As the American Expeditionary Force began to arrive in large numbers in the spring of 1918, the German high command was confronted with a critical choice: The spectacular military and economic gains in the east might be preserved and even extended by a negotiated settlement of the war in France. Peace feelers had been extended sporadically from London, Paris, Washington, and Berlin during 1917 and early 1918. The German quartermaster general, Erich Ludendorff, toyed with the idea of exploiting the Western powers' ideological fear of Bolshevism once the Allies began supporting the counterrevolutionary forces in Russia that had taken up arms against the new Communist government. But a separate peace in the west, with Germany posing as the defender of Western civilization against the Bolshevik peril, would require that Germany renounce its expansionist ambitions in Belgium and eastern France. And this it could not do. A militarily powerful and economically viable France, together with an independent Belgium serving as a vehicle for British interference in continental affairs, would hamper the operation of the Mitteleuropa project. Hence preparations were resumed for a final offensive on the western front. On March 21, 1918, sixty-two divisions of German military forces launched what was expected to be the long-awaited breakthrough that would drive France out of the war and Anglo-American forces out of the continent.

It is noteworthy that all of the major political organizations in Germany had fully supported the program of German military and economic expansion up to the period of this last great offensive. The Reichstag ratified the Treaty of Brest-Litovsk by a large majority, with even the Social Democrats choosing to abstain rather than to oppose what the Russian government, signing under protest, justifiably denounced as a "dictated peace." The Center and Progressive parties defended the treaty as consistent with the principle of "no annexations, no indemnities" (the formula adopted by a majority in the German Reichstag on July 19, 1917) because it did not involve the formal annexation of Russian territory. The Conservative and National Liberal parties criticized the treaty as too weak. On July 13, 1918, just before the failure of the final German offensive in France, the Reichstag once again registered its approval of the high command's offensive in France by passing the twelfth military appropriation law of the war.

The German offensive ground to a halt on July 15, and three days later the Allied armies mounted a counteroffensive that by August 8 began to take on the characteristics of a rout. With the German armies retreating along a broad front during the remainder of August and September, the military leaders recognized for the first time that victory in the west was an impossibility. Ludendorff and his associates thereupon dusted off the alternative strategy that had been under consideration ever since the conclusion of the Treaty of Brest-Litovsk: the exploitation of the Bolshevik peril as a means of securing a moderate settlement with the Allies. Ironically, this new policy of retrenchment in the west received the enthusiastic endorsement of the very spokesmen for German heavy industry who had previously pressed for extensive annexations in Belgium and eastern France. In September 1918 German industrialists such as Hugo Stinnes, Albert Ballin, and Gustav Krupp, in league with National Liberal leader Gustav Stresemann (also a former annexationist), urged the government to preserve Germany's economic and military gains in the east by renouncing its ambitious aims in the west. They also called for the introduction of domestic political reforms that would appeal to public opinion in the Allied camp by removing the stigma of autocracy from the German political system. The internal democratization of Germany would satisfy Wilsonian opinion abroad and progressive critics at home. A Germany serving as the bulwark of Western civilization against the menace of Bolshevism could expect to receive considerable sympathy in France, with its enormous investments in Russia threatened by the Communist revolution, and in Great Britain, with its millions of colonial subjects susceptible to infection by the revolutionary ideas circulating in Moscow and Petrograd.

The continuing deterioration of the German military position in France in the autumn of 1918 caused the high command to adopt parts of this strategy in one final effort to salvage the gains in the east. On October 4, less than a week after Ludendorff had informed the emperor of the need for an armistice as soon as possible, a "parliamentary government" headed by the liberal Prince Max of Baden was formed with the support of the parties of the center and left. On the same day, the German government appealed to President Wilson for an armistice of moderation on the basis of the principles enunciated in his famous "fourteen points." When Wilson replied that he would negotiate only with a genuinely democratic government, the military and political elite in Berlin realized that the cause was lost. Ludendorff resigned on October 27, the kaiser abdicated on November 9, and on the same day the Social Democratic leader Phillip Scheidemann proclaimed a German democratic republic. On November 11 the German delegates who had been negotiating with Allied military representatives in a forest north of Paris signed an armistice. It provided for the immediate evacuation of all French and Belgian territory as well as all German territory west of the Rhine River. It also stipulated, as a final blow to the hopes of the anti-Bolshevik faction in Berlin, that Germany renounce the treaties of Brest-Litovsk and Bucharest and withdraw all of its military forces from Russia, Romania, Austria-Hungary, and Turkey.

Like the "revolution" that had created a united German Empire in 1871, the "revolution" that established the German republic in November 1918 was accomplished from above, without the participation of the mass of citizens. The part of the German kings and princes in the coronation of William I at Versailles forty-seven years earlier was played by former supporters of the empire such as Erzberger and Stresemann and moderate leaders of the Social Democrats such as Scheidemann and Ebert. The military leadership did not lift a finger in defense of the repudiated Hohenzollern monarch, who slipped ignominiously across the Dutch border into exile on November 10. The German Republic was not forged by a revolutionary movement fired by democratic enthusiasm and hatred for the authoritarian regime that had brought the nation to defeat. It was created by political leaders who had either supported or acquiesced in the expansionist policies of the empire to the very end. It was tolerated by a military class that was pleased to see the civilian representatives of the democratic parties take responsibility for accepting the humiliating armistice terms dictated by the French generalissimo in the railroad car in the French forest at Compiègne after defeat in the war of conquest that the German high command had planned, waged, and lost.

THE SIGNIFICANCE OF THE AMERICAN INTERVENTION

At the outbreak of the war in Europe, the United States government had declared its intention to pursue a policy of strict neutrality. No American interests were directly threatened by the fighting across the Atlantic, and no American commitments, even of an informal nature, had been made to any of the belligerents. In the early stages of the war, considerable sympathy for both sides was expressed by various groups within the United States. There was widespread sentimental support for Great Britain for reasons of linguistic and cultural identification. French publicists effectively revived the fading memory of the great debt Americans owed France for its assistance in the War of Independence. On the other hand, this pro-Entente attitude was balanced by the pro-German or anti-British sentiment of the two largest ethnic groups in the United States, the German-Americans and the Irish-Americans. But as the war in Europe developed into a stalemate, the naval and economic policies of the belligerents caused a gradual modification of the American commitment to absolute neutrality in the direction of more active support for the Entente. By the spring of 1915 the British navy, profiting from the overwhelming numerical superiority of its surface fleet, succeeded in driving German warships and merchantmen from the high seas. Except for one inconclusive engagement in May 1916 off the Jutland peninsula of Denmark, the German High Seas Fleet was to cling to its home bases for fear of facing total destruction at the hands of the British Grand Fleet. Left unprotected by armed warships, the German merchant marine remained confined to port for the remainder of the war. This forced Germany into total reliance on neutral shipping for its foreign trade. But Great Britain proceeded to impose a blockade on Germany that effectively severed its access to neutral sources of supply and precluded its use of neutral means of transport.

The generally accepted custom of blockade in wartime prescribed the stationing of warships near the ports of the enemy country just outside the three-mile territorial limit. The blockading power was entitled to intercept and inspect the cargoes of merchant vessels seeking admission to the enemy port. Those ships found to be carrying articles of contraband, narrowly defined as weapons, ammunition, and other articles of war, could be denied entry to the port until they disposed of the objectionable cargo. But the British navy violated these regulations in three important respects. First, the blockade flotillas took up their stations on the high seas, invoking as justification for this unorthodox behavior the exceptional menace posed by long-range harbor artillery. This "loose blockade" enabled them to intercept neutral ships headed for neutral countries contiguous to Germany (such as Denmark and the Netherlands) and to confiscate contraband on the pretext that it could easily find its way into enemy hands. Second, the British government declared the entire North Sea a "military area" in November 1914 and proceeded to mine it so thoroughly that neutral merchantmen were compelled to stop at British ports for navigational directions. Such instructions were systematically withheld if their cargoes included articles of contraband. Third, claiming that in total war practically every important product, including foodstuffs and textiles for clothing, was of potential value to the enemy, the British extended the definition of contraband to include virtually every item that Germany was required to import.

As a consequence of this calculated policy of economic strangulation, Germany's foreign trade with neutral countries such as the United States slowed to a trickle, while the nations in the anti-German coalition took up the slack by importing huge quantities of munitions, food, and other necessities from Germany's traditional foreign suppliers. In the absence of surface shipping to contest British naval supremacy, Germany was driven to rely on the use of submarines, which could not be easily detected beneath the surface of the sea, to harass British merchant shipping in retaliation against the blockade. The international rules of naval warfare required submarines to surface and issue a warning to a vessel flying the enemy flag in order to afford passengers and crew the opportunity to abandon ship before the torpedo was released. But many of the British merchant ships were armed and their captains were under instructions to open fire on or ram German submarines that complied with this custom. After several incidents of armed resistance and ramming by British merchant ships, the German government issued on February 4, 1915, the definition of a "war zone" around the British Isles, within which all enemy ships would be liable to destruction without warning. Neutral merchant ships were advised to stay out of the zone to avoid cases of mistaken identity (a distinct possibility in view of British merchant ships' practice of hoisting neutral flags to confound enemy submarine commanders). Between February and May 1915, ninety ships went to the bottom in this newly defined zone. On May 7 the British passenger liner *Lusitania*, laden with ammunition and other contraband material purchased in the United States, was sunk by a German submarine off the coast of Ireland. The death of 128 American citizens in this incident prompted such vigorous protests from Washington that Berlin was induced to moderate its policy of unrestricted submarine warfare. Thereafter submarine commanders were instructed to issue warnings to enemy passenger liners before mounting an attack. In May 1916 this modification was extended to merchant ships as well, on the tacit understanding that the American government would persuade Britain to relax its "starvation blockade" of Germany.

The United States, which possessed the third largest navy in the world in 1914, could easily have convoyed its own merchant ships across the Atlantic and compelled Britain to halt its flagrant violations of established naval practices. That it chose not to do so, while continuing to protest German transgressions of the rules of submarine warfare, reflected two considerations that predisposed the Wilson administration to favor the Entente cause. The first of these was the strong sense of kinship with British traditions and institutions felt by key members of the American government, beginning with the president himself. The American ambassador to the Court of Saint James, Walter Hines Page; Secretary of State Robert Lansing (who had replaced the pacifist William Jennings Bryan in 1915); and President Wilson's intimate adviser, Colonel Edward House, all privately championed the Entente cause and opposed efforts to treat British and German violations of international law on an equal basis. The second and more important consideration was that since the British blockade had diverted the American export trade from Germany and adjacent neutral countries to Britain and France and their allies, American economic prosperity and corporate profits had become increasingly dependent on orders from Germany's enemies for munitions, machinery, textiles, grain, oil, copper, steel, and other products.

Once the nations of the anti-German coalition had exhausted their supply of dollar credits in the United States by liquidating their holdings of American securities, the only means of financing future imports was to obtain loans from the American banking community. Since trade with the Allies had become a critical element in America's recovery from the cyclical recession of 1913–14, the Wilson administration authorized the opening of the Wall Street capital market to the Allied governments. The investment banking firm of J. P. Morgan & Company became the official commercial agent in the United States for the British and French treasuries, coordinating Allied purchasing from American suppliers and organizing banking consortia to furnish the credits required to finance these operations. By the time of the American intervention in the war, private American financial institutions had advanced approximately $2.3 billion in loans and credits to the Allied states compared to only $27 million to the Central Powers. The House of Morgan had placed over $3 billion worth of contracts with American export firms on behalf of the British and French governments. In this way the trading partnership between American exporters and Anglo-French importers, reinforced by the financial relationship between Wall Street investment banking concerns and the state treasuries of Paris and London, gave American economic interests an important stake in the successful prosecution of the Allied war effort.

It was this inequality of economic treatment, together with the American government's failure to exert diplomatic pressure on London to relax its illegal "loose" blockade of Germany, that prompted the Berlin government to announce the resumption of unrestricted submarine warfare on January 31, 1917. Concluding that the United States could hardly be more helpful to the Anglo-French cause as a cobelligerent than it was as a neutral supplier of munitions and food paid for with American credits, German political and naval authorities chose to risk provoking American intervention. They confidently assumed that the disruption of Britain's transatlantic supply line would force that country out of the war within six months, before an American expeditionary force could be mobilized, trained, and transported through submarine-infested waters to Europe. The Wilson administration responded to the resumption of unrestricted submarine warfare by severing diplomatic relations with Germany and arming American merchant vessels. Hesitant to resume their perilous trade with the Allies, most American shipping firms kept their vessels in port, causing widespread fear of economic depression as products intended for export began to pile up on the wharves of east coast harbors. Many of those that risked the Atlantic crossing were sent to the bottom by German U-boats as they entered the war zone. This disruption of the American export trade, together with evidence of a German plot to entice Mexico into a war with the United States, supplied Wilson with a sufficient pretext for requesting a congressional declaration of war against Germany, which was granted on April 6, 1917.

During the first year of the American state of belligerency the United States army played no role in the Allied war effort. In April 1917 the American regular army of 130,000 officers and men was smaller than the Belgian army and poorly trained. It was only in the early summer of 1918, after the introduction of conscription and the advent of a military training program, that the American military and naval forces (which by the end of the war had swollen to 4.8 million persons) began to make a critical contribution to the Anglo-French effort on the western front. In the meantime, however, financial assistance from Washington enabled the Allied governments to expand their purchases of American supplies. Upon the American declaration of war, the financing operations of the New York banks were taken over by the Treasury Department. A large proportion of the proceeds from the war bonds that were sold to patriotic American investors were advanced to the Allied governments to finance their purchases in the American market. The German navy's hope of halting the transport of American supplies to France was dashed by British success in convoying merchant ships across the Atlantic.

The years 1914–18 witnessed a massive international transfer of wealth from the eastern to the western shore of the Atlantic. The liquidation of British and French investments in the United States in the first year of the war erased the debt owed by Americans to European lenders. The subsequent borrowing by Allied governments in the American money market transformed the United States from a debtor to a creditor of the European powers that had depleted their financial resources to pay for a war that seemed as though it would never end. Accompanying this shift of financial power from Europe to the United States was a revolutionary transformation in the system of world trade. While Germany was prevented from pursuing its commercial interests abroad by the British blockade, Britain and France were forced to divert their industrial production and their merchant shipping to wartime purposes. In the meantime, the United States expanded its export trade to capture many of the markets previously dominated by European firms. The American economic penetration of Latin America, which had begun at the turn of the century, accelerated during the war. Similarly, the Japanese Empire, which grabbed Germany's possessions in the Far East, expanded economically in that region at the expense of all three of the principal European belligerents. From an economic point of view, the First World War was won by the United States and Japan, both of which avoided territorial destruction and loss of life on a large scale while acquiring economic predominance within their respective geographic regions.

But the long-term implications of this fundamental shift in global economic power away from Europe passed largely unnoticed amid the emotionally charged atmosphere of the months following the armistice. Trade patterns and capital flows meant nothing to a

European population that was preoccupied with the more immediate concerns of postwar security and recovery. The choice of the capital city of victorious France as the site of the peace conference that would formally terminate the war reinforced the illusion that Europe, despite its commercial and financial decline during the war years, remained the center of the world.

2

THE PEACE OF PARIS AND
THE NEW INTERNATIONAL ORDER

The Paris Peace Conference, which was convened in January 1919, at the French Foreign Ministry (popularly known by its location, the Quai d'Orsay), constituted the largest and most important diplomatic gathering since the Congress of Vienna of 1814–15. Seventy delegates representing the twenty-seven victorious nations, accompanied by hundreds of advisers, clerks, and journalists, descended on the French capital to participate in the process of peacemaking that customarily follows the conclusion of great wars. The enormity of the human and material devastation recently witnessed hung like a cloud over the deliberations: Ten million lives had been lost during the previous four years. Another twenty million people had sustained war-related injuries. The total direct cost of the war was estimated at $180 billion and the indirect cost at over $150 billion. The four great empires that had exercised authority over hundreds of millions of people in the old world—Hohenzollern Germany, Habsburg Austria-Hungary, Romanov Russia, and Ottoman Turkey—had either disappeared or, in the case of the latter, were soon to expire. From their ashes arose politically unstable, economically backward states whose viability remained problematical. The agenda of the conference was twofold: to repair the political and economic fabric of half the world, and to prevent a recurrence of the type of organized violence that had recently been brought to an end.

The president of the United States, Woodrow Wilson, astonished his compatriots by deciding to attend the peace conference in person, becoming the first American chief executive to visit a foreign country while in office. All the more shocking, and infuriating to his critics at home, was his insistence on remaining in Europe (except for a brief return journey) for six consecutive months while subordinates in Washington were left to contend with the pressing domestic problems of postwar readjustment. Wilson had arrived in Europe in mid-December 1918 armed with more moral authority than any other national leader in history. His periodic exhortations on behalf of a new world order that would forever banish the scourge of war represented an entirely novel approach to the conduct of international relations, or so it seemed to the millions of war-weary European citizens who greeted him with unrestrained enthusiasm. In those intoxicating weeks before the opening of the conference, it appeared as though an exhausted continent, bled white by the most destructive war yet endured by mankind, had received a savior from across the sea untarnished by the discredited practices of traditional statecraft that had brought Europe to its present plight.

Insofar as one could judge from his public pronouncements on the subject, the American president believed that war in general, and the recent war in particular, was traceable to three principal causes. The first was the practice of secret diplomacy, whereby political leaders surreptitiously concluded military alliances and diplomatic engagements to further their own nation's ambitions. The second was the tendency of politically dominant nationality groups to oppress the ethnic minorities under their control. The third was the political system of autocracy, which enabled a privileged elite to monopolize political power at the expense of the population at large. Remove these impediments to the unfettered expression of the public will, Wilson seemed to be saying, and you will have abolished forever the causes of war. Secret diplomacy would give way to free and open discussion of international issues, a process certain to maximize the beneficent influence of public opinion and minimize the role of secretive intrigues by imperialistically inclined national leaders. The map of Europe was to be redrawn according to the principle of national self-determination so as to accommodate the long-suppressed aspirations of nationality groups whose struggle for independence had caused most of the wars of recent memory. And finally, the internal political institutions of Europe would be democratized so as to remove the autocratic constraints on public opinion that had permitted the ruling elites of the Central Powers to wage their war of aggression. Crowning this new achievement of internal and international democratization would be a world organization of free and independent nations empowered to resolve international disputes by negotiation and compromise, just as parliaments in democratic societies adjudicated the conflicting claims of their citizens.

It is easy to appreciate the appeal that this Wilsonian program exercised on the "generation of the trenches" in Europe. It engendered almost limitless hopes and expectations in the minds of a traumatized population craving for assurances that peace would endure. The two slogans most often associated with Wilson's name, "the war to end all wars" and "the war to make the world safe for democracy," both symbolized the widespread anticipation that the recent bloodbath had not been fought entirely in vain: People hoped that eternal peace and universal liberty would become its two unintended legacies.

The disappointment of these optimistic expectations represented one of the most tragic episodes in modern world history. So high were the hopes, so bitter was the disillusionment, that the genuine accomplishments of the Paris Peace Conference (which, as we shall see, were considerable, in view of the complexity of the problems that it confronted) have receded far into the background of historical memory. What is recalled instead is the enormous gap between intention and achievement. Because the American leader chose to express his foreign policy in the moralistic language of humanitarian idealism, he raised expectations that could not fail to be disappointed. The vague prescriptions for peace and liberty that filled Wilson's speeches crashed on the shoals of political reality in Paris, where fallible human beings assembled to undertake the momentous task of redrawing of the political map of Europe and organizing the economic recovery of the world.

The contrast between Wilsonian theory and practice came to light in the opening sessions of the peace conference, when the heads of government endeavored to establish effective procedures for peacemaking. The principle of equality among sovereign nations, born of the pervasive distrust of great-power diplomacy, dissolved in the decision-making process of these organizational meetings. The two ranking delegates of the five great powers—the United States, Great Britain, France, Italy, and Japan—preempted for themselves the right to adjudicate the important issues before the conference as the "Council of Ten." The leaders of the other twenty-two states in attendance were reduced to pleading their case, either in writing or in person, before these ten plenipotentiaries. When even this truncated decision-making apparatus subsequently proved too unwieldy, the leaders of the four great powers (minus Japan) began to meet in Wilson's quarters as the "Council of Four" to decide among themselves the fate of the world.

The preeminent position of the great powers at the Peace Conference was subsequently extended to the Covenant of the League of Nations, Wilson's cherished scheme for a world organization that was unveiled before the delegates on April 28. While each member state was to be represented by one vote in the General Assembly of the new organization, the principal decision-making body, called the Council, included permanent seats for delegates of the five great powers. A requirement of unanimity assured that each permanent member could veto any proposal that threatened to impinge upon its national interests. Other features of the League Covenant effectively preserved the inequality of power among the member nations. The British and French colonial empires were treated as single political units (except for Britain's self-governing Dominions, which obtained separate representation); at the behest of the American delegation, the Monroe Doctrine was specifically excluded from the purview of the League Covenant (thereby preserving the exclusive prerogative of the United States to maintain the peace in its hemisphere). The right to national self-determination, which was to be applied to the successor states of the German, Austro-Hungarian, and Russian empires in Europe, went unrecognized insofar as the non-European populations of the colonial world were concerned. Attempts by Latin American delegates to invoke the League's protection against interference by the United States in their internal affairs fell on deaf ears, as did efforts by spokespersons for the oppressed nationalities of the British and French empires in Asia to obtain recognition of their right to self-government. The application of Wilsonian principles was evidently to be restricted to the white nations of the Western world, and among those favored states, the four great powers of the victorious coalition were to preserve their preeminent position.

The much-heralded Wilsonian principle of open diplomacy was likewise an early casualty of the peacemaking process. It rapidly became evident that the American president's lofty promise of "open convenants of peace, openly arrived at" implied merely that the final texts of diplomatic agreements should be published (unlike those reviled "secret treaties" that had codified the various alliances of the great powers before and during the war). What it definitely did *not* mean, as revealed by Wilson's behavior in Paris, was that diplomacy ought to be subject to the influence of public opinion as expressed by press or parliament. The Council of Four conducted its deliberations in the utmost secrecy, at first even without taking minutes. When the British delegation finally insisted that a written record of the proceedings be preserved, a secretary was admitted on the condition that his notes be withheld from public scrutiny. The press, denied direct access to the decision makers, was compelled to rely on sanitized summaries of the daily deliberations. Most of what we know about the negotiations behind these closed doors comes from the notes taken by the British secretary and the French interpreter, which were published long after the end of the conference.

If the press had minimal access to and influence on the decision-making process in Paris, the elected legislative representatives of the four great powers had even less. Wilson in particular took little account of public opinion in his own country as recorded in the midterm elections of November 1918, which had returned Republican majorities in both houses of Congress. Instead of selecting a peace delegation that reflected this new shift in public sentiment, he chose men who either shared his own views on world affairs or lacked the authority to speak for the new Republican majority in the Senate (whose votes were required for legislative consent to the agreements reached at the conference). In his relations with the other Allied representatives he relied heavily on his hand-picked associate, Colonel Edward House, a behind-the-scenes political operator who reported directly to his old friend in the White House. Public expressions of legislative opposition to Wilson's policies in Paris, such as the famous "round robin" resolution signed by a sufficient number of senators or senators-elect to deny congressional consent to the treaty, had no apparent effect on the president.

The other Allied leaders were similarly insulated from the influence of domestic public opinion. The French premier, Georges Clemenceau, imposed a rigid censorship on the Parisian press and denied the Chamber of Deputies any role in the peacemaking process. Like Wilson, he ignored the advice of his foreign minister (and all other senior members of his government), preferring to consult his loyal personal assistant, André Tardieu, on most crucial matters. British Prime Minister David Lloyd George, though more sensitive to political pressures at home, often took positions in the privacy of the conference room that directly contradicted his public utterances. Not only were the covenants not "openly arrived at," they were fashioned amid an atmosphere of secrecy reminiscent of the diplomatic practice of the prewar years that had supposedly been repudiated.

These deviations from the lofty standards of Wilsonianism were prompted not merely by the demands of procedural efficiency: If the complexity and sensitivity of the problems confronting the peace conference required that decision-making authority be centralized in a group of four men meeting in private, then its membership might have been chosen by lot from among the twenty-seven delegations. That it was these particular four men who successfully arrogated unto themselves the function of drafting the peace treaties with the defeated enemies reflected the political realities of the postwar world. No amount of lip service to the principle of the equality of nations could conceal the glaring inequality of power relationships among the sovereign states whose leaders deliberated in Paris. The United States, Great Britain, France, and, to a lesser extent, Italy and Japan (the latter's representatives participated only when issues relating to East Asia were on the agenda) dominated the peace conference because they dominated the world after the defeat of Germany and the collapse of Russia. It was these nations that had raised armies of millions of men, mobilized their considerable economic resources, and imposed military defeat on the Central Powers. It was these nations that collectively exercised economic and political dominion over most of the land surface of the globe and naval control over its waterways. It was inconceivable to expect them to relinquish their prerogative to preside over the realignment of international power relationships that nec-

The "Big Four" take a break from the deliberations at the Paris Peace Conference: Left to right, British Prime Minister David Lloyd George, Italian Prime Minister Vittorio Orlando, French Premier Georges Clemenceau, and U.S. President Woodrow Wilson. These four leaders of the victorious powers met in utmost secrecy to draft the peace treaty with Germany. *(National Archives)*

essarily follows major wars. It was equally unrealistic to assume that their policies at the peace conference would reflect anything other than their own governments' conception of what their respective national interests required.

This intrusion of national interest into the decision-making procedures became particularly apparent during the deliberations concerning the redistribution of the territory, resources, and populations of the regions previously under the political control of the defeated powers. For reasons presently to be discussed, the victorious Allies held sharply conflicting views regarding the appropriate means of accomplishing the ultimate objective that they all shared, namely, the reestablishment of peace and security in Europe and economic prosperity in the world. This conflict over means eventually shattered the spirit of unity that had cemented the victorious wartime coalition. The Paris Peace Conference, which had opened with such high hopes, ended amid an atmosphere of inter-Allied acrimony that was to hamstring future efforts to enforce the provisions of the peace treaties that it produced.

The two essential goals of the French delegation at the peace conference were the definitive removal of the menace of German military aggression in Europe and the acquisition of financial assistance to defray the costs of restoring the territory in northeastern France that had been devastated by the German army during the war. All of the other French objectives at the conference were negotiable. These two were not.

France's preoccupation with obtaining ironclad guarantees against a revival of German military power derived from its vulnerable geographical and demographic situation at the end of the Great War. The long frontier with Germany, unprotected in its northern sector by natural impediments to military aggression such as wide rivers or high mountains, remained a source of grave concern to French military strategists. This sense of vulnerability was heightened by the loss of Russia as an eastern counterweight to German power. Equally alarming were the comparative statistics of population and natality in the two countries. There were 40 million Frenchmen facing over 65 million Germans, even with the addition of the nearly 2 million citizens of the provinces of Alsace and Lorraine that were restored to France. The decline of the French birthrate that had begun long before the war was accentuated by the death of 1.4 million potential fathers on the battlefield. Soon the Germans would be increasing in number at twice the rate of the French. The mid-1930s, when Germany could be expected to renew its bid for continental hegemony, would mark the beginning of a drastic reduction in the pool of French manpower available for military service.

How security against a German military revival could best be obtained became a matter of intense debate within the French government as well as in the country at large. Strident spokesmen for the nationalist Right demanded a return to the policies of Richelieu and Mazarin in the seventeenth century, which had kept France strong and secure by keeping Germany weak and divided. Such a policy implied the forcible partition of the German Reich into the pre-Bismarckian hodgepodge of some two dozen independent political units. The spontaneous emergence of separatist sentiment in the predominantly Catholic regions of southern and western Germany, which pressed for liberation from Protestant, Prussian domination, represented sufficient temptation for the French government to tender surreptitious support to these centrifugal forces within the enemy's frontiers. But the traditional French maxim that German unity was incompatible with French security was a relic of the "old diplomacy" and its balance-of-power doctrine. It was altogether inappropriate to the "new diplomacy" associated with the Wilsonian program, which valued the right to national self-determination (even when invoked by a former enemy) higher than the claims of continental security. Correctly anticipating vigorous opposition from the American delegation, French Premier Clemenceau presented a scaled-down version of this punitive scheme at the peace conference.

The focus of Clemenceau's strategy for ensuring French security was the region of western Germany strategically situated between the French frontier and the Rhine River, popularly known as the Rhineland. Geographers and military strategists on all sides agreed that control of this buffer zone separating the two ancient adversaries in Western Europe would determine the future power relationship between them. A German military force ensconced in the Rhineland would find no geographical obstacles between itself and France's major industrial sector in the northeast (including the iron-producing region of Lorraine that had been the prime object of German expansionist ambition during the war) and the center of French administrative authority in Paris. A French military contingent stationed in the Rhineland and on the bridgeheads on the opposite side of the river would be within striking distance of the industrial heartland of Germany located in the adjacent Ruhr Valley. So decisive was the strategic position of the Rhineland that military occupation of it by one of these two powers would almost certainly deter the other from daring to pursue an aggressive foreign policy on the continent.

In recognition of this geopolitical imperative, Clemenceau proposed at the peace conference that the Rhineland be severed from Germany and reconstituted as an independent sovereign state under French military protection. Fortunately for the French, the separatist group that had sprouted in this region after the armistice was the most ambitious and vocal of the "anti-Prussian" liberation movements in the predominantly Catholic portions of Germany. Unfortunately, it had failed to secure the support of the vast majority of the Rhenish population, which remained loyal to the national state with which it shared a common language and heritage. The forcible separation of the Rhineland from Germany would not only violate the principle of national self-determination (since a plebiscite in the region would certainly have resulted in the rejection of independence); it would also, particularly in the eyes of British Prime Minister Lloyd George, have created another Alsace-Lorraine, that is, a perpetual source of friction between Germany and the victorious powers responsible for depriving it of its "lost province."

In the face of intense Anglo-American pressure, which at one point included a veiled threat by President Wilson to abandon the peace conference in midsession, the French premier acquiesced in a compromise arrangement on the Rhine. In return for France's acceptance of German political sovereignty over the Rhineland, the American and British leaders consented to the following set of protective guarantees: the prohibition in perpetuity against the deployment of German military forces or the construction of fortifications on the territory west of the Rhine as well as on a strip fifty kilometers wide on the east bank of the river; the inter-Allied military occupation of the Rhineland for a fifteen-year period (at the end of which, it was presumed, the militaristic spirit of the old Germany would have been snuffed out by the forces of German democracy that had recently come to power); and, just in case, the permanent reduction of the German army to a token force of 100,000 men, prohibition of the manufacture of military aircraft, tanks, and other offensive weapons by Germany, and an unprecedented commitment by the United States and Great Britain to defend France by force of arms in the event of unprovoked German aggression. These measures satisfied Clemenceau as minimally acceptable guarantees against a future German military threat.

No less important than this search for security was France's economic objective of postwar reconstruction. It was a cruel irony that defeated Germany emerged from the Great War with its national territory virtually untouched by the ravages of combat while the most productive region of victorious France lay in ruins. The ten northeastern *départements* of France that had served as the battleground on the western front had been devastated during the four years of combat. To add insult to injury, the retreating German army had deliberately laid waste to the territory they were forced to evacuate; there is some evidence to suggest that this was done not only to deny its resources to the advancing Allied armies, but also to accord German economic interests a competitive advantage over their French counterparts after the war by crippling France's capacity for economic recovery. Coal mines flooded, railways and telegraph lines destroyed, farmland pockmarked with shell holes and honeycombed with trenches, livestock slaughtered, homes put to the torch—such was the somber scene that greeted the Allied armies as they liberated the war zone in the autumn of 1918. This destruction of industrial plant, agricultural acreage, and communication and transportation facilities in the northeastern region, together with the severe labor shortages caused by the wartime casualties, had gravely undermined France's productive capacity. To make matters worse, the liquidation of the major portion of France's foreign investment portfolio to finance the war effort, the incurring of massive foreign indebtedness, and the loss of the extensive prewar investments in Russia, Austria-Hungary, and Turkey had strained the country's financial resources almost to the breaking point. The necessity to reconstruct the devastated regions; to accommodate the needs of the millions of refugees, widows, orphans, and disabled veterans; and to service the enormous foreign debt incurred during the war required an immense effort of national economic recovery that clearly could not be sustained by the nation's depleted financial resources. It was evident that a massive infusion of capital from abroad was needed to defray the costs of France's postwar economic rehabilitation.

Historians of the Paris Peace Conference have almost invariably portrayed French authorities as united in the expectation that the costs of French economic recovery could and should be borne by Germany. But historical research has revealed that key officials in the Clemenceau government entertained the hope that national reconstruction would be financed not by the defeated enemy, but rather by France's two English-speaking associates that had been spared the trauma of military occupation and material destruction. What led France's economic planners to anticipate such assistance from the wartime partners across the Channel and the Atlantic was the development of a remarkable degree of economic cooperation among the Allied nations during the last year of the war. A number of inter-Allied organizations had been established in London to pool and allocate available cargo space on ships, raw materials, and munitions essential for the prosecution of the war. In this way France received from the United States and the British Empire deliveries of coal, oil, wheat, and dozens of other commodities that she was unable to produce domestically in sufficient quantities. The French minister of commerce, Etienne Clémentel, assisted by his enterprising young representative in London, Jean Monnet, mounted a vigorous campaign during the winter of 1918–19 to persuade American and British officials to extend this system of wartime economic cooperation to the postwar period. In Clémentel's scheme, France's economic reconstruction would be treated as an inter-Allied responsibility to be borne jointly by the governments of the victorious coalition on the basis of their financial capacity.

To a certain degree this program of postwar economic cooperation incorporated the spirit of the proposals tentatively adopted by the European Allies at the Paris Economic Conference of 1916 (see page 53). In the course of the intervening two years it had become unmistakably evident that the United States alone possessed sufficient financial resources to underwrite such an ambitious undertaking. At the time of the armistice, therefore, the Clémentel plan revived the idea of a permanent economic bloc of the victorious Allies originally envisioned by the Paris program of 1916, with the critical difference that the United States was to be included within rather than excluded from the proposed system. Furthermore, after the economic revitalization of France and Belgium was completed, Germany would be gradually integrated into what might be called a new Atlantic economic order after it had been severed from the Central European economic bloc that had begun to take shape after the signing of the Treaty of Brest-Litovsk. In this respect the French plan represented a modified version of Germany's wartime scheme for Mitteleuropa, with the roles reversed. There was originally little serious talk in French government circles about compelling Germany to foot the bill for France's economic recovery, for reasons presently to be sketched. Germany would be expected to contribute its share to the rebuilding of the territory that its armies had devastated, but only as part of a global effort of postwar recovery to be financed in large part by the United States.

The expectation that the American government would commit substantial public funds to the reconstruction of war-ravaged Europe was ill founded. Throughout the period of America's participation in the war, President Wilson had scrupulously insisted on his nation's separate and distinct status as an "associate" of the European Allies. The United States government had only reluctantly and belatedly associated itself with the inter-Allied economic machinery in the last year of the war, and then mainly for the purpose of limiting and coordinating the European Allies' requests for American aid. Once the victory over Germany had been assured, the United States government saw the area of economic interest that it had in common with its European partners as having narrowed considerably.

The first overt indication of this transatlantic parting of ways appeared on the eve of the armistice, when the American government formally rejected the French proposals for an inter-Allied pooling of economic resources on the basis of need during the period of post-war reconstruction. Even the shrewd attempt by French officials to identify this scheme of international economic cooperation with Wilson's pet project for international political cooperation, the League of Nations, failed to sway American policymakers. The Wilson administration made it clear that it expected the European nations to rely on their own resources to finance their economic recovery; any additional funds required would have to be sought through private investment channels in the American money market. In December 1918, President Wilson dismantled the War Industries Board, thereby removing government controls on raw materials and industrial production in the United States, and within a month he had begun to reduce American participation in the inter-Allied economic committees. In the spring of 1919 the secretary of the treasury announced his intention to terminate all American government loans to the wartime partners. In the future, the European states would be expected to seek the loans and credits they required on Wall Street instead of in Washington. Thus the French scheme for inter-Allied sharing of economic and financial resources was torpedoed by the American government's insistence on the return to the peacetime conditions of the free market. It was to be American investors and American exporters, not American taxpayers, who would supply Europe with the investment capital, raw materials, and products it required, and at the going price. There would be no Marshall Plan for European recovery after the First World War, as Clémentel, Monnet, and other French officials had hoped.

In the face of this abrupt return to economic nationalism by the United States, France was driven to seek relief from its economic distress in the form of "reparation" payments from Germany. As expressed in the meetings of the Reparations Commission of the peace conference, France's claims upon German resources were essentially of two types. The first was deliveries in kind of certain vital raw materials that Germany possessed in abundance but France lacked, most notably high-grade coal. The second was a relatively moderate debt of cash payments that could be readily "mobilized" (that is, converted into negotiable securities available for purchase by foreign investors, presumably Americans, in the secondary bond market) so as to turn the long-term German debt to France into immediately usable American credits. A high reparation bill was a mixed blessing for France. It could be paid only from the surplus of German exports over German imports, which would require an expansion of Germany's foreign trade at the expense of France's own exporters who were eager to recapture foreign markets lost during the war. Moreover, France was willing to receive as payment in kind on reparation account only those German goods (such as coal and timber) that did not compete with the products of French industry. To receive manufactured articles from Germany would be to grant German industrialists an inroad in the French market to the detriment of their French competitors.

The French government was therefore originally willing to abide by the relatively moderate prescriptions of President Wilson's Fourteen Points, which confined Germany's obligation to the reparation of civilian damages. Such a formula would have resulted in a total German payment of only 19 billion gold marks, of which France would have received 70 percent based on the extent of the damage to its national territory. The fixing of a specific, moderate sum would have greatly increased the chances of German acceptance of the obligation to defray the costs of French reconstruction, which could have been discharged without a drastic reduction in the German standard of living.

But such a moderate settlement of reparation claims was foreclosed by the intransigence of the British delegation at the Paris Peace Conference. Since the damage to civilian property in Great Britain* had been minimal, Lloyd George persuaded Wilson to include the cost of veterans' pensions and separation allowances in the total bill to be submitted to Germany in order to maximize Britain's share of reparation payments. Although this modification affected only the distribution of receipts among the various recipient countries and did not increase Germany's total liability, it left a lasting impression of Allied greed and unfairness. To make matters worse, the peacemakers decided to postpone the establishment of a total figure for the German liability until May 1921, with the provision that Germany make a down payment of $5 billion in the interim. The ostensible reason for this delay was the necessity to verify the extent of civilian damages by on-site inspection. The real reason was the fear that public opinion in the Allied nations, which had been led to expect fantastic payments from Germany by the electoral rhetoric of the political leaders, would reject any figure as insufficient and take political revenge on any government foolish enough to accept it.

This failure to fix a precise sum of reparation payments produced widespread economic uncertainty and political resentment in Germany. Foreign and domestic investors were understandably reluctant to commit their savings to an economic system that was saddled with an uncertain, and potentially enormous, claim on its productive resources. Public opinion within Germany fulminated against the "blank check" that the Allies had issued on that country's capacity to resume its prewar prosperity. But the greatest source of German resentment against the reparations settlement was purely symbolic, suggesting that symbols are often more important than substance in the formation of public attitudes. The legal justification for the indemnity was enshrined in article 231 of the peace treaty, which established Germany's liability for the damage to civilian property, a responsibility the German government had freely and explicitly acknowledged during the prearmistice negotiations. Inserted at the behest of an American representative on the Reparation Commission, John

---

*Caused by bombs dropped by Zeppelin airships and Gotha bombers in cross-Channel raids.

Foster Dulles, this article was designed to *protect* Germany against any Allied claims for reimbursement of the total costs of the war: Germany was to be held *morally* responsible for the war and its consequences, but *legally* liable only for the narrowly defined damages specified in the treaty. Somehow this article was taken to imply the establishment of the principle of Germany's unilateral "war guilt." Such an interpretation was entirely baseless. The word "guilt" does not appear in the article. Nor was there any evidence of a "unilateral" indictment of Germany: Almost identical language was incorporated in the treaties subsequently signed with Germany's allies, Austria, Hungary, Bulgaria, and Turkey. Yet the myth of the "war-guilt clause," repeated by successive German governments in the 1920s and later used to good effect by Hitler, was to become as great a source of resentment in Germany as were the actual financial exactions.

It may seem ironic, in view of the British delegation's role in forestalling a moderate and definitive settlement of the reparation issue at the peace conference, that Lloyd George returned from Paris with the reputation as the most vigorous advocate of a peace of moderation. In fact, this reputation was based largely on British opposition to the harsh territorial (as opposed to economic) penalties for Germany that had been sought by France. We have already noted Lloyd George's role in blocking French efforts to establish an independent client state in the Rhineland on the grounds that such a territorial amputation would supply grist for the mill of German revisionism. For the same reason Britain clashed with France in regard to the issue of the territorial settlement along Germany's eastern frontier. In the unsettled borderland of Eastern Europe, with its hundred million people precariously lodged between Germany and Russia, France's policy was to promote a degree of regional security and stability that would enable the newly created or enlarged successor states of the Habsburg and Romanov empires to preserve their independence from their two temporarily weakened but potentially powerful neighbors. The group of small and medium-sized states stretching from the Baltic to the Balkans were thought by French officials to hold the key to the future balance of power on the continent. The geographical barrier that they collectively formed between Germany and Russia seemed to represent the most effective means of preventing a rapprochement between those two dissatisfied powers at the expense of the victorious Allies. The new nations of Poland, Czechoslovakia, and Yugoslavia, together with the newly enlarged state of Romania, proudly asserted their right to national identity. But the mere declaration of national independence proved much simpler than the task of delimiting national frontiers in a region where the intermingling of populations throughout multinational empires during centuries of migration precluded the formation of ethnically homogeneous states. To complicate matters even further, economic and strategic considerations dictated several egregious violations of the principle of national self-determination. Thus, a million German-speaking citizens of Posen and West Prussia were incorporated into the new state of Poland in order to satisfy that fledgling nation's need for access to a seaport on the Baltic. In order to provide Czechoslovakia with defensible frontiers, 3.25 million German inhabitants of the borderlands of Bohemia were included in that new state. The German-speaking citizens of the rump state of Austria were expressly forbidden to join Germany proper, because the unification of those two Germanic states was deemed an intolerable menace to the security of the newly formed nations of Eastern Europe. As in the case of the Rhineland, but this time with no success, Britain opposed many of these violations of German nationality claims on the grounds that they were likely to incite perpetual German dissatisfaction with the peace settlement.

The principal motivation for this conciliatory policy toward Germany in territorial matters may be traced directly to the British government's conception of its nation's vital interests. Lloyd George's strategy at the peace conference was dictated by the overriding objective of assuring that Germany would never again threaten the sea-lanes of the empire and Britain's access to supplies in the western hemisphere. Such a guarantee was obtained through the reduction of the German navy to a token force of six warships and a corresponding number of auxiliary craft, the prohibition of submarines, and the redistribution of the German colonial empire in Africa and the Pacific among the victorious Allies as mandates under the auspices of the League of Nations. This naval and colonial settlement terminated the *Weltpolitik* inaugurated by the ill-fated William II. Thus restored to the continental position that it had occupied under Bismark, Germany ceased to pose a menace to British imperial and maritime interests. Accordingly, Great Britain reverted to its traditional policy of promoting continental equilibrium in order to free it to play a global role. Specifically, this implied a moderate territorial settlement in Europe that would preserve Germany as a counterweight to French power on the continent. The reestablishment of such a balance between the former ally and the former foe became all the more necessary in British eyes as France began to court the new successor states in Eastern Europe. The prospect of a French-dominated coalition on the continent was hardly less distasteful to British officials than had been that of a Europe under the German yoke.

Because of the divergent national interests of the British and the French, the wartime coalition did not survive the advent of peace. Soon after the signing of the peace treaty with Germany at the royal palace in the Parisian suburb of Versailles on June 28, 1919, the fissures in the Anglo-French Entente became a matter of public record. As successive French governments struggled to enforce strict adherence to the peace treaty, successive British governments chose to interpret its provisions in the broadest and most lenient sense. The most notable cause of Anglo-French friction over the application of the Versailles Treaty concerned the reparations section. While Lloyd George had forcefully advocated the imposition of a heavy indemnity on Germany at the peace conference, British financial officials were apprehensive about the consequences of such a punitive reparation settlement for their country's economic interests. Inspired by the writings of John Maynard Keynes, a disillusioned treasury official attached to the British delegation in Paris, British public opinion came to believe that a prosperous Germany was essential to the resumption of Britain's prewar trading patterns with Europe. Various arguments were advanced in London to justify drastic reductions in Germany's reparations bill even before a specific sum was fixed in May 1921. The first of these centered on Germany's prewar position as a major market for British manufactured products. Large reparation payments to France would inevitably reduce Germany's capacity to import and thereby deprive British industry of a potentially valuable customer on the continent. The second related issue revolved around the so-called transfer problem that had confounded the financial authorities at the peace conference: Germany could transfer her real wealth to France only by generating a foreign trade surplus at the expense of British and other Allied commerce. Britain's export trade, on which it depended so desperately for its economic well-being, would be severely damaged if Germany were permitted to capture foreign markets in order to earn sufficient foreign exchange to discharge its reparation debt to France. During the first half of the 1920s when the British economy suffered a prolonged crisis of industrial stagnation and high unemployment, this manner of thinking inspired the reparations policy of the British government, to the continual consternation of the financially hard-pressed French. The reparations imbroglio, aggravated by Anglo-French policy differences concerning Eastern Europe, the Rhineland occupation, and the Middle East,* effectively dissipated the wartime spirit of cooperation.

This Anglo-French wrangling transpired in the absence of the only power that possessed the economic resources and political influence to ease the world's transition to peacetime conditions. The explanation of America's abrupt withdrawal from world affairs after the close of the Paris Peace Conference is beyond the scope of this book. Suffice it to say that one group of historians emphasizes the shortsightedness and narrow-mindedness of the Republican majority in the Senate, which emasculated President Wilson's program of peace in order to avoid the unprecedented global commitments that it entailed; others blame the president's own unbending intransigence in the face of domestic political realities. Whatever the cause, the refusal of the United States Senate to accord its constitutionally prescribed consent to the three pacts signed by President Wilson at Paris—the peace treaty with Germany, the bilateral security treaty with France, and the Covenant of the League of Nations—resulted in the termination of America's participation in the peacekeeping machinery. (The only exception to this across-the-board American retrenchment was the maintenance of American military forces in the inter-Allied occupation army in the Rhineland, and even that token commitment was prematurely withdrawn in 1923.) America's return to diplomatic isolation left its wartime associates with the entire responsibility for supervising the peace settlement that Wilson had played such a prominent role in fashioning. With the reduction of Britain's commitments on the continent and the temporary disappearance of Russia from the European scene, that responsibility devolved by default upon France, in association with such small states in Eastern Europe as she could enlist in a coalition committed to the preservation of the postwar political status quo.

But American abstention from European peacekeeping operations did not signify the disappearance of American power and influence in the world. It merely marked a change in the way that that power and influence was exercised. The United States had entered the Great War with no territorial or financial goals and came to the peace conference with no demands for land or money. All it had hoped to achieve, beyond the vague philosophical goals propounded by Wilson, was the restoration of peace and stability in the world. It was under just such normal peacetime conditions that the United States had become the strongest economic power on earth by the beginning of the twentieth century. It was widely assumed in American government and business circles that the resumption of normal patterns of international trade and investment would stimulate a resurgence of economic growth in the postwar era. The removal of American support for the new political order in Europe coincided with a spectacular expansion of American economic power in the world that will be treated in subsequent chapters. As will become evident, what pol-

---

*France and Britain pursued divergent policies during the Greco-Turkish conflict of 1920–22, Paris supporting the Turks, London backing the Greeks. In addition, France suspected Britain of undermining French authority in Syria, which it acquired in 1920 as a mandate under the League of Nations.

Vladimir Ilich Lenin (1870–1924): A tireless orator, the Russian Bolshevik leader sought to mobilize public support for his fragile new regime. After signing a separate peace with Imperial Germany in March 1918 that deprived Russia of most of its vital resources, the new regime faced hostility from counterrevolutionary armies within the country and allied military forces that had landed in many of the country's ports. But Lenin and the Bolsheviks survived these challenges to the new revolutionary government of Russia and founded what was to become the Union of Soviet Socialist Republics. *(Courtesy of the Library of Congress)*

icymakers in Washington failed to realize during the 1920s was the extent to which the very conditions of international economic stability from which the United States was bound to profit depended on an effective solution to the simmering national antagonisms on the continent of Europe.

America's withdrawal from the new international order forged at the end of the First World War had been preceded by the disappearance of Russia as an active participant in world affairs. The fledgling Bolshevik regime that seized power in November 1917 had been forced to pay a high price for the separate peace it concluded with Germany four months later: The Baltic states, Finland, Russian Poland, part of White Russia, Ukraine, Bessarabia, and part of Trans-caucasia were detached from Russia and brought under German influence or control. This amounted to a quarter of Russia's territory and over a third of its population. It meant the loss of its most fertile food producing region and its most productive industrial areas. This extraordinary sacrifice was defended by Lenin against the anguished protests of many of his comrades on the grounds that it would provide a breathing spell for the new regime as it consolidated its power. He was also supremely confident that the revolutionary forces that had been unleashed in Russia would spread westward like wildfire across war-torn Europe, inciting the oppressed populations of all countries to overthrow their capitalist masters and establish Soviet republics on the model of the one recently formed in his own country. The free, independent, socialist states that would emerge from the ashes of the old empires of Europe would thereupon establish fraternal relations with the Russian regime from which they had gained their inspiration.

In the meantime, however, Lenin's authority over the shrunken remnant of the tsarist empire was forcefully contested by armed groups of counterrevolutionaries that had spontaneously sprouted all along the periphery of Bolshevik-controlled territory. Tsarist officers raised southern Russia in revolt against the Bolsheviks while simultaneously trying to drive the Germans out of Ukraine. In Siberia several anti-Bolshevik "governments" sprang up under the protection of a 50,000-man legion of Czechoslovak prisoners of war and defectors who had served in the tsarist army against Austria before Russia's withdrawal from the war. In September 1918 a "provisional all-Russian government" uniting the various anti-Bolshevik factions in Siberia was formed and eventually came under the control of Admiral Alexander Kolchak, former commander of the tsar's Black Sea Fleet. Kolchak assumed the title of "Supreme Ruler" of Russia and obtained the allegiance of most of the leaders of the other White armies operating in the region. In the north, an anti-Bolshevik regime was established in the Arctic port of Murmansk. The tsarist General N. N. Yudenich assembled a counterrevolutionary army in Estonia to mount an assault on nearby Petrograd (from which Lenin had prudently withdrawn in March 1918 to set up his capital in Moscow).

The outbreak of the Russian civil war presented the Allied governments with the opportunity to exploit the situation in the interests of prosecuting their war against the Central Powers. The Americans and British feared that the military supplies they had sent to the previous Russian regime, which were stacked up on the wharves of Russian seaports on the Arctic and the Pacific, might find their way into German hands. To prevent this from happening, a small British force was landed at Murmansk in March 1918; British, American, and French troops occupied Archangel in August for the same purpose; Japanese troops that had been landed at Vladivostok in April were eventually joined by a much smaller American contingent. These Allied military forces cooperated closely with the anti-Bolshevik governments that had been formed in the hinterlands of the port cities that they occupied. The Americans and the British confined their activities to protecting the army stores and were reluctant to become embroiled in the civil war between Reds and Whites. But the French government had much more ambitious plans. It hoped that the various groups that had taken up arms against Lenin's regime could unite to form a strong, stable Russian government willing and able to overthrow the Bolsheviks, resume the war against Germany, and relieve the pressure against the Allies caused by Ludendorff's spring offensive. As it turned out, the anti-Bolshevik factions were never able to unite on a common program for Russia's future because they spanned the entire political spectrum, from tsarist reactionaries on the right to Mensheviks and Socialist Revolutionaries on the left. Hobbled by internecine ideological conflicts and clashes of personalities, the Whites gradually surrendered all the territory they had gained. By the end of 1920 the Russian civil war had come to an end, with the Red Army having defeated its counterrevolutionary enemies on all fronts.

The purely military rationale for the Allied intervention in the Russian civil war disappeared with Germany's capitulation in November 1918. But Allied troops remained in the northern Arctic ports until the autumn of 1919 and the Japanese did not evacuate Siberia until the end of 1922. By the latter year the Bolsheviks had freed Russia of all foreign troops and recovered the frontiers of the former tsarist empire on all sides except in the west. There they faced the unrelenting hostility not only of the great powers that had defeated Germany, but also of a string of small independent states that had been carved out of former Russian territory lost at Brest-Litovsk: Finland, Latvia, Lithuania, and Estonia retained their independence under the protection of British warships operating in the Baltic. The greatly enlarged Kingdom of Romania preserved control of the former Russian province of Bessarabia that it had seized during the revolution. And, most ominous of all, a proud, assertive, strongly anti-Communist state of Poland had been reconstituted at Russia's gateway to Europe, with an eastern frontier extending far into former Russian territory.

Lenin's original plans for a Europe-wide Communist revolution that would liberate the masses from their oppressors and remove the threat of aggression against the Soviet state from the west went up in smoke during the first few months after the armistice. The few attempts that had been made by indigenous revolutionary movements in Central Europe to establish Communist regimes on the Russian model were ruthlessly crushed by the forces of counterrevolution with the sympathetic approval of the victorious allies. In January 1919 an insurrection in Berlin sponsored by the Sparticist League, a group of left-wing socialists inspired by the Bolshevik success in Russia, was quelled by the German government with the assistance of the army. A Soviet republic established in Bavaria in April was forcibly overthrown. The Hungarian Communist regime set up in Budapest by Béla Kun (a veteran of the Bolshevik Revolution in Russia) succumbed to a bloody counterrevolution supported by the invading army of Romania. In short, the Bolsheviks' triumph in Russia proved to be an isolated event rather than the beginning of the worldwide socialist revolution that its architects had confidently anticipated. The ideological hostility of the victorious Allies, coupled with the energetic opposition of the anti-Communist elites that assumed control of the successor states of the defunct empires of Central and Eastern Europe, succeeded in halting the spread of communism. The Allied statesmen meeting in Paris to make peace as the revolutions in Central Europe collapsed in the winter and spring of 1919 could take heart from the fact that, though the triumph of Lenin's movement seemed imminent within Russia in spite of counterrevolution and allied intervention, the "bacillus" of Bolshevism was being quarantined at the western border of the new Soviet state.

It is tempting for the historian of today, fortified with the wisdom of hindsight, to render a negative judgment on the Paris Peace Conference and the five treaties with the defeated powers that were signed in various Parisian suburbs in 1919–20.* The last great diplomatic gathering of comparable importance, the Congress of Vienna, had established a framework for international order that had prevented the outbreak of a Europe-wide war for a century. The Peace of Paris collapsed within a generation, ushering in a terrible

---

*The Treaty of Versailles with Germany, the Treaty of Saint-Germain-en-Laye with Austria, the Treaty of Trianon with Hungary, the Treaty of Neuilly with Bulgaria, and the Treaty of Sèvres with Turkey.

Boundary Changes in Europe after the First World War

cycle of totalitarianism, genocide, and war on a scale previously unimagined. Nonetheless, it must in fairness be recorded that the Treaty of Versailles proved to be a failure less because of the inherent defects it contained than because it was never put into effect. It is impossible to imagine a Germany that had been compelled to fulfill its treaty obligations in their entirety endangering the peace of Europe. Effectively reduced to a token force and excluded in perpetuity from the Rhineland, the German army would have posed no military threat to France or the newly independent successor states to the east. Payment in full and on schedule of the relatively modest reparation sum fixed in May 1921 would doubtless have defused France's anxiety about its precarious economic condition and probably would have considerably reduced Franco-German tension. Archival evidence of a genuine French desire to cooperate economically with Germany, particularly in the critical metallurgical sector (where French iron ore complemented German coking coal), suggests an opportunity for Franco-German reconciliation that was tragically lost.

It is difficult to conclude from a brief review of the territorial losses suffered by Germany after the Great War that the Versailles Treaty was unduly harsh on that score (see map on page 81). The cession of Alsace-Lorraine to France merely restored the status quo ante of 1870 and was never seriously disputed by anyone of consequence in German official circles. The loss of the Baltic port of Danzig and the "corridor" connecting it to Poland was more objectionable because it separated the German province of East Prussia from the main body of the nation and therefore caused considerable inconvenience in regard to overland transportation to the severed province. But such inconvenience was nothing in comparison to the economic disadvantages that would have been suffered by a landlocked Poland. Furthermore, the formation of the corridor was scarcely a blatant violation of German nationality claims since a majority of its inhabitants were Polish. Nor did it entail the loss of valuable natural resources that could not easily be compensated elsewhere. The same may be said for the cession to Poland of Upper Silesia, a coal-mining region of mixed Polish-German nationality. Coal output in the Ruhr and Saar covered Germany's domestic needs as well as its reparation obligations to France. Without the coal mines of Silesia, Poland would have been compelled to import enormous quantities of this expensive but essential fuel at a time when that fragile new state was struggling to put its financial house in order. Together with minor border rectifications to the profit of Denmark and Belgium, this constituted the totality of German territorial amputations after the war. Germany lost less territory at the peace conference than did any of its allies save Bulgaria. If any of the defeated nations deserved to complain of immoderate territorial losses, these were Austria, Hungary, and Turkey. But their complaints were of no consequence because they had ceased to be great powers and had lost all chance of regaining their former stature. Germany's treatment at Paris in 1919 was considerably less severe than the project for postwar European reorganization that had been endorsed by all significant political forces in Germany during the war and had been partially implemented in Eastern Europe after the collapse of Russia through the provisions of the Treaty of Brest-Litovsk. Despite its decisive military defeat, Germany emerged from World War I as potentially the most powerful nation on the continent. Its industrial heartland, in contrast to that of victorious France, survived undamaged and intact because the war had been fought beyond its frontiers. Its territorial losses did not decisively curtail its capacity for recovery, as did those of its hapless allies.

Similarly, the final reparations obligation imposed on Germany hardly constituted the barbaric exploitation that German publicists made it out to be. The London Schedule adopted in May 1921 reduced Germany's total reparation bill so drastically that it could have managed the payments with but a moderate reduction of domestic consumption. That the German government, and the German people, refused to accept the reparations schedule and the economic sacrifices it entailed had little to do with the country's "capacity to pay." Rather, it reflected the German belief that *any* reparations, like *any* diminution of national territory, was by definition unjust. They were judged to be unjust because of the prevalent tendency to deny that Germany had lost the recent war. Its armies in the east had defeated the Russian colossus and thrust it back out of Europe, according to plan. Its armies in the west had marched home in orderly formation after their leaders had negotiated what had been fraudulently advertised as an armistice based on the principle of "no annexations, no indemnities." There had been no destruction or military occupation of German land during the four years of the war. Under such conditions, it comes as no surprise that the German people proved responsive to the allegation, repeated ad nauseum by a succession of national leaders after the war, that their fatherland had been deceived and betrayed by the victorious Allies. When all was said and done, the critical shortcoming of the Versailles Treaty was not that it was unjust and unworkable, but that the Germans thought it was and were able to win widespread support for that view at home and abroad.

Once Anglo-American confidence in and support for the peace settlement of 1919 evaporated, the burden thrust upon France and the other continental beneficiaries of the treaty gradually became unbearable. In time the new political order in Europe took on the appearance of an unstable system. By preserving intact the political and economic structure of the German Reich while surrounding it with a collection of politically immature, militarily vulnerable, economically unstable states, the peacemakers had mandated a potentially explosive imbalance of power on the continent. The presence of substantial German-speaking minorities in the eastern successor states and the German majority in the new Austrian Republic constituted a perpetual temptation to the advocates of German expansionism. Their plaintive pleas for the liberation of their oppressed compatriots and the recovery of this "lost" territory challenged the legitimacy of the political settlement of postwar Europe long before Hitler embarked upon his campaign to revise it. With Russia temporarily absent from Europe, the only effective deterrent to German revisionism would have been the preservation of the wartime coalition of the United States, Great Britain, and France, fortified by the presence of the inter-Allied military force in the Rhineland. As we shall see, the disintegration of the victorious diplomatic coalition at the beginning of the postwar decade and the premature disappearance of the military deterrent force in the Rhineland at the end of it removed the sole practical means of enforcing the treaty that was supposed to keep the peace in Europe for all time.

3

THE WESTERN WORLD
IN THE TWENTIES: THE ERA
OF ILLUSIONS

THE ILLUSION OF ECONOMIC RESTORATION

The extensive economic dislocations caused by the First World War and the painful read-justment to peacetime conditions prompted widespread nostalgia in the Western world for the familiar system of international economic intercourse that had operated with relative effectiveness before 1914. As governments sought, with much wishful thinking, to resurrect the tried-and-true practices of the prewar epoch, a handful of perspicacious observers warned that the revolutionary transformation of the political and economic structures of the world wrought by the war precluded a simple return to the "good old days." But these ominous admonitions went unheeded. A superficial economic recovery during the second half of the 1920s effectively concealed the cracks in the edifice of international economic relations that had been rebuilt on the shaky foundations of the postwar world. The return of prosperity enabled national leaders to ignore the grave systemic weaknesses in the world economy and to avoid fashioning bold new policies to fit the new realities. It required the total unraveling of the network of international trade and investment that occurred in the 1930s to convince the political leaders that the First World War had signified the end of an era and that a new mechanism for the allocation of the world's productive resources was required.

For the purposes of historical analysis, the postwar decade may conveniently be divided in two. The first five years of peace were marked by severe depression in some countries, hyperinflation in others, and in general a slowdown of international economic activity. The cause of this poor performance was not a decline in production. The physical capacity of the world to produce goods and services had not been appreciably reduced by the destructive effects of the war, except in those unfortunate regions of northeastern France and European Russia that had served as the principal theaters of combat. The problem lay rather in the defective channels for the distribution of productive factors throughout the world, that is, in the international network of trade, investment, and migration. In the most general sense, the principal impediment to postwar economic recovery was the disappearance of the relatively efficient mechanism for the international exchange of products, resources, capital, and labor that had eased the Western world's transition to an international industrial order in the second half of the nineteenth century (see pp. 33–35).

The sluggish recovery of world trade in the early postwar years was directly related to developments in the political and economic relations among the nations of continental Europe. Among the most important of these problems was the spread of economic nationalism. This phenomenon was a natural outgrowth of the war, which had ostensibly revealed the military advantages of economic self-sufficiency and the danger of dependence on foreign markets and sources of supply. Most economic experts, and many political leaders, had recognized the folly of pursuing the elusive goal of autarky in the context of the narrow economic base of the individual nations of Europe. None of the belligerents in the Great War had possessed sufficient food-producing land, raw materials, or markets within their borders to meet its national needs. The recognition of the pressing necessity for some type of continental economic cooperation had prompted such multinational schemes as the German Mitteleuropa plan and the French proposal for an inter-Allied economic bloc. But these wartime projects for European economic integration had been thoroughly discredited by the end of the war. Instead, as we have seen, the political reorganization of Central Europe proceeded according to the principle of national self-determination; the territorial settlement codified in the Treaty of Saint-German-en-Laye with Austria and the Treaty of Trianon with Hungary set in motion the opposite trend, economic disintegration. The number of independent economic units in Europe—within which productive factors could circulate without restriction—increased from twenty to twenty-seven as the integrated economic systems of Austria and Hungary were shattered and parceled out among seven states (including three newly created ones), while five new nations were carved out of the western borderlands of Russia.

A negative economic consequence of this territorial distribution was the disruption of previously complementary regions: Urban centers (such as Vienna) were severed from their food supply in the agricultural hinterlands; industrial sectors (such as the Bohemian region of Czechoslovakia) were separated from their traditional sources of raw materials in those parts of the Habsburg empire that had been allocated to other states; the new frontiers often cut across the existing and most efficient means of transportation (thus, the railway system of Czechoslovakia was centered on Vienna rather than on the Czech capital, Prague, causing considerable confusion and inefficiency in the economic relations between rump Austria and the new Czechoslovak Republic). Unlike the national unification process of Western Europe in the nineteenth century, which enlarged economic units and increased productivity, the nation-building in Eastern Europe after the First World War reduced the size of existing economic units and thereby decreased the efficiency that has traditionally resulted from economies of scale. The products, resources, capital, and labor that had circulated relatively freely within the two political subdivisions of the Austro-Hungarian Empire before the war encountered all manner of political restrictions enacted by the successor states. For reasons of insecurity and national pride, the political elites of these new nations sought to nurture their infant industries by the usual discriminatory practices—tariffs, import quotas, and government subsidies—thereby inhibiting the revival of Europe-wide trade after the war. To make matters worse, access to the extensive natural resources and potentially lucrative markets of Russia was impaired on account of the intense ideological hostility evoked by the Soviet regime.

The clogging of the traditional channels of trade within Europe was a microcosmic version of the commercial crisis that gripped the entire world during the first half of the 1920s. The spirit of economic nationalism that inspired the governing classes of the new or newly enlarged nations in the center of the European continent also appeared in regions far removed from the battlegrounds of the recent war. Nations in the western hemisphere and the Far East had established or expanded domestic industries during the war in order to produce substitutes for the manufactured products that were no longer obtainable from the European belligerents. By the end of the war, several countries in Latin America, Canada, Japan, India, and Australia boasted highly developed industrial sectors that produced goods in direct competition with Europe's principal exports. It is no surprise that investors, managers, and labor groups that had acquired a stake in the profitability of those fledgling enterprises clamored for government protection against the anticipated influx of products from an economically revitalized Europe. Even the victorious powers of Western Europe, which had the most to gain from a revival of world trade because of their superior productive capacity, retained a number of wartime restrictions on imports of "luxury items" (defined in the broadest possible sense) to preserve the domestic market for national enterprises struggling to restore their productivity after four years of war-induced economic distortions.

But the necessity of protecting infant industries or to revive economic institutions devastated by war scarcely explains the protectionist policy pursued by the United States after the war. The Emergency Tariff Act of May 1921 and the Fordney-McCumber Tariff of the following year raised duties to their highest level in modern American history. These restrictionist commercial measures were the result of intense pressure exerted on the United States Congress by domestic agricultural and manufacturing interests that feared future competition from the replanted farmlands and reequipped industries of Europe. Moreover, in conjunction with this new protectionist policy, successive American administrations waged a vigorous campaign to promote the American export trade. The Webb-Pomerene Act of 1918 had exempted American export firms from the Sherman Anti-Trust Act in order to enable them to join forces and compete on equal terms with the European cartels. Under the Harding administration, Secretary of Commerce Herbert Hoover intensified this government-sponsored effort to increase sales of American products overseas. The State Department, as always devoted to the hallowed American dogma of the Open Door, vigorously supported the efforts of American firms to obtain access to markets and resources previously controlled by European concerns. A prime example of this partnership of business and government to expand American economic power overseas was the successful campaign by American petroleum companies, strongly backed by the State Department, to break the British monopoly on the oil reserves of the Middle East. In the meantime the United States mounted a spirited challenge to British domination of the international carrying trade. The Merchant Marine Act of 1920 authorized the sale of government-owned vessels to private shipping companies at bargain prices, while subsequent legislation granted public subsidies for the construction of new merchant ships. Economists warned that it was counterproductive for the United States to compete with European merchant fleets, since shipbuilding in the United

States was more expensive than it was elsewhere because of higher labor costs. It would have made much more sense economically to purchase the services of the established European lines at lower prices. But this argument did not deter the advocates of a merchant fleet second to none, who countered with appeals to national pride: American goods should be carried by American ships, regardless of cost.

In addition to the relatively slow recovery of international trade caused by the revival of protectionism and economic nationalism, there occurred an important change in the structure and direction of world trade. We have already noted that the European powers' wartime diversion of productive capacity to the fabrication of munitions and military supplies caused a drastic decline in their export trade, a condition that was aggravated by the blockade policy of Britain and the submarine warfare of Germany. We have also noted that this cutoff of European supplies compelled those neutral nations that possessed the means to do so to create or expand new industries to compensate for the shortfall in imports. But those underdeveloped nations that lacked the productive factors that would have permitted them to replace European imports with their own domestic output increasingly turned to the United States or Japan as alternative sources of industrial products. Consequently, the United States replaced Great Britain as the principal trading partner of Latin America and surged far ahead of Germany and France, while Japan (whose output of manufactured goods doubled between 1913 and 1921) made substantial inroads into British markets in Asia for textile products made of cotton and wool. Similarly, the opening of new coal mines in the United States, India, and South Africa and the emergence of Middle Eastern petroleum as an alternative source of energy caused a serious decline in British coal exports, which, together with textiles, had accounted for the bulk of Britain's prewar export trade. These new commercial relationships persisted after the war. When the European powers sought to recapture their traditional markets abroad, they found themselves excluded by a combination of political restrictions and economic competition from upstart economic powers. During the same period, Europe's share of the previously lucrative American market declined precipitously: Throughout the 1920s, the percentage of the total value of United States imports supplied by Europe averaged about 30 percent compared to over 50 percent before the war.

The extent of this dramatic shift in the direction of international trade away from Europe and toward North America and Japan is recorded in other revealing statistics as well. Between 1913 and 1929, the total value of all of the world's exports increased by two-thirds. During the same period, the total value of British, German, and French exports grew by 15, 33, and 50 percent, respectively. But the total value of American exports doubled while Japan's trebled. What these figures reveal is that Europe was gradually losing its position as the undisputed master of world trade. The acceleration of the two principal prewar trends in international economic development—the economic penetration of Latin America by the United States and Japan's commercial expansion in East Asia—required drastic readjustments in the structure of international economic relationships. Such spectacular shifts in the locus of world economic power need not have produced international economic instability. But they were bound to cause serious disruption unless the newly emergent economic giants of the world grasped the extent of their international responsibilities and displayed a willingness to discharge them in such a way as to promote harmony in international economic exchange.

Unfortunately, the United States proved unwilling to bear its new burden as the leading exporter and international investor of the world. The first sign of this American reluctance to assume its new world obligations was the retreat into political isolation after the legislative rejection of the peace settlement of 1919. Apart from a few minor exceptions, the United States government declined to join the numerous international organizations that had been established to enforce the peace treaties and preserve collective security. American delegates did not participate in the succession of international conferences held in the course of the 1920s to address economic and security problems. The absence of an American voice in these deliberations both diminished their effectiveness and reduced Washington's ability to coordinate its foreign economic policies with those of the other industrial powers of the world.

The second sign of this reluctance, as will be seen, was in the financial and commercial practices of the United States in the postwar years, which were mutually contradictory and served to undermine America's dominant position in the world economic order. It is wholly inaccurate to apply the term "isolationism" to American foreign economic policy in the 1920s: While America's military and diplomatic presence abroad was drastically reduced, its banking and trading interests were engaged in strenuous economic expansion that definitively established the United States as a world financial and commercial power of the first rank. But the way in which this expansion was managed produced a number of problems that were to damage and eventually unravel the fragile fabric of international economic exchange that was being refashioned after the war.

We have already had occasion to note the resurgence of commercial protectionism in postwar America and its deleterious effect on world trade. But this trend became all the more injurious to the health of the international economy because it occurred at a time when the United States had become the major source of investment capital for the world. In the course of the war, the principal movement of capital had ceased to be from Western Europe to primary producing regions for the purposes of developing underutilized resources; it went instead from the United States to Europe to finance human and material destruction. In 1914 the United States was a net debtor on international account by $3.7 billion. By 1929 it was a net creditor by more than $10 billion. Though the use to which American foreign lending and investment was put changed after the restoration of peacetime conditions, its direction remained largely the same, namely, to the European continent. That meant that America was lending to and investing in countries whose exports directly competed with American products. Consequently, the protectionist commercial policies adopted by postwar American governments, together with the vigorous campaign to expand American exports and to wrest control of foreign raw materials and the shipping trade from the European nations, made it increasingly difficult for America's European debtors to earn sufficient foreign exchange to repay their creditors across the Atlantic. Throughout the 1920s the United States maintained a balance-of-trade surplus with Europe that averaged a billion dollars annually and continually enjoyed balance-of-payments surpluses as well.

Unlike Great Britain in its heyday as the world's premier trading nation, the United States was reluctant to receive large quantities of raw materials, foodstuffs, and semifinished industrial products from abroad in exchange for its continually expanding exports of finished manufactured goods. The source of this "closed door" policy can be traced to the unique advantage of the American economy: privileged access to a vast internal market and virtual self-sufficiency in manufactured goods, basic foodstuffs, and most indus-trial raw materials. Foreign trade therefore accounted for a small proportion of its gross national product—less than 10 percent in 1929. Since American productivity was not sig-nificantly affected by the surpluses and deficits in international accounts, there was little incentive for officials in Washington to devise foreign economic policies that would pro-mote the kind of commercial and financial stability that had been one of the principal objectives of British foreign economic policy in the nineteenth century. Instead, Wash-ington responded to domestic pressures to insulate the domestic market even further from foreign competition at the same time it encouraged the expansion of American exports. This combination of import protectionism and export expansionism violated an elemen-tary principle of international economics: Trade is a two-way street; but customers can-not afford to buy your products unless they can sell you the fruits of their own labor. Sim-ilarly, your debtors cannot repay you unless they can acquire a sufficient amount of your currency by selling you their products or services.

As unsettling as this simultaneous pursuit of protectionism and export expansion by the United States proved to be, an equally debilitating influence on international eco-nomic stability was price inflation in the industrial countries of the world. During the First World War most of the belligerent and many of the neutral nations had abandoned the gold standard in order to conserve scarce reserves of gold and foreign exchange. The suppression of the free international movement of gold during and immediately after the war disrupted the customary connection between national price systems and permitted prices to fluctuate independently in each nation. Some hapless countries, such as Ger-many, Austria, and the Soviet Union, suffered such a destructive bout of hyperinflation in the early postwar years that their currencies collapsed altogether. But the scourge of inflation also hit France, whose wholesale prices after the war increased by eight times their 1913 level, and Italy, where they rose about sevenfold. On the international level, exchange instability increased the risks of short-term lending to finance trade and long-term lending to promote economic development: Investors understandably hesitated to transfer their assets into a foreign currency whose value fluctuated wildly against their own. Exporters were reluctant to exchange valuable goods for paper money rendered increasingly worthless by the rise in domestic prices.

In addition to these obstacles to the free international exchange of surplus capital and production, the international movement of labor was severely curtailed by politically imposed restrictions. Just as American producers strove to exclude foreign products from their domestic market, American labor organizations pressed their government to stem the influx of foreign immigrants in order to reduce competition for employment. In 1924 the United States Congress established immigration quotas that discriminated against the very regions of the world (Eastern and Southern Europe and Asia) that suffered from overpopulation. Before World War I, people inhabiting densely populated areas with poor economic prospects such as Italy and the Austro-Hungarian Empire migrated to underpopulated regions with plentiful resources and land such as the United States in search of employment opportunities. During the 1920s average annual immigration to the United States dropped by over 50 percent from its prewar level. This meant that over-populated areas could no longer rely on the safety valve of emigration to relieve internal pressures on land, food, and natural resources. As in the analogous case of tariff protec-tion, this also meant that wages in the United States remained at a higher level than would have been the case had immigrants been permitted to enter the country to compete for jobs.

Free trade and free immigration—the unrestricted international exchange of resources and labor—remained unfulfilled hopes of those who wished to restore the prewar system of international economic relations in the 1920s. But the one significant achievement of this period was the successful restoration of a considerable degree of financial stability in the world. The only obvious solution to the scourge of inflation and exchange instability in the early twenties was a return to the international financial arrangements of the prewar epoch: In that comparatively benign period, a single nation blessed with substantial capital reserves (Great Britain) supplied the necessary liquidity to balance international accounts, while the gold standard assured that national currencies would be convertible into one another on the basis of a fixed relationship to gold.

The temptation to return to the gold standard eventually proved so powerful as to overcome all objections to linking the economic fortunes of the world to what the British economist John Maynard Keynes once contemptuously referred to as "that barbarous relic." The return to gold was not easy for many nations, particularly those whose currencies had drastically depreciated in value during the war; the restoration of the gold standard at prewar parities would have reestablished exchange rates that considerably overvalued their currencies, thereby rendering their exports prohibitively expensive in foreign markets. This was precisely the position of Great Britain, which committed the error of returning to the gold standard at the prewar parity of $4.86. Other nations, such as France and Italy, took the precaution of devaluing their currencies in terms of its prewar parity, so as to bring their external value down to the level of their depreciated value and retain the competitive price advantage of their exports. Between 1925 and 1929 more than forty nations, including all of those with a significant stake in international trade, returned to the gold standard. By the end of the decade, the familiar method of adjusting international accounts had been universally reestablished. But, as always, it depended on the solidity of the principal reserve currencies (in this case, the British pound and the American dollar) and the willingness of the two governments that issued them to buy and sell gold at a specified price to preserve the convertibility of the world's currencies.

Equally important for international monetary stability as the return to the gold standard was the revival of long-term foreign investment. By the middle of the 1920s the total amount of foreign lending had surpassed its prewar level, with the United States replacing Great Britain as the principal source of this international capital flow. Between 1920 and 1929 American private lenders furnished $7.6 billion in dollar loans abroad, of which $7.3 billion were outstanding at the end of 1929. Though on a much more modest scale, Great Britain and France resumed their role as net exporters of capital in the early 1920s. This revival of foreign lending supplied the foreign exchange required for the conduct of international trade, the repayment of existing debts, and the stimulation of economic development.

But the new international financial system forged in the 1920s differed from its prewar predecessor in a number of important respects. The law of supply and demand should have dictated the resumption of large-scale capital flows from those nations with a surplus of savings over domestic investment opportunities as well as high labor costs to regions with abundant but underutilized resources and cheap labor. That would have meant the export of capital from the United States and, to a lesser extent, Great Britain and France, to the primary producing regions of the earth (particularly Latin America and East Asia, which had already begun to receive substantial infusions of investment capital before the war). But as Wall Street replaced the City of London as the "banker of the world," the volume, character, and direction of foreign investment underwent an important transformation.

First of all, the United States lent abroad a much smaller proportion of its gross capital formation than had Great Britain before 1914. The resulting accumulation of gold and foreign exchange in the United States was in large part due to the speculative boom on Wall Street, which drove stock prices to lofty heights entirely unrelated to the real assets that those securities represented. The prospect of selling these stocks at higher prices in a short period of time attracted an inordinate amount of domestic and foreign capital that otherwise would have been available for short-term lending to balance international accounts and long-term credits to increase the productive capacity of America's trading partners and debtors. In short, the lure of spectacular capital gains on the American stock market prevented the New York banking community from assuming its rightful role as the supplier of liquidity in international economic transactions. To make matters worse, the periodic attempts by the Federal Reserve Board to dampen the speculative boom by increasing interest rates precipitated a flood of foreign capital into the American money market in search of higher returns.

Second, the foreign lending that the United States did undertake in the 1920s differed from previous British lending policy in both character and direction. In the prewar years, most European foreign investments were channeled into the development of productive enterprises and transportation systems (such as railroads, roads, and ports) in developing countries in order to improve their ability to produce, transport, and export products that were desired in Europe. By contrast, most American foreign loans in the 1920s went to European governments and municipalities to finance public works projects such as bath houses, parks, urban housing, and the like. Such consumption-oriented amenities, however much pleasure they may have brought to European citizens weary of their wartime sacrifices, did not increase the productive capacity of the recipient countries or improve their ability to earn the foreign exchange required to finance their imports and service their foreign debts. The proportion of American lending that did go to productive enterprises tended to take the form of short-term loans financing long-term projects. This anomalous arrangement left the debtor countries vulnerable to default in hard times and dependent on the perpetual renewal of American credit.

A great deal has been written about the role of inter-Allied debts and German reparations as disruptive factors in the international economy of the 1920s. It has often been asserted that these intergovernmental obligations left over from the recent war inhibited postwar economic recovery by generating international capital movements that were entirely unrelated to commercial transactions or investment opportunities. Before the war, as we have seen, capital exports resulted from the free choice of individual investors, or of the banks in which they deposited their savings, as they sought the highest return for their funds consistent with safety. But after the war many of the governments of the world owed considerable sums to other governments for debts (either contractual or moral) incurred in the course of the war. In order to discharge these obligations, the debtor governments would have had to raise the funds domestically and then convert them into the currencies of the creditor nations. Thus, these politically defined debts represented distortions in the normal flow of international payments.

The first category of these intergovernmental debts comprised the roughly $10 billion that had been lent by the American Treasury Department to the governments of twenty nations during or immediately after the First World War. Over 90 percent of these debts were owed to the United States by its three principal associates in the war: Great Britain, France, and Italy. These sums had been raised by the sale of war bonds to American citizens after the intervention of the United States in April 1917. As we have seen, the proceeds of these bond sales were used to finance Allied purchases of American supplies required for the prosecution of the war and, after the armistice, for the beginning of postwar reconstruction. Though these debts appeared on the books as sight obligations and therefore were theoretically payable on demand, in the spirit of wartime cooperation the American government did not raise the issue of repayment during the war or its immediate aftermath. But beginning in 1922 the Harding and Coolidge administrations prodded the European debtors to enter into negotiations with the Treasury Department to devise repayment schedules.

America's erstwhile wartime associates resisted this pressure with vigor. They contended that these loans represented America's contribution to the joint war effort and therefore should be drastically reduced or written off altogether. The United States had basked in isolation during the first three years of combat and then took over a year to field a fully trained and equipped army on the western front while the European Allies bore the brunt of German military power at great cost to themselves. The French, British, and Italians could not retrieve their dead soldiers. Why should the United States be entitled to recover the funds that it had originally sent in place of men?

To this moral argument were added numerous economic ones. The claim that these loans represented an economic sacrifice on the part of the United States came under harsh criticism. The proceeds had been spent almost entirely in the United States to purchase American products. They therefore increased American profits and employment and even indirectly benefited the American treasury through the income taxes and excess profits taxes generated by these sales. Moreover, it was universally predicted in Europe that the cancellation of inter-Allied debts would redound to the commercial benefit of the United States. European treasury officials repeatedly reminded their American counterparts that Great Britain had forgiven the debts on the loans it had advanced to its continental allies during the war against Napoleon and had thereafter been repaid many times over by a prosperous Europe that imported British manufactured goods. From a financial point of view, it seemed pure folly for a major creditor nation, which had lent billions of dollars abroad through private channels, to expect repayment of these government obligations. The rules of international financial conduct suggested that the surplus funds that had accumulated in the United States during and after the war ought to be recycled into those war-ravaged countries that required working capital for reconstruction; instead, Europe was being asked to increase the American capital surplus even further through debt payments that would be exceedingly difficult to manage.

The most cogent argument advanced by the European debtors in favor of cancellation centered on the inherent contradiction between America's postwar commercial policy and its insistence on debt repayment. On many counts it resembled the case against reparations presented by Germany and other interested parties. The European debtors possessed insufficient gold reserves to effect payment in that precious metal, and in any case such massive gold outflows would destroy the value of their currencies. But even if they could raise the domestic paper currency equivalent of the amount owed to America, the European debtors lacked the balance-of-payment surplus to purchase the foreign currencies required to service the debt. Their dollar receipts from "invisible exports," such as shipping and insurance services, tourist expenditures, and remittances of European immigrants abroad, were far below the level required to make up the difference. Therefore, the Europeans argued, the only way that they could accumulate the necessary amount of dollars to discharge their obligation was by maintaining a continuously favorable balance of trade, especially with the creditor country. But, as we have seen, the combination of protectionism and aggressive export promotion pursued by the Republican administrations of the 1920s made it difficult for European firms to gain access to the American market, while throwing open European markets to American products. Economists on both sides of the Atlantic scratched their heads to figure out how the European nations, in the midst of this chronic "dollar shortage," could possibly satisfy American demands for debt repayment.

All of the economic arguments in favor of debt cancellation made good sense. What they failed to take into consideration was the extent of America's insulation from the operation of the international economic system in the 1920s. As we have noted in regard to the postwar commercial policy of the United States, the absence of a sense of economic interdependence enabled domestic pressure groups to exercise a decisive influence on their government's foreign economic policy. The same was true with regard to the dispute over inter-Allied debts. American taxpayers refused to bear the burden of higher taxation that would be required to redeem the war bonds at maturity if the European governments failed to pay. Sensational news reports from Europe of lavish spending for armaments and luxury items reinforced this parsimonious state of mind. American war veterans clamored for a "bonus" as a belated reward for services rendered to the Allied cause. They bitterly recalled that their government had generously chosen to forgo the liberal separation allowances and veterans' pensions that had been written into the reparation section of the treaty for the benefit of their British and French counterparts. Agricultural and manufacturing interests in the United States were deaf to the technical arguments of economists about the necessity of permitting European access to the American market in order to facilitate the repayment of the intergovernmental debt. Most importantly, American officials saw no distinction between public and private debts. These loans were regarded as normal business transactions. "They hired the money, didn't they?" asked President Calvin Coolidge. To forgive these intergovernmental obligations would undermine the sanctity of contracts and set a dangerous precedent that European recipients of American private loans might be tempted to invoke at some future date.

Responding to these domestic pressures, the United States Congress established the World War Foreign Debt Commission on February 9, 1922, and instructed it to reach agreement with the European debtors at a minimum interest rate of 4.25 percent and a maximum maturity of twenty-five years. Bilateral negotiations on the debt settlement dragged on for several years, while the State Department pressured recalcitrant governments to come to terms by encouraging an informal embargo on private loans to the guilty parties. As a result, all of the major debtors had signed funding agreements by 1926. The total interest charges more than doubled the original debt, though the rates were much lower and the maturities much longer than had been stipulated in the act creating the commission. The annual debt payments came to approximately a third of a billion dollars a year, which represented a significant portion of Europe's current dollar income from merchandise exports to the United States.

France, the major holdout, finally signed a funding agreement in April 1926, but the French parliament delayed ratification until the summer of 1929, when Germany's acceptance of the Young Plan promised sufficient reparation payments to France to cover France's debt payments to the United States. It was the issue of German reparations, more than any other, that poisoned the atmosphere of international relations during the decade of the 1920s. Though studies have shown that the actual economic consequences of the reparations settlement of 1919 were considerably less dramatic than was supposed at the time, the political passions that this issue engendered on all sides played a major role in undermining the structure of European security that had been fashioned at the Paris Peace Conference. Most of the issues that emerged in the course of France's effort to collect reparation payments from Germany in the first half of the 1920s had already been aired at the peace conference. The first of these, raised repeatedly at the numerous international economic discussions held during this period, was the familiar question of Germany's "capacity to pay." How much of the German people's income could be taxed by its government and applied to the payment of the reparation debt without impoverishing the nation and destroying its productive capacity? No one doubted that a bankrupt, unproductive Germany (however attractive a prospect that might have appeared to neighboring nations fearful of the military consequences of German economic recovery) would be incapable of paying anyone anything. But it was also universally understood that in order for Germany to discharge its reparation obligation, its people would have to reduce their consumption and bear the burden of higher taxes. These measures of austerity would release domestically produced goods for export and reduce domestic demand for imports. This would generate a trade surplus that would enable Germany to accumulate sufficient foreign exchange to pay the annual reparation installment.

This sacrifice the German people, and the German government, refused to accept. Far from submitting to the deflationary fiscal and monetary policy that such belt-tightening required, the Weimar Republic experienced in the early postwar years one of the most extraordinary bouts of hyperinflation that the world has seen. Whether, as some historians have suggested, that inflation was deliberately engineered by the German government to sabotage the reparations settlement, or whether it was caused by economic forces beyond anyone's control, the result was unmistakable: The nation that was supposed to consume less and produce more in order to indemnify France and other countries for their wartime losses began falling behind on its reparation deliveries as its currency depreciated and its domestic prices soared. It may have been unrealistic for the French to suppose that a people would freely consent to a reduction in its standard of living in order to compensate former enemies for damage claims it regarded as inflated and unjust. But the only alternative to a mutually acceptable contractual obligation is one based on coercion. When Germany repeatedly defaulted on reparation payments throughout the year 1922, the government of French Prime Minister Raymond Poincaré chose the path of military force as a means of compelling payment. On January 9, 1923, the French-controlled Reparation Commission officially declared Germany in default on coal deliveries. Two days later, on the express instructions of the commission, French, Belgian, and Italian technicians protected by a small military force entered the industrial heartland of Germany in the Ruhr Valley to procure the coal owed as reparations. When the Berlin government ordered the miners and railway workers to withhold their cooperation, a much larger contingent of French and Belgian troops was sent in to seal off the Ruhr from the rest of Germany and preserve domestic order while the technical personnel mined the coal and operated the railroads that transported it to the frontier.

All nations concerned profited handsomely from the Ruhr occupation. France obtained the coal it required as the German campaign of passive resistance petered out and finally ended in September 1923. British exports of coal and pig iron soared as continental customers who were cut off from their traditional suppliers in the Ruhr rushed to adopt British substitutes. The German government as well as private heavy industry discharged much of its domestic debt in the worthless currency debased by Berlin's profligate printing of paper money to pay unemployment benefits to the striking workers of the Ruhr. The only major losers amid the resulting hyperinflation that engulfed Germany in 1923–24 were the members of the German middle class living on fixed incomes, who lost their life savings and their confidence in the future.

But the short-term benefits of French coercion in the Ruhr did not alleviate the structural weaknesses of the European economic system. Though there was little evidence that the slow pace of postwar economic recovery was caused by the reparations dispute, official opinion in Great Britain and the United States increasingly came to accept this explanation. In addition to the problem of Germany's capacity to pay, the transfer problem that had bedeviled the financial experts at the Paris Peace Conference (see page 73) loomed large in the thinking of Anglo-American officials as they observed the unilateral French intervention in western Germany. The nature of the problem, according to contemporary financial opinion, had not changed since the debates over reparations at the peace conference: The transfer of such massive quantities of real wealth across national boundaries would inevitably disrupt the economies of debtor and creditor countries alike, discourage foreign investment, and endanger world trade. Domestic producers in Great Britain feared an influx of cheap articles "made in Germany," while British exporters shrank from the prospect of German competition in foreign markets that they were striving to recapture. American trading interests, eagerly eyeing the German market, worried about the decline in Germany's capacity to import that such large reparations payments would inevitably entail. Wall Street investment houses hesitated to commit funds to Germany so long as its government was saddled with a huge reparations burden.

By the end of 1923, a consensus had formed in financial circles of the English-speaking world in favor of a comprehensive reparations settlement that would resolve the problem of Germany's capacity to raise and transfer funds to her creditors. The onset of a severe financial crisis in France at the beginning of 1924—caused mainly by the French government's refusal to increase domestic taxation once it became evident that substantial German reparation payments to finance reconstruction of the devastated districts of the northeast would not be forthcoming—afforded British and American bankers the leverage they needed to impose a new reparations regime on the reluctant authorities in Paris. A committee of economic experts, headed by the American banker Charles Dawes, had been appointed by the Reparation Commission to study the problem and propose a solution. The Dawes committee report, submitted on April 9, 1924, proposed a complex system of annual payments that could be adjusted to Germany's capacity to pay, provided for a large private international (but mainly American) loan to Germany in order to facilitate the payment, and effectively destroyed France's controlling position in the Reparation Commission. National elections in France during the spring of 1924 led to the replacement of the Poincaré government, which had carried out the occupation of the Ruhr and consistently refused all compromise with Germany, with a cabinet headed by the more conciliatory Edouard Herriot. Alarmed by the collapse of the franc and tempted by the prospect of Anglo-American financial assistance, the new French government officially accepted the Dawes Plan at the London Conference of July 1924.

The Dawes Plan constituted a fundamental modification of the reparation section of the Treaty of Versailles by abolishing France's legal authority to compel German payment by unilateral fiat. The emasculation of the Reparation Commission and the evacuation of French military forces from the Ruhr in August 1925 removed forever the threat of military force as an option in French reparation policy. Through an elaborate financial sleight of hand, voluntary American capital investment had replaced the coerced diversion of German production as the engine of European economic reconstruction. In a certain sense, this represented a modified version of the original French plan for European recovery unveiled at the peace conference and subsequently rejected by the United States. The only major difference was in the source and direction of the capital movements involved. The funds would be supplied by private investment firms in New York instead of by the Treasury Department in Washington. They would be recycled through the German economic system instead of flowing directly to the Allied nations in need of working capital for reconstruction and debt service. Between 1924 and 1931 private American investors lent $2.25 billion to Germany. Germany resumed its reparation payments to the Allied states. The latter in turn forwarded about $2 billion to the United States in repayment for the wartime loans.

There were two important long-term consequences of this modification of the reparation system. First, the economic recovery of Europe became directly dependent on the willingness or ability of American investment banks to maintain this continuous flow of private funds to the national and municipal governments of Germany. Second, the targeting of Germany for the major portion of the American lending effort enabled the defeated nation in the war to discharge its annual reparation debt and reequip its industries almost entirely with capital supplied by its former enemy.

The apparent settlement of the reparations dispute, coinciding as it did with the influx of American capital, greatly assisted Europe in recovering rapidly from the debilitating effects of the Great War. By the end of 1925 industrial production and real wages in most continental nations had returned to their prewar levels and continued to rise for the remainder of the decade. The Europe that in 1923 seemed mired in economic crisis and torn apart by the Franco-German altercation over reparations embarked upon a period of prosperity and economic expansion in the middle of the decade. The only countries that failed to participate in this burst of economic activity were located in the food-producing regions of the southern hemisphere and Eastern Europe. These nations suffered from a persistent problem of agricultural overproduction that so exceeded world demand for foodstuffs as to cause a catastrophic drop in the price of such commodities as wheat, corn, sugar, coffee, and cocoa.

The causes of this agricultural overproduction can be traced directly to the First World War: The sharp decline in European food production during the war drove up commodity prices on the world market, which in turn prompted farmers on other continents to increase their acreage. After the war the fertile farmlands of France and Eastern Europe were quickly restored to their prewar level of agricultural output, in part because the introduction of better fertilizers and mechanization sharply increased the yield per acre. The resulting agricultural surpluses accumulated unsold because of income inelasticity in the industrial world. That is, as incomes rose in the developed countries of Western Europe, North America, and Japan, people did not spend their additional money on more food. At the same time, those regions of the southern hemisphere with large malnourished and even starving populations lacked sufficient income to purchase the agricultural production even at depressed prices. It was a tragic paradox of the interwar period that the food-producing regions of the earth, such as the newly independent countries of Eastern Europe, brought to the world market more of their cash crops than the industrial nations could consume and more than the hungry masses of the world could afford to buy. The resulting agricultural depression in turn applied a brake on the economic expansion of the industrialized nations of Western Europe, which found it increasingly difficult to sell their surplus manufacturing output to the hard-pressed primary producing areas of the world. Thus, the remarkable economic growth experienced by the industrial nations of the North Atlantic region during the second half of the 1920s concealed the ominous global implications of the chronic agricultural crisis that gripped the southern hemisphere and Eastern Europe during the same period. The illusion of Western prosperity survived so long as the engine of American financial power and industrial productivity continued to operate at peak efficiency.

THE ILLUSION OF CONTINENTAL SECURITY

Before examining the diplomatic maneuvering of the great powers in the decade after the Great War, we must pause to take note of the birth of the League of Nations, an institution that promised to revolutionize the conduct of foreign relations by establishing procedures for international cooperation that had not existed before. There had been a few earlier efforts to establish rules of international cooperation on specific issues, such as the formation of the International Telegraphic Union (1865) and the Universal Postal Union (1874), as well as two Hague Peace Conferences (1899 and 1907) that attempted to place limits on the arms race in Europe and to devise laws of war that would be respected by all combatants. The Covenant of the League of Nations, which entered into force on January 10, 1920, went much further than these earlier efforts by charging the new organization with a set of heavy responsibilities in almost every sphere of international affairs: the promotion of world disarmament; guarantees of the territorial integrity of member states and the imposition of sanctions against aggressors; the establishment of the Permanent Court of International Justice to adjudicate disputes among states; the supervision of colonial mandates in the former overseas possessions of Germany and the Ottoman Empire; and many others. The headquarters of the new organization was established the following November in Geneva, Switzerland. It housed a secretariat to manage the day-to-day business of the League as well as two deliberative bodies to make policy: The League Assembly consisted of all member nations, which originally included the victors in the war (with the exception of the United States, whose Senate refused to consent to U.S. membership in the organization) and most of the neutral countries. With the withdrawal of the United States, the League Council consisted of four permanent members—those great powers whose armies had played the most important role in defeating Germany and its allies (Great Britain, France, Italy, and Japan)—as well as four non-permanent members.

The League was successful to resolving a number of minor territorial disputes that did not engage the interests of the great powers, such as one between Sweden and Finland over the Aland Islands (1920–21) and one between Greece and Bulgaria in 1925. Moreover, its specialized agencies launched a number of initiatives to improve the lives of people that set important precedents for international cooperation in the future. The new World Health Organization established by the League coordinated an international response to the spread of typhus, influenza, and other infectious diseases after the war. It later pioneered new approaches in international health cooperation by sponsoring research on the effects of such socioeconomic factors as nutrition and housing on particular diseases. The International Labor Organization of the League campaigned for the improvement of working conditions, the regulation of child labor and hours of work, the provision of adequate wages, and the protection of workers against occupational disease and injury and of women and children against maltreatment. An agency of the League received and assessed complaints from representatives of ethnic and religious minorities in several European states about repression by their government.

In addition to this humanitarian work, the League of Nations will be remembered for having established the principle that the world cannot and must not depend on the anarchic rivalry among sovereign states to preserve the peace and security of the world. The horrible carnage of the recent war had inspired a new spirit of internationalism that sought to replace the alliances, ententes, and arms races of the past with institutions of international cooperation. Proponents of the new organization hoped that rules of international behavior recognized by all nations would replace the law of the jungle in world affairs. The principle of collective security would replace regional security arrangements as the guarantor of a nation's freedom from attack by its neighbors. The alliance of all members of the League against an aggressor would render unnecessary the discredited practice of accumulating allies to deter and, if need be, defeat potential enemies.

The credibility and effectiveness of this new form of international security were undermined by a number of weaknesses in the League of Nations that were apparent from the very beginning. First, the absence of the United States dealt a crushing blow to the prestige of the new organization, which had been established largely at the insistence of President Woodrow Wilson and whose members had expected to rely heavily on American diplomatic and economic support to make the bold experiment in international cooperation work.* Second, the requirement of unanimity in the voting rules of both the Assembly and the Council empowered a tiny minority of states, or even one by itself, to block effective action against an aggressor. Third, even if unanimity could be achieved

---

*Germany and the Soviet Union were originally excluded from the League, which further tarnished its reputation as the organization of the peoples of the world, but they would later join in 1926 and 1934, respectively.

A discussion at the League of Nations: When the United States failed to join the new world organization that President Wilson had expected to serve as the principal mechanism for the peaceful resolution of international disputes, Great Britain and France became the most influential members of the League. When matters affecting their vital interests arose, these and other great powers preferred to circumvent the League and deal with each other directly. But the League of Nations did establish a number of new international organizations that tackled a number of important world problems. *(Courtesy of the Library of Congress)*

in response to aggression, the organization lacked both a military force of its own and the power to raise one from its member states in order to back up its word.*

   The major weakness of the organization in Geneva was the unwillingness of the governing elites of the great powers of Europe to entrust to the League of Nations decisions affecting the security and economic well-being of their own people. They all continued to pursue their own vital interests as they saw them and promptly reverted to the prewar methods of state-to-state diplomacy that had supposedly been abandoned amid the new spirit of internationalism. Most of the important policies concerning the political and eco-

---

*The French delegation had proposed the establishment of a general staff and military force for the League at the peace conference, but that idea was rejected by the American president.

nomic future of Europe during the 1920s were developed and executed outside the auspices of the League.

The diplomatic history of this crucial decade in Europe may be reduced to a few essential themes: the German Republic's effort to dismantle the peace treaty that restricted its economic, diplomatic, and military power; the attempt by France and its continental allies to enforce those treaty limitations; and the effort by Great Britain, with the tacit encouragement of the United States, to remove the objectionable features of the peace treaty that were thought to be responsible for Germany's refusal to accept the new European order created at Versailles.

Throughout the first half of the 1920s, French governments of diverse political tendencies devoted their diplomatic skill to the achievement of one overriding objective: the resurrection of the alliance with Great Britain that had lapsed in 1920 after the United States Senate failed to consent to the French security treaty signed by President Wilson in Paris. The ostensible reason for Britain's repudiation of its commitment to defend France against unprovoked German aggression was purely legalistic; the Anglo-French security pact was to become operational only as an integral component of the ill-fated Franco-American agreement. The explanation of London's subsequent refusal to replace this moribund treaty with a strictly bilateral guarantee of France's frontier with Germany requires a cursory review of Great Britain's conception of its national interest.

As always, British foreign policy after World War I was dictated by the interrelated objectives of protecting the British Isles, preserving the empire, and controlling the sea communications between them. When Germany's "world policy" after the turn of the century had endangered those vital interests, Great Britain composed its differences with France and Russia in North Africa and South Asia, respectively, in order to form a common front in opposition to any further accretion of German power. As a result of the First World War and the peace conference that terminated it, the principal threats to the security of Great Britain and its empire had been removed: The abolition of the German air force, the reduction of the German navy to insignificance, and the dissolution of the German colonial empire had the combined effect of denying Germany the capacity to project its power beyond the European continent. The internal disarray of Russia removed the other potential menace to British imperial interests, namely, aggression by land against India, disruption of the British lifeline to Asia, and pressure against British-controlled petroleum resources along the Persian Gulf. In fact, as long as Germany was disarmed and deprived of its naval power and colonial bases, Russia was blocked in Southeastern Europe and South Asia, and Japan remained content to confine its expansionist aspirations to the region north of the Yangtze River in the Far East, the only conceivable peril to Britain's imperial communications came from France itself. France's ambitions in its newly acquired mandates in Syria and Lebanon and its intrigues in Turkey caused considerable friction with Great Britain, which insisted on preserving its undisputed position of dominance in the eastern Mediterranean.

In conjunction with its "empire first" strategy, London reverted to its traditional policy of promoting a balance of power in Europe while striving to prevent any one of the great continental nations from amassing sufficient military might (especially air and naval power) to pose the threat of an invasion across the English Channel. This policy inevitably inspired British opposition to France's quest for an overwhelming margin of military superiority over Germany. It is easy to forget, in light of the subsequent debacle of 1940, that France in the 1920s possessed the most formidable land army and air force in the world. With military disarmament in Germany by diplomatic fiat and in Great Britain and the United States by choice, France was the only one of the former belligerents to retain land and air forces of wartime dimensions. Though unmistakably intended for defense of the eastern frontier, French air power alarmed British strategists, who realized that the English Channel no longer provided the security from attack that it had before the advent of the air age, particularly since Britain had begun to dismantle its own air arm shortly after the armistice.

In light of Germany's disarmament and France's acquisition of undisputed military preponderance in Europe, it comes as no surprise that Great Britain systematically rebuffed French attempts in the early 1920s to secure a British commitment to defend by force of arms the territorial settlement in Western Europe. This refusal to accord France the promise of the military assistance she so ardently sought did not signify any willingness on Great Britain's part to tolerate German aggression against France. On the contrary, officials in London repeatedly reaffirmed that the inviolability of France's eastern frontier was an extension of Britain's own security interests. "Britain's frontier is on the Rhine" appropriately became the slogan of the new era. The problem lay in the conflicting views in Paris and London of how French and therefore British security could best be preserved. The French tenaciously clung to the notion that the only effective means of preventing Germany from endangering the peace of Europe was by compelling its strict adherence to the Versailles Treaty; any modification of the military, territorial, or reparation sections of the treaty was considered inadmissible in Paris on the grounds that it would encourage further efforts at revision. And a Germany freed from the restrictions imposed upon it at the peace conference would inevitably threaten the political status quo on the continent because of its position as the most populous and potentially the most economically powerful nation in Europe. By contrast, British policymakers contended that European security could best be assured by removing those irritants embedded in the Versailles Treaty that prevented Germany from accepting its reduced status in the world. Hence the British refusal to promise military aid to France against Germany as well as Britain's campaign to reduce Germany's reparations burden. Hence also British opposition to French efforts to compel German adherence to the Versailles Treaty by the threat or actual application of military sanctions. Underlying this British approach to European affairs was the conviction that a productive, stable, secure Germany could be enticed to rejoin the community of great powers as a peaceful, cooperative member. A Germany torn by economic chaos, political instability, and military insecurity could be expected to harbor sentiments of resentment and revenge.

The disappearance of the Anglo-American guarantee of France's border with Germany in 1920 prompted France to begin a compensatory quest for allies among the states on the European continent that shared with it a common interest in preserving the postwar political settlement. On September 7, 1920, France concluded a military alliance with Belgium, whose acquisition of the frontier districts of Eupen and Malmédy from Germany and whose strategic location astride the historic invasion route in Northern Europe rendered it a likely object of German aggression in a future war on the continent. This terminated that small country's long-standing status of neutrality and formed the basis of close Franco-Belgian cooperation to enforce the provisions of the Versailles Treaty.

On the opposite flank of Germany lay those states of Eastern Europe that been formed or enlarged at the expense of the Central Powers after the war and therefore were prime candidates for inclusion in the emerging continental coalition organized by Paris during the first half of the twenties. Foremost among these was Poland, which had been carved out of German, Austrian, and Russian territory to form an independent republic on November 3, 1918. Poland had obtained Allied recognition of its western frontiers with Germany in the Treaty of Versailles, acquiring thereby large parts of West Prussia and Posen (the corridor along the Vistula River to the Baltic Sea) as well as special economic privileges in the port city of Danzig (Gdansk), which became a "free city" under the authority of the League of Nations. German resentment of Poland's acquisition of this territory and a portion of Upper Silesia (an important industrial region of mixed German-Polish population that contained Germany's largest coal reserves), predisposed the government in Warsaw to seek the military protection of France. Paris responded favorably to these overtures from a fellow opponent of German revisionism; on February 19, 1921, the two states concluded a military alliance that was followed by extensive French economic assistance to Poland for armaments and national reconstruction.

In the meantime, the three nations in the Danube region that had acquired territory from Hungary after the war—Czechoslovakia, Romania, and Yugoslavia—concluded bilateral alliances with one another to deter Hungarian attempts to regain this lost land. Though this diplomatic association (which came to be known as the Little Entente) was directed against Hungary rather than Germany, French officials actively promoted it in the expectation that its three member states, in combination with Poland, could replace Russia as a counterweight to German power in Eastern Europe. French hopes for such an eastern bloc were pinned on Czechoslovakia, the only signatory of the Little Entente that shared a common frontier with Germany and possessed the industrial and military wherewithal to pose a credible deterrent to German aggression in the region. The presence of over three million German-speaking inhabitants in western Czechoslovakia and the efforts by nationalist elements in Germany to exploit their grievances against the Czech state guaranteed a sympathetic response in Prague to the French attempts at alliance making. On January 25, 1924, the two countries concluded a bilateral pact that provided for mutual assistance in the event of unprovoked aggression. Subsequent treaties of friendship between France and Romania (June 10, 1926) and between France and Yugoslavia (November 11, 1927) completed France's ambitious campaign to compensate for the absence of the Russian alliance by surrounding Germany with a collection of small states committed to the maintenance of the political status quo in Europe.

Though formidable on paper, this informal bloc of Eastern European countries linked to France was beset with defects that severely undermined its potential value as a peace-keeping coalition on the continent. All of France's partners in the east were multinational states whose discontented ethnic minorities represented an omnipresent threat to their political unity and social stability. Worse still, all of them were locked in bitter conflict over disputed territory either among themselves or with foreign powers other than Germany: Poland had wrested land from Russia after launching an invasion of Ukraine in 1920. Romania had seized the Russian province of Bessarabia during the latter stages of the World War. Yugoslavia clashed with Italy over competing territorial claims along the Adriatic coast. Czechoslovakia had obtained the coal-mining district of Teschen despite the presence of a Polish majority there, touching off a bitter altercation between Prague and Warsaw that poisoned relations between Paris's two premier allies in Eastern Europe. These internal difficulties and external tensions, legacies of the Paris Peace Conference's hopeless task of reconciling conflicting nationalist aspirations in a region of heterogeneous populations, guaranteed perpetual instability in Eastern Europe that could only redound to the benefit of Germany once it succeeded in emancipating itself from the strictures of Versailles.

To compensate for the fragility of the French alliance system in Eastern Europe, some French officials favored a supplementary security arrangement with Italy. But France's former wartime ally and "Latin sister" to the south had paradoxically become an opponent rather than a defender of the territorial status quo in the early postwar years. Despite its substantial territorial gains in the Alps and along the northeastern shore of the Adriatic, Italy left the Paris Peace Conference dissatisfied with the new international order and intent on revising it for her own benefit. This revisionist proclivity was not even tempered by the satisfactory resolution of Italy's principal grievance against the peace settlement: The Adriatic port of Fiume, which the peacemakers wanted to assign to the new state of Yugoslavia despite vehement Italian protests, was established as an independent city in November 1920 and then transferred to Italy by a bilateral agreement between the two rival claimants in January 1924. Many Italians nonetheless continued to complain that their country had been denied the fruits of victory while Britain and France had enriched themselves with commercial advantages and colonial spoils. The deepening economic crises, social tensions, and political instability that afflicted postwar Italy fanned this smoldering nationalist resentment against the Versailles system.

The ease with which the socialist-turned-nationalist demagogue Benito Mussolini took power in 1922 and established a Fascist dictatorship within three years was due to the aforementioned domestic and international conditions in postwar Italy. The Duce's promises to spur economic growth, abolish class conflict, and restore political unity under a one-party state appealed to Italians disillusioned with the country's parliamentary system and its manifold deficiencies. He also capitalized on the widespread patriotic fervor that craved relief from the country's domestic difficulties through diplomatic dynamism and military bravado. Italy consequently became a power on the make during the 1920s, nurturing ambitions of naval predominance in the Mediterranean and colonial expansion in Africa as part of Mussolini's preposterous reverie of recreating the Roman Empire. The result was an escalating rivalry with France that posed obstacles to Franco-Italian cooperation against Germany in Europe.

In the face of British disinterest, East European weakness, and Italian competition, why did France not probe further east to seek an understanding with Russia, the historic counterweight to German power on that half of the continent? First of all, the ideological antipathy for bolshevism engendered in the Western world by the October Revolution and its aftermath did not abate even after the failure of the Bolshevik-inspired insurrections in Central Europe during the early postwar years. The establishment in March 1919 of the Communist International (or Comintern), together with the subsequent emergence in all European countries of Communist parties that affirmed their allegiance to the Soviet Union and its Marxist-Leninist doctrines of social revolution, struck fear in the hearts of governing elites everywhere. In France this ideological hostility to the Soviet Union, which was particularly acute during the tenure of right-wing governing coalitions during the early 1920s, was reinforced by lingering resentment at the Bolshevik government's premature withdrawal from the war against Germany and its repudiation of the enormous debt owed to foreign (and mainly French) lenders and investors by the tsarist regime. Thus France had been the most vociferous advocate of the Allied intervention in the Russian civil war of 1918–20, lending its support to a succession of counterrevolutionary groups that tried in vain to strangle the infant Bolshevik regime and encouraging the Poles during their thrust into Ukraine in the spring of 1920.

Even more significant than this ideological element in Russia's tense relations with foreign powers was the geopolitical condition that not only rendered it unsuitable as a prospective member of the anti-German bloc, but in fact guaranteed Russian opposition on purely nationalistic grounds to the postwar political order that France was striving to uphold. Russia had lost much more territory and population as a result of the Great War than had Germany. Finland, Estonia, Latvia, and Lithuania had been formed out of Russian territory along the Baltic. Romania had been enlarged by the forcible acquisition of the Russian province of Bessarabia. The eastern frontier of the reconstituted state of Poland, which was fixed by the Treaty of Riga between Poland and the Soviet Union in 1921, included within it large numbers of White Russians and Ukrainians who had previously been subjects of the tsar. The Soviet regime was obliged to acquiesce in these territorial amputations by its smaller neighbors to the west because it was preoccupied with the immediate tasks of internal recovery and reconstruction in the wake of civil war and economic collapse. But the Bolshevik government remained unreconciled to the loss of these European borderlands and therefore shared with Germany a determination to destroy the territorial settlement of 1919 when conditions permitted. The revisionist grievances of Germany and Russia converged over Poland, which had been reconstituted at the mutual expense of these two states and therefore served as a potential basis for cooperation between them. Indeed, the permanent nightmare of Western statesmen throughout the 1920s was an alliance between these two dispossessed powers against the beneficiaries of the peace settlement. Thus the chain of successor states from the Baltic to the Balkans served in the eyes of French officials not only as a *cordon sanitaire* to shield Western Europe from the infection of Bolshevism but also as a means of keeping the two dissatisfied and potentially most powerful states of Central and Eastern Europe apart.

The rapprochement between the Weimar Republic and the Soviet Union had begun in the winter of 1920–21 in the realm of military cooperation (see p. 106), but these contacts were unknown to Allied leaders at the time. The first overt indication that the two pariah powers of the continent had joined forces hit the world like a bombshell in the spring of 1922 during an international economic conference in Genoa, to which Soviet representatives had been invited for the purpose of discussing means of promoting the economic recovery of Europe in general and Russia in particular. After French officials made it clear that Russia could expect no foreign economic assistance until it had recognized its prewar debt and provided compensation for nationalized foreign property, the German foreign minister, Walter Rathenau, and the Soviet foreign commissar, Georgi Chicherin, retired to the nearby town of Rapallo to sign a bilateral agreement providing for the establishment of diplomatic relations and economic cooperation between the two states. The specific terms of the Treaty of Rapallo—the mutual repudiation of claims for war costs and damages, Russia's renunciation of reparations from Germany, and Germany's renunciation of claims arising out of the nationalization of German property in Russia—were less important than the fact of the signing itself. It put the Western world on notice that the two most populous (and potentially most powerful) countries in Europe, though temporarily hobbled by internal economic problems, territorial losses, and the animosity of their neighbors, were committed to the pursuit of friendly diplomatic and economic relations with each other that could only strengthen their respective positions on the continent.

The normalization of relations between the Weimar Republic and the Soviet Union and the strengthening of their mutually beneficial economic links during the years after Rapallo reinforced other developments that were undermining France's attempt to isolate Germany and compel her to fulfill her obligations under the Versailles Treaty. We have already noted how Washington and London had successfully prodded Paris into granting substantial concessions to Berlin in the matter of reparations. The Dawes Plan, by effectively reducing the German debt and abolishing the coercive power of the French-dominated Reparations Commission, represented the first major revision of the peace treaty to Germany's advantage. But the lightening of the reparation burden in 1924 did not produce the sudden improvement in German behavior that the British and Americans had confidently anticipated and the French had cautiously hoped for. On the contrary, it soon gave way to a drumfire of German invective against the two other major restrictions on German sovereignty incorporated in the treaty: the clauses on disarmament and the inter-Allied occupation of the Rhineland. These two questions were closely interlinked, at least in the minds of French policymakers. In anticipation of American and British repudiation of the security treaties that had been offered to France in place of a permanent occupation of the Rhineland, Clemenceau had insisted on the insertion of article 429 in the Versailles Treaty; this clause stipulated that in the absence of adequate guarantees against unprovoked German aggression, the evacuation of the Rhineland could be delayed until such guarantees were forthcoming. The logic of this precautionary article was peculiar; it seemed to penalize Germany for decisions taken in London and Washington over which Berlin had no control. Nevertheless, French leaders wielded the threat of an indefinitely prolonged Rhineland occupation as a sheathed sword to cajole Germany into fulfilling its disarmament obligations under the treaty; in the absence of the Anglo-American guarantee, only a disarmed Germany would render a perpetual occupation of the Rhineland unnecessary.

The process of effecting the disarmament of Germany presented difficulties that had not been anticipated by Allied statesmen at the peace conference. First of all, the rapid demobilization of hundreds of thousands of young men whose only marketable skill was the bearing of arms placed an intolerable burden on the economic system of the Weimar Republic in its formative years. Even more disturbing was the threat to internal security posed by the existence of organized bands of unemployed veterans who detested the republican regime and periodically conspired to topple it, often with the tacit encouragement of their former superiors in the officers' corps. At the same time, these paramilitary vigilante groups performed a useful function in the service of the German state: They waged a pitiless campaign of intimidation and violence against the revolutionary Left, which itself was plotting to overthrow the parliamentary republic and replace it with a Communist regime modeled on the one recently installed in Russia. The Western powers were prepared to tolerate neither a right-wing military putsch that would rekindle the flame of German expansionism nor a Communist revolution that might inspire proletarian uprisings throughout the continent. The political leadership of the Weimar Republic skillfully exploited both of these Allied fears to extract concessions on the matter of disarmament. In June 1920, after an abortive military coup in Berlin followed by a Communist insurrection in the mining districts of the Ruhr Valley, the German government persuaded the Allies to authorize an increase in the size of the German police forces from 60,000 to 150,000 in order to protect the fledgling republic from its enemies on both extremes of the political spectrum. This beefed-up internal security apparatus, equipped with artillery and armored vehicles and soon quartered in barracks, was to supplement the regular army of 100,000 whose existence had been justified by the need to preserve internal order. Together they represented a potential force of a quarter of a million men under arms. In addition to this formal increase in the level of military manpower to meet the needs of internal order, the formation of numerous private paramilitary organizations, rifle clubs, veterans' organizations, and the like enabled Germany to evade the prohibition against universal military training.

The task of verifying German compliance with the disarmament provisions of the Treaty of Versailles fell to the Inter-Allied Military Control Commission (IMCC). This unarmed inspection team met with continual efforts at concealment by German military authorities and instances of intimidation by the general population. But even without deliberate German harassment, the process of disarmament inspection was rendered exceedingly difficult by the increasingly blurred distinction between the military and civilian sphere. The potential strength of modern armies could no longer be measured simply by the number of men in uniform. Modern warfare depended to a high degree on technology that was equally beneficial to industry, as we have seen in our own time that nuclear energy can be used both to generate electricity and to fabricate weapons of mass destruction. The postwar German chemical industry manufactured substances that could be used for either fertilizers or explosives. German aeronautics firms built commercial aircraft that could easily be converted to bombers. The Allies found it impossible to discover a justification for prohibiting Germany from producing fertilizers for its farms or developing its civilian aviation industry, especially at a time when the country was expected to recover economically in order to pay reparations. As a consequence, the IMCC was impelled to grant numerous exemptions to those sections of German heavy industry that possessed the capability of developing products that could be readily converted to military use.

The preservation of Germany's technological capacity to wage war was enhanced by secret military arrangements between the Weimar Republic and the Soviet Union. Collaboration between German and Soviet military authorities had begun in the winter of 1920–21 and was expanded after the signing of the Rapallo Treaty in 1922. Deep in the Russian interior, the German army was able surreptitiously to engage in the production and testing of military aircraft, tanks, poison gases, and other weapons outlawed by the Versailles Treaty, as well as the illegal training of military personnel in their use. Though this program of clandestine rearmament was organized and financed entirely by the German military out of secret funds placed at its disposal, its existence was known to and tacitly approved by German governments throughout the 1920s.

In spite of the geographical, political, and economic obstacles to the verification of German disarmament, the IMCC persisted in its thankless task. It had been forced to suspend activities during the Ruhr occupation when the Berlin government refused to guarantee the personal security of its members; it resumed its inspection only after Britain and France informed the German government that the impending evacuation of the Cologne zone in the Rhineland, which was scheduled for January 10, 1925, according to the timetable of the Versailles Treaty, would not begin until the control commission was permitted to verify German compliance with the disarmament sections of the treaty. In December 1924 the commission issued an interim report detailing flagrant German violations of most of the disarmament clauses. As a consequence, the Allies notified Berlin that the evacuation of Cologne would be delayed.

The German government was thereby faced, at the beginning of 1925, with a major foreign policy dilemma: how to achieve the liberation of the Rhineland without interrupting the clandestine rearmament that all of the major political leaders of the Weimar Republic deemed essential to Germany's return to the ranks of the great powers. It was to the solution of this dilemma that Foreign Minister Gustav Stresemann, the architect of German foreign policy during the second half of the 1920s, devoted the remainder of his career. Soon after he became chancellor of the German Republic in the summer of 1923 and terminated the passive resistance in the Ruhr, Stresemann acquired a reputation in Western capitals as a trustworthy advocate of "fulfillment" of the Versailles Treaty. In November 1923 he was replaced as chancellor and assumed the office of foreign minister. For the next six years until his premature death in October 1929 this astute diplomat became the symbol of those democratic forces in the Weimar Republic that ostensibly sought peaceful relations with the victorious Allies and the reintegration of Germany into a stable, prosperous Europe. In reality, Stresemann was an unreconstructed German nationalist who had never accepted his country's defeat in war and reduced status in peace. His preeminent objective in foreign policy was the destruction of the detested treaty requirements of 1919 that kept Germany in chains. But unlike the nationalist firebrands on the extreme right, Stresemann wisely recognized that Germany's temporary military inferiority in Europe dictated that the first attempts to revise the Versailles Treaty be conducted with diplomatic finesse rather than sterile militarist bluster. He identified two tempting soft spots in the armor of the Anglo-French entente which, if properly probed, might lead to the weakening of the French stranglehold on Germany. To begin with, he accurately surmised that Great Britain would welcome the opportunity to obtain a peaceful resolution of the Franco-German dispute in Western Europe, even if such a settlement were to erase France's margin of military superiority over Germany. He also understood that France, because of its chronically unstable financial situation and fear of diplomatic isolation, would be incapable of resisting British pressure to reach an accommodation with Germany over the most egregious sources of friction.

In accordance with these views, the German foreign minister mounted a bold diplomatic initiative carefully crafted to attain his own country's major foreign policy goals while satisfying the minimum security requirements of Germany's chief antagonist. France craved assurances of security in the form of (1) Germany's acceptance of the territorial status quo in Western Europe as well as the demilitarized status of the Rhineland, and (2) a British guarantee of these two arrangements. Germany sought the evacuation of Allied troops from the Rhineland, but without having to submit to the stringent treaty requirements for disarmament. Throughout the winter and spring of 1925, Stresemann approached London about the possibility of breaking the half-decade-long deadlock between Germany and France. He hinted broadly that Germany was prepared to acknowledge its loss of Alsace-Lorraine to France and affirm the inviolability of the Rhineland demilitarized zone in return for Allied concessions on a number of points. These conciliatory overtures, coming as they did after six years of German intransigence, were received with great enthusiasm in London and were promptly communicated to Paris with the British seal of approval. The consequent flurry of diplomatic activity eventually led to the convocation of the foreign ministers of France, Great Britain, Germany, Italy, and Belgium at the Swiss resort city of Locarno in October 1925. The pact initialed at this gathering and later signed in London committed France and Germany, and Belgium and Germany, to the formal acknowledgement of their mutual frontiers. It also included Germany's endorsement of the permanent demilitarization of the Rhineland. The political status quo in Western Europe and the demilitarized status of the Rhenish buffer zone, thus officially recognized by the three powers concerned, was in turn guaranteed by Great Britain and Italy. In return for acknowledging its territorial losses in the west (Alsace-Lorraine to France and the small frontier districts of Eupen and Malmédy to Belgium), Germany received from France the quid pro quo it had so earnestly sought: the promise of a prompt evacuation of the Cologne zone of the Rhineland, the scaling down of the occupation forces in the two remaining zones, and a reduction in the size and authority of the Allied inspection team, all to begin once Germany displayed some measure of good faith in regard to its disarmament intentions.

The Locarno agreement was universally hailed as an almost miraculous resolution of the conflict between the two powers on the Rhine that had unsettled Western Europe since the end of the war. After six years of disappointment and frustration, France had obtained what it wanted most: from Germany, freely tendered assurances that the Franco-German frontier as well as the demilitarized condition of the Rhineland were inviolate; from Great Britain (as well as Italy), the precious guarantee that had eluded French statesmen ever since the end of the Paris Peace Conference. Germany's prize was the promise of the eventual liberation of the Rhineland plus the assurance that French troops would never return to German soil. Almost as important as the actual text of the treaty was the atmosphere of cordiality that pervaded the meetings that produced it. German, French, and British officials dined together, exchanged pleasantries during festive boat cruises on Lake Maggiore, and gave every indication that the acrimony of the past had been buried in a universal enthusiasm for detente. The British foreign secretary, Austen Chamberlain, foreshadowing the misplaced optimism of his younger half-brother thirteen years later at Munich, confidently boasted that his conciliatory influence at Locarno had produced peace for his time. He shared the Nobel Peace Prize with Stresemann and the French foreign minister, Aristide Briand, the following year for this collective achievement of reconciliation.

But the euphoria engendered by the Locarno pact concealed serious deficiencies that were to be found not in what the treaty contained, but in what it omitted. Most important of all, the German foreign minister had adamantly refused to affirm the inviolability of Germany's borders with Poland and Czechoslovakia. By acknowledging its territorial losses to France and Belgium while refusing to recognize the political settlement in Eastern Europe, Germany had in effect reserved the right to seek redress of its grievances in that region at some future date. By freezing Germany's frontiers in the west without extracting equivalent pledges to respect the territorial status quo in the east, Briand and Chamberlain seemed to be tacitly acquiescing in Germany's eventual search for territorial compensation in that direction. The fact that neither Poland, Czechoslovakia, nor the Soviet Union had participated in the drafting of this important agreement on European security aroused fears in those countries that the Western powers had settled with Germany at their expense.

Equally as ominous was the absence of a specific German commitment to fulfill the disarmament provisions of the Versailles Treaty. Berlin had consistently objected to the principle of unilateral disarmament on the grounds that it left the German people perpetually exposed to invasion from a vindictive France armed to the teeth. By agreeing to the reduction of the military control commission to a token force, the Allies had effectively entrusted to Germany itself the responsibility of self-supervision without requiring even an innocuous verbal commitment to the principle of unilateral disarmament. The clandestine rearmament initiated in the early twenties proceeded thereafter without even the threat of detection by Allied military observers. In the meantime the Allies scrupulously adhered to their part of the bargain. The evacuation of the Cologne zone began on December 1, 1925, the day of the official signing of the Locarno pacts in London, and was completed by January 31, 1926. In time the French and British were moved to increase the concessions made at Locarno in their eagerness to appease Germany.

The most important diplomatic prize that Briand took home from Locarno, the British guarantee of the Franco-German frontier, was rendered worthless by the multilateral character of the commitment: For British military power to be effective in assisting France against unprovoked German aggression, extensive Anglo-French military preparations would have been required. But such privileged contacts would have prejudiced Britain's position as an impartial guarantor of the territorial status quo in Western Europe. Hence London systematically declined to authorize prior military arrangements with any of the beneficiaries of the Locarno guarantee. The most bizarre aspect of the situation was to be found in the fact that the British guarantee could be invoked by Germany against France in the event of a future French military operation in the Ruhr Valley. This meant that Germany was theoretically free to default on reparation deliveries, violate the disarmament restrictions, and exert pressure against France's allies in Eastern Europe, just so long as it refrained from sending troops into France, Belgium, or the Rhineland. Any French military response to these provocations would give rise, according to the language of Locarno, to British (and Italian) intervention against France on Germany's behalf.

The Locarno treaties were to enter into force upon the admission of Germany into the League of Nations. This remarkable event took place on September 10, 1926, after several months of haggling over how to accommodate Stresemann's demand for a permanent seat on the League Council without antagonizing other aspirants for this prestigious position among the second-rank powers. To French critics of Briand's conciliatory policy toward Germany, Stresemann at Geneva seemed equivalent to the fox in the chicken coop. How could an organization dedicated to the maintenance of the political status quo in Europe operate effectively with the most notorious proponents of territorial revision occupying a powerful place in its midst? In fact, the question was moot since the League had ceased to function as the forum for the discussion of matters relating to European security. On the model of the Locarno consultations, the important issues of the day were thereafter settled by the representatives of the four great European powers in private meetings in Geneva hotel suites. No longer a pariah among nations, Germany would participate on an equal footing with the victorious Allies in the deliberations concerning the future of Europe. The recently elected German head of state, Field Marshal Paul von Hindenburg, was a troublesome reminder of the imperial past. The German foreign minister, Stresemann, never concealed his disdain for the territorial settlement in Eastern Europe. But these were matters of little import in the eyes of a European world basking in the agreeable atmosphere of prosperity and peace. Armies were no longer on the march, intergovernmental debts were being repaid on schedule, production and employment had reached and surpassed the prewar levels. "Away with the rifles, the machine guns, the cannon!" Briand had exclaimed in his welcoming speech on the occasion of Germany's admission to the League. "Make way for conciliation, arbitration, and peace." The almost hysterical enthusiasm that greeted these words signified that the French foreign minister was expressing the hopes of an entire generation weary of war and intent on enjoying the fruits of European detente.

Yet the shrewd Briand, unjustly reviled by his nationalist critics at home as a gullible dupe of Stresemann, was fully aware of the grave shortcomings of the Locarno settlement as a guarantee of France's security. Indeed, his concessions to Stresemann had been reluctantly given, and only after persistent prodding from Chamberlain. Historians may never discover the true motivations of this incomparably enigmatic architect of French foreign policy in the second half of the 1920s. He seldom committed his most intimate thoughts to writing; even if he had done so, most of his private papers were destroyed. But his foreign policy initiatives after Locarno reveal the persistence of a profound skepticism about the good intentions of the German leadership with which he had recently made peace. To supplement the new Franco-German rapprochement he had helped to inaugurate, Briand took a number of compensatory steps to enhance France's diplomatic and military position vis-à-vis Germany as insurance against the day when Stresemann's conciliatory policy might be repudiated.

The first of these precautions was taken toward the end of the Locarno Conference itself. After his failure to obtain Stresemann's formal affirmation of Germany's borders in Eastern Europe, Briand hastened to reassure France's nervous allies in that region. He concluded mutual assistance pacts with Poland and Czechoslovakia that reaffirmed and strengthened the bilateral military commitments previously undertaken in 1921 and 1924, respectively. In June 1926 he added a treaty of friendship with Romania and in November 1927 a similar pact with Yugoslavia. By the end of the decade, as we have seen, Briand's passion for bilateral instruments to deter German aggression had provided France with military alliances or political understandings with Poland and the three countries of the Little Entente. Considered in conjunction with the Franco-Belgian alliance of 1920, this eastern alliance system seemed to represent for France a formidable supplement to the Locarno accords. Despite the aforementioned disputes among themselves (see p. 102), all of the members of the French-led diplomatic system on the continent shared a common interest in preserving the territorial settlement in Europe from which they all benefited. Moreover, these military and political links between France and the nations to Germany's east and south were reinforced by economic connections as well. French capital investment was directed to these countries both to enhance their value as allies and to secure their economic independence from Germany.

On two other occasions after Locarno, Briand attempted to reinforce the Franco-German detente by enlisting outside assistance on behalf of European peace and security. The first of these initiatives was launched on April 6, 1927, when the French foreign minister inserted in his message of gratitude to the American people on the tenth anniversary of the United States intervention in the Great War a suggestion that the two nations sign a bilateral treaty forswearing war between them. Since the likelihood of armed conflict between France and the United States was nil at the time, the State Department correctly suspected an ulterior motive behind this curious emanation from the Quai d'Orsay: Briand apparently hoped to ensnare the United States in a privileged relationship with France that might eventually evolve into some kind of commitment to bolster French security in Europe. Consequently, Briand's overtures received a cool reception from Secretary of State Frank Kellogg, who had no intention of permitting his nation to be lured into signing a disguised version of the ill-fated Franco-American security treaty negotiated by Wilson at Paris. But an effective publicity campaign orchestrated by prominent American pacifists, who saw in the French proposal an opportunity to launch a campaign to promote peace through international agreement, forced the State Department to respond. The shrewd Kellogg thereupon seized the initiative in December 1927, dispatching to Paris a draft treaty that transformed Briand's project for a bilateral pact into a universal declaration against war that all nations would be invited to sign. In place of the bilateral agreement between Washington and Paris that he had originally sought, the disappointed Briand obtained a multilateral renunciation of war rendered entirely innocuous by the absence of precise commitments and enforcement machinery. With great fanfare the representatives of fifteen nations signed the Pact of Paris on July 27, 1928, solemnly pledging to "condemn recourse to war for the solution of international controversies and renounce it as an instrument of national policy." Eventually sixty-two nations adhered to what became known as the Kellogg-Briand Pact, including all of those whose aggression was to produce a second world war in the near future.

Foiled in his surreptitious effort to obtain American support for French security, the energetic French foreign minister unveiled an even bolder scheme for the maintenance of European peace. In an historic oration from the rostrum of the League Assembly on September 5, 1929, Briand issued a vaguely worded but dramatic appeal for the creation of some kind of supranational arrangement linking the sovereign states of Europe. This urgent plan for European union sprang from the same motivation behind the earlier proposal to the United States: Briand hoped to restrain Germany from relapsing into its former aggressiveness, in this instance by submerging that nation in a supranational Europe that would become economically integrated and politically interdependent. He was thereupon invited by the surprised European members of the League to draft a detailed memorandum specifying the organizational structure and function of the "federation" alluded to in his speech. On May 17, 1930, he unveiled a formal proposal for the establishment of inter-European political institutions, a general system of arbitration and security, and a "common market" in which "the circulation of goods, capital, and persons would be facilitated." What appeared for a brief moment to be an imaginative prescription for European union proved instead to be one of the last gasps of the old order established at Versailles. As the delegates at Geneva debated the Briand plan with ever-decreasing enthusiasm, the German legislative elections of September 14, 1930, increased the Nazi party's representation in the Reichstag from 12 to 107, making Hitler's wrecking crew the parliament's second largest political party. Within a few months the Briand proposal had been permanently pigeonholed in a committee of the League Assembly. The juxtaposition of these two events at the beginning of the 1930s constituted an ominous portent for the future: The continent of Europe was to be unified within a decade not by the free consent of democratic nations, but by the military might of a rejuvenated Germany. Briand's project for European union, like his abortive effort to secure an American commitment to European security, was a generation ahead of its time. It required a second world war before the United States would come to regard Europe's security as an extension of its own and before the nations of the old continent would recognize the advantages of economic integration and political cooperation.

While the Quai d'Orsay sought to bolster France's diplomatic position in Europe through bilateral alliances and multilateral guarantees during the second half of the 1920s, the French Ministry of War was hard at work devising a military strategy that would protect France in case Briand's intricate network of diplomatic safeguards failed to deter German expansionism. The daunting strategic challenge that confronted French military planners was the following: All but one of the restrictions on German military recovery that had been written into the Versailles Treaty were of limited duration. Allied inspection of German disarmament was to end (and did end, in 1927) once the inspection commission judged the process of disarmament complete. Allied military occupation of the Rhineland was to be phased out in stages (the Cologne zone in 1925, the Coblenz zone in 1930, the Mainz zone in 1935). But the timetable for withdrawal from the last two zones was shortened in response to a combination of German complaints and pledges of good behavior. Coblenz was evacuated ahead of schedule on November 30, 1929, and the Mainz zone on June 30, 1930, both in exchange for Germany's acceptance of the Young Plan, an American-inspired proposal for the definitive resolution of the reparations problem. The sole permanent guarantee of French security was the demilitarized status of the Rhineland. This, it will be recalled, was the consolation prize awarded to Clemenceau in 1919 after his failure to fix Germany's western frontier at the Rhine. However, the Versailles Treaty did not oblige any nation to render France military assistance in the event of a German move to remilitarize this buffer region. Even the explicit Anglo-Italian guarantee of the demilitarized status of the Rhineland contained in the Locarno treaties was to become operational only in cases of "flagrant violation" of the provisions of the pact. Cases of "non-flagrant violation" were to be referred to the League Council for consideration. It soon became evident that London and Rome defined "flagrant violation" in the narrowest possible sense, namely, the entrance of German troops into the demilitarized zone preparatory to an actual military invasion of France. Before the ink was dry on the Locarno pacts, Great Britain made known her intention of using this semantic loophole to avoid any obligation to assist France against the isolated act of remilitarization itself.

The phased withdrawal of Allied troops from the Rhineland deprived France of its last line of defense against a resurgent Germany. With the Ruhr Valley no longer within range of French heavy artillery and mechanized infantry in the Rhineland, Germany's industrial heartland could no longer be held hostage to Berlin's pacific behavior. The French strategy of offensive military action in western Germany to compel German adherence to the Versailles Treaty, developed by Marshal Foch after the armistice and employed by Poincaré in 1923, underwent a radical transformation during the second half of the twenties. By the end of the decade, the decision was taken to replace the disappearing natural defensive barrier of the Rhine with a manmade substitute: a continuous stationary fortification covering the entire length of the Franco-German frontier, which came to be known, after the war minister who authorized its construction, as the Maginot Line.

So much ridicule has been heaped upon this military strategy since the demonstration of its inadequacies in May–June 1940 that it is worth pausing to review the underlying motivations for its adoption. Above all, there was the striking disparity in human and material resources between the two antagonists along the Rhine: There were 40 million

Frenchmen facing over 65 million Germans who were endowed with superior industrial (and therefore military) potential. French strategists accordingly concluded that in the event of a future conflict with Germany, France's only hope for survival as a nation lay in a defensive posture designed to spare as many French lives and as much industrial plant as possible. This inclination was reinforced by the putative lessons of the Great War: The suicidal offensives of 1914–17 were universally blamed for having needlessly squandered precious French manpower and resources. The superiority of firepower afforded by modern weapons, such as the machine gun and heavy artillery, was taken to mean that the war of movement was a relic of a bygone era. In future conflicts the advantage would unmistakably rest with the defensive, as it had during the war of recent memory. Instead of improvising underground shelters to protect against the devastating firepower of the advancing enemy, as had been necessary in 1914, France would construct in advance a permanent network of subterranean fortifications equipped with all of the supplies and amenities that had been lacking in the cramped, disease-ridden trenches of the western front: barracks, mess halls, ammunition dumps, even movie theaters and canteens, all interconnected by an underground railroad. In these comfortable surroundings the French infantry, protected by shields of concrete and fortified with powerful artillery pieces, would lie in wait for any German military force rash enough to risk a repetition of the bloody offensives of the Great War. The valuable time purchased by this defensive strategy would enable Great Britain to rearm, gather its military forces from their faraway imperial outposts, mobilize its extensive economic resources, and enter the fray alongside France. It was even contemplated, though without good reason, that the establishment of a stationary front along France's eastern frontier would once again result in an influx of the enormous industrial resources of the United States to tip the scale against the German aggressor.

From a purely military point of view, the Maginot Line was brilliant in conception and effective in practice. It functioned precisely according to plan when the German offensive finally came in May 1940. Nowhere along the Franco-German border was it penetrated by Hitler's armies. It was circumvented and taken from behind. France's defensive strategy failed to prevent the German breakthrough not because it was defective but because it was not carried to its logical conclusion. The fatal flaw in the Maginot system was the decision to terminate construction of the continuous fortified line at Longwy, leaving the entire Franco-Belgian border unprotected. This omission was a striking one in view of historical precedent and geographical reality, both of which suggested that the Belgian lowland would be the most likely path of a German assault against France, as in 1914.

The decision not to extend the Maginot Line the entire length of the Franco-Belgian frontier to the English Channel was dictated by considerations of foreign policy and domestic politics. To begin with, the military alliance that France had concluded with Belgium in 1920 made it diplomatically inopportune even to discuss the possibility of leaving a trusted ally outside the French defense perimeter. The French war plan presumed that Belgium would request French military assistance at the slightest hint of an impending German invasion; a Franco-Belgian line of defense could easily be improvised behind the only natural barrier to military aggression on the Belgian plain: the confluence of the Meuse River and the Albert Canal. What rendered this theoretically astute strategy fatally vulnerable was that it depended entirely on the willingness of a weak little neighboring state to maintain its commitment to joint defense with France in the face of German intimidation. But even in the unlikely event that Belgium would have cheerfully tolerated the establishment of a fortified line separating it from its ally and protector, the northward extension of the Maginot Line would have presented serious complications in the northeastern corner of France. This highly industrialized, densely populated region was entirely unsuitable for the permanent emplacement of heavy artillery, which requires long stretches of uninhabited territory to operate without obstruction. It was unthinkable, and politically impossible, to locate these weapons of destruction behind or within one of France's principal industrial, urbanized regions. These negative reasons for halting the Maginot Line at the intersection of the French, Belgian, and Luxembourgian frontiers were reinforced by a positive consideration: French military authorities judged the densely wooded hills of the Ardennes Forest that roll across the Franco-Belgian frontier impassable to tanks, armored personnel carriers, and other mechanized vehicles of modern warfare.

The construction of the costly Maginot Line had to await the definitive stabilization of France's financial situation in 1928. Begun in the following year as French troops prepared to evacuate the Rhineland, it was completed in the midthirties; the elaborate fortifications produced in the security-conscious French a feeling of relative safety amid an increasingly dangerous international environment. It also helped to erase the pejorative image of postwar France, by then widely viewed in the English-speaking world as a vengeful nation bent on perpetually intimidating a disarmed Germany with its overwhelming military superiority. What more conclusive demonstration of France's defensive intentions than a military strategy of passively awaiting events behind an impregnable fortified line? But the sentiments of security in Paris and relief in London were not shared in Prague and Warsaw. France's adoption of a defensive military strategy so soon after the Franco-German reconciliation at Locarno reinforced the skepticism of the Czechs and the Poles about the value of their bilateral alliances with their French protector. The presence of French military forces in the Rhineland during the 1920s had served as an effective deterrent to German meddling in the affairs of France's eastern allies. The evacuation of the Rhineland and the establishment of a stationary position behind the Maginot Line seemed to undermine the basic assumptions of France's ambitious diplomacy in Eastern Europe. Germany's recently acquired immunity from the threat of offensive military action by France seemed an open invitation to maintain a defensive posture on the Rhine while conducting an aggressive policy on the Danube and the Vistula.

The reduced likelihood of effective military assistance from France compelled the Eastern European states to reassess their strategy for protecting themselves from the consequences of German revisionism. Czechoslovakia, the most highly industrialized and financially secure nation in the region, was able to bear the costs of constructing its own miniature version of the Maginot Line. Unfortunately for the ill-starred Czechs, geographical considerations dictated that this defensive line be established in the mountainous region along the Bohemian frontier known in Germany as the "Sudetenland," an enclave of ethnic German settlement that served as a potential object of irredentist ambition across the border. Poland, which possessed neither the economic resources to finance elaborate defensive fortifications nor the natural geographic barriers on which to base them, responded to the devaluation of its French alliance by desperately seeking an accommodation with its two menacing neighbors. As will be seen, nonaggression pacts concluded with the Soviet Union in July 1932 and Germany in January 1934 represented desperate efforts by Warsaw to preserve a precarious balance between the two neighboring powers that harbored designs on Polish territory.

The first two years of the 1930s were dominated by the spreading economic crisis and the attempts by various governments to develop means of coping with it. These economic policies, both foreign and domestic, inevitably had important consequences in the political and military realm. This was particularly so in Europe, where political stability and military security were so heavily dependent upon the efficient operation of the international network of trade, investment, and intergovernmental debt service. The breakdown of this system in the early thirties delivered a devastating blow to the European security system that had been fashioned in the middle of the previous decade. The death of Gustav Stresemann in the same month (October 1929) that the American stock market began its downward slide was an eminently symbolic coincidence: The era of European detente associated with his name came to a close as the international economic order upon which it so heavily depended began to disintegrate. The man whose deceptively conciliatory diplomacy from 1924 to 1929 had relieved Germany of the burden of military occupation and inspection, drastically reduced its reparation debt, and restored it to the ranks of the great powers had bequeathed to his successors a golden legacy. They had only to bide their time while the deterioration of the international economic order enabled them to complete what he had begun: the liberation of Germany from the remaining fetters of Versailles.

Yet it would be a grave mistake to conclude that the disappearance of the "spirit of Locarno," the revival of German revisionism, and the advent of the Nazi dictatorship were direct results of the international economic collapse of the early thirties that will be discussed in the next chapter. The assumption of a causal relationship between economic prosperity on the one hand and political democracy and international stability on the other, widely held by government officials, business people, and financiers in the English-speaking world during the postwar period, may well explain the peaceful, prosperous, democratic years of Europe in the second half of the twenties. But the converse of that causal proposition fails to account for subsequent events. Germany began to terminate its brief experiment with international conciliation and political democracy in 1930, before the effects of the Great Depression had taken their toll. The legislative election campaign of that year, which resulted in the spectacular success of the Nazi party, was fought largely on issues of foreign rather than domestic policy. All of the major parties competed for votes with nationalistic denunciations of the Versailles system: strident demands for an end to reparations, the restoration of the former colonial empire, the recovery of territories lost to Poland, and the unrestricted right to rearm. Chancellor Heinrich Brüning's proposal for a customs union with Austria in March 1931 was less a measure for economic recovery than a political assault on the Versailles system and a threat to the security of Czechoslovakia. This move toward an economic *Anschluss** (which was torpedoed by France), together with the launching of a heavy cruiser construction program in the same year, were both justified to the apprehensive British and French as necessary ploys to outbid the Nazis in chauvinism in order to win over their supporters in the German electorate. So too were Brüning's insistent demands for a revision of Germany's eastern frontiers and his succes-

---

*German for "union," used in the 1930s to designate the German annexation of Austria.

sor Franz von Papen's decision to default on reparation payments in September 1932. In December of that year German pressure finally obtained from the nervous members of the League formal recognition of Germany's right to achieve equality of armaments. In short, the main features of the foreign policy program of the Nazi party were adopted by the very German statesmen, such as Brüning, Papen, and Hindenburg, who advertised themselves as the only alternative to Hitler.

The stage for Germany's internal evolution from democracy to dictatorship was likewise set during the three years prior to Hitler's accession. On July 16, 1930, after the Reichstag had rejected the government's budget bill, Hindenburg authorized it by presidential decree, dissolved the Reichstag, and called the new elections that produced the stunning Nazi gains. Within a year Brüning was circumventing the elected legislators altogether, invoking emergency powers to enact unpopular measures of economic austerity. The fierce political infighting of the year 1932, during which Brüning, von Papen, and General Kurt von Schleicher occupied in succession the chancellor's office, represented abortive attempts to patch together a governing coalition that would preclude Hitler's assumption of power. But the legislative elections of July 1932, in which the Nazis won 37 percent of the vote to become the largest party in the Reichstag, demonstrated the extent of Hitler's popularity among all segments of German society. Though a subsequent election in November of the same year reduced somewhat the Nazis legislative representation, the handwriting on the wall was unmistakable. The guardians of the old order read it accurately and acted accordingly. Their reluctance to embrace the upstart leader of the Nazis did not stem from any distaste for his revisionist foreign policy goals, still less from concern about his antipathy for democratic political institutions. It was the radical social program of National Socialism that alarmed these conservative politicians and the social elites they represented. Once assured of the purely rhetorical nature of the "socialist" element in the Nazi creed, and of Hitler's intention to leave intact the existing socioeconomic hierarchies, the East Prussian landowners, Ruhr and Rhenish industrialists, and upper-echelon military officers hastened to make their peace with him. The Junkers craved assurances that their vast estates would not be expropriated and redistributed to indigent veterans, as had been suggested by some as a means of combating the effects of the depression; the Krupps, Thyssens, and their fellow magnates of heavy industry coveted assured markets and sources of supply in Europe; the military leaders longed for a trained and equipped mass army; all three sought protection against what they feared to be the rising tide of communism in Germany, as reflected in the improved performance of the Communist party in recent legislative elections. These things Hitler promised, either directly or through intermediaries, as part of his program of foreign expansion, rearmament, and domestic dictatorship. In return he received the support, both political and financial, of these powerful interest groups in his bid for power. Hitler's appointment as chancellor on January 30, 1933, was engineered by men who believed that they could manipulate him and his extremist movement to obtain what they wanted and prevent what they feared. Instead, as will be seen, the Nazi leader turned the tables on his allies among the industrial, agricultural, and military elites, using them and the resources under their control to realize his ambitious plans for the future of Germany and Europe.

4

THE WESTERN WORLD
IN THE THIRTIES:
THE ILLUSIONS DISPELLED

THE COLLAPSE OF THE WORLD ECONOMIC ORDER

Since the wave of economic prosperity that swept Europe in the second half of the 1920s rested in large part on the industrial and financial strength of the United States, it was inevitable that the crash on the American stock market in the autumn of 1929 would have profound and deleterious effects on the other side of the Atlantic. The new role assumed by the United States in the postwar decade as the largest producer, lender, and investor in the world had rendered the international economic order acutely sensitive to the operation of the American economy. When that economy flourished, as it did with a few minor corrections and adjustments from 1922 through 1929, it served as an engine of prosperity for the rest of the industrial world. During the second half of the twenties, the United States, with about 3 percent of the world's population, accounted for 46 percent of its total industrial output. During the same period it produced 70 percent of the world's oil and 40 percent of its coal. Moreover, the flow of American surplus capital to Europe provided a relatively painless solution to the acrimonious disputes over German reparations and inter-Allied debts and supplied the necessary liquidity for the trading nations of the world to balance their international accounts.

We are familiar with the symptoms of weakness in the international economy that were already apparent in the boom years of the second half of the 1920s: the speculative fever on Wall Street that diverted capital investment away from those regions of the world that needed it most to the nation that needed it least; the tendency of those American investments that did go to postwar Europe to be short term rather than long term and speculative rather than productive; declining prices of foodstuffs, metals, and other primary products that prevented the countries of the nonindustrial world from earning enough to pay for imports from industrial countries; the problems of exchange instability, commercial protectionism, and immigration restrictions, which hindered the free flow of capital, resources, and labor across national frontiers. Once the American engine of world prosperity faltered and proceeded to burn out between 1929 and 1932, all of these ominous symptoms of economic instability, which had been either discounted or ignored during the boom years, developed into a full-blown crisis of the international economic order.

The causes of the precipitous decline in the prices of securities on the New York Stock Exchange need not detain us here. What is important for our purposes is the effect of the "Great Crash" on the economic health of the United States and then of the entire industrial world. The mere recitation of United States economic statistics for the three years after 1929 tells the story: Industrial production and national income declined by half; the real gross national product dropped by a third; the unemployment rate approached 25 percent of the work force; one-third of the nation's banks closed their doors; wholesale prices fell by 32 percent. Workers without work, banks without deposits, investors wiped out, home mortgages foreclosed, farmers and small business people unable to sell their wares and therefore unable to pay off their commercial debts—such was the domestic economic condition of the nation on whose prosperity the entire world had grown accustomed to depend.

The international effect of this sudden and pronounced economic downturn in the United States was devastating. The first and most obvious consequence was the abrupt termination of long-term foreign lending and the repatriation of existing foreign loans as they came due. Long-term foreign lending by private American investors declined 68 percent between 1929 and 1933, then ceased altogether for the remainder of the decade. From 1934 to 1939 there was actually a net liquidation of foreign assets held by Americans. This massive withdrawal of American funds had an immediate impact on the economies of those nations, particularly in Central Europe, that had become vitally dependent on an uninterrupted influx of American capital for the balancing of their budgets, the expansion of their industrial production, the financing of their trade, and the payment of their foreign debts. The repatriation of American foreign loans and investments was soon followed by a massive transfer of foreign gold holdings to the United States in response to the political instability in Europe. Between 1931 and 1938 American banks received a net inflow of gold amounting to roughly $6.6 billion. This liquidation of American assets abroad, the acquisition of American assets by foreigners, and the accumulation of foreign-owned gold in American banks resulted in a total capital inflow into the United States far in excess of the amounts required for the settlement of the world's current account deficit with the United States. This anomalous trend drastically reduced the supply of desperately needed gold and dollars in Europe.

To make matters worse, the decline of purchasing power in the United States sharply curtailed the ability of Americans to pay for imports from abroad. American merchandise imports dropped from $4.463 billion in 1929 to $1.343 billion in 1932, representing a 40 percent decline by volume. Furthermore, to compensate for the collapse of domestic prices, agricultural and manufacturing interests in the United States pressured the Congress into enacting the steepest protective tariff in the twentieth century, the Hawley-Smoot Tariff of 1930, which raised the average duty on protected goods to 59 percent. The combination of reduced demand and tariff protection in the United States precipitated a drastic decline in incomes and widespread unemployment among America's trading partners.

The contraction of world trade during the early 1930s also caused an abrupt decline in British foreign investment. France, the other great international lender, had already begun to divert a substantial portion of its surplus capital to gold purchases in order to bolster its recently stabilized currency. The simultaneous curtailment of foreign lending by the few nations of the world with surplus savings forced the recipient countries to acknowledge a fundamental weakness in their economic position that had been conveniently overlooked during the recent years of prosperity: their inability to service their enormous foreign debt (both private and governmental) without the continued receipt of additional foreign loans.

At first, the major European nations and the United States sought to ride out the storm by reverting to the traditional cure for such economic crises. Instead of repudiating the gold standard and permitting the exchange rate of their currencies to depreciate in order to preserve the competitive price advantage of their exports, they tenaciously clung to the system of fixed exchange rates and prepared to endure the severe deflation that was certain to result. But before this deflationary medicine had a chance to take effect, Europe was plunged into a full-fledged financial panic in the spring of 1931: The largest commercial bank of Austria, the Creditanstalt, was found to be on the brink of insolvency due to the withdrawal of foreign short-term funds. The Austrian government's decision to freeze the remaining assets of the beleaguered bank prompted a precautionary stampede on the financial institutions of Germany and the other nations of Central Europe as foreign lenders scrambled to recover their deposits before those governments followed the Austrian example. After failing to stem the outflow of foreign funds by the traditional means of raising interest rates to entice foreign investors to keep their assets in marks, the German government imposed exchange controls to halt the capital flight and preclude further bank closings. By the end of the year, eleven other European nations had enacted various types of restrictions on the transfer of capital abroad. In the meantime, political and financial authorities had taken steps to relieve the deteriorating economic condition of the Central European nations in general and the German Republic in particular. On June 21, 1931, President Herbert Hoover proposed a one-year moratorium on the payment of reparations and inter-Allied debts to afford Germany sufficient breathing space to get its financial house in order. The central banks of the United States, Great Britain, and France extended short-term loans to Germany, while international bankers undertook a study of the feasibility of arranging new long-term private loans to shore up the faltering economies of Central Europe.

But the financial storm brewing on the continent rapidly crossed the English Channel to engulf Europe's bulwark of monetary stability. Public awareness that British banks were heavily invested in the nations of Central Europe that had frozen foreign-owned assets or imposed exchange controls caused a widespread loss of faith in sterling. So too did the abrupt termination of German reparation payments after the announcement of the Hoover moratorium, which came during a period of chronic budget deficits in Britain. At the same time the need to make large international payments forced foreign creditors to withdraw foreign exchange and gold on deposit in London. What all of these considerations added up to, in the summer of 1931, was a run on the pound sterling that depleted Britain's reserves of foreign currencies and gold. When a large loan to the Bank of England from the Federal Reserve Bank of New York and the Bank of France failed to stem the tide, the

British Parliament on September 21 took the extraordinary step of suspending the obligation of the Bank of England to sell gold in exchange for the national currency.

Great Britain's repudiation of the gold standard was a landmark in the economic history of the modern world. It exposed the fundamental economic weakness of the nation that had presided for so long over the international monetary system: London was shown to be incapable of retaining sufficient reserves of gold and foreign currencies to function as one of the two financial centers of the world. The explanation of Great Britain's ignominious descent from its previous position of financial preeminence can be found in the shifting patterns of world trade during and after the First World War. The failure to recapture overseas markets lost during the four years of combat prevented the British export trade from resuming the spectacular rate of growth that had attracted the financial reserves of the world to the London banking system during the nineteenth century. The consequence of Britain's abandonment of gold on that historic day in September 1931 was the crumbling of the international monetary system that had been reestablished after the First World War.

The decision in April 1925 to return to the gold standard at the prewar parity of $4.86 was, by the beginning of the 1930s, generally blamed for having aggravated Britain's chronic trade deficit by making British exports too expensive in nations that had returned to the gold standard at a devalued level. Accordingly, British treasury officials hoped that once the exchange rate of the pound was free to fluctuate on world money markets it would drop to a level that would restore the competitive position of British exports. On being cut loose from gold, the British currency rapidly fell from par ($4.86) to about $3.50. But those nations for which Britain was a major customer and British banks the principal center for their surplus reserves could ill afford to allow sterling to continue to depreciate against their currencies for fear that their own exports would be priced out of the British market and the value of their sterling deposits in London would dwindle. Twenty-four such countries were therefore compelled to leave the gold standard and allow their currencies to float freely by the spring of 1932. Thereafter, the trading nations of the world were left to their own devices to adopt temporary expedients to finance their international transactions. The system of fixed exchange rates linked to gold, one of the pillars of postwar economic recovery, was in shambles.

The international monetary system soon disintegrated into three distinct groups of nations, each of which cautiously embraced its own preferred expedient. One set of five countries blessed with relatively healthy financial conditions—the United States, France, Belgium, the Netherlands, and Switzerland—remained on the gold standard while striving to reduce imports by erecting protectionist tariff barriers and imposing restrictive import quotas. A second group, composed of Britain and its major trading partners (including all of the member states of the empire except Canada, together with twelve other nations) followed Britain's flight from gold and tied the value of their currencies to the pound sterling. Exchange stability within this "sterling bloc" was maintained through the buying and selling of the British currency by the member governments, while Britain drew upon a stabilization fund to moderate exchange fluctuations between this sterling bloc and the "gold bloc." The third group, dominated by Germany and including many of the impoverished nonindustrialized nations of Central Europe and Latin America, imposed rigid exchange controls that rendered their currencies inconvertible. Since the protectionist policies of the gold bloc countries and the depreciation of the currencies of the sterling bloc countries had the identical effect of reducing imports, the only alternative open to the "exchange control states" was to seek new markets and sources of imports in other nations that had adopted exchange controls. This expedient of bilateral trade was increasingly adopted by Germany after the advent of the Nazi regime. On account of the drying up of foreign loans, the closure of markets abroad, and the inconvertibility of the mark, Germany lacked the means of accumulating foreign exchange to finance the imports of raw materials and foodstuffs that it required. It therefore increasingly strove to obtain its imports from those countries (mostly in Central Europe) that were indebted to Germany on current account or were willing to receive payment in marks that could not leave Germany because of the exchange restrictions. As a consequence, Germany's suppliers of raw materials and foodstuffs were required to import as much from her as they exported to her in order to avoid allowing the marks that they earned from their sales to accumulate unused in German banks. The German government also experimented with old-fashioned bilateral barter arrangements with various countries to circumvent the problem of currency inconvertibility. Thus German coal was shipped to Brazil for an equivalent value of coffee while German fertilizer was exchanged for Egyptian cotton.

The gold bloc and sterling bloc countries themselves turned away from the traditional system of multilateral payments through the London money market in favor of bilateral arrangements for the balancing of international accounts. Great Britain, France, and the Netherlands stepped up their imports from those parts of the world (in particular, their colonial empires) where their extensive capital investments supplied the necessary foreign exchange to pay for those imports. As a consequence, trade between the three large financial-commercial blocs of the earth continued to dwindle.

A related cause of the decline of world trade was the universal appearance of politically imposed restrictions on international commerce that made the protectionist measures of the 1920s pale in comparison. In response to the Hawley-Smoot Tariff of the United States, the major trading nations of Europe hastened to enact protectionist legislation to halt the precipitous decline of prices and the increase of unemployment in their domestic industries. France and Germany erected high tariff walls and imposed strict quantitative restrictions on imports. Even Great Britain, the perennial champion of free trade, succumbed to the protectionist pressures of the era. The Import Duties Act of 1932 terminated three-quarters of a century of free trade by raising duties on a variety of items. At the Ottawa Conference in the summer of the same year, this protectionist policy was extended to embrace the self-governing Dominions of the empire. Britain raised duties on foreign agricultural commodities that competed with Dominion exports to the metropole such as Canadian wheat, Australian wool, and New Zealand dairy products. In return, British manufactured goods received preferential treatment in Dominion markets. Meanwhile, France and the Netherlands had devised similar preferential arrangements with their colonial possessions. The turn toward imperial preference, the protectionist legislation that insulated the vast continental market of the United States from foreign competition, and the bilateral trading arrangements of the exchange control countries, signaled the disintegration of the network of international trade into a half dozen virtually self-enclosed commercial blocs. By 1931 tariff rates in some fifteen European nations had increased 64 percent above the 1927 level. Throughout the 1930s trade in manufactured products among Germany, France, and Great Britain declined to half the level of 1913.

International cooperative efforts to rectify this situation by reviving world trade and the international monetary system on which it depended were uniformly unsuccessful during the 1930s. This was so largely because domestic pressures in each major nation inhibited government officials from adopting policies which, though painful in the short run, might have promoted long-term recovery of international trade and investment. The most graphic instance of this shortsighted, narrow-minded response to the world economic crisis was the initial monetary policy adopted by the new administration of Franklin D. Roosevelt in the United States. In early 1933, the League of Nations issued invitations to an international economic conference to devise a multilateral solution to the chronic instability of the world's currencies caused by the collapse of the gold standard. The United States had previously declined to participate in the international economic conferences at Brussels (1920) and Genoa (1922) and most recently at Lausanne (1932). Moreover, though private American financial experts had played an important role in devising the economic recovery programs of the 1920s, such as the Dawes and Young plans, the United States government had expressly declined any official connection with those measures. It was with considerable relief that European officials learned of the decision of the new American administration to send high-level representatives to the conference scheduled to convene in London during the summer of 1933. But before the conference got under way, Washington cast a pall over the forthcoming talks, first by refusing to permit any discussion of intergovernmental debts and then, on April 19, by abandoning the gold standard. The new president and his advisers, alarmed by the collapse of domestic commodity prices and subject to intense political pressure from the farm bloc, erroneously concluded that American prices could be boosted by deliberately reducing the foreign exchange value of the dollar in order to stimulate demand for American commodities abroad. Roosevelt feared that any agreement on exchange stability reached in London would inhibit his ability to employ monetary measures at home to raise the domestic price level. He therefore jolted the London conference with a July 3 message expressing his unwillingness to consider even a temporary linkage of the dollar exchange rate to any international standard until domestic prices could be raised.

Once the world's major currency was cut loose from gold and permitted to depreciate on world markets, the London Conference's plan for international currency stabilization was nipped in the bud. The United States soon saw the error of its ways and renewed its commitment to exchange stability by returning to a gold exchange standard* in January 1934, but at a fixed price of $35 per ounce compared to the predepreciation price of $20.67. It was only a matter of time before the other gold bloc nations were forced to devalue their own currencies in order to preserve the competitive position of their exports and finally to abandon gold altogether. In the meantime the United States signed the so-called Tripartite Agreement with Great Britain and France, later joined by Belgium, the Netherlands, and Switzerland, by which the member nations agreed to sell each other gold in exchange for the seller's own currency at an agreed upon price. This temporary expedient kept the exchange rates of the world's strongest currencies within the narrow

---

*The gold exchange standard differed from the traditional gold standard in one fundamental respect: Under the old gold standard, each nation's currency was freely convertible to gold on demand; under the gold exchange standard, American citizens were legally prohibited from owning gold.

range of the announced gold support price of each country. This agreement, though serving as an important precedent for the revival of international monetary cooperation after the Second World War, failed to operate as a satisfactory alternative to the gold standard on account of its limited application. In response to these financial machinations, the exchange control countries of Central Europe and Latin America tightened their restrictions on capital transfers to protect their domestic reserves. The absence of a universally recognized mechanism for the convertibility of national currencies, together with the drying up of international lending to facilitate the adjustment of international payments, prevented the recovery of world trade (which at the end of 1936 stood at 10 percent below its 1929 level) and the repayment of existing debts (most of which remained in default for the rest of the decade).

Just as the Tripartite Agreement represented the only significant American initiative to restore exchange stability in the 1930s, the Reciprocal Trade Agreement Amendment to the Hawley-Smoot Tariff Act was the sole American effort to unclog the channels of world trade. This legislation, which went into effect on June 12, 1934, authorized the president to reduce existing duties up to 50 percent of their current level in exchange for reciprocal tariff concessions by America's trading partners. It was also based on the unconditional most-favored-nation principle, which meant that any concessions made to one country were automatically extended to imports of the same commodity from all other countries. By 1940 bilateral reciprocal agreements to reduce duties had been signed with twenty-one countries representing 60 percent of the volume of American foreign trade. In principle, this should have produced a general reduction in commercial restrictions and a corresponding expansion of world trade. In practice, American tariff negotiators attempted to limit concessions to items that did not compete with American products. Moreover, even the maximum concession of 50 percent preserved a high degree of protection since the rates established by the 1930 tariff act had been so steep in the first place. Finally, a number of quantitative restrictions (such as an import quota on sugar) were introduced by the Roosevelt administration. A federal law of March 1933 required United States government agencies to purchase American-made products in preference to foreign imports. In sum, the reciprocal reduction of tariff barriers during the New Deal was motivated less by a recognition of the critical relationship between the United States balance of payments and world economic recovery than by the expectation that reciprocity would stimulate American exports and therefore hasten domestic recovery. The bilateral character of these agreements further reflected the American government's reluctance to participate in a genuinely international effort to revive world trade.

The same can be said about the creation of the Export-Import Bank in March 1934. Despite the second term in its title, this government-funded agency initially confined its operations largely to the supplying of credits to American exporters of agricultural commodities and industrial equipment. Its comparatively modest lending for import purposes was dictated by considerations of national interest, such as the procurement of strategic raw materials or the cementing of friendly relations with the primary producing countries of Latin America that sought access to the American market. It was not until 1940 that the bank began to disburse long-term development loans to stimulate industrialization in selected Latin American countries such as Brazil, and then primarily for the national security goal of combating the growing economic influence of Germany in the western hemisphere. The expansion of this policy of long-term American government lending to develop the productive capacity of present or prospective trading partners had to await the end of the Second World War and the full recognition of America's veritable global responsibilities.

Finally, the United States government's stubborn refusal to modify its policy regarding the troublesome issue of inter-Allied war debt repayment confirmed the narrowly nationalistic character of American foreign economic policy in the 1930s. It was inconceivable that the economically battered nations of Europe could have been expected to continue to make these large capital transfers once the lubricant of American foreign investment in Central Europe had dried up. Consequently, as Hoover's one-year moratorium on the payment of these government obligations approached its expiration in the summer of 1932, the European powers issued an invitation to the United States to attend the economic conference at Lausanne, Switzerland, to discuss ways of removing these irksome impediments to European economic recovery. After the refusal of the United States to participate, the European debtors proposed what amounted to a mutual cancellation of German reparations and inter-Allied debts. The Hoover administration, which, like its predecessors, had consistently denied the connection between German reparations and the European war debts to the United States, indignantly refused. Since Germany had failed to resume the reparations payments that had been interrupted (temporarily it was thought but permanently as it turned out) by the Hoover moratorium, the European debtors of the United States were forced to the wall. When the next installment on the war debts came due on December 15, 1932, six nations (including France and Belgium) defaulted for the first time. In June 1933 Great Britain and Italy made drastically reduced payments, and within a year all of the European debtors except Finland had ceased payment altogether.

Instead of writing off these intergovernmental obligations left over from the First World War, the United States Congress retaliated with the Johnson Act of April 1934, which prohibited American citizens from purchasing the securities of governments in default on their war debts. All that was accomplished by this measure was the closure of American financial markets to Great Britain and France as they undertook programs of industrial expansion and rearmament to meet the Nazi menace. Similarly, the Neutrality Act of 1935, which banned the sale of munitions to belligerents and required cash payment for all exports to nations engaged in hostilities, denied the Western democracies American supplies on credit once they went to war with Germany in September 1939. As a consequence Britain and France were forced to reduce their imports from the United States to conserve their dwindling gold and dollar reserves. As American public support for the Anglo-French cause increased, Congress lifted the arms embargo in November 1939, but this belated reversal of isolationist policy did not come in time to be of much assistance to France, which collapsed before the Nazi blitzkrieg in June 1940. The cash-on-delivery requirement was finally supplanted on March 11, 1941, by the Lend-Lease program, which authorized American exports to countries deemed vital to the security of the United States, for which payment was postponed until the end of the war.

In sum, to the extent that the New Deal of Franklin Roosevelt rescued the United States from economic collapse—and historians have increasingly challenged that conventional judgment—it did so by pursuing narrowly conceived domestic remedies rather than by cooperating with the industrial nations of Western Europe to fashion a coordinated program of international recovery. The resumption of industrial expansion in Europe was precipitated by international strategic factors rather than by remedial economic measures: The intensive campaign of rearmament that got under way in the late 1930s generated demand for manufactured products, raw materials, and labor that far surpassed in stimulative effect the modest public works projects and domestic spending programs undertaken earlier in the decade by the Western democracies. It is perhaps the most tragic irony of modern history that organized violence on a large scale, or the preparation for it, has proved to be the most effective remedy for the economic problems of underconsumption and unemployment.

The causal connection between military preparedness and economic recovery was most graphically demonstrated in Hitler's Germany, where strict state control of political and economic life permitted the most efficient mobilization of capital, labor, and resources for military purposes and consequently generated phenomenal economic growth throughout the second half of the 1930s. The Nazi Four-Year Plan of economic development instituted in 1936 was designed to make Germany entirely independent of markets and resources outside its political and economic orbit. As will be seen in greater detail below, this goal of economic self-sufficiency, or autarky, was to be attained through the combination of two strategies: First, the German chemical industry developed a number of synthetic products to substitute for raw materials, such as rubber, cotton, and wool, that could not be produced domestically in sufficient quantity. Second, Germany tightened its economic grip on its weaker neighbors in Eastern Europe that possessed valuable mineral and agricultural resources. By expanding its bilateral trade relations with such countries as Poland, Hungary, and Romania, Germany obtained access to enormous supplies of wheat, lumber, oil, and other raw materials it required as well as markets in which it could dispose of its surplus industrial production.

THE COLLAPSE OF THE EUROPEAN SECURITY SYSTEM

As we have seen, the rearmament of Germany was already well advanced by the time of Adolf Hitler's rise to power in January 1933. The dramatic announcements of March 1935 confirmed the existence of, rather than the intention of creating, a German army and air force that had been a decade and a half in the making. The patient, subtle efforts of the Weimar Republic to evade the disarmament prescriptions of the peace treaty without provoking Allied retaliation had forged an institutional structure of military power that Hitler inherited intact: a general staff, effectively concealed within a labyrinth of government agencies and military bureaus; the nucleus of a well-trained army of several hundred thousand men dispersed among various police forces, paramilitary organizations, veterans' associations, and rifle clubs; the kernel of an air force in the form of hundreds of commercial airline pilots with thousands of hours of flying time; and an elaborate infrastructure of munitions plants, first located in Russia during the period of Allied inspection and later reassembled in the Ruhr, that were capable on short notice of turning out huge quantities of the implements of war that had been proscribed by the peace treaty, including aircraft, tanks, artillery pieces, shells, and poison gas.

The full extent of this German military buildup was not known to the Allies, but enough evidence had been uncovered to cause grave apprehension in European capitals about the consequences of an unlimited increase in Germany's war-making potential. The removal of the Allied inspection team in 1927 and the evacuation of the Rhineland three years later left the victors of 1918 with little leverage to apply against a Germany that was determined to rearm. As the feasibility of enforcing the unilateral disarmament of Germany began to recede at the end of the 1920s, the alternative of general disarmament began to exert an increasingly powerful attraction on peace-loving folk everywhere. This was particularly true of public opinion in Great Britain and the United States, two countries which had unilaterally demobilized their large land armies, dismantled their munitions industries, and voluntarily accepted limitations to their naval strength in the early years after the war. The concept of universal disarmament had been endorsed by the Versailles Treaty in accordance with the popular presumption that the very existence of stockpiles of munitions and large standing armies made war more likely. But no progress toward that end had been possible during the first half of the twenties because of France's refusal to relinquish its military superiority over Germany in the absence of an ironclad guarantee of the security of its eastern border.

The insertion of just such a guarantee from Great Britain and Italy in the Locarno treaties paved the way for the convocation of a preparatory commission on disarmament in Geneva in May 1926 to study means of reducing the level of armaments in the world. The tangible results of these deliberations were minimal because of French suspicions of Germany's good intentions. The commission closed up shop in January 1931 with little to show for its five years of disputatious deliberation. But public interest in universal disarmament was revived soon thereafter when the effects of the economic crisis that originated in the United States began to be felt in Europe. As governments hastened to reduce expenditures and shore up their faltering finances, the enormous costs of maintaining defense establishments came under heavy attack from advocates of austerity. It began to seem senseless to divert an ever-increasing proportion of a nation's ever-decreasing supply of resources to the unproductive purposes of military preparedness while businesses failed, banks closed their doors, and the unemployment lines lengthened. Hence, the economic crisis of the early 1930s, together with mounting apprehension about the clandestine, unilateral rearmament of Germany, prompted the great powers to convene an international conference on land armaments in Geneva in February 1932 in the hope of reaching a definitive agreement on the size of national armies.

At this conference the German delegation reiterated the position that it had taken in informal exchanges with the Allied governments throughout the twenties: either universal disarmament as envisaged by the Versailles Treaty or equality of arms between Germany and the other great powers of Europe. When this demand foundered on the shoals of France's insistence on security prior to disarmament, the German delegates abruptly left the conference on September 16. Desperately intent on getting the German government back to the bargaining table, Britain and France promised on December 11 to grant Germany "equality in a system which would provide security for all other nations." Though this formula simply restated the insoluble dilemma that had prevented previous agreement, it was conveyed in sufficiently conciliatory language to lure Germany back to the conference in February 1933.

But the German delegation that returned to Geneva was under orders from Adolf Hitler, designated chancellor the previous month. The new German leader had already decided on a massive program of unilateral rearmament, which he communicated to the highest-ranking military and naval officers of the Reich on February 3, the day after the reappearance of his delegates in Geneva: Germany would go through the motions of negotiating an agreement for equality of arms with the other great powers while secretly constructing a military force superior to that of all potential enemies. The ostensible purpose of this ambitious rearmament program was principally economic in nature. In the short run, the vast government expenditures for military purposes would stimulate employment and industrial production and therefore rescue the German economy from the depression into which it had recently plunged. The huge government outlays required for this program would be furnished through deficit financing. More than one historian has noted the similarities between the remedial measures adopted by the National Socialist government to combat the depression and those of the new Roosevelt administration in the United States, whose domestic recovery program was getting under way at the same time. The key difference, of course, was the object of the deficit financing and stimulative government spending in the two countries. In the German case, it was directed not toward domestic recovery but rather toward the overriding priority of achieving military superiority in Europe.

The long-term objective of this military buildup, as expounded by Hitler with perfect consistency in his major writings and speeches, was also superficially economic in character. To summarize this objective briefly, Germany, with its existing frontiers, suffered from the Malthusian curse of insufficient arable land with which to feed its expanding population. If the territory under German sovereignty were to remain constant, the only solutions to this dilemma were a reduction of the birthrate through measures of population control such as contraception or abortion (which was repellent to Hitler because it signified a deliberately engineered form of racial suicide) or emigration. But the type of emigration that he envisioned differed, both in its object and its methods, from that employed by Great Britain to ease its population pressures in the nineteenth century. Instead of directing German settlers to overseas lands, where they were likely to assimilate and lose their sense of national identity and therefore represent a net loss to the mother country, they were to be relocated in the adjacent land area to Germany's east that was populated by "inferior" races that would be subdued and then expelled or annihilated to make way for the German pioneers. The Nazi leader never deviated from his insistence that the living space, or *Lebensraum,* that Germany required was to be found in Eastern Europe and the western part of the Soviet Union. The fertile agricultural land and valuable mineral resources located in this region could supply Germany with the food and raw materials it needed to survive and prosper as well as affording an outlet for its surplus population. It was inhabited by two "racial" groups that, for personal reasons, Hitler detested and was determined to subjugate: He considered the majority population of Slavs so racially decadent as to be incapable of organizing this valuable territory politically, exploiting it economically, or defending it militarily; and he regarded the minority of Jews dispersed throughout the region, together with their coreligionists in Germany itself, as a cancer on the body of Europe that had to be removed.

Hitler's policy toward the other great powers of Europe in the early months of his rule reflected this single-minded goal of extending Germany's living space eastward at the expense of the Slavs and Jews in Eastern Europe and Russia. Since France was the self-appointed guarantor of the existing territorial distribution in Europe and protector of those states in the east that stood in the way of Germany's *Drang nach Osten,* Hitler's foreign policy envisioned the prior destruction of France as a prelude to his eastern conquests. With England the German dictator had no quarrel so long as it could be induced to remain disinterested in continental affairs. Indeed, his project of eastward expansion on land was entirely compatible with the maintenance of friendly relations with the British. Recalling the disastrous consequences for Germany of the kaiser's bid to challenge Britain's position outside Europe, Hitler hoped that Germany's abstention from an aggressive colonial and naval policy would remove any basis for Anglo-German friction and therefore any reason for British support of France. As for Italy, Hitler's ideological affinity for his fellow Fascist dictator, Benito Mussolini, who had taken power in 1922 as an opponent of the Versailles system, was reinforced by realistic reasons for Italo-German friendship: Italy was in perpetual conflict with France over naval and colonial matters in the Mediterranean, while Germany's ambitions in Eastern Europe and Russia posed no direct threat to Italy's vital interests (save Hitler's designs on Austria).

It is worth pausing at this juncture to remark upon the extent to which this program for continental domination diverged from the foreign policy objectives of the political elite of the Weimar Republic. The superficial similarity between the immediate foreign policy goals of Stresemann and Hitler has led some historians to emphasize the continuity of German foreign policy throughout the interwar period. Some have been tempted to view Hitler as a traditional German nationalist pursuing the policy that had been adopted in the 1920s by his republican predecessors: the recovery of the territory lost by Germany at the Paris Peace Conference, the annexation of adjacent regions with substantial German populations on the basis of the principle of national self-determination, and the restoration of military parity for Germany with the other powers of Europe. The plausibility of this interpretation stems from the incontestable fact that all of Hitler's official diplomatic initiatives from his accession in January 1933 to March 1939 were aimed at securing these traditional objectives of German foreign policy. What this interpretation overlooks are Hitler's numerous unofficial references to the expansionist program delineated above. The reversal of the "unjust" verdict of the Paris Peace Conference, which implied the recovery or annexation of all German-speaking regions of Central Europe, was but the first step in Hitler's grand design. In truth he cared nothing about the fate of the German-speaking citizens who had been incorporated within half-a-dozen neighboring states in the peace settlement of 1919–20. Their grievances merely served as a pretext for destroying the territorial settlement, and therefore the balance of power in Europe, as a prelude to conquering and exploiting the vast expanses of territories to the east where few Germans lived but where German colonists were to be sent in some distant future. Though his grandiose ambitions beyond the regions of German settlement were not openly pursued until as late as March 1939 with the absorption of the non-German sector of Czechoslovakia, they were frequently and forcefully expressed in speeches and writings that were well-known to the world's political leaders.

In the light of this program of eastward expansion, the disarmament talks in Geneva to which the German representatives returned in February 1933 were exercises in futility. Even the compromise plan drafted by British Prime Minister Ramsay MacDonald that projected parity of national armies in Europe at 200,000 men each, to be achieved by the gradual reduction of French forces over five years, failed to secure the approval of Hitler's hand-picked delegation, which had been instructed to reject any multilateral restrictions on the German rearmament program already underway. When the German demand for the immediate right to construct proscribed weapons and increase the size of the standing army encountered the anticipated French opposition, Hitler summarily withdrew Germany from the disarmament conference and the League of Nations on October 14. Germany's simultaneous withdrawal from the disarmament conference and the League of Nations dealt a devastating blow to the principle of collective security that was soon to prove fatal. Though that principle had already been severely undermined in the Manchurian affair (see p. 213), an incident in far-off Asia that did not involve the vital interests of the great powers in Europe and therefore could be conveniently overlooked. But the advent of an aggressive German foreign policy in the autumn of 1933 compelled French officials to abandon whatever hopes they may have entertained of restraining Germany by the application of the pressure of world opinion through the instrument of the world body in Geneva.

Following closely on the heels of Hitler's abandonment of Geneva was an equally dramatic reversal of German foreign policy that dealt a severe blow to France's defensive alliance system in Europe: the conclusion of a German-Polish nonaggression pact on January 26, 1934. Berlin's approach to Warsaw for an improvement of their traditionally frosty relations was prompted by Hitler's realization that in its present condition of partial rearmament Germany was unprepared for war. A relaxation of tension with its traditional adversary in Eastern Europe would facilitate Germany's internal consolidation and military preparation. The main source of friction between the two countries was the political conflict between the German-speaking majority of the free city of Danzig and the Polish government, which maintained a customs union with the city as well as authority over its relations with foreign states. The German dictator promoted a temporary resolution of the Danzig issue by imposing tactical restraints on the National Socialist municipal government that had been elected in 1933 by the German-speaking majority. Warsaw's desire to improve its relations with Berlin, in order to enhance its balancing act between its two powerful neighbors as well as to gain access to the German market for its coal and agricultural surpluses, cemented the friendship. The pact of January 1934 committed each signatory to a bilateral resolution of their mutual problems and the avoidance of the use of force against each other for a period of ten years. The German-Polish rapprochement inaugurated a diplomatic revolution in Europe. In his first foray into bilateral diplomacy since divesting Germany of the constraints imposed by membership in the League, Hitler had punched a hole in the French alliance system and obtained what appeared to be a considerable measure of security on Germany's eastern flank.

The dramatic announcement of the German-Polish nonaggression pact prodded the Quai d'Orsay into action. The successors of Briand, whose death in March 1932 had marked the end of an era in French diplomacy, hastened to bolster France's sagging security arrangements on the continent through bilateral approaches to two great powers that had been allies of France in the Great War but had been alienated from it ever since.

The first of these was Italy. Even before the advent of the Fascist regime in 1922, Italy had nurtured deeply felt grievances against France. All of these were related in one way or another to the frustration of Italian aspirations to become an imperial power in the Mediterranean basin. Italian Prime Minister Vittorio Orlando's failure to obtain Allied support for Italy's territorial ambitions along the Dalmatian coast at the Paris Peace Conference, though largely due to President Wilson's endorsement of Yugoslavia's competing claims, had caused a serious breach in Franco-Italian relations because of Clemenceau's reluctance to champion the Italian cause. The long-simmering Italian resentment at France's acquisition of Tunisia, a North African territory across the Mediterranean from Sicily, came to a boiling point after the war when France repudiated its earlier pledge to respect the special privileges of the large Italian population there. Reinforcing these territorial and colonial disputes was an intense Franco-Italian naval rivalry that developed in the course of the 1920s. Though France had been compelled to accept parity in capital ships with Italy at the Washington Naval Conference of 1921–22 (see p. 204), it offended Italian sensibilities by insisting that the necessity to divide the French fleet between the Mediterranean and the oceanic routes to the French empire in Africa and Asia entitled it to superiority in auxiliary craft such as cruisers and submarines.

In spite of these obstacles to Franco-Italian cooperation, the two countries shared one common objective that French officials hoped would serve as the basis of reconciliation. This was the preservation of the political independence of the German-speaking rump state of Austria. The periodic calls for the political unification of Austria and Germany, or *Anschluss,* that had emanated from pan-German circles since the end of the war had caused considerable alarm in Rome throughout the 1920s. That sense of alarm was increased after January 1933 when a pan-German zealot of Austrian birth came to power in Berlin. The source of Italy's anxiety about the extension of German sovereignty to its northern frontier was its potential effect on the German-speaking inhabitants of the south Tyrol region in the Alps that had been ceded by Austria to Italy at the Paris Peace Conference. France opposed the *Anschluss* both because of the threat that it would pose to its ally Czechoslovakia (which would be caught in the vise of an enlarged Germanic state) and because of the increase in Germany's population and industrial potential that such a union would entail.

Officials at the French foreign ministry hoped that this shared interest in preserving Austria's independence would serve as the basis for Franco-Italian cooperation in the defense of the territorial status quo in Central Europe. The prospects for such a Rome-Paris axis were enhanced by Italy's reaction to the Austrian crisis of July 1934, during which local Nazis in Vienna assassinated Chancellor Engelbert Dollfuss (a determined foe of *Anschluss*) and appealed to Hitler for assistance in their prospective coup d'état. Italian troops that had coincidentally been on maneuvers near the Austrian border staged a show of force at the Brenner Pass, prompting Hitler to repudiate the plot that his own embassy in Vienna had played a role in hatching. The ignominious collapse of the venture enabled Mussolini to take credit for having deterred Germany from interfering in Austria's internal affairs. Suitably impressed, Parisian authorities hastened to seek formal arrangements with Italy to deter any future German initiatives of similar stripe. In January 1935, Foreign Minister Pierre Laval of France journeyed to Rome to sign an agreement with Mussolini, which settled most of the outstanding Franco-Italian differences in Africa to the Duce's satisfaction in return for an Italian pledge to consult with France in the event of German violations of the Versailles clauses on disarmament and the independence of Austria.

The emerging Franco-Italian entente received its first test in March 1935, when Hitler formally repudiated the disarmament provisions of the Versailles Treaty. It had long been apparent that the military forces that the German dictator considered essential for his foreign policy objectives could no longer be forged in secrecy. The construction of a navy, an air force, and a mechanized army could not escape detection. Thus, on March 9 Hitler revealed the existence of a German air force as well as plans to expand its size and strength. On March 16 he decreed the reintroduction of universal military conscription with the announced goal of creating a thirty-six-division army (compared to the seven divisions permitted by the Versailles Treaty and the thirty divisions of the existing French army). A week later the French, British, and Italian prime ministers met to fashion a coordinated response to Germany's flagrant repudiation of the Versailles military restrictions. At the conclusion of this conference, held from April 11 to 14 at the Italian resort city of Stresa, the three powers issued a joint communiqué that sternly condemned the German action and threatened joint opposition to any further treaty violations. Moreover, France and Italy secretly exchanged pledges of military assistance to counter German violations of either the Rhineland demilitarized zone or the independence of Austria. Italy's commitment to cooperate with France in resisting further German revisionist bids reached its apex in June 1935, when Franco-Italian military conversations were resumed for the first time since the end of the war.

These fruitful French approaches to Fascist Italy were paralleled by simultaneous overtures to the Soviet Union. From the vantage point of ideological consistency, it may seem astonishing that a parliamentary democracy such as France could hope to base its system of continental security upon diplomatic links with Fascist and Communist dictatorships. But the realities of international power in Europe seemed to dictate just such an ideologically contradictory policy during the interwar period. In its frantic search for an effective anti-German coalition in the mid-1930s, France expressed an eagerness to obtain allies wherever it could find them, regardless of the character of their domestic political institutions. The approach to Italy, though distasteful to democratic opinion in France, was pursued with minimal domestic opposition. The overtures to Soviet Russia predictably provoked some agitation in the ranks of the anti-Communist right in France, but not enough to derail the Quai d'Orsay's efforts to reach an accommodation with the Kremlin. The national interest, which was thought to require a diplomatic strategy of encircling Germany with hostile powers associated with France, prevailed over the promptings of ideological preference in the minds of all but the most vociferously anti-Fascist and anti-Communist Frenchmen.

The possibility of a diplomatic understanding with Russia had long tempted Parisian officials because of the obvious advantages of confronting Germany with the prospect of a war on two fronts after the fashion of 1914. But the obstacles to a resurrection of the prewar Franco-Russian alliance were even more formidable than those that had hindered a Franco-Italian rapprochement: On the French side there was lingering resentment at the Soviet government's conclusion of a separate peace with Germany during the First World War and its repudiation of the enormous debt to French investors that had been contracted by the tsarist regime; on the Russian side there was bitterness at France's anti-Bolshevik posture in the Russian Civil War and its support of Poland's military offensive against Soviet Russia in 1920. Added to these historical animosities was the underlying incompatibility of foreign policy between the two states throughout the 1920s. As the major beneficiary of the peace settlement of 1919, France vigorously defended the postwar status quo in Europe by extending its financial support and political protection to the states of Eastern Europe that had also profited from the defeat of the Central Powers. Russia, which had lost a considerable portion of its territory in Europe to these new or enlarged states on its western frontier, accordingly favored the destruction of the postwar European system and had not hesitated to cooperate with the other great revisionist power, Germany, throughout the twenties.

But the rise of Hitler and the stalling of the disarmament talks in Geneva precipitated a simultaneous reversal in official French and Soviet attitudes toward each other. Hitler's oft-stated intention of seeking living space in Eastern Europe at Russia's expense, together with his frequent denunciations of communism as a political philosophy, were well-known to the leaders of the Kremlin. In February 1933, the Soviet foreign minister, Maxim Litvinov, officially reversed his government's long-standing support for revision of the peace treaties by openly endorsing the French position on collective security at the disarmament conference. In subsequent remarks the Russian diplomat clearly enunciated his government's new official line: Treaty revision meant war and therefore had to be avoided at all costs. The French government responded with alacrity to this stunning Soviet volte-face. For the first time since Russia's withdrawal from the world war, a French military attaché was dispatched to Moscow on April 8, 1933, as a gesture of interest in the Kremlin's new anti-German orientation. By the summer of 1933 the secret collaboration between the German and Soviet armies came to a halt, all German military facilities in Russia were closed, and visits of Soviet officers to Germany were cancelled.

The accession of Louis Barthou as French foreign minister in February 1934 marked the real beginning of the French quest for a Russian connection. A conservative lawyer with impeccable nationalist credentials, Barthou was ideally suited to the task of allaying right-wing suspicions of a closer relationship with the Soviet regime. He concocted the scheme of a dual alliance system in Eastern Europe designed to refurbish the existing French security arrangements in the region that had been weakened by Poland's accommodation with Germany in the month before he took office. The first part of this proposed association was a pact of regional assistance in Eastern Europe, modeled on the Locarno treaties for Western Europe, in which Germany, Russia, Poland, Czechoslovakia, Finland, and the Baltic states would mutually guarantee their frontiers. The second part of the proposal was a bilateral agreement between France and Russia in which Russia would render a commitment to France as though it were a signatory of the Locarno treaties while France would offer a guarantee to Russia as though it were a member of the proposed eastern pact.

Barthou's diplomacy in Eastern Europe failed because of the Polish government's announcement on September 27, 1934, that it would refuse to grant Soviet troops transit rights across Polish territory to fulfill Moscow's commitments under the proposed eastern security pact. Polish motives for this obstructionist posture were not difficult to discern. For Warsaw to permit a Soviet military advance across Polish territory to engage the forces of a nation with which Poland had just signed a nonaggression pact would have contradicted Poland's policy of balancing Germany against Russia. Moreover, no one, least of all France at the other end of the continent, could guarantee that a Red Army on Polish soil would not take the opportunity to enforce Russia's own extensive territorial claims against the Polish state. The assassination of the French foreign minister on October 9 in Marseilles ended for good the quest for an "Eastern Locarno."

But Barthou had always intended to pursue the bilateral pact with the Soviet Union regardless of the fate of the multilateral scheme for Eastern European security. The continuing recalcitrance of the Poles, together with the announcement of German rearmament, brought the issue to a head in the spring of 1935. Barthou's successor at the Quai d'Orsay, Pierre Laval, was profoundly skeptical of the desirability of an alliance with Russia. He favored instead a policy of cementing relations among France, Great Britain, and Italy as a prelude to luring Germany into a four-power pact to manage the affairs of Europe that had first been proposed by Mussolini in March 1933 but never acted upon. But the declaration of German rearmament in March 1935 frightened the French government into forcing the reluctant foreign minister to complete the arrangements with Moscow that Barthou had begun: On May 2, 1935, France and Russia concluded a pact of mutual assistance that was followed on May 16 by a similar agreement between the Soviet Union and France's principal Eastern European ally, Czechoslovakia. For a brief moment, Germany seemed isolated by a powerful coalition of states determined to resist further violations of the peace treaty. This impression was enhanced by a dramatic policy reorientation at the Seventh Congress of the Comintern, the international organization of Communist parties loyal to the Soviet Union, in August 1935. Whereas the Communist parties outside Russia had previously been instructed to refuse all political cooperation with "bourgeois parties" (including the Socialists), Hitler's liquidation of the German Communist party had revealed the dangers of this sectarian strategy. The new Comintern line called for Communist participation in a "Popular Front" with all political groups opposed to fascism at home and German expansion in Europe.

But the revival of Franco-Russian cooperation to restrain Germany was a pale shadow of the military alliance that had compelled the kaiser's armies to fight a war on two fronts in 1914–17. Laval had taken the precaution of ensuring that the bilateral agreement was strictly compatible with the multilateral provisions of the League Covenant and the Locarno treaties. What this meant in practice was that military assistance could be rendered by one signatory to the other only after an allegation of unprovoked aggression had been submitted to the League and only after prior approval of the other signatories of the Locarno Pact (Great Britain, Italy, and Belgium) had been obtained. The effectiveness of the pact was undermined even further by the French government's insistent refusal to accept a military convention stipulating the way in which the two armies would coordinate actions in the event of war with Germany. The effectiveness of the Czech-Soviet Pact was similarly weakened by a provision subordinating it to the prior application of the Franco-Soviet Pact as well as by the failure to resolve the problem posed by the absence of a common border between the two signatories.

The issuance of the Stresa declaration in April 1935, the signing of the Franco-Soviet Pact in May, and the advent of Franco-Italian military talks in June collectively gave the impression that France was well on the way toward fashioning the system of European security that had eluded it since the end of the last war. In addition to its alliances with Belgium, Poland, and Czechoslovakia and its treaties of friendship with Romania and Yugoslavia, France finally seemed about to resurrect the old wartime coalition of Great Britain, Russia, and Italy in an effort to prevent further German transgressions of the peace treaty.

Yet within less than a year, that coalition was in shambles as a result of the defection of Great Britain, Italy, and Belgium, France's three Western friends. The first chink in the armor of the anti-German coalition appeared on June 18, 1935, the 120th anniversary of the Battle of Waterloo, the date the British government tactlessly chose to unveil a bilateral naval agreement that it had secretly negotiated with Germany behind the backs of the French. The accord permitted Germany to exceed the naval limitations of the Versailles Treaty in exchange for a promise not to increase its total tonnage beyond 35 percent of that of the combined fleets of the British Empire. This Anglo-German naval agreement torpedoed the Stresa front by providing for precisely what the Stresa declaration had forbidden, namely, a further violation by Germany of its treaty obligations. London's motivation for acquiescing in Germany's repudiation of the last remaining armament restriction of the Versailles Treaty was obvious: It was known from intelligence sources that while Hitler planned to build a navy that would eventually enable Germany to play a global role, the German naval construction program for the immediate future was geared to the limited objectives of assuring control of the Baltic against the Soviet Union and harassing France's oceanic communications with its colonies and foreign sources of supply. In April 1935 the German government had informed the British of a construction program of twelve destroyers, two cruisers, and twelve submarines. Faced with this evidence of Hitler's intention to violate the treaty restrictions with impunity, the British judged it opportune to obtain at least the assurance that Germany would not threaten Great Britain's supremacy in the Mediterranean and the North Atlantic. The agreement had no effect whatsoever on Germany, which constructed as many ships as its resources permitted and continued to develop plans for ultimately contesting British naval power on the high seas once its predominance in Europe had been assured.

The second dramatic defector from the anti-German front established in the spring of 1935 was Italy. This defection was caused by Mussolini's invasion of the East African empire of Ethiopia, one of only two African states (the other being the Republic of Liberia) that had successfully resisted absorption by European powers during the imperial expansion of the prewar years. Italy's interest in Ethiopia dated from the last two decades of the nineteenth century. After a humiliating military defeat at the hands of Ethiopian warriors in 1896, Italian colonial forces had retreated to the coastal enclaves of Eritrea on the Red Sea and Somaliland on the Indian Ocean. But by the mid-1930s, Mussolini's grandiose design for a new Roman Empire around the Mediterranean inspired a revival of the dormant territorial claims against the independent East African state. Great Britain and France, which had minimal interests in the area and were intent on securing Italian support for resistance to German adventurism in Europe, did nothing to discourage Italy's belated colonial aspirations. During his meeting with Mussolini in Rome in January 1935, Foreign Minister Laval of France formally renounced his country's minor economic interests in Ethiopia and gave the Italian leader verbal assurances of a free hand there. At the Stresa Conference in April, Mussolini's intimations of Italian ambitions in East Africa elicited no objections from the French and British heads of government. In August 1935 London and Paris went so far as to offer Rome a privileged economic position in Ethiopia together with the right to appoint Italian advisers to the country's civil service, army, and police, the traditional prelude to the establishment of a protectorate.

These extensive Anglo-French concessions to Italian ambitions in Ethiopia clearly indicate that Mussolini could have obtained effective control of that country through patient diplomacy. But the prospective leader of the new Roman Empire was intent on obtaining military glory with a minimum of risk. He therefore launched a full-scale armed attack against Ethiopia on October 3 with the expectation that Italy would encounter little military resistance from the ill-equipped forces of the Ethiopian emperor, Haile Selassie, and no diplomatic opposition from the European powers. On the first count he was correct. The rugged mountains in the interior slowed the Italian advance, but the introduction of air power and poison gas routed the Ethiopian forces in the spring of 1936. But on the diplomatic front in Europe, the Duce was to be first disappointed and then outraged by the unsympathetic response of his friends in London and Paris. Since Ethiopia was a member of the League of Nations, public opinion in Great Britain lashed out at this overt violation of national sovereignty and pressured the government into invoking the principle of collective security. To Mussolini's astonishment, Britain and France prodded the League into condemning the Italian offensive as an act of aggression and voting for the imposition of economic sanctions against the aggressor state on October 18. The hypocritical policy of the two powers that had divided up most of the continent of Africa between them before the First World War, and had recently given Italy the green light belatedly to obtain its share of the spoils, left a lasting negative impression on the Italian leader. His feelings of betrayal and annoyance were not assuaged by subsequent efforts by London and Paris to undermine the very policy that they had promoted at Geneva. A secret Anglo-French agreement in December providing for the cession of most of Ethiopia to Italy and the reduction of the remainder to the status of an Italian client state had to be disavowed when its embarrassing contents were leaked to the press by unsympathetic personnel at the Quai d'Orsay. But the abortive Hoare-Laval Pact, named for the British and French foreign ministers who devised it, accurately reflected the true policies of the two governments, as had the earlier efforts to placate Mussolini. This is shown by their refusal to extend the economic sanctions to an embargo of oil, which Italy required to fuel its mechanized army and air force in Ethiopia and which it had to import from foreign sources.

The most important consequence of the Ethiopian affair, apart from the military defeat of Haile Selassie's empire and its annexation by Italy in May 1936, was the deterioration of relations between Italy and her erstwhile partners in the Stresa front against Germany. By supporting economic sanctions against Italy and verbally condemning its actions in the League, Britain and France had antagonized Mussolini without succeeding in denying him the objectives he sought in East Africa. The Hoare-Laval scheme and the half-hearted application of sanctions also undermined the principle of collective security. If such an unmistakable instance of aggression against a member of the League could go unpunished, what was to prevent the more subtle forms of aggression practiced and planned by Germany in Europe?

In the meantime, Hitler remained neutral in the Italo-Ethiopian struggle while expressing his willingness to supply Mussolini with iron, coal, steel, and other scarce materials. Berlin's benevolent neutrality was greatly appreciated in Rome. Thus, with the two guarantors of the Locarno treaties (Great Britain and Italy) at loggerheads over East Africa and Mussolini grateful for Germany's acquiescence in his imperial policies, the Führer correctly gauged that the time was right for a daring probe of the anti-German diplomatic coalition. The submission of the Franco-Soviet Pact to the French Chamber of Deputies for ratification in February 1936 supplied the perfect pretext for Hitler's first provocative move since his announcement of German rearmament a year earlier. The Führer warned that he would regard the Franco-Soviet alliance as a violation of the multilateral agreement signed at Locarno and a grave threat to Germany's security; he would therefore feel free to renounce Germany's end of the Locarno bargain by reintroducing German military forces and fortifications into the demilitarized zone of the Rhineland. In fact Hitler regarded the Franco-Soviet Pact as a great advantage for German foreign policy. Useless to France as a military deterrent because of its geographical contradictions, it was immensely valuable as a propaganda tool to Germany. Its unpopularity in anti-Communist circles in all

European countries, especially England, enabled the German dictator to raise the bogey of the "red menace" while citing the innocuous pact as justification for tearing up the Locarno Pact. After the French Chamber ratified the treaty, three battalions of German infantry, accompanied by antiaircraft guns and air force squadrons, moved into the Rhineland on March 7.

As we have seen, the demilitarized status of the Rhineland was widely regarded as the most important guarantee of German good behavior in Europe. It was thought to preclude a German advance against France and Belgium and, by exposing Germany to invasion from the west, to deter German aggression eastward. Its disappearance in March 1936 ought therefore to have elicited a strong response from France. But no such response was forthcoming. French military strategy as developed over the past several years dictated just such a posture of passivity. By constructing the Maginot Line France had in effect already written off the Rhineland as indefensible. It would make little difference on which bank of the river German forces were situated so long as France retained its impregnable bastion of concrete and gun emplacements along the Franco-German frontier. Accordingly, the French army possessed no mobile force that could be dispatched to the Rhineland to expel the German battalions and had devised no advance plan for such an operation. The creation of such a force and the development of such a plan, suggested a year earlier by the politician Paul Reynaud on the advice of Colonel Charles de Gaulle, was rejected as incompatible with the defensive strategy so tenaciously pursued by the French general staff. So long as the German forces in the Rhineland did not give any indication of preparing for a military attack against France, which Hitler shrewdly forbade them to do, the French high command warned the government in Paris that a military response to the recent German action would be both unnecessary and foolhardy. It was thought unnecessary for the strategic considerations mentioned above. It was deemed foolhardy because of the exaggerated estimate of German military strength in French military circles at the time.

The civilian government in Paris, a caretaker ministry in power pending the legislative elections scheduled for the following month, displayed greater interest in an offensive operation to expel the German forces from the Rhineland than did the military authorities. Foreign Minister Pierre-Etienne Flandin flew to London to discuss the possibility of a joint Anglo-French countermove. He was greeted with the news that the British government did not view the remilitarization of the Rhineland as a "flagrant" violation of the treaty of Locarno because it was not accompanied by menacing German moves toward the French frontier; consequently Britain would neither participate in any military response nor approve of a unilateral French action. Beneath this narrow, legalistic interpretation of the language of Locarno lay the real reason for Britain's hesitation: its desire to avoid at all costs the European war that it believed would inevitably result from a French or Anglo-French advance into the Rhineland. Consequently, the response of London and Paris was confined to the issuance of stern protests, the sponsorship of a pro forma condemnation of the action by the League of Nations, and the authorization of joint Anglo-French military conversations. Though the latter development satisfied a long-standing objective of French foreign policy, these staff talks were confined to meaningless generalities because of British reluctance to discuss detailed plans of operations. Even the advent of British rearmament in the aftermath of the Rhineland crisis gave little comfort to France since it concentrated on upgrading naval and air forces for home and imperial defense instead of on establishing a land army that could be dispatched to the continent. Thus the remilitarization of the Rhineland was rapidly to become a fait accompli.

As noted above, the remilitarization of the Rhineland did not appreciably alter the strategic balance between France and Germany in Western Europe since France's previously adopted defensive posture along her eastern frontier had rendered the Rhenish buffer zone irrelevant to French military calculations. Nor did it suddenly negate the value of France's security commitments to Poland and Czechoslovakia. Those had previously been rendered incapable of realization once construction of the Maginot Line had begun half a decade earlier. But the failure of France to react firmly to Hitler's unilateral repudiation of the Locarno Pact had a devastating psychological impact on all of the smaller countries on the continent that had expected France to take the lead in restraining Germany.

The result of this French abstention was a radical reorientation of the foreign policies of all of these minor powers. The chiefs of staff of the Little Entente, meeting in June 1936 to reassess the strategic situation in Central Europe in the light of recent events, concluded that their countries' future security might well require a choice between subservience to Germany or to Russia. The Polish government, which faced that unpleasant predicament even more directly, resumed with greater enthusiasm its policy of detente with Germany that had been inaugurated at the beginning of 1934. Belgium, France's neighbor in Western Europe and its earliest and staunchest ally against Germany, also drew the appropriate conclusions from French inaction during the Rhineland crisis and acted accordingly. On October 14, 1936, the Belgian government formally renounced its military alliance with France and reverted to its prewar status of neutrality. The dramatic Belgian reversal stemmed in part from domestic political tension between the French-speaking Walloons and the Flemish population, the latter of which had long resented their country's diplomatic subservience to France. It also reflected the reluctance of anti-Communist elements to see their nation dragged into a war with Germany on behalf of France's new Russian ally. But the principal reason was the belief that neither France nor Great Britain could or would afford Belgium the kind of protection it required for the preservation of its security. The military consequences of the Belgian defection were critical: Anglo-French forces were no longer guaranteed transit rights across Belgian territory in case of war with Germany. Franco-Belgian military coordination, a key element in France's strategy for the defense of her unfortified northeastern frontier, was abruptly terminated.

By the autumn of 1936, Germany had thus obtained geographical protective screens on its western and eastern borders that effectively insulated it from the threat of military intervention by the great powers in alliance against it. In the west, a neutralized Belgium and a remilitarized Rhineland (which was in the process of being reinforced by the construction of elaborate fortifications along the French frontier) shielded Germany's industrial heartland in the Ruhr Valley from French military power. To the east, an increasingly cooperative Poland served as a barrier against the Soviet Union. To the south, the nations of the Little Entente, geographically separated from their undependable French patron, were driven to seek improved relations with Germany in the hope of stabilizing the political situation in that region. Hitler wasted no time in profiting from Germany's enhanced position on the continent to expand his nation's economic and diplomatic influence in those nations of Central and Southeastern Europe whose cooperation or acquiescence he desired in the fulfillment of his short-term objectives in foreign policy, which were the annexation of Austria and the destruction of Czechoslovakia. At the same time he took steps to accelerate the pace of German rearmament and to reorient the economy in such a way as to prepare his nation for the major war that he planned to launch in the more distant future.

The failure of the Western powers to recognize the implications of this process of consolidation, both within Germany and between Germany and its neighbors to the south and east, was in large part due to the fixation of world attention on the civil war that erupted in Spain in the summer of 1936. On July 17 of that year, military officers in command of the garrisons in Spanish Morocco rebelled against the left-leaning government in Madrid that had been elected the previous February and proceeded to organize an uprising on the Spanish mainland. When the navy and air force remained loyal to the Republican government, the leader of the coup, General Francisco Franco, was compelled to look abroad for assistance in transporting his forces in North Africa across the Straits of Gibraltar to the Iberian peninsula. This appeal from the Spanish rebels, or Nationalists as they called themselves, received a sympathetic response in Berlin and Rome. By the end of July German and Italian planes were ferrying Franco's troops to the mainland, where they quickly established contact with the rebel-held sector in the northeast. By the autumn of 1936 the quantity of German and Italian aid markedly increased. Hitler dispatched a special air force unit, the Condor Legion, to provide air cover for the rebel forces while Mussolini contributed large contingents of Italian infantry in the guise of "volunteers."

Hitler's decision to assist the military rebellion in Spain was determined by a number of factors. The most important military advantage to be gained, apart from the opportunity to test the tactic of terror bombing of civilian population centers that would later be used against Warsaw, Rotterdam, and London, lay in the promise of access to Spain's abundant supply of strategic raw materials. With Germany engaged in a massive rearmament program at a time when it suffered from a severe shortage of foreign exchange, Hitler hoped to obtain Spanish iron and copper ores without having to pay for them in scarce foreign currency. An arrangement to this effect was reached in the summer of 1937, once the major iron- and copper-producing regions of Spain had fallen under Franco's control. Large quantities of these strategic materials, which had previously been exported to Great Britain, were diverted to the German rearmament program in payment for the military supplies that Hitler was furnishing Franco. In addition to this expectation of economic advantage, two diplomatic considerations dictated Germany's active support of the Nationalist insurrection in Spain. The first was the likelihood that cooperation with Italy on Franco's behalf would cement the friendly relations between Berlin and Rome that had been established during the Ethiopian affair. This became all the more apparent when France and Great Britain organized a nonintervention committee in September 1936 to curb all foreign involvement in the Spanish conflict. Once Mussolini had committed his personal prestige to a rebel victory in Spain, the Western democracies' expressions of displeasure at the Italian intervention, though no more effective than their exhortations during the Ethiopian affair, dashed whatever chances may have existed of reconstituting the Stresa coalition and drove Mussolini even closer to Hitler. But the most obvious benefit that Germany derived from the Spanish civil war was the diversion of French and British attention from the process of German rearmament and continental economic consolidation that was underway. For this reason it was to Hitler's advantage to prolong the military conflict on the Iberian peninsula as long as possible instead of helping the rebels to achieve a quick victory. This was accomplished by refusing Franco's urgent request for large German infantry units after the failure of the rebel offensive against Madrid at the end of 1936, as well as by restricting the Condor Legion to its original size for the duration of the conflict.

The ideological overtones of the Spanish civil war were apparent from the outset and contributed to its image in the popular imagination as an epic confrontation between the forces of international fascism and the defenders of the democratic cause. Franco's tactical alliance with the small Spanish Fascist movement, the Falange, viewed in the context of his dependence on Mussolini and Hitler for military support, seemed to herald the spread of the ideological doctrine hatched in Italy and perfected in Germany to the western tip of Europe. Conversely, the arrival in Spain of the "International Brigades," groups of left-wing volunteers organized in various foreign countries to fight on behalf of the beleaguered Republic, expressed the democratic world's commitment to oppose fascism in all its forms. The conspicuous presence of the small Spanish Communist party in the Popular Front coalition in Madrid and the flow of military aid from the Soviet Union to the Spanish government reflected the Kremlin's newly adopted policy of defending parliamentary institutions against the Fascist menace.

In fact, this ideological dichotomy was deceptive. Franco and the military, clerical, and landowning groups that formed his base of support were reactionary devotees of a premodern era who shared little in common with the Falangist firebrands, who were reduced to insignificance when the marriage of convenience with them had outlived its usefulness. Once Franco's military victory in the spring of 1939 relieved the Spanish dictator of the need to rely on German and Italian assistance, he displayed little interest in joining a "Fascist crusade" in league with Hitler and Mussolini. Fears of a menace to France from a Nationalist regime across the Pyrenees proved ill founded. The Spanish Caudillo was to remain neutral for the duration of the Second World War despite strenuous German efforts to secure his active cooperation with the Axis war effort.

In the opposite camp, all manner of internal tensions and contradictions undermined the political unity and ideological consistency of the anti-fascist cause. Within Republican Spain itself, Communists, Anarchists, Trotskyists, Socialists, and Liberals repeatedly clashed over matters of political ideology and military strategy, with differences often settled by a burst of machine-gun fire. Outside of Spain, the nations supposedly committed to the defense of democratic government against the menace of fascism behaved in ways ill suited to that objective. The Conservative government in Great Britain could scarcely conceal its distaste for the leftist regime in Madrid and refused to lift a finger in its defense. Even the recently elected Popular Front government in France, dominated by Socialists with Communist support, refused Spanish Republican appeals for military supplies for fear of antagonizing Great Britain and further inflaming domestic Catholic opinion already agitated by reports of monasteries looted and nuns murdered by defenders of the regime in Madrid. The Soviet Union, though the only European power to furnish supplies to Republican Spain, kept the flow of aid to a minimum and demanded immediate payment in gold or raw materials. It is possible, as some historians have speculated, that Stalin's parsimony was prompted by the same considerations that caused Hitler to restrict his assistance to Franco, namely, to keep the Spanish pot boiling as a diversion from domestic turmoil, in Russia's case the purge trials that began a month after Franco's insurrection.

While the Spanish civil war occupied the attention of the world, Germany proceeded to inaugurate a program to put its economy on a wartime footing while mounting a diplomatic offensive in several directions to facilitate the realization of Hitler's two immediate objectives: the annexation of Austria and the annihilation of Czechoslovakia.

The economic situation of Germany in 1936 was marked by superficial signs of prosperity that concealed a structural weakness of alarming proportions. The major achievement of the Nazi economic policy was the elimination of unemployment by the rearmament boom fueled by the deficit financing of the government. But an underlying weakness of the German economy began to occupy the attention of Hitler's economic policy makers at the beginning of 1936: Because of its heavy reliance on foreign imports of raw materials required by the rearmament program, Germany had begun to suffer from a severe shortage of foreign exchange. If present trends continued, the remilitarization of Germany and the economic recovery that it had stimulated risked being halted in its tracks by the inability of the German government to pay for the continued importation of strategic raw materials that could not be produced domestically.

The crisis of raw material imports that loomed in the winter and spring of 1936 reminded the Nazi leaders of Germany's plight in the Great War, when its dependence on foreign supplies had exposed it to the crippling effects of the British blockade. Hitler's proposed solution to this threat to his future plans took the form of a short-term program of economic development designed to render Germany self-sufficient in the strategic materials she required to prepare for the European war that was expected to begin no later than the summer of 1940. The Four-Year Plan, launched on October 18, 1936, under the supervision of Hermann Göring, aimed at establishing Germany's absolute independence from foreign trade by fostering the production of synthetic materials as substitutes for the natural resources unobtainable domestically. In time the German chemical industry developed artificial rubber, textiles, and plastics. A synthetic fuels program was expanded, whereby oil was extracted from Germany's abundant coal supplies. The utilization of Germany's low-grade iron ore for the production of steel was intensified in order to reduce the nation's dependence on the high-grade ores of Sweden and Spain.

The unfolding of Hitler's military strategy in the mid-1930s reflected the precarious position of the German economy at that time. The shortage of raw materials, even with the compensation provided by the development of synthetic substitutes, meant that Germany could not hope to win a long war of attrition against Russia and the British Empire, especially if American assistance were eventually thrown in the balance against it. Such was the lesson of the 1914–18 war. Hence the adoption of the strategy of "blitzkrieg," a series of short, swift engagements against isolated opponents. The principal weapons to be used were tanks and airplanes, both of which required large quantities of oil, rubber, and other products that Germany was preparing to produce synthetically. But the brief duration of these "lightning wars" would permit victory with only a modest mobilization of Germany's economic power. The territory conquered by Germany in these mechanized thrusts against isolated opponents would eventually afford it access to the raw materials of the European continent that would bring self-sufficiency at last.

The diplomatic counterpart of this economic-strategic program developed by Hitler in the course of 1936 was the campaign to weaken the French alliance system in Eastern Europe and to discourage the other great powers—Italy, England, and Soviet Russia—from joining France and its remaining Eastern European clients in resisting Germany's bid for hegemony in that region. Since the annexation of Austria was the first item on Hitler's agenda for Germany's continental expansion, it is no surprise that he endeavored to solidify Germany's friendly ties with Italy, the traditional guarantor of Austrian independence, that had been established during the Ethiopian invasion and the early stages of the Spanish civil war. On October 26, 1936, the two governments announced the conclusion of an agreement on Italo-German cooperation that was soon being touted as the "Rome-Berlin Axis." This agreement in effect signaled the Italian leader's tacit acceptance of Germany's freedom of action in Austria in particular and Southeastern Europe in general. The reorientation of Italian foreign policy toward an accommodation with Germany reflected Mussolini's conversion to Hitler's conception of the geopolitical basis of Italo-German cooperation: the complementary expansion of Italian power southward into the Mediterranean basin and of German power eastward into the heartland of Central Europe and beyond. The formation of the Rome-Berlin Axis on this basis afforded Hitler two crucial advantages: It removed the Italian veto of Germany's annexationist designs on Austria, and it increased the likelihood of tension in the Mediterranean and North Africa between Italy and the two dominant powers in that region, Great Britain and France.

Throughout the year 1937 Hitler steadily increased the pressure on the Austrian government to align its foreign and domestic policies more closely with those of the Third Reich. In the meantime he encouraged the Austrian Nazis to step up their subversive activities in preparation for a peaceful takeover in Vienna that would lead to a voluntary unification with Germany. But when the Austrian chancellor, Kurt von Schuschnigg, authorized police raids on the headquarters of the Austrian Nazis that uncovered embarrassing evidence of collusion with their counterparts in Germany, Hitler reversed his earlier strategy for an evolutionary move toward *Anschluss* and prepared to achieve that result quickly through direct intimidation of the government in Vienna. In a meeting between Hitler and Schuschnigg at Berchtesgaden on February 12, 1938, the Führer berated the Austrian chancellor for failing to pursue pro-German policies and threatened immediate military intervention unless Schuschnigg allowed the Austrian Nazis to play a major role in his government. Though the Austrian leader acceded to this demand on the advice of Mussolini, he boldly decided to preempt Hitler's plans for a peaceful takeover of his country by seeking an expression of national support by means of a plebiscite to be held on March 13 in which the Austrian people would be asked to vote on the question of their nation's independence. Though a plebiscite conducted before the advent of the Nazi regime in Germany would probably have resulted in an overwhelming vote for unification of the two German-speaking states, anti-Nazi sentiment in Austria was sufficiently strong to prevent Hitler from risking the embarrassment of a negative vote. Thus, after securing the tacit consent of Mussolini, the Führer sent German troops into Austria on March 12, where they met no resistance from Austrian military forces. Schuschnigg's request for advice from the British and French governments had revealed that neither London nor Paris was any more willing to risk a European war by intervening on Austria's behalf than was Mussolini. On April 10 a rigged plebiscite resulted in an overwhelming vote for the unification of Hitler's adopted nation and the land of his birth.

Germany's success in securing Italian consent for its expansionist policy in Central Europe was matched by the gradual evolution of a cordial relationship with the rising imperial power in the Far East (see p. 215). By encouraging Japanese imperial ambitions in East Asia, Germany stood to benefit from the pressure that such expansion would exert

Adolf Hitler (1889–1945) with Hermann Goering at the Reichs Chancellery, 1938: This native Austrian has just engineered Germany's absorption of German-speaking Austria and is preparing to annex the German-speaking region of Czechoslovakia. Both acts were justified on the grounds of President Wilson's hallowed principle of national self-determination. *(Courtesy of the Library of Congress)*

on the Asian possessions of Germany's principal antagonists in Europe. Great Britain would be less likely to interfere with Germany's eastern policy on the continent if confronted with the simultaneous challenge to its imperial interests from Japan in the western Pacific and from Italy along its Mediterranean lifeline. The ratification of the Franco-Soviet Pact by the French parliament in February 1936 also highlighted the obvious congruity of interest between Tokyo and Berlin. In combination, Germany and Japan could restrain the Soviet Union on its European and Asian flanks to the benefit of both. Accordingly, on November 25, 1936, the two governments unveiled with much fanfare an agreement designated as the Anti-Comintern Pact. Its ostensible purpose was to promote cooperation to combat the subversive activities of the Communist International and its political apparatus in each country. But since both Germany and Japan had long since suppressed their domestic Communist parties, the agreement was widely and correctly suspected of containing secret provisions directed against the Soviet Union. With the adhesion of Italy to the agreement on November 6, 1937, the world was confronted with the nightmare of an impending global alignment of the three expansionist powers.

While Fascist Italy and imperial Japan gradually gravitated toward the German orbit in the years 1936–38, Hitler mounted a successful campaign to accelerate Germany's tactical rapprochement with Poland in order to secure that country's acquiescence in his plan to destroy Czechoslovakia. To achieve this result, Hitler had only to remove the major source of friction between Berlin and Warsaw while emphasizing the one issue that was likely to foster Polish-German cooperation against his intended victim. The principal source of friction was the city of Danzig, where the Nazi municipal government caused considerable trouble for Polish authorities. Directives from Berlin had effectively restrained the anti-Polish agitation of the Danzig Nazis during the period that Hitler solicited Warsaw's friendship. The positive basis for German-Polish cooperation at the expense of Czechoslovakia was the Teschen district of Silesia, a rich industrial area awarded to Czechoslovakia in 1920 despite the presence of almost eighty thousand Poles. At Hitler's urging the Polish government added its demand for Teschen to Hitler's insistence that the German-speaking Sudetenland be ceded by Czechoslovakia to Germany. It may have seemed hypocritical if not dangerous for the Poles, who presided over a collection of discontented minorities in their own multinational country, to issue territorial demands on the basis of the principle of nationality. But this inconsistency caused them little concern at a time when the prospects seemed excellent, as a silent partner of Germany, to acquire economically valuable territory at Czechoslovakia's expense.

Simultaneous German efforts to detach Romania from Czechoslovakia were facilitated by the bitter territorial struggle between Romania and Czechoslovakia's ally, Russia, in regard to Bessarabia, a former province of the tsarist empire annexed by Romania during the Russian Revolution. Just as Poland, with its large holdings of former Russian territory, needed little prodding from Germany to block Soviet access to Czechoslovakia, Romania's own national interest prompted it to deny the Red Army the ability to circumvent the Polish barrier to Central Europe.

Hitler's diplomatic campaign to isolate Czechoslovakia from its neighbors was bolstered by a series of commercial policies designed to subordinate the shaky economic systems of the nations of Central Europe to the expanding economy of Germany. This economic advance into Central and Southern Europe had begun in the early 1930s when the predominantly agricultural economies of those regions had began to suffer from the catastrophic collapse in world commodity prices. Germany, with its chronic deficit in food production, became the major customer for the agricultural surpluses that were piling up in these nations. With the advent of the Nazi regime, as we have seen, the introduction of exchange controls and bilateral barter arrangements compelled these nations to import an ever-increasing quantity of German industrial products in exchange for their agricultural exports. Subsequent political developments increased this dependence on Germany as a market for their primary products and a supplier of their industrial needs. The German annexation of Austria, a major trading partner of Yugoslavia and Hungary, increased Germany's domination of those nations' foreign trade. German economic penetration of Romania was prompted by increasing interest in that nation's abundant supplies of oil, which was required by the mechanized army and air force that Germany was constructing. A German-Romanian agreement of December 1937 provided for the exchange of German military equipment for Romanian oil to supplement the synthetic

petroleum production quota of the Four-Year Plan. These commercial connections between Germany and the nations of Central and Southern Europe, though developed for
rational economic reasons that promised benefits to both partners, helped to smooth the
path toward more cordial political relations at a time when German diplomacy was loosening the bonds of the Little Entente to isolate the Czechoslovak prey.

Germany's diplomatic and commercial offensive in Central Europe severely undermined the security of Czechoslovakia. The enlistment of Poland in Germany's campaign
of territorial revision and the de facto collapse of the Little Entente left the Czechoslovak
state bereft of defenders and surrounded by predators. Its bilateral alliances with France
and the Soviet Union, though technically operational, had been gravely weakened by the
diplomatic revolution wrought by Hitler in the two and a half years after the remilitarization of the Rhineland. Profiting from the Belgian-Rhenish screen in the west, the
Polish-Romanian screen in the east, and the deterrent effect that the new alignment with
Italy and Japan could be expected to exercise on Great Britain, Hitler proceeded to lay
the political groundwork for his projected blitzkrieg against Czechoslovakia.

The furious propaganda campaign that the Nazi leader unleashed against the Prague
regime in the summer of 1938 was directed at its alleged persecution of the three million
German-speaking inhabitants of the Bohemian borderlands. The Sudeten Germans' principal grievance was the preference accorded Czech-speaking citizens in the recruitment of
government employees, a discriminatory practice that engendered considerable resentment among the German-speaking minority during the Depression years and was skillfully exploited by Berlin. But Hitler cared little about the plight of the Sudentenlanders.
The last thing he wished was an amicable resolution of their dispute with Prague that
would remove the pretext he required to destroy the Czechoslovak state by force. He
accordingly instructed the leader of the Sudeten German party, Konrad Henlein, to
demand from the Czechoslovak government what he knew it could not grant, namely, concessions that would lead to the political autonomy of the German-speaking region as a
prelude to secession and eventual annexation by Germany. The loss of the Sudetenland
would deprive Czechoslovakia of its defensible frontiers and the elaborate border fortifications constructed behind them, leaving the truncated nation exposed to invasion by a
German military force unimpeded by natural or artificial barriers; it would also set a precedent for similar demands by the other national minorities in the polyglot republic—the
Poles of Teschen, the Hungarians in southern Slovakia and the Carpatho-Ukraine, even the
increasingly dissatisfied Slovaks. The result was bound to be the dissolution of the multinational state erected in 1918.

As German intimidation of Czechoslovakia intensified, and as it became increasingly
evident that Hitler was fully prepared to resort to force in pursuit of his annexationist
aims, the French and British governments were compelled to clarify their policies toward
the impending crisis in Central Europe. In July the Czech minister in Paris was privately
informed that France was unwilling to go to war over the issue of the Sudetenland, though
it would remain publicly committed to the Franco-Czechoslovak alliance for the sake of
appearances. The deplorable condition of the French air force, the refusal of Belgium to
allow the transit of French troops to Germany's most vulnerable industrial targets, and
exaggerated estimates of the size of Germany's army and the strength of its Rhineland
fortifications all contributed to this French failure of nerve. The British government,

unaware of Paris's repudiation of its obligation to Prague, became greatly alarmed at the prospect of being dragged into a war between France and Germany over an issue of no importance to British national interests. British leaders exerted every diplomatic effort to avert a war that might bring German air attacks on British cities still inadequately protected by the antiaircraft artillery system and radar installations then under construction. Anglo-French pressure on Prague to reach a settlement with the Sudeten party compelled Czech President Eduard Beneš to grant all of that party's main demands in a major concession on September 5. But since war rather than a political settlement on *any* terms was Hitler's goal, he instructed the Sudeten German party to fabricate a new list of grievances that could be exploited when preparations for the invasion were complete.

The German dictator was deprived of his goal of military conquest because of the eagerness of the British prime minister, Neville Chamberlain, to take him at his word. Like many British statesmen of his generation in both major parties, Chamberlain was profoundly influenced by memories of the two major events of his younger years, the Great War and the Paris Peace Conference. He shared the widespread conviction that the great powers had blundered into a terrible war that might well have been averted by a more skillful, active diplomacy. He also believed that the victorious Allies had mistreated Germany at the peace conference by refusing to apply the principle of national self-determination to the delimitation of the defeated nation's eastern frontiers. The convergence of these two issues during the Czechoslovakian crisis of September 1938 prompted Chamberlain to make one last effort to prevent a second world war by means of face-to-face negotiations with Hitler to reach a definitive solution of what he conceded to be Germany's just grievance against Czechoslovakia. On September 15, two days after Hitler approved the Sudeten German leader's withdrawal from the negotiations with the Czechoslovak government in preparation for war, Chamberlain boarded an airplane for the first time in his life and flew to Hitler's private retreat at Berchtes-gaden in a frantic quest for a settlement.

He received there Hitler's demand for the transfer of the Sudetenland to Germany on the basis of national self-determination and returned to London to try to persuade the representatives of France and Czechoslovakia to accept this peaceful solution. In order to obtain the support of the skeptical French premier, Edouard Daladier, for this plan, Chamberlain dramatically reversed a century of British foreign policy by promising to guarantee Czechoslovakia's redrawn frontiers. The government in Prague angrily rejected the Anglo-French proposal but was quickly forced into line by the threat of an end to British peacemaking efforts and a bluntly repeated refusal of French assistance if war broke out. When Chamberlain returned to the German city of Godesberg on September 22 to inform Hitler that his demands had been accepted by all interested parties, the Führer reneged on the agreement that he himself had earlier proposed; the deteriorating political situation in the Sudetenland required immediate German intervention. The German retraction at Godesberg turned many British and French appeasers into hard-liners and momentarily stiffened the resolve of Chamberlain and Daladier to hold to their position even at the risk of war. France began to mobilize its army and Great Britain announced the mobilization of its fleet on September 27. In London and Paris trenches were dug in parks, gas masks were distributed, and children were evacuated to the countryside. Hitler ordered the attack on Czechoslovakia to begin on the morning of September 30.

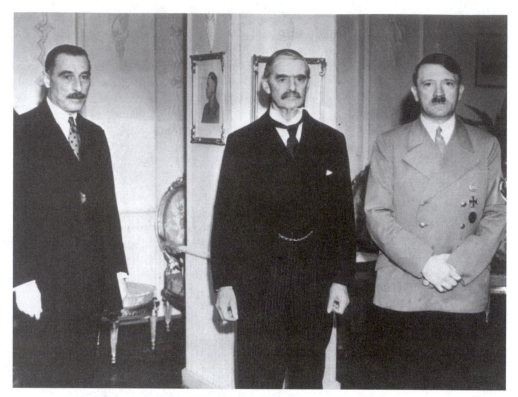

Hitler and British Prime Minister Neville Chamberlain (1869–1940) meet for the second time in Hitler's hotel room at the German city of Bad Godesberg, September 22, 1938: The man at the left is Sir Neville Henderson, the British ambassador to Germany, who was a leading proponent of the policy of appeasement. *(Courtesy of the Library of Congress)*

Few doubted that war would eventually lead to the defeat of Czechoslovakia for the strategic and geographical reasons summarized above. The French war plan envisioned a token advance into the Rhineland to be followed by a tactical withdrawal behind the Maginot Line for the winter. The British government could only hold out the possibility of sending two underequipped divisions to the continent. The Soviet Union, whose treaty with Czechoslovakia was due to go into effect once France had come to that country's assistance, had no way of assisting its ally except by air because of the Polish-Romanian barrier and therefore did not even take the precaution of a general mobilization. As the hopelessness of Czechoslovakia's position regardless of British, French, and Russian support became apparent, the tragic absurdity of the situation began to dawn on officials in Paris and London: Czechoslovakia was about to be crushed and Europe about to be embroiled in a war over the trivial details of how and when a previously agreed upon plan of territorial transfer was to take place.

While resuming their preparations for war, therefore, Chamberlain and Daladier desperately cast about for ways to arrange a negotiated settlement. The British prime minister persuaded Mussolini to intervene with Hitler to arrange for a final meeting to avert war. For reasons known only to himself, the Führer agreed to postpone his mobilization plans and to host a conference of the leaders of Britain, France, and Italy at Munich on September 29. His decision to stop at the brink of war may have been influenced by the hesitations of Mussolini, the reluctance of his generals, or the refusal of Chamberlain and Daladier to stand idly by if Germany attempted to settle the Sudeten crisis by military means. In any event, he had every reason to assume that his Godesberg demands would be accepted and he knew that their implementation would spell the early demise of the Czechoslovak state.

The Munich conference, from which both Czechoslovakia and its ally the Soviet Union were excluded at German insistence, produced an agreement that provided for the evacuation of Czechoslovak military forces from the Sudetenland between October 1 and 10 to be followed by its occupation by German troops in four stages. An international commission would administer plebiscites in disputed areas and fix the new frontier. Britain and France undertook to guarantee the redrawn borders of Czechoslovakia against unprovoked aggression while Germany and Italy promised similar guarantees once Polish and Hungarian territorial claims had been satisfactorily adjudicated. The Czechoslovak government was presented with this agreement in the form of an ultimatum on September 30 and denied even the right to submit written objections that Germany had enjoyed at the Paris Peace Conference in 1919. Abandoned by its Western allies and threatened with a war it could not hope to win if it resisted, the Prague government dutifully signed what its leaders knew to be its death warrant.

Upon their return to their respective capitals, Chamberlain and Daladier received euphoric expressions of public gratitude for having prevented the arcane dispute in far-off Czechoslovakia from plunging Britain and France into a war with Germany that neither nation wanted nor was prepared to fight. For those who believed Hitler's oft-repeated assurances that his objective in Eastern Europe was the absorption of territory populated by citizens of German descent, the Munich Pact promised the end of Germany's claims against what remained of Czechoslovakia and seemed to herald the advent of stability in the region. They ignored those passages in the Führer's speeches and writings that clearly enunciated his ultimate goal, which was not to liberate oppressed Germans from foreign rule, but rather to subject the non-German peoples of all of Eastern Europe and western Russia to direct or indirect domination from Berlin. There were those in England and France who were willing to tolerate and even to encourage the diversion of Germany's expansionist energies eastward at the expense of states for which they had little concern or, in the case of Soviet Russia, considerable aversion. But the leaders of Great Britain and France who struck the bargain with Hitler at Munich did not belong to this group of enthusiastic appeasers. They appear genuinely to have believed, Chamberlain with greater confidence than the more skeptical Daladier, that the annexation of the Sudetenland would remove the last obstacle to the peaceful reintegration of Germany into the Versailles system thus modified to its benefit.

Far from securing the territorial status quo on the continent, the Munich settlement accelerated the process of disintegration that would tip the balance of power in Eastern Europe toward Germany. The territorial amputations had condemned the rump state of Czechoslovakia to such a precarious existence as to preclude its operating as an independent political unit. Germany's annexation of the Sudetenland, together with the subsequent acquisition of the Teschen district by Poland and parts of Slovakia by Hungary, shattered the political authority of the government in Prague. The Slovaks, who inhabited the eastern region of the state and resented the politically dominant Czechs, seethed with separatist agitation that was actively encouraged by Berlin. The loss of the formidable string of fortifications along its western frontier exposed the truncated Czechoslovak state to unimpeded military invasion from Germany. Once the Munich Pact was put into effect, the political disintegration of Czechoslovakia and its gravitation toward the German orbit could have been prevented only by Hitler's willingness to abide by its terms or the determination of the Western powers to enforce them. The first possibility was ruled out by the German leader's plan to destroy Czechoslovakia preparatory to waging a war in the west to crush France and forcibly remove Britain from the continent in order to free German military forces for the land grab in the east that remained the ultimate goal of his foreign policy. The second prospect—that of an effective Anglo-French military deterrent to German violations of the Munich accord—was precluded by the geographical and strategic impossibility of bringing such Anglo-French military power as existed to bear against Germany.

The devastating consequences of the Munich Pact for rump Czechoslovakia were also felt in the other countries of Eastern and Southern Europe. France's willingness to sacrifice its strongest and most trusted ally in the region encouraged Czechoslovakia's partners in the Little Entente to hasten the reorientation of their foreign policies toward greater cooperation with the emerging German colossus. Shocked by France's abandonment of Prague and uneasy about threats to its own territorial integrity from Hungary and the Soviet Union, Romania resumed its rapprochement with Germany that had begun in response to earlier indications of the recession of French power in Eastern Europe. An economic agreement signed on December 10, 1938, guaranteed German access to Romanian oil (to supplement the insufficient synthetic production from domestic coal) as well as surplus wheat (to help compensate for Germany's annual shortfall in agricultural output). Yugoslavia, also subject to Hungarian revisionist demands and alarmed at the perpetual threat of Italian territorial ambitions along the Adriatic, strengthened its economic ties with Germany and solicited Hitler's restraining influence on its two revisionist neighbors. Hungary rapidly adjusted to the new political realities in Eastern Europe, dramatically demonstrating its alignment with Berlin's foreign policy by joining the Anti-Comintern Pact and withdrawing from the League of Nations. As a reward it received Germany's approval to annex Czechoslovakia's easternmost province, the Carpatho-Ukraine (Ruthenia), which contained numerous Hungarians.

The process of German economic and political domination of the smaller states of Eastern and Southern Europe was completed by Hitler's destruction of the Munich Pact on March 15, 1939. On that day the grievances of the Slovak minority against the Czech ruling elite were seized upon as a pretext for the German military occupation of Prague. The western half of the country, inhabited by the Czechs, was promptly transformed into a German protectorate while the eastern half was converted into the satellite state of Slovakia. In response to this spectacular and effortless extension of German military power into the Danube basin, all of the states of Eastern and Southern Europe, with one important exception, were either seduced or intimidated into accepting German hegemony on the eastern half of the continent. Romania and Yugoslavia, the former allies of Czechoslovakia and clients of France, relapsed into a policy of diplomatic and economic sub-

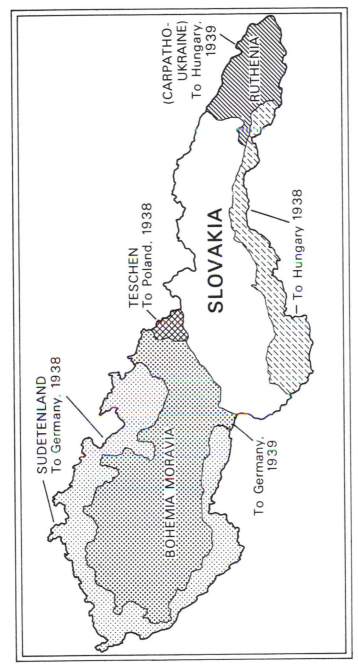

SUDETENLAND
To Germany, 1938

TESCHEN
To Poland, 1938

BOHEMIA MORAVIA

To Germany,
1939

SLOVAKIA

To Hungary 1938

(CARPATHO-
UKRAINE)
To Hungary,
1939

RUTHENIA

The Partition of Czechoslovakia, 1938–1939

servience to Germany. Hungary and Bulgaria, already firmly in the German orbit, resumed their active support for Hitler's aggressive moves.

It is ironic that the single exception to this pro-German reorientation in Eastern Europe after Munich was the policy conducted by the earliest supporter and principal beneficiary of Germany's eastern revisionism: Poland. Berlin's tactical flirtation with Warsaw, inaugurated by the nonaggression pact of 1934 and confirmed by the two governments' collaboration in the territorial amputation of Czechoslovakia in the autumn of 1938, reflected Hitler's intention of using Poland first as an accomplice in removing the Czech menace and later as a geographical barrier to possible Soviet interference with his planned military offensive in the west. But the government in Warsaw consistently rebuffed Hitler's demands that Poland publicly confirm its subservience to German foreign policy by adhering to the Anti-Comintern Pact. Though staunchly anti-Communist and implacably hostile to the Soviet Union, the Polish ruling elite stubbornly withheld this symbolic gesture because it would signal the end of the precarious balancing act between Germany and Russia that Poland had conducted since its rebirth as a nation after the Great War. For reasons of national pride, the Poles were unwilling to accept the same fate as the Czechs.

Poland's refusal to affirm its subservience to German foreign policy after the German march on Prague caused Hitler to revise his attitude toward Poland and therefore to reverse his timetable for European domination. With an unreliable Poland to the east, he could ill afford to resume his preparations for the war against France and Great Britain that he had originally planned to launch after removing the military threat of Czechoslovakia and obtaining that country's valuable munitions plants and raw materials for the German war machine. The Führer accordingly decided that the war in the west would have to await the prior defeat of Poland, the only recalcitrant power on Germany's eastern flank. Since the authorities in Warsaw could be neither enticed nor intimidated into acquiescing in Germany's plans for continental conquest, as all of its neighbors in Eastern Europe had been, Poland would have to be eliminated before rather than after the inevitable showdown with the Western democracies. Once the decision to attack Poland ahead of schedule was taken in the spring of 1939, the old grievances that had been deemphasized during the period of German-Polish detente were suddenly revived. The alleged maltreatment of the Germans in Danzig and the economic difficulties caused by the separation of East Prussia from the rest of the Reich once again gave rise to heated protests from Berlin. German demands for the restoration of Danzig to German sovereignty and an extraterritorial road and railroad across the corridor to East Prussia were met with the same polite but firm refusals in Warsaw that had greeted Hitler's earlier efforts to obtain Polish adherence to the Anti-Comintern Pact. Alone among the nations of Eastern and Southern Europe, Poland seemed prepared to defend its territorial integrity and national independence.

A major factor contributing to the stiffening of Polish resolve after the collapse of the Munich settlement was the abrupt change of British and French foreign policy from appeasement to resistance. Shortly after returning from Munich, Chamberlain and Daladier had taken a number of precautions against the possibility that the recent agreement to preserve the peace in Eastern Europe would come unglued. In the early months of 1939, Great Britain greatly accelerated the pace of its rearmament and finally began to formulate precise plans for the deployment of a large expeditionary force on the continent. France took steps to rectify the serious deficiencies in its air power by placing orders for warplanes in the United States after obtaining the tacit consent of the Roosevelt government. But it was the German occupation of Prague that precipitated the fundamental reversal of Anglo-French policy toward Hitler's Germany. Unlike all previous instances of German territorial expansion during the thirties, this one was executed at the expense of non-Germans and therefore could not be justified by the principle of national self-determination that Hitler had previously invoked in regard to the Rhineland, Austria, and the Sudetenland. Public opinion in Britain and France had rallied behind the Munich agreement because it was advertised by all of its signatories as the definitive resolution of Germany's nationality grievances in Eastern Europe. Its unilateral repudiation by Hitler less than half a year later produced a profound sense of betrayal in London and Paris as well as the determination not to repeat the same mistake in the future. As the principal architect of the Munich settlement, Chamberlain abruptly recalled the British ambassador to Berlin and issued a stern note of protest. On March 18, only three days after the fall of Prague, Britain and France approached the governments of Russia, Poland, Romania, Yugoslavia, Greece, and Turkey about the possibility of forming a coalition to oppose further German aggression. It rapidly became evident that the most likely victim of Hitler's next aggressive move was Poland, the only nation in Eastern Europe that had refused to align its policies with Germany and therefore denied Hitler the luxury of concentrating the bulk of German military forces in the west. In accordance with this perception, the British government took two unprecedented steps in the spring of 1939 that expressed its new-found determination to halt German aggression in its tracks. On March 31 it publicly pledged to guarantee the territorial integrity of Poland. On April 26 it announced its intention to request parliamentary authorization for the introduction of conscription. Never before had Great Britain been willing to promise military assistance to a nation in Eastern Europe and to institute a draft during peacetime. Such measures were unnecessary for France, with its existing treaty commitment to Poland and its large conscript army.

The minor powers of Southeastern Europe whose adhesion to an anti-German bloc Great Britain belatedly sought in the spring of 1939 were by then entirely unsuited for such service. Romania and Yugoslavia had drawn too close to Germany, both economically and politically, to be willing to help defend Poland, whereas Greece and Turkey were too geographically remote to do so. Only the Soviet Union was in a geographical position, and had previously expressed the willingness, to join Britain and France in a common front against Germany. But the Anglo-French overture of March 18 was foredoomed by the refusal of Poland and Romania to be associated with the Soviet Union and the reluctance of London and Paris to press them on this point. A month later, on April 17, Stalin offered the alternative of a military alliance among France, Great Britain, and Russia—the old Triple Entente of 1914—to guarantee all of the independent nations of Central and Eastern Europe against German aggression. On the same day, however, he authorized the Soviet ambassador to Berlin to broach the subject of a Russo-German rapprochement to officials in the German Foreign Office. In short, a month after the German absorption of Czechoslovakia, the Soviet leader had simultaneously floated two trial balloons to assess the intentions of the two contending blocs that were forming in anticipation of the impending showdown over Poland. The two conflicting traditions of postwar

Soviet foreign policy, the Popular Front-collective security strategy of cooperation with the Western powers to restrain Germany and the Rapallo policy of collaboration with Germany against the West, hung precariously in the balance.

Moscow had many reasons to fear the consequences of German hegemony in Europe. Hitler's brutal suppression of the German Communist party, his periodic outbursts against the menace of international communism, and the well-known project sketched in his book *Mein Kampf* and reiterated frequently thereafter for the seizure of Russian land for German agricultural development and resettlement—all of this had made a profound impression on Stalin and converted him to the cause of collective security and the Popular Front during the period 1935–38. But the refusal of the French to transform the Franco-Soviet Pact into a military alliance, the hesitation of Great Britain to commit itself to guaranteeing the territorial status quo in Eastern Europe, and the exclusion of the Soviet Union from the Munich conference left Stalin with the impression that the Western powers looked with favor on Germany's eastward expansion. Some influential publicists and statesmen in France and England believed that their nations stood to profit from, and therefore should promote, a struggle to the death between Teuton and Slav in the expanses of Eastern Europe. Anti-Communist sentiment in the Western democracies made the London and Paris governments reluctant to respond to the numerous overtures for cooperation against Germany that had emanated from the Kremlin. The private comments of key policymakers in Great Britain and France suggest that a lack of faith in the efficacy of the Red Army, with its decapitated command structure* and its inadequate transportation facilities, together with the refusal of Poland and Romania to tolerate the presence of Russian troops on their soil, complemented ideological hostility as a motive for this cautious posture. In any case, by the time the British and French governments had overcome this reluctance to make common cause with the Kremlin against Hitler in the spring of 1939, Stalin had decided, for a number of reasons to be summarized presently, that the best hope for Russia to protect the security of its western frontier lay in rapprochement with rather than resistance to Germany.

The first of these reasons was the Kremlin's discovery of evidence that Hitler's plans for the destruction of Poland were preparatory to a war not against Russia but rather against the Western powers. This conclusion emerged from intelligence reports from a well-placed Soviet spy in Tokyo, which detailed the acrimonious dispute between Germany and Japan during secret negotiations to transform the Anti-Comintern Pact into a triparte military alliance of the Axis powers. As we have seen, the Japanese steadfastly insisted that any such association be directed specifically and exclusively at the Soviet Union (their primary antagonist on the mainland of Asia), while Berlin had tried and failed to lure Tokyo into a military alliance aimed solely at France and Great Britain. Had the impending assault against Poland represented merely the first stage of a German invasion of Russia, a Germano-Japanese alliance against the Soviet Union would have obviously represented the most effective means of diluting Moscow's military strength by forcing it to fight a war on two fronts. Yet this was precisely the alignment that Hitler, in spite of unmistakable indications of Japanese interest, was unprepared to contemplate at this time. The announcement of the "Pact of Steel" between Germany and Italy on May

---

*Four hundred officers from the rank of colonel up had been executed during the purges of 1937–38.

22 confirmed the breakdown of the German-Japanese negotiations and signaled Hitler's intention to direct his aggressive policies against France and Great Britain (the only powers against which Italian assistance would count).

Thus the Soviet Union could hope to escape the trauma of an immediate German invasion, which did not fit into Hitler's plan for a westward advance after the destruction of Poland. It followed that Russia had much to gain from assuming a defensive posture on its western frontier and much to lose from joining a military alliance with Britain and France that might provoke the German dictator into revising his timetable for European conquest and dispatching his forces eastward after Poland's demise. Herein lies the obverse of the sinister intention that Stalin imputed to Western leaders after Munich. An accommodation with Hitler in Eastern Europe would deflect German aggression westward. Russia could obtain considerable advantage by abstaining from a war between the capitalist powers that was likely to result in their mutual exhaustion. In the meantime, such an abstention would afford a precious breathing spell that would enable Stalin to reorganize the command structure of the Red Army that had been decimated by his own paranoic purges of 1937–38; it would also permit the gearing up of the Russian economy for the war with Germany that was bound to come once Hitler had secured his western flank by defeating France and forcibly removing British power from the continent.

It was these considerations of national advantage that determined the Kremlin's double game in the spring and summer of 1939, when Britain and France belatedly solicited Soviet assistance in the containment of Germany. Russian criticism of the German occupation of Prague, followed up by the intimations of Soviet interest in the formation of a new Triple Entente, kept the door to London and Paris open. But various exploratory gestures from the Kremlin simultaneously kept the door to Berlin ajar. On May 3 the Soviet foreign minister, Maxim Litvinov, whose Jewish ancestry and passionate advocacy of the pro-Western policy adopted in the mid-1930s rendered him inappropriate for the task of negotiating an accommodation with Nazi Germany, was abruptly replaced by Stalin's loyal henchman Vyacheslav Molotov. This unmistakable signal to Hitler that Stalin was prepared to do business was followed up by an intensification of the contacts between Moscow and Berlin initiated in April. On May 20 Molotov himself informed the German ambassador of Stalin's interest in exploring a "political basis" for greater Russo-German cooperation. For the next three months, as Hitler's propaganda war against Poland reached a fever pitch, the low-level discussions between the Germans and the Russians resumed their leisurely pace. Britain and France finally agreed on July 25 to dispatch military missions to Moscow to explore the basis of an alliance with the Soviet Union against Germany. The German ambassador to Moscow was convinced that the Kremlin was at that time "determined to sign with England and France, if they fulfill all Soviet wishes."

But the manner in which the two Western governments conducted their negotiations with the Kremlin conveyed neither a sense of urgency nor a determination to secure Soviet membership in the anti-German coalition as an equal partner. The departure of the Anglo-French negotiating team was postponed for eleven days and then sent on its way not by airplane, which would have got the mission to Moscow in a day, but rather by the slowest possible means of sea transport, a 9,000-ton passenger-cargo vessel. When it finally reached Moscow on August 11 the mission consisted of low-ranking officers uncertain of their negotiating powers. When the talks got underway, the Anglo-French delegates evaded searching questions from the Soviets about troop strength, military

The signing of the Nazi-Soviet Non-Aggression Pact, August 23, 1939: Left to right, German Foreign Minister Joachim von Ribbentrop, Stalin, Wilhelm Gauss (legal adviser to the German Foreign Ministry who drafted the agreement), Gustav Hilger (counselor to the German Embassy in Moscow who served as interpreter), Soviet Foreign Minister Vyacheslav Molotov, and German Ambassador Friedrich Werner Count von der Schulenburg. Evidence of the "secret protocol" partitioning Poland and establishing a Soviet sphere of influence in the Baltic states did not come to light until after the war. *(Courtesy of the Library of Congress)*

plans, and means of persuading Poland and Romania to permit the passage of Russian military forces across their territory. The Russians could not help but compare the desultory behavior of the British and French governments to the eagerness of Chamberlain and Daladier to fly to Munich to deal directly with Hitler. It also contrasted dramatically with the strong expressions of interest in a Russo-German rapprochement that had begun to emanate from Berlin during the first three weeks of August. The strenuous efforts by the German foreign minister, Joachim von Ribbentrop, to secure an audience with Stalin as soon as possible were prompted by Hitler's concern about the timing of the Polish campaign, which had to be completed before the onset of winter would interfere with mechanized transport and aerial operations.

Stalin's decision to receive Hitler's foreign minister on August 23 marked the end of the double game that Russia had played since the spring of 1939. During the two meetings conducted in the Kremlin on that historic date, the German and Russian representatives reached a series of understandings that were codified in two documents—one for public consumption, the other for the confidential reassurance of the two signatories. The public document committed Germany and Russia to the observance of strict neutrality toward one another should either become involved in war. Hitler thereby secured Russian acquiescence in Germany's forthcoming campaign against Poland as well as relief from the threat of a two-front war once he turned his forces westward against France and Britain. Stalin obtained what Chamberlain and Daladier had earlier secured at Munich: the postponement of a war with Germany that their countries were at the time unprepared to fight, which afforded them precious time to upgrade their strategic capabilities as best they could. The "secret additional protocol" confirmed the geopolitical reality that had, since the end of the Great War, represented a potential basis of collaboration between Germany and Russia and an obstacle to Moscow's rapprochement with the West: While France and, belatedly, Britain, had been driven by the dictates of national interest to support the independence of the successor states in Eastern Europe, Germany and Russia were impelled by the promise of territorial aggrandizement to cooperate in their destruction. Thus the two signatories secretly agreed to the fourth partition of Poland. Finland, Latvia, and Estonia—all, like the eastern sector of Poland, former provinces of the tsarist empire—were allotted to the Russian sphere of influence.* Germany recognized Russia's right to recover the province of Bessarabia, whose seizure by Romania during the Russian Revolution had never been recognized by the Soviet regime. Except for the reannexation of Bessarabia, the motive for this Soviet expansionism may be summarized in a single phrase: the quest for security. Soviet domination of Finland and the two northernmost Baltic states would reduce the vulnerability of Russia's second capital, Leningrad, by providing it with a defensive buffer in the path of the traditional northern invasion route. The recovery of the territory lost to Poland in the war of 1920–21 would restore the historic buffer between the Germanic and Russian populations in Eastern Europe.

The Nazi-Soviet Pact of August 23, 1939, sealed the fate of Poland and enabled Hitler to launch the European war he had planned since coming to power. Last minute British efforts to promote a peaceful resolution of the German-Polish crisis had no chance of success: Hitler's military timetable required the war against Poland to begin no later than early September in order to permit the annihilation of that country before the autumn rains could interfere with the operations of his tanks and dive bombers. He would not again be cheated out of a victorious war against a despised victim as he had been at Munich. His evasive reply to Britain was therefore designed to split the Western powers from Poland—since he preferred to engage his enemies seriatim if that could be arranged—rather than to serve as the basis for a negotiated settlement he was determined to avoid at all costs. On the eve of August 31, a fabricated border incident was used as the justification for mounting a massive armor and air assault against Poland the following morning. The British and French governments, which had previously warned Berlin that the rapprochement with Russia would not alter their determination to honor their

---

*Lithuania, assigned to Germany's sphere in the Nazi-Soviet Pact, was transferred to the Soviet sphere in a subsequent agreement on September 28.

commitment to Poland, dutifully declared war on Germany on September 3 following the expiration of their ultimatum demanding the evacuation of German forces from Polish soil. With the temporary abstention of Russia and Italy (the latter on the grounds of unpreparedness), only four European powers were involved in the military drama that unfolded at the beginning of September 1939 on the Polish plains. But the limited number of participants and the geographically localized theater of combat did not prevent journalists from soon referring to a second world war.

5

GERMANY'S SECOND BID FOR EUROPEAN DOMINANCE (1939–1945)

The six-year war that began in the autumn of 1939 may be conveniently divided into three chronological periods. The first phase started with the successful blitzkrieg against Poland and ended with the establishment of a deceptively stable front along Germany's western frontier during the winter of 1939–40. The second phase opened with a German offensive in the west through the Low Countries, which resulted in the rapid collapse of France and the evacuation of British military forces from the continent according to plan, and ended with the failure of direct German aerial bombardment to knock Great Britain out of the war. The third phase marked the transformation of the European war into a world war, in which first the Soviet Union and then the United States were drawn into the global conflict that eventually destroyed Nazi Germany and its two Axis allies, Fascist Italy and imperial Japan.

The collapse of Poland after less than a month of fighting was foreordained by the Nazi-Soviet Pact, which denied Poland the hope of military assistance from Russia against Germany and partitioned that geographically cursed nation between the two powerful states to its east and west. Though the Russo-German agreement of August 23, 1939, did not stipulate Soviet participation in the military destruction of Poland, Stalin prudently dispatched troops westward on September 17 to lay claim to the territory allotted to the Soviet Union. Following the surrender of Warsaw on September 27, Poland once again simply disappeared from the map of Europe as Germany and Russia absorbed their respective shares of the spoils.

Both Great Britain and France were obliged by their treaty commitments to mount a military offensive against Germany if it attacked Poland. Such an offensive failed to materialize. The French general staff had devised no operational plans for a drive into western Germany, believing as it did that such a strike against Germany's heavily fortified French frontier was inconceivable and knowing that an offensive against Germany's greatest point of vulnerability in the Rhineland bordering Belgium was precluded by the latter country's refusal to compromise its neutrality by granting transit rights to French troops. As for the British, they had begun to rearm in earnest and to organize a land army on the basis of compulsory military service less than six months before the outbreak of the war in Poland. They therefore possessed neither the weaponry nor the manpower to mount a credible deterrent on Germany's western flank even if they could have solved the geographical riddle of how to project such military force as they did possess into enemy territory.

The efficacy of the blitzkrieg—the rapid thrust of massed tank formations supported by aerial assaults from dive bombers—was so brilliantly confirmed in the Polish campaign that Hitler issued an order on October 9 for the preparation of an early offensive with identical tactics through the Low Countries against France. Originally scheduled for November 12, then twice postponed on account of bad weather, the date for the great western offensive was eventually set for the second week in May to take advantage of the spring thaw. As the winter set in, German military forces transferred from the Polish front massed along the Dutch and Belgian frontiers while British and French forces dug in along France's eastern border. The absence of actual fighting led journalists to dub this second phase of the European struggle for hegemony the "phony war." Blitzkrieg, observed one wag, had given way to "sitzkrieg" ("sitting war").

Amid this eerie atmosphere of inactivity in the west, world attention was suddenly turned to events in the frozen terrain of Northern Europe. In September and October the Soviet Union began to exercise the prerogatives accorded it by the secret protocols of the Russo-German Pact to reassert Russian authority over the former European domains of the tsarist empire that had been lost after the revolution. The governments of the Baltic states of Latvia, Estonia, and Lithuania were compelled to authorize the garrisoning of Russian troops on their territory and to sign treaties of mutual assistance with the Soviet Union. When Finland refused both to grant Russia the strategic bases it sought for the protection of Leningrad and to regard itself as part of the Soviet "sphere of interest," Stalin launched a military attack against that country on November 30 in the expectation that Finnish resistance would collapse in short order after the fashion of Poland. But sub-zero temperatures and rugged terrain—advantages that had been unavailable to the hapless Poles—helped the Finns to hold out for over three months against a Russian army three times larger than their own.

With public opinion in Britain and France clamoring for military intervention on behalf of valiant little Finland, authorities in London and Paris concocted a scheme ostensibly designed to relieve the Finns but in reality aimed at a soft spot in the strategic arsenal of Germany. As noted earlier, Germany depended heavily on imports of high-grade iron ore from Sweden for its armaments production. During the winter months, when much of the Baltic Sea was frozen, the ore had to be transported overland by rail to the ice-free port of Narvik in Norway for transshipment through Norwegian territorial waters to ports in northern Germany. Plans were drawn up for an Anglo-French expeditionary force to be landed at Narvik and sent across Norway and Sweden to assist Finland while seizing the Swedish ore fields along the way. When the Finnish capitulation on March 12 foreclosed this project, it was replaced by an earlier British scheme to mine Norway's territorial waters in order to cut Germany off from its iron ore supplies. Though both of these schemes were fraught with diplomatic complications caused by the refusal of Norway and Sweden to compromise their neutrality, the British proceeded with the plan anyway. But the day after the British mining operation began, German amphibious and paratroop forces seized the capital and major ports of Norway and occupied Denmark on April 9. Contingents of Anglo-French troops hastily landed on the Norwegian coast failed to secure defensible beachheads and eventually had to be withdrawn. Germany had instantaneously obtained at virtually no cost a string of strategically located bases in Scandinavia that would subsequently be used for submarine warfare against Great Britain in its home waters. By refusing to coordinate their defense plans with Great Britain and France, and by denying the Anglo-French armies transit rights across their territory, the Nordic neutrals facilitated the abrupt expansion of German power into Northern Europe. Norway and Denmark paid for their policy of aloofness by being forced to submit to German military occupation and all of the privations that that entailed. On account of its previously demonstrated willingness to cooperate economically with Germany, Sweden was spared the agony of its neighbors. From its posture of absolute neutrality it continued to supply the German war machine with all of the high-grade iron ore it required at a handsome profit.

After Germany had secured its northern flank, the long-awaited western offensive finally unfolded on May 10. The buffer states of the Netherlands and Belgium, which like their Scandinavian counterparts had consistently rebuffed Anglo-French overtures for joint military planning, were rewarded for their scrupulous adherence to neutrality with a brutal combination of aerial bombardment and mechanized invasion that rivaled the Polish campaign in its rapidity as well as its destructiveness. On paper the two sides were of roughly equal strength in manpower (134 German divisions versus 94 French, 10 British, 22 Belgian, and 8 Dutch divisions). Germany's three-to-one advantage in air power was partially offset by the numerical superiority of the Western Allies in the decisive weapon of the moment: 3,200 Anglo-French versus 2,500 German tanks. But sheer numbers of men and machines do not tell the whole story. The training and equipment of the German motorized infantry units were vastly superior to that of the Western powers. Moreover, the Allies squandered their numerical superiority in armor by dispersing their tank formations among the regular infantry divisions as support groups instead of concentrating them in separate armored divisions to serve as spearheads for motorized infantry units. It is supremely ironic that this tactic for the most efficient use of armor in offensive warfare had been conceived by a British military theorist, B. H. Liddell Hart, and popularized by a young French tactician, Colonel Charles de Gaulle, only to be put into practice by the German Generals Fritz Erich von Manstein and Heinz Guderian. Dutch resistance collapsed in five days and Belgian forces retreated in total disarray before the German juggernaut as it rolled toward the French frontier. Panzer spearheads with divebomber support cleared the way for motorized infantry units to slash through the Ardennes hill country in southern Belgium (which had been considered "impassable" to armor by those French military planners who vetoed the extension of the Maginot Line to the North Sea). The German forces breached the French defenses at Sedan on May 16, then veered northward toward the Channel coast to sever the supply lines and communications of the main Anglo-French armies in northeastern France and Belgium. After reaching the sea on May 20, this advance German tank contingent swung eastward toward the isolated Allied forces that had reassembled at the French port of Dunkirk near the Belgian frontier.

On the same day that the German western offensive began, the thoroughly discredited British prime minister, Neville Chamberlain, had been replaced by Winston Leonard Spencer Churchill, who had been a vocal critic of the policy of appeasement throughout the 1930s. In one of his first important decisions as Britain's wartime leader, Churchill on May 28 turned down the urgent request of the French prime minister, Paul Reynaud, that the remainder of the Royal Air Force be dispatched to the continent for the defense of France. Churchill also ordered the evacuation of the Anglo-French troops trapped in the vicinity of Dunkirk. During the next eight days 200,000 British and 130,000 French soldiers were ferried across the Channel by a hastily improvised flotilla of vessels while the German armies turned southward to deliver the knockout blow to the remnants of the French army. By June 16 the French cabinet, which had abandoned Paris five days earlier and headed south, reluctantly concluded that further resistance was pointless. Reynaud resigned in favor of the octogenarian hero of the Great War, Marshal Henri-Philippe Pétain, who assembled a ministry favorable to a prompt end to the fighting. On June 22 the French government capitulated after less than six weeks of resistance, signing an armistice that provided for the disarmament of the French forces and the delivery of the northern three-fifths of the country to German military occupation.

Brigadier General Charles de Gaulle had been a prewar critic of the French high command's defensive military doctrines and had served briefly as an undersecretary of defense in the Reynaud government. Opposed to the decision for an armistice, he fled to London, and four days before the French capitulation, broadcast a message to the French people over British radio urging resistance to the German occupation and inviting French military and political authorities to join him in England to resume the struggle against the invader. When no one in high office responded to this appeal, he promptly formed the French National Committee in London, which operated alongside the other governments in exile that had fled the overrun countries of the continent. Great Britain subsidized and encouraged this "Free French" movement and severed relations with the collaborationist regime of Marshal Pétain established on July 2 in the unoccupied sector of southern France at the resort city of Vichy. Unlike the other European governments in exile that had reassembled in London after the defeat of their armies in the field, de Gaulle's organization had no claim to political legitimacy since the legally elected French parliament had voted to confer emergency powers on the Pétain regime on July 9. Nonetheless, de Gaulle assembled a ragtag military force, composed of French soldiers, sailors, and airmen who had escaped from the continent, that participated in several campaigns against the Axis during the rest of the war.

The fall of France in the summer of 1940 completed the revolution in the balance of power in Europe that had begun with the remilitarization of the Rhineland. In just four years Germany had come from nowhere to dominate the entire continent, controlling either directly or indirectly almost as much territory as Napoleon at the height of his power. Nine formerly independent states had submitted to the domination of Berlin in various guises, ranging from outright annexation in the case of Austria to a fictitious independence in the case of the Vichy regime in France. The remaining nations of the continent had become either military allies or economic vassals of Germany, except for a handful of states—Spain, Portugal, Switzerland, and Sweden—that managed to cling to a precarious neutrality. The sympathetic collaboration of the Soviet Union in Germany's drive toward the west, originally confined to the joint partition of Poland but soon expanded to include the exchange of Russian grain and oil for German manufactured products, seemed to afford Germany the advantage it had gained too late in the last war:

protection against economic strangulation by the British blockade through access to Russia's inexhaustible supply of food and fuel.

The end of the Battle of France on June 22 was followed by hasty preparations for the Battle of Britain. Plans for a Channel crossing were drawn up on July 2: Germany assembled troop transport ships along the French Channel coast and organized thirteen divisions in preparation for what Hitler christened "Operation Sea-Lion," the first attempted invasion of the British Isles since the Norman Conquest. But Churchill's decision to hold in reserve the bulk of the Royal Air Force (RAF) during the French campaign forced a postponement of the projected amphibious landing until the Luftwaffe could remove the threat of aerial harassment of the trans-Channel invasion force. Emboldened by its astonishingly effective performance against Poland and France, Air Marshal Hermann Göring assured his Führer that the numerically superior German fighter force, after several days of precision bombing of the British fighter bases, could remove the enemy's air arm from the skies within a month.

Apart from the courage and skill of its pilots, three technological factors enabled the RAF to foil German plans for achieving the control of the air deemed necessary for a successful amphibious invasion. The first was the qualitative superiority of British air power that helped to compensate for its numerical inferiority. In this respect, Britain's belated entry in the aerial arms race had proved to be an advantage; the new Spitfire and Hurricane fighters fresh off the assembly line were faster, more maneuverable, and possessed greater firepower than the older German Messerschmidts. The second was radar, the technique of employing the reflected echo of radio waves to detect distant objects in the atmosphere. Perfected in 1935 by the British scientist Robert Watson-Watt, this technological breakthrough resulted in the construction of twenty early warning stations along Britain's Channel coast by the spring of 1939 from which observers could locate approaching aircraft soon after their departure from continental bases and measure their range with uncanny accuracy. This radar network enabled the RAF fighters to conserve precious fuel by remaining on the ground until an attack was underway and then heading straight for the incoming German planes, whose limited fuel supply often forced them to return prematurely to their French or Belgian bases. The third factor in the British air victory was the development by British intelligence of an electrically operated cipher machine capable of decoding German radio messages. This device, based on a code machine that had been stolen in Germany by the Polish Secret Service and transported to England in utmost secrecy before the war, enabled British cryptographers to crack the German code and therefore gave the RAF occasional bits of useful advance knowledge about the German air force's operational instructions.

But the major responsibility for the Luftwaffe's failure to gain control of British air space in the autumn of 1940 must be placed squarely on the shoulders of Hitler himself. When the RAF raided Berlin in retaliation for the accidental bombing of London by German planes, the Führer angrily ordered round-the-clock bombardment of the major British metropolitan areas as punishment. He apparently persuaded himself that such brutal tactics would serve a good military purpose by sapping British morale and inciting civilian opposition to Churchill's policy of resistance. Hitler's faith in the efficacy of massive aerial bombardment of civilian population centers (rather than military installations) was shared by an entire generation of strategists inspired by the writings of the Italian general Giulio Douhet, who had forecast the total breakdown of social order and mass uprisings leading to demands for capitulation by the terrorized civilian victims of such air power. Though German bombing raids killed 51,509 British civilians and damaged or destroyed one out of five British homes, they did not produce the widespread demoralization and civil unrest that the theorists of strategic bombing since Douhet had predicted. On the contrary, the Blitz, as these bombing raids were collectively called in Britain, galvanized the population behind its leadership and stiffened its resolve to carry on the war. The campaign to terrorize the metropolitan centers of Britain proved counterproductive in strategic terms also because it diverted German air power from the military targets that really counted: the fighter bases of the RAF, which had been severely damaged by the initial onslaught and might very well have been wiped out by a continuation of the precision bombing that Göring had initiated in the late summer.

The postponement of Operation Sea-Lion and the dispersal of the cross-Channel invasion flotilla in mid-September did not signify the end of the Luftwaffe's bombardment of British cities, which continued through the spring of 1941. But the air war in the British skies thereafter took second place to the project that had remained the touchstone of Hitler's foreign policy: the annihilation of the Soviet Union. On July 31, two weeks before the beginning of the bombardment of Britain, Hitler informed his generals of his plan to invade Russia the following May. In the early autumn the redeployment of German forces from occupied France to the east began. But "Operation Barbarossa" against Russia was unexpectedly delayed when Mussolini, who had entered the war against France and Britain in June, imprudently embroiled Italy in conflicts in the Balkans and North Africa, which required the diversion of German forces southward in rescue operations. Italian troops based in the recently acquired protectorate of Albania had attacked Greece in October 1940 in search of a quick, cheap victory. Instead they encountered fierce resistance from the Greek army and by March 1941 faced the prospect of a humiliating military defeat when British troops landed in Greece at the invitation of the Athens government. The sudden reappearance of a British army on the continent elicited a swift response from Berlin. When the new government of Yugoslavia bravely repudiated its predecessor's pledge to grant transit facilities to the German army, Hitler launched an invasion from bases in Hungary and Bulgaria that crushed Yugoslav and Greek resistance in three weeks and forced a hasty evacuation of the British force from the Greek peninsula.

In the meantime, an offensive mounted in mid-September by Italian forces in Libya against the lightly defended British garrison in Egypt (which protected the Suez Canal and the Middle Eastern oil fields) ground to a halt and then was transformed into a rout as British forces counterattacked deep into Libyan territory. In February 1941 Hitler was compelled to dispatch an armored "Afrika Korps" under General Erwin Rommel to relieve the battered Italian forces in North Africa. Within two months Rommel's panzers had hurled the British back to the Egyptian frontier. Though successful in the short run, these two Mediterranean diversions caused a six-week delay in Hitler's timetable for the invasion of Russia. The loss of precious time during a season of favorable weather caused little concern in Berlin because of Hitler's confident expectation, based on the French precedent, that Russian resistance would crumble within three months, before the onset of winter. So confident was the German military command of a speedy victory in the east that it had ordered winter clothing only for the small contingent of troops that were to remain in Russia for occupation duty after the withdrawal of the victorious invasion force.

Inspecting the damage: British Prime Minister Winston Churchill (1874–1965) inspects property damage in London caused by the German bombing campaign against British cities in the autumn of 1940. "The blitz," as it was popularly known, had the opposite effect on the British people than the one that Hitler had intended. It bolstered their commitment in support of the government's war effort. *(Courtesy of the Library of Congress)*

The German invasion of the Soviet Union began on June 22, 1941, the 129th anniversary of the launching of Napoleon's ill-fated expedition to Moscow. Four million men, 3,300 tanks, and 5,000 aircraft were sent eastward to wage what was to become the greatest land war in history. Ignoring warnings from British, American, and even Soviet intelligence sources about the impending attack, Stalin and his military advisers were totally unprepared for the German onslaught. As the Soviet armies reeled in confusion before the offensive in the summer and fall of 1941, the consequences of Stalin's purge of the officers' corps in 1937–38 were graphically revealed in the tactical incompetence of the inexperienced junior officers who had replaced the executed members of the high command. In the first three months of battle, over half of the Soviet army was killed, wounded, or captured. At the farthest extent of the German army's three-pronged advance—toward Leningrad in the north, Moscow in the center, and the Ukrainian grain fields and Caucasian oil wells in the south—almost half of Russia's industrial resources and cultivated land were under enemy control.

It has often been asserted in justification of Stalin's separate peace with Hitler in August 1939 that the Soviet Union gained valuable space and time to prepare for its defense. But the space gained in the Baltic states and eastern Poland proved of no strategic value and was overrun by the invading German armies in the first few days of the eastern offensive. The time gained by Stalin for the reorganization of the Red Army and the construction of munitions factories far to the east of Russia's exposed western frontier was also time gained by Hitler that the latter put to good use. Freed from the threat of a two-front war by Russia's indulgence, Germany forcibly acquired the economic and strategic resources of a dozen countries for use against the Soviet Union. With the fall of Kiev and the siege of Moscow and Leningrad in the autumn of 1941, the benefits of Russia's abstention from the war in Europe that had begun in September 1939 were difficult to identify. Space and time counted for little in the type of war that Germany was waging against the Soviet Union—a blitzkrieg whose aims were to rout the Red Army and topple the Stalinist regime before the arrival of the winter snows.

The failure of the German army to deliver the decisive blow before the Russian winter ground its mechanized offensive to a halt in December 1941 has been traced by some military historians to the six-week delay caused by the Balkan and Mediterranean diversions of the previous spring. Others have blamed Hitler's decision to detach armored divisions from the Center Army Group advancing along Napoleon's road to Moscow in order to bolster the drive against Leningrad in the north and Ukraine in the south. But whatever its tactical cause, the strategic result of the stalled eastern offensive was unmistakable: Hitler's swift war of annihilation became a long war of attrition. This change upset the calculations of the German leader, which rested on the presumption of total victory in Russia within three months. It also enabled Stalin's Machiavellian diplomacy during the 1939–41 period of Russian abstention to yield its anticipated dividends. Shielded from the effects of the European war by the nonaggression pact with Hitler, the newly constructed factories east of the Urals began to compensate during the winter of 1941–42 for the lost production in the regions of European Russia that had been overrun by the invading German armies. The nonaggression pact that Stalin had signed with Japan on April 13, 1941, freed Russia from the threat of a war on two fronts and permitted the redeployment of large numbers of troops from the Far East to replenish the depleted ranks of the defenders of Moscow. Once the promise of a quick German triumph was buried in the snows of December, the scales gradually began to tip in favor of the Soviet Union, whose seemingly inexhaustible reserves of military manpower and strategic raw materials represented a formidable advantage in a long-drawn-out struggle.

The potential vulnerability of Germany in a conflict of long duration became evident during the six months that it waged war against two powers, Great Britain and Russia, which together commanded almost a quarter of the world's resources. The imbalance became all the more pronounced with the transformation of the European conflict into a world war upon the entry of the United States a few days after the Russian counteroffensive from Moscow began. Though the brunt of America's military power could not be hurled against the Third Reich for another two and a half years, its vast economic resources were placed at the disposal first of Great Britain and then of Russia just as they had been in the period before the active participation of the American Expeditionary Force in the earlier war against Germany.

During the twelve months after the fall of France when Great Britain faced Germany alone, the isolationist policy of Washington gradually evolved into a pro-British strategy as the damaging consequences to American national interest of a German victory against England became apparent to Roosevelt and his foreign policy advisers. On September 2, 1940, as the Luftwaffe began its furious air assault on the British Isles, the United States transferred fifty overage destroyers to Great Britain in exchange for a ninety-nine-year lease of naval and air bases on eight British possessions in the western hemisphere. This arrangement supplied the Royal Navy with desperately needed ships with which to wage the Battle of the Atlantic against German submarines, while the sale of surplus American munitions enabled the British army to replace the materiel abandoned on the beaches of Dunkirk. On December 20 Roosevelt established a defense board to plan and coordinate American assistance to the embattled British, a move that was denounced by the German government as an unwarranted intervention in the European war that compromised America's neutral status. But the "cash-and-carry" provisions of American neutrality legislation, which prohibited American merchant vessels from entering the war zone in Europe and required advanced payment for purchases by belligerents in the American market, had brought Britain to the brink of bankruptcy by the end of the first year and a half of the war. The decline of Britain's foreign trade, caused by the conversion from production for export to production for warmaking and aggravated by German submarine attacks on British merchant shipping, left that country without a sufficient reserve of dollars to finance its mounting purchases from the "arsenal of democracy" across the Atlantic. Even the sale of its remaining foreign assets and the depletion of its gold stocks would not bridge the gap for very long. The American response to the exhaustion of British dollar reserves was the enactment on March 11, 1941, of the so-called Lend-Lease Act. This legislation repealed the "cash" part of the cash-and-carry requirement, authorizing the sale of American products on credit to "any country whose defense the President deems vital to the defense of the United States." Under the authority granted by this law, a million tons of American agricultural surpluses were shipped across the Atlantic between April and December 1941 to alleviate Great Britain's serious food shortage caused by the German submarine campaign. On November 6, 1941, the Roosevelt administration extended a $1 billion Lend-Lease credit to the Soviet Union, which was struggling to defend its major cities against the German attack that had been launched that previous summer. In this way a considerable proportion of the strategic arsenal and economic resources of the United States was made available to the two major powers in the anti-Axis coalition during the remaining months of American neutrality.

The intervention of the United States in the Second World War was precipitated not by any quarrel with Nazi Germany, but by Japan's surprise attack on the American Pacific fleet based at Pearl Harbor, Hawaii, on December 7, 1941.* By the spring of 1942, all of East Asia had come under the domination of Japan. American forces had been

---

*Germany and Italy declared war on the United States on December 11, 1942.

expelled from the Philippines, Britain's major East Asian base at Singapore had surrendered, and Japanese military and naval power began to fan out in three directions—toward Australia, India, and the Aleutian Islands off Alaska (see p. 223). Despite the expanding power of Japan across the Pacific and the absence of any immediate German threat to America's vital interests, Roosevelt resolved to pursue a "Europe-first" strategy in the war. By the summer of 1942 the United States had replaced Britain as the major foreign supplier of the Soviet Union, shipping foodstuffs, clothing, and mechanized vehicles across the Atlantic to the northern ports of Murmansk and Archangel as well as to the Persian Gulf for transshipment by rail across Iran to the embattled cities of European Russia. The menace of German submarines, which had sunk a third of Britain's merchant fleet tonnage by the time of the Pearl Harbor attack, was removed by the spring of 1943 with the help of American convoys and reconnaissance planes equipped with microwave radar to detect U-boats. In April German naval authorities conceded defeat in the Battle of the Atlantic by recalling the submarines to their bases along the Norwegian and French coasts. Anglo-American control of the sea-lanes to Europe enabled Allied strategists to envision for the first time an invasion of the continent.

But that invasion was not soon in coming. For three full years—from June 1941 to June 1944—the Soviet army fought the German army on the continent virtually unaided. The British government's enthusiastic expressions of solidarity with and tendering of economic assistance to its newly acquired ally against Germany* were not translated into concrete actions on behalf of the common struggle in the form of direct military intervention. Despite urgent pleas from Stalin for some kind of diversionary action in Western Europe to relieve the pressure on the Soviet armies, Churchill steadfastly declined to risk such a direct assault on the western flank of the German-controlled continent. The British preferred to engage the vulnerable Italians in their ersatz empire in the Mediterranean basin rather than challenge the formidable German forces ensconced in their *Festung Europa,* except for long-range bombing raids on German cities that had no discernible effect on Germany's capacity to wage its land war in the east. The American intervention did not change the situation, in spite of Roosevelt's professed enthusiasm for an Anglo-American landing in northern France, for the British prime minister was able to persuade the American president that such an operation was inopportune. The extensive inter-Allied discussions about the opening of a "second front" in France appear to have been intended mostly to placate the increasingly insistent Stalin. Why it took the Western powers so long to organize and execute such an operation has remained a point of intense historiographical controversy. Defenders of the Soviet Union detected a cynical motive behind this Anglo-American hesitation, namely, the desire to see Russia bled white while its Western allies conserved their military and economic resources in order to step in at the last moment to replace defeated Germany and preempt exhausted Russia in order to dominate the continent. To judge from the statements of the principals themselves, what prompted Churchill to oppose an early Allied landing in Western Europe, and what persuaded Roosevelt to acquiesce in this postponement, were two considerations. The first was the insufficient number of landing craft, the risks of transporting large numbers of American troops to Britain while German submarines still roamed the North Atlantic with impunity, and the

---

*On July 13, 1941, London and Moscow concluded a pact of mutual assistance.

entrenched position of the German forces along the French Channel coast. This caused Churchill to fear that a premature landing of ill-equipped, undermanned Allied forces in northern France would suffer the same fate as the suicidal amphibious operation at Gallipoli, for which he had been blamed during the First World War and which had almost cost him his political career. The second consideration was the existence of a much more attractive alternative: an Allied landing in the lightly defended North African colonies of Vichy France, which could then serve as a springboard for the invasion of Fortress Europe through its back door in the Mediterranean.

The revival of the German offensive in Russia in the summer of 1942 placed a considerable strain on the Grand Alliance,* as Stalin vainly badgered the Anglo-American leadership to open the much-discussed second front in the west. The invasion of French North Africa, which took place in November 1942, was a spectacular success from the Western Allies' point of view. It led to the surrender in the following May of the Axis armies in Libya, which were caught in the vise between the Allied forces landed in Morocco and Algeria and the British army in Egypt that had pierced the German-Italian front at El Alemein. It also brought southern Italy within range of Allied bombers stationed in Tunisia just across the Mediterranean narrows. But the liberation of North Africa was accomplished at the expense of the long-delayed cross-Channel invasion of France. To the suspicious Stalin it seemed a disappointing diversion of Anglo-American military power from where it was needed in Western Europe. The trans-Mediterranean landing on Sicily in July, which paved the way for the Allied invasion of the Italian mainland in September, did little to calm Soviet anxieties about the implications of Allied strategy. It merely increased Stalin's exasperation at his allies' reluctance to engage the German army directly while Soviet troops were mounting their own ferocious counterattack in the east.

The professed objective of the Anglo-American Mediterranean strategy was to force an Italian surrender and to pin down as many German troops as possible on the Italian peninsula in preparation for the invasion of France. In this the British and the Americans were signally successful. The landing of Allied troops in Sicily, coming as it did amid desperate shortages of food, fuel, and munitions and mounting evidence of social unrest in Italy, compelled Mussolini to convene on July 24, 1943, a meeting of the Fascist Grand Council, his rubber stamp "parliament" that had not met for years, to shore up the deteriorating prestige of his regime. Instead, the Council voted to confer emergency powers on King Victor Emmanuel, who the following day replaced Mussolini with Marshal Pietro Badoglio and had the Duce arrested. The new Italian leader promptly dissolved the Fascist party, approached the Allies for an armistice (which was finally concluded on September 8), and announced his country's adherence to the Allied cause. The German military forces in Italy, which had been increased to twenty-five divisions in anticipation of just such a turnabout, proceeded to disarm the Italian army, occupy the northern two-thirds of the peninsula, and install Mussolini as head of a new "Italian Social Republic" in the northern city of Saló after his spectacular rescue from prison by German paratroopers. The subsequent squandering of Anglo-American lives and supplies in the long and costly advance up the Italian peninsula, which took more than a year after the land-

---

*The popular term for the American, British, and Soviet coalition against Germany.

ing in Sicily, was unquestionably one of the greatest strategic blunders of the Allied campaign in Europe.

As the Anglo-American forces cleared North Africa of Axis troops, gained effective control of the Mediterranean, and began their Italian campaign, the Soviet armies in the east finally turned the tide of battle against the German invaders. The German army in southern Russia had been advancing toward the strategically situated city of Stalingrad on the Volga throughout the summer of 1942, threatening to sever the direct railway and river connections linking the major Soviet armies to their sources of fuel in the oil wells of the Caucasus. By mid-September the German Sixth Army had reached the outskirts of the city that bore Stalin's name, the industrial and communications hub of southern Russia, and proceeded to place it under siege. But the gradual buildup of a numerically superior Russian defense force in the autumn prompted the German commander, General Friedrich von Paulus, to request authorization to fall back to a more defensible position. Refusing to countenance what would have been regarded as a humiliating retreat, Hitler ordered a fight to the finish. After three months of what one military historian has called "the most senseless example of human slaughter in history," von Paulus disobeyed his Führer's orders and surrendered the tattered remnant of his army on February 2, 1943. The loss of half a million Axis soldiers dead, wounded, or captured and the opening of a massive Soviet counteroffensive in the spring signaled the beginning of the end of Hitler's obsessive drive for German *Lebensraum* in the European part of the Soviet Union. By the end of the year two-thirds of the Soviet territory under German occupation had been liberated by the advancing Red Army.

As the Soviet counteroffensive from the east gathered momentum, Roosevelt, Churchill, and Stalin met together for the first time at Teheran, Iran, in November 1943 to plan the timing and strategy of the projected invasion of Western Europe. Churchill, true to form, unveiled an elaborate proposal for an Anglo-American landing at selected points in the Balkans that would have once again deferred the long-delayed invasion of France. Stalin had little difficulty in persuading Roosevelt and his military chiefs that such an indirect assault on Hitler's Europe was a poor substitute for a cross-Channel operation on France's Normandy coast, which would place the Anglo-American armies on the shortest and most direct route to the center of Germany's industrial and warmaking power in the Ruhr. Thus the American and Soviet heads of state turned aside the British leader's Balkan scheme in favor of an amphibious landing in northern France to be followed by a crossing from North Africa to the French Mediterranean coast. On June 6, 1944, five seaborne and three airborne divisions of American, British, and Canadian troops were put ashore along the Normandy coast, quickly securing four beachheads. They were supplied in part by a massive floating dock that had been prefabricated in England and towed across the Channel to compensate for the absence of good harbors in the invasion zone. Within a week and a half the initial Allied invasion force had swollen to 640,000 well-equipped soldiers. The greatest amphibious operation in history was facilitated by the absence of effective resistance from the two arms of Hitler's war machine that had enabled it to subdue the entire continent of Europe four years earlier: the air force and the armored divisions. The Luftwaffe had been driven from the skies for lack of gasoline by the U.S. Army Air Corps' precision bombing of Germany's oil supply in the spring of 1944. The German tank units in northern France had been held in reserve until it was too late on the mistaken assumption that the Normandy invasion was an elaborate feint to lure the panzers into a trap. At the end

Men examining bodies amid the rubble of the Altmarkt in Dresden, Germany, after British firebombing raids killed 135,000 on the night of February 13, 1945: Immortalized in Kurt Vonnegut's novel *Slaughterhouse Five,* the firebombing of Dresden, together with earlier raids on the Baltic port city of Hamburg that killed over 40,000 people, had been prompted by the widespread belief among advocates of strategic air power that such massive death and destruction would sap the enemy's will to resist. A survey completed after the war by American investigators concluded that the Allied bombing campaign against German population centers did not significantly affect the German war effort. *(Courtesy of the Library of Congress)*

of July the Allied forces smashed out of their coastal enclave and began a relentless offensive, which, in conjunction with the northeastward advance of Anglo-American and Free French forces landed in southern France on August 15, cleared France of the German occupation army by the end of the year.

After flirting with the idea of subjecting liberated France to an Allied military occupation on the grounds that Marshal Pétain's collaboration with Germany had qualified his country for treatment as a defeated enemy, the United States government reluctantly recognized de Gaulle's French Committee of National Liberation as the de facto civil government of France on July 11. Roosevelt had long been contemptuous of the imperious leader of "Free France," suspecting him of harboring authoritarian plans for postwar France scarcely less objectionable than the current policies of Pétain. For his part, de Gaulle deeply resented the American president's decision to maintain diplomatic relations with the Vichy regime after the fall of France, his refusal to inform de Gaulle in advance of the Normandy invasion or to assign Free French forces a prominent role in it, and his ill-disguised efforts to promote the candidacies of rivals to de Gaulle within the French army. De Gaulle succeeded in elbowing his way into a position of supreme political authority in liberated France during the summer of 1944 and forced the United States to acknowledge his fait accompli. But his wartime dispute with Roosevelt left a legacy of bitterness and ill will which, as we shall see, was to have an unsettling effect on Franco-American relations in later years.

As the American, British, and Free French armies approached Germany's western frontier in the autumn of 1944, Soviet forces overran Bulgaria and Romania and advanced deep into Polish territory. In the winter of 1944–45, desperate German counteroffensives against the Western Allies in Belgium and against Soviet forces approaching Hungary temporarily postponed the inevitable collapse of Hitler's tottering empire in Central Europe. But in February 1945 the offensives on Germany's two flanks resumed. In early March the Anglo-American armies became the first military force to cross the Rhine in combat since Napoleon's day. The Soviet army in Southern Europe took Budapest on its way to Vienna, while Soviet forces in the north decimated retreating German contingents along the Baltic coast in preparation for the march on Berlin.

The disintegration of the exhausted German armies before the advancing forces of the United States and its allies from the west and the Soviet Union from the east produced a vast military vacuum in the center of the European continent. The question inevitably arose: Which of the two invading armies would fill it? This was a question that was fraught with political as well as strategic overtones. In light of the radically dissimilar political, social, and economic systems of the Anglo-Americans and the Russians, which had given rise to intense mutual antagonism before they were thrown together in the joint crusade against Nazi Germany, it was inevitable that this ideological hostility would resurface once the military collapse of Germany removed the only important reason for them to continue to cooperate. On the Russian side, as we have seen, Stalin's distrust of his Western allies had originally been engendered by their hesitation to open a second front in France while the Red Army engaged nine-tenths of the German army in the east. Neither the stellar performance of the American army in crushing German resistance in the west nor Washington's repeated promises to observe the policy of unconditional surrender, adopted by Roosevelt and Churchill at the Casablanca conference of January 1943, appeared to allay Stalin's fear that the Western capitalist powers planned to allow the doomed German army to engage Soviet forces in the east while Anglo-American troops prepared to thrust deep into the continent and dictate a political settlement in Eastern Europe at Russia's expense. Had Churchill's been the decisive voice in Allied military planning, the Russian dictator's assessment would not have been wide of the mark. Fervently anti-Communist and alarmed at Soviet designs on Eastern Europe, the British prime minister wanted the Allied forces that had penetrated western Germany to march as far east as Berlin and as far south as Prague, whence they would be in a strong position to bargain with the Russians over the political future of the former Nazi satellites.

But the American government rejected the Englishman's plan, as it had earlier turned down his project for a Balkan landing during the conference in Teheran, on the grounds that it was unwise from a military point of view. The American president was counting on Russian assistance in the war against Japan in the Far East, which his generals told him could not be won before November 1946. He also assumed that the American people would not tolerate a continued American military presence in Europe for very long after the war and therefore regarded the Red Army as a useful deterrent to the resurgence of German military power. Consequently, Eisenhower's forces in Germany were

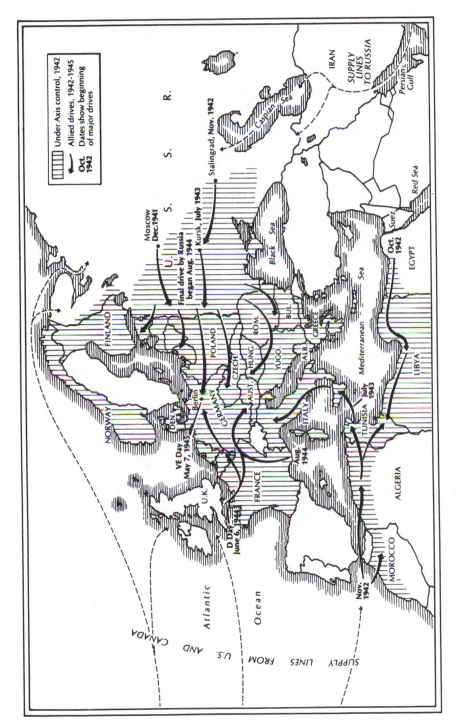

The Second World War in Europe, 1941–1945

instructed to halt their eastward march at the Elbe River while the Soviet army proceeded to liberate Berlin and Prague. On April 25 American and Russian soldiers shook hands at Torgau on the Elbe just northeast of Leipzig, and on May 1 Eisenhower and the Russian commanders agreed on a temporary military occupation line that left Soviet forces in control of all of Eastern Europe including the eastern halves of Germany and Austria. Hitler's suicide on April 30 in his Berlin bunker brought his thousand-year Reich to an end twelve years after its birth. German military authorities surrendered unconditionally at Eisenhower's headquarters in Rheims, France, on May 7 and again to the Russians in a separate ceremony in Berlin two days later.

The last year of the war against Hitler brought to the fore the question of how Germany and the vast territory on the continent that it had subjugated should be politically reorganized. It is scarcely surprising that little serious thought was devoted to the question of the postwar political settlement in Europe while the outcome of the military struggle remained in doubt. Before the summer of 1943, when the defeat of Germany looked likely with the Anglo-American landings in southern Italy and the Russian counteroffensive in Eastern Europe, the war aims of the Allies were confined to vague generalities. Meeting at sea off the coast of Newfoundland in August 1941, Churchill and Roosevelt had signed the Atlantic Charter, which committed the two English-speaking powers to work for a postwar international order reminiscent of the one that Wilson had vainly attempted to forge a generation earlier. They agreed to oppose all postwar territorial changes that violated the wishes of the populations concerned, to support the establishment of democratically elected governments in the regions emancipated from German rule, and to favor the creation of an international peacekeeping organization to supplant the moribund League of Nations. It was easy enough for the Soviet Union to endorse these neo-Wilsonian platitudes as a gesture of solidarity with its new British partner in the common struggle against Germany. But when London sounded out Moscow on its attitude toward specific matters, such as the principle of territorial transfer, it encountered Stalin's blunt assertion of his nation's right to retain the territory in Eastern Europe that it had forcibly acquired under the terms of the Nazi-Soviet Pact. Churchill reluctantly agreed to this concession to Stalin's understandable obsession with the security of Russia's western frontiers, even though it violated the Atlantic Charter's prohibition of forcibly imposed territorial changes. After Pearl Harbor the American government, while shrinking from an official endorsement of Soviet claims on the Baltic states, eastern Poland, Romania, and Finland, tacitly accepted them as inevitable in recognition of Russia's critical role in the Grand Alliance against Hitler.

The turning of the tide of war in the summer of 1943 forced the leaders of the anti-German coalition to confront seriously for the first time the long-deferred question of Europe's postwar political future. At the first joint meeting of Allied foreign ministers in Moscow in October 1943, plans were drawn up for the inter-Allied military occupation of Italy after the war. Despite Soviet efforts to obtain equal participation, effective power was placed in the hands of Anglo-American administrative authorities who accompanied the American and British armies on their northward march up the Italian peninsula. At the Teheran conference a month later, Stalin stubbornly reiterated his intention to retain Russia's territorial acquisitions of 1939–41 in Eastern Europe. The two Western leaders grudgingly gave way, on the condition that Poland's territorial losses in the east to Russia be compensated by the annexation of German territory in the west. No one thought to propose a plebiscite to consult the Poles earmarked for inclusion in the Soviet Union or the Germans to be incorporated in the reconstituted Polish state as it "moved west." Thus did the high-sounding idealism of the Atlantic Charter succumb to the practical requirements of Realpolitik in the midst of total war.

Once Roosevelt had definitively rejected Churchill's proposal at Teheran for an Anglo-American landing in the Balkans as a prelude to an offensive into the Danube Valley, Soviet domination of Southeastern Europe was assured, just as Western primacy in Italy, France, the Low Countries, and Scandinavia had been foreordained by the liberation of those countries by American and British forces. By September 1944 Romania and Bulgaria had capitulated to the Red Army, which was poised for an advance into Yugoslavia, Hungary, and Greece. The British prime minister thereupon hastily flew to Moscow in October to confirm and extend an informal understanding with the Russian leader on the future political orientation of the Balkan nations that had first been suggested by the British in June 1944. The architect of the Atlantic Charter and its principled commitment to national self-determination obtained Stalin's consent to a "percentages agreement" allotting Romania, Bulgaria, and Hungary more or less to the Soviet sphere of influence, Greece to the Anglo-American sphere, with Yugoslavia to be split between them. President Roosevelt, though prevented from attending the Moscow conference by political obligations in his reelection campaign, was kept fully informed of the proceedings by his ambassador to Moscow, W. Averill Harriman. Roosevelt's subsequent failure to raise objections to this cynical bargain may be taken as a signal of Washington's tacit acceptance both of the sphere-of-influence approach to the political future of Southeastern Europe and of the specific geographical divisions agreed to by Churchill and Stalin.

But the spirit of cooperation that had enabled the Allies to agree on the de facto partition of the Balkans and to recognize Russia's right to retain her western borders of 1941 in Eastern Europe began to evaporate when the question arose concerning the fate of Germany and Poland, the two nations whose quarrel had precipitated the conflict in Europe that was drawing to a close. When the question of Germany's future status had been informally addressed at Teheran, the Big Three had seemed to agree that partition represented the only effective solution to the "German problem" that had plunged Europe into two great wars in the first half of the century. Reviving proposals aired by French hardliners during the Paris Peace Conference in 1919, Churchill spoke of detaching from Germany its industrial heartland in the Rhineland-Westphalia region and of establishing a Central European federation linking the south German states, Austria, and Hungary. Stalin forcefully pressed for the political dismemberment of the nation whose expansionist policy had brought such ruin to his own country. The original American proposal to solve the German problem was equally harsh, but characteristically focused on the economic sources of German power. At the Anglo-American conference in Quebec in September 1944, Roosevelt obtained Churchill's tentative agreement to a scheme devised by Treasury Secretary Henry Morgenthau that envisioned the destruction of Germany's industrial plant and the reduction of the country to agricultural status.

By the time of the summit meeting at the resort city of Yalta on Russia's Crimean peninsula in February 1945, the Anglo-American position on the political and economic future of Germany had undergone a fundamental shift from the vindictive schemes entertained at Teheran and Quebec. With Allied military forces deep in German territory and the Third Reich on the brink of collapse, British and American officials began to have second thoughts about the consequences of Germany's political and economic disintegration. Some of the same considerations that had prompted Wilson and Lloyd George to oppose Clemenceau's harsh plans for postwar Germany at Paris a quarter of a century earlier inspired Roosevelt's and Churchill's resistance to Stalin's stringent demands for reparations and political dismemberment at Yalta: The total disappearance of German power in Central Europe would leave a vacuum in that region that the nearby Russian colossus was bound to fill; and the crippling of the German economic system through excessive reparation demands would have a deleterious effect on the rest of the industrial world as it struggled to recover from the war. While no definitive decision was reached on the twin issues of reparations and the political future of Germany, the Yalta Conference produced an agreement on the temporary partition of the country into military occupation zones. The Soviet army would occupy the territory east of the Elbe that it was in the process of liberating from Hitler's retreating forces. The remainder would be occupied by the armies of the United States, Great Britain, and France (whose participation Churchill demanded for fear that American military forces would be withdrawn from Europe as they had been after the last war, leaving Britain facing Russia alone). As in 1919, the volatile issue of reparations was postponed, though the figure of $20–22 billion (with half going to the U.S.S.R.) was mentioned as a basis of discussion.

The long-simmering dispute over the political future of Poland became the major bone of contention between the western and eastern members of the Grand Alliance at Yalta. In April 1943 Stalin had abruptly withdrawn diplomatic recognition of the pro-Western Polish government in exile headquartered in London when it appeared to give credence to Nazi accusations that Soviet military forces in Poland had massacred more than ten thousand Polish officers during the Soviet occupation of eastern Poland. Shortly thereafter Stalin gave his official blessing to a rival group of Polish exiles in Russia that disputed the London Poles' claim to political legitimacy. On July 23, 1944, a pro-Soviet Polish Committee of National Liberation was established in the Polish city of Lublin after its capture by the Red Army. On August 1, in response to an appeal from the London Polish group, the forty six thousand members of the Warsaw underground rose against the German occupation army and were joined by most of the city's civilian population. At the time of the Warsaw uprising the Red Army had smashed through the German defenses to within six miles of the city while Radio Moscow broadcast messages of support for the insurrection. But the Soviet forces abruptly halted their advance and stood by while the German army of occupation brutally crushed the uprising by the end of September. Churchill's appeal to Stalin for permission for Anglo-American planes based in Italy to land on Soviet airfields after bomb attacks and parachute drops in support of the Warsaw uprising fell on deaf ears in the Kremlin. The consequent death of thousands of Polish partisans wiped out the impressive political and military organization that the London Poles had succeeded in establishing in the occupied country, thereby paving the way for the pro-Soviet rival group that accompanied the advancing Red Army. In January 1945, with Soviet military forces in occupation of the entire prewar territory of Poland, the Kremlin installed the pro-Russian Polish faction in Warsaw and accorded it formal diplomatic recognition.

At Yalta in the following month, Roosevelt and Churchill obtained Stalin's agreement to add non-Communist resistance leaders to the recently established provisional government. They also wrested from him the pledge that free elections, Western style, would be conducted in Poland after the end of the war to enable that country to determine its own

The Big Three during a break at the Yalta Conference, February 1945: With the Red Army in occupation of most of Eastern Europe, Stalin was in a strong position to assert his claim to predominance in that region. The only concession that Roosevelt and Churchill could obtain from the Soviet leader was a promise of free elections in Poland and his acceptance of the vaguely worded "Declaration on Liberated Europe" promising self-determination for the countries of the continent after Germany's defeat. *(Courtesy of the Library of Congress)*

future form of government. This promise was subsequently extended to the entire continent through the adoption by the Big Three of the American-sponsored Declaration on Liberated Europe. Roosevelt returned home to die on April 12 from the mortal illness that was already in evidence during the Crimean meeting. He went to his grave apparently convinced that the "spheres of influence" formula adopted by Stalin and Churchill at Moscow four months earlier had been superseded by a neo-Wilsonian principle of national self-determination that revived the spirit of the Atlantic Charter. His successor, Harry S Truman, believed even more resolutely in this version of the wartime agreements concerning the political future of Europe.

Stalin left the Crimean summit conference apparently assuming that the informal understanding on the spheres of influence previously reached with Churchill remained in effect and that the Yalta declaration represented nothing more than rhetorical window dressing, perhaps to placate voters of East European descent in the United States. Western journalists and politicians had often spoken of the need to establish a postwar consortium consisting of the three great powers in the anti-German coalition, each of which would ensure peace and stability by exercising paramount influence in its own orbit. At Teheran, Roosevelt had broached to Stalin his neo-Metternichian project of the "Four Policemen"—the United States, Great Britain, the Soviet Union, and China—that were to maintain order in the world after the defeat of the Axis. The decision at Teheran to permit the Soviet army to liberate the Balkans and the bargain in Moscow delineating the victors' respective spheres of influence in that region seem to have led Stalin to believe that the old concept of the concert of great powers would continue to operate in peacetime as it had during the war.

On the basis of this assumption, the Soviet leader proceeded to execute the provisions of the Moscow percentages agreement, which had formed the basis of the armistice accords concluded with the former Nazi satellites in Eastern Europe. Russian members of the control commissions in Romania, Bulgaria, and Hungary bypassed their Anglo-American colleagues to assure Soviet predominance, just as the British and Americans ignored Moscow's representatives on the control commission in Italy, which, although not covered by the percentages agreement, clearly lay within the Western sphere of influence. When a civil war spontaneously erupted in Greece during the winter of 1944–45 between Communist and anti-Communist factions within the resistance movement, Stalin withheld support from the Greek Communist insurgents, thereby enabling the pro-Western government in Athens to retain its power with British military assistance. The Communist parties in France and Italy, whose ideology had previously prevented them from participating in "bourgeois" political administrations, were instructed by the Kremlin to accept subordinate positions in non-Communist coalitions and to behave with unaccustomed moderation despite their temporary status as the most popular political parties in their respective countries. This was because Stalin recognized those two countries, which had been liberated by Anglo-American military forces, as belonging within the Western zone of influence. The impending military triumph of the Grand Alliance necessitated a resolution of these contradictory versions of the wartime decisions regarding the political reorganization of liberated Europe. Would the spirit of Metternich or of Wilson prevail?

As the European war drew to a close in the early months of 1945, the singular brutality of Nazi occupation policy came to light. The Red Army's capture of the Nazi extermination center at Auschwitz in Poland in January, followed by the Anglo-American liberation of the death camps such as Buchenwald and Bergen-Belsen in Germany in April, revealed the full extent of the Third Reich's horrendous campaign to exterminate the Jewish inhabitants of German-occupied Europe. The deliberate slaughter of more than 6 million of Europe's 12 million Jews, now widely known in the English-speaking world as "the Holocaust,"* was carried out largely by the S.S. Hitler's strategy for ridding the continent of its Jewish population developed in three stages from his accession in 1933.

---

*Ironically, the term's original meaning was "a sacrifice by fire offered only to God."

The first stage, which lasted until the summer of 1941, was marked by attempts to organize the mass expulsion of Jews from Germany as well as from the territories overrun by its armies. By the advent of the Second World War in September 1939, more than half of the Jews of Germany and Austria had emigrated to such foreign havens as would receive them. When the conquest of Poland brought an additional 1.8 million Jews under German control, these hapless souls were assembled in concentration camps in preparation for deportation to some distant dumping ground after Germany's anticipated military triumph. The defeat of France spurred discussion of the possibility of transferring Europe's Jews to the French-owned island of Madagascar off the east coast of Africa.

The second phase of Hitler's Jewish policy began in the summer of 1941 as German military forces invaded the Soviet Union. Following on the heels of the army were small, mobile S.S. units known as *Einsatzgruppen* ("emergency squads"). It became the task of these bloodthirsty marauders to enforce the Führer's "Commissar Order" of May 1941, which stipulated that all Communist government officials captured during Operation Barbarossa be executed on the spot in order to obliterate the political infrastructure of the Soviet state. Amid this war of annihilation the *Einsatzgruppen* massacred approximately 1.4 million of the Soviet Union's 5 million Jews. This was done on the pretext of eliminating suspected Communist partisans from the rear of the German armies that were driving toward Leningrad, Moscow, and Stalingrad. While the S.S. contingents were rounding up and murdering every Jew they could lay their hands on, Air Marshal Hermann Göring ordered the S.S. official Reinhard Heydrich to devise a more efficient and systematic method of dealing with the millions of Jewish survivors who were concentrated in urban areas across occupied Europe. By the time Heydrich had drafted his diabolical scheme, the German offensive against the Soviet Union had ground to a halt in December 1941. With the onset of winter it became evident that the war in Russia would drag on much longer than anticipated with no end in sight.

The failure of Operation Barbarossa prompted the Nazi leadership to revise both the method and the timetable for what Hitler and his henchmen thought of as "the final solution of the Jewish problem." At the end of 1941 the Nazi regime abruptly reversed its policy of promoting mass Jewish emigration and forbade Jews to leave German-occupied Europe. A top secret meeting of senior Nazi officials on January 20, 1942, in the Berlin suburb of Wannsee ushered in the third and most barbaric phase of what one historian has called "the war against the Jews." Heydrich secured approval of a proposal to replace the haphazard assassination techniques that were being employed by the roving bands of S.S. thugs behind the German lines in Russia with a systematic campaign of extermination that would apply the modern methods of scientific technology. Those who did not gradually succumb from disease and starvation through forced labor would be instantly dispatched en masse in gas chambers and crematoria. The death camps were established at various sites throughout Germany and occupied Poland, to which Jews and other groups considered subhuman by the Nazis—such as gypsies, homosexuals, and Poles—would be transported during the years 1942–44.

After irrefutable evidence of the extermination campaign reached foreign countries in November 1942, the response of Allied leaders was circumspect and ineffective. Insisting on according absolute priority to the war effort against the Axis, the U.S. War Department refused to divert planes conducting raids near Auschwitz to bomb the gas chambers and the railway lines leading to the death camp. It was only after the liberating

Two Jewish inmates standing at the Ampfing subcamp of the Dachau concentration camp near Munich, Germany, after its liberation by American troops, May 4, 1945: The concentration camps (as opposed to the death camps such as Auschwitz, whose inmates were promptly and methodically exterminated) were used for slave labor, though hunger, disease, and maltreatment caused many deaths in these camps as well. *(Courtesy of the Library of Congress)*

armies uncovered the remains of the victims and confronted the emaciated survivors that the governments of the victorious coalition began vigorously to insist that the Nazi leadership be held accountable for its record of genocide. The prosecution of twenty-two top Nazi leaders in the Bavarian city of Nuremberg from November 1945 to September 1946, which resulted in sentences ranging from ten years' imprisonment to death save for the three who were acquitted, contributed a new term to the vocabulary of international law: "crimes against humanity."

6

THE CONFIRMATION
OF UNITED STATES SUPREMACY
IN LATIN AMERICA

THE ERA OF DIRECT DOMINATION (1914–1932)

We have earlier noted how the Caribbean Sea was transformed into a veritable American lake between the end of the Spanish-American War and the beginning of World War I. Through a combination of financial supervision, commercial penetration, diplomatic agreements regulating regulations with foreign nations, and the occasional application of military force, the United States had acquired effective control of the political and economic systems of some of the islands in the Caribbean and the mainland republics of Central America that had achieved independence from their European colonial masters in the course of the nineteenth century. The European powers acquiesced in this extension of American hegemony because their national energies were absorbed by their own colonial rivalries in Africa and Asia as well as by the power struggles on the old continent that resulted in the First World War. It was the war itself that confirmed American supremacy in the Caribbean region and facilitated the expansion of American economic power to the continent of South America as well, for reasons presently to be discussed.

It is ironic that Woodrow Wilson, champion of national self-determination and critic of his Republican predecessor's "dollar diplomacy" in Latin America, conducted more military and diplomatic interventions south of the border than any American president before or since. He had genuinely persuaded himself of the essential morality of his interventionist policies in the Caribbean: A passionate proponent of good government, he cringed at the widespread corruption, inefficiency, autocracy, and social unrest that was conspicuously in evidence among America's southern neighbors. Just as he had sought to cleanse the political institutions of New Jersey and then of Washington, this progressive idealist set out to impose order, honesty, and efficiency on the Caribbean republics for their own good.

179

But beneath this disinterested idealistic position lay the same preoccupation that had prompted the interventionist policies of Roosevelt and Taft in the era of Republican supremacy: the fear that political revolution, social instability, and financial collapse in the Caribbean region would tempt the great powers of Europe to intervene to protect the lives and investments of their citizens. The prospect of European powers militarily ensconced, or even financially engaged, in a region critical to the security of the Panama Canal, which had been opened in the summer of 1914 as the war clouds appeared in Europe, was more than any American president could tolerate.

And so, behind a smokescreen of progressive rhetoric about America's obligation to foster good government in its own hemisphere, Woodrow Wilson resumed the Roosevelt-Taft policies of military intervention and dollar diplomacy in Latin America. The first beneficiary of this new form of American heavyhandedness couched in the language of Wilsonian benevolence was Nicaragua. The Bryan-Chamorro Treaty (signed on August 5, 1914, and ratified two years later) transferred supervisory authority over the finances of that nation from American private banking interests to a commission controlled directly from Washington. The United States government advanced funds to the financially strapped Nicaraguan regime to reduce its public debt in return for an exclusive concession to construct a trans-Isthmian canal and to establish naval bases at its two termina. The object of this agreement was to protect the northern land approach to the Panama Canal, preclude any future European-constructed canal along the alternative Nicaraguan route, and rehabilitate the finances of this perpetually insolvent nation so as to remove any possible pretext for European intervention. The American marine contingent that had been landed in 1912 was retained and augmented to provide the requisite armed support for this policy of financial reorganization.

Similar instances of social unrest and financial instability in the adjacent states of the Dominican Republic and Haiti on the island of Hispaniola elicited similar intimations of European intervention and, consequently, a similar preemptive response from Washington. A default on foreign loans by the Dominican government in 1904 had resulted in the establishment of a customs receivership in the hands of an agent, appointed by the president of the United States, who was empowered to distribute the customs receipts of Dominican ports to foreign creditors. As in so many of previous and subsequent instances of American financial intervention in the Caribbean, this policy was motivated by the obsession with removing any pretext for intervention by European nations on behalf of their aggrieved bondholders. The rapid breakdown of social order and the attendant possibility of financial collapse in the Dominican Republic during Wilson's first term once again raised the prospect of European intervention in that unstable country. To avert such a possibility, the United States undertook to supervise national elections in 1914 and then to dispatch marines in 1916 to preserve order and assure American financial control.

In the contiguous Republic of Haiti, the possibility that Germany would exploit that nation's perennial political unrest and financial difficulties by seizing control of its customs houses to ensure the service of its large foreign debt inspired great unease in Washington. So too did the prospect of German naval bases in Haiti that would command the passage between Hispaniola and Cuba to the Panama Canal. When revolutionary disorders continued to rage, Wilson resolved to act unilaterally to preempt any such European

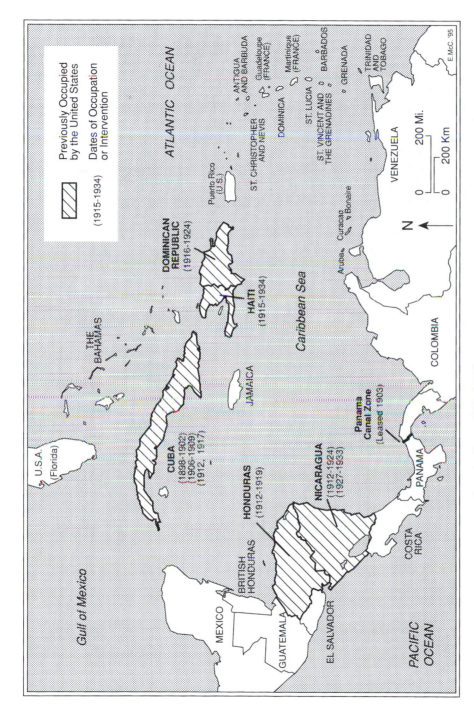

Central America and the Caribbean Before the Second World War

The U.S. high command at U.S. field headquarters near Casas Grandes, Mexico, in 1916 during the expedition to capture Francisco "Pancho" Villa (1878–1923): General John J. Pershing is the fourth from left. Behind him at the right is Lieutenant George S. Patton. *(Courtesy of the Library of Congress)*

involvement in Haitian affairs. Marines were dispatched in 1915 to protect foreign lives and property, American banks were persuaded to lend funds to the Haitian government to enable it to consolidate and refund its foreign debt, an American financial adviser assumed control of the national finances, an American receiver-general was installed to supervise the collection of customs receipts, and American military officers took charge of the Haitian police forces. A new constitution (drafted by Assistant Secretary of the Navy Franklin D. Roosevelt) transformed Haiti into an American protectorate. In the same year the Wilson administration reintroduced military forces into Cuba (from which they had been withdrawn in 1909) and purchased the Danish West Indies (renamed the Virgin Islands) from Denmark under the implied threat of seizure, all in the interest of keeping the European belligerents out of the "American lake."

Wilson's most spectacular intervention in Latin America ironically took place in a nation that had been relatively well disposed to the United States and was scarcely in danger of falling under the sway of the European powers. Of all the nations of Latin America, Mexico had retained the most cordial relations with its northern neighbor since the end of the American Civil War. Resentment at the territorial losses to the United States in the mid-nineteenth century had been attenuated by the American government's decisive role in pressuring France to withdraw its military forces from Mexico in 1867. This led to the overthrow by Mexican nationalists of the French satellite empire headed by the Austrian archduke Maximilian. As we have seen, between 1876 and 1910 Mexican dictator Porfirio Diaz eagerly solicited American capital investment in Mexican land, natural resources, railroads, and public utilities. But the Mexican Revolution of 1910–11 that ousted Diaz had plunged the nation into a social and political upheaval that seriously menaced these American properties and investments. The assumption of dictatorial power by President Victoriano Huerta in February 1913 offended the democratic sensibilities of President Wilson, who withheld diplomatic recognition and attempted to topple the new Mexican strongman by permitting American arms shipments to his "Constitutionalist" enemies, who controlled most of the northern sector of the country. The arrest in April 1914 of American sailors on shore leave in the Caribbean port of Tampico, though in fact nothing more than a spontaneous indiscretion by an overly zealous subordinate, was viewed in Washington as a retaliatory action by the Mexican president that deserved and required punishment. Consequently, American naval units occupied the port of Vera Cruz and war between the two countries was narrowly averted before a compromise settlement facilitated their evacuation seven months later. In March 1916 one of the Constitutionalist leaders, Pancho Villa, eager to provoke American intervention in the Mexican civil war so that he could unite his divided country against the common enemy to the north, launched a raid on an American border town in New Mexico. In retaliation, Wilson dispatched a punitive military expedition under General John J. Pershing deep into the Mexican interior in pursuit of the "bandit" leader. The ostensible purpose of this quixotic adventure was to impress upon the Mexicans the necessity of establishing a democratic government capable of preserving social order. After angry protests from the Mexican government and clashes with Mexican military forces, the American troops were finally withdrawn on February 5, 1917, a few days after Washington's severance of diplomatic relations with Berlin over the issue of unrestricted submarine warfare, which foreordained America's intervention in the European war.

The Wilson administration's resumption of the Roosevelt-Taft policy of military intervention and financial supervision in the Caribbean occurred at a time when the United States was rapidly expanding its economic power to the continent of South America. In the aftermath of the Spanish American War, United States commercial and financial involvement in Latin America was concentrated almost exclusively in the neighboring Caribbean islands and the nations of Central America. Between 1898 and 1914, American investment south of the border had increased from $320 million to $1.7 billion, with Mexico and Cuba together accounting for almost a third of the total. Despite the beginning of American economic activity in the larger nations of South America, the foreign trade and financial relations of those republics were still centered on Europe. At the turn of the century, Great Britain remained the prime source of foreign capital for Latin America as a whole, its direct and portfolio investments in the region totaling $2.5 billion. By 1914 total British investment in Latin America had increased to about $3.7 billion, with Argentina and Brazil receiving 60 percent of the total and Chile, Peru, Mexico, and Uruguay taking most of the remainder. France became a major investor in Latin America after 1880, increasing its total commitment in the region threefold between 1900 and 1914 to $1.2 billion. Approximately $900 million of German foreign investment was in Latin America by 1914, principally in Argentina, Brazil, Chile, and Mexico. Thus, at the beginning of the First World War, the value of Britain's investment in the region roughly equaled that of her three principal foreign competitors combined.

Collectively, the major European economic powers supplied the Latin American republics with the largest proportion of their investment capital and manufactured products while receiving in exchange the bulk of their agricultural and mineral exports. But World War I abruptly severed these financial and commercial connections between Latin America and the old world. The British blockade and the German submarine campaign, together with the diversion of European industrial production, capital investment, and merchant shipping to war-related purposes, deprived Latin America of the foreign trade and financial assistance that had previously flowed across the Atlantic.

Into the economic vacuum in Latin America produced by the reduction of European trade and investment during the war stepped the powerful, prosperous, neutral state from the north. American manufacturers captured markets previously dominated by European exporters. American agricultural, mining, and petroleum interests wrested control of Latin American land and subsoil resources from British, French, and German firms. When Great Britain and France were forced to curtail their investments in Latin America in order to finance their war effort and German holdings in the region were either sold or confiscated, American lenders promptly replaced their European competitors as the prime source of investment capital. During the war the dollar value of American investments in the region increased by about 50 percent. By the end of the war, the influx of American capital had paved the way for the spectacular expansion of United States investment in and trade with Latin America during the 1920s as the European powers found it impossible to regain their prewar position as bankers and trading partners of the region.

The spurt of American investment in the economies of the Latin American republics after the war was facilitated by the passage in 1919 of the Edge Act, which authorized for the first time the establishment of foreign branches of American banking institutions. This legislation afforded American investors, who had previously been required to conduct their financial operations through the British banking system and its vast network of international affiliates, direct access to the money markets of the various Latin American states. Wall Street banks lent ever-increasing sums to national and municipal governments, as well as to private corporations, whose securities could no longer find a market in a Europe struggling to satisfy its own substantial capital requirements in the period of postwar reconstruction. During the second half of the 1920s Latin America absorbed 24 percent of the new capital issues floated for foreign account.

Accompanying this notable increase in United States portfolio investment in Latin American countries was a spectacular upsurge in direct investment. Channeled principally into electrical utilities, railroads, mining, petroleum, and tropical plantation agriculture, American direct investment in Latin America increased almost threefold between 1914 and 1929. By the latter date it had come to represent 44 percent of total United States direct investment abroad. The combined total nominal value of American direct and portfolio investment in Latin America had more than doubled in the decade after 1919, while British investments in the region remained roughly unchanged and those of France and Germany declined dramatically.

This strong investment position enabled the American financial community to acquire a large measure of control over the fiscal and monetary policies of the recipient nations. The effects of this economic power were naturally felt most directly in those countries, such as Nicaragua, Haiti, and the Dominican Republic, whose financial institutions had come under direct American supervisory control. But even such nominally independent states as Cuba, Brazil, Chile, and Venezuela became so dependent on American investment that most of their tax revenues were generated from economic activities directed by

American banks and corporations. Decisions taken in the boardrooms of these American-based institutions often had an immediate and decisive impact on the budgetary policies of Latin American governments (and therefore on the distribution of national wealth). This sharp increase of American capital investment in Latin America during the First World War transpired amid a remarkable expansion of inter-American trade. The three years of American neutrality hastened the process whereby the United States replaced Britain as the region's principal trading partner for the reasons sketched above. After the war, operating under the provisions of the Webb-Pomerene Act (which exempted firms engaged in the export trade from the application of antitrust laws), American conglomerates continued to supplant weaker European export firms in the Latin American market. United States exports to Latin America tripled in value from 1914 to 1929, and by the latter year accounted for almost 40 percent of the region's total imports. In exchange for its sales of manufactured goods, the United States became the major customer for Latin America's primary products (principally subsoil minerals and tropical foodstuffs), taking almost a third of Latin America's total exports by the end of the 1920s.

In different circumstances this inter-American commercial relationship might have matured into a mutually beneficial exchange of surplus products between complementary economic systems. Instead, it degenerated into a neocolonial relationship from which one party derived extensive benefits while the other became locked into a system of abject dependence. The unequal nature of inter-American trading patterns that emerged in the postwar period can be traced to several sources. The first of these was the tendency of American firms and their financial backers to acquire through direct investment a controlling interest in the principal export industries of many Latin American nations. Examples of this overwhelming domination abound. American capital came to represent 92 percent of the total investment in Chilean copper mines. American oil companies, after forcing out their European competitors, acquired control of over half of Venezuela's petroleum production. Two-thirds of the Cuban sugar crop was owned by American producing and refining corporations. Two American firms, the United Fruit Company and the Standard Fruit Company, together enjoyed a monopoly of the banana plantations of Guatemala, Honduras, Nicaragua, and Panama. This extraordinary degree of foreign ownership resulted in the repatriation of profits generated from the exploitation of these national resources rather than reinvestment in the infrastructure of the host country. This diverted scarce capital that might otherwise have financed projects of domestic economic development that would have increased the nation's productive capacity and raised the standard of living of the indigenous population.

The second adverse feature of this pattern of inter-American commercial exchange from the Latin American point of view was the propensity of United States direct investment to promote the intensive development of a single export crop or commodity in each country at the expense of product diversification. This tendency to "put all one's eggs in one basket" rendered most Latin American nations tragically vulnerable to the wild fluctuations of commodity prices that characterized the 1920s. When the world prices of sugar, coffee, copper, and other commodities dropped precipitously, as they frequently did during this period, the national economies for which exports of these primary products represented virtually the only source of hard currency were plunged into severe crises.

Finally, the commanding share of the Latin American export trade acquired by the United States during and after the First World War created a relationship of dominance-subservience that naturally extended to other matters as well. The extent of this export dependence was to reach incredible extremes in some cases: In the year 1937 the United States was purchasing 80 percent of Cuba's exports, 88 percent of those of Honduras, and 91 percent of those of Panama. No nation whose domestic prosperity depended so heavily on unimpeded access to the American market could be expected to withstand pressure from Washington to adjust their foreign and internal policies to the requirements of the national interest of the United States.

Were the independent states of Latin America condemned to languish in a position of perpetual subservience to their powerful northern neighbor? As noted earlier, the reduction of Europe's economic stake in Latin America as a consequence of World War I removed whatever advantage the Latin republics had derived from United States-European rivalry in the region. In light of the striking imbalance of economic and military power in the western hemisphere, the only alternative to a destiny of continual inferiority for the individual states south of the North American giant was progress toward the type of political and economic integration on a continental scale that the United States had achieved in North America.

Sentiment for the unification of Latin America had surfaced soon after the expulsion of Spanish and Portuguese authority in the first quarter of the nineteenth century. Under the inspiration of the great liberator, Simon Bolívar, the Congress of Panama in 1826 produced a number of resolutions aimed at amalgamating the Spanish and Portuguese successor states in order more effectively to combat the anticipated menace of intervention by the European powers. But only four Latin American republics sent representatives to that conference, and only Bolívar's Colombia ratified the agreements on continental cooperation that were concluded. Three more Latin American congresses met during the nineteenth century, usually in response to the threat or reality of foreign intervention in the hemisphere. But these four conferences (1826, 1847–48, 1856, and 1864–65) produced nothing more promising than a single, innocuous consular convention ratified by the few states that bothered to send delegates. Instead of advancing toward some form of continental integration, the successor states of Latin America were plagued by the opposite tendency of political disintegration after the withdrawal of Spanish and Portuguese authority. The United Provinces of Central America seceded from Mexico in 1823, then shattered into five small republics in 1840. The Gran Colombia of Bolívar eventually split into Venezuela, Colombia, and Ecuador, and the rump state of Colombia subsequently lost its province of Panama in 1903. The Dominican Republic seceded from Haiti in 1844. As we have seen, Mexico lost half its territory to the United States at midcentury. The combination of geographical isolation, poor communications, and fierce national rivalries nipped in the bud all integrationist tendencies, even when the advantages of Latin American cooperation became so apparent during the achievement of United States supremacy in the twentieth century.

The persistence of these centrifugal forces suggested that the unification of Latin America stood the best chance of success under the aegis of one or the other of those regional powers that exhibited some of the characteristics traditionally associated with a leadership role. Brazil, comprising almost half of the territory and over a third of the population of the South American continent, was the obvious candidate to become the "Prussia" of Latin America. But Brazil's historic rivalry with the other potential unifier of the continent, Argentina—not to speak of the linguistic barrier separating the only

Portuguese-speaking nation of the hemisphere from its Spanish-speaking neighbors—prevented it from assuming continental leadership. Instead of becoming an instigator of Latin American integrationist sentiment in opposition to North American domination, Brazil was to become the United States' most loyal supporter in the region. This political cooperation was enhanced by a profitable economic relationship based on American purchases of Brazil's principal export crop, coffee, a commodity that enjoyed great popularity in the United States and was not grown domestically.

Brazil's reluctance to spearhead a movement of Latin American solidarity in resistance to American hegemony left Argentina as the sole aspirant to such a position after the First World War. The special geographical and economic advantage enjoyed by Argentina enabled it to adopt an independent posture in hemispheric affairs that frequently brought it into direct conflict with Washington. Its geographical location at the southern extremity of South America rendered it less susceptible to American military and naval intimidation. Moreover, unlike any other South American country, its major exports (beef and grain) competed with rather than complemented American exports and therefore precluded the type of cooperative economic relationship that had developed between the United States and Brazil. On the contrary, American farmers obtained extensive tariff protection against Argentinian grain and Western ranchers were insulated against competition from Argentinian cattle in the form of a stringent sanitary prohibition of beef imports from regions infected by foot-and-mouth disease (a persistent condition in the pampas). This closure of the American market impelled Argentina to preserve and extend its commercial relationship with Europe during the very period that its sister republics were submitting to the domination of American trade. As late as 1937, Argentina's imports from the United States accounted for only 16.1 percent of its total foreign trade while it received 59.1 percent of its imports from Europe. In the same year Argentina shipped only 12.8 percent of its exports to the United States compared to 74.3 percent to Europe. This European commercial orientation was reinforced by the presence of substantial numbers of immigrants in Argentina from countries of the old world (principally Germany and Italy) who retained close ties to their homelands. The combination of these geographical, economic, and cultural factors helped to place Argentina beyond the reach of American power in Latin America and enabled it to mount a spirited challenge to American hemispheric hegemony.

The rallying cry of Argentina's campaign to organize Latin American sentiment in opposition to United States domination was the ideology of Pan-Hispanic solidarity, which it trumpeted as a preferable alternative to the Pan-American ideology that the United States had employed since the end of the nineteenth century as a means of mobilizing its Latin American clients. But in light of the patent inequality of power in the western hemisphere, the likelihood of Latin American solidarity and independence was problematical so long as the United States continued to enjoy the prerogative of intervening directly in the domestic affairs of Latin American nations to protect the lives of American citizens, preserve social order, and collect public debts from governments that refused to submit disputes with foreign investors to international arbitration. Consequently, it was the issue of the right of intervention that became the focal point of the Argentinian-led assault on United States hegemony that enlivened the periodic Pan-American conferences of the 1920s. This prerogative, which was both generally recognized in international law and specifically codified in the Roosevelt Corollary of the Monroe Doctrine, was periodically reasserted by the American government. The right of foreign intervention was deeply resented by the nations of Latin America as a humiliating limitation to national sovereignty much in the same way that the principle of extraterritoriality engendered fierce opposition in China (see p. 208). In vain did the southern republics endeavor to secure acceptance by the United States of the Calvo Doctrine (after the Argentinian jurist Carlos Calvo), which asserted the principle of a sovereign state's absolute immunity from external intervention and recognized the judicial system of the host nation as the final authority in disputes involving foreign citizens or corporations. Though most Latin American nations customarily inserted a "Calvo clause" in contracts signed with foreign investors (to preclude their appealing to their home governments for diplomatic support in disputes with the host government), the United States stubbornly declined to relinquish its right to intervene on behalf of its aggrieved citizens if the host country refused to arbitrate.

The Latin American states just as resolutely refused to recognize the obligation to submit to international arbitration disputes between a host government and citizens of a foreign government, denouncing it as an intolerable infringement on national sovereignty. They pressed instead for the codification of an inter-American system of international law that would enshrine the principle of absolute equality and sovereignty of the nations of the western hemisphere. The United States, for its part, opposed the concept of a regional international law that would deprive it of the traditional right of intervention sanctioned by international legal precedent. Between 1889–90 (the meeting of the first Pan-American Conference) and 1928 (the sixth conference at Havana), the Colossus of the North and its Latin American clients periodically sparred over this divisive issue. At the Havana conference, in response to the introduction of a formal resolution prohibiting intervention, United States delegate Charles Evans Hughes mounted his country's last defense of its absolute right to intervene in its hemisphere to preserve internal stability and national independence. That this dispute represented more than mere legalistic wrangling was attested to by the conspicuous presence of American military forces in Nicaragua and Haiti as well as by the legal constraints on the sovereignty of Cuba and Panama that remained in force as the delegates deliberated.

In addition to this Latin American campaign on behalf of the doctrine of absolute nonintervention, there were other indications of mounting resistance to American hemispheric hegemony. The first of these was the refusal of most Latin American states to follow the lead of the United States in the First World War. In contrast to the British Dominions, which enthusiastically rallied to the side of the mother country and made important contributions to the British victory, only eight of the twenty Latin American republics (of which seven were tiny Caribbean and Central American nations under direct American domination) declared war on Germany. Such geographically strategic states as Mexico, Colombia, and Venezuela maintained a position of strict neutrality.

This spirit of independence from American foreign policy resurfaced in the postwar period. All of the Latin American republics joined the League of Nations at one time or another after that world body had been repudiated and shunned by the United States. Fifteen of them sat in the first Assembly of the League; the presidency of the Assembly was often occupied by a Latin American delegate; Latin American nonpermanent seats in the League Council increased from one to three in the course of the 1920s. The very fact of Latin American membership and active participation in the international organization signified a defiant repudiation of the United States' conception of a self-enclosed inter-

South America Before the Second World War

American security system. But Latin American efforts to employ the League as a counterweight to United States power in the western hemisphere were uniformly unsuccessful. It was precisely such a possibility that had inspired American insistence on the inclusion in the League Covenant of article 21, which specifically denied League jurisdiction over matters within the purview of the Monroe Doctrine. Latin American attempts to persuade the League to repudiate this endorsement of American hegemony in the western hemisphere failed to budge the cautious European governments that dominated the League Council and were reluctant to antagonize the United States. As a consequence, the League was able to intervene in inter-American conflicts on only two occasions (and then only after having secured the prior approval of Washington), successfully in the Letitia conflict between Peru and Colombia (1932–35), unsuccessfully in the Chaco War between Bolivia and Paraguay (1928–38).

To recapitulate: Between 1914 and 1932 the United States definitively replaced Great Britain as the dominant commercial and financial power in Latin America after having successfully challenged British diplomatic and naval supremacy in the region at the end of the nineteenth century. Direct American military domination and financial control of Cuba, Panama, Haiti, the Dominican Republic, and Nicaragua, together with the acquisition of the Virgin Islands from Denmark, completed the process of domination of the Caribbean region begun before the First World War. The establishment of undisputed strategic mastery of the Caribbean and economic preponderance in South America was facilitated by the weakening of European economic power in the western hemisphere during the war and then confirmed by the inability of the exhausted European states to recapture their prewar position in the 1920s. Latin American efforts to counter the southward advance of American power through some form of continental cooperation were frustrated by Brazil's reluctance to renounce its privileged relationship with the United States and the unwillingness of the other republics to follow Argentina's lead in directly challenging American encroachments on Latin American sovereignty. The promise of collective security represented by the League of Nations proved illusory because of the European powers' hesitation to risk Washington's displeasure by supporting the extension of the League's protection to the nations within the inter-American security system formed and dominated by the United States.

THE ERA OF INDIRECT HEGEMONY (1933–1945)

The United States' acquisition of undisputed hegemony over Latin America during the First World War and the succeeding decade removed the traditional justification for the employment of military force to forestall European intervention in the western hemisphere. This new situation of absolute immunity from transatlantic threats, which was confirmed by the abolition of the German navy at the Paris Peace Conference of 1919 and the limitations on naval construction adopted by the other maritime powers at the Washington Naval Conference of 1921–22, enabled Washington to adopt less overtly coercive means of preserving its position of hemispheric dominance. As Latin American criticism of heavy-handed American intervention and the legal principles on which it was based reached a crescendo toward the end of the 1920s, the direct methods of military force and diplomatic intimidation gradually gave way to a more subtle, but scarcely less effective, mechanism for maintaining control of the client states south of the border.

The first direct challenge to American power in Latin America was to come from the contiguous nation of Mexico, which had lost half of its territory to the United States in the middle of the nineteenth century, endured American military and naval interventions between 1914 and 1917, and seen most of its natural resources and valuable land fall into the hands of American investors and corporations. Memories of past humiliations, mingled with the daily experience of economic subservience, rekindled resentment toward the powerful neighbor north of the Rio Grande. These long-suppressed grievances bubbled to the surface as the last contingent of American troops that had been dispatched southward by President Wilson to combat "banditry" was withdrawn in February 1917 once the American chief executive was satisfied that representative government was about to be restored. It is supremely ironic that the democratic government that Wilson had insisted upon with such unbending determination proceeded in one of its first official acts to adopt a national constitution that contained a number of articles designed to liberate Mexico from the economic domination of foreign nations in general and the United States in particular. The most controversial of these constitutional safeguards vested in the Mexican nation ownership of all the subsoil resources of the country (of which petroleum was indisputably the most valuable). Soon thereafter this constitutional provision was judged by the Mexican government to apply retroactively: This signified the loss of title to hundreds of millions of dollars worth of oil reserves owned by American petroleum companies. It is worth pausing to record that this unilateral action by the Mexican government constituted a landmark in the history of the relations between the developed and the underdeveloped world; it was the first attempt by a country whose economic system had fallen under the de facto control of foreign interests to assert its prerogative to exercise exclusive legal authority over its own natural resources.

This unprecedented gesture of defiance did not immediately produce the desired result. The American government, under intense pressure from petroleum interests with extensive Mexican holdings, wielded every diplomatic weapon short of economic retaliation—including the policy of nonrecognition—to induce Mexico City to reverse its course. A compromise of sorts was reached in 1923, whereby the United States acknowledged Mexico's right to exercise authority over its subsoil resources in return for Mexican acknowledgment of the legal sanctity of contracts held by American oil companies prior to the adoption of the 1917 constitution. A similar compromise was struck in 1927, following a temporary revival of the dispute over retroactivity, which remained in force until 1938. In the latter year the Mexican government settled the matter for good by expropriating the property of British, Dutch, and American oil companies after they refused to abide by the ruling of the Mexican judicial system in a labor dispute.

Efforts by the expropriated American oil companies to organize an international boycott of Mexican crude in retaliation failed because of the eagerness of Germany, Italy, and Japan to purchase this critical source of energy as their rearmament programs got into high gear. American concern about the potential threat to national security posed by the development of intimate economic ties between Mexico and the Axis powers eventually took precedence over the parochial interests of the oil firms. A mutually acceptable agreement was signed a few weeks before Pearl Harbor whereby Mexico retained control of its oil reserves in return for a promise of financial compensation to the dispossessed American companies. Having extracted this major concession from the United States, Mexico was to become a loyal supporter and supplier of the American war effort, in sharp contrast to its defiant posture of absolute neutrality during the First World War.

Mexico's persistent (and eventually successful) campaign to reassert control of its national economic resources became an inspiration for burgeoning nationalist movements in other Latin American countries, which brought increasing pressure to bear on their governments to challenge the United States' refusal to acknowledge the prerogative of a sovereign nation to exercise political authority over people and property within its borders. We have seen how Latin American attempts to gain American recognition of this right at the Pan-American conferences of the 1920s met with failure. At the sixth conference of the American states in 1928, United States delegate Charles Evans Hughes's reference to a "breakdown of government" as sufficient justification for American intervention seemed so broad and imprecise as to justify virtually unlimited interference in the domestic affairs of the sovereign states of Latin America.

Yet, by the early 1930s, the presence of American military forces in the Caribbean region had become a source of acute embarrassment to the United States as it endeavored to mobilize world opinion against Japan's expansionist policies in the Far East. The Japanese incursion in Manchuria had been officially justified by Tokyo as a necessary step to protect Japanese citizens and property endangered by Chinese lawlessness; such language was uncomfortably reminiscent of the rationale invoked by the United States in defense of its military interventions south of the Rio Grande. Sensitive to the mounting allegations of hypocrisy that emanated from the world community, the new administration of Franklin Roosevelt that took office in 1933 inaugurated a dramatic modification of the Latin American policy of the United States. The groundwork for this change had been laid by the Hoover administration in 1930, when the State Department published a lengthy memorandum composed by Under Secretary of State J. Reuben Clark that repudiated the Roosevelt Corollary to the Monroe Doctrine as a justification for the American right of intervention in Latin America. Though the Clark Memorandum was replete with qualifications and did not receive much serious attention from American officials, it heralded a new attitude toward inter-American relations that had begun to crystallize in Washington. Before leaving office, the Hoover administration undertook a thorough reevaluation of the interventionist policy that had been pursued by every American president since Theodore Roosevelt.

In his inaugural address on March 4, 1933, Franklin Roosevelt declared that in the field of foreign policy he "would dedicate this Nation to the policy of the good neighbor who resolutely respects himself, and, because he does so, respects the rights of others." There was no reason for his listeners to believe that this innocuous phrase applied specifically to Latin America since no geographical region was mentioned in the speech. But a month later, speaking at the office of the Pan-American Union, the new American president mentioned the need for hemispheric cooperation in such conciliatory tones that commentators were soon hailing the new "Good Neighbor Policy" of the United States toward Latin America. Later in 1933, at the seventh conference of the American states in Montevideo, Uruguay, this presidential rhetoric was translated into government policy. The new secretary of state, Cordell Hull, abruptly reversed a long-standing American policy by supporting a resolution prohibiting any nation in the western hemisphere from intervening "in the internal or external affairs of another." By this historic act the Calvo Doctrine, resisted so long by the United States, was incorporated in an official document endorsed by Washington. Though Hull insisted on reserving the rights of the United States conferred by international law, the American reversal at Montevideo marked a turning point in inter-American relations. Soon thereafter, the United States proceeded to relinquish, one by one, its treaty rights to intervene in the de facto protectorates in the Caribbean basin. During the first two years of the Roosevelt administration, American military forces were withdrawn from Nicaragua and Haiti. In 1934 the United States Senate abrogated the notorious Platt Amendment of 1901, which had restricted Cuba's treaty-making power and established the prerogative of American military intervention to protect the island's independence and preserve domestic order. In July 1935 an agreement was concluded with the government of Haiti enabling it to regain control of its finances by purchasing the Haitian national bank from the National City Bank of New York. A year later a treaty with Panama terminated the American right of military intervention outside the Canal Zone (though Senate ratification was delayed until 1939, when an exchange of notes authorized "emergency" military action by the United States to protect the canal).

The Roosevelt administration had thus resumed and accelerated the radical transformation of the traditional policy of the United States toward Latin America initiated by President Hoover. By 1934 no American troops were stationed in sovereign countries in the region (except at the bases retained in Guantanamo Bay, Cuba, and the Panama Canal Zone). Washington had specifically relinquished its claim to the right of intervention to protect persons and property. Financial supervision of Haiti, the Dominican Republic, and Nicaragua was phased out between 1936 and 1940. Mexico had successfully nationalized American-owned petroleum properties without suffering the effects of American retaliation. It truly seemed that the previous relationship of dominance and subservience between North and Latin America had been replaced by a relationship of equality and mutual respect.

But the modification of American policy toward Latin America was more apparent than real. While the Good Neighbor Policy terminated the practices of military intervention and financial supervision, it replaced this discredited diplomacy of the gunboat and the dollar with a more indirect form of American control. In essence this consisted of the utilization of noncoercive means of enlisting the assistance of indigenous political, military, and business elites in preserving the United States' grip on the economic resources of the region. The judicious use of American Export-Import Bank loans to tie the economic systems of the individual Latin American republics even more closely to the American economy, the training and equipping of national constabularies to suppress social insurrection against pro-American regimes, and financial assistance to autocratic governments to balance budgets and stabilize currencies—these were the alternative means for perpetuating American hegemony once the employment of direct military force and financial control were abandoned.

The experiences of Nicaragua and the Dominican Republic furnish typical illustrations of this evolution from direct to indirect control. The United States had retained military forces in Nicaragua from 1912 to 1933 (except for a brief interlude in 1925–26). During the last years of the American occupation, U.S. officials trained and equipped a national guard to assume the function of preserving internal security upon the withdrawal of American troops. After the American evacuation in 1934, Cesar Augusto Sandino, leader of the rebel forces that had been harassing American marines throughout the twenties, signed a truce with the Nicaraguan government only to be murdered by members of the national guard. Two years later the head of the American-trained security forces, General Anastasio Somoza, seized power and instituted a dictatorial regime that brutally repressed revolutionary elements in the country and maintained close relations with the United States. The Somoza family remained in power either directly or through surrogates until being overthrown by the ideological heirs of Sandino in 1979.

A similar transfer of power from American military occupation authorities to a U.S.-trained indigenous elite occurred in the Dominican Republic. Having ruled that nation under martial law since 1916, the United States withdrew its military forces in 1924 after establishing a national constabulary to replace the departing marines. In 1930 General Raphael Trujillo, who had moved up the ranks of the national guard to become its chief in 1928, assumed the presidency after a fraudulent electoral campaign. With the financial assistance of American sugar interests, the National City Bank, and the government in Washington, Trujillo ruled his country with an iron fist for the next thirty-one years until his assassination in 1961. Within a few days after Pearl Harbor all four of the former American protectorates—Nicaragua, Cuba, Haiti, and the Dominican Republic—displayed their continuing loyalty to the United States by declaring war on Japan, Italy, and Germany.

In conclusion, it may be said that Franklin Roosevelt abandoned the "big stick" first wielded by his cousin in the years before World War I for a number of economic and strategic reasons. First of all, the economic recovery of the United States in the depths of the Depression required guaranteed and continuous access to the raw materials and markets of Latin America. This became all the more important as the revival of economic nationalism and the increased likelihood of war in Europe and Asia threatened to disrupt American trade with those distant continents. Second, the rearmament of Germany, not to speak of the increasing belligerence of Italy and Japan, revived the long-dormant issue of foreign interference in the Americas. In order to counter this new menace posed by the informal "unholy alliance" of Nazi Germany, Fascist Italy, and Imperial Japan, the United States sought to strengthen the peacekeeping machinery of the Pax Americana. But the traditional methods of military coercion and diplomatic intimidation had been rendered increasingly difficult to countenance in the face of sustained resistance from the Latin American republics and the accusations of hypocrisy from the world community. By substituting indirect for direct methods of hemispheric domination, the Roosevelt administration cast off the embarrassing albatross of old fashioned imperialism. It was thereafter free to act as the defender of peace and national sovereignty in the world at large as well as to mobilize its clients in Latin America in a hemispheric security system based on the voluntary cooperation of juridically equal nations.

After the announcement of German rearmament and the Italian invasion of Ethiopia in 1935, the United States government launched its first initiative aimed at establishing a system of hemispheric solidarity amid the collapse of collective security across the Atlantic. On January 30, 1936, President Roosevelt proposed the convocation of a special inter-American conference to devise procedures for protecting the western hemisphere from the new threat to world peace brewing in Europe. At this conference, held in Buenos Aires in December 1936, the American and Argentinian delegations clashed head on over the question of how such hemispheric security could best be assured. Foreign

General Cesar Augusto Sandino (1893–1934): Sandino and his followers harassed U.S. marines who sought to bolster the conservative government of Nicaragua from 1927 to 1934. After his assassination in 1934 by agents of the head of the country's national guard, Anastasio Somoza Garcia (1896– 1956), Sandino became a cult hero among Nicaraguan opponents of the Somoza family and their U.S. allies. *(Courtesy of the Library of Congress)*

Minister Carlos Saavedra Lamas of Argentina, the leading proponent of Latin American resistance to United States domination, trotted out a proposal for cooperation with the League of Nations to implement sanctions against aggressor states anywhere in the world. Predictably, the Argentine plan struck at the very heart of the Pan-American ideology propounded by the United States. It linked the security of the western hemisphere to the international organization headquartered in Europe, dominated by the European powers and repudiated by the United States. The American plan, introduced by Secretary of State Cordell Hull, preserved the principle of Pan-Americanism by seeking to organize the republics of the Americas in a common defense of hemispheric security. It proposed the creation of an inter-American consultative committee comprising the foreign ministers of the twenty-one republics, which would be authorized to hold consultations during international emergencies. In the event of war involving any of the member states, the neutral nations of the Americas would be obliged to enforce an embargo of credits and arms supplies on all belligerents.

Determined Argentine opposition to this United States effort to circumvent the League of Nations by establishing an exclusively inter-American security system resulted in the passage of a seemingly innocuous compromise: The principle of mutual consultation in the event of a threat to the peace of the Americas was embodied in the Treaty for the Maintenance, Preservation, and Reestablishment of Peace, but no institution was designated to hold such consultations and the obligation to embargo credits and munitions to belligerents was dropped. The absence of effective peacekeeping machinery notwithstanding, the mere affirmation of the principle of inter-American consultation represented a significant victory for Washington in its diplomatic confrontation with Buenos Aires. It established the precedent for the policy of hemispheric neutrality and collective defense that was later to be adopted by the American states at the outbreak of war in Europe. The price that the United States had to pay for this unanimous declaration of hemispheric solidarity was the Special Protocol Relative to Non-Intervention, which overrode the Hull reservation to the Montevideo resolution by prohibiting any of the signatories from intervening "directly or indirectly, and for whatever reason," in the internal or external affairs of the others. It was unimaginable that the United States, which was earnestly endeavoring to mobilize its Latin American clients against the menace of aggression from abroad, could cling to the last vestige of its own prerogative to violate their national sovereignty. The abrogation of all of the treaty rights authorizing United States military intervention and financial supervision in the Caribbean by the end of the 1930s fulfilled the solemn promises of the Buenos Aires protocol.

In the two years after the Buenos Aires Conference of December 1936, the deteriorating political situation in Europe underlined the necessity of institutionalizing the principle of hemispheric security that had been endorsed by the American republics. The failure of the League of Nations to restrain Italian aggression in East Africa and the inability of Great Britain and France to halt German revisionism in Central Europe raised the possibility of a new European war that would inevitably affect the economic and strategic interests of the western hemisphere. Most ominous of all was the apparent increase of Axis-inspired subversion in those Latin American states, such as Argentina, Brazil, and Uruguay, with substantial numbers of first-generation immigrants from Germany and Italy. Hitler's agents had seized control of the major organizations and publications of the Latin Americans of German descent. In some cases German immigrants were blackmailed into serving the Nazi cause under the threat of reprisals against their relatives at home. The resulting upsurge of subversive activity in these countries was accompanied by a propaganda broadside launched from Berlin in the form of radio broadcasts, press subsidies, and cultural exchange programs that was aimed at promoting Latin American support for German foreign policy. In the meantime, the Nazi regime made a determined effort to improve Germany's economic position in the region through the granting of foreign credits to and the conclusion of barter agreements with a number of Latin American states.

In the aftermath of the Munich Conference, the Roosevelt administration began to exert pressure on the Latin American republics to tighten the bonds of hemispheric solidarity in the face of the threat of war in Europe and the increase in German political and economic activity in the Americas. At the Eighth Conference of the American States in Lima, Peru, in December 1938, Secretary of State Hull obtained unanimous consent to a pledge of joint cooperation to defend against "all foreign intervention or activity" that might threaten any of the twenty-one American republics. To facilitate the process of joint consultation endorsed at the Buenos Aires Conference, a consultative organ composed of the foreign ministers of the signatory states was formed to handle emergencies. As was customary, Argentina resisted this United States-inspired movement toward closer hemispheric cooperation and held out for the maintenance of close relations with Europe; but the mounting anxiety in Latin America about the threat of a European war enabled Secretary Hull to win the day while the Argentine delegate remained incommunicado after having prematurely stalked out of the conference.

The consultative machinery established by the Declaration of Lima was first put into operation in response to the outbreak of the European war in September 1939. The first ad hoc meeting of the foreign ministers, held in Panama September 23–October 3, 1939, produced a series of recommendations that were unmistakably detrimental to the Axis and favorable to the Anglo-French cause. These included the proscription of domestic activities on behalf of any belligerent state (a measure aimed at German and Italian nationals residing in Latin America) as well as the revision of maritime legislation to enable neutral ports in the western hemisphere to receive armed merchant ships (thereby affording an advantage to Great Britain's large surface fleet) and to exclude belligerent submarines (thereby discriminating against the principal naval weapon of Germany). Less successful was the Panama conference's designation of a neutral zone around the western hemisphere extending several hundred miles from shore as far north as Canada. This presumptuous redefinition of the laws of naval warfare deterred none of the European belligerents as they launched the Battle of the Atlantic in the winter of 1939–40.

In addition to passing these blatantly anti-Axis resolutions, the Panama conference strengthened the existing machinery of hemispheric solidarity by creating an inter-American Financial and Advisory Committee to promote economic cooperation among the American republics. Behind the euphemism of inter-American cooperation lay a concerted (and ultimately successful) campaign waged by the United States to reduce Latin American trade with the Axis powers and to reserve for itself the markets and the strategic raw materials of the region. This American effort to forge a hemispheric economic bloc was the culmination of a long and bitter trade dispute that had threatened to undermine United States commercial predominance in Latin America. During the second half of the 1920s, the traditionally protectionist Republican administrations in Washington had resisted Latin American initiatives, led by Argentina, to eradicate artificial trade barriers (such as the notorious sanitary prohibition that excluded most Argentine beef from the American market). The Hawley-Smoot Tariff of 1930 placed additional obstacles in the path of Latin American exports to the United States. This upsurge of American protectionism ultimately forced many of the states of Latin America (with Argentina typically leading the way) to turn to Europe for alternative trading partners. The Roca Convention of May 1, 1933, established a privileged commercial relationship between Argentina and the British Empire (which had recently been reorganized into a virtually closed economic bloc by the imperial preference agreements signed in Ottawa in the summer of 1932). Great Britain agreed to purchase a prescribed annual quantity of Argentine beef and grain in return for assurances that Argentina would spend the proceeds from these sales on British manufactured products. This preferential trade arrangement, which adversely affected both American agricultural exports to Britain and American exports of manufactured goods to

Argentina, was followed by other bilateral commercial agreements between various Latin American states and the increasingly closed economic systems controlled by Britain, France, and Germany.

It was in response to this threat to inter-American commercial relationships that American Secretary of State Hull promoted his pet project for the reciprocal lowering of trade barriers to revive foreign commerce in the midst of the Depression. Though originally proposed to all of the major trading partners of the United States, the lack of enthusiasm on the part of the European powers (which were busy forming autarkic trade zones out of the extensive territory under their political control) caused Hull to concentrate on reducing trade barriers between the United States and the twenty other American republics. The American secretary of state tirelessly pressed for the adoption of reciprocity at the conferences of the American states, first in Montevideo in 1933, and with even more determination after the passage by the United States Congress of the Reciprocal Trade Agreements Act in June 1934, which authorized the president to negotiate reciprocal reductions in tariff duties with individual countries. During the last half of the 1930s a number of such bilateral agreements were signed with the nations of Latin America. This lowering of barriers to trade, together with the extension of commercial credits by the Export-Import Bank, forged a tight-knit commercial relationship between the United States and its Latin American clients that intensified the economic solidarity of the western hemisphere.

The sudden collapse of the Low Countries and France in May-June 1940 presented the first direct challenge to the security and neutrality of the Americas. The uncertain fate of the Dutch and French possessions in the Caribbean and on the northeast coast of South America raised the unnerving possibility of Germany's extorting rights to bases in this region from the helpless Dutch and French authorities. To avert such an eventuality, the U.S. Congress passed a joint resolution on June 18, 1940, reaffirming America's traditional opposition to the transfer of territory in the western hemisphere from one non-American power to another. The hastily convened second conference of foreign ministers of the American states, held in Havana July 21–30, 1940, endorsed the "no transfer" principle and authorized the seizure and joint administration by the American republics of any European possession judged to be in danger of falling into hostile hands. The most momentous act of the Havana conference was the Declaration of Reciprocal Assistance and Cooperation for the Defense of the Americas, which defined an act of aggression by a non-American state against any one of the twenty-one republics as an act of aggression against them all. This declaration in effect represented the formal multilateralization of the Monroe Doctrine. The principle of regional collective security, based on the mutual consent of the twenty-one American republics, thereby replaced the unilateral prerogative of the United States to prevent foreign intervention in the hemisphere.

The Declaration of Reciprocal Assistance enabled Washington to proceed with its plans to organize the defense of the Americas in the face of the Axis threat. The way in which hemispheric defense was to be managed became a subject of intense debate within the Roosevelt administration in the year before Pearl Harbor. The State Department, led by Undersecretary Sumner Welles, advocated the extension of the multilateral principle underlying the Good Neighbor Policy to the realm of regional military cooperation. Such an approach would furnish a solid foundation for the recent trend toward hemispheric unity in political and economic matters by giving all twenty Latin republics an equal stake in the cause of regional defense. The War and Navy departments preferred to organize the defense of the Americas on the basis of the United States' own special security requirements as defined by its service chiefs. This implied a series of privileged bilateral military relationships with a handful of countries (Mexico, Panama, Ecuador, and Brazil) strategically situated along the southern extension of the United States' defense perimeter (which was thought to run from the Galapagos Islands eastward to the Brazilian bulge). This approach would avoid overextending American resources to the peripheral southern portion of Latin America, which in any case contained two countries (Argentina and Chile) that maintained relatively cordial relations with the Axis powers and therefore were unlikely to be reliable partners in a hemisphere-wide security system led by the United States. It would permit military planners in Washington to concentrate on the two most pressing objectives of American strategy: the defense of the Pacific approaches to the Panama Canal against Japan and the protection of Brazil's northeastern bulge from the potential naval threat from bases that Germany might obtain in French West Africa.

Even before the entry of the United States in the Second World War, it became apparent that American military authorities were prevailing in their bureaucratic struggle with the advocates of a genuinely multilateral or collective security system for the defense of the hemisphere. The Roosevelt administration concluded bilateral defense agreements with the strategically situated republics within the United States' defense perimeter. Bilateral commissions modeled on the United States-Canadian Joint Board of Defense were established with Mexico and Brazil to coordinate those two countries' contribution to hemispheric defense. Negotiations were begun with Brazil and several states in the Caribbean region to secure air and naval base facilities for the United States to supplement those obtained in the British possessions in the new world by virtue of the destroyers-for-bases exchange of September 1940. American military and naval missions were dispatched southward to assist the individual states in their defense preparations while Latin American army and navy officers were invited to either the United States or the Panama Canal Zone for training. Lend-Lease agreements for the delivery of military supplies were eventually signed with every Latin American nation except Argentina and Panama (which received American aid under a separate arrangement for the protection of the canal zone).

Washington's success in assuming the role of the sponsor of strategic and economic coordination in the western hemisphere was facilitated by the common sentiment of danger from Axis-controlled Europe that gripped the ruling elites of Latin America after the fall of the Low Countries and France. That sense of a foreign menace, together with the abandonment of overt coercion within the hemisphere by the United States, secured the cooperation of the Latin American republics (always excepting Argentina) in the cause of hemispheric solidarity that was championed and dominated by the senior partner to the north.

This is not to suggest that this wartime expansion of America's hegemonic position in its hemisphere occurred without any resistance on the part of the weaker nations to the south. Even two such pro-American states as Brazil and Panama, for example, dragged out for many years their negotiations with the United States for base rights on their territory. But the behavior of Latin America as a whole after the United States' entry in the Second World War exhibited a cooperative spirit unprecedented in the history of inter-American relations. In contrast to the First World War, all twenty republics of Latin America eventually followed the United States into war, although Chile and Argentina held out until the last minute. At the third conference of foreign ministers in Rio de Janeiro, January 15–28, 1942, all of the American republics except Argentina and Chile severed diplomatic relations with the Axis powers, undertook to cooperate in the suppression of German espionage in the Americas, and adopted an extensive program of inter-American economic coordination and the pooling of strategic materials. Strategically located states such as Ecuador, Brazil, and the Caribbean republics eventually furnished base facilities to American military and naval forces, which accommodated over 100,000 United States troops by the end of the war.

These developments collectively reflected the unequal distribution of inter-American military and economic power that had been evident for so long. Notwithstanding the ubiquitous references to multilateral cooperation and collective security in the rhetoric of American officials concerned with Latin America during the war, the Roosevelt administration engineered the military buildup in the western hemisphere according to the specific strategic requirements of the United States. The most notable exception to the general trend toward bilateralism in the United States' security relations with its Latin American clients was the establishment in 1942 of the Inter-American Defense Board. But that sole surviving symbol of the State Department's original project for multilateral hemispheric defense was reduced to an innocuous advisory role as the United States military establishment pursued its preferred policy of bilateral links with the military elites of the individual states to the south.

Though Brazil sent an infantry division to the Italian theater in the summer of 1944, and the Mexican air force flew in support of U.S. infantry in the Philippines in the spring of 1945, Latin America's most important contribution to the war effort was economic rather than military. Under the procurement programs drawn up by the War Department in Washington, the Latin nations were induced to step up production of raw materials essential to the struggle against the Axis and to export them northward at artificially low prices in exchange for the provision of Export-Import Bank loans. This emergency program of wartime production led to the almost total reorientation of the economies of the Latin American states toward the United States, placing them in a position of great dependence on the American market for the specific strategic commodities involved. Once the demand for these war-related exports abruptly declined after 1945, most of the supplier countries were condemned to endure a painful readjustment to peacetime conditions. In the meantime, the reciprocal trade agreements (which reduced Latin American tariff barriers to United States exports) and Export-Import Bank loans strengthened the bilateral commercial ties between each of the individual Latin American countries and their powerful and prosperous neighbor to the north at the expense of the region's former trading partners in wartorn Europe and Asia. Thus the Second World War and the intense inter-American cooperation it generated reinforced the long-term trend toward United States dominance of economic relations in its hemisphere and launched the process of bilateral military cooperation between the armed services of the individual Latin states and their sources of military aid and training in Washington.

7

THE CONFIRMATION OF JAPAN'S SUPREMACY IN EAST ASIA

THE PERIOD OF PEACEFUL PENETRATION (1914–1930)

The First World War afforded the Japanese Empire a golden opportunity to consolidate and expand its economic penetration and political domination of East Asia without incurring the diplomatic risks that would earlier have accompanied such an aggressive policy. In its capacity as an ally of Great Britain, Japan had declared war on Germany in August 1914 and proceeded to seize all of the German possessions in the Far East. By the end of the year, Japanese military forces were in occupation of Tsingtao and the province of Shantung on the Chinese mainland as well as the German-controlled island chains in the northern Pacific (the Marianas, Marshalls, and Carolines).

The effortless absorption of the former German colonial possessions in Asia and Oceania, when added to the territories and privileges previously obtained as the spoils of victory after wars with China and Russia, enabled Tokyo to direct its expansionist energies toward the historic object of Japanese designs: China itself. The Chinese Revolution of 1911–12, which overthrew the decrepit Manchu dynasty, had sparked Japanese fears of losing the economic toehold on the mainland that had been acquired as a result of those earlier military triumphs. While the Manchu regime had relied heavily on Japan for financial assistance and political advice, the successor government in Beijing turned to Europe for support in an apparent attempt to loosen the mainland's ties of dependency to its powerful island neighbor. Anxious about losing its privileged position in southern Manchuria and Inner Mongolia, Japan profited from the military stalemate in Europe (which distracted the powers that had previously combined to restrain Japanese ambitions in East Asia) to present the Chinese government with the infamous "Twenty-One Demands" in January 1915. In its original form, this harsh ultimatum stipulated Japanese control of China's principal natural resources (especially the extensive iron and coal reserves located in the central part of the country) as well as the establishment of a de facto protectorate in the form of Japanese advisers attached to the Chinese government. Though energetic protests from the United States and Great Britain induced Tokyo to rescind its demand for a protectorate, it succeeded in extracting a number of economic concessions from the helpless Chinese government that significantly improved Japan's economic position on the mainland.

By 1916 Japan's major European allies, Great Britain, France, and Russia, granted formal recognition of Tokyo's wartime gains in East Asia, thereupon conferring the stamp of legitimacy on this unilateral extension of Japanese power. The sole obstacle to Japanese expansionism was the United States, which had expressed profound displeasure at the imposition of the Twenty-One Demands on China. Washington's mounting concern about the developments across the Pacific was not due to any fear for the security of the American homeland. The opening of the Panama Canal in the summer of 1914, which permitted the rapid concentration of American naval power in the eastern Pacific, had virtually eliminated a Japanese naval threat to the American west coast. But America's longtime commitment to the preservation of the territorial integrity of China and the "Open Door" for trade and investment in that country, coupled with the concern for guaranteeing the security of the Philippines, gave rise in 1916 to the passage of an ambitious naval construction program designed to ensure American naval supremacy in the western as well as the eastern Pacific. Japan's equally insistent preoccupation with securing its privileged position in Manchuria and northern China seemed to preclude an amicable resolution of this impending transpacific rivalry. Finally, on November 2, 1917, a mutually satisfactory compromise was reached by the American secretary of state and the Japanese ambassador to Washington. The so-called Lansing-Ishii Agreement affirmed the territorial integrity of China and the principle of the Open Door while recognizing Japan's "special interests" in China that were conferred by geographical proximity. This ambiguous accommodation— an executive agreement that was not submitted for legislative ratification—enabled the two countries to cooperate in the common struggle against Germany while postponing the inevitable showdown over China until after the end of the war.

In Japanese eyes, this reference to the "special interest" in China represented something akin to the Asian counterpart of the Monroe Doctrine, with Japan playing the role of hegemonic power in this instance. Such an interpretation gained even wider acceptance in Tokyo after the military collapse and political disintegration of Russia, Japan's traditional rival for the Chinese spoils. Following the Bolshevik Revolution and the signing of the Treaty of Brest-Litovsk, the French government persuaded President Wilson to approve a Japanese military intervention in eastern Siberia; its ostensible purpose was to restore order and promote the reconstitution of a Russian political and military authority capable of renewing offensive operations against Germany's eastern front in order to relieve the embattled Allies in the west. Japanese expansionists welcomed the opportunity to strengthen Japan's economic and political position in eastern Siberia and to create a buffer zone between Russia and Japanese-dominated Manchuria. Wilson reluctantly bowed to French pressure for a Japanese intervention on the condition that the expeditionary force be limited to seven thousand soldiers, approximately the size of the American contingent that was earmarked for the Siberian campaign. But the Japanese army in eastern Siberia mushroomed to seventy two thousand by the end of the war. There it was to remain until 1922, long after the defeat of Germany and the evacuation of the small American contingent that had been stationed in Vladivostok. The political authority of

Russia, the traditional counterweight to Japan in the northern borderlands of China, was virtually nonexistent in the region just as Japanese power there reached its height.

Japan's conspicuous presence at the Paris Peace Conference as one of the five dominant powers was a fitting tribute to that small island nation's remarkable rise from backwardness and obscurity in less than half a century. Though disinterested in the redistribution of territory and resources in far-off Europe, the Japanese delegation pressed for and obtained substantial advantages within its own geographical sphere. These included the acquisition of the former German Pacific islands north of the equator in the form of a League of Nations mandate as well as Germany's former economic privileges on the Shantung peninsula of China. The latter region was viewed by expansionist business elites in Tokyo as a stepping stone for further economic penetration of China similar to the one acquired earlier in Korea, the other peninsula extending from the mainland toward the Japanese islands. These territorial and economic gains firmly established Japan as a major economic force on the Asian mainland and the principal naval power in the western Pacific at a time when Russia still reeled from the effects of civil war and economic chaos and Great Britain was struggling to recover financially and commercially from the consequences of the Great War.

Once again, it was the United States that posed the most formidable challenge to Japan's expansionist moves in the Far East. America's growing apprehension about Japan's imperial ambitions across the Pacific was caused not only by the latter's territorial and economic gains at the peace conference but also by the alarming growth of Japanese naval power. The Tokyo government's spending on naval construction tripled from 1917 to 1921 and came to represent over a third of the imperial budget. Though possessing a fleet that ranked a distant third behind the formidable armadas of Great Britain and the United States, Japan's distance from North America rendered it virtually immune to the deterrent effect of American naval power (which in any case had to be divided between two oceans) while its alliance with Great Britain (concluded in 1902 and renewed in 1905 and 1911) neutralized the Royal Navy as a potential constraint on Japanese imperial ambitions. In response to the increase of Japanese naval strength, the United States transferred the bulk of its fleet from the Atlantic to the Pacific after the end of the war in Europe (in order to achieve virtual parity with Japan in that ocean) and proceeded to open the dry dock at Pearl Harbor in Hawaii. Relieved of the German naval menace in the Atlantic by the disarmament provisions of the Versailles Treaty, American naval strategists began for the first time to develop contingency plans for the projection of American naval power across the Pacific to the vicinity of Japan.

The prospect of a costly naval race so soon after the termination of the world war was anathema to all powers concerned. Great Britain, still the mistress of the seas but in danger of being surpassed by the United States and equaled by Japan in the near future, was plagued by chronic unemployment and industrial stagnation; these domestic ills dictated a policy of austerity and budgetary restraint that was incompatible with a large naval construction program. The American administration of President Warren Harding presided over a serious postwar recession in the early twenties and was dominated by conservative isolationists committed to drastic reductions in taxation and government spending as well as retrenchment from President Wilson's ambitious global commitments. Japanese leaders, while continuing to believe that national prosperity depended on privileged access to markets and raw materials abroad, displayed a willingness to adopt a strategy of peaceful economic expansion and cooperation with the two great English-speaking powers rather than incur the domestic costs and foreign policy risks of a naval arms race. It was in the context of this widespread apprehension about the economic and strategic consequences of unrestrained naval rivalry that President Harding invited the foreign ministers of eight maritime nations to the first international conference on naval arms control in the history of the world. Held in Washington during the winter of 1921–22, this unprecedented conclave produced a number of agreements to limit the naval arms race in general and to reduce Pacific tensions in particular.

The principal achievement of the Washington Naval Conference, the so-called Five Power Treaty, established a tonnage ratio for existing capital ships (defined as warships over 10,000 tons carrying guns larger than eight-inch) of 5:5:3:1.67:1.67 for Great Britain, the United States, Japan, France, and Italy, respectively, and decreed a ten-year moratorium on the construction of new ships in the same category. The three great naval powers agreed to refrain from building new fortifications on their Pacific possessions (excluding Singapore and Pearl Harbor, the principal forward bases of Britain and the United States, respectively). Japan consented to evacuate eastern Siberia, to restore to China sovereignty over the Shantung peninsula, and to permit its bilateral alliance with Great Britain—which was strongly opposed by the United States—to be replaced by a multilateral agreement to respect the political status quo in Asia. The Washington Naval Conference was widely acclaimed as the opening of a new era in international relations. Never before had the great powers freely consented to limit the size of a portion of their armed forces and to refrain from constructing new fortifications. Advocates of universal disarmament regretted the exclusion of land armaments from the agenda—a concession to the nervous French, who insisted on the right to retain undisputed military superiority over Germany in the absence of effective security guarantees. But this omission did not dampen the spirit of exhilaration that greeted the publication of the Washington treaty provisions. The vague commitment to universal disarmament that had been inserted in the Paris peace treaties finally resulted in concrete action, at least in the limited sphere of naval power.

The agreements specifically relating to East Asia also engendered considerable optimism about the prospects of peace and stability in that unsettled region, in Washington as well as in Tokyo. American Secretary of State Charles Evans Hughes, the host and guiding spirit of the conference, had achieved his three principal objectives—the termination of the Anglo-Japanese alliance, the recognition of American naval parity with Great Britain and superiority over Japan, and the evacuation of Japanese military forces from eastern Siberia. Tokyo had accepted the inferior position in the 5:5:3 ratio for capital ship tonnage because the nonfortification agreement seemed to represent an adequate guarantee of Japan's security in its home waters as well as its control of the sea approaches to the Asian mainland. These mutually acceptable compromises in strategic matters were supplemented by a series of informal pledges by Japan to abandon its unilateral quest for preferential rights in China in favor of a multilateral approach to the economic development of that country in cooperation with the Western powers.

Domestic developments within Japan after the conclusion of the Washington Conference appeared to confirm the new orientation of Japanese foreign policy and facilitated the rapprochement between Tokyo and the Western powers possessing colonial holdings in East Asia. The passage of progressive social legislation and the adoption of universal male suffrage in 1925 helped to dispel the lingering image of Japan in the Western democracies as an authoritarian, militaristic society. This apparent evolution toward enlightened administration and representative government caused many American bankers and business executives to reassess their attitudes toward economic opportunities in the Far East. China, the traditional object of American commercial and financial interest in the region, seemed hopelessly mired in political chaos and social unrest and therefore came to be regarded as a poor risk for trade and investment. By contrast, Japan acquired the well-deserved reputation as an island of stability in a turbulent part of the world that offered a much more hospitable environment for American economic interests. A close Japanese-American commercial relationship had developed during the First World War, when American exports to Japan increased fivefold and Japanese exports to the United States almost tripled. These economic contacts were expanded throughout the 1920s, during which the United States remained Japan's biggest customer and supplier. Throughout the decade the United States was exporting to Japan most of the island empire's automobiles, machinery, building-construction materials, and oil. Conversely, the American market absorbed 40 percent of Japan's total exports, including 90 percent of its raw silk products (a major source of foreign exchange for the export-dependent Japanese economy). During the same period American banks supplied Japan with 40 percent of its foreign investment. These commercial and financial connections, reinforced by the mutually advantageous agreements on naval arms limitation concluded in 1922, produced an atmosphere of cordiality and cooperation between Tokyo and Washington which in turn promoted stability in the western Pacific for the remainder of the 1920s.

But the structure of economic interdependence and multilateral security for East Asia depended, in the final analysis, on Japan's willingness to continue to pursue its national aspirations by peaceful means; that is, through economic rather than military rivalry with the Western powers. The limitations written into the Five Power Treaty at Washington confirmed Japan's naval superiority in its geographical sphere. By agreeing not to construct additional fortifications between Pearl Harbor and Singapore, the United States and Great Britain had significantly reduced their capability of deterring future Japanese aggression on the Chinese mainland or in southeast Asia. The vulnerability of British and American possessions in the Far East was increased by the advent of air power as a decisive factor in naval warfare. Four months before the opening of the Washington Naval Conference, the United States Army Air Corps had sunk a captured German battleship in an experimental test off the Virginia capes with foreign (including Japanese) military observers in attendance, conclusively demonstrating that gravity-propelled bombs could send a heavily armored vessel to the bottom. In strategic terms, this suggested that capital ships could no longer safely operate in waters within range of land-based enemy aircraft or aircraft carriers. Gone were the days when great battle fleets could roam about the oceans with impunity, intervening anywhere at will. Anglo-American superiority in battleships, which Japan had conceded at Washington, was therefore a deceptive advantage. The comforting vision of the great white fleet advancing westward from Pearl Harbor to liberate the Philippines and blockade the Japanese home islands, the basis of American naval strategy since the early 1920s, was chimerical. Japan had obtained a string of potential air bases in the form of the German mandate islands that lay sprawled across the western Pacific between the Philippines and Hawaii. From these safe bases, or from the aircraft carriers that were under construction, Japanese bombers could conceivably block

American naval access to the western Pacific, thereby isolating the vulnerable Philippine Islands from the principal American Pacific base at Hawaii.

This potential imbalance of power in the western Pacific, though continually decried by American naval authorities, generated little concern among policy-makers in Washington. Preoccupation with European and Latin American affairs in the 1920s resulted in a relatively nonchalant attitude toward Asia. American trade with and investment in Japan continued to increase, while Tokyo gave every indication of honoring its pledges to refrain from exploiting the advantage conferred by geographical proximity and technological innovations in naval warfare to upset the balance of power of the region. But the demographic, geographical, and economic sources of Japanese expansionism that had prompted the foreign adventurism of the past remained. The fatal combination of a rapidly expanding population, a limited supply of arable and habitable land, and a dearth of mineral resources and fossil fuels represented in the minds of worried officials in Tokyo a potentially insuperable barrier to future Japanese economic growth. Unless a remedy to this predicament could be devised by the ruling elite of the nation, Japan faced the prospect of a drastic reduction in its standard of living and the social tensions and political instability that often accompany economic stagnation and decline.

The solution to this dilemma sought by the Japanese government in the 1920s was reminiscent of the path chosen in the previous century by Great Britain, another island nation plagued during its developing phase by overpopulation and inadequate natural resources. This involved: (1) the encouragement of emigration to relieve domestic pressures on land, food, and natural resources; (2) the promotion of exports of manufactured products to finance imports of essential raw materials and foodstuffs; and (3) the pursuit of political accommodation with the other great powers in order to facilitate this policy of peaceful economic expansion. During the period of the so-called Taisho—a democracy, a progressive governing coalition of bankers, industrialists, and civil servants successfully combined a domestic program of social and political reform with a conciliatory foreign policy toward the other great powers and a drastic reduction in military expenditures.

But this turn toward moderation never commanded the support of the powerful military, naval, and bureaucratic elites in Japan that had shaped the expansionist policies of the recent past. Like their counterparts in Weimar Germany, these defenders of the old order remained unalterably opposed to their government's domestic reform program and its foreign policy of accommodation. They continued to dream of an East Asia dominated by an authoritarian Japanese empire free of Western influence. Their cause was strengthened by a series of international developments in the course of the 1920s that gradually undermined the basis of the government's cooperative relationship with the Western powers and enabled its military critics to mobilize popular opposition to that policy. The first of these was the appearance of legal restrictions on Japanese immigration in the English-speaking world. Opposition to Oriental immigration in the United States, Canada, and Australia, which had surfaced at the turn of the century, sharply curtailed the opportunity of Japanese nationals to migrate to low-population-density countries bordering the Pacific. In 1924, the American Congress went so far as to enact legislation that singled out Japanese immigrants as ineligible for American citizenship.

Though the practical effect of this punitive legislation was minimal—the previously existing quota system had allowed only a few hundred Japanese immigrants a year—its emotional impact on the proud Japanese people was considerable. Not only did it imply an American assumption of racial inferiority. Considered in the context of similar exclu-sionary restrictions imposed in Canada and Australia, it suggested a white man's con-spiracy to deny Japan the opportunity to relieve its population pressures through emigra-tion to the underpopulated regions of English-speaking settlement across the Pacific. Earlier Japanese hopes for the large-scale colonization of Korea, Formosa, and Man-churia after those nearby areas had been brought under direct or indirect Japanese con-trol before the war had failed to materialize. Less than half a million Japanese had migrated to Korea in the decade following its annexation and less than 200,000 had set-tled in Formosa. Twenty years after the acquisition of special privileges in Manchuria, less than a quarter of a million Japanese had resettled there. The reluctance of Japanese citizens to relocate to these neighboring areas, in spite of lavish inducements from their government, has generally been attributed to the overpopulated conditions and unsuitable climate that were to be found there. But whatever the explanation, and regardless of the alternatives to emigration that were available, expansionist-minded zealots in Japan began to raise the alarm: Their country and its people were being boxed in by the racist policies of the white, English-speaking nations.

The erection of barriers to the exportation of surplus population was soon followed by the appearance of obstacles to the expansion of Japanese trade with the English-speaking world. Commercial intercourse between Japan and the United States, which (as we have seen) increased steadily since the end of the war, began to decline sharply at the begin-ning of the 1930s because of the sudden collapse of purchasing power in Depression-ridden America. By 1930 Japan's raw silk prices had fallen to one-fourth of the previous year's level and silk exports to the United States fell by over 40 percent, causing the ruination of many peasants who depended on this important cash crop for their liveli-hood. The abrupt decline of the Japanese export trade caused by the contraction of demand in the United States was aggravated by the increase in American protectionism during the world economic downturn. Producers for the domestic market and labor organizations in the United States sponsored boycotts of Japanese goods and waged a "buy American" campaign to protect domestic profits and jobs. The Hawley-Smoot Tar-iff of 1930 raised duties on Japanese products by an average of 23 percent. The govern-ment in Tokyo made matters worse by returning to the gold standard at the existing exchange rate in January 1930. Intended as a measure to integrate the Japanese economy more closely into the international monetary system that was dominated by other nations that had long since returned to gold, this belated decision caused a dramatic overvalua-tion of the yen and therefore increased the price of Japanese exports at the very moment that the decline in purchasing power and the rise of protectionism abroad was closing for-eign markets. All of these developments contributed to a rise in unemployment, a sharp decrease in the real income of agricultural and industrial workers, and the beginnings of social unrest in Japan.

As opportunities for increased trade and emigration across the Pacific vanished, cer-tain interest groups in Japanese society revived the old dream of establishing a neocolo-nial relationship with the gigantic neighbor on the Asian mainland. At the end of the Great War, Japan had seemed ideally positioned to exploit the political divisions and eco-nomic distress of China to establish its predominance there. Though the Western powers had induced Tokyo to join them in reaffirming the Open Door Policy concerning equal-ity of commercial opportunity in China, the agreement lacked an enforcement mechanism. This meant that Japanese economic domination of China, even if it were to violate the protections agreed upon at the Washington conference, was unlikely to elicit more than verbal protests from the other great powers.

The internal political situation in China constituted an open invitation to Japanese intervention. The Chinese Revolution of 1911–12 had failed to establish a viable government capable of unifying the country and liberating it from foreign interference. From 1912 to the mid-1920s, administrative authority in China was divided among a number of regional military commanders or political leaders, most of whom passively tolerated the humiliating system of economic and legal privileges enjoyed by Japanese, European, and American trading companies. Manchuria was dominated by a local figure beholden to the Japanese; an ineffectual regime in Beijing, recognized by the Western powers as the nominal "government" of China, was powerless to prevent foreign restrictions on Chinese sovereignty and the assumption of regional authority by local warlords. Only Sun Yat-sen, the spiritual leader of the 1911 revolution who had established a rival "government" in Canton in 1917, represented a potential inspiration for Chinese national unity and sovereignty. But his regime lacked the military strength to enforce its will on the regional warlords and to command the respect of the foreign powers.

Enfeebled by these centrifugal forces, China submitted to an ever-increasing degree of Japanese economic domination. In the course of the 1920s Japanese capital accounted for 90 percent of all new foreign investment in China while 25 percent of Japan's total exports went to that country. The offshore island was rapidly developing a neocolonial relationship with the mainland analogous to that of the United States with Latin America, exchanging manufactured goods and investment capital for coal, iron, rice, soybeans, and other mineral and agricultural resources. Japan's economic penetration of China was facilitated by the system of commercial privileges inherited from the previous century. Restrictions on China's tariff autonomy prevented increases of duties on imports without the approval of the great powers. The principle of extraterritoriality exempted foreign residents of China from the jurisdiction of Chinese legal authorities and permitted foreign powers to maintain their own infrastructure (such as postal, communications, and transportation services) within their concessions. Both constraints on Chinese sovereignty were justified by the foreign powers on the grounds that China's chronic political instability prevented it from exercising the legal authority that is normally associated with sovereign states. Though the European nations and the United States also benefited from these privileges, Japan drew the greatest economic advantage from them and accordingly became the principal object of Chinese resentment against these blatant instances of foreign intrusion.

Chinese demands for the restoration of tariff autonomy and the abolition of extraterritoriality fell on deaf ears in Western circles whenever they were voiced. Despite the high-sounding endorsement of Chinese administrative and territorial integrity at the Washington conference, none of the great powers was prepared to accord China the full political sovereignty it craved. The United States was concerned almost exclusively with the preservation of the principle of equal opportunity for foreign nations seeking to trade with China and displayed little interest in restoring tariff and judicial autonomy to that country. Frustrated by the Washington treaty powers' refusal to recognize China's sovereign rights, Sun Yat-sen turned for support to the Soviet Union, which had not been invited to the Washington conference and which had renounced all of the special privileges in China that it had inherited from the tsarist regime. The Canton government's overture to Moscow came at a propitious moment in the evolution of Soviet foreign policy after the First World War. Surprised and disappointed at the failure of the Communist revolution to spread to the industrialized countries of Europe, Lenin and his successors turned their attention to the nonindustrialized regions of Asia in the hope of exploiting for Russia's benefit the anti-imperialist discontent of the subjugated masses there. In 1924 Russian representatives of the Communist International (Comintern) were dispatched to Canton to reorganize Sun's political movement, the Kuomintang, into a disciplined revolutionary organization capable of leading a mass movement in alliance with the small Chinese Communist party that had been founded three years earlier. The death of Sun Yat-sen in 1925 eventually brought to power in Canton a young military officer named Chiang Kai-shek who had visited the Soviet Union and remained in close touch with the Comintern agents in China. Chiang promptly mounted a campaign to unify the country as well as to liberate it from the detested system of foreign economic privileges. He proclaimed the Kuomintang the national government of China and on July 4, 1926, formally launched a northern military expedition to destroy the power of the regional military authorities, promote the administrative unification of the country, and expel foreign interests from Chinese territory. In the same year popular outbursts of xenophobia resulted in attacks on foreign citizens and property, revealing widespread support for Chiang's dynamic policy of national unification and liberation.

But unlike the Communists in his Nationalist coalition, Chiang was willing to distinguish among the various foreign powers that were encroaching on Chinese sovereignty. He expressed an eagerness to negotiate bilaterally with any one of them that was prepared to consider phasing out the despised treaty privileges. As it happened, public and official attitudes toward China in the United States had been gradually evolving toward greater sympathy for China's predicament. This new departure in American policy was publicly confirmed on January 27, 1927, when Secretary of State Frank Kellogg issued a statement affirming Washington's willingness to consider granting tariff autonomy to a central government of China that could command the allegiance of the Chinese people and protect American lives and property. The new Chinese strongman soon began to pursue policies and display personal traits that endeared him to public opinion in the United States. In April 1927 he turned against his erstwhile Communist allies, expelling Comintern advisers from the country, ruthlessly suppressing the Chinese Communist party, and denouncing the Soviet Union as a "red imperialist." At the end of the year he married a Wellesley College-educated daughter of a wealthy Christian businessman from Shanghai, who converted him to the Christian faith. In July 1928 Kuomintang forces successfully completed their northern expedition by occupying Beijing and bringing most of China under their effective control. In the meantime, the Nationalist government had caused a furor in Tokyo by announcing plans to construct a railroad in Manchuria in competition with the existing Japanese line, actively encouraging thousands of Chinese to emigrate to the northeastern province, and harassing Japanese economic interests there. Soon thereafter boycotts were organized against Japanese goods, and on December 29, 1928, Manchuria was formally reunified with China.

This nationalist revival hastened the process whereby the United States revised its paternalistic attitude toward China. The military successes, administrative reforms, and anti-Communist political orientation of the Nationalist regime appealed to those elements in American society that had longed for a stable, pro-Western, Christianized China open to American trade and investment. In recognition of these changed circumstances, the United States unilaterally accorded tariff autonomy to China on July 25, 1928, in exchange for a reciprocal most-favored-nation agreement; thus ended one of the humiliating economic privileges that had been extracted from the impotent Chinese during the age of imperial expansion. American business executives and bankers began once again to ponder the potential value to American trade and investment represented by the vast mainland of China, politically unified and protected from internal instability by a vigorous national government.

This revival of Sino-American friendship, together with the impending collapse of the system of foreign privileges in China and the challenge to Japanese interests in Manchuria, inflamed expansionist opinion in Tokyo. Japan's privileged position on the mainland seemed in danger of being swept away by a resurgent Chinese nationalism aided and abetted by the United States, which could be expected to obtain economic advantages from its recent rapprochement with Kuomintang China to the detriment of Japanese interests. Indeed, Japanese exports to China dropped by one half between 1929 and 1931, and by the latter year the United States had supplanted Japan as China's principal supplier of foreign products. The collapse of Japan's export trade in Asia, together with the sharp decline in Japanese-American commerce noted above, provoked widespread anxiety among merchants, bankers, and government officials. Their principal concern was the prospective loss of foreign exchange to pay for the supplies of coal, iron, oil, rubber, rice, and soybeans from the Chinese mainland and the offshore islands of southeast Asia that Japan depended on for survival. The deepening of the world economic depression prompted the United States and the industrialized nations of Europe to insulate their domestic markets from foreign competition, while the Asian and African empires of the European powers were rapidly becoming inaccessible to Japanese commercial penetration. The United States and the Soviet Union with their vast continental domains, and Britain and France with their worldwide empires, boasted a sufficiently diverse base of raw materials and sufficiently large markets to ride out the storm. Japan, by contrast, seemed isolated and economically vulnerable, without a market and resource base equal to its needs at a time when closed economic blocs were being formed throughout the world.

Added to this fear of economic strangulation was a growing concern about Japan's security interests in the western Pacific. At the London Naval Conference of 1930, which had been convened to reduce naval competition in categories of ships not covered by the Five Power Treaty limitations—destroyers, cruisers, and submarines—the Japanese delegation was persuaded to accept a compromise agreement that was viewed in Japanese naval circles as a serious threat to Japan's position of naval superiority in its region. Patriotic organizations in Japan bitterly denounced this "sellout" to the Western powers and mounted a nationwide campaign against the government for compromising the safety of the nation. The military and naval critics of the civilian government's conciliatory policy at London effectively exploited the widespread social discontent that had been caused by falling farm incomes and expanding urban unemployment. High-ranking military and naval officers perceived an ominous connection between the economic and security problems that the empire faced at the beginning of the thirties: Many were convinced that a global war was inevitable in the not-so-distant future; they believed that Japan's only hope of defending its interests lay in forging a domestic consensus behind a program of foreign expansion in order to create a self-sufficient strategic-economic bloc in East Asia controlled from Tokyo. In short, the conciliatory, pro-Western orientation of Japan's postwar civilian leadership appeared in the eyes of its naval, military, and nationalist critics to be leading Japan down the path of national suicide and economic decline.

THE PERIOD OF MILITARY EXPANSION (1931–1941)

The collapse of Japanese democratic political institutions and the abandonment of the moderate foreign policy of the Taisho   a period did not occur overnight. There was no march on Rome, no Reichstag fire, whereby the antidemocratic elements in Japanese society abruptly overthrew the democratic regime. The transformation of the Japanese political system from a Western-type parliamentary system into a military dictatorship transpired in almost imperceptible gradations between 1931 and 1936. There were ample domestic reasons for the collapse of Japanese democracy amid the social tensions and economic distress caused by the Depression. The plight of the peasantry in particular rendered it susceptible to demagogic appeals from political groups that promised deliverance from the deepening agricultural crisis. But the substance of the militaristic movement's program was concentrated on foreign policy issues because the world outside was seen both as the cause of Japan's mounting economic problems as well as the most promising source of salvation. The weak, vacillating policy of the government had brought the empire to its current perilous position. National renewal and economic prosperity were to be found in the rediscovery of Japanese pride at home and in the reassertion of Japanese power abroad.

The spearhead of this revolt against the established political order in Japan was a conspiratorial coterie within the officers' corps of the army known as the "Imperial Way" faction (so called because of its devotion to the principle of emperor-worship); it was composed mainly of younger officers stationed in Manchuria to guard the Japanese-owned South Manchurian Railway together with their supporters and promoters at home. This cadre tended toward ideological fanaticism, conceiving of foreign conquest as the most effective mechanism for the spiritual regeneration of a Japan that had become corrupted by Western cultural and commercial influences and was a menaced by Western naval power. Passionately intent on purifying their society and restoring national glory, the young zealots of the Imperial Way launched a number of violent attacks on the political leadership and its foreign policy that paved the way for the collapse of the Japanese parliamentary regime and the abandonment of its conciliatory foreign policy.

The first of these challenges to the political elite came on September 18, 1931, when middle-echelon officers on duty in Manchuria blew up a section of the South Manchurian Railway, attributed that act to Chinese terrorists, and proceeded to use it as a pretext for occupying the rest of the Chinese province. This plot, which had been hatched in consultation with sympathetic officers in the war ministry in Tokyo, represented a response to the encroachments in Manchuria by the reinvigorated Chinese government of Chiang Kai-shek. Though the emperor, the business leaders, and high government officials continued to preach caution and restraint in Japan's relations with the mainland, an outpouring of public support for the army's independent action forced the political authorities to acquiesce in the military fait accompli. In March 1932 a "Manchurian independence movement" financed and controlled by the Japanese occupation army established the sovereign state of Manchukuo, which was detached from China and placed under Japanese military protection. This virtually bloodless subjugation of Manchuria, a region with a land area greater than that of Japan, a population of 30 million, and valuable agricultural and mineral resources, had a profound repercussion on Japanese domestic politics. The wave of euphoria that swept the country confirmed the army's predominance in political affairs and relegated the elected government officials to a subordinate role, particularly in the formulation of foreign policy.

The response of the Western powers to this egregious violation of the principle of collective security was timid and vacillating. The American president, Herbert Hoover, was averse to the imposition of economic sanctions against Japan, fearing that they would lead to war (an attitude evidently shared by the majority of the American people at the time). Instead, Secretary of State Henry Stimson dispatched a note to Tokyo on January 7, 1932, expressing the American government's refusal to recognize any "treaty or agreement" that was brought about by means contrary to the Kellogg-Briand Pact. This nonrecognition doctrine enabled the Hoover administration to uphold the sanctity of international law without running the risk of imposing economic sanctions. This cautious American response was dictated by a number of considerations. To begin with, American economic and strategic interests in northern China were minimal; they certainly were insufficiently important to warrant retaliatory measures against Japan that might result in a diplomatic and perhaps even military showdown. Second, as noted above, American commercial and financial concerns had developed a substantial stake in the Japanese economy in the course of the 1920s; they were understandably reluctant to jeopardize their current trade and investment interests, not to speak of future opportunities, and did not hesitate to make their views known to the American government. Third, congressional refusal to appropriate funds to bring American naval strength up to the Washington and London treaty limits had deprived the United States of a credible deterrent force in the western Pacific to back up a strong diplomatic response to the Japanese action.

The circumspect policy adopted by the Hoover administration was resumed by President Franklin Roosevelt upon his inauguration in March 1933. The ambitious program of economic reconstruction launched in the first few years of the New Deal absorbed the attention and energies of the new administration, leaving little room for bold initiatives in foreign affairs. Moreover, the advent of the Nazi regime in Germany distracted world attention from the expansion of Japanese power in East Asia. Consequently, rumors of clandestine Japanese efforts to fortify the mandated Pacific islands in violation of the Five Power Treaty went uninvestigated. The State Department continued to discourage American trade with and investment in the vulnerable remnant of China under Kuomintang control. American exports of strategic materials to Japan continued unabated throughout the remainder of the 1930s.

Great Britain displayed even less of an inclination to risk antagonizing Japan by seeking to dislodge it from an area of no particular importance to Britain's national interests. Some officials in London even welcomed Tokyo's increasing military involvement in northern China as a useful diversion from the region of East Asia—which stretched from Hong Kong southward to Singapore—that was of substantial concern to Britain on economic and strategic grounds. Throughout the Manchurian episode British policy toward

Japan's Emperor Hirohito (1901–1989) on horseback, reviewing his troops in northern China, 1933: Historians still debate whether the emperor was an ally or a tool of the militaristic faction in Tokyo that launched Japan's aggressive campaign against China in the 1930s. *(Courtesy of the Library of Congress)*

East Asia was dominated by the aspiration to reach a mutually satisfactory division of the entire region into Anglo-Japanese spheres of commercial and strategic interest. The tame condemnation of Japanese aggression in Manchuria by a League of Nations commission headed by Britain's Lord Lytton reflected London's inclination to placate Tokyo: On the basis of the Lytton Commission report, the League's "sanctions" against Japan were confined to symbolic gestures of disapproval, such as the refusal to recognize the passports and postage of the newly installed Japanese puppet state of Manchukuo that Tokyo had imposed on the Manchurians.

But it soon became evident that the Japanese military's thirst for foreign conquest could not be quenched by the de facto absorption of Manchuria. The collapse of parliamentary democracy in many nations of Europe and the deepening of the Depression had undermined the credibility of that section of the Japanese ruling elite that had attempted to transplant Western-type political and economic practices to Japan and to cooperate with the Western powers in fostering international stability and prosperity. In its place emerged the dynamic young cadre of the army—the Imperial Way faction—that had launched the spectacularly successful coup in Manchuria. Gradually the power of the political parties and the Diet waned. Real authority was assumed by a small group of cabinet ministers beholden to the military chiefs. Army and naval officers infiltrated the middle and upper echelons of the civil service in increasing numbers, bringing great pressure to bear on the surviving remnants of the old governing elite to adopt more authoritarian measures at home and aggressive policies abroad. Internal repression mounted. Leftist politicians and labor leaders were imprisoned, newspapers were censored, and Western influences in Japanese culture came under attack from the proponents of the new nationalism.

But the beneficiaries of this political transformation in Japan were not to be the fanatical young officers of the Imperial Way. Their romantic reverie of a purified Japanese society untainted by the evils of the industrialized West was patently inappropriate to the launching of the war of conquest that all significant factors of the Japanese ruling elite had come to favor by the middle of the 1930s. The more sober and practical-minded members of the Japanese military establishment recognized that the time had long since passed when spiritual virtues were sufficient to win wars, nor could they promote the economic growth on which military success in the modern world depended. The more conservative modernizers among the army leaders, while equally committed to the cause of military grandeur, realized that discipline, organization, and technological innovation were the most suitable means of achieving that end. The so-called Control Faction of older, maturer officers therefore resolved to harness the energies of their exuberant younger colleagues and redirect them into more effective channels. The opportunity for coopting the program of the radical firebrands of the Imperial Way arose in February 1936, when fifteen hundred junior officers and soldiers in Tokyo seized government buildings and assassinated several current and former government leaders and a high-ranking army general before being captured by loyalist forces in the military. This abortive putsch provoked a response by the modernizing faction of the army high command, which hastened to restore discipline in the armed forces and suppress the Imperial Way cabal.

The modernizing faction of the military, while acting against the excesses of the junior officers, had been converted to the cause of foreign conquest that the latter group so energetically espoused. Domestic authoritarianism and foreign expansion were endorsed by the army leaders not as a means of spiritual renewal, but rather as means of mobilizing domestic support for military modernization and an increase in the political power of the army high command. Similarly, the business and financial oligarchy that had presided over Japan's industrial revolution was gradually won over to the cause of rearmament and foreign expansion for reasons of economic self-interest. The Zaibatsu elite—comprising the conglomerates Mitsui, Mitsubishi, Sumitomo, and Yasuda—which had previously cooperated with the civilian governments' policy of domestic liberalization and peaceful economic expansion abroad, joined forces with the modernizing sector of the army to form a vast military-industrial cadre devoted to massive rearmament in preparation for overseas conquest. The army leaders recognized the necessity of obtaining the services of this business elite for the exploitation of the extensive economic resources of Manchukuo. Japanese heavy industry in turn reaped lavish rewards from the remilitarization of Japanese society and the increased economic penetration of the mainland. Industrial production skyrocketed from 6 billion yen in 1930 to 30 billion yen in 1941. The four Zaibatsu conglomerates more than tripled their total assets during the same period. It is ironic that a movement of national regeneration launched by a radical faction of disgruntled junior officers who sought to realize their nostalgic vision of a return to the preindustrial way of life was appropriated by the technologically minded elite of the army and heavy industry. Historians have drawn the parallel between the February 1936 abortive coup in Japan and the "Night of Long Knives" of Nazi Germany in 1934, when Hitler turned against the anti-capitalist, romantic youth of the Sturm Abteilung (S.A.) and forged an alliance with the conservative elite in the officers corps and the business community.

Once the Control Faction of military technocrats and their allies in the Zaibatsu industrial and financial empires consolidated their authority in Tokyo, plans were laid for the extension of Japanese power in East Asia beyond the frontiers of the new client state of Manchukuo. In August 1936 the cabinet adopted the "Fundamental Principles of National Policy," which foresaw the economic integration of Japan, Manchukuo, and northern China, the economic penetration of Southeast Asia, and the acquisition of undisputed naval primacy in the western Pacific. In order to protect its northern flank from possible Soviet interference with this southward expansion, the Japanese government signed the so-called Anti-Comintern Pact with Nazi Germany in November 1936 to intimidate Moscow.

The first stage of this plan for regional hegemony was put into operation in July 1937, when an accidental clash between Chinese and Japanese troops on maneuvers near Beijing escalated into a full-fledged (though undeclared) war between the two states. Japanese military forces swept south and west from their bases in northern China, defeating the best divisions of the Kuomintang army around Shanghai and capturing Chiang's capital city of Nanking in December. Hankow and Canton fell in the autumn of 1938, by which time all of the major cities, ports, railway lines, and productive parts of northern and central China had fallen under Japanese control. On the heels of the victorious Japanese armies followed industrial officials who organized "development companies" to exploit the mineral resources and run the basic industries of the newly occupied regions. In December 1938 the Nationalist Chinese government retreated to the mountain redoubt of Chungking in the west to carry on the fight, while a guerrilla resistance movement was organized by the Communist party in Yenan in the northwest. The Japanese occupation authorities established a puppet government in northern China and then in March 1940 formed a collaborationist regime in Nanking to rival the Nationalist stronghold in Chungking.

It is surprising that the United States government continued to pursue a wait-and-see attitude toward Japanese aggression in China. Japan had launched an ambitious program of naval construction after the expiration of the London Treaty in 1936 that unmistakably upset the balance of naval power in the western Pacific. The economic penetration in north and central China that followed in the wake of the military advance clearly endangered existing American commercial interests and foreclosed future opportunities there. Yet the Roosevelt administration persistently rebuffed British entreaties for joint diplomatic pressure against Tokyo to force a halt to the southward advance in China. The American president was content to issue stern verbal warnings, such as the vaguely worded "Quarantine the Aggressor" speech of October 5, 1937, in which he called for "positive endeavors to preserve peace." This phrase, linked as it was to the quarantine metaphor, was taken to imply Washington's willingness to consider the imposition of economic sanctions against Japan, until the public outcry from isolationists in the United States forced the president to beat a hasty retreat. But within a year, the Japanese onslaught in China precipitated a change in American policy toward the undeclared war in the Far East. By purchasing Chinese silver, the American government supplied the hard-pressed Nationalist government with dollars to pay for American military equipment. Secretary of State Hull announced a "moral embargo" on aircraft sales to Japan. Congress authorized the construction of two new aircraft carriers and a twofold increase in the number of naval aircraft.

But the greatest leverage that the United States exercised over Japan was its ability to mount a full-scale campaign of economic retaliation. Despite the drop in Japanese exports to the United States during the 1930s, Japan remained America's third best customer in world trade (behind Great Britain and Canada), receiving over 40 percent of its imports from the United States. We have noted how these close commercial ties constituted one of the main causes of Washington's reluctance to consider the imposition of economic sanctions on Japan in retaliation against the Manchurian invasion. American export interests feared the loss of lucrative markets that would result from an American embargo. But this commercial interdependence worked both ways: Japan's heavy reliance on American suppliers for strategic materials such as petroleum, iron, copper, steel, and industrial machinery rendered that nation vulnerable to American economic pressure. A cutoff of these supplies would seriously jeopardize the continuation of Japan's economic expansion and rearmament.

After a fierce struggle within the Roosevelt cabinet between supporters and opponents of economic retaliation, the advocates of sanctions prevailed. On July 26, 1939, the United States gave Japan the required six-months notice of its intention to abrogate the Japanese-American commercial treaty of 1911, thereby removing the legal obstacles to the adoption of trade restrictions. Before the expiration of the six months, the outbreak of the European war in September 1939 presented the Japanese with a fortuitous opportunity similar to the one they had enjoyed in 1914. Events across the world again diverted attention from Tokyo's expansionist designs in the Far East. The Asian colonies of Britain, France, and the Netherlands were left virtually undefended as most available forces were redeployed to Europe to participate in the forthcoming confrontation with Hitler's armies. Then the fall of the Netherlands and France in May-June 1940 enabled the Japanese to extort extensive economic and strategic concessions from those weakened European powers. The Dutch government finally bowed to Japanese pressure in June and removed many restrictions on petroleum exports from the Dutch East Indies to Japan. In the same month the Vichy government of France was pressured by Japan into closing the supply route through Indochina to Chiang Kai-shek's besieged regime in Chungking. In September Japanese forces occupied the northern half of French Indochina for the ostensible purpose of ensuring the isolation of the Chinese Nationalists' stronghold. Recognizing that further expansion southward risked a confrontation with the United States, Tokyo sought and obtained the conclusion of a Tripartite Pact with Germany and Italy in the hope of intimidating Roosevelt into granting Japan a free hand in Asia.

Confronted with this unmistakable Japanese bid for primacy in the Far East, the American government mounted a campaign of retaliation that unfolded in graduated stages in response to each Japanese transgression. Reports of Japanese efforts to corner the market on American oil exports prompted President Roosevelt to impose an embargo on aviation fuel and the highest grades of iron and scrap steel in July 1940. As Japanese troops poured into northern Indochina in September, the embargo was extended to include all scrap metals. While Japan consolidated its position in northern Indochina, the American president finally agreed in October 1940 to authorize joint Anglo-American naval staff talks (though he stubbornly resisted London's suggestion that the American Pacific Fleet be transferred from Pearl Harbor to Singapore to bolster British naval power in the Far East).

Japan's objectives in pursuing its southward campaign were both economic and strategic in nature. The economic planners in Tokyo hoped to achieve national self-sufficiency in strategic materials by obtaining control of the oil, rubber, tin, and nickel resources located in the European colonial possessions in Southeast Asia (British Malaya, French Indochina, and the Dutch East Indies). When the Dutch government rebuffed Japanese demands for the right to import unlimited quantities of oil from the East Indies, the Imperial Council adopted on July 2, 1941, a grandiose scheme for the definitive expulsion of European power from Asia and the establishment of a confederation of Asian nations under the economic control, political tutelage, and military protection of Japan. In the minds of officials in Tokyo, this "Greater East Asia Co-Prosperity Sphere" would concretize the Oriental Monroe Doctrine that had been ineffectually advanced by earlier Japanese officials: The vacuum produced by the withdrawal of European power from East Asia, like the vacuum produced by the withdrawal of European power from Latin America in the nineteenth century, would be filled by the regional power whose cultural, economic, and military superiority entitled it to exercise hegemony in its geographical sphere. In pursuit of this objective, fifty thousand Japanese troops began to advance into the southern part of Indochina on July 24, 1941. The acquisition of naval and air bases on the Indochinese coast immediately posed a grave menace to the British naval base at Singapore and the petroleum reserves of the Dutch East Indies. The American government's retaliatory response to this dramatic extension of Japanese power marked the decisive turn in relations between Tokyo and Washington: President Roosevelt froze Japanese assets in the United States and imposed an embargo on high-octane (military) gasoline, effectively terminating all trade between the two countries and depriving Japan of the fuel she needed to resume mechanized military operations on the Asian mainland.

The mounting concern in Washington about the deteriorating situation in the Far East was accompanied by growing public support in the United States for the embattled population of China. Pearl Buck's best-selling novel, *The Good Earth,* later made into a popular motion picture, evoked widespread sympathy through its portrayal of the sturdy, virtuous Chinese peasant. Such an image stood in glaring contrast to wire service photographs and news stories of Japanese troops looting and pillaging throughout China. The American support for China had come in the form both of official government loans ($20 million in the spring of 1940, $100 million in November 1940) and of unofficial expressions of solidarity with the suffering Chinese. In 1937 Captain Claire Chennault, a retired Army Air Corps officer, had become the chief adviser to the Chinese Air Force; he brought with him a group of mercenary American pilots, the "Flying Tigers," whose services on behalf of a foreign power were tacitly tolerated by the American government. In April 1941, Roosevelt signed an executive order legalizing this mercenary activity and in October 1941 dispatched an official American military mission to Chiang's government in Chungking.

The imposition of the American embargo, together with the stepped-up American economic and military support for the Chinese resistance, left Japanese officials in a quandary: Japan possessed less than a two-year supply of oil at a time when the seemingly interminable struggle on the Asian mainland absorbed huge quantities of aviation

Generalissimo Chiang
Kai-Shek (1887–1975)
and his wife, Madame
Chiang Kai-Shek (neé
Mayling Soong) (1897–
2003) in Chungking, the
temporary capital of
Nationalist China during
the Second World War:
*Educated at Wellesley Col-
lege, a devout Christian,
fluent in English, Madame
Chiang served as the liaison
between her husband and
his U.S. supporters during
and after the Second World
War. (Courtesy of the
Library of Congress)*

and motor fuel. In light of severe shortages of other vital minerals, the cutoff of American oil exports forced Tokyo to consider the alternative of seeking a negotiated settlement with China and evacuating Indochina (the conditions on which American oil shipments would be resumed). Such a reversal would have constituted a return to the policy
adopted during 1914–18 of peacefully seeking advantages in Asia by capitalizing on the
Western powers' involvement in the European war. This option unmistakably represented the most promising one from a purely economic point of view.

But withdrawal from the mainland would have caused a humiliating loss of face for
that group of army officers that had spearheaded the expansionist policy of the thirties. It
would also have weakened the domestic position of the military and would have abruptly
halted the momentum of the movement of national regeneration launched in the aftermath of the Manchurian expedition.

The second option available to Japan was a southward thrust to break the American-
imposed embargo by seizing the petroleum reserves of the Dutch East Indies and the
other raw materials of Southeast Asia. In the end the lure of the extensive natural
resources and territory in Southeast Asia left unprotected by the European colonial powers induced the military party in Japan to risk war with the United States.

It is necessary here to review the conflicting pressures operating in Tokyo and Washington during the evolution of foreign and military policies toward East Asia. In Japan army planners were continually preoccupied with the traditional victim, China, and the traditional rival on the Asian mainland, Russia. Japanese military leaders, together with most of the prominent civilian leaders, favored the preservation of normal relations with the United States. They failed to realize, or realized too late, that the offensive operations in China were likely to alienate American opinion and provoke measures of retaliation from Washington. Even after the decision to expand toward Southeast Asia was taken, high-ranking generals in Tokyo hoped to exclude the Philippines from the new Asian economic bloc that would be formed under Japanese leadership out of the former British, French, and Dutch possessions in the region. They entertained the hope that the new East Asia bloc would thereafter compete peacefully with the Russian, American, and European economic systems on relatively equal terms.

The Japanese navy, on the other hand, had regarded the United States as the most probable enemy since the end of the First World War. After the London Naval Conference of 1930, naval authorities in Tokyo forcefully pressed for parity with the United States in order to assure undisputed Japanese control of the western Pacific and permit an eventual advance southward. The army's lack of enthusiasm for this "southern" strategy was prompted by its obsession with protecting the newly acquired empire on the Chinese mainland from the predatory grasp of Russia. An advance toward the South Seas would necessarily denude Japan's northern defenses and conceivably tempt Moscow to intervene at the Japanese rear.

But two developments in the spring and summer of 1941 relieved this source of anxiety about Russian intentions. In April 1941 the Japanese government succeeded in signing a neutrality treaty with the Soviet Union in order to remove the possibility of a two-front war. Two months later Hitler launched his full-scale military assault on Russia from occupied Europe, compelling Stalin to transfer several divisions from Siberia to European Russia to repel the Nazi advance against its major metropolitan areas. These two events removed the threat of Soviet pressure in Manchuria and helped to convert the Japanese military to the cause of the southern strategy championed by the navy. The cabinet's decision in July 1941 to acquire the bases in Indochina preparatory to a strike against Singapore and the East Indies reflected this confluence of strategic opinion in the two services.

American policy toward East Asia was subjected to similar pressures from various sources within Roosevelt's entourage. The internecine struggle in the cabinet between advocates of economic sanctions (led by Treasury Secretary Henry Morgenthau and Interior Secretary Harold Ickes) and opponents (such as Secretary of State Cordell Hull and his undersecretary, Sumner Welles) was reenacted within the leadership of the armed services. Naval authorities had targeted Japan as America's most likely enemy since the early twenties. War plan "Orange," formulated in 1924, envisioned a westward sweep of the American battle fleet from Pearl Harbor to liberate the lightly defended Philippines, destroy the Japanese navy, and blockade the home islands. But the spectacular increase in German naval power in the North Atlantic astride the critical trade route to Western Europe forced a reversal in American naval thinking. In the spring of 1939 American naval officials began to shift toward a defensive strategy in the Pacific: They took it for granted that economic pressure would suffice to deter Japanese aggression in that ocean.

The military collapse of France and the German air assault on England hastened this reorientation. On November 4, 1940, a revised war plan, dubbed "Plan Dog," became the official basis of American naval strategy. It identified Germany as the foremost naval threat and presumed that Japan would never risk war with the United States by attacking its possessions in the Pacific. Even in the event of a Japanese invasion of the Philippines, the combination of economic warfare and a defensive naval task force was deemed sufficient to protect American interests in the region while the brunt of American power was to be deployed against Germany. The Lend-Lease agreement with the European powers fighting Germany, the acquisition of bases in Greenland, the increase in the American naval presence in the North Atlantic, and the refusal to dispatch the American fleet to Singapore constituted additional evidence of the European orientation of American naval strategy and the hesitancy to become embroiled in Asian complications. As Roosevelt himself graphically put it, in response to the pleas of those favoring a hard-line policy toward Japan: "I simply have not got enough navy to go around—and every little episode in the Pacific means fewer ships in the Atlantic."

By the time of the seizure of the Indochinese bases and the imposition of the American oil embargo in the summer of 1941, negotiations between Tokyo and Washington to reach a mutually acceptable compromise had been dragging on with no end in sight. Japanese-American contacts had been set in motion toward the end of 1940 through the intervention of a small group of private citizens in both countries that the State Department code-named the "John Doe Associates." It included two American Catholic prelates—Bishop James Walsh and Father James Drought, a former missionary in China, who met with Japanese officials in Tokyo and with U.S. officials in Washington (including Secretary of State Cordell Hull and President Roosevelt himself) in an energetic campaign to promote high-level negotiations to reach a settlement of Japanese-American differences that would prevent military conflict. When the president gave the green light to his secretary of state, Hull met with Japanese Ambassador Kichisaburo Nomura on March 8, 1941, for the first of fifty face-to-face discussions to seek an agreement. In the course of these talks, the incompatability of the Japanese and American demands became apparent. The United States insisted on the prior withdrawal of Japanese forces from *all* of the territories occupied since 1931 as a *precondition* to a settlement in East Asia. Certain sections of official opinion in Tokyo, aware of the increasing naval cooperation between Great Britain and the United States, disheartened by the failure of the German army to deliver the knock-out blow against Russia, and anxious about Japan's dwindling oil reserves, were prepared to support a retreat from Indochina and even South China in exchange for a resumption of trade with the United States and the assurance of an adequate flow of strategic raw materials. But no Japanese leader in a position of authority was prepared to relinquish the special position in Manchukuo that they believed belonged rightfully to Japan. Yet American Secretary of State Hull stubbornly reiterated the original American demand for a total Japanese withdrawal from the Asian mainland. In short, the Roosevelt administration remained rigidly faithful to the principles of American diplomacy in Asia established by Secretary of State John Hay's "Open Door" notes at the turn of the century and reiterated by Welson's opposition to Japan's Twenty-One Demands on China (1915) and Secretary of State Henry Stemson's nonrecognition of the Japanese puppet state of Manchukuo (1932). This policy clashed directly with Japan's conception of its right to dominate China in general and Manchuria-Manchukuo in particular.

By the autumn of 1941 the Japanese naval forces in the western Pacific had attained virtual parity in the region with the combined fleets of the United States and Great Britain. At the same time, the productive capacity, and therefore the war-making potential, of the Western powers was many times greater than that of the island empire. Moreover, the United States had recently embarked on a massive naval construction program that threatened to erase Japan's margin of safety in the western Pacific within a few years. Such a fatal combination of short-term advantage and the prospect of long-term inferiority, as we have seen in the case of imperial Germany in the years before 1914, tends to increase the temptation to resort to preventive war. While the Japanese diplomats sought to moderate the more extreme features of the American negotiating position in the fall of 1941, the military and naval commands prepared for the worst. On October 16 General Hideki Tojo, a hard-liner and former chief of staff of the Japanese occupation forces in Manchuria, replaced Prince Fumumaro Konoe as prime minister. The new strongman in Tokyo proceeded to set a deadline for a settlement with Washington that would lift the embargo on strategic materials and would lead to a temporary suspension of U.S. aid to Chiang Kai-shek's government in China. If an acceptable agreement was not forthcoming by November 29, a proposal for war would immediately be submitted to the emperor. The Japanese negotiators in Washington issued their latest proposal, which called for a resumption of American oil deliveries and an end to U.S. aid to China, but the main quid pro quo was merely a pledge to withdraw from Indochina after a peace agreement with China had been concluded by Japan. Hull responded with a ten-point note on November 26 demanding a withdrawal from Indochina and all of China. This blunt restatement of Washington's original uncompromising position was the last straw for the hard-liners in Tokyo, who had been engaged in an intensive debate with advocates of a peaceful solution to the Japanese-American conflict. On December 1 the Imperial Conference formally approved the initiation of hostilities against American, British, and Dutch possessions in Asia in order to secure the oil and other strategic raw materials that Japan required to resume its campaign to achieve hegemony in East Asia. The next day the government ordered the Japanese navy to execute the plan carefully worked out earlier by Admiral Isoroku Yamamoto for a surprise attack on the American Pacific fleet at its base in Pearl Harbor, Hawaii. A task force of six aircraft carriers and two battleships steamed toward the Hawaiian island of Oahu in strict radio silence to evade detection. A few minutes before 8:00 a.m. (Hawaiian time) on Sunday, December 7, the 353 airplanes transported by this flotilla struck the American air base as well as the naval vessels moored in the harbor. Within two hours eight battleships went to the bottom and the rest were severely damaged, depriving the United States of the bulk of its Pacific fleet. Though the Japanese attack force had failed to destroy the three U.S. aircraft carriers stationed at the base—two were at sea and the other was at San Diego—the elimination of the U.S. battleship fleet in the Pacific in a single day was one of the greatest naval disasters in history.

American intelligence, thanks to the cracking of the Japanese code in August 1940, was aware of Tokyo's plans to move against Singapore, the Dutch East Indies, and Thailand. There was also some evidence in these intercepts that Japan planned an assault on the Philippines. But no one in a position of authority in Washington expected an attack on Pearl Harbor; the Japanese government's instructions to its consul in Honolulu contained strong hints of an impending attack against the nearby naval base, but code machines (which had been dispatched to the Philippines) had unaccountably not been sent to Hawaii.

The U.S.S. ARIZONA in flames at Pearl Harbor, December 7, 1941: The remains of many of the 1,177 crewmen who lost their lives were preserved in the sunken battleship at the bottom of the harbor. The 184-foot-long memorial structure spanning the midsection of the submerged ship is visited by thousands of tourists each year. *(National Archives)*

Intercepted instructions cabled to Japanese negotiators in Washington contained sufficiently menacing language that Chief of Staff General George Marshall dispatched a last minute warning to Pearl Harbor on December 7, but he sent it by Western Union instead of by the overloaded government cable; the messenger boy carrying the news was pedaling his bicycle toward the American military compound when the Japanese planes struck. Simultaneous Japanese attacks against the American air base at Clark Air Field in the Philippines, British Malaya, Singapore, Hong Kong, and other outposts of Western power in Asia represented a vast preemptive attack to cripple Japan's adversaries as it sought to secure its dominance in the region. That there were numerous examples of mistaken judgment on the part of American officials in the Pearl Harbor affair is indisputable. But despite the claims of conspiracy-minded critics, there is no evidence that President Roosevelt knew in advance of the plan to attack Pearl Harbor and deliberately exposed the Pacific fleet to destruction in order to bring the United States into a war against Japan and its European allies. It was diplomatic and military miscalculations about Japan's intentions and capabilities that explain the American disaster at Pearl Harbor.

It is safe to conclude that neither the United States government nor the Japanese government looked forward to a Pacific war. Influential sections of the governing elites in both countries had good reason to press for a restoration of the amicable diplomatic relations and reciprocally profitable economic intercourse that had transpired during the 1920s. But it is equally true that the two governments developed foreign policies in the course of the following decade that guaranteed an eventual confrontation. The ruling elite in Tokyo, despite Japan's spectacular economic advances of the interwar period, came to regard hegemony over China and the French, British, and Dutch empires in East Asia as the only alternative to economic decline and subservience to the European powers that controlled the vital resources of the region. Conversely, a consensus gradually developed in Washington that the addition of China and the European possessions in Asia to the Japanese empire would constitute an unacceptable alteration of the balance of forces in the western Pacific as well as a severe menace to American economic interests in the region. Once these mutually incompatible perceptions of national interest became the basis of foreign policy, it was only a matter of time before the two powers on opposite sides of the Pacific would come to blows.

THE WAR IN ASIA (1941–1945)

Japan's surprise carrier raid on the American naval base at Pearl Harbor effectively erased the naval power of the United States in the western Pacific. Three days later land-based Japanese planes sent two of Great Britain's premier battleships to the bottom off the coast of Malaya. In his memoirs Winston Churchill recalled that in those dark days of December, "There were no British or American capital ships in the Indian Ocean or the Pacific except for the American survivors of Pearl Harbor, who were hastening back to California. Over all this vast expanse of waters Japan was supreme, and we everywhere were weak and naked." These crippling blows to Anglo-American naval strength in East Asia were soon followed up by rapid Japanese military advances against the Western powers' imperial outposts in the region. On February 15, 1942, Britain's naval base at Singapore, the supposedly impregnable Gibraltar of the Far East, was taken from behind by a Japanese land army that had advanced down the jungles of the Malay peninsula. By the spring of 1942 the major colonial possessions of the Western powers in Asia—the Philippines, Malaya, most of the Dutch East Indies, and Burma—had come under Japanese military occupation, while nominally independent Thailand became an ally and subservient client state of Tokyo. An area encompassing 100 million people and sufficient food-producing land, strategic minerals, and petroleum reserves to assure Japan the economic self-sufficiency it had previously lacked and had desperately sought was organized as the Greater East Asia Co-Prosperity Sphere. With Japanese forces advancing westward toward India and southward toward Australia, the remnant of the British Empire in Asia was exposed to mortal danger at a time when Britain's power was concentrated in the North Atlantic and the Mediterranean to combat the German threat closer to home. America's only ally in Asia, the Chinese Nationalist government holed up in its Chung-

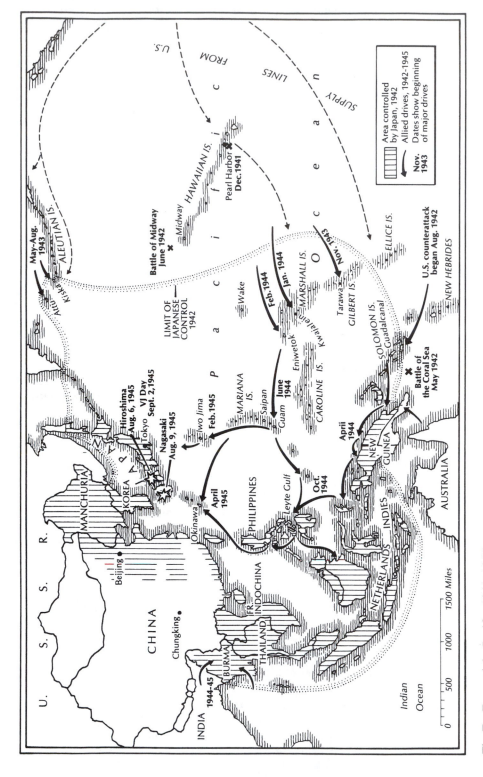

The Far East and the Pacific, 1941–1945

king mountain redoubt, was cut off from land communications with the outside world when the Japanese closed the Burma road to India.

From the beginning of the Pacific war it was certain that Japan could pose no serious threat to the national existence of Great Britain and the United States. Britain's Mediterranean-Indian Ocean lifeline to Asia had been superseded in importance by her Atlantic lifeline to North America, which was kept open by Allied convoys and antisubmarine warfare against Hitler's U-boats. Not even the most fanatical warlord in Tokyo deluded himself into believing that Japan had the capability of projecting its power across the Pacific to the American west coast. That delusion was confined to politicians on the American coast, who persuaded the Roosevelt administration to authorize in February 1942 the forced evacuation and internment of 120,000 Japanese-Americans in California, Oregon, and Washington on the grounds that they represented a fifth column of potential value to a Japanese invasion force.

The day after the Pearl Harbor attack, the United States Congress declared war on Japan with only one dissenting vote.* Great Britain soon followed with declarations of war against Japan. Nazi Germany was not required by its alliance with Japan to enter a war that Japan had initiated and Hitler had no military plans to fight the United States while his armies were fully engaged with the Red Army deep in Soviet territory. But the German dictator decided for his own reasons to demonstrate solidarity with his Japanese allies by ordering the Reichstag to declare war on the United States on December 11. Germany's Italian ally promptly followed suit. The American and British governments agreed that Germany was the main enemy and must be dealt with first. The Europe-first strategy relegated the Pacific war to the background. The Anglo-Americans waged their bombing campaign against Germany in preparation for the cross-Channel assault on Hitler's Fortress Europe, while the Soviet Union honored its nonaggression pact with Japan in order to concentrate its forces against the German armies in European Russia.

The expanding Japanese empire reached its limit within the first year of the Pacific war. In June 1942 the Japanese fleet suffered its first major defeat at the hands of the American navy as it vainly attempted to seize Midway Island west of Hawaii. From September 1942 to February 1943 Japanese efforts to reach Australia, the principal base of Anglo-American operations in the South Pacific theater, were turned back in a fierce jungle campaign in New Guinea and Guadalcanal. The strategy of the American counteroffensive against Japan consisted of a two-pronged drive. The first was an island-hopping campaign by the navy across the central Pacific spearheaded by the aircraft carriers that had been missed at Pearl Harbor by the Japanese bombers. The American fleet commanded by Admiral Chester Nimitz sailed across the central Pacific to gain control of the Marshall, Mariana, and Caroline islands (which Japan had received from Germany as mandates at the 1919 peace conference and used as bases for its eastward naval assaults). The second was a drive by the American army under General Douglas MacArthur along the northern coast of New Guinea and other islands in the vicinity toward the Philippines. By the summer of 1944 American naval forces advancing westward had reached the island of Saipan in the Marianas, from which the first land-based bombing raids of Japa-

---

*Congresswoman Jeanette Rankin of Montana, a pacifist who had voted against the resolution declaring war against Germany in 1917, cast the sole "no" vote.

nese cities were launched by the autumn of that year. In October MacArthur's forces landed on Leyte Island in the Philippines, and retook Manila in February. The two prongs of the American counteroffensive converged on the island of Okinawa in April; then, as the defeat of Germany in Europe permitted the redeployment of Allied troops and material to the Pacific, the Americans used the Okinawa base to launch the greatest air offensive in history against the major cities of Japan. During the spring and summer of 1945 these land- and carrier-based raids by the U.S. Army Air Force's enormous new B-29 bombers, supported by shelling from United States battleships operating with impunity off the Japanese coast, destroyed or immobilized the remnants of the Japanese navy, shattered Japanese industry, and cut off the Japanese home islands from their supplies and military forces abroad.

Despite the military setbacks that the Japanese forces faced on all fronts, they fought back with a tenacity and a bravery that have rarely been equaled in the history of warfare. This extraordinary fighting spirit was amply demonstrated in the last two major battles of the Pacific War. The first took place on the small island of Iwo Jima, which is located 660 miles south of Tokyo. The island was a prime target for U.S. military strategists because it had served as an early warning station that radioed reports of approaching enemy aircraft to the mainland, enabling Japanese air defenses to prepare for the bomber raids that the American Army Air Force had been conducting from its bases in the Mariana islands. The 22,000 Japanese soldiers stationed on the little island were instructed by their superiors in Tokyo to inflict heavy casualties on U.S. forces in order to discourage an invasion of the home islands. After massive bombardment and shelling from naval guns, 30,000 U.S. Marines waded ashore on the island on February 19, 1945, and engaged the Japanese defenders in a bloody campaign that finally ended on March 26. U.S. casualties totaled more than 25,000, including 7,000 dead. Of the 22,000 Japanese defenders of Iwo Jima, only 1,000 were taken prisoner. The rest had gone down fighting for the fatherland and the emperor.

The second decisive battle in the latter stages of the Pacific War began less than a week after Iwo Jima was conquered by the Americans. It was fought on the island of Okinawa in the Ryukyu chain running southwest from the Japanese home island of Kyushu toward Taiwan. As noted above, Okinawa was sought by the U.S. military command as a base for the launching of a strategic bombing campaign against the cities of the Japanese mainland. The invasion force of 60,000 U.S. Marine and Army troops that landed on Okinawa on April 1 met no resistance: The commander of the 100,000 Japanese troops on the island had assembled his men in caves and tunnels in ridges above the landing beaches in preparation for a fight to the death that would inflict heavy casualties on the invader. In the meantime, hundreds of Japanese suicide aircraft (kamikaze) attacked the American fleet of over 1,300 vessels that was shelling the island in support of the ground troops, sinking 30 ships and damaging 164 others. After a furious campaign of hand-to-hand combat, the American forces finally claimed victory at the end of June. But more than 38,000 American soldiers had been wounded, and 12,000 were killed or missing. More than 100,000 Japanese defenders perished, including several (including the commanding general) by ritual suicide (kari-kiri).

The fanatical determination of the Japanese military forces to die in defense of these two small islands, together with the very high casualties that the U.S. forces had to endure in order to defeat them, caused great apprehension in Washington. With the casualty fig-

Japanese soldier walks through Hiroshima after the atomic bomb devastated the city on August 6, 1945: The bomb, nicknamed "Little Boy,'" was created using uranium-232. Hiroshima was one of four cities chosen as possible targets because they had been relatively untouched by the war and would therefore provide unmistakable evidence of the new weapon's destructive force, prompting the Japanese government to surrender unconditionally. *(National Archives)*

ures of Iwo Jima and Okinawa fresh in their minds, officials worried about the price that might have to be paid in American lives during the amphibious invasion of the Japanese mainland that was already being planned in the event that the Japanese government refused to read the handwriting on the wall and capitulate. Meanwhile, forces were at work in Tokyo to bring an end to the war before the Americans arrived on the beaches of the Japanese mainland. Acknowledging the certainty of defeat, the emperor formally urged the Supreme Council in June to approach the Allied governments for peace terms. The military and naval leaders in power refused to face the inevitability of the collapse of their grandiose dreams: They vainly attempted to arrange for Soviet mediation in favor of a conditional surrender that would enable them to preserve their positions of prestige and authority. In the meantime, a peace faction within Japan cautiously advocated ending the war on the sole condition that the titular authority of the emperor be preserved. But the United States government reaffirmed its demand for the unconditional surrender of Japan that had been formulated at the wartime conferences in Casablanca and Cairo in 1943. The formal definition of this unconditional surrender was issued on July 26, in the so-called Potsdam Declaration: Japan was to be stripped of its empire and occupied militarily until it had been transformed into a peaceful nation. The future status of the emperor, that symbolic issue of such emotional importance to the Japanese people, was left ambiguous, but the consequence of a Japanese refusal was not: It was to be "prompt and utter destruction."

The government in Tokyo failed to respond to this ultimatum, probably because such ominous threats were common fare in the propaganda warfare of the time. In any case, the military and naval policymakers who wielded decisive authority in Japan were determined to wage a pitiless struggle to the finish in defense of the home islands, while the position of the moderate peace faction had been undermined by the uncompromising language of the Potsdam Declaration. The United States thereupon proceeded to unleash upon Japan a devastating weapon of destruction that had been developed in total secrecy by American and European émigré scientists in the course of the war. On August 6 the first atomic bomb was detonated over Hiroshima, Japan's eighth largest city, with a population of 200,000, instantly killing over 70,000, seriously injuring as many more, and leveling four square miles of homes and factories. Three days later a second bomb was dropped on Nagasaki with similar results. In the meantime the Soviet Union, honoring its pledge made at the Yalta Conference to enter the conflict in the Far East within three months of Germany's surrender, declared war on Japan and dispatched military forces to Japanese-occupied Manchuria.

The atomic bombardment of the two Japanese cities, unlike the conventional bombing of German cities and the firebombing of Tokyo earlier in the war, had a devastating effect on civilian and military morale. For the first time since the beginning of the Pacific War, the Japanese ruling elite was stunned into the realization that the conflict must be ended immediately. Spurred by these devastating events into assuming authority he had previously shrunk from exercising, Emperor Hirohito broke a deadlock in the Supreme Council on August 10 by voting to accept the Potsdam Declaration as the basis for Japan's surrender. The sole condition specified by Tokyo was that the emperor's right to retain his throne as the titular leader of his people not be prejudiced. Upon receiving American assurances to this effect, the Japanese government accepted the terms of surrender on August 15 and formally capitulated to General MacArthur on September 2 aboard the American battleship *Missouri* in Tokyo Bay.

President Truman's decision to drop two atomic bombs on Japan in August 1945 ushered in the nuclear age. It was the first and, thus far, only time that nuclear weapons have been used. The question of whether, once available, they would be employed seems never to have been raised by officials in Washington from the advent of the $2 billion nuclear weapons research program in August 1942—the so-called Manhattan Project—to the first successful test explosion in the arid desert in New Mexico on July 16, 1945. Truman had been solemnly warned by his military advisers that an amphibious invasion of the Japanese islands would cost many thousands of American casualties and prolong the war for another six months. The temptation to terminate the conflict immediately in a manner that would sacrifice not a single American life outweighed whatever moral qualms American policymakers may have entertained about the particular type of weapon used. In any case, the indiscriminate slaughter of civilian populations by conventional aerial bombardment had become an acceptable form of warfare during the Second World War. More people perished in the conventional bombing raids on Dresden and Tokyo than at Hiroshima or Nagasaki.

Subsequent critics of Truman's decision have contended that the same military objective could have been achieved by unveiling the new weapon in a demonstration test on an uninhabited Pacific atoll in the presence of Japanese observers. Defenders of the decision counter this argument with the reminder that (1) the scientists who had developed the two bombs were unable to guarantee that they would detonate, and (2) at the time the Nagasaki bomb was dropped no others were immediately available; the highly publicized testing of a "dud" would, according to this argument, have seriously damaged the credibility of American military power, stiffened Japanese resistance, and prolonged the war. Apart from these hypothetical disagreements about the feasibility of a demonstration nuclear test as a means of terminating the Asian war without the devastation that actually transpired, one thing is certain: The capitulation of Japan could have been assured by the imposition of a total naval blockade coupled with bombing of its internal transportation network. This would most likely have starved it into submission within a few months by depriving its people of the food and fuel they needed to survive.

But in two or three months time the United States might well have been compelled, as it had been in Europe, to share the prerogative of filling the power vacuum created by the collapse of the defeated enemy with the Soviet Union. By the end of the war, the Red Army had swept into Manchuria and into Korea down to the 38th parallel, and had occupied the Kurile Islands and the southern half of Sakhalin Island. Stalin's conditions for Russian entry in the war against Japan, which had been earnestly sought by the United States before the development of the atomic bomb, included the recovery of all of the territory and privileges that had been lost by Russia after its defeat by Japan in 1905.

Thus, in addition to the demonstrable military advantages of compelling a Japanese capitulation without the necessity of mounting a costly invasion of its home islands, a diplomatic factor may have reinforced the American government's determination to employ its powerful new weapon as soon as it was demonstrated to be operational by the successful test explosion in New Mexico in July 1945. The diplomatic tug-of-war between the United States and its Russian ally concerning the political reorganization of the postwar world had already begun. Upon learning of the test during the Potsdam Conference of the Big Three wartime leaders, Truman informed Stalin that the United States had developed a new weapon "of unusual destructive force," a fact already known to the Russian leader through his espionage network. Some historians have suggested that Truman was eager to wield the atomic weapon against Japan in order to frighten the Soviet Union into granting political concessions in Europe as well as to terminate the war in the Far East before Russia could participate in the victory in that theater and therefore claim a role in the postwar military occupation of Japan.

In contrast to the situation in defeated Germany, the United States was able to assert its unchallenged position of primacy in defeated Japan. Beginning on August 28 American military forces were landed on the home islands to occupy key cities and supervise the disarmament of Japanese military forces. With the formal surrender on September 2, supreme authority passed into the hands of General Douglas MacArthur in the name of the Allied powers. Soviet requests for the right to share in the occupation of the northern Japanese island of Hokkaido, which lay only twenty-five miles from the Russian-occupied Sakhalin

Island, were turned aside. Though ostensibly acting on behalf of the victorious coalition, the United States proclaimed its intention to manage the occupation of Japan without the assistance of its wartime allies and administer it as a single political unit. The acrimonious Soviet-American disputes over the treatment of postwar Germany would not be reenacted over the treatment of postwar Japan: The overwhelming American air and naval superiority in the western Pacific enabled Washington, through its powerful proconsul in Tokyo, to enjoy undisputed supremacy there.

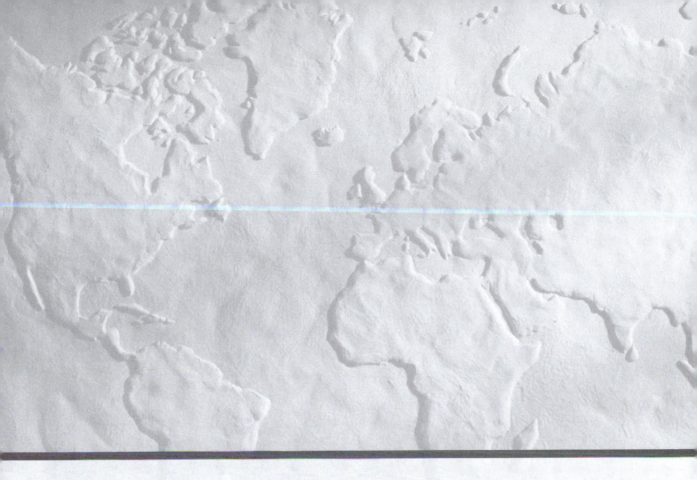

Part Two

THE COLD WAR BETWEEN THE SUPER-POWERS (1945–1985)

8

THE FORMATION OF THE BIPOLAR WORLD IN THE TRUMAN–STALIN ERA (1945–1953)

THE POLITICAL DIVISION OF EUROPE

When the advancing armies of the United States and the Soviet Union met at the Elbe River in the heart of Germany on April 25, 1945, the exhilarating prospect of victory and peace momentarily overshadowed the political disagreements between their respective governments that had surfaced at the Crimea conference two and a half months earlier. Within a week word had arrived of Hitler's death by his own hand and the capitulation of the German armies in Italy and Austria. The formal surrender by German military authorities on May 7 merely confirmed what had been known for months to be a foregone conclusion: the collapse of the Nazi imperium in Europe. Though the American soldiers encamped along the bank of the Elbe River and in other liberated regions of the continent anticipated redeployment to the Far East for the final drive against the receding military forces of Japan, the end of the most destructive military contest in history was, at long last, in sight.

The convergence of American and Russian military power at the center of the devastated continent of Europe in the spring of 1945 signified something of critical significance for the future of the world beyond the immediate reality of Germany's defeat. Amid the universal expressions of relief on "Victory in Europe" (VE) day, there remained a number of disturbing facts about the way in which the war against Hitler's Third Reich had been brought to a close that were to prevent the restoration of the peacetime conditions for which all of the belligerent populations of the war-ravaged continent desperately yearned.

Foremost among these postwar realities was the disappearance of all forms of indigenous political authority and military power in Central Europe as the German state disintegrated and its war machine ground to a halt. This condition had been foreordained by the Allied leaders' decision to impose upon the vanquished enemy an unconditional surrender that would assure the instantaneous destruction of all German political and military institutions. The unprecedented brutality of the Nazi occupation of Europe had inspired in the victorious coalition the determination to rid the continent once and for all of the scourge of German power. The war against Hitler had assumed the character of a moral crusade against a monstrous evil that had to be subdued and then permanently eliminated for the benefit of humanity. In striking contrast to Wilson's discriminating policy at the end of the First World War, Roosevelt declined to distinguish between the objectionable regime of the enemy state and the civilian population that it had ruled. The Führer was regarded merely as the agent of a German people whose instinctual propensity for aggression disqualified it from playing any role whatsoever in the postwar reorganization of Europe. The dissolution of the German administrative and military apparatus by the Allied powers, followed by their refusal to countenance the prompt reconstitution of a German successor regime, produced the vacuum in Central Europe that Churchill had foreseen before the Yalta Conference. This vacuum was inevitably to be filled by the military power of the advancing armies that converged on the center of the continent from west and east in the spring of 1945.

In this way the informal partition of liberated Europe into Western and Soviet spheres was dictated by the military situation at the moment of Germany's collapse. Each of the two zones eventually adopted political institutions, economic practices, and foreign policies that reflected the preferences and influences of its liberator. France, Belgium, Greece, and Italy, in spite of the presence of powerful Communist movements that had played a significant role in resisting the German occupation of their countries, reestablished Western-style parliamentary systems and capitalist economic structures while adapting their foreign policies to the Anglo-American vision of the postwar world. The states on the eastern half of the continent, despite their historic hostility to communism and nationalistic antipathy for Russia, adopted Soviet political and economic models and supported the Kremlin's foreign policy goals under the watchful eyes of the Russian occupation armies and their civilian collaborators among the indigenous population.

This ideological bifurcation of Europe did not occur overnight. In the Soviet sphere, non-Communist political parties were permitted to operate and non-Communist leaders to participate in coalition governments in all of the Eastern European states for a few years after the war; similarly, the Communist parties of France, Italy, and Belgium were not only tolerated but allowed to hold cabinet posts in the early postwar coalitions in those countries. But one salient feature of the postwar political situation in Europe eventually caused the division of that continent into two mutually antagonistic blocs of states respectively identified with the superpower whose military forces had emancipated them from German rule: This was the unwavering determination of the Soviet government to establish a ring of subservient client states in Eastern Europe along the broad invasion route stretching from the western shore of the Black Sea to the eastern shore of the Baltic that had brought marauding armies to the heart of Russia twice within the memory of most of its citizens still alive in 1945.

We have seen how Stalin's insistence on securing border rectifications at the expense of Finland, Poland, and Romania to enhance the security of Russia's western frontier had won the reluctant assent of the Western powers. But the Kremlin's subsequent attempt to promote, through political intimidation backed by the presence of the Red Army, the installation of pro-Soviet regimes in the states of Eastern Europe beyond the newly expanded frontiers was to provoke increasing opposition from Washington. In time a momentous evolution in the strategic thinking of policymakers in the Truman administration took place. American officials began to ponder the implications of the developments unfolding on the eastern half of the European continent in light of historical precedent and geographical context. Great Britain and, belatedly, the United States had intervened in the two European wars of the twentieth century to restore the balance of power that had been upset by Germany. The temporary elimination of German power at the end of the First World War had been preceded a year earlier by the temporary disappearance of Russian power. The simultaneous weakness of Germany and Russia in the decade of the 1920s had enabled the small states of Eastern Europe to preserve their independence from both of their potentially powerful neighbors with the support and encouragement of France. Hitler's subsequent bid for German hegemony in Europe had also resulted in the erasure of German power, but this time Russian power had been projected into the political and military void of Eastern Europe at a time when no nation or coalition of nations on the Western half of the continent was strong enough to balance it. The tough-minded realism of geopolitics, so familiar to European strategists and statesmen, began to replace the Wilsonian reveries of Roosevelt in the minds of the foreign policy advisers of the new American president: Russia was rapidly acquiring control of the heartland of Eurasia. The military exhaustion and economic distress of the nations along the western rim of Europe exposed them to the threat of Soviet domination as well. A Russian-controlled continental empire stretching from the Sea of Japan to the Atlantic and from the Arctic to the Aegean would be better positioned to mount a drive for world dominion than Nazi Germany had been at the height of its power. What may have appeared to Stalin as a legitimate attempt to bolster the security of Russia's vulnerable western frontier by the formation of compliant buffer states beyond it was increasingly interpreted in Washington as the beginning of a Russian drive for continental hegemony on the road to mastery of the globe. The ominous prophecy of the geopolitical theorist Mackinder returned to haunt those who had confidently expected that the end of the fighting would bring peace and security: "Who rules east Europe commands the Heartland; who rules the Heartland commands the World-Island; who rules the World-Island rules the world."

The establishment of Russian hegemony over the reconstituted states of Eastern Europe after the war occurred because the only nation capable of preventing it had disengaged militarily from the European continent. At the time of Germany's defeat the numerical strength of the armed forces of the United States exceeded 12 million. By the end of 1947 that number had fallen to 1.4 million as a consequence of the abolition of universal military conscription and a drastic reduction in the size of the professional armed services. The demobilization of America's military forces and the dismantling of its war industries transpired at a time when the Soviet Union kept over 4 million battle-seasoned veterans under arms and retained the formidable arsenal of weaponry with which it had driven the German army from Moscow to Berlin.

The reasons for this precipitous disengagement of American military power from Europe after the Second World War are easy to appreciate. The American public, accustomed to small volunteer armies in peacetime, had no inclination to tolerate the retention of an American military presence in postwar Europe beyond the token forces required for occupation duty in Germany and Austria. The United States had entered the European war for the purpose of destroying the Nazi regime and eliminating German military power from the continent. Once those two objectives had been achieved, only an American government endowed with superhuman powers of persuasion could have induced its war-weary citizens to bear the enormous costs and manifold inconveniences of maintaining large military forces across the Atlantic solely for the purpose of balancing the undiminished military might of a nation that had so recently been hailed as an indispensable ally against Hitler.

The American public's inclination to "bring the boys home," reflected in expressions of congressional sentiment and recorded in the opinion polls of the period, was entirely consistent with the Roosevelt administration's master plan for the political organization of the postwar world. The American commander in chief during World War II shared the optimistic expectation of his predecessor during World War I that the defeat of Germany would herald a new era in which international conciliation would supplant the operation of the balance of power as the mechanism for the preservation of world order. The United Nations Organization (UN), conceived by American, British, and Russian representatives at the Dumbarton Oaks Conference in the autumn of 1944 and formally established by the delegates of fifty states meeting in San Francisco from April through June 1945, was designed to supersede the discredited League of Nations and resume its noble purpose with more effective means. Since both the United States and the Soviet Union shared, along with Great Britain, France, and China, permanent representation on the new organization's decision-making body, the Security Council, it was widely assumed that such disagreements as might arise among the great powers over the postwar political settlement could be amicably adjudicated in the United Nations without recourse to the old practices of power politics and regional alliance systems that had been so decisively discredited in the recent past.

Furthermore, the American monopoly on nuclear weapons in the early postwar years reinforced the traditional sense of invulnerability to external aggression that had long nourished the national proclivity for isolationism. The United States had intervened in the two world wars on the assumption that the subjugation of Europe and the control of its resources and Atlantic bases by a single aggressive power would pose an unacceptable threat to the security of the western hemisphere. In the first few years after Hiroshima and Nagasaki, America's ability to devastate the principal cities of any potential aggressor with no risk of retaliation against its own territory seemed to afford a greater degree of protection than even the Atlantic Ocean ever could. Such a condition of strategic omnipotence was scarcely conducive to the sentiment of national insecurity that would have been required to generate broad public support for the assumption of extensive military commitments abroad so soon after the end of the war. Particularly in light of Roosevelt's tacit endorsement of Soviet predominance in the half of Europe that was liberated by the Red Army, his successor was in no position to contest the Kremlin's exercise of that prerogative beyond innocuous expressions of displeasure at the inevitable violations of the rights of the populations concerned.

The Truman administration forcefully challenged the expansion of Soviet power only when it appeared to cross the demarcation line separating the two spheres of influence that had been tacitly recognized by the Allied leaders at the wartime conferences. During the years 1946 and 1947 a series of political developments along the southern rim of

Eurasia was viewed by Western leaders as evidence of a coordinated Soviet effort to attain one of the traditional objectives of Russian foreign policy: expansion southward toward the eastern Mediterranean and the Persian Gulf, a region historically under the sway of British power.

The site of the first direct confrontation between the Soviet Union and the Western powers was Iran, a country whose strategic location had rendered it the object of Russian and British rivalry at the end of the nineteenth century. As we have seen, these two imperial powers had jointly partitioned the country into spheres of influence in the decade prior to the First World War. The collapse of the tsarist empire and the advent of the Bolshevik regime had temporarily resulted in a diminution of Russian influence in Iran; Great Britain proceeded to exploit the vast reserves of petroleum that had recently been discovered there and attempted to establish predominant political influence over the government in Teheran. In August 1941, as Hitler's armies advanced deep into the Soviet Union, Russian and British military forces simultaneously entered Iran and replaced the increasingly pro-German regime of Reza Shah with a more compliant government nominally headed by his young son, Mohammed Reza Pahlevi. According to the terms of an Anglo-Russian-Iranian treaty concluded on January 29, 1942, Russian troops were stationed in northern Iran and British troops in the south to protect the vital supply route from the Persian Gulf to the Russian frontier along which British and American arms were transported to the Soviet Union. Both foreign occupation forces, as well as the American contingent that later joined the British troops in the southern zone, were to be withdrawn within six months of the end of the war. A few months after Germany's surrender, Soviet-backed insurgents launched a separatist revolt in the northwestern province of Azerbaijan bordering on the Soviet Union. The Russian occupation army prevented the Iranian government from suppressing the insurgency by denying its military forces access to the rebellious province. In November a provincial assembly in Azerbaijan declared its autonomy, a move that was widely regarded as the first step toward the absorption of the province by the Soviet Republic of Azerbaijan across the border. In the meantime, the Iranian government had received a Soviet request for a concession to prospect for oil in the northern part of the country.

Interpreting these Soviet moves as the beginning of a campaign to obtain effective control of the entire country, including its rich petroleum reserves and its ports on the Persian Gulf, the British and American governments applied vigorous diplomatic pressure on the Kremlin to terminate its Iranian adventure. But the Red Army, alone among the three wartime occupation forces, delayed its evacuation beyond the March 2, 1946, deadline. The resulting firestorm of criticism from the British and American governments compelled the Kremlin to negotiate a settlement with the Iranian prime minister: In exchange for Iran's pledge to grant Azerbaijan a substantial degree of autonomy and to award a concession to a Soviet-Iranian company to search for oil, Stalin withdrew his forces from the northern province on May 9. After the Red Army's withdrawal, the Iranian parliament, emboldened by the vociferous expressions of Anglo-American support, declined to ratify the agreement that had been concluded under duress with the Kremlin. In the meantime an American military mission had arrived in Teheran and arrangements had been made for the purchase of American military equipment by the Iranian government. The diplomatic setback suffered by the Soviet Union in the Iranian crisis of 1946 was a direct consequence of the Truman administration's decision to join Great Britain in protecting this historic object of Russian expansionist ambition. Washington's determination to bolster the Pahlevi regime set the stage for the establishment seven years later of an intimate security link between Washington and Teheran that was to last for a quarter of a century. In a more general sense, it heralded America's determination to resist the expansion of Soviet influence throughout Eurasia.

Just as Soviet activities in northern Iran during 1946 were viewed in Washington as evidence of the Kremlin's renewal of traditional Russian expansionism toward the Persian Gulf, simultaneous Soviet pressures on Iran's neighbor Turkey appeared to rekindle Russian ambitions for a geo-political offensive into the eastern Mediterranean. On March 19, 1945, Moscow had formally denounced the Turko-Soviet treaty of friendship concluded in 1925, which had established close political and economic collaboration between these two historic enemies and included reciprocal pledges of nonaggression. On June 7, 1945, Foreign Commissar Vyacheslav Molotov presented the Turkish ambassador to Moscow with a set of demands, spelled out in more detail the following June, that collectively constituted a substantial infringement on Turkish sovereignty. These included the cession of territory in the Caucasus annexed by Russia in 1878 and reacquired by Turkey after the First World War, the revision of the Montreux Convention of 1936 governing the Turkish Straits so as to establish joint Russian-Turkish jurisdiction over this vital waterway, and the leasing of Soviet bases on its shores to ensure its defense.

Readers of these pages need no reminder of Russia's historic interest in obtaining effective control of the outlet of the Black Sea to the Mediterranean. As had been the case with Soviet advances in Eastern Europe at the expense of Finland, the Baltic states, Poland, and Romania, as well as in Manchuria at the expense of China, Stalin's diplomatic offensive against Turkey represented an attempt to restore territory or privileges previously possessed by or promised to the Russian state. Not even the demand for de facto control of the Dardenelles was new. In a different form it had been secretly granted to the tsarist regime by its Anglo-French allies during the First World War before the Bolshevik Revolution resulted in its repudiation. More recently, Molotov had tried in vain to secure Germany's endorsement of Russian designs on Turkey's Caucasian frontier and the Straits during the period of the Nazi-Soviet Pact. Stalin had insistently raised the matter of the Straits with Churchill at Moscow in October 1944, with Roosevelt at Yalta, and with Truman at Potsdam, all without concrete result. His argument was framed in entirely defensive terms: Turkey, which had remained neutral during the war despite British and Russian bids for an alliance and permitted the sale of strategically important chrome to Germany for fear of antagonizing Hitler, was too weak to prevent powers unfriendly to the Soviet Union from sending their warships into the Black Sea. But to the United States, Stalin's demand represented nothing less than the revival of the old dream of a Russian breakthrough to the Mediterranean at Turkey's expense, and therefore had to be resisted with the same firmness that had been displayed by Great Britain in the days when it was still capable of playing such a role.

In short, the Truman administration's response to the Turkish crisis of 1945–46 reflected the same determination to replace Britain as the principal guarantor of Russia's confinement along the southern rim of Eurasia that had prompted its vigorous resistance to Soviet pressure on Iran. To Washington, as to London during the era when the "eastern question" had preoccupied the architects of British foreign policy, Russian control of the Straits would entail domination of the eastern Mediterranean. This in turn would signify command of the vital commercial waterway linking Europe to the Orient and afford easy access to the valuable mineral resources of North Africa and the Middle East. Accordingly, when Ankara's indignant rejection of Moscow's demands precipitated a violent campaign against Turkey in the Soviet press and the deployment of twenty-five Russian divisions on the Caucasian frontier, the Truman administration resolved to bolster the beleaguered Turkish regime. In the summer of 1946 Washington reinforced the U.S. naval task force in the eastern Mediterranean as a demonstrative show of force and later announced that a portion of the American fleet would be permanently stationed there. In the face of this ostentatious display of American naval power, which was implicitly reinforced by the American monopoly on atomic weapons, Moscow backed down at the Turkish Straits just as it was being dislodged from northern Iran, though the extent of the Soviet retrenchment was not apparent until much later.

During the Russian-American showdown over Moscow's demands on Ankara, acute domestic unrest across the Aegean in Greece was viewed in London and Washington as a third theater of the putative Russian campaign of southward expansion already in evidence in Iran and Turkey. It will be recalled that upon the evacuation of German occupation forces in Greece in November 1944, a fierce internal struggle had erupted between the conservative faction of the Greek resistance movement loyal to the monarchy and the Communist partisan organization. The intervention of British military forces in the winter of 1944–45 resulted in a truce concluded between the two factions in February 1945 as well as an agreement stipulating a referendum on the question of the restoration of the monarchy and national elections under Allied supervision. The elections of March 1946 were boycotted by the leftist political organizations and therefore produced a comfortable majority for the royalist party that was actively supported by the British. In the summer of 1946, at the height of the Turkish crisis, thousands of Greek Communists concentrated in the north renewed their guerrilla warfare against the pro-Western government in Athens with the encouragement and material assistance of the newly installed Communist regimes across the border in Yugoslavia, Albania, and Bulgaria. When the national referendum in September resulted in a large majority in favor of the restoration of the monarchy, the conflict raging on the Greek peninsula assumed the aspect of an ideological confrontation pitting the British-backed royalist regime in Athens against the Communist guerrilla movement in the north that was supplied and supported by the adjacent Communist states.

In this sense the Greek drama was reminiscent of the earlier struggle in Poland between the pro-Western and pro-Soviet factions of the resistance movement. But there were two critical differences between the Polish and Greek situations that determined their divergent outcomes. First of all, the geographical position of Greece was decisively favorable to the pro-Western government and its British protectors. Whereas Poland's common border with Russia and its forbidding distance from the Western powers foreordained the triumph of the pro-Soviet Polish faction backed by the Red Army, the proximity of the Greek peninsula to the British bases in the Mediterranean constituted a major liability for the Communist partisans in their struggle with the Athens regime. Moreover, it will be recalled that Stalin had excluded Greece from the Russian sphere of influence in his wartime bargain with Churchill and had displayed no enthusiasm for the Communist insurrection there in the winter of 1944–45. On the contrary, the Soviet leader instructed the Greek Communists to cooperate with the British-backed government in the same way that he had urged restraint on the Communist parties of France and Italy that were participating in governing coalitions dominated by pro-Western groups. The principal foreign supporter and supplier of the Greek Communist insurgency was Yugoslavia, which, under the leadership of its charismatic strongman, Marshal Tito, was already displaying the taste for independent activity that was soon to result in a total break with Moscow.

It may be supposed, from what is now known about the postwar foreign policy goals of the Kremlin, that the motivation for this Soviet caution in the Greek civil war was twofold. It reflected Stalin's disinclination to favor the establishment by indigenous partisan forces of an independent Communist state beyond the effective reach of Russian military power and political control. This tendency appears to have determined his simultaneous reluctance to offer unqualified support to the Communist forces of Tito in Yugoslavia and Mao Zedong in China in their respective struggles for power against anti-Communist rivals. An additional source of Soviet hesitation seems to have been the apprehension that a Communist takeover in a country specifically allotted to the Western sphere of influence was certain to provoke sharp reactions from Washington and London with potentially unpleasant consequences for the Soviet Union.

As it turned out, the capacity of Great Britain to fulfill its historic function as the guardian of Greek independence had been severely impaired by the economic crisis that gripped this erstwhile world power at the end of the Second World War. The drain on British reserves of gold and foreign exchange occasioned by the requirements of financing the war against the Axis had been partially mitigated by lend-lease assistance from the United States. Following the termination of this wartime aid, an American emergency loan of $3.75 billion was extended to Britain in 1946 on the assumption that this would suffice to cover its short-term needs until the restoration of its export trade would produce the foreign exchange required to finance essential imports. But the proceeds of this loan were used to pay for emergency food and fuel imports, depleting British reserves amid the worst weather conditions in recorded history during the winter of 1946–47. The national transportation system ground to a halt, the shortage of coal forced the closing of factories and temporary cutoffs of electricity, and the freezing of winter crops led to the rationing of food.

A nation in such dire straits was hardly in a position to furnish the military and economic assistance required by the Greek government to quell the Communist insurrection in the north. On the twenty-first of February 1947, the British Foreign Office officially informed the American State Department of its intention to terminate all financial assistance to Greece and Turkey and to remove the forty thousand British troops from Greece as of the following March 31 on account of Britain's own economic trauma. Remarking that both of the recipient countries were desperately in need of foreign aid to stave off total economic collapse as well as to finance the reorganization and reequipment of their armed forces to preserve their security, the British government expressed the hope that the United States would be able to assume the obligation it was about to relinquish. In this dramatic diplomatic communication the government of the greatest empire the world had ever seen conceded the beginning of its demise. The recession of British power along the vulnerable lifeline to that empire, from Gibraltar to Singapore, had produced a vacuum along the southern shores of Eurasia comparable in importance to the vacuum in Eastern Europe produced by the crumbling of German power there. Britain's inability to continue to bear the financial burden of maintaining its far-flung garrisons and bolstering friendly regimes along the lifeline seemed to present the United States with the choice of substituting American for British power in that region or of passively permitting Soviet power to fill the void.

The American president took up the challenge on March 12, 1947, in a historic address before a special joint session of Congress: The United States government declared its intention to supplant Great Britain as the guarantor of the economic viability and military security of Greece and Turkey. Congressional authorization was sought, and duly obtained, for the disbursement of $250 million and $150 million worth of military and economic assistance to the governments of Athens and Ankara, respectively, as well as for the dispatch of American advisers to these countries to assist in their economic stabilization and military reorganization. As noted above, the Soviet claims on Turkey simply disappeared from public discourse after the American show of force in the eastern Mediterranean. In Greece, the civil war petered out during the years 1948–49, as the Royal Greek Army, organized in close collaboration with the American military mission and lavishly supplied with American munitions, swept northward to occupy all of the rebel strongholds in the mountains and force the Communist partisans into exile in Bulgaria and Albania. The Greek Communists' chief benefactor, Tito's Yugoslavia, had sealed their fate by closing its frontier and terminating all assistance to the insurgents in July 1948 after its exclusion from the international Communist movement the previous month.

Embedded in Truman's speech of March 12 was a single sentence that affirmed that the American government had no intention of confining its newly adopted program of foreign assistance to the narrow objective of helping the governments of Greece and Turkey to overcome their immediate difficulties: "I believe," Truman declared, "that it must be the policy of the United States to support free peoples who are resisting subjugation by armed minorities or by outside pressures." Implicit in this presidential declaration, which subsequently acquired the designation "Truman Doctrine," was the pledge to employ the economic resources of the United States to bolster friendly nations all along the periphery of the Soviet bloc that appeared susceptible to pressure from their powerful neighbor or to insurgency by domestic Communist movements connected by ideological affinity to the Soviet Union. The power vacuum in the Balkans and Southwest Asia created by the collapse of the Pax Brittanica seemed in danger of becoming filled by Soviet power. This circumstance presented the Truman administration with an emergency that was promptly met, as we have seen, by the dispatch of American assistance to the governments of Greece, Turkey, and Iran. But the power vacuums at the two opposite ends of the Soviet empire, in Europe after the collapse of Germany and in East Asia after the defeat of Japan, represented even more serious threats to American security than did the prospect of Soviet domination of the eastern Mediterranean and Southwest Asia in the eyes of those highly placed officials in the Truman administration who were engaged in this fundamental reshaping of American foreign policy.

It therefore became the task of this handful of men—led by George Kennan, Dean Acheson, and William Clayton at the State Department and James Forrestal at the Pentagon—to develop a rationale for a coordinated response to Soviet expansionist pressures wherever they might occur that would persuade the Republican-controlled Congress and the American public at large of the pressing necessity to abandon the tradition of peacetime isolationism and retrenchment. The most articulate and influential enunciation of the

George Frost Kennan (1904–2005): As the first director of the State Department's Policy Planning Staff from 1947 to 1950, Kennan provided the intellectual justification for the Truman administration's strategy of "containment" of the Soviet Union in the early days of the Cold War. He later complained that his emphasis on economic and political measures to thwart Soviet expansion had been superseded by a preoccupation with military power. *(Courtesy of the Library of Congress)*

case for an activist American foreign policy appeared anonymously in the July 1947 issue of the journal *Foreign Affairs* under the heading "The Sources of Soviet Conduct." Composed by Kennan, the director of the newly created Policy Planning Staff of the State Department who had observed Soviet behavior at firsthand in his former post as deputy chief of mission at the American embassy in Moscow, it summarized official government policy as distilled from the high-level discussions conducted in Washington during the recent crises in Iran, Turkey, and Greece. Its message was straightforward and simple: The Soviet Union, for reasons related more to the traditional Russian sense of insecurity than to the messianic goals of Marxist-Leninist ideology, could be expected to probe the weak points beyond its frontiers in an effort to extend the reach of Soviet power in the world. It is in the national interest of the United States to conduct a firm but patient policy of containing the expansion of Soviet power beyond the limits informally established at Yalta by strengthening the political, social, and economic institutions of those countries that had or might become subject to such expansionist pressures. Through the application of such counterpressure the Kremlin would gradually be brought to realize that the cost of such aggressive policies would greatly outweigh any conceivable benefits they might yield. The ultimate result, Kennan confidently predicted, would be the attenuation of the Soviet threat to the vital interests of the United States and the frontline nations, which his policy of resistance was designed to protect.

While this bold reformulation of American policy toward the Soviet Union was being put in press, a dramatic public statement by Secretary of State George C. Marshall delivered at the Harvard University graduation ceremonies on June 5, 1947, directly addressed the particular problem that had preoccupied Kennan as he drafted what came to be known as the doctrine of containment: This was the vulnerability of the Western European countries to Soviet domination caused by their inability to recover from the war-induced dislocations of their economic systems. We have already had occasion to ponder, in connection with the Greco-Turkish crises of 1946–47, the catastrophic consequences of the postwar financial crisis in Great Britain for the recovery of that country's industrial productivity and the resumption of its foreign trade. Economic conditions were far worse in those nations on the continent that had been occupied and economically exploited by Germany and had served as the final battleground for the war in Europe. The continued impoverishment of the countries of Western Europe seemed an open invitation to the Soviet Union to extend its political dominion over them with the connivance of the powerful Communist parties and Communist-controlled labor organizations in countries such as France, Italy, and Belgium. To meet this presumed threat the American secretary of state invited the nations of Europe, including the Soviet Union and its satellites, to prepare a plan for European economic recovery with massive American assistance on the basis of permanent economic cooperation among themselves.

The inclusion of the Soviet bloc in this unprecedented offer of foreign economic assistance from Washington prompted the governments of France and Great Britain to solicit the Kremlin's participation in a conference in Paris at the end of June to draw up a collective response to the American initiative. On June 26 Soviet Foreign Commissar Molotov arrived in the French capital accompanied by eighty-nine economic specialists, apparently prepared to give serious consideration to the American proposal. But after a few days of fruitless negotiation, Molotov and his entourage abandoned the conference while the Soviet government denounced the project and forbade the governments of its East European "protégés" to have anything to do with it.

The grounds for the Soviet rejection of what came to be known as the Marshall Plan were twofold. First, in order to collect the pertinent economic statistics and to ensure that the funds disbursed were spent for the purposes intended, the American government had insisted on access to, and some degree of advisory authority over, the internal budgets of the recipient states. These are conditions customarily required of impoverished countries by their prudent foreign bankers, from the era of financial imperialism before the First World War to the current tight-fisted lending policies of the International Monetary Fund. But it was too much to expect of a victorious great power, particularly one as secretive and suspicious as the Soviet Union, to open its books to the prying eyes of American financial officials and to adjust its budgetary policies to spending priorities established in Washington. This requirement was denounced in Moscow as an intolerable infringement on the national sovereignty of the participating states. The investigations of the Marshall Plan administrators would doubtless have revealed how vulnerable the postwar economy of the Soviet Union was, a circumstance that the Kremlin was desperately trying to conceal for reasons of Communist ideology as well as national pride. Moreover, the proviso that most of the Marshall aid be spent for the purchase of American exports prompted Soviet suspicions of an ulterior motive beneath the facade of humanitarian largesse. It appeared to confirm the Leninist prediction of the impending collapse of capitalism and the capitalists' frantic efforts to prevent it: American corporate monopolies, squeezed by the drastic decline in domestic demand for their products as war-related orders dried up, now strove to save themselves by obtaining markets in Europe and subjecting the shattered economies of that continent to American commercial domination. This interpretation even received some confirmation from the mouths of American officials themselves, who tried to sell the Marshall program to Congress by warning that Europe's huge trade deficit with the United States was bound to cause serious difficulties for American exporters unless the chronic "dollar shortage" across the Atlantic could be rectified through the granting of government credits.

Responding to the invitation of the foreign ministers of Britain and France, representatives of all the sixteen European nations outside the Soviet sphere except Spain* assembled in Paris on July 12 to lay the groundwork for a coordinated response to the American government's offer of economic assistance. On September 22 a committee formed at this gathering submitted a plan for a four-year recovery program, which specified the anticipated combined budget deficit of the sixteen participating states. On the basis of the plan, the United States Congress voted by lopsided majorities on April 3, 1948, to appropriate $6 billion to cover the combined deficit for the first year and agreed to make three annual grants later. In mid-April the recipient nations established the Organization for European Economic Cooperation to supervise the allocation of the American aid and promote coordination among the nations that were to receive it. Between 1948 and 1952 the European Recovery Program (as Marshall's brainchild was officially known) supplied grants and credits totaling $13.2 billion, including $3.2 billion to Great Britain and its dependencies, $2.7 billion to France, $1.5 billion to Italy, and $1.4 billion to what in 1949 was to become West Germany.

The economic consequences of the Marshall Plan surpassed the most optimistic expectations of its authors. By 1952, the termination date of the American aid program, European industrial production had risen to 35 percent and agricultural production to 10 percent above the prewar level. From the depths of economic despair the recipient nations of Western Europe embarked on a period of economic expansion that was to bring a degree of prosperity to their populations unimaginable in the dark days of 1947. In the meantime, the donor nation derived great commercial benefits from its financial benevolence, as the Marxist-Leninist critics had forecast; more than two-thirds of the European imports under the plan came from the United States, which meant higher profits for American firms engaged in the export trade as well as more jobs for the workers they employed. It is doubtful that the phenomenal growth of the American economy in the prosperous era of the fifties and early sixties would have occurred without the stimulus provided by orders for its goods and services from the other nations of the industrial world across the Atlantic that were rebuilding their war-torn economies. One must not exaggerate the extent of the American economy's export dependence in the early postwar years. With a huge internal market still capable of absorbing most of its industrial production and a considerable proportion of its agricultural output, the United States still exported less than 10 percent of its gross national product compared to much higher percentages for the genuinely export-dependent nations of Western Europe and Japan. Nevertheless, postwar America had begun to develop an important stake in international trade for the first time in its history. In 1946 America's total exports were almost four times the prewar average of $4 billion per year, and certain sectors of the economy had come to depend on foreign sales for a major proportion of their earnings. The dollars lent or given to the importing nations to finance this expansion of transatlantic trade were repaid many times over in the form of a mutually

---

*Spain was excluded from participation in the Marshall Plan on account of its autocratic political system as well as its pro-Axis sympathies during the Second World War.

The Italian government and the Economic Cooperation Administration that supervised the Marshall Plan join forces to build a new housing project in Matera, Italy: The appearance of the Marshall Plan shield on such construction projects reminded the citizens of the recipient nations of American benevolence, a valuable weapon in the campaign to combat the appeal of communism in Western Europe. *(National Archives)*

beneficial system of commercial links between Western Europe and the United States that complemented their increasingly intimate political ties.

The postwar recovery of the industrialized countries of the Western world was facilitated by the relatively efficient operation of the new international monetary system that had been established at a meeting of forty-four allied nations at the Bretton Woods resort in the White Mountains of New Hampshire during July 1944. Recognizing that the low level of international trade and investment represented a serious impediment to postwar economic growth in all countries, the financial representatives of the states at war with the Axis devised at Bretton Woods a number of measures to promote the resumption of world trade and capital movements. The International Monetary Fund (IMF) was created to restore the network of multilateral international payments that had broken down in the early thirties as countries left the gold standard and adopted temporary expedients, such as exchange controls and devaluations, that disrupted world trade. The IMF consisted of a pool of currencies contributed by member states upon which any member could draw in order to correct temporary balance-of-payments difficulties without having to resort to exchange controls or devaluation. The chronic problem of exchange instability was addressed through the reestablishment of a modified system of fixed exchange rates: The dollar became the world's principal reserve currency and was rendered freely convertible into gold at a fixed price. The exchange rates in operation at the opening of the Bretton Woods conference were recognized as the par values for the new system, and any subsequent adjustment of the exchange value of a member country's currency required the prior approval of the governing board of IMF. Many of the West European economies were not strong enough to accept convertibility of their fixed-rate currencies until the late 1950s, and there were occasional exchange problems for Britain and France. Nonetheless, Bretton Woods ushered in a quarter century of relative exchange stability, which facilitated international trade, lending, and investment by removing the uncertainty of currency values.

An additional stimulus to the postwar recovery of world trade was the creation of a multinational institution empowered to establish rules for the international exchange of goods and services to replace the protectionist policies of the thirties. America's increasing involvement in world trade after the war had led the Truman administration to importune other nations, particularly those wartime allies who were deeply in debt to the Treasury Department and therefore particularly susceptible to Washington's pressure, to dismantle the trade barriers inherited from the Depression years that blocked American access to foreign markets. The major trading nations of the world were finally induced by the United States to adhere in the autumn of 1947 to the General Agreement on Tariffs and Trade (GATT). GATT would later sponsor negotiations among the major trading nations of the world to lower barriers to trade based on the most-favored-nation principle, which stipulated that trade concessions negotiated bilaterally would automatically be extended to all GATT members. The reduction of tariffs and other trade barriers during GATT bargaining sessions nourished a remarkable increase in the international exchange of goods and services after almost two decades of stagnation.

The political consequences of the Marshall Plan were to prove as far-reaching as the economic ones for the future of Europe. The Soviet bloc's repudiation of the program not only foreclosed the possibility of restoring prewar economic, and therefore political, relations between Eastern and Western Europe; it also accelerated the ideological polarization within each European state. The deterioration of political relations between Communist and non-Communist parties in all countries of the continent had already begun by the time of Secretary Marshall's offer of economic assistance. In the spring of 1947, the Communist ministers in the coalition governments of France, Italy, and Belgium were either excluded from or chose to leave office because of mounting ideological differences with the dominant pro-American parties. In the meantime, the Communist parties of Eastern Europe were systematically eliminating all non-Communist organizations from positions of power. The advent of the American-sponsored European Recovery Program hastened this trend toward the ideological bifurcation of the continent. In an effort to present the U.S. economic penetration of Europe, Moscow established on September 22, 1947, the Communist Information Bureau (or Cominform), a formal organization of European Communist parties designed to ensure their subservience to Moscow. Though successful in liquidating all non-Communist political forces in Eastern Europe that might prove susceptible to American influence, the Cominform failed to generate effective opposition to the Marshall Plan in Western Europe. Strikes and disorders fomented by the Communist-controlled labor organizations of France and Italy in the autumn of 1947 failed miserably. The governing coalitions in those two countries, from which the respective Communist parties had been expelled the previous spring, resumed their eager solicitation of American economic assistance and tendered active support for the new anti-Soviet foreign policy adopted in Washington.

Thus, by the beginning of 1948 the European continent had been reorganized into two political and economic blocs, the one dependent on the United States, the other subservient to the Soviet Union. This was soon to be followed by the division of the continent into two military blocs joined in a commitment to common defense against the other and backed by the overwhelming armed might of their respective patrons. Since the end of the war, Western and Soviet representatives had engaged in regular if not cordial communication in successive conferences at the foreign minister level, in the Allied Control Council for Germany and in the United Nations, in an effort to settle by diplomatic negotiation the outstanding matters in dispute. But the February 1948 Communist takeover in Czechoslovakia, which symbolically and literally blocked the last major avenue in Europe linking East and West, precipitated the final rupture in relations between the two victorious powers that had been building up since the end of the war. Thereafter, the economic reconstruction of Western Europe that was about to get under way seemed futile unless the nations of that region could adequately protect themselves against what had come to be viewed, in the aftermath of the Communist-inspired unrest in France and Italy and the Prague coup, as Moscow's imminent bid to project its power westward beyond the sphere of interest informally allocated to it at the end of the war.

On March 17, 1948, two events occurred on opposite sides of the Atlantic that together signified the determination of the Western nations to supplement their emerging transatlantic economic partnership with a commitment to collective self-defense. The first of these was the signing of the Brussels Pact and the formation of the Brussels Pact Organization, a military alliance of fifty years' duration, binding Great Britain, France, and the three small countries now collectively designated as Benelux (Belgium, the Netherlands, and Luxembourg) in a joint pledge to repel "an armed attack" against any one of the signatories. The second was President Truman's special message to the U.S. Congress requesting authorization to reinstate conscription and universal military training, which had been allowed to expire after the war in keeping with the traditional American preference for a small volunteer army during peacetime. These two simultaneous actions were obviously not unrelated. The Brussels Pact was designed to demonstrate the West European nations' willingness to cooperate in their own defense and therefore facilitate Truman's task of securing congressional approval of American participation in that effort.

These first tentative steps toward American rearmament and West European collective defense were to provoke a Soviet response of such belligerence as to confirm the worst fears of the Western leaders and therefore to accelerate the trend toward military preparedness and transatlantic cooperation in security matters. The site of the first direct confrontation between Western and Soviet power was, appropriately, the region of Europe where it collided head-on: occupied Germany. The partition of Germany, Austria, and their respective capitals into four military occupation zones under American, British, French, and Soviet jurisdiction had been intended as a temporary expedient pending the emergence of indigenous political elites untainted by Nazi connections that would be prepared to undertake the governance of their reunified sovereign state. In the meantime Germany (like Austria) was to be administered as a single political and economic unit by the Allied Control Council sitting in its capital, Berlin, which itself, though divided into four occupation sectors, was to be governed as a single municipal unit.

But a number of developments during the three years after the end of the war had converged to sabotage the Potsdam plan for eventual German unification. Most of these were related to the determination of the Soviet Union to profit from its military control of the eastern part of Germany to procure from its own zone the reparations that it had expected, after Yalta, to obtain from all of Germany. The Soviet occupation authorities peremptorily requisitioned German machinery, power plants, railway track and rolling stock, as well as substantial quantities of coal and other raw materials for delivery to Russia. They also repudiated their pledge to furnish agricultural products from their own zone to the three Western zones in exchange for the industrial equipment they had already received from them. These unilateral measures, as understandable as they may have been in light of the desperate economic condition of the Soviet Union that had been caused by the German invasion, elicited sharp criticism from the American government and its representative on the Control Council in Berlin. The Truman administration had no intention of permitting the Russians to seize the economic assets of their own zone and continue to receive reparation deliveries from the Western zones while the United States was paying for the sustenance of the impoverished populations of postwar Germany. Convinced that Germany's economic recovery was vital to the economic recovery of Europe as a whole, the United States pressed the Soviet Union in vain to treat the matter of reparations as part of a comprehensive plan for the orderly management of the entire economy of the country. When the Russians resumed their unilateral requisitions, the United States terminated the transfer of reparations to the Soviet zone in May 1946. In the meantime, the Russians had introduced measures of economic reform in their own zone—such as the confiscation without compensation and the redistribution of all large landholdings—which not only contradicted American principles of free enterprise, but also further undermined the original policy of treating all of Germany as a single economic entity.

Then, in an abrupt shift in strategy, the Kremlin abandoned its vindictive policy toward Germany in favor of a conciliatory approach. At the Paris meeting of Allied foreign ministers in July, Molotov violently accused the United States of reintroducing in disguised form the long-since repudiated Morgenthau Plan for the deindustrialization of the Reich by imposing restrictions on Germany's coal and steel production. The Soviet foreign commissar proposed the establishment of a single German government and denounced the French plan for the separation of the Ruhr from Germany. Molotov's remarks apparently signified a Soviet bid to curry favor with the starving and suffering German masses by posing as their defenders against the three Western allies.

Not to be outbid in the "struggle for Germany," American Secretary of State James Byrnes responded to Molotov's ploy in a speech before an audience of 1,400 German dignitaries in Stuttgart on September 5 that signified a critical turning point in American policy toward the occupied country. He announced his government's intention to promote the economic rehabilitation of Germany in order to enable it to contribute to the economic recovery of Europe as a whole. He rejected the idea of splitting off the Ruhr from the rest of the country. He called for the prompt formation of a provisional government with authority to administer the entire country so that Germans could once again manage their own affairs. Most important of all, from the standpoint of German public attitudes toward the Soviet Union, Byrnes specifically refused to recognize the Oder-Neisse frontier between Germany and Poland. That boundary, which deprived Germany of a considerable portion of its prewar territory, had been unilaterally established by the Russians in 1945 in order to compensate Poland for the 70,000 square miles of its own territory

Germany Between East and West

that it had been forced to cede to the Soviet Union. By throwing American support behind the German people's complaints about that territorial amputation, Byrnes had shrewdly smoked out the Kremlin, forcing it to choose between its client state in Poland and its prospective friends in Germany. Stalin sided with Poland, thereby antagonizing the German public that Moscow had earlier attempted to woo.

The Truman administration proceeded to make good on the commitments to the German people that had been sketched by Byrnes in his Stuttgart speech. It promoted greater coordination of the occupation policies in the three western zones and granted a greater measure of economic and political authority to the pro-Western German elites that were emerging there. On January 1, 1947, the Americans and the British formally merged their two zones into a single economic unit, and in the following May established an economic advisory committee consisting of fifty-two delegates from the regional (*Land*) assemblies that the two occupying powers had permitted to be elected in their zones. In July the United States decided to extend Marshall Plan aid to the three Western occupation zones. The French, who had at first steadfastly opposed all measures favoring German political or economic integration (for obvious historical reasons), acceded to Anglo-American pressure in the summer of 1947 and began to participate in a common economic policy for the three Western zones. Soon the rudiments of a West German administration appeared in the form of the Supreme Economic Council, which adopted a bold plan for industrial recovery that was to pave the way for the West German economic "miracle" of the fifties. On March 1, 1948, a central bank serving all three western zones came into being; on June 18 France finally agreed to fuse its zone with the Anglo-American zone; and on June 20 an all-West German currency, the deutsche mark, was established to cure inflation, curb black market activities, and restore faith in paper money after three years of quasi-barter in which cigarettes had been the hardest currency. These reforms signified the allies' acknowledgement that Western European prosperity depended on Germany's economic recovery, that the reunification of the entire country was impossible under current circumstances, and that the most suitable alternative was to integrate the American, British, and French zones into a single entity.

This process of economic integration in western Germany—the removal of all restrictions on the circulation of labor, capital, and products within the three zones, the formation of German-controlled trizonal economic bodies with broad decision-making powers, and the establishment of a trizonal central bank and currency backed by American financial power under the Marshall Plan—can only have been interpreted by Moscow as what indeed it proved to be: a prelude to the political integration of the three western zones in the form of a West German state dependent on and loyal to the United States. Since the newly consolidated western occupation zones of Germany contained three-quarters of that country's population as well as the most productive industrial region of prewar Europe (the Ruhr-Rhineland-Westphalia complex), the prospect of a politically unified, economically advanced west German state associated with the United States produced predictable uneasiness in the Kremlin: It might exert a magnetic attraction on German nationals within the eastern zone, which was being drained of its resources and compelled to endure acute economic privation by its Soviet occupiers; it might serve as a center of Western intrigue against the East European satellites; worst of all, in light of the simultaneous request by Truman for the restoration of conscription in the United States and the formation of a West European military alliance, the emerging West German state might become a launching pad for aggression by America and her West European clients in the Brussels Pact against the Soviet motherland.

Moscow chose to counteract the American decision to establish a west German political and economic entity by applying pressure at the point of greatest Western vulnerability: the western sector of Berlin, situated 110 miles inside the Russian zone and tenuously linked to the western zone by a highway and a railroad. On June 24, 1948, the Soviet authorities in Germany halted all surface traffic crossing from the western zone through the Soviet zone to West Berlin, whose 2.5 million inhabitants thereupon faced the prospect of starvation, having food stocks for only thirty-six days. Though ostensibly undertaken in retaliation against the establishment of a strong currency in the western zone (which was bound to destroy the weak German currency in the Soviet zone), the evident purpose of the Berlin blockade was to expel the Western occupation forces from the city. If the formation of a west German state could not be forestalled, at least the last open hole in the "iron curtain" that Churchill had decried in his famous address in March 1946 could be plugged. But the American and British government responded to this direct challenge to their occupation authority in Berlin by organizing an airlift, which supplied the beleaguered citizens of the city with the food, fuel, and other basic commodities they required. On May 12, 1949, Stalin acknowledged the failure of the blockade and terminated it with a face-saving gesture that fooled no one. (The Kremlin announced that the roads and railroads, which had been closed "for repairs" for a year, would be reopened to traffic from the West.) The soviet Union's failure to remove this anomalous island of Western influence within a region firmly under its control and subject to its overwhelming military superiority was due to a single overriding fact: The United States possessed nuclear weapons that could be dropped on Russian cities by the sixty B-29 bombers that had been transferred (though without being converted to carry atomic bombs) to British bases at the height of the crisis.

The Berlin blockade accelerated the progressive involvement of the United States in the defense of Western Europe that had begun on the rhetorical level with the proclamation of the Truman Doctrine and the adoption of the containment policy during the Greek and Turkish crises in 1947. On April 23, 1948, a few weeks after President Truman's request to the United States Congress for the reintroduction of conscription and universal military training and the simultaneous formation of the Brussels Pact in Europe, Foreign Secretary Ernest Bevin of Britain had sounded out the State Department about the possibility of forming a North Atlantic security system linking the United States, Canada, and the five signatories of the Brussels Pact. The imposition of the Berlin blockade in June strengthened the position of those officials within the Truman administration who had reached the conclusion that the United States had to make a clean break with its isolationist heritage and supplement its support for European economic recovery with some kind of concrete commitment to European defense.

The two measures that were required for the United States to assume such an unprecedented foreign commitment were both in the hands of the legislative branch of the government, as had been the case thirty years before, when a Democratic president's plans for America's global responsibilities were dashed on Capitol Hill. American participation in European defense required a sufficiently powerful military force to assure the credibility of the pledge as well as legislative authorization to adhere to whatever system of regional defense that Bevin and his European colleagues had in mind. As it turned out, congressional Republicans who had been converted to the cause of "internationalism" outnumbered the remaining guardians of the isolationist heritage by a wide margin. On June 24, 1948, the congress repudiated the tradition of a small volunteer peacetime army by enacting the euphemistically named Selective Service Act. This legislation laid the basis for a sharp increase in American military manpower by subjecting all able-bodied males from nineteen to thirty-five years of age to compulsory military service of twenty-one months. Like their counterparts in the Brussels Pact nations, which had also reinstituted conscription after the war, millions of American young men would be trained in the martial arts not to fight a war in Europe, but to deter the Soviet Union from starting one there.

The concept of extending American military protection to the European signatories of the Brussels Pact that came under active consideration in Washington during 1948 seemed to contradict the essential purpose of the United Nations Organization, which was to provide a global network of collective security that would render such regional defense arrangements superfluous. Whereas the British wartime government had pressed for the decentralization of the projected world body in the form of regional associations, it had been overruled by an adamant Roosevelt who had insisted on the Wilsonian concept of a single universal organization without regional subdivisions. But shortly after Roosevelt's death, as delegates from fifty countries assembled in San Francisco to draw up a charter for the United Nations Organization, American officials concerned with Latin American affairs expressed the fear that the projected global system of collective security might endanger the United States' special relationship with its clients south of the border. Just as the Wilson administration had insisted on exempting the region covered by the Monroe Doctrine from the purview of the League of Nations Covenant, the Truman administration arranged for the insertion of article 51 in the United Nations Charter, which preserved the right of member states to cooperate to provide for their self-defense outside the United Nations. The first such regional agreement to be concluded was the Rio Pact of September 2, 1947, which established the principle of collective self-defense for the western hemisphere by defining an attack against one of the American republics as an attack on them all and providing for a joint response to aggression. The aforementioned Brussels Pact for Western Europe's joint defense was also based on the provisions of Article 51. Armed with the precedent of the Rio and Brussels pacts, Republican Senator Arthur Vandenberg (a former isolationist turned internationalist who had helped to formulate article 51 and had subsequently become chairman of the Senate Foreign Relations Committee) introduced a resolution in the United States Senate that was designed to circumvent the Soviet veto in the United Nations Security Council on matters relating to European security without violating the United Nations Charter. The Vandenberg resolution in effect repudiated the hallowed U.S. belief in the priority of the western hemisphere in times of peace by affirming Washington's willingness to join the Western European regional security system that was in the process of formation.

Acting under the authority of the Vandenberg resolution, which passed the Senate with only four dissenting votes, the State Department began negotiations on July 5 with representatives of the Brussels Pact countries and Canada, which were later joined by officials from Italy, Norway, Denmark, Iceland and Portugal. Finally, on April 4, 1949, delegates of these twelve nations signed the North Atlantic Treaty, a regional security arrangement modeled on the Rio Pact, that obligated each signatory to render assistance to any of the others that sustained an armed attack. The Senate ratified the North Atlantic Treaty by the lopsided margin of 82 to 13 and President Truman signed it on July 25. On the same day he requested congressional approval of the Mutual Defense Assistance Program, a one-year military aid package of $1.5 billion that represented the financial underpinning of the military commitment to America's new European partners in what was to be called the North Atlantic Treaty Organization (NATO).

Thus was born the mythical concept of a North Atlantic community. It was a myth because it included countries such as Italy (not to speak of Greece and Turkey, which adhered to the pact in 1952) whose shores were far removed from the waves of the Atlantic Ocean. It was a myth because it did not include geographically eligible states such as Spain (on account of its authoritarian government and its past associations with the Axis powers)* and Sweden and Ireland (which insisted on retaining their traditional neutrality). Nor could it be represented as a coalition sharing a cooperative spirit of long standing since it was to comprise two states, Italy and later West Germany (which joined in 1955), with which most of the other members had recently been at war. The new myth of Atlanticism superseded, at least in the minds of the American proponents of the alliance, the older myth of hemispheric solidarity that had governed American diplomatic behavior from the promulgation of Monroe's Doctrine to the pursuit of Roosevelt's Good Neighbor Policy. The Atlantic Ocean ceased to be regarded as an aquatic buffer between two distinctly separate if not mutually incompatible civilizations, the old world and the new, which protected the latter from the nefarious influences of the former. Instead the sea was seen as uniting the peoples of European heritage, those whose forbears had traversed it and those who had remained at home, in a community of shared principles and values. In fact the Atlantic alliance, as we have seen, was forged not by a common devotion to shared beliefs, but rather by the sentiment of danger: What united the signatories of this pact was the fear of Soviet aggression, which had been exacerbated by the Berlin blockade, and the determination to deter or resist it with the assistance of the American guarantee bolstered by the atomic bomb.

Another important consequence of the Berlin blockade was the formal partition of Germany into two separate political entities, each intimately linked to one of the two superpowers. Shortly after the formation of the North Atlantic alliance and during the final week of the blockade, in May 1949, the three western occupation powers permitted the establishment of the Federal Republic of Germany with its capital in the Rhenish city of Bonn. The first postwar elections conducted on August 14, 1949, throughout the three Western zones brought to power the conservative, pro-Western Christian Democratic party, whose fervently anti-Communist leader, Konrad Adenauer, became chancellor of the new state. Adenauer was firmly convinced that the path to national recovery for the new country lay in close cooperation with the Western allies against the Soviet bloc. The

---

*Though Franco's Spain was denied membership in NATO largely at the insistence of the British Labour government, the United States and Spain concluded a bilateral agreement in September 1953 that provided for the establishment of American naval and air bases on Spanish territory as well as American military and economic assistance to Franco. After the death of the dictator and the restoration of a constitutional monarchy, Spain was admitted to NATO in 1982.

United States came to regard West Germany as an integral part of its policy of containment, lifting restrictions on the country's economic production and increasing Marshal Plan aid. Washington also applauded the free market economic policy of Adenauer's economics minister, Ludwig Erhardt, whose promotion of domestic savings and investment as well as exports generated a spectacular increase in productivity that came to be known as the West Germany "economic miracle."

In the meantime, the Soviet zone had been transformed into the nominally independent state of the German Democratic Republic. Hitler had set out to unify all of Europe under German auspices. Instead, his policies resulted in the division of Europe, the division of Germany, and the division of the city where he had directed his armies and finally met his own end.

THE REARMAMENT OF THE WEST

It would be premature to designate the Berlin blockade and the formation of NATO as the decisive events that produced the rearmament, remobilization, and remilitarization of the United States and its allies in Western Europe. The North Atlantic Treaty represented merely a statement of intention, and a rather vague one at that. Though obliging each signatory to take up arms "immediately" in the event of an armed attack on any of them, it left each member to decide for itself if an armed attack had in fact occurred, whether it threatened the security of the region covered by the treaty, and what appropriate responses (if any) were called for. In light of the overwhelming conventional military superiority in Europe that the Soviet Union and its clients were thought to enjoy at the time—175 divisions compared with 14 divisions for the Western powers*—it was unclear how the promised American protection would be extended to the transatlantic allies in the event of a Soviet attack. It was originally assumed that by throwing a "nuclear cloak" over Western Europe, the United States could dissuade Moscow from interfering with the economic recovery and political stabilization of the countries receiving Marshall Plan assistance. The grossly outnumbered armed forces of the European members of NATO would serve as the "shield" of the Western alliance that would slow up a conventional Soviet assault until the "sword" represented by the American nuclear arsenal could be unsheathed and plunged into the heart of Russia. But the deterrent power of America's ultimate weapon was compromised before the ink on the North Atlantic Treaty was dry. On August 29, 1949, the Soviet Union exploded its first atomic bomb, signalling the end of the American nuclear monopoly on which the "shield and sword" strategy of the alliance was based and that American intelligence experts had expected to last for several years.

Shocked by the Soviet nuclear test and apprehensive about its implications for the future of Western defense, President Truman ordered the National Security Council to undertake a comprehensive reevaluation of American policy toward the Communist bloc. The product of this high level investigation was a top secret document known as NSC-68, which was submitted to the president in April 1950. It portrayed the Soviet Union as

---

*Intelligence estimates of Eastern bloc troop strength at this time were grossly exaggerated, as the American government itself conceded many years later. But the disparity between the two blocs was still significant.

an inherently aggressive power whose unquenchable thirst for expansion had led to the subjugation of Eastern Europe and China and threatened to engulf the rest of Eurasia. Moscow's acquisition of atomic weapons would enable it to bully its nonnuclear neighbors into submission unless the United States took immediate steps to remedy this potentially catastrophic imbalance of power in the world. A continuation of the containment policy adopted in 1947 would no longer suffice. The economic reconstruction of Western Europe and Japan and the stockpiling of American atomic weapons thousands of miles from the flashpoints of East-West confrontation had failed to stem the inexorable advance of communism in the world. What was called for instead was a global offensive against the Soviet bloc that would restore the initiative to the non-Communist world.

The specific recommendations of NSC-68 included the prompt development of the thermonuclear (hydrogen) bomb, the expansion of American and West European conventional forces, the mobilization of America's economic resources to sustain this military buildup, and the tightening of the bonds between the member states of the Western alliance system in order to meet the Communist threat. Three proposals designed to strengthen NATO and give more concrete form to the American military commitment to Western Europe had been under active consideration ever since the explosion of the Soviet bomb. The first of these was the stationing of large numbers of American ground forces in Europe (beyond the two divisions in West Germany) to supplement Allied manpower as well as to enhance the credibility of America's pledge to participate in the defense of the western half of the continent. The second was the installation of air bases on the continent to accommodate the bombers that carried the American nuclear deterrent. The third was the closer integration of the national armies of the alliance and the development of procedures for joint military planning in order to remove the logistical inefficiencies that are endemic to a loosely organized coalition of sovereign states. The general proposals included in NSC-68, together with its specific prescriptions for the buildup and projection of American military power abroad, implied nothing less than a revolutionary transformation of the manner in which the United States had managed its national defense in peacetime. Some opponents of the new proposal within the administration argued that it overstated Soviet territorial ambitions beyond the Communist bloc. Others worried that the enormous increase in defense spending called for in the memorandum would harm the nation's economy.

After considering the arguments of his advisers, President Truman pondered the politically charged question of whether to present the case for a substantial increase in American military power in peacetime. His ruminations were abruptly interrupted by the unexpected outbreak of hostilities between Communist and anti-Communist armies thousands of miles from Europe in June 1950 (see page 327). Though the peninsula of Korea was terra incognita to most Europeans, enough was known about its political situation to cause widespread uneasiness about its similarities to the postwar position of Germany. Formerly a part of the Axis coalition, Korea had been partitioned in 1945 between the United States and the Soviet Union. After three years of fruitless Soviet-American efforts to agree on measures of reunification, each occupying power had established in its own zone a government that claimed authority over the entire country. Now, the Communist half, armed and supported by the Soviet Union, had attacked the non-Communist half. Like South Korea, West Germany confronted an adversary who enjoyed decisive military superiority. The Soviet command in East Germany had recruited over fifty thousand "military police" from its occupation zone and had reorganized these paramilitary units into a powerful fighting force that could be hurled against the disarmed Federal Republic. Consequently, the diffuse feeling of anxiety about the theoretical possibility of nuclear annihilation aroused by the Soviet atomic test in the summer of 1949 was instantaneously replaced by a more precisely focused apprehension about the prospect of a Korea-type conventional assault across the north German plain that could radically transform the balance of power on the continent.

Whether the Kremlin ever seriously entertained the notion of making such an aggressive move in Europe—and no evidence has ever surfaced to indicate that it did—is beside the point. What mattered is that the governing elites of the NATO powers at the time made the mental connection between Korea and Germany at the height of the Korean emergency in the summer and fall of 1950. Moreover, the Truman administration's prompt and effective response to the North Korean invasion removed any lingering doubts in Europe about the capacity and determination of the United States to honor its commitments abroad: A nation that did not hesitate to fight a war in an obscure country that had been excluded from its defense perimeter in the western Pacific could scarcely be suspected of reluctance to defend the European members of the Western alliance system to which the United States had enthusiastically adhered.

The transformation of the Cold War into a shooting war in Asia led to the militarization of the containment policy in Europe. The Truman administration seized upon the alarm caused by the aggression in Korea to push forward the drastic increase in military spending as well as the extension of unprecedented American security pledges to Western Europe that had been contemplated during the high-level discussions of the NSC-68 memorandum. The provisions of the North Atlantic Treaty, as we have seen, represented little more than a vaguely worded commitment to common defense, implicitly fortified by the existence of the American atomic arsenal and the large pool of American military manpower produced by the introduction of peacetime conscription. But the concrete American contribution to European defense was initially to be confined to the provision of munitions and matériel, and even those were in short supply because of the reduction in American military spending in the years after the Second World War. The Korean War abruptly changed all of this. In September 1950, the council of NATO foreign ministers assembled in New York and unanimously adopted a "forward-looking strategy" for the defense of Western Europe, which was to be facilitated by the formation of an integrated military force under a unified command. In the same month President Truman dispatched four divisions of American combat troops to Europe and announced plans to augment even further the size of the American military contingent on the continent. In December the NATO foreign ministers announced the creation of an integrated defense system under the supreme command of General Dwight D. Eisenhower. On April 4, 1951—two years to the day after the signing of the NATO Pact—the United States Senate approved the principle of an integrated command and Eisenhower's nomination and endorsed the transfer of the four divisions of American ground troops to Europe.

In the meantime the Truman administration had taken dramatic steps to upgrade America's nuclear and conventional capability as well as to furnish the European allies with the military equipment that they required. In the last year of the Truman presidency, the institutional structure of the Western alliance system was rationalized: The Lisbon conference of the Atlantic Council in February 1952 created a NATO secretariat under a secretary general and centralized all alliance activities in headquarters located in and around Paris. Plans were drawn up to increase the number of divisions from fourteen to fifty, the combat readiness of existing forces was improved, and concrete steps were taken to centralize the command structure and integrate the national armies of the alliance. Negotiations were begun, and a number of agreements concluded, with various European states for the establishment of bases for American ground, air, and naval forces.

It is impossible to exaggerate the precedent-shattering significance of the new American defense policy that gradually unfolded from the formulation of the Truman Doctrine in 1947 to the establishment of a full-fledged American military presence in Europe by 1952. By assuming the supreme command of NATO, by furnishing armaments to its allies, and by stationing its own ground forces on the other side of the Atlantic, the United States had undertaken the task of preserving the postwar political status quo in Europe. The original emphasis on containing Russia's westward expansion by promoting the economic recovery and political stability of the nations of Western Europe was superseded by the commitment to project American military power to the very heart of the continent in an effort to achieve the same objective.

But the assumption of such unprecedented global responsibilities was not without cost. The American economy, notwithstanding its spectacular rate of growth in the early fifties, could not have been expected to sustain unlimited demands on its productive capacity. Particularly during the Korean War, when the American public was required to endure austerity measures such as wage and price controls and various restrictions on consumption, it was not surprising that the Truman administration began to press the European allies for greater contributions to their own defense. It soon became clear that Europe's greatest reserve of potential military strength was West Germany, with its large pool of manpower and its latent economic capacity. Why should the Germans themselves not be expected to contribute to their own protection, especially since any conceivable Soviet military advance in Europe would of necessity take place on German territory?

At the height of the Korean emergency American officials began to prod the West European governments to confront the issue that they had previously preferred to postpone: the rearmament of West Germany and its admission to the Atlantic alliance. On September 12, 1950, Secretary of State Acheson forcefully entreated America's European allies to agree to the inclusion of West German divisions in NATO. Though resolutely opposed by the governments of those nations, such as France, that had recently endured the painful consequences of German military power, German participation in Western European defense had been informally discussed since the formation of the alliance. "Germany's rearmament is contained in the Atlantic Pact as the embryo is in the egg," warned the Parisian newspaper *Le Monde* on the very day the NATO treaty was signed. French officials remained resistant to the idea of resurrecting German military forces, even with the assurance that their guns would be pointed east this time. "Germany has no army and cannot have one," declared French Foreign Minister Robert Schuman during the parliamentary debates on the ratification of the pact. "It has no armaments and it will not have any." But the increased pressure from Washington had its effect on Germany's apprehensive neighbors in the West. Particularly in France, public opinion began to accommodate itself to the idea of Germany's reintegration into the Western European system. Many French people had ceased to regard Germany as the hereditary enemy as they began to view Russia as the principal threat to national security. Moreover, that por-

Jean Monnet (1888–1979), the "Father of Europe": The brilliant Frenchman was a behind-the-scenes operator and visionary. He drafted the Schuman Plan for the European Coal and Steel Community (the forerunner of the European Economic Community and the European Union) and the Pleven Plan for the European Defense Community (a failed scheme for a European army that was later resurrected as the European Security and Defense Policy). A tireless campaigner for European economic and political integration, he constantly repeated the refrain "Continue, continue, there is no future for the people of Europe other than in union." *(Courtesy of the Library of Congress)*

tion of Germany under Western influence, which contained over three quarters of the country's industrial plant, came to be regarded as a valuable economic asset to Western Europe as a whole: The enormous productive potential of the Federal Republic, if permitted to develop to its full capacity, could serve as the engine of economic recovery for the entire western half of the continent. All that remained was to devise some means of assuring that West Germany's economic recovery would be managed without endangering the security of its non-Communist neighbors.

Even before the stimulus provided by the Korean War, the French government had launched a bold initiative that was eventually to provide such assurance. On May 9, 1950, French Foreign Minister Robert Schuman formally proposed that the coal and steel production of France and West Germany be combined and supervised by a supranational authority, which would be open to the participation of the other countries of Western Europe. Great Britain declined the invitation to join in discussions of this proposal because of its reluctance to compromise its privileged relationship with North America and the Commonwealth. But representatives of West Germany, Italy, and the Benelux nations joined French officials in negotiations that produced in 1951 an agreement to form a European Coal and Steel Community. When the Schuman Plan officially went into effect in the summer of 1952, the new supranational entity had been endowed with a political organization to complement its economic apparatus: an executive body, a parliamentary assembly, and a court of justice. Moreover, the specified objective of gradually abolishing all politically imposed obstacles to trade within the community (such as tariffs, quantitative restrictions, and import quotas) in coal and steel products implicitly established a precedent that could (and would) be extended to other and eventually all sectors of the economy. Thus the Schuman Plan contained the seeds of European economic integration that would later germinate during the second half of the fifties.

But the Schuman Plan was pregnant with strategic implications as well: it seemed to offer a masterly solution to the question of German rearmament that had been insistently raised by the United States since the beginning of the Korean War. Schuman's proposal, like the abortive scheme for European union advanced by another French foreign minister, Aristide Briand, a generation earlier, had been prompted by the hope of enmeshing Germany in a web of European economic integration that would forever remove both the incentive and the opportunity to make war on its partners in such a cooperative enterprise. It was inevitable that a proposal to domesticate Germany's industrial power by integrating it into a European economic community would give rise to the idea that Germany's warmaking potential could similarly be harnessed to the cause of joint European defense. Schuman's original hope was that an economically integrated, politically unified Europe, led by France and its junior partner across the Rhine, could emerge as a "third force" capable of managing its own defense without depending on either of the two superpowers or becoming embroiled in their global struggle for hegemony. But the outbreak of the Korean War five days after representatives of the six interested states had assembled in Paris to consider the French proposal abruptly transformed the nature of the discussion. The concept of Franco-German partnership within a Europe disengaged from the two superpowers vanished amid the prospect of all-out war with the Communist bloc. On October 24, 1950, as the governments of Western Europe groped for a constructive response to Acheson's proposal for the addition of West German divisions to NATO, French Premier René Pleven unveiled a plan that was carefully crafted to satisfy the

American demand for German rearmament while allaying the fears that such an event was bound to engender in Germany's West European neighbors. The Pleven Plan provided for the formation of a combined European military force, equipped and financed by the member states, with the integration of national contingents at the lowest possible level. The advantage of the scheme was that it would mobilize French, German, Italian, and Benelux forces without actually creating a German army or a German high command. Instead, German soldiers would be spread throughout a genuinely European army.

The American government initially hesitated to endorse the French proposal for a unified European military force for fear that it was merely a diversionary maneuver to delay or forestall German entry in NATO. But Washington was gradually won over to the Pleven Plan as the most suitable formula for including Germany in the common European defense effort without inspiring apprehension in the other allied countries. At a time when the conflict in Korea was widely regarded as a prelude to a general war, the governments of Western Europe displayed a remarkable willingness to accept the restrictions on their national sovereignty implied by the Pleven Plan. On May 27, 1952, after long and arduous negotiations, representatives of the six nations concerned signed the treaty establishing the European Defense Community (EDC). Thus was born the concept, if not yet the reality, of a supranational military organization under the supreme command of NATO, with common armed forces wearing a common European uniform, a common defense budget, and common political institutions including a council of ministers, an assembly, and a court of justice. The EDC treaty diverged from the original Pleven Plan in one important respect: Instead of providing for the dispersion of national forces in small units throughout the military organization, it established national contingents on a divisional scale (ostensibly for reasons of efficiency). This meant that German divisions would contribute to the defense of Western Europe after all, belonging to a multinational force and taking orders from "European" commanders. In recognition of West Germany's proposed adherence to the military alliance directed against Russia, the three Western occupying powers took the requisite steps to remove the anomalous reminders of its status as a vanquished enemy. A day before the signing of the EDC pact in Paris, the American, British, and French governments concluded an agreement with the Adenauer regime in Bonn ending the military occupation and restoring political sovereignty to the Federal Republic upon the entry into force of the treaty.

As the parliaments of the six member states of the EDC ratified or began debate on the ratification of the treaty to create a European army, two momentous political transformations occurred almost simultaneously in Washington and Moscow. In January 1953, the Democratic administration of Harry S Truman, which had inaugurated the policy of containing the Soviet Union and brought America into the Atlantic alliance, turned over the reins of power to the Republican administration of Dwight D. Eisenhower. On March 6, less than two months after the new American president took office, the Kremlin announced that Joseph Stalin had died of a stroke the previous day. It soon became evident that the upper echelons of the Soviet government and Communist party had undergone the most sweeping reorganization since the purges of the late thirties and that the Soviet dictator would be replaced by a cadre of political and military personalities who would rule on the basis of collective leadership. The disappearance of the two governing elites that had between them presided over the destinies of the entire globe since the end of the Second World War engendered a universal sense of uncertainty in the world. No one could predict with confidence whether the foreign policies conducted by Truman and Stalin would be perpetuated by their unfamiliar and untested successors.

What *was* certain, however, was that Truman had left an extraordinary legacy of achievements in the realm of foreign policy. The underlying objective of that policy, the containment of Soviet expansion beyond the regions that had come under Russian military domination at the end of the war, had been met everywhere. In Iran, Turkey, Greece, West Berlin, South Korea—wherever the Soviet Union probed or was thought to have probed Western intentions—American diplomatic, economic, or military power had been exercised in such a way as to preserve the non-Communist character and pro-Western inclinations of those disputed regions. The countries of Western Europe, on the brink of economic collapse and vulnerable to Soviet military pressure in 1947, had made spectacular strides toward economic recovery and collective defense under American inspiration. And American economic assistance to Yugoslavia after its defection from the Soviet bloc in 1948 facilitated Marshal Tito's campaign against Moscow's primacy in the Communist world.

In view of the remarkable success of this containment policy it must be regarded as ironic that the Republican party's victory in the presidential election of 1952 was in large part due to its success in portraying the Truman administration as "soft on communism." The strength of this paradoxical assertion rested on the supposed advance of Soviet power in Asia rather than in Europe. China, the most populous country on earth, was widely thought to have been absorbed into the Soviet empire. The Korean War dragged on inconclusively while American soldiers continued to die. The Communist insurgents in Indochina threatened to dislodge America's French allies and open all of Southeast Asia to the domination of the Kremlin and its puppets in the region. Added to this perception of Soviet gains across the Pacific was the widespread suspicion, incited by legislative demagogues such as Wisconsin's Senator Joseph R. McCarthy, that Communist agents had infiltrated America's domestic political institutions and were promoting Soviet interests there. The new American administration promised in certain ill-defined ways to remedy these defects in American policy toward the Soviet bloc and to halt what was viewed by the Republicans as the trend toward retrenchment and retreat.

9

COEXISTENCE AND CONFRONTATION (1953–1962)

EISENHOWER'S "NEW LOOK"

After having languished in impotent political opposition for twenty years, the Republican party took control of the White House at the beginning of 1953 ostensibly committed to a reversal of the foreign policy of its Democratic predecessor. But it was not to be a reversal toward the direction of isolationism and "America first." That wing of the party, led by Senator Robert Taft, had been decisively defeated by the "internationalist" faction that had adopted General Eisenhower as its standard-bearer and chosen as its foreign policy spokesman the New York attorney John Foster Dulles, who was to become Eisenhower's secretary of state. Prior to and during the presidential campaign, Dulles had articulated his party's alternative to the Truman administration's foreign policy. He denounced the containment doctrine as excessively passive in the face of the greatest threat of global aggression that the world had ever faced; moreover, it represented an immoral abandonment of the populations of Eastern Europe that had been permitted to fall under Soviet domination. Instead of striving to preserve the balance of power in Europe that had been established at the end of the war, Dulles asserted, the United States should make every effort to "liberate" the satellite states and "roll back" Soviet power to the Russian frontier. Inspired by a Manichean conception of good and evil and a messianic devotion to advance the boundaries of what he called the "free world," the new American secretary of state challenged all foreign nations to choose between enlisting in the American crusade for global righteousness or submitting to Soviet domination. Observers at the time did not fail to detect the similarity between this ideologically charged conception of American foreign policy and the orthodox doctrines of Marxist-Leninism. Both regarded the other side as so intrinsically evil as to preclude mutual accommodation, and each exhibited the unshakable confidence that its eventual triumph over the other was inevitable.

Such a dynamic vision of America's role vis-à-vis its principal rival in the world obviously implied a considerable augmentation of American military power. Yet the requirement of a drastic increase in defense spending to lend credibility to the American challenge to Soviet power contradicted the orthodox economic platform of the Eisenhower presidential campaign, which promised tax relief, a reduction in government expenditures, and a balanced budget. The resulting paradox was resolved by a high-level decision to inaugurate what was dramatically labeled a "new look" in America's defense policy. In January 1954, Dulles spelled out the Eisenhower administration's bold innovation in strategic doctrine that was designed to increase American military power while reducing defense expenditures: Since the most expensive component in the defense budget was represented by spending on conventional forces (mainly pay and equipment for the army and navy), this would be reduced in the interests of cost efficiency. The old idea of increasing NATO's troop strength to fifty divisions, which had been formally adopted by the alliance in 1952, would be abandoned because it cost too much. Instead, the United States would place greater reliance on its nuclear arsenal and delivery system (which at the time consisted of a powerful bomber force based in the United States and abroad). In this way a parsimonious Republican administration could plan to hold down the costs of defense without sacrificing the security interests of the Atlantic alliance. The inferiority of the Western allies' conventional forces in Europe would be compensated for by upgrading the capacity of American strategic airpower to deliver a retaliatory nuclear blow "instantly, by means and at places of our own choosing," in Dulles's own forceful formulation. The new American defense policy would be much more cost effective by providing, in the candid expression of Defense Secretary Charles Wilson, "more bang for the buck."

The strategy of "massive retaliation," as it came to be known, could remain a credible deterrent to aggression only so long as the Soviet Union lacked the means to retaliate in kind. At the time that Dulles proclaimed his policy, the United States possessed the wherewithal to inflict extensive damage to Russian territory by means of long-range bombers based at home or medium-range bombers deployed in allied countries along the periphery of the Soviet empire. The Soviet Union had exploded its own hydrogen bomb on August 20, 1953, only nine months after the first successful American thermonuclear test. But it possessed neither long-range bombers capable of making the round-trip flight from Russian territory to North American targets nor air bases in the western hemisphere. Thus the United States could count on devastating the major urban areas and industrial sectors of its enemy without fear of reprisal.

The deterrent value of massive retaliation also depended on the ability of the United States to assure its adversary that aggressive activity in certain strategically situated areas of the globe would automatically trigger an American nuclear response. The dynamic military strategy associated with Dulles's name therefore also gave birth to an equally aggressive diplomatic strategy intended to ring the Soviet bloc with hostile powers linked to and protected by the United States through a series of mutual defense treaties. The Atlantic alliance and its emerging regional subgroup, the European Defense Community, that had been inherited from the Truman administration formed the keystone of the global security system that Dulles was striving to construct. Confronted with a rearmed West Germany within a rearmed Western Europe backed by the invulnerable American

President Dwight D. Eisenhower (1890–1969) and his secretary of state, John Foster Dulles (1988–1959): Dulles's heated rhetoric during the 1952 presidential campaign about "liberating" the populations of Eastern Europe and "rolling back" communism proved hollow when the United States refrained from intervening during uprisings against Soviet power in East Germany (1953) and Hungary (1956). But the new administration's heavy reliance on nuclear deterrence fueled the nuclear arms race with the Soviet Union, while Eisenhower's energetic secretary of state crisscrossed the globe to forge regional alliances against the Communist bloc. *(National Archives)*

nuclear deterrent, the Soviet Union would be dissuaded from risking further probes of the soft spots beyond the Western borders of its empire.

But the Dulles strategy for Europe was dealt a devastating blow on August 30, 1954, when the French parliament declined to ratify the treaty establishing the European Defense Community two years after it had been signed by the leaders of the six member states. The grandiose project for a supranational West European military force came to an ignominious end at the hands of the very nation that had originally proposed it. French opposition to EDC sprang from a variety of impulses, apart from the predictable hostility to the restrictions on national sovereignty implied by the treaty. Foremost among these was the apprehension that Great Britain's refusal to adhere to the pact signified a return to the traditional aloofness of that island nation that would condemn France to a lonely and vulnerable position of inferiority on the continent vis-à-vis a rearmed, prosperous, self-confident Germany. London's pledge on April 13, 1954, to assign to the projected European army one armored division as a token of British involvement was to no avail. Neither was Dulles's veiled threat in December 1953 of an "agonizing reappraisal" of American support for European defense if France rejected the EDC. An additional cause of France's dwindling enthusiasm for the project it had initiated was the mounting hope of detente with the Soviet Union that had been stimulated by the death of Stalin and the increasingly amicable comportment of his successors. During a period when Soviet and Western statesmen cordially negotiated a settlement to the Indochinese war at Geneva and no less an avid anti-Communist than Winston Churchill was urging East—West discussions to settle the world's problems, it was more difficult to preserve the cohesion of the Western bloc than in the period of high tension during the Stalin years.

For a brief moment the French rejection of the EDC threatened the unity of the Atlantic alliance, upset the plan of integrating West Germany into the system of European defense, and derailed the movement toward European unity. But after the initial flurry of recriminations, the interested parties settled down to explore alternative arrangements for salvaging the cause of Europe's common defense. This time the initiative was to come from London. British Foreign Secretary Anthony Eden suggested, as a practicable alternative to the supranational defense organization that had recently been repudiated, the enlargement of the more conventional type of military alliance that had been created by the Brussels Pact of 1948 to include Germany and Italy. Since Britain was a charter member of the Brussels Pact and maintained four infantry divisions and air force units on the continent in that capacity, such a transformation would entail the British commitment to European defense that the French had so earnestly sought as a counterweight to German power. In October 1954, representatives of the Brussels Pact nations plus Germany and Italy signed an agreement enlarging the moribund five-member security organization into the seven-member Western European Union (WEU). Britain, France, and the United States formally agreed to terminate the occupation regime in West Germany and restore full sovereignty to the Federal Republic (including the right to rearm, on the sole condition that it promise never to manufacture atomic, biological, or chemical weapons on its territory). Thus did Germany finally cease to be treated as an "enemy" by the three Western powers that had occupied it since 1945, though the "state of war" technically continued in the absence of a formal peace treaty. Installed as a full-fledged member of the expanded WEU, West Germany was forthwith proposed for membership in NATO, which it officially joined on May 9, 1955, exactly ten years after the Nazi regime's surrender.

The Soviet Union responded to these momentous events five days later by convening representatives of its seven East European satellites in Warsaw for the signing of a twenty-year mutual defense treaty that established a formal military alliance as a counterpart to NATO. Though formally a military alliance protecting the eastern bloc against a threat from the Western bloc, and particularly from its newest member, the Warsaw Pact Organization, as this new Communist security system came to be called, functioned principally as an instrument of Soviet political domination of Eastern Europe.

Thus only a few months after the collapse of the ambitious scheme for a supranational West European army, the cause of joint European defense had been rescued by the more modest alternative of a traditional alliance of sovereign states fielding national armies under the aegis of NATO. From the ashes of the EDC emerged a reinvigorated Western

Europe in the Cold War

alliance system of which a rearmed West Germany, contrary to every expectation, had become a member on an equal basis.

But the objective of military collaboration against the Soviet Union had been reaffirmed at the cost of sacrificing the cause of European unity that many had hoped would be facilitated by the formation of the EDC. Exponents of the European idea such as France's Jean

Monnet, though chastened by this setback, redirected their energies toward promoting *economic* integration as a prelude to political integration by strengthening and expanding the sole survivor of their earlier integrationist hopes, the European Coal and Steel Community. The relative ease with which the six member states of the ECSC (France, West Germany, Italy, and Benelux) had consented to the removal of most restrictions on the exchange of coal and steel products within the community inspired considerable optimism among the proponents of supranationalism about the prospects of extending the concept to other economic sectors. Intensive negotiations were conducted during the mid-fifties to that end. Finally, on March 25, 1957, representatives of the six ECSC states signed the Treaty of Rome establishing the European Economic Community (EEC).

The two overriding purposes of the EEC, which formally entered into operation on January 1, 1958, were the gradual elimination of all legal restrictions on trade, capital movements, and labor migration within the community as well as the establishment of a common external tariff to protect member states from foreign competition during the difficult transitional stage leading to the creation of a genuine free trade zone. As had been the case during the formation of the ECSC, Great Britain declined to join the emerging economic bloc on the continent for fear of jeopardizing its "special relationship" with the United States as well as its preferential trade arrangements with Commonwealth countries (which enabled it to import cheap food and other commodities). The long-range goal of political integration was facilitated through the creation of a complex apparatus of embryonic political institutions as well. The most important of these were the Council of Ministers representing the six countries; the Commission, thirteen "European" civil servants appointed by the member governments, and a "European" parliament, empowered to oversee the Commission's activities. Though originally endowed with minimal authority and budgetary autonomy, the institutions of what would later merge into a single entity renamed the European Community presided over a process of economic integration that survived all subsequent attempts by some member states (especially France) to reassert the old prerogatives of national sovereignty. Though the goal of political federation proved much more elusive, the "idea" of Europe continued to exercise a powerful attraction on Europeans weary of the old national antagonisms and cognizant of the advantages that West European political unity would bring in the global contest for power, influence, and prosperity.

THE ERA OF PEACEFUL COEXISTENCE

It was a considerable feat for NATO to absorb West Germany without sacrificing its internal cohesion during a period of reduced tension with the very power whose ostensibly aggressive behavior had given rise to the formation of the alliance in the first place. Ever since Stalin's death in March 1953, signals had been emanating from the new collegial leadership in the Kremlin that implied compromise and conciliation. One by one, divisive issues that had given rise to acrimonious exchanges between East and West during the Stalin era suddenly proved susceptible to settlement. The armistice negotiations in Korea, which had been hopelessly deadlocked for two years, were expeditiously completed in July 1953 on terms that denied the Soviet client state in the north the political gains it had sought in the south. In the spring of 1955 the Kremlin impressed even the most truculent anti-Communists in the West with a flurry of conciliatory gestures. The Austrian State Treaty, which was signed on May 15, 1955, after a decade of bickering, stipulated the withdrawal of all Allied (including Soviet) occupation forces from Austria, on the condition that the newly sovereign country observe strict neutrality between the two blocs. The Porkkala naval base that Stalin had wrested from Finland in 1947 was returned to that country. The Manchurian naval base at Port Arthur (Lüshun) obtained in exchange for the Russian declaration of war against Japan in 1945 was evacuated and turned over to China. Normal diplomatic relations were restored with Tito's Yugoslavia and the initiative was taken to establish them for the first time with West Germany. This series of dramatic diplomatic concessions prompted speculation in Western capitals that the Soviet Union had renounced its aggressive intentions and was prepared to negotiate a settlement of East-West differences.

This new Soviet posture of accommodation appears to have been prompted by a number of considerations. Foremost among these was the uncharacteristic primacy of domestic politics over international affairs in the thinking of the post-Stalinist governing elite during the succession struggle of 1953–57. While the first secretary of the Communist party, Nikita Khrushchev, gradually prevailed over half a dozen rivals to secure the top leadership post, he was obliged to bargain with and sometimes concede to various blocs and constituencies within the Soviet political hierarchy in order to amass and then consolidate his power.* At the same time, the fluidity of the political situation during the transitional phase following the death of a despot in a country with no institutionalized mechanism for succession permitted the emergence of a kind of public opinion, which clamored for better living conditions and a relaxation of the stifling political repression inherited from Stalin. In such an uncertain domestic political environment, the Soviet leadership was understandably inclined to avoid confrontation and conflict with its foreign antagonists in the West, particularly after having failed to forestall the emergence of a rearmed Germany allied to the United States. The Kremlin's quest for stability in Europe during the mid-1950s reflected a positive consideration as well: the opportunity to exploit and possibly profit from the mounting difficulties experienced by the European powers in Africa and Asia occasioned by the outburst of revolutionary agitation in those regions that remained under their control (see p. 272). A Soviet diplomatic offensive in the colonial world on behalf of the subject populations that were struggling to rid themselves of British or French rule dictated a defensive strategy in Europe to avoid antagonizing the United States and its continental protégés.

This trend toward the relaxation of East-West tensions in Europe reached a crescendo at the first postwar meeting of the Soviet and Western heads of government in Geneva during July 1955. The four days of personal conversations among the four plenipotentiaries—President Eisenhower for the United States, Premier Nikolai Bulganin of the Soviet Union, Prime Minister Anthony Eden of Great Britain, and Premier Edgar Faure of France—transpired amid an atmosphere of cordiality that contrasted dramatically with the rhetorical fulminations of the previous ten years. As titular head of the Western coali-

---

*Khrushchev acquired political primacy in June 1957 by engineering the expulsion of his three principal rivals, Malenkov, Molotov, and Kaganovich, from the Presidium and the party Central Committee, though he did not become head of government until March 1958.

tion, President Eisenhower set the tone of the conference with an earnest appeal for a cooperative new approach to the substantive problems of European security that would obviate the arms race and dispel the fear of nuclear annihilation. His "Open Skies" proposal, which envisioned a full exchange of blueprints of American and Soviet military installations and mutual aerial photoreconnaissance, was designed to circumvent the traditional Soviet objection to on-site inspection. Bulganin in turn unveiled a project for disarmament stipulating an absolute prohibition of the fabrication and use of atomic weapons as well as a ceiling on the size of the conventional forces of the world's principal military powers.

Neither arms limitation proposal was acceptable to the other side for the usual reasons—the Soviets were not about to expose their secretive military planning to intelligence reconnaissance by air, while the Americans were averse to participating in reciprocal prohibitions or limitations of military capability without adequate provisions for inspection. But despite the absence of any concrete achievements, the face-to-face bargaining with polite language represented a significant departure from the acrimonious exchanges of the past. The sweet reasonableness of Eisenhower won him accolades at home and abroad as a "man of peace," while the Soviets conveyed an uncharacteristic image of sincerity and trust. To Eisenhower's earnest pledge that "the United States will never take part in an aggressive war," Bulganin solemnly replied, "We believe that statement." Newspaper columnists in the West waxed lyrical about the "spirit of Geneva" while the Soviet press repeated the catchword "peaceful coexistence" that had become the watchword of the early post-Stalin years.

The new conciliatory gestures emanating from Moscow in the mid-fifties reflected the beginning of what appears to have been a genuine change of attitude at the highest levels of the Soviet hierarchy. As Khrushchev began his bid for uncontested authority toward the end of 1955, he inaugurated a fundamental reassessment of Soviet policy, foreign as well as domestic. This reassessment rapidly developed into a full-scale indictment of the Stalinist legacy as well as of those Soviet political personalities who sought to perpetuate it. The ambitious party secretary, sensing the prospect of political victory, eagerly embraced the cause of "de-Stalinization" as a weapon in his campaign for primacy within the collective leadership. Once the transformation had been effective and the new Soviet line displayed in public view, it was to shake the Communist world to its very foundations. At a closed meeting of the Twentieth Congress of the Communist Party of the Soviet Union on February 24, 1956, Khrushchev delivered a long late-night address that startled the assembled delegates and then the entire world once its contents had been leaked to the press. The titular head of the international Communist movement berated Stalin for his repressive policies and called for the establishment of less arbitrary rules of political procedure in the Soviet Union. Implicit also in his speech was an endorsement of liberalization in the satellite states of Eastern Europe and a relaxation of the Soviet Union's tight grip over their domestic politics. This impression was confirmed two months later by the dissolution of the Communist Information Bureau (Cominform), which had been created by Stalin at the beginning of the Cold War to ensure the subservience of the Communist parties of Europe to Moscow.

Even before Khruschev's denunciation of Stalinist repression and the dissolution of the Cominform in 1956, the post-Stalinist leadership had taken tentative steps to relax the rigid economic and political constraints on the satellites of Eastern Europe in an effort to placate the patently discontented subject populations of that region. The objective seems to have been the setting in motion of a gradual, orderly process of retrenchment and liberalization that would remove the most objectionable features of Russian control over the daily lives of the subject populations without impairing the status of the satellites as ideological confreres and military allies of the Soviet Union. But Khrushchev's dramatic repudiation of the Stalinist legacy nearly transformed this orderly retreat into a rout. He had undermined the credibility of the Soviet Communist party as the undisputed and infallible interpreter of Marxist-Leninist doctrine and keystone of the international Communist movement. In so doing he unleashed the forces of "polycentrism," which meant that individual Communist parties throughout the world were free to pursue their separate paths independent of dictates from Moscow. The challenge of Communist pluralism that Tito had hurled at Stalin in 1948 now seemed to have received the tacit endorsement of Stalin's successor, who invited the renegade Yugoslav leader to Moscow four months after the "secret speech" and received an urgent appeal from Tito for liberalization in the satellites.

The anti-Stalinist rhetoric in the Soviet Union quickly spread to Eastern Europe and became a source of acute danger to Soviet interests there. In June 1956 labor unrest engulfed the Polish city of Poznan as thousands of workers noisily demonstrated for better economic conditions. By October this isolated outbreak of social protest had evolved into a nationwide expression of resistance to Soviet interference in Poland's internal affairs. The trials of the Poznan rioters ended abruptly, several Communist leaders publicly urged that Soviet officers be removed from the Polish army, and Wladyslaw Gomulka, a symbol of nationalist Communism who had been jailed in 1951 by the pro-Soviet puppet regime in power for "Titoism," rejoined the central committee of the Polish Communist party. On October 20 Khrushchev hastily flew to Warsaw to nip the incipient insurgency in the bud, only to be rebuffed by Gomulka, whose election as first secretary of the Polish Communist party the following day signified the advent of "national communism" in Poland. As Russian tanks rolled toward Warsaw and the Polish government began to distribute arms to the workers of the city, the Soviet leader recognized the imminence of a national war between two Communist neighbors and decided to back down after receiving reassurances from Gomulka. He announced full support of the reformist Polish Communist leader, arranged for the return of Soviet troops stationed in Poland to their barracks, and flew back to Moscow. The consequences of the Polish October were the removal of many restrictions on individual liberties, the curtailment of Russian military authority within Poland, and the formation of a de facto alliance between the "national" Communist party of Gomulka and the Polish Catholic church headed by Stefen Cardinal Wyszynski, who, like Gomulka, had been released from prison during the upsurge of political unrest. Recognizing that Poland's geographic position between Germany and Russia precluded a totally independent course, Gomulka prudently sought to consolidate the gains of October while affirming his country's loyalty to the Soviet bloc. By preventing the newly won domestic liberalization from getting out of hand and by remaining committed to the goals of Soviet foreign policy, this shrewd Polish patriot preserved for his country a considerable measure of independence and dissuaded the Kremlin from resorting to military means to enforce its will.

Not so prudent, and not so fortunate, was the political leadership of Communist Hungary that had assumed power in October amid circumstances superficially similar to those in Poland. Hungary had been one of the last Eastern European states to succumb to Soviet domination, and the Communist system had never succeeded in enlisting mass support there. The Communist party barely managed to cling to power, as its economic policies resulted in a lowering of living standards and therefore generated considerable resentment among the population. The anti-Stalinist revelations at the Soviet Communist party congress in 1956 undermined the authority of the hard-line, pro-Soviet leadership in Budapest; then the events in Poland inspired a popular insurrection in Hungary that rapidly exceeded the limits to dissent that had been imposed by Gomulka. The new Hungarian prime minister, the liberal Communist Imre Nagy, promptly formed a coalition government that, for the first time since the advent of the Cold War, included non-Communist elements. He then announced his intention to conduct in the near future free elections that threatened to end the monopolistic position of the Communist party. On October 30, Nagy obtained from the Kremlin a remarkable public pledge of support for Hungary's national independence, which included promises to remove immediately the Soviet troops that had been dispatched to Budapest to quell the incipient insurrection and eventually to evacuate all Russian military forces from Hungarian territory. For a fleeting moment it appeared that the trend of the previous decade had been reversed, that the liberal policies adopted by Stalin's successors might actually result in a significant degree of political independence for the nations in Russia's East European satellite empire.

But as Soviet troops streaming out of Budapest halted their evacuation on November 1, Nagy panicked and abruptly announced Hungary's withdrawal from the Warsaw Pact, the military alliance concluded in May 1955 between the U.S.S.R. and the seven Communist satellites of Eastern Europe in response to the inclusion of a rearmed West Germany in NATO. The prospect of a politically independent and militarily neutral Hungary was evidently too much for the Soviet leadership to entertain with equanimity: It would establish a dangerous precedent that, if followed by the other East European states, could only bring about the disintegration of the buffer zone between Russia and the West that Moscow had so insistently established after the collapse of Hitler's Reich. The "liberation" of the Soviet East European empire and the "rollback" of Communist power to the Russian frontier suddenly seemed imminent not because of American pressure, but because of the explosion of unrestrained nationalism in Hungary. Thus on November 4, the 250,000-man Russian army returned to Budapest with 5,000 tanks and inaugurated a reign of terror that undid all that had been accomplished during the previous month: The Nagy regime was forcibly replaced by a puppet government under János Kádár, whose authority rested entirely on the presence of Soviet troops that were to remain, at the request of that compliant regime, to guard against a repetition of the recent unpleasantness.

The Kremlin's decision to abandon the policy of gradual retrenchment in Eastern Europe that had begun after Stalin's death and was confirmed by Khrushchev's famous speech was occasioned not only by apprehension about the dangerous precedent of a defiant Hungary, but also by the tempting opportunity fortuitously presented by the simultaneous eruption of the crisis along the Suez Canal in October 1956 (see p. 278). With the United States and its allies preoccupied with events in Egypt, the Soviet Union could risk a military intervention in Hungary with greater confidence that it could be accomplished without opposition from the Western powers, despite all of the talk on Western transmitters pledging support for the anti-Soviet resistance.

The relaxation of Moscow's iron grip on Eastern Europe and the recession of Soviet power in the Far East in the years after Stalin's death coincided with the revival of Rus-

Hungarian Prime Minister Imre Nagy (1896–1958) (center) at an emergency meeting in parliament after issuing an appeal for foreign assistance against invading Warsaw Pact military forces, November 4, 1956: After his ouster Nagy received asylum in the Yugoslav embassy in Budapest. On receiving assurances of safe passage from his pro-Soviet successor, he left the embassy only to be arrested by Soviet security officers. After a secret trial he was executed two years later. *(Getty Images)*

sian ambitions in those regions of the Middle East and southern Asia that were emancipating themselves from the colonial domination of Great Britain and France. Earlier Soviet attempts to establish an ideological affinity between Russian communism and the cause of national liberation in the colonial world during the 1920s had met with failure and were virtually abandoned during the Stalin years. But the Leninist doctrine of imperialism, according to which the capitalist nations of the West were ineluctably driven by the dynamics of their own internal economic development to seek markets for their surplus capital in the nonwhite regions of the earth, remained a potentially powerful weapon in the ideological arsenal of the Soviet leadership should it attempt anew to compete for influence there. In the fall of 1955 Khrushchev and Soviet Premier Nikolai Bulganin dusted off this old Leninist doctrine during an extended sojourn in southern Asia. The two Soviet leaders vociferously denounced the evils of European imperialism; endorsed the principle of national liberation; and extended the promise of Russian economic, technical, and military assistance to the newly independent nations that were struggling to overcome the debilitating legacy of European rule. This new Soviet ideological offensive toward the south, and the American effort to counter it, was destined to drag the region stretching from the eastern Mediterranean to the Indian Ocean into the Cold War between East and West. Just as the collapse of German power in Europe and Japanese power in

Asia in 1945 had left power vacuums in those areas that invited Soviet-American competition for influence, the retreat of British and French power in the Middle East and Asia during the 1950s resulted in a politically unstable situation that inevitably tempted the two superpowers to intervene to promote their respective interests there.

The ruling elites of the newly independent nations of the postcolonial world were confronted with the choice of either declaring their allegiance to one or the other of the two global coalitions or remaining formally nonaligned in the East-West struggle. None of them except North Vietnam (see page 338) chose to throw in their lot with the Soviet bloc in the course of the 1950s, in spite of the Kremlin's determined efforts to curry their favor. On the other hand, a number of them were induced by the United States and its European allies to join Western-oriented regional security systems that were specifically directed against the Soviet Union and its allies. In the aftermath of France's military defeat in Indochina (see pp. 340), Secretary of State Dulles masterminded a collective defense system for Southeast Asia to contain Soviet and Chinese expansion in that region. Established on the NATO model (though without provisions for automaticity of defense collaboration), the Southeast Asia Treaty Organization (SEATO) embraced the United States, Great Britain, France, Australia, New Zealand,* Pakistan, Thailand, and the Philippines.† In the Middle East, the pro-Western states of Turkey and Iraq concluded the Baghdad Pact in 1955 (reorganized in 1959 as the Central Treaty Organization, or CENTO, after a revolution in Iraq that brought to power an anti-Western regime). This regional security organization was later joined by Iran, Pakistan, and Great Britain (which still exercised influence in the region through military and naval bases in the Persian Gulf). The formation of this Southwest Asian defense system was actively encouraged by the United States, which acquired observer status in the new regional organization's policy-making body. In this way the Atlantic powers had succeeded by the mid-1950s in forging a network of alliances that linked many of their former dependencies or client states in the common purpose of containing the Soviet Union in that region. The states of the Middle East and of southwestern and southeastern Asia that adhered to these Western-sponsored regional pacts received, in addition to the pledge of protection in the event of an external threat to their security, an increasing amount of technical assistance to promote their economic development and enhance their military capability.

The alternative of nonalignment in the Cold War was most articulately expressed by the principal spokesman for the developing world, the prime minister of India, Jawaharlal Nehru. Long regarded as Great Britain's most valuable colonial possession, the Indian subcontinent had obtained its independence on August 15, 1947, following its partition into the predominantly Hindu state of India and the separate Muslim state of Pakistan. Though embroiled in a costly regional conflict with its Muslim neighbor over the disputed province of Kashmir and plagued by religious strife between its Hindu majority and its Muslim minority, Nehru's India aspired to a world role commensurate with its size and population. Its remarkable prime minister, who acted as his own foreign minis-

---

*The United States, Australia, and New Zealand had already concluded a tripartite security treaty (ANZUS) in September 1951.

†The United States had been granted a ninety-nine-year lease of Philippine military and naval bases in March 1947. The two countries concluded a bilateral mutual defense treaty in August 1951.

ter throughout his long tenure in office, attempted to steer clear of the East-West struggle and urged the other newly independent nations of the southern hemisphere to do likewise. He tirelessly warned of the misfortunes that were bound to befall states that were enticed to join one or the other of the two blocs in their global contest for power. Nehru sought to extract tangible benefits for his own poverty-stricken country from the Soviet-American competition for influence in the postcolonial world, so long as it was understood that no political strings were attached to the economic assistance. In January 1952 he signed a five-year "Point-Four" agreement with Washington for development aid for the Indian subcontinent.* In December 1953 he concluded a five-year trade pact with Moscow and in June 1955 a long-term agreement for Soviet economic and technical assistance to India. The Nehru's ultimate objective was the formation of a cohesive bloc of Third World nations recently emancipated from European rule that would promote the cause of world peace by declining all participation in the Cold War between the superpowers. Such was the message emanating from the first international conference of independent African and Asian nations held at Bandung, Indonesia, in April 1955.

A very different version of Third World neutralism was espoused by the charismatic military officer who had acquired dictatorial power in Egypt by the midfifties, Colonel Gamal Abdel Nasser. Whereas Nehru preached nonalignment as a means of promoting world peace, the soldier Nasser considered it as a means to two very different objectives, one short-term and the other long-term, that he had embraced with an all-consuming passion. His immediate goal was the promotion of a crash program of economic development and military rearmament for his own country that would establish it as the dominant power in North Africa and the Middle East in the wake of the Anglo-French withdrawal from that region. In the long term he envisioned a vast Pan-Arab empire from the Atlantic to the Persian Gulf under his own leadership. In pursuit of these goals the Egyptian strongman shamelessly played off the two superpowers against one another, soliciting economic and military assistance from both while hinting to each that he was about to strike a bargain with its rival in order to increase the total amount obtained. From the Communist bloc he procured in September 1955 a pledge of military supplies to equip the Egyptian army in exchange for cotton and rice. From the United States and Great Britain came a joint offer of financial assistance in the amount of $70 million for Nasser's pet project of economic development, the construction of a new dam at Aswan on the Nile that would increase Egypt's cultivable land by one-third and its electric power by one-half. Egypt rapidly developed into a microcosm of the East-West competition for influence in the Third World, with American and Soviet missions vying for the privilege of furnishing Nasser the funds he sought to modernize his backward country and its primitive armed forces.

At the same time the Egyptian leader devoted his energies to removing from North Africa and the Middle East three political forces that constituted the principal obstacles to the realization of his Pan-Arab dreams. The first of these was French colonial authority in Algeria, which had been forcefully contested since the autumn of 1954 by a guer-

---

*The "Point Four" program, named after the fourth point in Truman's 1949 inaugural address, was the first U. S. government foreign and program aimed at developing countries. It was intended to were their support against the Soviet bloc.

Champion of the cause of nonalignment in the Cold War: Prime Minister Jawaharlal Nehru of India (second from right) shaking hands with President Eisenhower in the White House, December 1956. At the extreme left is Nehru's daughter, Indira Gandhi, who later served as prime minister (1966–1977, 1980–1984). During his tenure as prime minister (1947–1964), Nehru walked a tightrope between the two superpowers, successfully seeking economic aid from both Washington and Moscow. *(Courtesy of the Library of Congress)*

rilla movement dedicated to the cause of national independence. Unlike France's other overseas territories, Algeria contained a large French colonial population—estimated to exceed one million by the 1950s—that had traversed the Mediterranean to settle as early as the mid-nineteenth century in the coastal cities and their agricultural hinterlands. These Christian, Caucasian "French Algerians" dominated the economic life of the country through ownership of its urban businesses and its fertile agricultural land. The monopoly of political power by these *colons* was assured by a complicated electoral system that, although granting legal equality to all citizens, had the practical effect of disenfranchising most of the Arab Muslim majority. Thus the insurrection against French rule that erupted in 1954 assumed the character of a bloody civil war between two peoples of different ethnic and religious heritage, both of whom claimed Algeria as their homeland as well as the right to control its political and economic life. To the Muslim Arab insurgents, Nasser of Egypt promptly furnished all manner of assistance including sanctuary for their political leaders, acquiring thereby immense prestige in the Arab world as the champion of its liberation from European colonial rule. The granting of independence to France's two other North African possessions, Morocco and Tunisia, in March 1956 appeared to confirm the inevitability of decolonization in the region, a prospect Nasser anticipated with undisguised alacrity.

In order to remove a second major vestige of colonialism, this one in his own country, the Egyptian strongman wrested from Great Britain on October 19, 1954, a pledge to relinquish its right to maintain a military base on the Suez Canal and to evacuate the canal zone entirely within twenty months. In exchange, Egypt guaranteed freedom of navigation through the waterway and promised to permit the reentry of British military forces in the canal zone in the event of an armed attack by an outside power against any Arab state or Turkey. By the summer of 1956, therefore, Anglo-French colonial authority in the Arab world had either disappeared or, in the case of Algeria, was challenged by a powerful insurrection whose ultimate triumph was doubted by no one save the most unrealistic devotees of Algérie française. The future seemed to hold the promise of Arab self-determination and unity after so many years of subservience and disunity under various European masters and their strategy of divide and conquer; such, at least, was the vision of the ambitious soldier-statesman in Cairo.

The third stumbling block to the realization of Nasser's Pan-Arabist dream was the state of Israel, formed in May 1948 by Jewish refugees from European oppression out of the territory of Palestine previously administered by Great Britain under a mandate from the League of Nations. A resolution by the United Nations General Assembly on November 29, 1947, proposing the partition of Palestine into two sovereign political entities, one Jewish and the other Arab, had been rejected by the neighboring Arab states. Consequently, the proclamation of the Jewish state of Israel upon the termination of the British mandate resulted in a war between Israel and the Arab states that was temporarily interrupted by an uneasy truce in the summer of 1949. To its Jewish inhabitants and their coreligionists abroad, the new state represented the fulfillment of a two-thousand-year-old dream of returning to the land of their ancestors. In more concrete terms, it offered a haven from the type of persecution they had encountered in Central and Eastern Europe, from the pogroms of the Russian tsars to the Holocaust of Hitler. The political movement of Zionism, founded in the 1890s by the Austrian journalist Theodor Herzl in reaction to the resurgence of European anti-Semitism during the Dreyfus affair in France, was based on the conviction, reinforced by the indelible memory of the concentration camps of the Third Reich, that the Jews scattered throughout the world would never enjoy security in any nation where they constituted a minority. Their only hope lay in the establishment of a state populated, controlled, and defended by Jews. But to the proponents of Pan-Arabism, the emergence in 1948 of a state dominated by citizens of European descent in the very heart of the Arab world signified a return to the colonial past and posed a serious challenge to the cause of Arab unity. Thus, Nasser took the lead in organizing the Arab states in opposition to Israel, barring Israeli ships from passing through the Suez Canal or the Straits of Tiran and providing bases for the Arab refugees from Palestine who launched hit-and-run raids across the Israeli border.

In the summer and fall of 1956 these disparate developments converged in an international crisis that was to damage the solidarity of the Western alliance at the very moment that the unity of the Soviet bloc was being shaken by the events in Poland and Hungary. On June 13, 1956, Great Britain evacuated the Suez Canal Zone as required by the Octo-

Egyptian President Gamal Abdel Nasser (1918–1970): Revered in the Arab world for his denunciation of Israel and European imperialism in the Middle East and North Africa, he tirelessly campaigned for the unity of the Arab peoples while playing off the two superpowers against each other to gain advantages for his country. His prestige abroad was severely diminished by the humiliating military defeat of Egypt and its Arab allies in the Six-Day War of 1967. *(Getty Images)*

ber 1954 agreement, leaving Egypt with full responsibility for the defense of that important waterway. On July 20 the United States government, annoyed at Nasser's increasing dependence on military assistance from the Soviet bloc and attentive to pro-Israel sentiment in Congress, abruptly withdrew its offer to finance the construction of the Aswan Dam. Stung by this threat to his personal prestige and his plans for the economic development of his country, the Egyptian ruler retaliated six days later by nationalizing the Suez Canal Company (which had remained under the financial control of British banking interests) and announcing his intention to employ the revenue from the canal to defray the costs of building the dam. After three months of fruitless diplomatic efforts to bring the pressure of world opinion to bear on Nasser to accept multinational control of this vital artery through which the bulk of European trade and Middle Eastern oil shipments passed, the British prime minister, Anthony Eden, concluded that his only recourse was military force. He hoped to topple Nasser, whom he had come to view as an incarnation of Hitler who, if not restrained, would accomplish in the Middle East what Hitler had done in Europe. Nasser's prior support for the Algerian rebellion against France and the Palestinian guerrilla campaign against Israel guaranteed that the British leader's scheme would find a sympathetic audience in Paris and Tel Aviv. Without consulting their American ally in advance, the British and French governments concocted and executed an elaborate hoax involving three nations that was designed to achieve for each the objectives it sought at Egypt's expense. By prior arrangement the Israeli army attacked Egypt on October 29, 1956, and within a few days had routed the Egyptian army on the Sinai peninsula and ominously approached the Suez Canal. On November 5 British and French paratroops were dropped in Suez and Port Said for the ostensible purpose of separating the two armies and protecting the canal in the interests of its international clientele. The real goal of this coordinated military operation against Egypt was the forcible replacement of the Nasser regime with one that would abstain from menacing British interests in the canal, French authority in Algeria, and Israel's security along its western frontier. The Suez intervention failed not because of Egyptian military resistance, which crumbled before Israeli tanks in the Sinai and Anglo-French paratroopers along the canal, but rather because of the unexpected and vigorous opposition of the United States. For reasons related as much to personality conflicts between Dulles and Eden as to divergences of national interest, the American government exerted sufficient pressure on its two European allies to compel a humiliating withdrawal of the three military forces that had converged by prior arrangement on the Suez Canal at the end of October.

The Suez fiasco was pregnant with long-range consequences for the future of the international order. It spelled the end of Anglo-French pretensions to an imperial role in the Middle East. It undermined the political cohesion of the Atlantic alliance by revealing to the Europeans that they no longer enjoyed the prerogative of pursuing foreign policies that did not have Washington's blessing. It immeasurably bolstered the prestige of Nasser in the Arab world and solidified his reputation as the spokesman for the developing nations in their struggle to eradicate the remaining vestiges of European colonialism. The Soviet Union, which had energetically intervened on Egypt's behalf to the point of threatening nuclear retaliation against Britain and France at the height of the crisis, acquired a reputation as the champion of Arab aspirations at the expense of the Western powers and their Israeli ally. Thus, just as the Soviet Union's undisputed predominance in Eastern Europe appeared threatened by the outbreak of nationalist agitation in Poland and Hungary, the Suez affair enabled the Kremlin to renew its ideological offensive in the Third World under the most favorable of circumstances. Moreover, while the polycentrist tendencies within the Communist bloc were abruptly curbed through Polish prudence in Warsaw and Soviet repression in Budapest, America's abandonment of its allies at Suez strengthened those Western European forces, which were particularly strong in France, that favored the pursuit of military, diplomatic, and economic policies independent of the United States.

The transatlantic tensions generated by the Suez crisis were fed by the mounting anxiety felt in Western Europe about the reliability of American military protection against the Soviet menace. As we have seen, the strategy of nuclear deterrence embraced by the Eisenhower administration consisted of the threat of a massive nuclear strike against the population centers of Russia in retaliation against a conventional Soviet military advance into Western Europe. Its credibility rested on the capability of the United States to unleash its nuclear arsenal without fear of a Soviet counterblow against its own cities. During the first decade of the Cold War the Soviet Union had made considerable progress in narrowing the lead of the United States in the nuclear arms race; it exploded its first atomic bomb four years after the United States in 1949 and its first hydrogen bomb only

First battalion of Royal Scots marching into Port Said, Egypt, November 16, 1956: The military success of the Anglo-French-Israeli intervention in Egypt was negated by the diplomatic pressure applied by the United States, which forced a withdrawal of the three armies before they could achieve their governments' goal of toppling the regime of Gamal Abdel Nasser in Cairo. Most historians regard the Suez affair as the last gasp of British imperial ambitions in the Middle East. *(Getty Images)*

nine months after the United States in 1953. What Russia conspicuously lacked were either bases in the western hemisphere from which to threaten American territory with nuclear bombardment or an intercontinental delivery system to transport nuclear weapons from Russian territory to their targets in North America. During the second half of the 1950s the Soviet Union acquired just such a delivery system that promised to neutralize the American deterrent. By mid-1955 it had perfected a long-range bomber that had the round-trip capacity to strike at American territory, but the United States possessed five times as many such planes as well as an efficient radar system to detect those of the enemy. The major Soviet breakthrough in nuclear delivery systems occurred as a consequence of advances in rocketry associated with the early efforts at space exploration. On October 4, 1957, the Kremlin astonished the world with its announcement that

Russian scientists had successfully launched the first man-made space satellite, the Sputnik. It was obvious that a rocket capable of projecting a metal object into orbit around the earth would be capable of delivering a nuclear warhead to targets anywhere on the surface of the globe. Indeed, on August 21 of the same year the Soviets conducted the first successful test of an intercontinental ballistic missile (ICBM). The United States promptly caught up by testing a five-thousand-mile-range Atlas ICBM in December 1957 and then launching its first space satellite, the Explorer, in February 1958. But until the Americans could construct a large number of ICBMs, they would be forced to rely on obsolete long-range bombers (which, unlike the ICBMs, were vulnerable to interception by enemy aircraft before reaching their targets) and on intermediate-range ballistic missiles (IRBMs) launched from bases in friendly countries close to the Soviet Union.

Stung by its embarrassing inferiority in nuclear delivery systems, the U.S. government launched a crash program that rapidly bridged the gap. By the early 1960s it had begun to deploy its own ICBM system, upgraded its intercontinental bomber force, and expanded its arsenal of medium-range bombers and IRBMs based in allied countries. Nervous talk in Washington about a "missile gap" during the presidential campaign of 1960 proved excessively pessimistic, largely because Soviet nuclear technology was not up to the ambitious task assigned to it by the Soviet leadership. But the fact remained that, for the first time since the advent of the atomic age, the United States was vulnerable to a massive nuclear attack from missiles launched from Soviet territory. A U.S. nuclear response to a conventional Soviet thrust in Western Europe (whether by means of long-range bombers and ICBMs on American territory or medium-range bombers and IRBMs based on Allied soil) could severely threaten the United States by leaving its principal population centers exposed to annihilation. From this ominous transformation of the nuclear balance, America's European partners drew two conclusions, both of which were destined to create serious tensions in the Atlantic partnership. The first was the growing doubts that the U.S. president would sacrifice American cities for the sake of defending Western Europe. The second was that by consenting to the deployment of American medium-range missiles and bombers on their own territory, as several of the NATO allies had been persuaded to do by the end of the 1950s, the nations of Western Europe would be exposing their own populations to total nuclear destruction in the event of a Soviet-American nuclear exchange. In time, the realization that the densely populated countries of Western Europe that hosted American bomber bases or missile installations would be automatic targets for any surprise attack by Russia provoked widespread discontent within the Western bloc. In England, which had launched its own modest nuclear armament program in the midfifties and integrated it with the much larger American deterrent force, nongovernmental organizations (NGOs) such as the Campaign for Nuclear Disarmament and the Committee of 100 loudly demanded withdrawal from NATO, the removal of American air bases and missile sites, and the abandonment of British nuclear weapons. On the continent, official voices were raised in favor of a reciprocal disengagement of American and Russian forces from their forward positions in Central Europe in order to avert a superpower confrontation in that region that could lead to a nuclear holocaust. At the same time, skepticism about the reliability of the American "nuclear umbrella" prompted some Western leaders to call for greater European efforts at self-defense and independence from the United States.

THE ANOMALY OF BERLIN

These tensions within the Western alliance emboldened the Kremlin to test the resolve of the United States and its European partners by cranking up the pressure on West Berlin, which was militarily indefensible by the small American, British, and French garrisons stationed there. The former capital of Hitler's Reich once again became the focus of East-West tension in November 1958: Khrushchev abruptly demanded the total evacuation of all four occupation forces from Berlin within six months, failing which the Soviet Union would unilaterally transfer its functions in the city to its East German puppets sitting in the Berlin suburb of Pankow. Since the Allies had neither diplomatic relations nor an access agreement to Berlin with the Pankow regime, acceptance of the Soviet ultimatum would have isolated the Western enclave from its protectors and doubtless led to its absorption by East Germany. Khrushchev reopened the "Berlin question" that had lain dormant for a decade after the abortive blockade of 1948–49 in response to loud complaints from East German Communist boss Walter Ulbricht about the humiliating presence of allied military, political, and intelligence personnel in the city that lay 110 miles within East Germany as well as about the embarrassing economic prosperity of West Berlin that any East Berliner (who had the right to unrestricted travel throughout the city) could readily observe. But what alarmed the East German Communist leadership most of all was that the promise of a much higher standard of living and a less repressive political climate had induced over two million East Germans to escape to the Federal Republic during the first decade of its existence. The inordinately large proportion of highly skilled professionals in this mass migration westward jeopardized the economic recovery of the German Democratic Republic. By 1958 the long border separating the two Germanies had been effectively sealed. But the brain drain continued through the last remaining hole in the iron curtain: the unobstructed passage between the eastern and western sectors of Berlin.

The Khrushchev ultimatum on Berlin was not only designed to achieve the narrow objective of removing this irritating challenge to Soviet control over its East European satellite empire and East German opportunities for economic development. It was also intended to serve another ambitious purpose. That was to disrupt the increasingly intimate connection between the United States and West Germany. The Adenauer regime had come to regard Berlin as the preeminent test of America's determination to defend Bonn's security interests. If the Western allies, whose token garrisons in that city were outnumbered five to one by Communist military forces in the vicinity, could be pressured into surrendering their patently indefensible position deep within the Communist sphere, the emergent Washington-Bonn axis would be severely damaged, perhaps beyond repair.

But the Western powers unanimously rejected the Soviet ultimatum, reaffirming their access rights to Berlin and refusing to recognize the transfer of Russia's authority to the East German regime. Faced with this united front by the West, Khrushchev allowed his May 27 deadline for the transfer of sovereignty to East Germany to expire and proposed a summit meeting to settle the Berlin issue once and for all. In early August 1959, during a conference of foreign ministers in Geneva, Khrushchev accepted an invitation from President Eisenhower to come to the United States for one-on-one discussions to resolve the question of Berlin's future political status.

During the last two weeks of September 1959, Nikita Khrushchev became the first Russian leader in history to visit the United States. After a whirlwind tour of the American hinterland, the Soviet visitor settled down for a series of private discussions with Eisenhower at Camp David, the presidential retreat in the Maryland mountains. Nothing of substance seems to have resulted from these confidential talks, save a tacit agreement to put the Berlin problem on ice pending the convocation of a summit conference of the great powers in the following year and Eisenhower's acceptance of Khrushchev's invitation to visit the Soviet Union after the summit. Nevertheless, the state-controlled Soviet press hailed the "spirit of Camp David," just as it had celebrated the "spirit of Geneva" after the inconsequential exchange of pleasantries at the summit four years earlier. The tenor of cordiality that marked East-West communications greatly improved the prospects for genuine detente as the tension-filled decade of the 1950s drew to a close. The death in May 1959 of John Foster Dulles, the preeminent symbol of the Cold War mentality in the American government, seemed to signify the end of the era of Soviet-American confrontation. The moratorium on the Berlin question that had been effortlessly agreed to at Camp David provided a welcome respite from a tension-filled dispute. In a speech from the rostrum of the United Nations General Assembly in New York, Khrushchev unveiled a proposal for general and complete disarmament within four years—an appealing if unrealistic solution to the arms race that the Kremlin would periodically reiterate. A few months after his return to Moscow the Russian leader announced that the Soviet Union would reduce its standing armed forces by a third in an apparent gesture of goodwill. From the brink of conflict over Berlin, the two superpowers had advanced a considerable distance toward mutual accommodation.

The summit conference that was to transform the conciliatory spirit of Camp David into a comprehensive settlement of the remaining issues of the Cold War was scheduled to open in Paris in the spring of 1960. On the fifth of May, eleven days before the discussions were to begin, Khrushchev announced that a high-altitude U-2 American spy plane had been shot down over Soviet territory five days earlier and angrily demanded an explanation. After a clumsy effort by the State Department to deny the intelligence-gathering purposes of the flight, President Eisenhower accepted full responsibility for the embarrassing incident. After arriving in Paris, the Soviet leader insisted that Eisenhower formally apologize for the violation of Soviet air space, punish those responsible, and promise to discontinue the flights. Since the intelligence-gathering function of these high-altitude planes was soon to be assumed by satellites orbiting the earth, it was a small matter for the United States to accede to the final Soviet demand. But for reasons of domestic politics in an election year as well as of international prestige, the American president was in no position to apologize to the Russian leader, let alone to penalize subordinates who were merely following orders. This supplied Khrushchev with the pretext he had apparently been searching for to abandon the Paris summit conference on May 16 and cancel Eisenhower's invitation to the Soviet Union.

Khrushchev apparently decided to use the U-2 incident to sabotage the Paris summit because he had come under intense pressure from sources within the Communist camp to reverse the policy of rapprochement with the West that he had inaugurated in the late 1950s. Hard-liners in the Soviet Politburo strongly opposed a negotiated settlement of the German problem in general and the Berlin issue in particular for fear that Soviet concessions would further undermine Russia's hegemonic position in Eastern Europe that had earlier been challenged in Warsaw and Budapest. At the same time, the Communist regime in China had become openly antagonistic toward Khrushchev's conciliatory posture in world affairs. In the eyes of the Maoist leadership in Beijing, the prospect of a Soviet-American rapprochement in Europe violated the revolutionary principles of Marxist-Leninism, of which the Oriental branch of the international Communist movement had become the most orthodox devotee. In place of the relentless struggle for the triumph of world communism, Khrushchev had substituted the policy of peaceful coexistence through disarmament negotiations and summit talks with the enemy. To counter this apparent renunciation of the messianic goals of world communism, Beijing let it be known after the Camp David talks that it would not be bound by such international agreements to reduce tensions as might be concluded by the two superpowers and their partners. Reinforcing this ideological dispute was Beijing's mounting displeasure at Moscow's failure to support with sufficient vigor the Chinese position on a number of critical issues; these included its border dispute with India (a country with which Russia maintained excellent relations), its campaign to reacquire by military force the Chinese Nationalist offshore haven of Taiwan (which enjoyed the military protection of the United States), and its goal of acquiring nuclear weapons (a prototype of which had been promised by the Russians to the Chinese in October 1957 only to be cancelled by Khrushchev in June 1959). Herein lay the early indications of what was soon to be called "the Sino-Soviet split," which would shatter the monolithic unity of the Communist bloc (see pp. 335–336).

Thus, opposition to Khrushchev's policies within the Soviet ruling elite, combined with the Chinese threat to challenge Soviet leadership of the Communist bloc on the issue of Khrushchev's attempt to relax East-West tensions, had placed the Russian leader in a vulnerable position as the Paris summit conference approached. The U-2 incident fortuitously played into the hands of those in Moscow and Beijing who had been pressuring Khrushchev to abandon his campaign of peaceful coexistence. In any case, within a week of the Paris meeting's premature demise, the man who had virtually declared the Cold War to be at an end during his American tour issued a new threat to conclude a separate peace treaty with East Germany, repeated the warning to European nations hosting American bases that they were inviting nuclear destruction, and flew to Beijing to reassure his Chinese critics of Soviet toughness.

This brusque reversion to an aggressive posture continued for the remainder of Eisenhower's tenure in office. Khrushchev appeared intent on seizing every available opportunity to challenge the West, no doubt to disarm his critics at home and in Beijing, perhaps also to confront the new American president with a challenging set of foreign policy crises on his inauguration. Once again, the temptation to fish in the troubled waters of the Third World proved irresistible. In Laos, a landlocked kingdom in Southeast Asia formerly attached to the French Indochinese empire, the Soviet Union sent massive military supplies to the proCommunist guerrilla movement that challenged the authority of the right-wing government forces that were being trained and equipped by the United States. The Soviet leader even took the gamble of extending Russian influence to the heart of sub-Sahara Africa, a large portion of which was in the process of obtaining national independence from the European colonial powers. When civil war erupted in the former Belgian Congo soon after its independence in the summer of 1960, the Kremlin provocatively hinted at the possibility of Soviet military intervention on behalf of the central government against a secessionist regime in the mineral-rich province of Katanga that was backed by Belgian copper and cobalt interests. When an international police force under the auspices of the United Nations was dispatched at the request of the Congolese government to restore order and supervise the withdrawal of Belgian troops that bad been rushed back to the country to protect Belgian nationals, Moscow accused UN Secretary General Dag Hammarskjold of prejudice against the leftist regime of Patrice Lumumba. Khrushchev promptly sent the Congolese leader military equipment, technicians, and advisers while threatening to dispatch Russian "volunteers" in a bold plan to establish the first Soviet foothold beyond the Eurasian continent. The collapse of the Lumumba regime and the expulsion of Soviet personnel by its successor dealt Khrushchev's newly aggressive policy in Africa a humiliating setback. He retaliated with a spirited assault against the Western bloc's controlling position in the United Nations, proposing the dismissal of Hammarskjold and the replacement of the office of secretary general by a "troika" representing the Western, Communist, and nonaligned states.

Though nothing ever came of either project, Khrushchev's shoe-banging performance at the UN General Assembly meeting of October 1960 signified his appreciation of the revolutionary implications of the decolonization process then in full swing. By 1960 the membership of the United Nations had doubled, as newly independent states emerged from the ashes of the European colonial empires in the southern hemisphere. From an exclusive club dominated by the powerful white nations of the West, the world organization was becoming a forum for a bloc of newly sovereign political entities from Africa and Asia. Combined with the nations of the Communist bloc, these erstwhile victims of European imperialism formed a solid majority in the United Nations General Assembly that might prove useful in forthcoming diplomatic contests with the United States and its allies in that forum of world opinion.

Yet despite the emergence of the postcolonial developing world as an arena for Soviet-American competition, the center of the Cold War remained in Europe, and the center of Europe remained Germany, and the center of Germany remained Berlin. Accordingly, it was in that perennial trouble spot that Khrushchev strove to regain the initiative in foreign affairs that had been lost amid the abortive efforts to establish a Soviet foothold in sub-Sahara Africa and to reorganize the United Nations. In light of the simmering discontent within the Soviet leadership and the increasingly bitter recriminations from Beijing, Khrushchev desperately needed a triumph in foreign policy to shore up his faltering position at home and within the international Communist movement. The hemorrhage of East Germany's skilled labor force through the Berlin gap would continue so long as the Western allies remained in military occupation of the western sector of that city. With the new, untested administration of President John F. Kennedy recently installed in Washington, Khrushchev resolved once and for all to settle the Berlin issue on Moscow's terms. He took the occasion of a Soviet-American summit conference at Vienna in June 1961—the fourth such face-to-face encounter since the advent of the Cold War—to present the new American chief executive in the most menacing of terms with another ultimatum demanding a German peace treaty, an end to the occupation regime, and the transformation of West Berlin into a free city. Upon his return to Moscow he set the end of the year as the deadline for his ultimatum and announced a one-third increase in military spending to underline his determination to dislodge the Allied garrisons from Berlin. Kennedy reaffirmed America's commitment to defend West Berlin by armed force if necessary and announced plans for an additional $3 billion increase in defense expenditures and the tripling draft calls. At the end of the tension-filled summer of 1961, the Kremlin announced the resumption of nuclear tests that had been suspended by mutual agreement of the Soviet Union, the United States, and Great Britain since the fall of 1958; a series of Soviet nuclear tests in the autumn was capped by the detonation of a 58-megaton device, three thousand five hundred times more powerful than the Hiroshima bomb. American entrepreneurs promoted family-size fallout shelters to protect against the nuclear radiation that was sure to come, while the American and British governments responded by resuming nuclear testing to avoid falling behind in the arms race.

But in the meantime the Soviets and their East German clients had devised a stopgap solution to the Berlin problem that avoided the risk of a nuclear showdown. On the morning of August 13, East German police sealed the border separating the two sectors of the city and three days later began construction of a concrete-and-barbed-wire barrier that prevented all travel between East and West Berlin except through a handful of closely guarded checkpoints. The Western response to this imaginative method of unilaterally nullifying the intercity access arrangements was confined to sharp diplomatic protests and a token reinforcement of Allied garrisons in the western sector of the city. No attempt was made to remove the wall, which, though an embarrassing symbol of East Germany's prison-like status, solved Ulbricht's brain-drain problem: whereas over 103,000 East Germans had fled through the escape hatch of Berlin during the first six months of 1961, only a few thousand were able to escape thereafter.

The improvisation that had been intended as a temporary solution of the festering problem of divided Berlin accomplished its purpose. On October 17, by which time it had become evident that the Western allies had acquiesced in the fait accompli of the wall, Khrushchev again lifted his deadline for the resolution of the related issues of Germany and Berlin; Russian and East German authorities allowed the Allied military forces in the Western sector to remain unharassed and refrained from interfering with their access to the Federal Republic across the East German autobahn. In June 1964 the Soviet Union concluded a separate agreement with East Germany formally recognizing its sovereignty but without challenging the special status of West Berlin and the presence of the Allied military forces stationed there. Never again would the anomalous position of Germany and Berlin seriously disturb relations between the two superpowers. In the interest of averting a nuclear confrontation, Washington and Moscow had become reconciled to what appeared to be the permanent partition of the German nation and its erstwhile capital.

But the solution to the Berlin problem reached in 1961 had fallen far short of the spectacular success in foreign policy that Khrushchev had covered as a means of stifling the rumblings of discontent within the Communist bloc. Though the problem of East German emigration had been resolved, the Americans had stood firm in Berlin, with the unqualified support of their NATO allies (including even the increasingly independent-minded French regime of President Charles de Gaulle). The Kremlin's resumption of nuclear testing many be viewed as both a compensatory and an intimidating gesture: it was compensation for the patent Soviet strategic inferiority and vulnerability to the United State (as revealed by the U-2 flights over Russian territory and subsequently confirmed by the Pentagon's public references to the small number of ICBMs the Soviets had managed to produce since Sputnik) and intimidation of the increasingly hard headed Kennedy and the increasingly recalcitrant Mao Zedong. The resumption of nuclear testing during the

A group of West Berliners peers over the new Berlin Wall, 1961: Despite the East German government's claim that the wall was intended to protect its own citizens from aggression from the West, its real purpose was to prevent East Germans from leaving their country for the West. One hundred seventy one people died attempting to escape at the Berlin Wall between August 13, 1961, and November 9, 1989, when free travel through the wall's checkpoints was permitted for the first time. *(Courtesy of the Library of Congress)*

autumn of 1961 shattered the hopes for strategic arms control that had been nurtured by the 1958 moratorium and kept alive by the atomic disarmament negotiations conducted in Geneva. Thus, instead of serving as the first step in a comprehensive resolution of East-West differences, the stalemate over Berlin resulted in heightened international tensions and rekindled Soviet-American competition in nuclear weaponry.

It was in this context of strategic rivalry that Khrushchev felt impelled to take his most reckless gamble in foreign policy, one that brought the two superpowers to the brink of a nuclear exchange that could have annihilated a large proportion of the people in the two belligerent countries. In one of the most notable ironies in the history of international relations, the Soviet-American confrontation that came closest to transforming the Cold War into the nuclear Armageddon that the prophets of doom had been predicting since the advent of the atomic age occurred not in one of the usual distant flashpoints of East-

West conflict in Europe or the Far East, but in the one region of the world that had been entirely off limits to Soviet influence because of its proximity to and historic connections with the United States.

THE UNITED STATES AND LATIN AMERICA IN THE CRISIS YEARS

The position of the United States vis-à-vis the twenty independent republics of Latin America from the end of the Second World War to the beginning of the 1960s can best be characterized as one of undisputed domination. The world war and its aftermath had definitively confirmed the economic preeminence of the United States in the western hemisphere. Europe's commercial and financial stake in Latin America had declined dramatically as Great Britain, Germany, and France depleted their human and material resources during the war and then struggled to rebuild their own shattered economies after 1945. In the meantime, as we have seen, the economic systems of most of the Latin American countries had been closely tied to the expanding economy of the United States as it geared up for and then sustained the global war against Germany and Japan. American military power was projected southward with the explicit consent of the Latin American states for the purpose of protecting them from the menace of Axis aggression. As the end of the war approached, many Latin American governments expressed concern that the United States' new global responsibilities as well as its sponsorship of a new international organization for the maintenance of peace and security would undermine the solidarity as well as the effectiveness of the inter-American regional security system that had been forged during the war. In order to allay Latin American anxieties on this score, United States delegates at the founding conference of the United Nations Organization in the spring of 1945 inserted a provision in the UN Charter authorizing the formation of regional security organizations with powers of enforcement that would not be subject to the approval of the UN Security Council.

With the advent of the Cold War in Europe, the United States and its Latin American clients moved to give concrete form to the informal regional security arrangements agreed to during the war. The Inter-American Treaty of Reciprocal Assistance, signed in Rio de Janiero in September 1947 and eventually ratified by all of the twenty-one American republics, established a permanent defensive alliance against aggression originating both outside and inside the hemisphere. In the spring of 1948 the American republics endowed this military alliance with a formal political structure by transforming the loosely organized Pan-American Union into the Organization of American States (OAS). The peacekeeping machinery of the OAS thereafter operated with unanticipated effectiveness in settling a number of regional disputes between member states, such as those between Nicaragua and Costa Rica in 1949, 1955, and 1959 as well as a flareup between Nicaragua and Honduras in 1957.

But whereas the Latin American members of the OAS regarded the inter-American system as a multilateral mechanism for the maintenance of regional peace and security, the United States came to view it in much narrower and more explicit terms, particularly after the outbreak of the Korean War and the resulting American preoccupation with the spread of communism throughout the world. From Washington's perspective, the OAS-Rio Pact structure was designed to serve the same purpose that was being served by the other regional security systems that the United States had sponsored, namely, the defense of the non-Communist world against the expansionist ambitions of the Soviet bloc.

We have seen how the fear of Communist insurgency in the war-ravaged countries of Western Europe had led to the provision of large amounts of American aid to cure the socioeconomic ills on which communism was thought to thrive. But in spite of the persistence of such problems in Latin America on a scale much larger than in Western Europe, and in spite of urgent requests from Latin American countries for economic assistance to address them, there was to be no Marshall Plan for the western hemisphere in the early postwar years. Secretary Marshall himself had pledged at the Rio Conference of 1947 that serious attention would be devoted to Latin American pleas for development assistance. But no progress was made in the few discussions of inter-American economic affairs that were conducted in subsequent years. Whereas the Latin American countries hoped to secure United States government assistance after the fashion of the European Recovery Program, Washington insisted that such development aid as might be forthcoming would have to emanate from private sources.

The economic backwardness of Latin America, coupled with the coexistence of a tiny land-owning and commercial elite and large landless, destitute peasantry, was a recipe for social instability. Many Latin American countries experienced acute conflicts between reformist political movements backed by the lower classes and the defenders of the social and economic oligarchy. Because of extensive American economic involvement in the region, the U.S. government paid close attention to these political struggles.

This is precisely what was to happen in the Central American republic of Guatemala, where, after the thirteen-year-old dictatorship of General Jorge Ubico was overthrown in 1944, a mild-mannered university professor named Juan Arevélo was elected president on a program of sweeping social renovation. From 1945 to 1951 Arevélo undertook to narrow the enormous gap between rich and poor as well as to improve the educational and economic conditions of the large Indian population through a series of government-sponsored reforms that met with strong opposition from landowners and foreign investors. In March 1951 Arevélo was succeeded by the fiery spokesman for the ruling party's left wing, thirty-seven-year-old Colonel Jacobo Arbenz Guzmán. After pushing through the Guatemalan parliament a far-reaching program of agrarian reform, Arbenz announced his intention to expropriate 225,000 acres of undeveloped land belonging to the American banana concern, the United Fruit Company, for only taken compensation, and to redistribute it to the peasantry. As United Fruit solicited the support of its government against the Guatemalan regime, the new Eisenhower administration was becoming greatly alarmed at what its ambassador in Guatemala City was describing in ominous terms as the mounting influence of Communists in Arbenz's government.

By the beginning of 1954, representatives of United Fruit as well as agents of the Central Intelligence Agency was approaching right-wring Guatemalan exiles in Nicaragua and Honduras with schemes to overthrow Arbenz while Washington organized a boycott of arms to the country. When evidence surfaced that the Guatemalan leader had attempted to circumvent the boycott by contracting for a shipment of 2,000 tons of light arms from Czechoslovakia, Washington had the pretext it required for initiating remedial action to forestall the spread of Communist-bloc influence to its own backyard. In June the American-backed Guatemalan exiles reentered the country with air support furnished by planes piloted by CIA operatives and instigated a military coup that toppled Arbenz and sent him into exile. The new military junta that assumed power promptly revoked most of the land reforms enacted by its predecessor and inaugurated a campaign of repression against left-wing organizations in the country.

The unilateral intervention of the United State of Guatemala and been undertaken with the tacit acquiescence of the OAS, which had issues a declaration during the Caracas conference in March 1954 condemning thee domination of any member state by "the international Communist movement" as a "threat to the sovereignty and political independence" of them all. But this new inclusion of anticommunism in the definition of Pan-Americanism was opposed by most of the civilian-ruled republics, and even some of the military dictatorships had to be threatened with American economic reprisals before they cast their affirmative vote. The prospect of United States interference in Latin American, notwithstanding the principle of nonintervention enshrined in the OAS Charter, remained a much greater source of concern to the Latin republics than the remote danger of a Communist takeover. The CIA-sponsored coup in Guatemala seemed to demonstrate that the principle of nonintervention, for which Latin American governments had fought so hard and so long, had become a casualty of the Cold War.

As a symbol of the resurgence of unilateral, if covert, United States interference in the internal affairs of Latin American states, the overthrow of Arbenz rekindled widespread resentment among nationalists groups throughout the region. The central role of the United Fruit Company in the Guatemalan episode also played into the hands of left-wing political agitators, who mobilized mass support by attributing Latin America's chromic economic problems to the nefarious influence of United States corporations operating there. The extent of Latin American discontent with the United States came to light in dramatic fashion during Vice President Nixon's good-will tour to eight Latin American countries in May 1958. The startled vice president and his entourage were confronted by hostile demonstrations at every stop. In Caracas his motorcade was almost overwhelmed by angry, stone-throwing mods hissing "Yankee go home."

The embarrassment of the Nixon tour alerted the Eisenhower administration to the simmering grievances that the Latin American masses harbored against the United States. A few weeks later, an imaginative proposal issued by Brazilian President Juscelino Kubitscheck envisioning a joint program of economic development for the hemisphere caught the eye of United States officials alarmed by the upsurge of anti-American sentiments south of the border. The final year of the Eisenhower presidency was marked by a notable modification of United States economic policy toward Latin America. Washington finally withdrew its opposition to the formation of a government-funded regional financing agency, a longstanding objective of several Latin American states. In October 1960 the Inter-American Development Bank was established to disburse development loans to Latin American countries. Though it fell far short of the region's enormous financing requirements, the advent of IADB lending signified an important symbolic departure from Washington's traditional insistence on referring Latin American borrowers to the private capital markets.

The Kennedy administration went much further than Eisenhower's modest commitment to hemispheric economic development. In his inaugural address on January 20, 1961, the new American chief executive proposed an "alliance for progress" with the United States' sister republics to the south in order to help them overcome the debilitating effects of economic backwardness. In a speech on March 13 to an assembly of representatives from the Latin American states, Kennedy outlined in detail an ambitious project of United States public assistance to the region. At the Inter-American Economic and Social Conference in Punta del Este, Uruguay, the following August, the Alliance for Progress was formally brought into existence. As originally conceived, it included features that responded to two concerns that the Latin American countries had been voicing for decades. The first, and by far the most important, was the pledge of a ten-year, $20 billion project of United States government aid to promote the economic development of Latin America and to raise its per capita income 2.5 percent annually. The second was an agreement to seek means of preventing the wild fluctuation of foreign exchange earnings from commodity exports that had plagued the Latin American economies for so long.

This radical reversal of United States economic policy toward Latin America was undertaken with the enthusiastic support of all of the twenty republics to the south save one. Ironically, it was the one that had over the years been most closely linked, economically, politically, and militarily, to the Colossus of the North. In January 1959 the autocratic Batista regime in Cuba, which had preserved that impoverished nation's traditionally subservient relationship with the United States and with the private American sugar companies that controlled its single-crop economy, was toppled by an insurrectionary movement headed by a charismatic revolutionary in the Latin American style named Fidel Castro. Once ensconced in Havana, the new Cuban ruler took a number of steps to eliminate American economic influence in his country amid a flurry of rhetorical outbursts against "Yankee imperialism." In June 1960 he expropriated the extensive landholdings of the American sugar firms. The following October he nationalized all of the banks and large industrial enterprises on the island, a considerable proportion of which were American-owned. This egregious challenge to American economic interests in Cuba provoked a graduated response from Washington that was originally confined to measures of economic retaliation, including a 95 percent reduction of the sugar quota (by which Cuba's exports of its major cash crop were allowed to enter the United States at prices above those obtainable on the world market) on July 6 and an American embargo on all exports to the island except medical supplies and most foodstuffs on October 19. As the once-intimate economic relationship between the United States and Cuba approached the breaking point during 1960, the Soviet Union grasped this unprecedented opportunity to contest the hegemonic position of the United States in its own hemisphere. In February 1960 the U.S.S.R. agreed to purchase one-fifth of Cuba's sugar production, subsequently raising the proportion to a half in December of that year. It also granted $200 million in low-interest loans to the financially hard-pressed Havana regime. By the end of the year, Cuba was receiving substantial arms shipments from the Soviet bloc.

As President Eisenhower prepared to vacate the White House during the winter of 1960–61, it had become unmistakably evident that American economic pressure on the Castro regime was doomed to fail because of the Soviet Union's eagerness to replace the United States as Cuba's primary customer for its sugar and principal supplier of its foreign credits. Moreover, the Cuban leader had explicitly endorsed the general foreign policy goals of his new economic benefactors, most dramatically during a four-and-a-half-hour denunciation of yankee imperialism from the rostrum of the United Nations General Assembly on September 26, 1960. While the size of America's diplomatic representation in Havana was systematically reduced at Cuban insistence to such minimal levels as to provoke a rupture in relations in January 1961, thousands of Soviet technicians, military

Nikita Khrushchev (1894–1971) and Fidel Castro (1927–) at a meeting of the United Nations General Assembly, September 1960: The aging Soviet leader admired the dynamic young revolutionary who defied the United States in its own backyard. The Eisenhower administration was already devising plans to topple the new Cuban strongman, who had recently nationalized U.S. companies and farms and had begun to align himself with the Eastern bloc in the Cold War. *(Courtesy of the Library of Congress)*

advisers, and diplomatic personnel poured into the country to lend assistance to Castro's revolutionary regime. To nervous observers in Washington, it appeared that the small island that had long been regarded, in strategic and economic terms, as an extension of the Florida Keys in the Caribbean, was on the verge of becoming a client state of the Soviet Union.

To obviate that ominous possibility, the outgoing Eisenhower administration had bequeathed to its successor a plan for the forcible overthrow of the Castro government. Under the supervision of the American Central Intelligence Agency, an exile army composed of refugees from Cuba had been armed and trained at clandestine camps in Florida, Guatemala, and Nicaragua in preparation for an invasion of the island. The organizers of the expedition were confident that the mere appearance of these paramilitary freedom fighters would incite an internal uprising by the disgruntled victims of Castro's oppression. Though skeptical about its chances of success, the new American president authorized the projected invasion. On April 17 a brigade of about fifteen hundred Cuban exiles transported in American ships from training camps in Guatemala disembarked on the island and established a beachhead at a place called the Bay of Pigs. The anticipated

Cuban volunteers in Miami receiving physical exams to become recruits in the CIA-supervised exile army to overthrow Castro, April 1961: Five days before the Bay of Pigs invasion on April 12, Kennedy declared at a press conference that "there will not be, under any conditions, an intervention in Cuba by the United States Armed Forces. The basic issue in Cuba is not one between the United States and Cuba. It is between the Cubans themselves." *(Courtesy of the Library of Congress)*

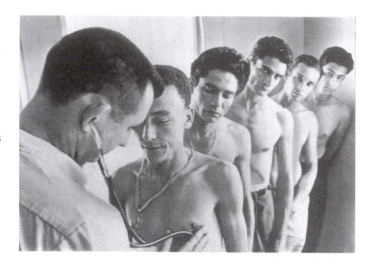

revolt against Castro failed to materialize, and within three days the entire invasion force had been either killed or captured by Castro's military forces.

As embarrassing as this misadventure proved to be to the new American president at the very beginning of his term, its most important consequences were felt in Cuba itself. Convinced that the abortive landing at the Bay of Pigs was merely the opening salvo in America's campaign to dislodge him, Castro earnestly solicited Moscow for what it had previously refrained from according him: the promise of military protection against the United States. But as U.S. plans to destabilize the Castro regime proceeded, the Kremlin decided in the spring of 1962 to accede to the request of its protégé in Havana for conventional weapons to defend the island. Soon thereafter, Khrushchev sweetened the offer by adding medium- and intermediate-range ballistic missiles as a deterrent to another American-sponsored invasion by Cuban exile commandos who were still being trained on American territory.

Notwithstanding all of its professions of concern for the security of its new client state in the Caribbean, Moscow's decision to begin the construction of sites for thirty-six medium-range ballistic missiles (MRBMs) and twenty-four intermediate-range ballistic missiles (IRBMs) in Cuba was also prompted by considerations directly related to the Soviet national interest. Some Soviet officials saw the missiles as potential bargaining chips in the global poker game that the Cold War between the two superpowers had become. Some imagined a Cuba-for-Berlin deal that would finally remove the embarrassing showcase of Western economic prosperity and political liberty from the center of East Germany. Most importantly, Khrushchev stood to regain for his country the strategic advantage that had been lost by the impressive buildup of American ICBMs since Sputnik: Missiles based in Cuba with ranges of 1,100 to 2,200 nautical miles would have constituted ersatz intercontinental missiles, reducing the American warning time to virtually nothing and exposing the entire territory of the continental United States save a corner of the Pacific Northwest to a Soviet nuclear attack.

In any case, the discovery of the Soviet missile sites by American reconnaissance planes overflying Cuba in mid-October 1962 provoked an American rejoinder of such unyielding firmness as to preclude whatever high-level horse-trading or strategic gains the Soviet leader may have had in mind. President Kennedy flung down the gauntlet to Khrushchev in a nationally televised address on October 22. After citing the irrefutable evidence of the missile sites in the process of installation, he announced his intention to impose an air and naval "quarantine"—avoiding the term "blockade" because it signified an act of war according to international law—to prevent the arrival of additional nuclear armaments in Cuba. He proceeded to warn Moscow that any nuclear missile launched from Cuba against any nation in the Western hemisphere would be considered a Russian attack on the United States and would be met with instant American nuclear retaliation against the Soviet Union. He demanded the prompt removal of the missile sites already completed or in the process of construction. After obtaining the unanimous support of America's allies in NATO and in the OAS, Kennedy ordered the naval blockade into effect on October 24. Warships of the American Second Fleet took their stations along the arc of a five hundred-mile radius around the eastern tip of Cuba under orders to intercept and search all vessels suspected of carrying the missiles to the island. On the same day, thirty Soviet or Soviet-chartered cargo ships were steaming across the Atlantic for Cuba while construction work on the missile sites continued at a hastily increased pace. Suddenly, after a decade of rhetoric about "massive retaliation" and "nuclear exchanges" in Washington and Moscow, the two superpowers appeared poised for an epic confrontation from which neither seemed able to back down.

Then, on the evening of the twenty-fourth, a dozen of the Russian ships en route to Cuba (presumably those carrying the contraband) either altered or reversed course. The remaining problem of the missile sites already in place was resolved in the following few days through an exchange of written communications between Kennedy and Khrushchev. Confronted with the genuine possibility of all-out-nuclear war, the Soviet leader capitulated to the Kennedy ultimatum on the basis of a single condition: The missile installations would be dismantled and returned to Russia in exchange for an American promise not to invade Cuba. By the end of the year, the Soviet missile sites had disappeared from the Cuban earth, the American naval quarantine had been lifted, and Moscow had signaled to Washington its earnest desire to settle all of the outstanding issues in dispute between the two superpowers across the globe. Both sides managed conciliatory gestures in recognition of the necessity to keep alive the spirit of cooperation that had been forged in the fires of the Cuban crisis. The Soviet Union, which could easily have blockaded Berlin in revenge for the American blockade of Cuba, refrained from even the slightest provocation in that region of maximum American vulnerability. In the following year the United States inconspicuously dismantled its Jupiter missiles based in Turkey, fulfilling a verbal pledge that President Kennedy had conveyed to the Kremlin through his brother Robert.

The Kremlin gamely attempted to put the best possible light on its humiliating setback in Cuba in order to reassure allies and prospective clients alike of its reliability as a patron: By extracting the no-invasion pledge from Kennedy, Khrushchev had rescued

"Eyeball to eyeball, they blinked first": That was the judgment of U.S. Secretary of State Dean Rusk at the end of the Cuban missile crisis. The photo shows the Soviet freighter *Anesov* being escorted by a U.S. navy plane and the destroyer U.S.S. *Barry* while leaving Cuba in October 1962 (probably loaded with missiles under canvas seen on the deck). An enraged Castro felt betrayed by the Soviet leader's decision to suspend the delivery of missiles to Cuba and to remove those that had already reached the island. *(Courtesy of the Library of Congress)*

Castro from a terrible fate. The missiles were therefore no longer required as protection against Yankee aggression. But the American secretary of state, Dean Rusk, character- ized the outcome of the Cuban missile crisis in a pitchy, unforgettable line that typified the spirit of machismo animating the Kennedy administration: "Eyeball to eyeball, they blinked first."

10

DETENTE AND MULTIPOLARITY (1962–1975)

If we define a global power as a state capable of exercising decisive influence anywhere in the world through economic, political, and military means, then the United States alone deserved that designation at the time of the Cuban missile crisis of 1962. With a gross national product three times that of its nearest competitor, the Soviet Union, America's economic preponderance in the world was beyond dispute. So too was the ubiquity and potency of its political influence in the non-Communist world. America's political preeminence in Western Europe had been secured once President Truman assumed the leadership of the Atlantic bloc at the end of the 1940s and Eisenhower reaffirmed the ideological unity of the non-Communist world during the 1950s. In the early 1960s the political influence of the United States was extended to the nations of the Third World by means of the elaborate projects of foreign assistance that had been inaugurated by the charismatic new occupant of the White House. As the unchallenged protector and benefactor of the non-Communist portions of the earth, the United States could, at least until the mid-1960s, confidently count on commanding a comfortable majority for its policies in the General Assembly of the United Nations to supplement the preeminent position occupied by itself and its three loyal allies among the permanent members of the Security Council.

In sum, Washington's political standing in the developing world had risen dramatically during the first half of the 1960s. The progressive rhetoric of the Kennedy administration endowed American foreign policy with a positive ideological component that it had lacked during the rigidly anti-Communist Eisenhower-Dulles years. The professed commitment to "nation building," to the provision of United States economic and technical assistance to promote modernization in the Third World, exerted a powerful attraction on the impoverished masses of the earth. The other part of the Kennedy policy toward the developing world was the counterinsurgency feature. This was designed to ensure that the sweeping socioeconomic reforms that were supposed to be catalyzed by the American aid programs would be managed in an evolutionary rather than a revolutionary manner. This aspect of American policy naturally appealed to the ruling elites of the developing countries who feared insurrection and welcomed American assistance in quelling it. As the United States behaved during the first half of the sixties as the champion of peaceful social reform and economic modernization in the developing world, Moscow had emerged from the Cuban missile crisis with the tarnished reputation of a patron who would not stand firm behind its client when the chips were down. It appeared, however briefly, that America was winning what President Kennedy was fond of calling the contest "for the hearts and minds of the underdeveloped and uncommitted peoples of the world."

ARMS CONTROL AND STRATEGIC PARITY

It was only in the realm of military power that the Soviet Union, could claim to challenge America's global supremacy, and even that challenge proved to be illusory. As we have seen, the alarmist talk about a "missile gap" following the firing of the first Soviet intercontinental ballistic missile in August and the launching of the Sputnik earth satellite in October of 1957 was based on a gross overestimation of the Russians' capacity to translate technological potential into strategic achievement. In December of the same year the United States launched its own five-thousand-mile-range Atlas ICBM, and promptly began to construct a formidable intercontinental missile force. Eisenhower's embarrassment over the U-2 affair of May 1960 was surpassed by Khrushchev's own humiliation at seeing the hollowness of his inflated strategic claims exposed: A nation that had launched the world's first earth satellite and tested the first ICBM could not prevent American spy planes from overflying its territory at 75,000 feet for four years until engine trouble forced one to descend. At the time of the showdown over Cuba, the Soviet Union was outclassed by the United States in every category of nuclear armament and delivery system; moreover, Russia boasted neither an oceanic navy capable of projecting Soviet power beyond its coasts nor overseas bases to accommodate such a "blue water" fleet, while the United States boasted a naval presence and base facilities all over the world. The Russian colossus remained the premier land power in Eurasia, capable of reaching the Rhine or the Mediterranean or the Persian Gulf in a few weeks by dint of its overwhelming conventional superiority vis-à-vis weak and vulnerable neighbors. But it was dissuaded from even seriously considering such a conventional military breakthrough by the American nuclear deterrent composed of ICBMs and long-range bombers based on American soil and IRBMs, MRBMs, and medium-range bombers arrayed along the Russian frontier in countries allied to the United States.

Khrushchev's attempt to leapfrog the American defense perimeter along the periphery of Eurasia by implanting a Soviet nuclear armament system in Cuba may have in part represented a desperate gamble to rectify this strategic imbalance in a single decisive blow. The humiliating conditions of the Soviet retreat in Cuba produced precisely the opposite effect from the one presumably intended. Instead of establishing a more stable balance of nuclear power between the two superpowers, the Cuban crisis graphically revealed to the world the extent of Soviet military inferiority. Instead of rallying the Communist bloc behind a newly invigorated Soviet Union, it prompted the Chinese leadership to accelerate its defection from the Soviet orbit that had begun two years earlier. Instead of enhancing Khrushchev's standing in the eyes of the Soviet military establishment and its allies in the civilian leadership, it aggravated the internal dissatisfaction that eventually led to his downfall.

The lessons learned by the Kremlin from the Cuban fiasco resulted in the adoption of two strategies—one diplomatic and the other military—that were to remain the basis of Soviet policy after Khrushchev's departure. The first was the resumption of the quest for "peaceful coexistence" with the Western bloc that had been initiated by Stalin's successors in the midfifties but had been interrupted by the bellicose Soviet probes in Berlin and Cuba during 1958–62. Its purpose was to minimize the possibility of a nuclear confrontation such as had almost occurred in 1962—a contest that the Soviet Union, in its current state of strategic inferiority, was bound to lose. The second was the acceleration of a long-range program, also begun in the mid-fifties but postponed for a variety of domestic reasons, to transform Russia from a Eurasian land power into a global sea and air power capable of defending its interests anywhere in the world. *Its* purpose was to achieve an approximate parity in nuclear and naval forces that would neutralize the American strategic deterrent and naval superiority that had been exercised so effectively at Russia's expense in the autumn of 1962.

The most dramatic consequences of the policy of peaceful coexistence were to become evident in the realm of strategic arms control. Since the end of the Second World War, fruitless discussions on nuclear disarmament had been conducted in the United Nations and proposals to that effect had periodically issued from Washington and Moscow. At the first meeting of the United Nations Atomic Energy Commission in June 1946, the United States, at the time enjoying a nuclear monopoly, offered to turn over its stockpile of atomic weapons to an international agency under United Nations auspices on the condition that all other countries pledge not to produce them and agree to an adequate system of inspection. The Soviet Union, hard at work on the development of a nuclear capability of its own, rejected the so-called Baruch plan on the grounds that the United Nations was dominated by the United States and its West European partners and therefore could not be trusted to exercise authority over atomic weaponry in an evenhanded manner. After the Soviet Union became a nuclear power in 1949, it became a convert to the cause of atomic arms control, particularly after the death of Stalin and the beginning of the pursuit of peaceful coexistence. On May 10, 1955, the Kremlin formally proposed a gradual reduction of conventional forces to specified levels, followed by the destruction of nuclear stockpiles. Khrushchev went one step further in a speech to the UN General Assembly in 1959, calling for general and total disarmament within four years. But all of these Soviet proposals foundered on the question of verification: Washington firmly insisted on the principle of onsite inspection to certify compliance with such disarmament agreements as might be concluded; Moscow resolutely refused to permit arms inspectors on its territory and, as we have seen, even rejected Eisenhower's proposal at the 1955 Geneva Conference for mutual aerial surveillance of military installations.

But if superpower disarmament in an unstable world proved to be an impossible goal, the nuclear alarm sounded by the Cuban missile crisis prompted the two sides to concentrate on a more modest and attainable objective: the imposition of limitations on the testing, deployment, and proliferation of nuclear weapons in the future. In August 1963 the Soviet Union joined the United States and Great Britain in signing the limited Test Ban Treaty, which prohibited nuclear tests in the atmosphere and in the sea. In January

1967 the same three nations together with France, which had become the fourth nuclear power in 1960, agreed to keep outer space free of nuclear weapons. Later in the same year, Latin America was declared a nuclear-free zone by a majority of its member states in the Treaty of Tlatelolco.

The establishment of direct teletype communications between the White House and the Kremlin after the Cuban missile crisis—the "hot line" agreement of June 20, 1963—was an expression of Soviet-American determination to reduce the risk of accidental nuclear war. But an even greater concern shared by the two superpowers was the potential threat to the delicate strategic balance posed by the acquisition of nuclear weapons by other countries. The Soviet Union had adamantly refused to share its nuclear technology with its European satellites and its Asian allies or even to supply them with nuclear weapons under Russian control. The United States had done its best to dissuade its Atlantic partners from developing nuclear capabilities of their own by refusing to share nuclear information while assuring them adequate protection under the American nuclear "umbrella." But the advance of scientific knowledge and the consciousness of national sovereignty were not limited to the United States and the Soviet Union. What had been a nuclear duopoly at the beginning of the 1950s had become a nuclear club of ominously expanding membership by the middle of the 1960s. Great Britain had tested its first atomic device in 1952 and its first hydrogen (or thermonuclear) bomb in 1957. France and China, two nations that began to pursue foreign and defense policies independent of the wishes of their erstwhile superpower allies in the early 1960s, joined the nuclear club in 1960 and 1964, respectively.

With the intention of curbing the further expansion of the nuclear fraternity, the United States, the Soviet Union, and Great Britain signed in July 1968 the Nuclear Non-Proliferation Treaty, which came into force on March 5, 1970, when ninety-seven countries had signed it and forty-seven (including the original signatories) had ratified it. According to its provisions, the nuclear powers (minus China and France, both of which refused to sign) pledged never to furnish nuclear weapons or the technology to fabricate them to nonnuclear powers, while the nonnuclear countries promised never to produce or acquire them. An international inspection team was established in Vienna under the auspices of the United Nations International Atomic Energy Administration to verify compliance with the treaty.

The spate of international agreements in the 1960s had the effect of forbidding the testing, development, or deployment of nuclear weapons by nonnuclear powers and by nuclear powers in certain specified regions. A much more challenging task was to impose limits on the nuclear arsenals of the only two nations that were capable of unleashing nuclear devastation on the entire world. The U.S.S.R. had had no incentive to endorse strategic arms control during the twenty-year period after the Second World War when it lagged far behind its Cold War rival in the quality and quantity of its nuclear arms. To freeze the nuclear forces of the two superpowers at a level of such strategic imbalance would have permanently relegated the Soviet Union to the position of military vulnerability that had enabled Dulles to threaten massive retaliation against conventional Soviet moves during the 1950s.

In the very period (the aftermath of the Cuban missile crisis) when the Soviet Union cooperated with other nations to impose limits on the nuclear arms race, it earnestly pursued the goal of strategic parity with the United States. When the Brezhnev-Kosygin faction toppled Khrushchev on October 15, 1964, it inherited an ambitious project for military expansion begun in 1960 that was designed to erase the Soviet Union's strategic inferiority by the end of the decade. This program included a buildup of the Strategic Rocket Forces (which were created as an independent arm of the military forces), the development of medium- and intermediate-range ballistic missiles for deployment in the European theater, and the upgrading of antiaircraft and civil defense capabilities. In all of the categories of military strength, the new leadership in the Kremlin achieved its goals. During the second half of the 1960s, while America's war in Vietnam swallowed up funds that might otherwise have been spent to increase the size of its nuclear arsenal, the Soviet Union tripled the number of its land-based ICBMs and greatly expanded the number of its submarine-launched ballistic missiles (SLBMs). Consequently, the missile gap that had forced Khrushchev to back down during the Cuban crisis had been bridged by the end of the decade: Whereas the United States had possessed 294 ICBMs compared to 75 for the Soviet Union in 1962, by 1969 the Soviet arsenal of long-range missiles numbered 1,050 as against 1,054 for the United States. In the meantime the Soviets had overtaken the United States in SLBMs and were challenging American superiority in long-range bombers. In short, the two superpowers had achieved what President Richard M. Nixon later termed "essential equivalence" in their strategic forces. In the chilling language of defense analysts, they had acquired the capacity for "mutual assured destruction" (MAD). This meant the ability to destroy a quarter of the enemy's population and over half of its industry in a nuclear exchange.

During the same period, Soviet naval power was expanded with the intention of contesting America's hitherto undisputed supremacy on the high seas. Since, unlike the United States, Russia's seaborne trade was insignificant and it could reach all of its major allies by land, the Soviet leadership had never before felt impelled to construct a fleet capable of operating on the oceans and remained content with a naval force geared to coastal defense. But in the course of the 1960s the Soviet navy acquired the capability to intervene far from its shores in defense of Soviet interests. This feat was accomplished under the leadership of Admiral Sergei Gorshkov, who had been appointed head of the navy by Khrushchev in 1957. In 1964 a Soviet Mediterranean squadron made its first appearance and in 1968 a regular Soviet naval presence was established in the Indian Ocean just as British naval power was being withdrawn from that region. A large Soviet nuclear submarine fleet was roaming the ocean depths by the late 1960s. By the early 1970s, the Soviet Union was able to project its naval power and its nuclear deterrent to all of the strategically important regions of the world. All that stood in the way of its becoming a global naval power was the lack of overseas bases and refueling stations to accommodate its oceanic fleet, a problem that would, as we shall see, be overcome in the course of the following decade.

This narrowing of the strategic gap between the two superpowers in the late 1960s supplied the stimulus for the first successful arms control negotiation since the advent of the Cold War. There had been some serious talk of convening Soviet-American arms limitation talks in the mid-1960s. But the American military escalation in Vietnam, the Arab-Israeli conflict in the Middle East, and the Soviet intervention in Czechoslovakia embittered relations between Washington and Moscow during the years when Lyndon Johnson occupied the White House and Leonid Brezhnev and Alexei Kosygin jockeyed for primacy in the Kremlin after Khrushchev's removal in 1964. It required the inauguration of a new American president, Nixon, and the emergence of an undisputed master of the Politburo, Brezhnev, in the year 1969 before the hopes of bilateral talks on strategic arms control could be translated into reality. For a complex set of political and economic reasons to be summarized below, Nixon and Brezhnev had simultaneously developed an appreciation of the numerous advantages that were likely to accrue to both sides from a relaxation of Soviet-American tensions in the world. The military context of the evolution toward improved relations between Washington and Moscow was the rough parity in strategic weaponry cited above: In the face of the certainty of mutual destruction, both superpowers shared a common interest in curbing an arms race that, it was now unmistakably plain, neither side could win. The economic advantages to be gained from a deceleration in military spending need scarcely be cited: The swollen defense budgets of both superpowers had diverted financial resources that might otherwise have been available for the funding of domestic social programs and productive enterprises that would increase the standard of living of the Russian and American people. Accordingly, on the day of Nixon's inauguration (January 20, 1969) the Kremlin publicly proposed Soviet-American negotiations for the reciprocal limitation of nuclear delivery vehicles and defensive systems. Nixon promptly endorsed the Soviet proposal in a speech that also contained a significant modification of the traditional American position concerning the strategic balance that was bound to smooth the path toward accommodation with the U.S.S.R.: For the first time, an American president accepted the principle of strategic parity in place of the customary insistence on American strategic superiority. On November 17, 1969, preliminary discussions began in Helsinki between Soviet and American officials. Six subsequent meetings were held alternately in Vienna and Helsinki with the designation Strategic Arms Limitation Talks (SALT).

After more than two years of tortuous negotiations over the complexities of strategic weaponry, an interim arms control agreement (officially known as the first Strategic Arms Limitation Treaty or SALT I) was signed on May 26, 1972, during President Nixon's unprecedented official visit to Moscow. Instead of attempting to impose limits on the number of nuclear weapons that had been stockpiled by the two superpowers in the course of the previous two decades, the SALT negotiators had concentrated on two other components of the strategic balance that proved more susceptible to agreement. The first was the delivery vehicles that would carry the warheads to their targets. A ceiling was placed on the number of ICBMs that each side could deploy for a period of five years (October 3, 1972, to October 3, 1977), freezing the number of American ICBMs at 1,054 while permitting the Soviet Union to increase its ICBMs from 1,530 to 1,618. A moratorium of equivalent duration was declared on the construction of submarine-launched missiles (SLBMs), leaving the Soviet Union with 950 missiles in sixty-two submarines compared to 710 American missiles in forty-four submarines. These two agreements represented the first successful effort by the two superpowers to establish quantitative limits on their strategic delivery systems.

The second weapons system that was restricted by the SALT I treaty was the so-called Antiballistic Missile (ABM) System that was designed to intercept and destroy incoming missiles before they reached their targets. The United States had been experimenting with a variety of antimissile defense systems since 1956, a year before the Soviets launched their first ICBM. The first successful test of an interceptor missile was conducted in New Mexico in 1959. Between 1962 and 1967 Robert S. McNamara, the secretary of defense

**U.S. President Richard Nixon and Soviet General Secretary Leonid Brezhnev during Brezh-
nev's visit to Washington, June 19, 1973:** The two architects of detente presided over a marked
improvement in Soviet-American relations during the first half of the 1970s. At the time of this
visit, Nixon was already embroiled in the Watergate crisis that would force him to resign the following year. *(National Archives)*

under presidents Kennedy and Johnson, presided over the development of an ABM system that consisted of a short- and a long-range missile designed to protect cities against
attacks from miner nuclear powers such as China (which had joined the nuclear club in
1964). This was a tacit admission that no antimissile system could protect America's
urban populations against the formidable nuclear arsenal of the Soviet Union: A single
missile eluding interception could destroy Washington, New York, or Los Angeles. In
recognition of this fact, President Nixon in 1969 abandoned the concept of defending
cities (except for Washington, the nation's command center) in favor of protecting America's land-based retaliatory missiles, which, because they were housed in concrete underground silos, could be expected to survive damage that would prove lethal to an entire
population of an unprotected urban area. The Nixon ABM system, which became partially operational by 1972, prompted great uneasiness in Moscow, while the simultaneous development of a Soviet ABM system (Galosh) aroused similar apprehension in
Washington. The reason that what appeared to be a purely defensive weapons system
evoked such anxiety on both sides is that it threatened to upset the delicate balance of
mutual deterrence that had been established by the end of the 1960s. The future deployment of an impenetrable ABM system by either side, capable of defending all of that
side's large cities from nuclear attack, could readily be interpreted by the other side as a

prelude to a surprise first strike that could be launched without fear of retaliation. To allay these concerns, the SALT I agreement limited each side to the deployment of 100 ABM launchers and interceptor missiles at two sites, one to be the national capital and the other to be an ICBM missile base (in the American case, the Minuteman silos located near Grand Forks, North Dakota). The logic underlying this feature of the SALT I agreement was that it preserved the stability of the strategic balance by reducing the incentive for either side to gamble on a first strike: If one side could protect its command center* and one of its land-based ICBM sites, it would thereby retain the capacity to retaliate in spite of the total destruction of its remaining nuclear arsenal by a surprise attack.

The preceding comparative figures reveal that the Soviet Union retained superiority in the total number of missiles covered by the SALT I agreement (ICBMs and SLBMs). Nevertheless, President Nixon was able to assure his domestic constituency that the United States enjoyed overall parity with its principal adversary because of American superiority in strategic weapons systems not covered by the treaty limitations. First of all, the United States retained a considerable advantage in the number of long-range bombers. Second, the Soviet Union had no counterpart in the western hemisphere to the American intermediate-range missiles stationed in Europe that could reach cities in western Russia. Third, the British nuclear forces provided an additional incremental advantage to the United States unavailable to the Soviet Union, which refused to permit its East European satellites to develop independent nuclear forces and could not count the Chinese nuclear armament on the plus side of its strategic ledger. But the decisive equalizer for the United States was the superior quality of its nuclear warheads. Many of the American land-based (Minuteman) and submarine-based (Poseidon) missiles had been fitted with multiple warheads, each of which was capable of striking different targets. These so-called Multiple Independently Targetable Reentry Vehicles (MIRVs) greatly increased the destructive power of the ICBMs on which they were fitted. Moreover, while it was relatively easy to detect through satellite reconnaissance the number of land-based and submarine-based missiles a nation possessed, it was virtually impossible to verify the number of independently targetable warheads each missile contained.

After the forced resignation of President Nixon in August 1974, continuity of policy was assured through the retention of Henry Kissinger as secretary of state by Nixon's successor, Gerald Ford. Ford and Brezhnev were able to conclude an interim agreement at the Vladivostok summit conference on November 24, 1974, which established guidelines for a SALT II treaty that would limit categories of strategic delivery vehicles not covered by SALT I (such as MIRVs and long-range bombers).† For the first time since the advent of the Cold War, officials in Washington and Moscow were confidently forecasting an end to the unrestrained competition for strategic superiority between the two superpowers.

The SALT I treaty froze the two superpowers into a position of approximate parity in strategic weapons systems and preserved the status of "mutual assured destruction" that

---

*A protocol signed in 1974 restricted each side to a single ABM deployment, thereby abandoning the original idea of protecting the two national capitals.

†In addition to placing an upper limit of 2,400 on each side's ICBMs, SLBMs, and heavy bombers, the Vladivostok agreement (which was never ratified) established a ceiling of 1,320 MIR Ved missiles.

its architects regarded as the most reliable form of insurance against a nuclear holocaust. Plans were promptly laid for negotiations to produce a successor agreement after the expiration of SALT I in 1977.

The development of Soviet-American cooperation to impose restraints on the nuclear arms race during the first half of the 1970s would have been inconceivable without prior success in the reduction of political tensions between the two superpowers in those parts of the world where their interests directly collided. The most visible flashpoint of super-power confrontation at the time was Southeast Asia, where half a million American troops combated a North Vietnamese army supplied and supported by the Soviet Union. The Nixon administration's decision to terminate America's direct involvement in the war in Indochina, however protracted that disengagement turned out to be, removed a major irritant in Soviet-American relations. But in the context of the global rivalry between Washington and Moscow, the war in Southeast Asia was overshadowed by the salient geopolitical feature of the 1960s, which was the gradual disintegration of the two rigid power blocs that had coalesced in the early years of the Cold War. Throughout the previous decade a majority of the countries of the world were aligned in one or the other of the two armed camps. The two superpowers had been able to count on the unswerving allegiance of those nations that remained under their tutelage and protection. The loosening-up of this bipolar international system during the 1960s was precipitated by three important developments in the world. The first, already alluded to in Chapter 9, was the appearance of dozens of newly independent nations in the Third World that swelled the ranks of the nonaligned bloc. The second was the increasingly assertive and independent posture of America's allies in Western Europe, who began to chafe at their position as pawns in the Cold War and eagerly sought a *modus vivendi* with the Communist states to the east in order to reduce the risks of nuclear annihilation. The third was the defection of China from the Communist camp and its emergence as an independent force in world affairs. These three converging developments helped to produce a more fluid international environment than had existed when two tightly organized blocs dominated by two superpowers confronted each other across the great ideological divide in Europe and Asia. In the end, as we shall see, the evolution of a multipolar international system enabled the United States and the Soviet Union to break the impasse of the Cold War and approach the hitherto impossible goals of arms control, disengagement, and detente.

FRANCE'S ASSAULT ON THE BIPOLAR WORLD

The first direct challenge to America's preeminent position in Western Europe was to come from France after the return to power in June 1958 of Charles de Gaulle, Roosevelt's old wartime nemesis who had disappeared from the political scene in 1946. The occasion of his reappearance was France's costly, foredoomed struggle to retain control of its North African territory of Algeria in the face of an insurrection by its majority Arab population. Armed with emergency powers to settle this bitter dispute, which had brought his own country to the brink of military insurgency and civil war, de Gaulle proceeded to cut France loose not only from Algeria but also from its remaining colonial possessions in Africa. By 1962 France's painful process of postwar decolonization was virtually complete, while a fundamental constitutional reorganization had placed extensive authority in the hands of the chief executive. These two developments rescued France from the debilitating political and colonial burdens of the recent past and set the stage for a series of bold diplomatic initiatives aimed at securing an objective that had been dear to de Gaulle's heart since the end of the Second World War: the transformation of a French-led Europe into a political, economic, and strategic bloc independent of both the United States and the Soviet Union and capable of acting as a third force in world affairs. Though the outcome of this bid for European independence of superpower domination fell far short of the excessively ambitious expectations of its architect, the foreign policy of Gaullist France from 1962 to 1969 left a lasting imprint an East-West relations by loosening the ties that had bound the signatories of the North Atlantic Treaty in a position of subservience to American authority and unqualified support for American global objectives.

De Gaulle's foreign policy stemmed from a fundamental dissatisfaction with the international order envisioned by the leaders of the United States and the Soviet Union during World War II and formalized during the early years of the Cold War. The postwar division first of Europe and then of the entire world into a bipolar system under the shared hegemony of the two non-European superpowers was regarded by de Gaulle as an intolerable condition for France in particular and Europe in general for a number of reasons.

First of all, it deprived the once proud and independent states of the continent of the freedom of action that de Gaulle regarded as the prerequisite of great power status. No nation condemned to rely on the military protection of another for its security, he declared, could hope to aspire to a role beyond that of compliant protégé. The understandable resentment that had been engendered by this condition of subservience was especially widespread in France, with its vivid memories of a glorious heritage as a continental and imperial power of the first rank. But de Gaulle's blatant appeal to national pride struck a sensitive nerve throughout Western Europe, whose postwar economic and political recovery had erased the sense of despair and vulnerability that had prevailed in the early years of the Cold War and led to its dependence on American military protection and economic assistance. The European Economic Community that had been formed in 1957 was developing into one of the most formidable economic blocs in the world. Many Europeans who basked in the economic prosperity and political stability of the 1960s began to wonder why they should continue to feel obligated to adapt their foreign and defense policies to the global strategy of their transatlantic patron, particularly at a time when the Soviet threat to Western Europe appeared to have receded.

In addition to this appeal to national pride, de Gaulle's denunciation of Western Europe's military dependence on the United States exploited the sentiment of fear stimulated by the nuclear arms race. Since the two superpowers were engaged in a global contest for hegemony, Soviet-American tensions in regions of secondary concern to Europe could readily escalate into a nuclear confrontation that would inevitably engulf the western half of that continent by virtue of its alliance with the United States and the presence of American military bases and missile installations on its territory. Dulles's saber rattling during the Quemoy crisis shortly after de Gaulle's return to power in 1958 raised the prospect of a nuclear showdown over a worthless island thousands of miles from France (see p. 362). The war scare over Cuba in 1962 reinforced such apprehensions, as did the subsequent American military escalation in Vietnam during the mid-1960s.

The obverse of this fear of being dragged by the United States into a nuclear Armageddon over issues unrelated to Europe's vital interests was the fear of being abandoned by the

President Charles de Gaulle of France (1890–1970): De Gaulle was the first European leader to challenge the undisputed dominance of the United States in the Western alliance. His dream of a Europe emancipated from the domination of the two superpowers did not materialize, but his independent policies, combined with those of China's Mao Zedong in the Communist world, chipped away at the bipolar international system that had been dominated by Washington and Moscow since the advent of the Cold War. *(Courtesy of the Library of Congress)*

United States in the case of Soviet aggression on the continent. Ever since the development of Soviet intercontinental ballistic missiles in 1957, the credibility of the American pledge to deter a Soviet attack in Europe by threatening nuclear retaliation against Russia itself encountered mounting skepticism across the Atlantic. During the last years of the Eisenhower administration, European doubts about the future of the American commitment were fed by the writings of influential American defense theorists who severely criticized the strategy of massive retaliation in favor of a more discriminating approach that would permit a graduated response to a Soviet attack in Europe. Under the Kennedy administration, the outmoded doctrine of massive retaliation was formally supplanted by a new approach of "flexible response," which envisaged reliance on a variety of military measures—conventional, tactical nuclear, or strategic nuclear—to counter Soviet aggression in Western Europe. The new strategy was a tacit acknowledgment that the threat of nuclear retaliation was no longer a credible deterrent when American cities were within range of

Soviet missiles. Its professed intention was to induce uncertainty, apprehension, and therefore caution in Moscow since the precise nature of the American response could not be known in advance. But by reserving maximum flexibility for the American president to determine the time, place, and manner of a military response to Soviet actions, it inevitably heightened insecurity among America's European allies, who had become accustomed to depending on the certainty of an unconditional American guarantee. Many observers in Europe interpreted the new doctrine as a thinly disguised effort to renege on the pledge of nuclear retaliation against a Soviet conventional attack.

In anticipation of the day when the risk of a nuclear response from Russia would weaken America's resolve to defend Western Europe, French officials had decided in the midfifties to pursue alternative means of providing for their country's defense in the form of an independent French nuclear force. Shortly before the demise of the Fourth Republic in the spring of 1958, the French government authorized preparations for the testing of a nuclear device. De Gaulle accelerated this weapons-related research program upon his accession in June, convinced as he was that no nation could hope to play an influential role in the modern world without a nuclear capability of its own. On February 13, 1960, France became the fourth member of the nuclear club with the announcement that it had tested its first atomic bomb in the Algerian Sahara.

Ever since the passage of the McMahon Act in 1946, the United States government had been legally precluded from assisting other countries, even its most trusted allies, in developing an independent nuclear capability. In 1957 this prohibition was modified in order to permit the sharing of nuclear technology with Great Britain, which had tested its first atomic bomb in 1952 and its first hydrogen bomb in 1957. But American support for the modest British nuclear force was tendered on the unstated condition that it remain under indirect American control and conform to American strategic doctrine. France's acquisition of a nuclear capability, on the other hand, posed a serious challenge to the incoming Kennedy administration because of de Gaulle's undiguised intention to develop a fully independent nuclear strike force, or *force de frappe*. The prospect of a French nuclear force operating under national rather than NATO (hence American) auspices directly contradicted the new strategic doctrine embraced by Kennedy and his defense secretary, Robert McNamara, which depended on a centrally controlled mechanism of retaliation against Soviet aggression.

Since the one component lacking in the British and French nuclear forces was a credible delivery system, Kennedy sought to exploit this weakness in order to ensure American control over them. At the Nassau conference in December 1962 between President Kennedy and Prime Minister Harold Macmillan, the United States offered to supply Great Britain with Polaris missiles for deployment on British submarines as a replacement for its obsolete and vulnerable long-range bomber force. The offer was contingent on Macmillan's pledge that the modernized British force would be assigned to a projected Multilateral Nuclear Force (MLF) within NATO. Upon Macmillan's acceptance, Kennedy tendered a similar offer to de Gaulle on the same condition, but was rebuffed with the reply that French military independence was incompatible with supranational control of its emerging nuclear armament. The American concept of an MLF for NATO was spelled out in March 1963 in the form of a proposal for a multinational fleet of surface ships armed with Polaris missiles under the joint supervision of the alliance's member states. To Washington this represented a concession to European misgivings about the American monopoly of NATO's nuclear decision-making authority. In Paris it was perceived as an attempt to dissuade France from proceeding with its plans to deploy an independent nuclear force by raising the frightening possibility of West German participation in an all-European nuclear force. The MLF proposal finally died in December 1964 on account of the reluctance of the other NATO powers to antagonize France for fear of provoking a full-fledged crisis in the alliance.

But by the time of the MLF's demise, France had already begun to deploy a rudimentary delivery system, which eventually consisted of long-range bombers as well as land-based and submarine-based missiles. The strategic rationale for France's *force de frappe* was the theory of "proportional deterrence" developed by General Pierre Gallois and implicitly endorsed by President de Gaulle. According to this doctrine, the two superpowers each required a massive deterrent capability because a deficiency in either one might tempt the other to risk the destruction of a large proportion of its population for the grand prize of total victory over its only global adversary and therefore absolute security in the future. But the modest nuclear force that France had begun to deploy was sufficient as a credible deterrent because the damage it could inflict on a few Russian cities represented a patently unacceptable sacrifice for the minimal rewards that Moscow could expect to obtain by the conquest of a second-rank power such as France.

The incompatibility of Gaullist nuclear policy and the American conception of a tightly knit Atlantic alliance under the centralized direction of Washington needs no reemphasis here. Underlying the esoteric Franco-American debate over technical matters of military strategy was a more fundamental divergence of views concerning the emerging supranational European entity. The formation of the European Economic Community in 1957 and the subsequent progress toward European economic integration inevitably posed the question of America's future relationship to this powerful West European economic bloc, with its potential for political and even military integration. The Kennedy administration had devised a "grand design" for the improvement of relations between the United States and Western Europe. It hailed the emerging economic community across the Atlantic as a welcome sign of vitality in valued allies, despite the potential menace to American commercial interests implied by the formation of an integrated, protectionist trading bloc on the continent. But in the realm of defense policy, as we have seen, the United States declined to relinquish its ultimate authority over the nuclear armament of the Western alliance. It was therefore on the sensitive issue of European military security that de Gaulle sought to mobilize his continental partners in support of his own competing "grand design," which envisioned the disruption rather than the strengthening of the transatlantic partnership.

It seemed ironic that the soldier-statesman of France whose career had been dominated by fear and distrust of Germany would turn first to his country's traditional adversary for assistance in his ambitious plan to emancipate Europe from American domination. As head of the provisional government of France in the immediate postwar years, de Gaulle had pressed for punitive measures against defeated Germany, including political dismemberment and harsh economic exactions, to ensure that it would forever remain subservient to France in Europe. After the establishment of the West German state, de Gaulle out of power strongly opposed its reintegration into the Western system on the basis of equality for the fear that it would one day overshadow France. But by the early 1960s, two aspects of the Franco-German relationship proved conducive to a political reconciliation of these two historic adversaries. The first was the strengthening of the economic ties between them during the 1950s to the point where they had become each other's most important trading partner by the end of the decade. The fond hopes of integrationists like Jean Monnet in France and Walter Hallstein in West Germany that mutually beneficial economic relationships would promote political reconciliation were confirmed as the ancient hostility between these two countries dissolved amid economic partnership and shared prosperity. The second factor favorable to a Franco-German rapprochement was France's newly acquired status as Western Europe's only nuclear power. Since West Germany was prohibited from acquiring a nuclear capability of its own by agreement with its allies, France was assured of a decisive advantage in military power to compensate for its eastern neighbor's superior economic strength. From this position of strategic preeminence de Gaulle felt secure enough to conclude with Chancellor Konrad Adenauer a Franco-German treaty of reconciliation, which was signed by these two elder statesmen in Paris on January 22, 1963. It specified bilateral cooperation on security matters (including regular meetings of defense ministers, exchanges of military personnel, and cooperation in arms production) and provided for prior consultation between Paris and Bonn on all important subjects relating to European defense. De Gaulle's motivation for establishing a privileged bilateral relationship with West Germany within NATO was the hope of weaning Bonn away from the American-controlled alliance as the first step toward the formation of a truly independent West European security system based on France's national nuclear deterrent. Adenauer's flirtation with de Gaulle's projected Paris-Bonn axis stemmed from his fears that the Kennedy administration's flexible response doctrine and its insufficiently belligerent posture during the Berlin crisis of 1961 heralded a weakening of America's resolve to defend West Germany's security and political interests in Central Europe.

To de Gaulle's disappointment, the Franco-German entente did not yield the benefits that he had anticipated; it lapsed into insignificance after Adenauer's replacement in October 1963 by the more resolutely Atlanticist Ludwig Erhard, who reaffirmed Bonn's close ties to Washington while holding Paris at arm's length. De Gaulle's project of a Paris—Bonn axis ultimately failed because he was unable to persuade the Germans that the independent French nuclear force, or any future European nuclear system that might evolve from it, would represent a more reliable source of protection than the American strategic deterrent. As French criticism of American preeminence in NATO mounted in intensity during 1964–65, West German officials began to fear that it might provoke a resurgence of isolationism in the United States that would result in an American withdrawal from Europe.

Frustrated in his attempt to cement a Franco-German partnership as a prelude to the reorganization of a French-led Europe detached from the United States, de Gaulle proceeded to provoke a serious crisis within the Atlantic alliance in pursuit of the same end. He denounced the intolerable infringement on France's national independence represented by the integration of its armed forces in a supranational military organization whose supreme commander had always to be an American general and whose nuclear armament was under the sole control of the American president. The general's escalating criticism of NATO's command structure prompted speculation that de Gaulle was laying the groundwork for a major proposal for a fundamental restructuring of the alliance that would transfer more decision-making authority to its European members. Thus the fourteen other NATO states were unprepared for the shock to allied unity administered by the French president in March 1966, when he announced the withdrawal of all French land and air forces from the NATO military command, demanded the removal of the alliance's military headquarters from the Paris region, and required the departure of all American and Canadian military bases from French territory.

As the Western governments reeled from these French blows to the cause of unified Western defense, de Gaulle provocatively embarked on a state visit to the Soviet Union in June 1966. In Moscow the renegade in the Western camp was showered with honors, including an invitation to become the first Western leader to visit the top secret space-launching site in Kazakhstan. Soviet Premier Kosygin returned the visit in December and received an equally cordial welcome in Paris. The Kremlin had actively encouraged France's estrangement from the United States in the expectation of deriving valuable benefits from the resulting turmoil in the Atlantic alliance. For his part, de Gaulle accompanied his broadsides against the United States, which included harsh criticism of the American interventions in Vietnam and the Dominican Republic, with an ostentatious bid for an improvement in France's bilateral relations with the Soviet Union.

By means of these two interrelated policies—disengagement from NATO and detente with Moscow—the French president dreamed of establishing his nation as the self-appointed spokesman for Western Europe in its relations with the Communist bloc. A French-dominated Western Europe detached from the United States would be in an advantageous position to negotiate directly with the Russians to resolve the outstanding political disputes on the continent that had perpetuated the Cold War, particularly those concerning the status of divided Germany and its eastern frontiers. The ultimate goal of this ambitious project was a mutual disengagement in Europe that would leave the Russian satellites in the east free to pursue their autonomous course as Western Europe resumed its evolution away from the United States. A continent partitioned into two rigid power blocs at Yalta and Potsdam would thereafter be free to regain its position of power in the world.

The military consequences of France's withdrawal from NATO were trivial: The headquarters of the alliance were transferred from Paris to Brussels with relative ease. Neither the forced evacuation of American and Canadian military personnel nor the loss of French territory as a staging area for the provisioning and reinforcement of Allied troops in West Germany caused serious difficulties. The bases in France had always played a subsidiary, supportive role in NATO strategy, which envisioned West Germany as the principal battlefield for a conventional engagement with Warsaw Pact forces and presumed a nuclear response before they reached the Rhine. Supplies could be and had for years been channeled through Benelux and West German ports to the forward area in Central Europe. The only three indispensable French contributions to NATO's defense capability—the stationing of French ground and air forces in West Germany as a guarantee of France's participation in the defense of that country, the granting of access to the pipeline across France that carried oil and fuel to NATO forces in Germany, and overflight rights in French air space that connected the northern and southern half of the alliance—were all preserved by special agreement. Moreover, France retained representation on the exclusively political organs of the alliance (the North Atlantic Council and its subsidiary bodies) as well as liaison officers attached to some of the military organs.

The attempt to forge a bilateral rapprochement with Moscow that accompanied de Gaulle's diplomatic warfare with Washington failed to produce the anticipated realign-

ment of power in Europe: The monetary and financial crisis that engulfed France following the student-worker unrest in the spring of 1968 revealed how poorly endowed that
country was to play the powerful, independent role envisioned for it by its leader. The
Soviet invasion of Czechoslovakia in the summer of the same year had the dual effect of
enhancing the cohesion of the Western bloc and undermining the assumption of Soviet
retrenchment in the east on which de Gaulle's hopes for a free and independent Europe
rested. The abrupt abdication of the idiosyncratic French president in April 1969 brought
to an end his grand design for France and Europe, which had overestimated French power
and Europe's willingness and ability to defend itself without American assistance.

THE POLITICAL SETTLEMENT IN EUROPE

But if de Gaulle's excessively grandiose conception of a new *international* system
proved ephemeral, the Gaullist vision of a new *intra-European* order survived the demise
of its author with profound consequences for Europe, Russia, and America. Beneath the
spectacular rhetorical flourishes of this quixotic advocate of a French-led Europe emancipated from superpower domination lay a much more practical prescription for the solution of the political antagonisms on that continent that had perpetuated its partition into
two political, economic, and military blocs. Foremost among these were the outstanding
matters of dispute between the Federal Republic of Germany and its Communist neighbors to the east. These nettlesome issues, de Gaulle asserted, had to be settled by patient
diplomacy before the Cold War in Europe could be brought to a close and the superpowers' grip on their respective halves of the continent loosened. The French president's mistake was to imagine that his own country, on the strength of its military supremacy and
powerful diplomatic influence in Western Europe, was capable of orchestrating such a
relaxation of tensions in the center of the continent as the West's privileged interlocutor
of the eastern bloc. This Gaullist strategy overlooked two fundamental elements of European power politics: The first was that the only continental state capable of granting the
Soviet Union and its satellites the assurances they required as a prerequisite for genuine
detente in Europe was West Germany; the second was that Bonn, unlike Paris, would
never dare to seek an accommodation with the Eastern bloc without obtaining the prior
consent of Washington, on whose military protection and diplomatic support it utterly
depended for its security.

The East-West struggle in Europe had begun over the issues of Germany and Berlin
and persisted into the midsixties because those two related questions remained unresolved. The principal obstacle to their resolution was West German Chancellor Konrad
Adenauer's stubborn refusal to abandon the dream of the reunification of the two German
states that had been established in 1949. This was a cause that continued to exercise great
emotional appeal on West German voters, but was anathema to the Soviet Union and its
East European satellites, particularly the East German regime that understandably feared
being submerged in the larger, more populous, and more prosperous West German entity.
Bonn's denial of East Germany's sovereignty and its insistence on enjoying the exclusive
right to represent all Germans was formally expressed in December 1955 with the promulgation of the Hallstein doctrine (named after the then-secretary of state of the West German foreign office). This declaration affirmed Bonn's intention to regard diplomatic

recognition of the East German regime as an unfriendly act because it implied acceptance of Germany's permanent division. Accordingly, West Germany severed diplomatic relations with the Eastern European states that recognized Pankow except for the Soviet Union, which it prudently exempted from the purview of the doctrine. A related source of antagonism between West Germany and its eastern neighbors was its refusal to recognize Germany's frontiers with Poland and Czechoslovakia that had been redrawn in 1945 to the advantage of those two countries; to acknowledge these territorial losses would be to antagonize the large and vocal political constituency composed of German refugees who had been expelled from these regions after the war and who insisted on compensation for their loss. The twin issues of East Germany's political status and Germany's eastern frontiers kept the embers of the Cold War burning in Central and Eastern Europe.

In December 1966 a governing coalition was formed in West Germany that included as foreign minister the Social Democratic leader Willy Brandt, who was fired by the determination to normalize his country's relations with the Communist bloc. Brandt's new "eastern policy," or *Ostpolitik*, reflected a profound shift in West German attitudes toward the other Germany and its Communist allies. Majority opinion within the two parties that formed the new coalition had concluded that the old "policy of strength" toward East Germany and Eastern Europe had failed to yield the desired results: Instead of promoting the collapse of the Communist system in Eastern Europe and the reunification of the German peoples, the unyielding approach inherited from the Adenauer years had left the Federal Republic isolated in the Western camp as the last stronghold of orthodox policies of the Cold War amid a general evolution toward the acceptance of the political status quo in Europe and the permanent division of the two Germanies. The alternative that Brandt proposed was the normalization of West Germany's relations with its East European neighbors as a means of facilitating a continent-wide relaxation of tensions that might eventually lead to the peaceful reunification of the two German states. In short, the once-central component of Bonn's foreign policy, the insistence that all-German reunification would have to precede a relaxation of East-West tensions, was abandoned and the priority reversed: Detente became the means of achieving the ultimate goal of the reconciliation of the two Germanies.

After prudently informing and obtaining the tacit approval of his NATO allies (including the United States), Brandt embarked on a cautious campaign to improve West Germany's relations with the nations of Eastern Europe. In January 1967 Bonn restored diplomatic relations with Bucharest in direct violation of the Hallstein doctrine. He proceeded to dispatch West German trade missions to several East European capitals to lay the groundwork for an unprecedented commercial penetration of the Communist bloc that was financed by West German banks. Then the West German elections of October 1969 brought Brandt to power as chancellor in a coalition cabinet dominated by his Social Democratic party. As head of government he promptly renewed and intensified his efforts to reach a comprehensive settlement with the East. In response to his earlier overtures, the Warsaw Pact states had specified the price for such a rapprochement: acknowledgment of the territorial status quo in Eastern Europe and the recognition of East Germany's sovereignty. Before tackling these difficult issues, the West German leader paved the way for a mutual accommodation by signing the Nuclear Non-Proliferation Treaty on November 28, 1969; he then concluded a nonaggression pact with the Soviet Union on August 12, 1970, by which both parties affirmed the existing frontiers in Eastern Europe and forswore the use of force against one another. These two gestures helped to alleviate Moscow's ultimate fear of a revisionist West Germany armed with nuclear weapons. The festering dispute concerning Germany's border with Poland was disposed of with astonishing ease in view of the quarter-century deadlock over this troublesome issue. On December 7, 1970, Brandt journeyed to Warsaw to sign a nonaggression pact with Poland that formally renounced Germany's territorial claims by recognizing the German-Polish frontier at the Oder-Neisse Line.

The more emotionally charged matter of East German sovereignty required more time and patient diplomacy to resolve. Since the establishment of the two German political entities in 1949, the West German people and their political leaders had steadfastly adhered to the principle of German reunification on the basis of Western-style free elections. If such a goal seemed within the realm of possibility during the 1950s, it had ceased to be anything but a chimera after the construction of the Berlin Wall in 1961 and the West's failure to contest its existence. No longer able to escape their condition of servitude by voting with their feet, the remaining inhabitants of East Germany had to resign themselves to permanent citizenship in the Communist state and build their future as best they could. In tacit acknowledgment of the irreversibility (at least in the near future) of Germany's partition into two sovereign states, Brandt had broached the novel suggestion that Germany be considered "two states within one nation." This concession failed to elicit the approval of East German leader Walter Ulbricht, who repeated his demand for formal recognition of his regime's sovereignty in exchange for improved relations with Bonn. But Ulbricht had been installed and maintained in power by his masters in the Kremlin, and therefore had no hope of conducting a foreign policy that contradicted their wishes. As we have seen, by the beginning of the 1970s Moscow was actively pursuing a policy of rapprochement with Washington, partly out of fear of China, partly in the expectation of obtaining economic assistance from the West; to complement the projected agreement on arms control between the two superpowers, Brezhnev and company pushed for political detente in Europe that would clear up all the sources of East-West friction there. Since Ulbricht's recalcitrance represented the major stumbling block to agreement with the new conciliatory government in Bonn, the old East German hardliner had to go. On May 3, 1971, he was replaced as first secretary of the party by the more compliant functionary Erich Honecker.

The removal of this aged symbol of the Cold War era paved the way for the European political settlement that both sides had come to favor. In September 1971 the four occupying powers in Berlin—the United States, the Soviet Union, Britain, and France—signed an agreement recognizing each other's existing rights in their respective sectors of the city and affirming the special political relationship between West Berlin and the Federal Republic. The Kremlin had thereby sacrificed in the interests of detente the long-standing demand of its East German client for total control of access routes to the city that had precipitated the Berlin crises of 1958–61. Finally, on December 21, 1972, East Germany was compelled to accept and sign the Basic Treaty with the Federal Republic that failed to accord the East German state the formal diplomatic recognition it had always demanded as a precondition for inter-German reconciliation. The Basic Treaty provided for increased commercial, cultural, and personal relations between the two German states as well as the exchange of permanent missions rather than embassies. In September 1973, twenty-four years after they had emerged as de facto nations, the two Germanies were admitted into the United Nations as separate sovereign entities. In this piece-meal, ad hoc fashion, the unresolved issues of the Second World War were settled inso-far as the countries of Central Europe were concerned.

All that remained was for the two superpowers who had won the war and were simul-taneously pursuing improved relations in other ways to put their seal of approval on the European settlement negotiated bilaterally between West Germany and its eastern neigh-bors. Ever since the midfifties the post-Stalinist leaders in the Kremlin had issued peri-odic proposals for the convocation of a European Security Conference to break the polit-ical impasse on the continent and reduce the likelihood of a military confrontation between NATO and the Warsaw Pact. The nations of Western Europe had consistently rebuffed these Soviet overtures on the grounds that political agreements were meaning-less unless accompanied by a mutual reduction of military forces on the continent; that was an idea that had little appeal in Moscow because of Soviet apprehension about the political consequences in Eastern Europe of such troop withdrawals. But by the early 1970s two developments in the global balance of power forced the West European nations on the one hand and the Soviet Union on the other to reconsider their incompat-ible positions in the interests of promoting an all-European conference that now seemed advantageous to both sides. Western Europe's enthusiasm for an agreement to reduce the size of the military forces on the continent was increased by the ominous signs of retrenchment that had appeared in the United States in reaction to the traumatic experi-ence of Vietnam. A resolution in the U.S. Senate calling for the withdrawal of most American military forces from Europe had elicited sufficient public and congressional support to cause anxiety in Europe about the future of the American military presence there. The abolition of American conscription after the Vietnam pullout foreshadowed a reduction in American military personnel that would require politically unpopular increases in European defense spending if the military forces of the two alliance systems were to remain at their current levels. The key to Russia's new conciliatory posture in Europe was to be found in Beijing. Russo-Chinese border clashes in March 1969 high-lighted the increasingly bitter territorial disputes between those two erstwhile Commu-nist allies; the spectacular visit to China in July 1971 by President Nixon's national secu-rity adviser, Henry Kissinger, forshadowed an improvement of Sino-American relations at Russia's expense (see p. 349). Confronted by a hostile, independent China on its Asian frontier, the Soviet Union could not fail to recognize the advantages of detente and sta-bility on its European flank.

Two months after Kissinger's China sojourn, Brezhnev agreed in principle to partici-pate in a conference on Mutual and Balanced Force Reductions (MBFR) in exchange for the Western nations' endorsement of the Soviet proposal for a European Security Con-ference (CSCE). After a year of preparatory discussions these two parallel conferences began, the CSCE in Helsinki on January 15, 1973, and the MBFR in Vienna on October 30. While the talks on military reductions bogged down in technical matters and led to nothing of consequence, the political discussions in Helsinki achieved remarkable progress largely because of the preparatory groundwork laid by the bilateral agreements concluded between West Germany and the Communist bloc. What Moscow hoped to obtain was the West's formal recognition of the postwar political status quo in Europe, including the sovereignty of East Germany that had already been conceded de facto by Bonn in the Basic Treaty.

In addition to these cherished political goals, economic considerations played an important role in the Soviet Union's bid for detente in Europe: Polish riots against food price increases in December 1970, which toppled Communist party boss Gomulka from power, marked the culmination of a decade of growing economic unrest within the Soviet Union's East European empire. In January 1949 Moscow had established the Council for Mutual Economic Assistance (Comecon) to develop an integrated economic bloc in Eastern Europe as a counterweight to the Marshall Plan and the Organization for European Economic Cooperation in the West. But as Western Europe edged toward genuine economic integration with impressive results during the 1950s, Comecon remained little more than an instrument for perpetuating the Soviet Union's stranglehold on the economic life of its Eastern European satellites. The economies of the region were exploited to accelerate the economic recovery of the Soviet Union by means of reparation exactions from former enemy states, the formation of joint stock companies under Russian control, and the forced diversion of trade on advantageous terms to the Soviet Union. Some Eastern European Communist leaders dared to express dissatisfaction with these commercial arrangements. These rumblings of discontent within the Communist bloc reflected a growing awareness of the marked disparity between the prosperity of Western Europe and the economic stagnation of Eastern Europe. From Molotov's abandonment of the Paris meetings on the Marshall Plan in 1947 through the 1960s, the Kremlin had strenuously opposed the only obvious solution to this problem, namely, the opening of its satellite empire to trade and investment from the West, for fear that economic penetration would bring ideological contamination and the attendant menace of political unrest within the bloc. But by the early 1970s Brezhnev and his associates had come to believe that the only hope of satisfying the mounting consumer demands of the Eastern European peoples, and indeed of the Russian population itself, was a massive influx of foreign industrial products, technology, and investment capital that only the advanced economic powers of the non-Communist world could provide.

Agreements on trade and technical cooperation concluded with France and West Germany in the early 1970s had set the stage for this economic opening to the West, which was given a tremendous boost by the conclusion on August 1, 1975, of the two-year-long European Security Conference in Helsinki. On that historic date, representatives of thirty-three European countries (all but the perpetually isolated Albania), the United States, and Canada signed the Final Act of the European Security Conference. Among its most important provisions were those that formally recognized the existing political frontiers of Europe (including the border separating the two Germanies), provided for an increase in economic and cultural relations between the two blocs, and specified prior notification of and the exchange of observers at large-scale military exercises conducted by the two alliance systems. The major concession made by Moscow in exchange for the West's implicit acknowledgment of its domination of Eastern Europe was the so-called basket three, which guaranteed respect for human rights and political freedoms in a manner reminiscent of the Yalta Declaration on Liberated Europe.* Thus, thirty years after the defeat of Hitler, the war he had started was brought to an end (though without the for-

---

*The "basket three" provisions encouraged dissidents within the Soviet bloc to campaign openly for measures of political liberalization during the remainder of the 1970s.

malities of a peace treaty, since the Final Act of the Helsinki conference was officially only a political statement of intent rather than a legally binding document). The political division of Europe, which had precipitated the Cold War between the two victors in the struggle against Nazi Germany, was finally acknowledged as a fait accompli. By obtaining international recognition of its preeminence in the East European buffer zone as well as the de facto division of Germany, the Soviet Union now enjoyed a degree of political security that reinforced the military security that had resulted from its acquisition of strategic parity with the United States in the course of the 1960s.

Complementing the political and military detente of the mid-1970s was an informal "economic detente" consisting of the unclogging of commercial and financial channels between East and West. The bifurcation of Europe into two closed economic blocs, itself both a cause and a consequence of the Cold War, gave way to a notable increase in trade and investment between them. West European banks poured hard-currency loans into the economies of Eastern Europe, which enabled these states to purchase Western consumer goods and industrial products in unprecedented quantities. Italy opened a Fiat automobile plant in the heart of Russia. The United States became the Soviet Union's principal foreign supplier of grain after the conclusion of a five-year sales agreement on October 25, 1975. But as political and economic intercourse between the two blocs in Europe intensified and Soviet-American negotiations on strategic arms limitation progressed during the first half of the 1970s, the deteriorating situation in that volatile part of the world known as the Middle East threatened to nip in the bud this promising trend toward East-West reconciliation.

THE MIDDLE EAST AS PERENNIAL HOT SPOT

The engagement of the two superpowers in this perennial trouble spot had begun toward the end of the 1950s. The United States sought to counter what it saw as Moscow's efforts to exploit for its own benefit Arab opposition to the lingering presence of European colonial power in the region and to the existence of the state of Israel that had been carved out of the former British mandate in Palestine. We have seen how the Suez crisis in the autumn of 1956 marked a critical turning point in the history of foreign involvement in the Middle East. Chastened by Washington's refusal to endorse their attempt to retain an influential position in the region, Great Britain and France were compelled to follow the lead of the United States as it strove to exclude the Soviet Union from this strategically located, oil-rich part of the world. This transfer of authority was formalized on January 5, 1957, by the proclamation of the Eisenhower Doctrine, which affirmed the responsibility of the United States to assist any nation in the Middle East that was judged to be threatened by Communist aggression. Since the Soviet Union at the time had neither the capacity nor, so far as was known, the inclination to expand militarily into the region, the Eisenhower Doctrine served as the justification for American action against the one power there that did entertain expansionist ambitions at the expense of states friendly to the United States and its European allies, namely, Nasser's Egypt. In July 1958 Anglo-American troops intervened to rescue the pro-Western regimes of Jordan and Lebanon from the presumed threat of a pro-Nasser coup such as the one that had recently toppled the government of the British client state in Iraq. It was Nasser's professed goal to unite all the Arab states of the Middle East and North Africa under his leadership, and his increasingly intimate political and economic relations with the Communist bloc made him appear in American eyes as the stalking horse for the Kremlin in what had come to be regarded as an area of vital interest to the United States.

Apart from the economic benefits that he obtained from the Soviet Union, such as development aid for the Aswan Dam project to replace the funds previously withheld by the United States and Great Britain, the Egyptian leader's principal reason for cultivating Russia's friendship was the hope that it would assist him, diplomatically and militarily, in removing what he considered the major roadblock to the realization of his Pan-Arab project: the state of Israel. In the aftermath of the Suez affair, and particularly after the promulgation of the Eisenhower Doctrine, the two superpowers had become indirectly embroiled in the bitter dispute between the Jewish state and its Arab neighbors that had festered ever since its formation in May 1948. The Soviet Union furnished military assistance to Egypt and dispatched Russian officers to train the army of Syria, Israel's northeastern neighbor, which had fallen under the control of an anti-Western ruling elite that cultivated close ties with Moscow. The fear that a pro-Communist Syria would also threaten the adjacent pro-Western regimes of Jordan, Lebanon, and Turkey prompted Washington to step up military assistance to those states, while American arms supplies flowed into Israel to counter the ominous buildup of Russian weaponry in Egypt.

When these links with the Soviet Union failed to produce the Middle East settlement that Egypt and Syria desired, these two states jointly endeavored to break the deadlock by force. Armed with Soviet tanks and planes, Nasser demanded and obtained the removal of the United Nations peacekeeping force that had been deployed between Egypt and Israel on the Sinai peninsula after the Suez incident in 1956. On May 22, 1967, he closed to Israeli shipping the Straits of Tiran, the narrow waterway that afforded access to Israel's only port on the Red Sea. Interpreting this partial blockade as a prelude to war, Israel launched a preemptive strike against Egypt and Syria on June 5. Within six days Israeli forces had captured the strategic buffer zones of the Golan Heights from Syria, the entire Sinai peninsula including the east bank of the Suez Canal from Egypt, and the west bank of the Jordan River including the Jordanian sector of Jerusalem (which had been partitioned after the 1948–49 war). By one bold stroke in three directions, Israel had decimated the military forces of its most determined adversaries and extended its borders on all sides. To these it defiantly clung for more than a decade, in spite of Resolution 242 passed by the United Nations Security Council on November 22, which called for Israel's withdrawal from the recently occupied territories in exchange for assurances from the frontline Arab states that its sovereignty within secure frontiers would be recognized and its freedom of navigation in international waters assured.

The Six-Day War of June 1967 represented a humiliating setback for the Soviet Union and its two client states in the Middle East. Moscow's credibility as a reliable and effective patron had been undermined. Its armaments in Egypt and military advisers in Syria had failed to halt the advance of the outnumbered Israeli forces in their victorious war of six days on three fronts. The United States, distracted by its war in Vietnam, was unwilling to be dragged into the Middle East dispute. But Washington's prior military assistance to Israel was sufficient proof of where its sympathies lay, as was the ostentatious sale of fifty American F-4 Phantom jets to Israel in December 1967 while Egypt and Syria were still licking their wounds inflicted the previous June.

Egypt's humiliation during the Six-Day War: A column of Israeli mechanized infantry approaches the Sinai front while a truck carrying Egyptian POWs in their underwear heads in the opposite direction, June 9, 1967. The Egyptian forces in the Sinai were defeated within four days, after about 300 planes of the Egyptian air force had been destroyed on June 5 by Israeli bombers.

Half of the Arab states severed diplomatic relations with Washington during the Six-Day War, and a number of them promptly granted the Soviet Union the use of their ports in retaliation against America's support for the hated "Zionist entity" in their midst. In early 1970 the Soviet Union supplied some three hundred surface-to-air missiles (SAMs) to Egypt to help it counter Israel's air superiority, which had been decisively demonstrated in the war three years earlier and more recently during Israeli raids over the Suez Canal. Moscow also dispatched twenty-one thousand advisers to reorganize Egypt's shattered military forces. The completion of the Russian-financed Aswan Dam in 1971 was followed by new Soviet commitments of economic assistance to Cairo. In exchange the Soviet Union obtained naval facilities at three Egyptian ports to accommodate its Mediterranean fleet as well as the use of an Egyptian airfield. On March 28, 1971, Egyptian President Anwar Sadat, who had succeeded to the presidency after Nasser's death in September 1970, concluded a fifteen-year treaty of friendship and cooperation with the Soviet Union

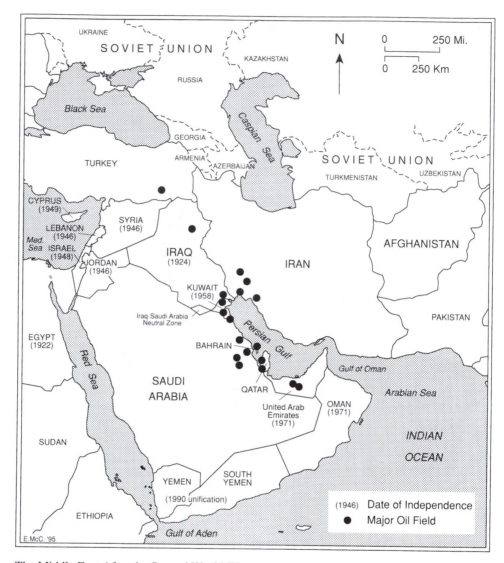

The Middle East After the Second World War

in the hope of obtaining much larger quantities of sophisticated weaponry that would enable his country to regain by force the Sinai territory it had lost to Israel in 1967.

Those Egyptian hopes were to be gravely disappointed, however, just as Israel failed to secure Washington's unqualified endorsement of its newly expanded frontiers. The two superpowers patiently attempted to restrain their respective protégés in the Middle East by restricting arms deliveries and prodding them into seeking a mutually acceptable resolution of their differences. Neither Washington nor Moscow wished to be dragged into a confrontation in this volatile part of the world at a time when Nixon and Brezhnev were jointly striving to reduce East-West tensions. But neither was capable of controlling its Mideastern client because the stakes in this regional conflict had become so high for both Cairo and Jerusalem. Sadat required a military success against Israel that would recover at least a portion of the lost land in the Sinai in order to shore up his sagging domestic popularity and divert public attention from the precarious state of the Egyptian economy. The leaders of Israel were driven by a sense of mistrust and anxiety to refuse any concession that might undermine the recently acquired security afforded by the newly occupied land. On the contrary, plans were drawn up to populate the occupied territories with Jewish settlers, a policy that was viewed by the Arab states bordering on Israel as a prelude to de facto annexation.

The tension between Egypt and Israel, which boiled over in intermittent skirmishing along the Suez Canal during the early seventies, was exacerbated by the plight of the 2.75 million stateless Palestinian Arabs, half of them refugees from the area incorporated in the new Jewish state after the 1948–49 war. The government of Israel had declined to permit their repatriation after the conclusion of the armistice, unwilling to allow the Jewish citizens of the new state to be numerically overwhelmed by more than a million discontented Arabs returning to a land they considered their own. Since no neighboring Arab state was prepared to resettle them permanently within its own frontiers, these hapless souls had been "temporarily" dispersed in squalid refugee camps located in Lebanon, Syria, Jordan, and the Egyptian-controlled Gaza strip, where they festered in poverty and idleness. The more politically active among them formed in 1964 the Palestine Liberation Organization (PLO), which operated from Jordanian territory until it was expelled in 1970–71 by the military forces of King Hussein, who feared that his kingdom would be overwhelmed by its Palestinian majority. As the PLO reassembled in Lebanon in the early 1970s, its commandos sponsored spectacular acts of terrorism to publicize the Palestinian grievances, such as the hijacking of airplanes and the murder of Israeli athletes at the 1972 Olympic games in Munich.

When President Sadat failed to secure from the Soviet Union the offensive weapons that would have assured Egyptian military superiority over Israel, he abruptly turned against his less-than-accommodating benefactors. On July 18, 1972, shortly after the Nixon-Brezhnev summit talks in Moscow appeared to confirm the Kremlin's commitment to East-West detente at the expense of its clients in peripheral regions such as the Middle East, the Egyptian leader angrily ordered most of the Soviet advisers and technicians out of his country. When the chastened Kremlin began to deliver the armaments it had previously withheld, the Egyptian leader became convinced that a renewal of armed struggle with Israel was necessary in order to involve the two superpowers in a Middle East peace settlement that would restore the Sinai to Egypt. Thus in early October 1973, on the Jewish holy day of Yom Kippur, Egypt in concert with Syria launched a well-coordinated surprise attack against Israel. Egyptian forces drove across the Suez Canal into the Sinai peninsula, overrunning Israel's Bar-Lev defense installation with furious infantry and artillery assaults. In the meantime a large Syrian force equipped with eight hundred tanks swarmed onto the Golan Heights overlooking Israeli settlements in the valley below. But after two weeks of fighting, an Israeli force counterattacked into Syria and drove to within twenty miles of Damascus, while another landed on the west bank of the

Suez Canal to encircle the Egyptian Third Army on the east bank in the Sinai, sever its supply lines, and block its retreat.

Washington and Moscow, though reluctant to become involved in another Middle East confrontation that might unravel the fragile fabric of detente fashioned by Nixon and Brezhnev, did not want to be defeated by proxy. They therefore supplied military equipment to their respective clients while vainly seeking to arrange a ceasefire in the United Nations. When an Egyptian defeat appeared imminent after Israeli forces crossed the Suez Canal on October 16, the Kremlin endorsed Sadat's request that the United States and the Soviet Union jointly intervene to separate the belligerents. Once President Nixon refused to countenance the unprecedented deployment of Russian troops in a region of such strategic and economic importance to the United States, the Kremlin thereupon declared its intention to introduce its own forces in the area unilaterally. In response, Nixon ordered a worldwide nuclear alert of American forces and the Soviet Union promptly reciprocated. For a moment it appeared that Moscow's desire to exploit the Arab-Israeli conflict in order to gain a foothold in the Middle East, and Washington's determination to prevent such a radical shift in the global balance of power, outweighed both superpowers' commitment to the Nixon-Brezhnev policy of detente.

But the escalation of the fourth Arab-Israeli war into a global confrontation between the United States and the Soviet Union was averted by a compromise resolution passed by the UN Security Council on October 22 that authorized the creation of a seven-thousand-man United Nations emergency force to supervise a cease-fire. In December 1973 the Israelis and Arabs, under intense pressure from the superpowers (and with American and Soviet participation), conducted their first face-to-face negotiations in a quarter of a century at a peace conference in Geneva. Thereafter, the energetic American secretary of state, Henry Kissinger, shuttled between Cairo and Tel Aviv intermittently for two years in an effort to bring Israel and Egypt together while freezing the Soviet Union out of the negotiating process. In September 1975, the two sides finally concluded an agreement that provided for a partial Israeli withdrawal in the Sinai to create a buffer zone manned by American and United Nations observers operating technical equipment to detect violations of the cease-fire. Though the Soviet Union did not recognize this American-sponsored interim solution to the Israeli-Egyptian conflict, it refrained from interfering with the peace process in the Middle East. Thus, the superpower detente appeared to have survived its first serious test, while the prospects for stability in the Middle East seemed more promising than ever before by the middle of the 1970s.

Despite the apparently satisfactory outcome of the October War from the standpoint of the United States and its Israeli client, the Western world's stake in the Middle East conflict had taken on an ominous new dimension during the most recent outbreak of violence. In retaliation against Washington's airlift of supplies to Israel to replace losses of tanks and planes, the oil-producing states of the Arab world imposed a five-month embargo on petroleum shipments to the United States, which caused gasoline shortages and considerable inconvenience to American consumers. More serious than the inconvenience of long lines at the gasoline pumps was the severe shock to the world economy administered by the oil-producing cartel, the Organization of Petroleum Exporting Countries (OPEC), which quadrupled the price of crude oil between 1973 and 1975.

The oil embargo and the precipitous price increases exposed the prosperous nations of the industrialized world (the United States and Canada, Western Europe, and Japan) to an

The gasoline crisis during the oil embargo, autumn, 1973: The embargo imposed by Arab oil-producing states demonstrated the vulnerability of the United States to politically motivated disruptions of the supply of vital economic resources. The subsequent sharp increase in oil prices dictated by the Organization of Petroleum Exporting Countries (OPEC) caused the worst worldwide economic downturn since the end of the Second World War. *(National Archives)*

unprecedented type of economic warfare waged by a coalition of impoverished nations of the developing world. OPEC's ability to increase at will the world price of its precious product highlighted the industrial world's dependence on foreign sources of energy—the United States imported 40 percent of its petroleum in the mid-1970s while the nations of Western Europe and Japan satisfied over 80 percent of their energy needs through purchases abroad. As the first commodity cartel to employ its raw material assets as an effective economic and political weapon, OPEC set a precedent that other primary producing nations could be expected to follow. The industrial world of the north depended on the nonindustrial world of the south for over half of its supplies of a whole range of raw materials—cobalt, copper, chrome, manganese, tungsten, tin, bauxite, aluminum, and others—without which its economic prosperity would grind to a halt. The specter of Third World producer cartels dictating sharp price increases of these essential commodities as a means of forcibly redistributing the world's wealth haunted officials in the non-Communist industrial world during the mid-1970s. Nervous statesmen in Western Europe began to call for the opening of a north-south dialogue to establish orderly procedures for the exchange of economic assets between the industrialized and the commodity producing regions of the earth. Others, especially naval and military strategists in the United States, reemphasized the necessity of safeguarding the sea-lanes to these vital mineral resources and ensuring the security and the pro-Western orientation of the regimes that controlled them through increased American military assistance and protection.

The danger of a Soviet-American confrontation in the Middle East in the mid-1970s was averted by the Kremlin's decision to refrain from interfering with the unilateral American effort to promote a reconciliation between Israel and Egypt. Both superpowers had apparently learned to appreciate the advantages of stability in the Middle East as a complement to the relaxation of tensions in Europe and the strategic arms control agreement recently achieved. Moscow seemed resigned to Washington's unilateral sponsorship of a Middle East peace, while the United States prodded its Israeli client to relinquish the Egyptian territory it held in exchange for security pledges from its Egyptian enemy.

11

THE RISE OF CHINA
AND THE COLD WAR IN ASIA

THE COMMUNIST VICTORY IN THE CHINESE CIVIL WAR

The total collapse of the Japanese Empire in August 1945 left a vast power vacuum in Asia comparable to the one created in Europe by the German capitulation three months earlier. But the political consequences of the Allied military victory in the Far East differed from the postwar situation in Europe in one crucial respect: The United States had waged the Pacific war almost singlehandedly and had been able to compel the enemy's surrender without having had to rely on the military assistance of the Soviet Union. By the time the Red Army had begun to consolidate control of its prescribed occupation zones on the Asian mainland (Manchuria and northern Korea) and its offshore islands (the Kuriles and the southern half of Sakhalin), the predominance of the United States and its European associates in the rest of Japan's former East Asian empire was assured. American forces under General Douglas MacArthur unilaterally undertook the military occupation and political administration of the Japanese home islands despite Soviet pleas to participate. British, French, and Dutch forces returned to their old outposts of empire in Southeast Asia either to reassert colonial authority or to grant political independence to successor regimes controlled by non-Communist, pro-Western indigenous elites.

The reestablishment of Western power in East Asia after 1945 appeared to thwart whatever ambitions Stalin may have entertained of extending Soviet influence over the populous, economically valuable region recently liberated from Japanese domination. A spectacular exception to this record of postwar Soviet setbacks in the Far East was the establishment in October 1949 of the People's Republic of China, a Communist state comprising a quarter of the world's population that promptly became a military ally and economic beneficiary of the Soviet Union.

The installation of a Communist government in China in late 1949 terminated a civil war that had raged intermittently in that country since 1927 between the pro-Western government of Chiang Kai-shek (Jiang Jieshi) and the Communist guerrilla movement operating in the countryside. Since the victory of communism in China occurred in the year following the Soviet-inspired coup in Czechoslovakia and the attempt to dislodge the Western allies from Berlin, the new regime in Beijing was viewed by many officials in Washington as an Asian counterpart of the Soviet satellite empire in Eastern Europe. But the American foreign service officers who had spent time with the Chinese Communist guerrilla forces in the city of Yenan in Shensi province during the war understood a signal fact about this movement that was entirely ignored by official and public opinion in the United States amid the indiscriminate anti-Communism of the 1950s: They knew it to be a thoroughly indigenous organization whose ideological affinity with and material dependence on the Soviet Union was minimal and whose political relations with the Kremlin and its representatives in Asia had long been marked by stresses and strains.

Such a conclusion was inescapable from a study of the history of the Chinese Communist party from the mid-1930s to its spectacular triumph in 1949. That history was replete with instances of ideological and tactical differences between the dedicated band of revolutionaries in China and the agents of the Comintern who had been dispatched there by Moscow to organize an insurrection on the Soviet model. Prominent among those was the ideological contradiction between the Marxist-Leninist emphasis on the revolutionary role of the urban working class and the growing recognition on the part of the Chinese Communist leadership of the revolutionary potential of the landless peasantry in a preindustrial country where few people toiled in factories. Lenin, who had relied on the impoverished rural masses of Russia to ensure the success of his own revolution, nevertheless had regarded the peasantry as only an auxiliary force in the proletarian revolution. The Soviet Comintern agents in China and their protégés in the Chinese Communist party therefore concentrated their energies throughout the 1920s on organizing labor in preparation for a workers' insurrection that would begin in the cities. But in China the workers' vanguard had no workers. This lesson had been learned at great cost to the Chinese Communist movement in 1927 when, at the suggestion of their Russian advisers, they incited proletarian uprisings in several cities that were easily suppressed by the government. In the same year a brilliant Communist organizer named Mao Zedong had independently concluded that the only hope for social revolution in his country lay in mobilizing its hundreds of millions of oppressed peasants against their exploitative landlords and the political and military elites who sustained them. By the middle of the 1930s Mao had effectively assumed control of the Communist party apparatus. Though he refrained from publicly disputing the applicability of Soviet Communist ideology to the peculiar conditions of his own country, Mao charted an increasingly independent course for the Chinese variant of communism. Such a posture was anathema to Stalin, who was accustomed to dealing with foreign Communist leaders who were entirely dependent on the Kremlin for their positions and respectful of its absolute authority within the international Communist movement.

The principal source of friction between the Communist regime in Moscow and the Communist revolutionary movement in the Chinese countryside was Stalin's subsequent determination to maintain friendly relations with the very government in China that Mao's movement was striving to overturn. The Russian leader's solicitude for the fervently anti-Communist Chiang during the 1930s stemmed from considerations of national interest, namely, the concern that the two strongmen shared about the increasing military menace to their respective countries posed by Japan. During that country's undeclared war against China from 1937 to 1945, the Soviet Union pressured the Communist guerrilla movement ensconced in northern Shensi province to observe a temporary truce in its insurrectionary challenge to Chiang's nationalist government in Nanking (and later Chungking) in the interests of waging a common struggle against the foreign invaders. The Kremlin supplied considerable military and financial assistance to the Nationalist forces and persuaded Mao to place his Red Army under the nominal jurisdiction of the Chinese government. The removal of the Japanese threat in 1945 neither dampened Stalin's enthusiasm for preserving cordial relations with Chiang nor produced an increase in direct Soviet support for the Chinese Communist movement. On August 14, 1945, the day before Japan accepted the Allied terms of surrender, the Soviet Union concluded a treaty of friendship and alliance with the Chinese Nationalist government. In this pact Moscow recognized Chiang's regime as the legitimate government of China and pledged to send it military and economic aid in exchange for joint Sino-Soviet management of the Manchurian railway network and the port of Dairen (Dalny), and the right to construct a Soviet naval base at Port Arthur (Lüshun). Moscow urged the Chinese Communists to dismantle their independent military apparatus and to form a political coalition with the Nationalists. By the time that Russian military forces evacuated Manchuria in 1946 (after having stripped it of all portable industrial equipment), it had become evident that Moscow was playing off the two rivals in the Chinese civil war against each other in order to prevent the creation of a unified China under a single political authority. Thus, the Soviet occupation forces transferred captured Japanese weapons to Mao's partisans in Manchuria while acceding to Chiang's request that the Soviet troops remain in the region until the Nationalist forces could arrive in sufficient numbers to prevent a Communist takeover.

Moscow's equivocal policy toward the Chinese civil war continued after hostilities resumed in 1946 following the failure of an American mediation mission headed by General George C. Marshall. As the Nationalist armies in northern China disintegrated before the Communist onslaught in 1948, Stalin urged Mao in vain to stop his military offensive at the Yangtze River in order to permit the regrouping of Chiang's forces and the creation of a non-Communist enclave in southern China. The reason for the Kremlin's reluctance to tender its unqualified support to the Communist insurrection in China was evidently the same that had prompted the recent exercise of its restraining influence on the Communist insurgents in Greece: the fear that a local Communist triumph over forces supported by the West would provoke an American response that could escalate into a global confrontation with the Soviet Union for which she was at the time entirely unprepared. It probably also reflected Stalin's concern that a vigorous new Communist regime established without the assistance of the Red Army in a country with almost three times the population of Russia would inevitably become a competing pole of attraction within the world Communist movement.

Ironically, while the Soviet Union attempted to restrain the Chinese Communists and preserved its diplomatic contacts with the doomed Chinese Nationalist regime as it collapsed during the summer of 1949, the United States announced on August 5 the termination of all economic and military assistance to Chiang Kai-shek on the grounds that through corruption and inefficiency his government had forfeited its claim to American support. Upon the establishment of the People's Republic of China on October 1, 1949, Washington appeared prepared to accept the fait accompli of a Communist victory in the Chinese civil war. In January 1950, a month after the last tattered remnants of Chiang's military forces and political administration had retreated to the island of Taiwan (then called Formosa), President Truman reaffirmed the Allied declarations of Cairo and Potsdam that Taiwan was to be regarded as an integral part of China and announced that he had no intention of resuming American military assistance to the Nationalist authorities that had been suspended the previous August. The implication of these declarations was that Washington would do nothing to prevent the new regime on the mainland from completing its victory by forcing Chiang's forces to surrender their vulnerable offshore redoubt.

The Communist leadership in Beijing, though triumphant in its twenty-two-year struggle without significant Soviet assistance and in spite of Soviet counsels of restraint, was compelled by the disastrous economic conditions it inherited to look toward Moscow for economic assistance to recover and rebuild. The extensive damage wrought by the Japanese occupation and the civil war required economic assistance from abroad. Accordingly, Mao left his country for the first time in his life at the end of 1949 to visit the Soviet capital hat in hand. On February 14, 1950, the two Communist leaders signed a thirty-year Treaty of Friendship, Alliance, and Mutual Assistance that included a mutual defense clause. By the terms of other agreements, Stalin secured recognition of Soviet management of the Manchurian railroad and of Soviet base rights in the two Yellow Sea ports of Dairen and Port Arthur until 1952. Mao also had to consent to the formation of joint stock companies to develop the mineral resources of Manchuria and Xinjiang, two historic objects of Russian economic ambition. Moscow thereby obtained the assurance of a friendly power on Russia's Asian frontier together with naval privileges and economic concessions that can only be labeled neo-imperialist in character. Such was the price that Mao had to pay for the Soviet economic assistance and pledge of military protection he desperately needed. Significantly, no military aid flowed from Moscow at a time when Chiang's armies were regrouping on Taiwan in preparation for an invasion of the mainland.

In light of this inauspicious beginning of the Sino-Soviet entente and Stalin's earlier tendency to hold the Chinese Communists at arms length, Washington might have been able to disrupt the emerging partnership between Moscow and Beijing by extending diplomatic recognition and economic assistance to the new ruling elite in China once its authority on the mainland had been confirmed in the early months of 1950. Mao entertained the possibility of establishing correct if not cordial relations with Washington at the end of the war, while he was still in close contact with American diplomatic and intelligence agents attached to the Chinese Communist movement during the common struggle against Japan. The Truman administration's cultivation of friendly ties with Yugoslavia after Tito's defection from the Soviet bloc in 1948 furnished an instructive precedent for Washington's willingness to temper its indiscriminate antipathy for Communist regimes. The United States government was in no hurry to join the East European Communist states, Scandinavia, Switzerland, and Great Britain* in extending formal recognition to the Beijing government at a time when it was mistreating American citizens and seizing American property in China. But officials in the State Department were patiently preparing for a time when, after a suitable interval, the Communist triumph in the Chinese civil war would receive explicit acknowledgment from the United States.

---

*London's prompt recognition of the People's Republic was motivated by concern about the status of the British crown colony of Hong Kong, a coastal showcase of Western capitalism that was tolerated by Beijing because of its value as a "window" to the non-Communist world. On Hong Kong's future status, see page 404.

THE KOREAN WAR AND AMERICA'S REENGAGEMENT IN THE FAR EAST

That acknowledgment would not come for two and a half decades because of the eruption of hostilities on the Korean peninsula in the summer of 1950, which eventually brought the military forces of Communist China and the United States into armed conflict. We have already noted the ways in which postwar Korea resembled postwar Germany: Temporarily partitioning the country along the 38th parallel of latitude into a northern Soviet zone and a southern American zone, the two superpowers failed to reach agreement on the conditions of reunification and thereupon permitted the establishment in their respective zones of a government that claimed sovereignty over the entire country. In August 1948, after free elections conducted under the supervision of the United Nations, the Republic of Korea was formed in the south with Seoul as its capital and the conservative anti-Communist Syngman Rhee as its president. The following September a People's Democratic Republic of Korea was established in the northern city of Pyongyang under the leadership of the revolutionary Communist militant Kim Il Sung. But whereas the mutual disengagement of Soviet and American military power from divided Germany proved to be an impossible goal, the two superpowers had little difficulty in withdrawing from divided Korea, the Russians by December 1948 and the Americans by June 1949. But what they left behind was a bubbling cauldron of political instability: two separate Korean governments, each armed and supplied by one of the two contestants in the Cold War, each claiming authority over the territory ruled by the other.

On the early morning of June 25, 1950, this unstable political situation on the Korean peninsula boiled over into war when 90,000 North Korean troops launched a surprise attack across the 38th parallel against South Korea. Profiting from their numerical superiority and the element of surprise, the North Korean forces hurled back the South Korean army, capturing the capital city of Seoul on June 27. On the same day the United Nations Security Council, meeting in the absence of the Soviet delegate (who had been boycotting its sessions since January 1950 to protest the refusal of the United Nations to assign the Chinese seat to the newly established Communist regime in Beijing), adopted an American-sponsored resolution that requested all member states "to provide the Republic of Korea with all necessary aid to repel the aggressors." Even before the adoption of this resolution, President Truman had instructed the commander of the American occupation forces in Japan, General Douglas MacArthur, to furnish naval and air support to a South Korean army that was reeling in disarray from the North Korean onslaught. On June 29, in the face of an imminent South Korean collapse, he ordered the transfer of two American infantry divisions from Japan to Korea. On July 7 the Security Council, still in the absence of the Soviet delegate, established a United Nations expeditionary force for deployment in Korea, which the following day was placed under MacArthur's command with instructions "to repel the armed attack and to restore international peace and security." By the middle of September twenty member states had contributed token ground forces to the United Nations army. The United States eventually supplied half of the ground forces, 86 percent of the naval forces, and 93 percent of the air forces.

President Truman's decision to intervene militarily in Korea was prompted by his conviction that the North Korean attack was a Soviet-inspired probe of Western resolve in Asia similar to those in Europe that had given rise to the American doctrine of containment. The evidence for Stalin's approval of the North Korean aggression came to light in the Soviet archives after the demise of the U.S.S.R. in 1991. The North Korean leader, Kim Il Sung, had lived in Russia for years, had returned to his country in the company of the Soviet liberation army in 1945, and had been installed in power three years later on the express orders of Stalin. Kim made the case for a speedy victory over the rival Korean regime in meetings with Stalin several months earlier, and the Soviet leader had given Kim the green light. The prospect of a rapid triumph at minimal cost for his Asian client state over the outmanned, underequipped South Korean army must have represented a nearly irresistible temptation to the Soviet leader. He had no reason to suspect that the United States would interfere with the Pyongyang regime's bid to unify the Korean peninsula under its auspices. On the contrary, in a highly publicized speech before the National Press Club in Washington on January 12, 1950, Secretary of State Dean Acheson had specifically refrained from including South Korea within America's "military defense perimeter" in the Far East.

The swift and massive intervention of the American-dominated United Nations army in Korea appears to have caught the Kremlin entirely off guard. Its failure to wield its veto in the Security Council to prevent the authorization for such an action can only be regarded as a serious blunder with unfortunate consequences for its North Korean protégés. By September 15 the North Korean forces had conquered practically the entire peninsula, driving the demoralized South Korean army into a small corner around the port of Pusan on the southern coast. But on the same day MacArthur's UN force executed a successful amphibious landing behind enemy lines at Inchon, the port of Seoul. Within two weeks MacArthur's troops had driven the North Korean army all the way north to the 38th parallel, killing or capturing half of its soldiers in the process. The expulsion of the North Korean invaders from South Korea fulfilled the United Nations instructions to "repel the armed attack." But the disorganized retreat of the North Korean invasion force presented the Truman administration with an opportunity too tempting to pass up: that of forcibly reunifying the peninsula by erasing the artificial dividing line that neither Korean regime had ever accepted as permanent and that had never been recognized by the United Nations. In pursuit of this objective, the United States pushed through the General Assembly of the United Nations on October 7 a resolution authorizing MacArthur to "take all appropriate measures to insure a stable situation in the whole of Korea." Though this resolution technically lacked the force of law because it had emanated from the General Assembly rather than the Security Council,* MacArthur ordered his troops to cross the 38th parallel into North Korea on October 9. Within three weeks they had occupied the northern capital of Pyongyang and were advancing toward the Yalu River separating North Korea from China's province of Manchuria.

Even before the ominous advance of MacArthur's forces toward Manchuria, the United States government had taken a decisive step that was guaranteed to provoke a hostile response from the new Communist government in Beijing. President Truman decided on the evening of June 26, 1950, to dispatch the American Seventh Fleet to the Taiwan strait

---

*The General Assembly possesses no decision-making power, according to the UN Charter. Once the Soviet Union, realizing its error in boycotting the Security Council, resumed its seat on August 1 it was in a position to veto any resolution presented to that body. Hence, the United States was driven to endow the General Assembly with an authority it did not legally possess.

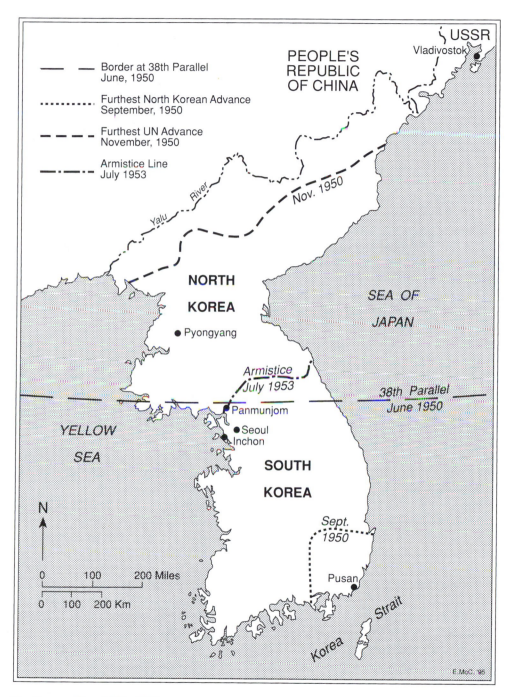

The Korean War, 1950–1953

between China and the island of Taiwan, where the battered armies of Chiang Kai-shek had reassembled after their expulsion from the mainland. He took this precautionary step to prevent mainland China and the Nationalist forces on Taiwan from further complicating the unstable situation in the western Pacific by renewing their own bitter conflict. But to the regime in Beijing this American action appeared as a flagrant intervention in the Chinese civil war that effectively prevented the victors from consolidating their triumph by invading the Nationalists' redoubt and restoring the island to Chinese sovereignty.

MacArthur's counteroffensive deep into North Korea and his rapid advance toward the Manchurian frontier finally spurred Beijing into action. On October 2, Chinese Premier Zhou Enlai warned the United States through an intermediary that if American forces crossed the 38th parallel, China reserved the right to defend its vital interests. When that warning was ignored by Washington, almost 200,000 Chinese troops crossed the Yalu River into North Korea during the month of October. After several inconclusive engagements with MacArthur's troops, an enlarged Chinese army attacked along a broad front in late November, forcing a United Nations retreat southward. By the end of the year Chinese and North Korean troops had crossed the 38th parallel and early in 1951 reoccupied Seoul.

The Truman administration was confronted with the equally unattractive alternatives of waging a protracted ground war on the Korean peninsula or of adopting MacArthur's strategy of extending the conflict to China itself by bombing the Manchurian sanctuary. Anticipating that the latter course would risk escalation of this regional conflict into a world war in view of China's alliance with the Soviet Union, Truman decided in early March to restrict UN military operations to Korea and to propose negotiations for a cease-fire. By the beginning of April the United Nations troops had halted the Communist offensive and counterattacked once again into North Korea. MacArthur publicly demanded that China agree to an armistice or be subject to U.S. bombing attacks in Manchuria. Then a provocative letter from him was read on the floor of the House of Representatives suggesting the possible use of Nationalist Chinese troops against the Communists and calling for an all-out victory. Truman responded to this egregious act of insubordination by firing his military commander on April 11 and replacing him with General Matthew B. Ridgway.

MacArthur's departure removed the major impediment to a negotiated settlement of the war that both side wanted to end. On June 25 Truman accepted a Soviet suggestion for a cease-fire and the beginning of armistice discussions. The first meeting between representatives of the United Nations and the Communist commands took place in July 1951. These talks dragged on intermittently for two more years until an armistice was finally signed on July 26, 1953, at the tiny village of Panmunjom near the 38th parallel. It provided for a demilitarized zone along the redrawn frontier separating the two Korean states and a joint UN-Communist military armistice commission to meet periodically for the purpose of resolving matters in dispute. The new boundary line was very similar to the one that had existed before the beginning of the three-year conflict that cost a million South Korean, a million North Korean and Chinese, and more than thirty-three thousand American lives.

The importance of the Korean War as a catalyst of rearmament and remobilization in Western Europe has already been remarked on. No less dramatic were its effects on the political and military situation in the Far East. Faced with what it regarded as a bid by the

President Harry S Truman (1884–1972) awards General Douglas MacArthur (1880–1964) the Distinguished Service Medal at Wake Island, October 14, 1950: Truman and his Joint Chiefs of Staff were already beginning to worry about the independent streak in Washington's proconsul in Asia. *(Courtesy of the Library of Congress)*

U.S.S.R. and China to extend the rule of Communism in Asia, the United States intervened to support and protect the non-Communist states of the region just as it had done to the non-Communist states of Europe in the previous decade.

The retention of American military forces in South Korea and the conclusion of a mutual security agreement with that country, which pledged American armed intervention in its defense, was merely one of a number of similar commitments that were undertaken in the early fifties. During the Korean emergency in 1951 the United States concluded in rapid succession military agreements with island nations in the western Pacific to bolster their security in the face of the presumed menace of Communist aggression. On August 30 the United States signed a mutual defense treaty with the Philippines, which had been granted its independence in 1946 and accorded the United States air and naval base rights the following year. On September 1 Washington concluded a tripartite security treaty with Australia and New Zealand (the ANZUS Pact), thereby replacing Great Britain as the protector of those two transplanted European states in the Pacific.

But the most important addition to the American-sponsored East Asian security system that was being formed in the autumn of 1951 was to be the country whose aggressive acts had brought the United States into the Far Eastern war a decade earlier. The American military occupation of Japan, like the American military occupation of Germany, had originally been established for the purpose of preventing the vanquished power from ever again threatening the security of its neighbors. This meant the total demilitarization of the country, the abolition of all nationalistic societies, the purging of public officials and business leaders who had cooperated with the military authorities in planning and waging the recent war, and the dissolution of the large industrial conglomerates that had prospered during the period of military expansion. It also meant the limitation on Japanese industrial production and the diversion of a portion of that production as reparations to the victims of Japan's aggression. The imperious commander of the American military occupation regime in Japan, General Douglas MacArthur, ordered his staff to write a new constitution for the country, which went into effect on May 3, 1947. It established a parliamentary form of government, safeguarded civil liberties, and included a provision renouncing war as well as the maintenance of land, sea, and air forces. But the Soviet-American confrontation in Europe at the end of the 1940s prompted the Truman administration to reconsider and eventually to reverse its stern occupation policy in Asia for fear that an economically weak, militarily vulnerable Japan would become a tempting target for Soviet intimidation once the American occupation forces had been withdrawn. Thus in 1948–49 the United States removed all restrictions on Japan's economic recovery, halted the requisition of capital equipment for reparations, abandoned plans for the forced decentralization of Japanese industry, and began to furnish financial assistance to promote Japan's economic growth and social stability.

The outbreak of the Korean War accelerated the transformation of Japan from impoverished enemy to prosperous ally by demonstrating that country's value to the United States as a counterweight to Soviet and Communist Chinese power in the Far East. American military procurement expenditures during the war stimulated an economic boom in Japan that by the midfifties was to bring its people the highest standard of living in Asia. Capital investment and technology transfers from the United States increased sharply, enabling Japanese industry to replace its war-damaged equipment with the most up-to-date machinery. Japan's export trade rapidly recovered, first in textiles and other light industries, and later in advanced sectors such as electronics, automobiles, and shipbuilding. The spectacular economic revival sparked by the Korean War was accompanied by an expansion of Japan's defense capabilities. In the summer of 1950 the government in Tokyo secured American authorization to create the seventy-five thousand-member National Police Reserve to replace the American occupation troops that were being redeployed in Korea. A rudimentary Japanese navy was created in August 1952 to ensure coastal defense. In February 1954 the existing ground and naval forces were expanded and a small air force was brought into being. All of these were designated as "self-defense" forces in deference to the constitutional renunciation of war and the means of waging it. But whatever their euphemistic designation, they collectively constituted the nucleus of Japan's rearmament during a period when the Cold War was being extended to Asia.

The rearmament and economic recovery of Japan during and after the Korean War transpired behind the protective shield of the United States, which hastened to terminate Japan's status as occupied enemy and restore it to full political sovereignty. On September 8, 1951, the United States and forty-eight other nations (excluding the Soviet Union and China) signed a peace treaty with Japan in San Francisco, which ended the state of war and brought the American occupation to an end on April 28, 1952. On the same day the United States and Japan signed a bilateral security treaty granting the United States the right to maintain military and naval forces in the defeated country. Thus the former enemy Japan, like the former enemy Germany at the other end of the Eurasian land mass, had come to be regarded by the United States as an indispensable asset in its campaign to contain the global expansion of Soviet power.

A similar function was soon to be fulfilled by the outpost of the anti-Communist Nationalist Chinese on the island of Taiwan. In the course of the Korean conflict, the United States had resumed the deliveries of economic and military assistance to Chiang's government in exile that had been suspended in the final stage of the Nationalist collapse on the mainland. On December 2, 1954, the Eisenhower administration signed a mutual defense treaty with Chiang's "Republic of China." Washington protected its claim to the Chinese seat in the United Nations. In 1955 the United States Congress voted by large majorities to authorize the president to commit American military forces to the defense of the island. When China in 1954–55 and again in 1958 shelled Quemoy (Jinmen) and Matsu (Mazu), two small islands a few miles off its coast that had been occupied by Nationalist troops and were used for commando raids against the mainland, the United States pledged to defend the islands by force. For the next two decades Washington forbade American citizen to travel to, or American corporation to trade with, mainland China. The exotic land that had once exercised such an irresistible attraction for American merchants in search of markets and American missionaries in search of converts abruptly disappeared from the public consciousness of the United States.

THE U.S.S.R. AND CHINA: FROM PARTNERSHIP TO RIVALRY

All of these measures understandably poisoned Sino-American relations and forestalled the rapprochement between Beijing and Washington that may have been a fleeting possibility during the brief interlude between the Communist victory on the mainland and the outbreak of the Korean War. In the meantime Moscow and Beijing drew closer together in the face of what they jointly viewed as Washington's attempt to erect an anti-Communist bastion in Asia composed of nations armed, assisted, and protected by the United States. The American-sponsored rehabilitation of Japan, the former enemy of Russia and China that had risen to power at their expense, was a special source of common concern. Though prohibited by its own constitution from ever again becoming a military power of the first rank, Japan's security pact with the United States, its willingness to host American bases on its national territory, and its rapid progress toward economic recovery raised fears in the Communist-controlled portion of East Asia similar to those simultaneously engendered in Eastern Europe by the revival of an economically powerful West Germany supported by the United States.

The Sino-Soviet partnership that matured during the first half of the 1950s took the form of Russian economic and diplomatic support for China in exchange for Beijing's continued recognition of Moscow's undisputed authority in the world Communist movement. The Soviet Union had supplied China with roughly $2 billion worth of military equipment during its undeclared war in Korea. Thereafter, by the terms of an agreement concluded by the two governments in September 1953, Soviet economic aid and technical advisers poured into China to assist that country in its crash program of industrialization. By the middle of the decade the Soviet Union had become China's principal trading partner, taking about half of its exports. On October 11, 1954, Moscow removed the last vestiges of Russian imperialism in China by pledging to evacuate the Soviet naval base at Port Arthur (Lüshun) by the end of 1955* and transferring to Beijing the Soviet share of the joint-stock companies that had been formed in 1950 to exploit Xinjiang's mineral resources. The Russians also consented to a long-term development loan of $250 million and promised to assist the Chinese in a number of industrial projects. In the meantime the Soviet Union led the unsuccessful campaign in the United Nations to transfer the Chinese seat from the "Kuomintang clique" on Taiwan to the People's Republic and strongly supported China's claim to sovereignty over the island. This strengthening of bilateral ties between the two giants of the Communist bloc confirmed American fears of a monolithic Communist conspiracy to conquer the world, fears that were aggravated by the spread of McCarthyite hysteria in the United States during the same period.

But as American Cassandras bemoaned the "loss of China," the "no-win policy in Korea," and the rising tide of communism in Asia, cracks were already evident in the supposedly sturdy edifice of Sino-Soviet friendship. As already noted, China drew close to the Soviet Union during the first half of the fifties because it needed Russian economic aid for its industrialization and Moscow's diplomatic support in its disputes with hostile neighbors, particularly the American-backed Nationalist regime on Taiwan. Throughout the entire period of the Soviet economic assistance program, however, the authorities in Beijing were disappointed with the amount furnished and the strings attached. The military aid during the Korean conflict had to be repaid in full at a time when China was struggling to recover from the effects of its civil war and launch its industrial takeoff. The economic aid that was forthcoming thereafter fell far short of Chinese expectations. Once Khrushchev mounted his campaign to extend Soviet influence in the nonaligned countries of the Third World in 1955, Russia was supplying more development assistance to non-Communist states such as India and Egypt than to its Communist neighbor in Asia. Similarly, Soviet support for China's military preparedness was halfhearted and always tendered on the condition of Beijing's absolute subservience to Moscow. After promising to help China develop a nuclear weapons program in 1957, Khrushchev abruptly cancelled the agreement two years later.

These disagreements and disappointments over the quantity and character of Soviet aid to China transpired against the background of a growing ideological dispute between Moscow and Beijing during the second half of the 1950s. Mao was convinced of the inevitability of war with the capitalist powers at a time when Khrushchev, fearful of the consequences of a nuclear exchange for his own country, was pursuing peaceful coexistence with the West. Each time Russian and American chiefs of state met face-to-face, in Geneva in 1955, at Camp David in 1959, in Paris (however briefly) in 1960, Beijing feared a rapprochement between the superpowers that would leave China exposed to the threats to its sovereignty and territorial integrity that emanated from its unfriendly neighbors. The most serious of these threats was thought to come from the Nationalist regime on Taiwan. When China resumed its heavy shelling of Quemoy (Jinmen) in August 1958 as part of its campaign to dislodge the Nationalists from their island fortress a few miles

---

*The Soviet withdrawal from Port Arthur, which had been scheduled to take place in 1952, was postponed by joint agreement because of the Korean War. The pullout finally took place in 1955.

from the mainland, President Eisenhower ordered American planes to airlift supplies to Chiang's troops and arranged for ships from the American Seventh Fleet to escort a Nationalist convoy to the beleaguered island. The State Department issued a veiled threat of an American military intervention should China seek to recapture Quemoy and Matsu. At the height of the Quemoy crisis, Beijing was displeased to note an official Russian silence instead of the customary expressions of support, a silence that was broken only after China had agreed to participate in direct negotiations with representatives of the United States at Warsaw to seek a peaceful solution to the crisis.

In the following year, Khrushchev's meeting with Eisenhower at Camp David reignited Chinese fears of a Soviet-American accommodation at their expense. This suspicion was not allayed by Khrushchev when, returning from his American tour via Beijing, he publicly warned Mao to avoid a confrontation with the United States over Taiwan. This admonition on behalf of peaceful coexistence, coming as it did three months after the Soviet leader had rescinded his pledge to help the Chinese develop a nuclear armament and only a few days after his cordial tête-à-tête with Eisenhower, brought into question the value of Russian support for China's grievances against the American-backed regime across the Taiwan Strait.

A simultaneous source of Sino-Soviet friction as the 1950s drew to a close was the conflict between China and India over Tibet, once a Chinese province that after 1914 had enjoyed de facto independence under its divine ruler, the Dalai Lama, until in 1950 it was forcibly restored to Chinese sovereignty by the new Communist regime. During the spring of 1959, China ruthlessly quelled an armed insurrection in favor of Tibetan independence and accused India, which had given sanctuary to the Dalai Lama and his entourage, of having fomented it. Sino-Indian border clashes were accompanied by conflicting territorial claims along the rugged Himalayan frontier. Suddenly in September 1959, as Khrushchev prepared for his American visit, Moscow infuriated Beijing by declaring its neutrality in the Sino-Indian dispute and then announcing its intention to grant New Delhi a loan much larger than any that had ever been furnished to its Communist ally in Asia. Just as Khrushchev had placed a higher priority on reaching agreement with the West over Berlin and Europe than on supporting China at the Taiwan Strait, he was apparently willing to sacrifice China's security in the Himalayas in the interests of cultivating closer relations with India, the titular leader of the nonaligned states of the Third World.

The Sino-Soviet quarrel first became public, albeit in disguised form, at the Third Congress of the Romanian Communist Party in June 1960. Responding to Khrushchev's defense of the policy of peaceful coexistence and his implicit criticism of the Maoist claim that war with the capitalist states was both inevitable and winnable, the Chinese delegate asserted that the recent U-2 incident and the breakup of the Paris summit meeting (to which China had not been invited) revealed the evil nature of imperialism and indirectly chided the Kremlin for attempting to coexist with it. This seemingly fraternal debate over the proper interpretation of Communist doctrine was soon followed up by direct action: Three months later, in August 1960, Khrushchev abruptly recalled the 1,390 Russian technicians who had been dispatched to China to assist in its economic modernization, ordering them to return with their industrial blueprints. At the conference of world Communist parties in Moscow in November 1960, the Chinese delegation assailed the Soviet Union for betraying the cause of world revolution.

The deterioration of relations between the two states remained an internal affair within the Communist bloc until the autumn of 1962, when the simultaneous outbreak of three unrelated crises strained the Sino-Soviet relationship to the breaking point. The outcome of the Soviet-American showdown over Cuba precipitated an outburst of criticism from Beijing, which in March 1963 denounced the Soviet Union's humiliating retreat before the imperialist aggressor. Mao assailed the Limited Nuclear Test Ban Treaty signed by the two superpowers and Great Britain in August 1963 for preventing China from providing for its own defense. Refusing to sign the treaty, China proceeded to explode its first atomic bomb on October 16, 1964 (coincidentally just as Mao's antagonist Khrushchev was being overthrown in the Kremlin). The second source of conflict between Moscow and Beijing was the renewal of hostilities between China and India along their common frontier in the Himalayas in October 1962. During the border skirmish the Kremlin again took pains to affirm its absolute neutrality, brushing aside Beijing's attempts to secure Soviet support. On February 27, 1963, the Chinese Communist party publicly denounced the Soviet Union for furnishing military assistance to its enemy India after having terminated its aid to China in 1960. The third occasion of Sino-Soviet tension was potentially the most ominous of all: a border dispute between the two Communist powers themselves in China's northwestern province of Xinjiang, which had formerly been within the Russian sphere of interest. This conflict marked the beginning of China's assertion of territorial claims against the Soviet Union, which had retained possession of almost a million square miles of former Chinese territory in central Asia and Siberia that had been forcibly acquired by the tsars under treaties imposed on imperial China in the nineteenth century.

By the end of 1964 the Sino-Soviet rift had become embarrassingly public and apparently irreversible. China's entry into the nuclear club as its first nonwhite member in October of that year had given a tremendous boost to its prestige in the Third World, where it was by then avidly competing with the Soviet Union for influence. Within the international Communist movement, pro-Chinese factions had broken away from the regular Communist parties and professed a more radical brand of Marxist-Leninism in practically every country in the world. Some of the Soviet satellites in Eastern Europe took advantage of these polycentric trends in the Communist world to follow a more independent course. Romania pursued an increasingly independent foreign policy, establishing diplomatic relations with West Germany and retaining them with Israel in 1967 in violation of Eastern bloc policy. Czechoslovakia during the first half of 1968 experimented with various forms of economic liberalism and political democracy that contradicted the basic tenets of Communist doctrine.

Romania's assertion of independence was tolerated by Moscow because the Romanian leader Nicolai Ceausescu maintained a harshly repressive political system that spared the Kremlin what it feared most: the proliferation of liberal ideas that could infect Romania's partners in the Warsaw Pact. It was the failure of the government of Alexander Dubček in Czechoslovakia to keep the lid on domestic dissent during the "Prague spring" of 1968 that precipitated the Soviet-led invasion of that country the following August and the termination of its brief flirtation with liberal communism and national independence. The Soviet intervention in Czechoslovakia predictably prompted a torrent of invective from Beijing against this blatant interference in the domestic affairs of a sovereign Communist state. So did the enunciation by the Soviet first secretary in November 1968 of the Brezhnev Doctrine, which justified intervention by Communist bloc forces in any Communist country threatened by internal or external elements "hostile to socialism." Though ostensibly directed at the Soviet satellites in Eastern Europe, this assertion of the right of intervention (or the "Doctrine of Limited Sovereignty," as it was euphemistically called) could easily have been interpreted as a veiled threat to China, then in the midst of a domestic "cultural revolution" with unmistakable anti-Soviet overtones.

From the vantage point of global power politics, the Sino-Soviet quarrel in the 1960s afforded the United States a rare opportunity: By playing off the two rivals for leadership in the Communist camp against one another, Washington might have been in a position to exploit to its own advantage the divisions within the formerly monolithic Communist bloc. Instead, as Moscow and Beijing were drawing apart by the middle of the decade, the United States became deeply involved, for the second time since World War II, in a military operation in Asia that temporarily reunited the entire Communist world against it.

THE UNITED STATES AND INDOCHINA

Between 1862 and 1897 France had established political control over the region of southeastern Asia known as Indochina (today's Vietnam, Laos, and Cambodia). The motives for the French colonization of this distant land were mixed. Commercial interests were attracted by the valuable raw materials of the region—rubber, tin, tungsten, and rice—that could be shipped to European markets. Catholic missionaries flocked to this outpost of empire on the other side of the earth in search of converts. Military and naval officials envisioned garrisons and bases that would enable France to challenge Great Britain's preeminence in the Far East. Indigenous resistance to French domination developed after the First World War under the leadership of a charismatic nationalist leader widely known by the pseudonym Ho Chi Minh. In 1919 Ho appeared at the Paris Peace Conference to press for the application of the Wilsonian principle of self-determination, currently being invoked on behalf of the former subjects of the Austro-Hungarian Empire in Europe, to the Indochinese victims of French colonial domination in Asia. On learning that the Wilsonian principle of liberal nationalism was to be restricted to white European peoples, Ho turned to the only alternative ideology that appeared to offer the promise of national liberation for his compatriots. He traveled to Moscow to receive instruction in the techniques of revolutionary agitation, and in 1930 he formed the Vietnamese Communist party. After the fall of France in 1940 and the Japanese occupation of Indochina with the tacit consent of the Vichy French administration, Ho organized in China a League for the Independence of Vietnam, or Vietminh, a coalition of nationalist groups led by the Communist party that spearheaded the underground resistance to the Japanese occupation. At the end of the war in the Far East, he appealed to the United States government to support the independence of his country on the basis of the neo-Wilsonian principles of national self-determination incorporated in the Atlantic Charter and reaffirmed in President Roosevelt's wartime pronouncements. In September 1945, following the surrender of Japan and the evacuation of its occupation forces from the Asian mainland, the Vietminh formally declared the independence of the Democratic Republic of Vietnam and established its capital in the northern city of Hanoi. But Great Britain, whose military forces had temporarily occupied the southern portion of the country, permitted French troops to reenter the zone under its jurisdiction. Throughout 1946, Vietminh efforts to negotiate national independence within the French empire (renamed the French Union in October of the same year) along the lines of the self-governing Dominions of the British Commonwealth foundered on the unwillingness of France to relinquish sovereignty. In November 1946, after the refusal of the Vietminh to obey a French order to evacuate Hanoi and its port of Haiphong, the French military and naval forces in the vicinity bombarded the two cities, causing six thousand casualties. The Vietminh responded by taking to the countryside, organizing a guerrilla movement modeled on that of Mao Zedong's in northern China, and engaging the French army in a full-fledged war of national liberation.

The policy of the United States toward the Franco-Vietnamese conflict underwent a profound transformation during the second half of the 1940s. President Roosevelt had opposed the restoration of European colonial power in Asia after the war. But the Truman administration turned a deaf ear to Ho Chi Minh's postwar appeals for American economic assistance and diplomatic support for the political independence of his country. Ho's Communist affiliations became a matter of great concern in Washington as the Soviet-American wartime partnership degenerated into the Cold War, despite the fact that Moscow had given little support or encouragement to the Vietminh. The victory of the Communist faction in the Chinese civil war in 1949 left the impression in Washington of a coordinated Communist advance in Asia masterminded by Moscow. France shrewdly exploited these American fears, arguing that its military operation in Vietnam, which shared a common border with newly communized China, represented the Far Eastern counterpart to the containment policy that the United States and its Western partners were currently pursuing in Europe.

Following the diplomatic recognition of Ho Chi Minh's government by China and the Soviet Union in January 1950, Washington established formal diplomatic relations with the puppet regime of Emperor Bao Dai in Saigon that had been established by the French in the previous year as a nominally independent state (along with Laos and Cambodia) within the French Union. Then the outbreak of the Korean War in June 1950 prompted the United States to intervene actively on behalf of the French against the Communist-led insurgency in Indochina. In the following autumn a team of American military advisers and $150 million in military equipment were dispatched to Vietnam to assist the French effort there.

By 1954 the United States was paying 78 percent of the costs of the French military operations and had over three hundred military advisers on the spot. By the spring of that year, in spite of the increase in American support for the French forces, the Vietminh had gained effective control of the countryside through daring guerrilla tactics borrowed from the teachings of Mao Zedong. The French military commander, General Henri Navarre, concluded that the only hope of crushing the enemy, who struck from ambush only to disappear into the jungles, lay in luring him out into the open to fight a conventional war that the French, with their superiority in artillery and air power, fully expected to win. Accordingly, the French deployed 13,500 of their best troops in the fortress of Dien Bien Phu on the Laotian border in the hope of engaging the Vietminh in a fight to the finish on open terrain. A fight to the finish it was, after a fifty-five day siege of the fortress, but it was the French army that was finished. Employing artillery furnished by the Chinese to shell the beleaguered French ground troops from the hills surrounding their self-made trap, and using Chinese antiaircraft guns to neutralize French air power, the Vietminh

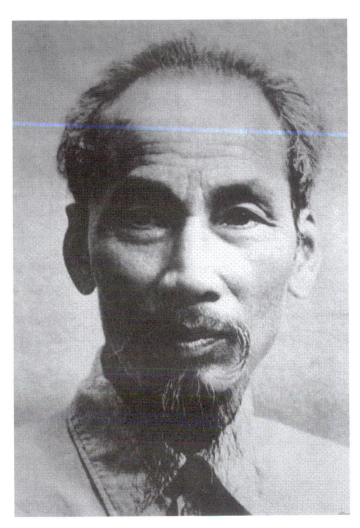

Ho Chi Minh (1890–1969): For fifty years he waged a campaign to secure the withdrawal of foreign forces from Vietnam. At the end of both world wars he appealed in vain to U.S. Presidents Woodrow Wilson and Harry S Truman, respectively, to support the independence of his country. He died four years before the American military withdrawal from Vietnam and six years before the defeat of the U.S.-backed government of South Vietnam. *(Courtesy of the Library of Congress)*

killed over 7,000 French soldiers at Dien Bien Phu and captured the remaining 11,000 on May 7.

During the siege of Dien Bien Phu, on April 26, a conference of the Big Four (the United States, the Soviet Union, Great Britain, and France) in Geneva was authorized to open negotiations for a cease-fire in Indochina, to which representatives of its three constituent states—Vietnam, Laos, and Cambodia—and China were invited. By a tragic coincidence (from the French perspective), the talks on Indochina began on May 8, the day after the fall of Dien Bien Phu. The United States had consented to participate in the Geneva conference in the hope of reaching a settlement that would preserve the non-Communist character of Indochina, with or without a continuing French presence there. But opinion polls and expressions of congressional sentiment clearly revealed the absence of public support for an American military intervention to assist the embattled French. Requests from Paris for the use of B-29 American bombers based in the Philippines, though endorsed by the chairman of the Joint Chiefs of Staff, were turned down by President Eisenhower in the face of congressional opposition and in the absence of British approval for such a rescue operation. Ironically, in light of subsequent events, one of the most outspoken opponents of an American intervention in Vietnam was the Democratic leader in the Senate, Lyndon Baines Johnson.

The final blow to France's imperial position in Southeast Asia came in mid-June when the Laniel government in Paris was replaced by one headed by Pierre Mendès-France, a longtime critic of the war who took office on the basis of a pledge to obtain a cease-fire within a month or resign. Acting as his own foreign minister, Mendès-France hastened to Geneva to seek the support of Moscow and Beijing for a settlement permitting France to exit gracefully from a lost cause. In conversations with Russia's Molotov and China's Zhou Enlai a deal was struck. On July 21 the Geneva Accords terminating the eight-year war in Southeast Asia were signed and sealed: Vietnam was to be temporarily partitioned along the 17th parallel of latitude; the Vietminh would administer the northern zone; the southern zone would be governed from Saigon, where the discredited Emperor Bao Dai would later be ousted by his American-educated Catholic prime minister, Ngo Dinh Diem. Neither sector was to sign military alliances with foreign powers or to permit foreign troops on its territory. In two years the country was to be reunified after elections conducted by secret ballot under the supervision of a United Nations Control Commission. The sovereignty of the royalist governments of Laos and Cambodia was formally recognized by all signatories.

Ho Chi Minh had thus been persuaded by his Soviet and Chinese patrons to surrender roughly 20 percent of the territory that he controlled to an anti-Communist regime in Saigon and to accept the temporary partition of his country as the exhausted colonial power prepared to withdraw. The post-Stalinist leadership in the Kremlin sacrificed the interests of the Communist movement in Vietnam to seek better relations with Washington. Beijing, recovering from its costly war in Korea, did not want to give the Americans an excuse for another military intervention on the Asian mainland. The United States promptly signaled its determination to prevent the unification of Vietnam and to protect the royalist regimes in Cambodia and Laos against insurgencies mounted by their own indigenous Communist movements. Having declined to sign the Geneva Accords, Washington felt under no obligation to honor their prohibition against foreign military involvement in Indochina. In September 1954 Secretary of State Dulles orchestrated the formation of the South East Asia Treaty Organization (SEATO), a regional security arrangement that committed the United States and other countries to the defense of Laos and Cambodia against Communist aggression or insurgency as well as of South Vietnam against North Vietnam. By the end of 1954. American military advisers were arriving in Saigon to train the South Vietnamese army while American economic assistance was flowing into Diem's coffers.

The South Vietnamese government had no intention of honoring the Geneva Accords' provisions for the holding of nationwide elections for the unification of the country. In the summer of 1955 Hanoi twice formally asked Saigon to designate representatives to the electoral commission envisaged by the accords. On August 9 Diem declined to do so on the grounds that such elections would be pointless as long as North Vietnam refused to grant democratic liberties to its own citizens. The United States government, convinced that the Vietminh would win all-Vietnamese elections, endorsed the cancellation

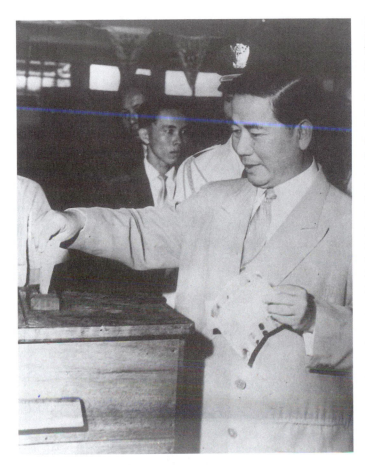

President Ngo Dinh Diem (1901–1963) of South Vietnam casting his ballot in elections, Saigon, 1961: A Vietnamese nationalist who had opposed French rule but was also a fervent anti-Communist who refused to cooperate with the Viet Minh, Diem returned from exile in the United States to take control of South Vietnam as French forces prepared to evacuate the former colony in the summer of 1954. His refusal to permit elections to unify Vietnam in 1956 satisfied the American government, which feared an electoral victory by Ho Chi Minh, but led to a Communist-led insurrection in South Vietnam that received support from North Vietnam. *(Courtesy of the Library of Congress)*

of the electoral provisions of the Geneva Accords. As the date for the projected elections passed in the summer of 1956, the provisional demarcation line along the 17th parallel became the boundary between two hostile states. By the end of the decade the 275 American military advisers attached to the South Vietnamese army in late 1954 had grown to 685, and about $300 million worth of U.S. military aid was provided to Diem annually. In the meantime, the Soviet Union and China began to furnish economic and military assistance to North Vietnam.

At the time of the ceasefire in 1954, thousands of Vietminh guerrillas had remained in the southern zone in anticipation either of political victory at the polls two years later or of a renewal of the armed struggle in the absence of a politically mandated national unification. The cancellation of the elections prompted a renewal of the guerrilla campaign, which took the form of the selective assassination of officials appointed by the Saigon regime. In the meantime the corruption, nepotism, and repressive policies of the Diem government had engendered widespread discontent among non-Communist interest groups in the south. In December 1960 a coalition of anti-Diem dissidents—Communist and non-Communist alike—formed the National Liberation Front, dedicated to social reform, political liberalization, and neutrality for South Vietnam. Capitalizing on this

N

| 0 | 100 | 200 Miles |
| 0 | 100 | 200 Km |

PEOPLE'S REPUBLIC OF CHINA

BURMA

NORTH VIETNAM

● Dienbienphu   ● Hanoi
● Haiphong

LAOS

Gulf of Tonkin

Hainan

● Vientiane

Demilitarised Zone

● Hue

● Da Nang

THAILAND

● Pleiku

● Bangkok

CAMBODIA

SOUTH VIETNAM

Phnom Penh ●

● Cam Rahn Bay

● Saigon

Gulf of Thailand

SOUTH CHINA SEA

MALAYSIA

E.McC '95

Indochina, 1954–1975

indigenous discontent, Hanoi extended support to this opposition group in the south, which was contemptuously labeled "Viet Cong" (Vietnamese Communist) by Diem.

The administration of John F. Kennedy had inherited from its predecessor a commitment to help the non-Communist regimes of the former French Indochina—particularly Laos and South Vietnam—to preserve their independence from the Communist regime in Hanoi and to protect them from domestic insurgencies mounted by the indigenous Communist organizations in their midst. Landlocked Laos, granted independence from France in 1954, had been torn by civil strife for the remainder of the decade. After a rapid succession of government changes, during which the United States furnished military assistance and advisers to various right-wing factions while Moscow and Beijing backed a coalition of neutralists and the pro-Communist Pathet Lao forces, the great powers reconvened the Geneva Conference on Indochina in May 1961 to explore a solution to the Laos problem. An agreement was finally concluded in June 1962 that guaranteed the neutrality of Laos (by prohibiting it from signing alliances with, furnishing bases for, or receiving military aid from foreign powers) under a coalition government composed of the three contending factions. But Washington resumed deliveries of arms to the coalition government and secretly bombed Pathet Lao training camps after the Communists had left the coalition government and renewed their insurgency.

While the Laos accords collapsed in the early 1960s, neighboring Vietnam degenerated into chaos. When President Kennedy took office in January 1961, almost 900 American military advisers were stationed in South Vietnam to train that country's army in the techniques of counterinsurgency warfare. By the end of the year that number had increased to about 2,600; at the time of Kennedy's assassination in November 1963 it had risen to 16,500. U.S. military aid to Saigon escalated dramatically. At the same time, Kennedy tried and failed to persuade the autocratic Diem to institute economic and political reforms to satisfy the discontented masses and the Buddhist majority that felt persecuted by the Catholic elite in power. As Vietnamese army units fired on unarmed protestors and stormed Buddhist pagodas in 1963, the Kennedy administration publicly expressed displeasure with its recalcitrant protégé by reducing economic assistance to Saigon. Assuming from this signal that Diem had lost Washington's favor, senior South Vietnamese military officers toppled his regime on November 1 with the tacit approval of the American ambassador in Saigon, Henry Cabot Lodge, and murdered Diem. Kennedy himself was to be assassinated three weeks later.

Between November 1963 and the end of 1965 Saigon saw twelve changes of government as military officers completed for power. The succession of generals and marshals who occupied the top post in South Vietnam displayed little inclination to seek public support for the regime by instituting land reforms or expanding political and religious liberties. Nevertheless, the new Johnson administration in Washington resumed and intensified the American military engagement in South Vietnam on behalf of the anti-Communist forces there. As the insurgents in the south began to receive large quantities of supplies from North Vietnam, China, and the Soviet Union, the character of the American involvement began to change. In February 1964 the American-advised South Vietnamese army launched covert commando raids into North Vietnam while air strikes were carried out in neighboring Laos to interdict the supply line from north to south. The following summer an incident occurred off the coast of North Vietnam that provided the president with a convenient pretext to disarm the Republican opposition by escalating the

Buddhist monk burning himself to death to protest government repression of his faith, Saigon, summer 1963: Discrimination against the Buddhist majority practiced by the regime of Ngo Dinh Diem, a devout Catholic whose brother was the archbishop of Hue, alienated many non-Communist citizens of South Vietnam and fed the Communist-led insurgency against the Saigon government. Photographs such as this one severely damaged the international reputation of Diem's government. *(Courtesy of the Library of Congress)*

American military involvement: On August 4, North Vietnamese torpedo boats allegedly fired on two American destroyers in international waters in the Gulf of Tonkin. Though the Vietnamese vessels promptly retreated and neither American ship suffered damage, Johnson took the occasion of this provocation to submit to the United States Congress a previously drafted resolution requesting congressional authorization to deal with North Vietnamese aggression by all appropriate means. On August 7 the Tonkin Gulf resolution passed unanimously in the House and with only two dissenting votes in the Senate. The president had the authority he required to intensify U.S. involvement in the conflict.

After his reelection in November 1964, President Johnson's plans for the intensive bombardment of North Vietnam were implemented. On February 7, 1965, when a Viet Cong mortar attack on an American barracks and airfield at Pleiku resulted in nine American deaths and over a hundred casualties, Johnson ordered retaliatory air strikes against North Vietnam from carriers of the Seventh Fleet. Less than a month after these first large-scale bombings, Washington announced (on March 6) that two battalions of marines were being dispatched to South Vietnam. By the end of 1965, the man who had promised during his reelection campaign that he would never send U.S. soldiers to Vietnam had dispatched over 184,000 American ground forces to that country. That number was to reach 385,000 by the end of the following year, 535,000 by the end of 1967, and a maximum of 542,000 in February 1969. Neither the bombing of the north nor the escalation of American troop strength in the south succeeded in quelling the insurrection against the South Vietnamese regime. Hanoi increased its flow of arms and men to the south while the indigenous forces of the Viet Cong gained effective control of almost all rural areas.

The turning point of the war in Vietnam came on January 30, 1968, which was the first day of Tet, the holiday marking the beginning of the lunar New Year. On that day Viet Cong guerrillas and North Vietnamese regulars launched an offensive against most of the provincial capitals of South Vietnam as well as Saigon itself, where they reached the presidential palace, the radio station, the airport, and even the grounds of the heavily fortified American embassy. The apparent military objective of the Tet offensive was to spark an uprising in the South Vietnamese cities against the Saigon regime and its American protectors. In this strictly military sense it was a failure, and a costly one at that. Over 45,000 Communist troops were killed compared to about 4,000 South Vietnamese and Americans. The insurgents were evicted from all of the cities they had overrun in the face of a furious American-South Vietnamese counterattack. But by invading the major cities of South Vietnam, Hanoi and its supporters in the south had won a public relations triumph of imposing dimensions by discrediting the excessively optimistic claims of the American government that the enemy was on its last legs in a war that was becoming increasingly unpopular at home.

As the increase in American troop strength required the dispatch of large numbers of conscripts in 1965–68, opposition to the war began to surface in Congress. The casualty figures and "body counts," meticulously recorded by American television correspondents reporting directly from the battlefield, helped to fan the flames of discontent at home. In 1966 and 1967 President Johnson, feeling the sting of political criticism from members of his own party, tried to induce Hanoi to negotiate an end to the conflict by temporarily suspending the bombing of North Vietnam. The North Vietnamese government consistently refused to enter into negotiations until Washington agreed in advance to a permanent bombing halt. After each bombing "pause" failed to lure the North Vietnamese to the conference table on American terms, the bombing was resumed on an even greater scale in an effort to force them to talk. Then the Tet offensive appeared to demonstrate that the ground war in the south was unwinnable, that the bombing of the north had done nothing to bring the contending forces closer to a negotiated settlement, and that the only way out of the quagmire in Southeast Asia was a halt to the bombing coupled with overtures to Hanoi.

The growing public opposition to the war was graphically symbolized by the strong showing of antiwar Senator Eugene McCarthy in the first of the state primary elections of the 1968 presidential campaign. When Senator Robert Kennedy, the younger brother of the slain president, entered the race for the Democratic nomination on an antiwar platform, the discouraged Johnson abruptly decided to reverse his course and leave the Vietnam mess to others. On March 31, 1968, he announced that he would not run for reelection, halted all bombing attacks against North Vietnam north of the demilitarized zone, and asked Ho Chi Minh to send delegates to a conference to end what he called "this ugly war." Peace talks opened in Paris within a few months, but little progress was made while Hanoi awaited the outcome of the U.S. presidential elections in November.

The new president, Richard Nixon, had spoken vaguely during his campaign of a "peace plan" that would bring an end to America's military involvement in Indochina. At Guam in July 1969 Nixon finally announced his new foreign policy for East Asia in general and Vietnam in particular. At the heart of this Nixon Doctrine was the concept of "Vietnamization," which meant the gradual strengthening of the South Vietnamese military forces in order to permit them to assume the burden of national defense that was gradually to be relinquished by the United States. The number of American military personnel in South Vietnam was reduced from 540,000 at the end of 1968 to 139,000 by the end of 1971 and 25,000 by the end of Nixon's first term. But in an effort to "buy the time needed to make our ally self-sufficient," the Nixon administration simultaneously escalated the level of violence in response to each North Vietnamese success on the battlefield. In April 1970 American ground forces invaded neutral Cambodia with the intention of interdicting the supply routes to the south and driving the North Vietnamese regulars from their Cambodian sanctuaries. In the spring of 1972 North Vietnamese infantry and armored units mounted an assault across the demilitarized zone against South Vietnam and directly menaced Nixon's Vietnamization program. The American president responded in May by issuing orders to bomb transportation facilities and military installations in North Vietnam and to mine the principal harbors of that country in order to cut off the flow of supplies from China and the Soviet Union. In December 1972, shortly after Henry Kissinger's announcement of the imminence of a peace settlement, Nixon ordered a massive B-52 bombing raid on Hanoi and Haiphong to force North Vietnam closer to the American negotiating position.

Since assuming his position as national security adviser to the president, Kissinger had met secretly with North Vietnamese negotiator Le Duc Tho to explore the basis for an agreement to end the war. By the end of 1972 the United States made the crucial concession: a cease-fire in place instead of the total withdrawal of North Vietnamese forces from the south that it had previously insisted on. Agreement was finally reached on January 27, 1973, shortly after Nixon began his second term after his reelection. The United States agreed to remove all of its armed forces from South Vietnam within two months. The two sides agreed on an exchange of prisoners of war. The vague political terms of the accord provided for a coalition government in the south that would conduct free elections there. No serious discussions to that end were ever held, and within two years of the American evacuation all three of the pro-Western regimes of Indochina were overthrown by their Communist enemies. The Saigon government fell to North Vietnamese forces on April 30, 1975, two weeks after the Cambodian Communist organization, the Khmer Rouge, toppled the pro-American government that had replaced the neutralist regime of Prince Norodom Sihanouk in 1970. On August 23 the third domino of the former French Indochina fell when the Communist Pathet Lao dissolved the non-Communist administration in Laos.

Between 1961 and 1973 almost fifty-eight thousand Americans died in the Indochina conflict, the country's longest and costliest foreign war. The United States Air Force dropped on Vietnam over three times the tonnage of bombs that had been dropped on Germany during the Second World War. The financial burden of the war, including military aid to Saigon, has been estimated at approximately $150 billion. The escalation of the American military involvement in Vietnam during 1965–68 coincided with a sharp increase in domestic government spending to finance the social programs of Johnson's "Great Society," yet he eschewed politically unpopular increases in taxation to pay for both "guns and butter." The resulting budget deficits produced a rampant inflation whose damaging effects on the American economy persisted for a generation. The social and political consequences of America's long involvement in Indochina were scarcely less significant: skepticism bordering on cynicism toward government, fueled by the enormous "credibility gap" between the idealistic, optimistic pronouncements of administration officials and the sordid reality in the Vietnamese jungles that could be seen on the daily television newscasts; a public distaste for foreign entanglements of any kind that threatened to revive the isolationist tradition of the distant past; a host of war-related social and psychological afflictions among returning veterans, such as drug abuse and a mental illness designated by psychiatrists as post-traumatic stress disorder.

In the light of the enormous costs paid by the United States for its abortive effort to prevent the three states of the former French empire in Southeast Asia from falling under Communist domination, how does one explain the tenacity and persistence with which this adventure was pursued by four successive administrations of divergent political tendencies? The lure of economic advantage does not come close to justifying the expenditure of money, lives, and prestige; neither the raw materials of the region nor the potential markets for American exports or capital investment played an important role in decision making concerning Indochina. The military threat—actual or potential—posed by a unified Communist Vietnam to the United States and its allies in Asia was nonexistent in light of the preponderance of American naval and air power in the region. Imponderables such as bureaucratic inertia, personal involvements of military and civilian policymakers, and concern about loss of prestige in the eyes of allies and adversaries alike all doubtless played their part in preventing the United States from extricating itself from the morass of Indochina for so many years. But one is also inevitably drawn to the conclusion that an important motivation for the American war in Southeast Asia was concern about China. In April 1965 President Johnson publicly accused Beijing of masterminding the North Vietnamese effort to absorb the south, and Secretary of State Dean Rusk repeated that allegation on several occasions during the legislative hearings on the Vietnam conflict conducted in 1966.

Though Beijing undeniably supplied Hanoi with military equipment during its war with the United States, it did so primarily to compete with the predominant Soviet influence in the north rather than to promote the establishment of a militarily powerful, politically unified Vietnam. Centuries of ethnic antagonism between the Chinese and Vietnamese peoples had left a legacy of mutual mistrust that even the common ideological bond of communism could not overcome. The very idea of Vietnam as a stalking horse for an expansionist China bent on conquering all of Southeast Asia and its offshore islands, so prevalent in the public pronouncements of American officials seeking to justify their nation's military intervention in Indochina, was an absurdity that would have astonished specialists in the region's history (of whom there were precious few in the State Department during the 1960s, owing in part to the McCarthyite purges of the previous decade following the "loss" of China). In any case, the rationale for the Vietnam intervention as a means of containing Chinese communism in Asia lost the last vestige of its credibility in the early 1970s, when Beijing severed the tenuous thread that still connected it to Moscow and began to explore the possibility of improved relations with Washington.

THE DEVELOPMENT OF THE SINO-AMERICAN RAPPROCHEMENT (1969–1975)

The split between the Soviet Union and China continued to widen during the second half of the 1960s in spite of their joint efforts on behalf of North Vietnam during its military struggle with the United States. In the autumn of 1966 Mao expelled all Soviet exchange students from China and the Kremlin promptly responded in kind. By the end of the decade the Sino-Soviet quarrel had degenerated from a doctrinal dispute between rival claimants to leadership of the Communist world into a fierce diplomatic, and, briefly, even military clash between two sovereign powers over traditional matters of territory and regional security. Into this breach between Moscow and Beijing plunged the new administration in Washington that had taken office in January 1969. After initiating the negotiations with North Vietnam that were to produce the American disengagement from Southeast Asia in 1973, the Nixon government undertook to profit from the Sino-Soviet split to open a dialogue with the Chinese Communist regime that had been ostracized by successive American administrations for the past twenty years. The result was a dramatic transformation of the global relationship between the Communist and non-Communist world.

The deterioration of Sino-Soviet relations finally erupted into violence on March 2, 1969, when Chinese military forces ambushed a contingent of Soviet troops near the disputed Damansky (or Chenpao) island at the confluence of the Amur and Ussuri rivers. Subsequent skirmishes in the same region as well as along the frontier of Chinese Xinjiang during the spring and summer were accompanied by a renewal of Chinese territorial claims against the Soviet Union. In response to these provocations, Moscow took a number of steps to reinforce its defenses on the Chinese border. In April 1969 East European military contingents were detached from the Warsaw Pact command and transferred to the Far East. The number of Soviet divisions deployed along the Chinese frontier was increased from fifteen in 1967 to twenty-one in 1969 and thirty in 1970. Tactical nuclear weapons were stockpiled in Soviet-controlled Mongolia, while officials in the Kremlin considered launching a preemptive strike against China's infant nuclear installation at Lop Nor in Xinjiang.* In the summer of 1969 Moscow sounded out the governments of India, Thailand, and Indonesia about the possibility of concluding an Asian defense pact directed against Beijing. Though neither the preemptive strike nor the diplomatic encirclement materialized, the nervous authorities in China ordered the construction of nuclear fallout shelters in anticipation of a Soviet attack. Negotiations over the disputed frontier, which had begun in September, broke down three months later. By 1972 forty-four Soviet divisions stood guard along the 4,500-mile border with China (compared to thirty-one divisions in Eastern Europe), while a quarter of the Soviet air force had been redeployed from west to east.

In the meantime, the new American administration of Richard Nixon had undertaken a fundamental reevaluation of American policy toward China in light of the Sino-Soviet split and the consequent breakup of the monolithic Communist bloc. In 1969 the first ten-

---

*China had exploded its first atomic bomb in October 1964 and its first hydrogen bomb in June 1967. But by the end of the 1960s its rudimentary delivery system left it vulnerable to a Soviet preemptive strike.

tative gesture of reconciliation emanated from the White House in the form of a relaxation of certain trade and travel restrictions that dated from the Korean emergency. The Chinese reciprocated a year later by reopening the informal Sino-American talks in Warsaw that had been suspended in early 1968 to protest the American bombing campaign in Vietnam. In April 1971 the Chinese government caused a minor sensation by inviting an American table tennis team competing in Japan to try its skills against the Chinese team. Beijing's "Ping-Pong diplomacy" prompted a vigorous U.S. response. In June Nixon formally revoked the twenty-one-year-old trade embargo on China. On July 9 Kissinger, after establishing contact with Chinese authorities through the government of Pakistan (which enjoyed cordial relations with both the United States and China), secretly flew to Beijing. Six days later President Nixon astonished the world with the announcement that he would personally travel to China to "seek the normalization of relations" between the two governments. To impress upon his future hosts the seriousness of his quest for an improvement in Sino-American relations, Nixon inaugurated a dramatic change in American foreign policy that was guaranteed to win approval in Beijing. On October 25, 1971, the United States allowed the United Nations to expel the Chinese Nationalist government on Taiwan and transfer its seat on the Security Council to the People's Republic.

Having smoothed his path to Beijing with these gestures of goodwill, Nixon journeyed over 20,000 miles in February 1972 to become the first American president in history to set foot on Chinese soil. After several days of intensive negotiations, punctuated by an hour-long meeting between top American officials and the ailing seventy-eight-year-old Mao Zedong, the two governments issued a joint communiqué in the city of Shanghai on February 27. The United States agreed to reduce its military installations on Taiwan, but it also insisted that the dispute between the two Chinas could be resolved only by peaceful means. While committing itself to the total withdrawal of American military forces from Indochina once a negotiated settlement could be reached in Paris, Washington reaffirmed its treaty commitments to South Korea and Japan. Both governments pledged to oppose any other nation's efforts to pursue "hegemony" in East Asia (a clear warning to the U.S.S.R.). The communiqué also endorsed the expansion of cultural and commercial contacts between the two nations to complement the normalization of political relations that was underway.

The visit by the preeminent symbol of American anticommunism to the center of militant revolutionary opposition to the capitalist world was in itself an almost inconceivable event. The respectful, almost deferential, behavior exhibited by each delegation toward the other during the public ceremonies stood in glaring contrast to the mutual distrust and ideological antipathy that had characterized Sino-American relations since 1950. American reporters observing Nixon and Kissinger embracing their Chinese hosts remarked how far the two governments had progressed since the Geneva Conference in 1954, where Secretary of State Dulles brusquely declined to shake the hand of Chinese Foreign Minister Zhou Enlai. It was evident that both Washington and Beijing had been prompted by the most compelling of motives to jettison the bitter legacy of two decades and seek a durable basis for rapprochement.

The primary concern that both governments shared, of course, was that of restraining and containing the Soviet Union. Nixon and Kissinger hoped that the Kremlin's willingness to reach agreement on strategic arms control and political detente in Europe would be hastened by the emerging Sino-American understanding in the Far East; that devel-

U.S. President Richard Nixon (1913–1994) and Chinese Communist Party Chairman Mao Zedong (1893–1976) shaking hands, February 29, 1972: "There is no reason for us to be enemies," the longtime American critic of the Chinese Communist regime and staunch supporter of the Chinese Nationalist government on Taiwan declared in this private meeting. "Neither of us seeks the territory of the other; neither of us seeks domination over the other; neither of us seeks to stretch out our hands and rule the world." *(National Archives)*

opment, in conjunction with the disengagement of American military forces from Vietnam, would increase Soviet uneasiness by releasing Chinese military forces in the southern region for redeployment along the northern frontier. Moscow's subsequent eagerness to conclude the SALT I treaty and settle the remaining East-West political differences in Europe was undeniably influenced by Nixon's willingness to "play the China card" and confront the Soviets with a potential threat from the east. For their part, Mao and Zhou welcomed the normalization of relations with Washington and the prospective American disengagement from Indochina and Taiwan for the same reason, that is, to permit the concentration of Chinese military strength in the north to counteract the massive Soviet buildup in Siberia, Mongolia, and the maritime provinces.

There were also powerful economic motivations for the Sino-American rapprochement. The hoary myth of the China market reasserted its almost magical attraction on

American business interests during the early 1970s, when the spectacular postwar economic expansion of the United States had begun to peter out. Increased competition from Japan and the European Economic Community had eaten into America's share of the world market for manufactured goods, while the deficit financing of the Great Society at home and the military intervention in Southeast Asia during the previous decade had generated the highest rates of American inflation since the Second World War. The suspension of the dollar's convertibility into gold in August 1971 shattered the edifice of international monetary relations erected at Bretton Woods in 1944 and exposed the weaknesses of America's financial position in the world. The prospect of gaining entrée to a virtually untapped market comprising a quarter of the world's population fueled extravagant expectations on the part of certain American export interests in the early years of the Sino-American courtship. Within months of Nixon's historic visit, American business executives were flocking to China in search of orders for their products. American exports to China increased from $5 million in 1969 to $700 million in 1973. From the Chinese perspective, the increase in trade with the United States, as well as with its ally Japan, offered an attractive alternative to the economic connection with the Soviet Union that had been severed at Moscow's behest in the 1960s. By January 1975 Chinese Premier Zhou Enlai was publicly advocating closer economic relations among China, Japan, and the United States.

Neither the Nixon administration nor the interim successor government of Gerald Ford was eager to take the final step of establishing regular diplomatic relations with Beijing for fear of traumatizing the already nervous Nationalist Chinese regime on Taiwan. Following the exchange of "liaison offices" in 1973, a rather clumsy "two Chinas policy" was attempted by Washington in lieu of the formal diplomatic recognition of Beijing that it was as yet unprepared to contemplate. But the remarkable increase in Sino-American trade; the influx of American journalists, scholars, and tourists to China; and numerous return visits by Kissinger and the Ford trip of 1975 confirmed the seriousness of America's courtship of China. No longer would the most populous country in the world be treated as a pariah by the most prosperous country in the world. No longer would China be regarded in the United States as the Far Eastern agent of a monolithic, Moscow-based Communist conspiracy intent on absorbing the remainder of non-Communist Asia. Instead, it would be viewed, and would come to view itself, as a middle-rank power of great potential but modest achievement pursuing regional rather than global objectives. When American military power was engaged on the mainland of Asia during the fifties and sixties, waging two wars against fraternal Communist states bordering on China and protecting the Nationalist Chinese regime on an island that Beijing regarded as its own, China's vital interests seemed most directly threatened by the capitalist superpower across the Pacific. But the American withdrawal from Asia and the simultaneous increase of Soviet military power along China's northern border during the first half of the 1970s brought the two Communist behemoths into direct conflict with one another and spelled the end of the Cold War in the Far East.

12

THE RESURGENCE OF EAST-WEST TENSION (1975–1985)

THE PROSPECTS FOR PLURALISM AND INTERDEPENDENCE

In the year 1975, as the Helsinki Conference formally recorded the end of the Cold War in Europe, the Cold War in Asia drew to a close as the pro-Western regimes in South Vietnam, Cambodia, and Laos succumbed in rapid succession to Communist-led insurgencies with only pro forma protests from the American government that had abandoned them to their fate two years earlier. In the meantime the People's Republic of China and the United States accelerated their rapprochement that had begun in the early years of the decade. Just as Washington tacitly recognized the permanence of Soviet hegemony in Eastern Europe, it acknowledged the triumph of national Communist movements in China and Indochina. The thirty-three thousand ground forces in South Korea and the token air units stationed in that country and in Thailand constituted the sole remnants of the once-formidable American military presence on the mainland of Asia that had been established for the ostensible purpose of containing Chinese expansionism in that part of the world. Most of the ghosts of the past three decades appeared to have been interred by the arms control agreements concluded between the two superpowers and the signs of political detente that surfaced almost simultaneously in Europe and Asia, the two historic flashpoints of the Cold War.

Underlying the American pursuit of stable relations with the two quarreling giants of the Communist world and the simultaneous reduction of America's overseas role during the first half of the 1970s was the Nixon-Kissinger vision of a new global order that rapidly acquired the designation of the "pentagonal multipolar system." In place of the rigid, ideologically defined bipolar system that had operated during the first quarter century following the end of the Second World War, Nixon and his influential foreign policy adviser envisaged a looser multipolar system in which five rather than two power centers—the United States, the Soviet Union, Western Europe, China, and Japan—would function as the principal actors on the stage of world politics. The split within the Communist bloc and China's bid to play an independent role in the world, together with the impressive economic power of the newly enlarged European Economic Community* and Japan, seemed to render obsolete the familiar conception of a world divided into two monolithic power blocs directed from Washington and Moscow.

In regard to Europe, we have seen how the Final Act of the Helsinki European Security Conference in 1975 resolved to the apparent satisfaction of all parties concerned the thorny disputes over borders and sovereignty that had poisoned East-West relations on the continent since 1945. Likewise, the economic benefits of this relaxation of political tensions proved so substantial to both sides that the process of conciliation set in motion by Willy Brandt in the early 1970s had acquired a momentum of its own during the second half of the "decade of detente." Trade contacts between East and West expanded significantly in the course of the 1970s. The new willingness on the part of Moscow and its satellites to abandon the traditional quest for bloc autarky in favor of foreign trade contacts outside the Communist world opened up markets and resources that had been virtually inaccessible to Western trading interests.

Accompanying this significant expansion of interbloc commercial relations was a remarkable increase in West European private and public lending to the Communist states to the east. These hard currency loans helped the Soviet satellites to pay for their imports of Western technology and industrial products; German, French, and British banks, whose reserves had been greatly expanded by the influx of petrodollar deposits from the OPEC states after the oil price increases of the midseventies, eagerly grasped the opportunity to recycle these funds through loans to Communist states. The combined foreign debt of the Soviet satellites to Western financial institutions increased from $19 billion in 1975 to about $62 billion by the end of 1981. These commercial and financial connections across the iron curtain had the effect of fostering an unprecedented degree of economic interdependence between Western and Eastern Europe (including the Soviet Union). According to the advocates of detente in the West, this web of interdependence would enhance the prospects of continued peace and stability in Europe by giving the West valuable leverage over the East: The economic benefits of trade, technology transfer, and hard currency credits would demonstrate to the Communist bloc the value of cooperation with the non-Communist world and would therefore discourage a reversion of Cold War policies.

THE RENEWAL OF THE ARMS RACE

The notable progress toward political conciliation and economic interdependence in Europe during the second half of the 1970s and beyond was accompanied neither by a reduction in tensions between the two superpowers nor by the successful conclusion of their earlier efforts to impose restraints upon the nuclear arms rivalry between them. As we have seen, the retention of the Kissinger foreign policy team following Nixon's ignominious departure enabled the process of Soviet-American detente to proceed on schedule during the interim administration of Nixon's handpicked successor. The Ford-

---

*In January 1973 Great Britain, Denmark, and Ireland joined the European Economic Community. Greece was admitted as the Community's tenth member in January 1981, Spain and Portugal followed in 1986.

Brezhnev interim agreement signed at the Vladivostok summit in November 1974 had sketched the basic outlines of a replacement for the SALT I treaty that was due to expire in 1977. But by the advent of the administration of President Jimmy Carter in Washington and the expiration of the SALT I treaty, negotiations for a successor agreement had been thrown off track by a number of technological innovations in the Soviet nuclear arsenal that were denounced by American congressional critics as a serious threat to the delicate balance of strategic forces that had been confirmed by SALT I: The U.S.S.R. had tested a MIRVed missile for the first time and deployed a new long-range bomber called the "Backfire," indicating that the Soviets were bent on competing with the Americans in the two categories of delivery vehicles in which the United States enjoyed a decisive lead to compensate for its inferiority in the size and number of ICBMs. To meet this new challenge, the Carter administration accelerated the development of several new weapons systems: the mobile "Missile Experimental" (MX) ICBM, thought to be virtually invulnerable to a preemptive strike; the small, inexpensive "cruise" missile, a pilotless miniature aircraft that could slide beneath radar and reach Soviet targets undetected; and the new Trident submarine intended to replace the aging Polaris, whose missiles could reach most important targets in the Soviet Union.

In spite of this U.S. arms buildup, the American and Soviet chiefs of state signed the SALT II treaty in Vienna on June 18, 1979. The agreement limited each side to 2,250 delivery vehicles of which no more than 1,320 could be MIRVed missiles. In theory this permitted the Soviet Union approximately nine thousand warheads on land-based missiles, more than enough to place the American Minuteman arsenal in jeopardy, a circumstance that confirmed the Carter administration's determination to accelerate development of the mobile (and theoretically invulnerable) MX missile system.

But as the second treaty on strategic arms control was being debated in the United States Senate in preparation for a ratification vote, the issue of intermediate-range nuclear weapons in Europe suddenly emerged as a controversial issue in East-West relations. In 1977 the Soviet Union had begun to deploy SS-20 land-based missiles whose 3,000-mile range put them within reach of any target in Western Europe. The SS-20 was MIRVed, with three independently targetable warheads, and was mobile and therefore difficult to locate and destroy. Viewing this as a prelude to Soviet nuclear superiority on the continent, the NATO Council decided on December 12, 1979, to deploy a new generation of intermediate-range missiles in Western Europe to offset the Soviet SS-20s, unless Washington could reach an agreement with Moscow to reverse its decision to deploy the missiles. According to this plan, 108 Pershing II missiles would be deployed in West Germany, while 464 land-based cruise missiles would be deployed in Great Britain, Italy, Belgium, the Netherlands, and West Germany by the end of 1983. In the absence of an arms control agreement, these new missiles would serve as a counter to the Soviet SS-20 force.

The NATO decision to modernize the nuclear weapon force in Europe provoked an agitated response from the Kremlin as well as an outpouring of antinuclear sentiment in those West European countries that were designated to receive the new missiles. This public opposition increased in intensity after January 1981 when the Reagan administration came to power. The new occupant of the White House was widely perceived to be much less committed than his predecessor to an agreement with the Russians that would remove the justification for deploying the controversial intermediate-range missiles.

But the new president surprised everyone by bringing the United States into the Intermediate-range Nuclear Forces (INF) talks with the Soviet Union in Geneva in November 1981. He put Brezhnev on the spot by proposing a simple, definitive solution to the nuclear arms race on the continent: the so-called zero option, whereby the United States would refrain from deploying the 572 cruise and Pershing II missiles in exchange for the dismantling of the 600 Soviet intermediate-range missiles. The Kremlin adamantly rejected this scheme, which would have required it to jettison an existing missile force in exchange for an American promise not to deploy missiles whose effectiveness had yet to be demonstrated and whose deployment was strongly opposed by a significant segment of public opinion in Western Europe. Little progress was made in the INF negotiations, in part because the Russians insisted on counting the 162 British and French intermediate-range missiles as part of the American atomic arsenal in Europe while the United States refused to negotiate on behalf of its allies. At the end of 1983, the Soviet delegates walked out of the INF talks when the United States began to deploy the Pershing and cruise missiles at the designated European sites.

While the two superpowers failed to reach agreement on nuclear weapons in Europe, the complex issue of strategic arms control also continued to elude a mutually acceptable solution. A spirit of ambivalence seemed to characterize the Reagan administration's attitude toward strategic arms control. On the one hand, the new American chief of state presided over the largest peacetime military buildup in history in an effort to overcome what he ominously described as the Soviet Union's commanding lead in nuclear weaponry, while officials in his entourage indulged in bloodcurdling rhetoric about the possibility of surviving a nuclear war and the necessity of preparing to fight one. In May 1983 the administration sought and won congressional approval for construction of a scaled-down version of the MX missile system to replace the ostensibly vulnerable Minuteman ICBM force. Two months earlier the president had raised eyebrows by floating the idea of abandoning the existing defense policy of reciprocal deterrence (or mutual assured destruction) in favor of constructing an air-tight antiballistic missile system composed of satellite-launched laser beams that could intercept and destroy all Soviet missiles before they reached the territory of America or its allies. Such an innovation—dubbed the Strategic Defense Initiative by its proponents—would not only have violated the ABM provisions of the SALT I treaty of 1972, but would also, according to many experts, have promoted acute instability in the strategic balance and therefore increased the possibility of preventive nuclear war.

On the other hand, the Reagan administration took two steps that indicated a willingness to find common ground with Moscow. First, Reagan agreed to abide by the provisions of the unratified SALT II treaty, which he had earlier criticized for leaving the United States at a strategic disadvantage. Second, he called for a resumption of strategic arms negotiations with the Soviet Union, under the title Strategic Arms Reduction Talks (START), to express his preference for deep reductions in, rather than limitations of, the nuclear arsenals of the two superpowers. The START talks, which began in Geneva on June 29, 1982, kept the process of arms control negotiations alive amid a deterioration of relations between the two superpowers. The failure of arms control talks during Reagan's first term was in no small measure due to the instability in the Soviet leadership. Yuri Andropov, who replaced Brezhnev in November 1982, died in February 1984. His successor, Konstantin Chernenko, in turn died in March 1985 to be succeeded by the unknown, untested Mikhail Gorbachev.

The poisoning of relations between the United States and the Soviet union began during the Carter administration, when officials determined that Moscow had reneged on its implicit pledge to pursue peaceful coexistence with the West and promote stability in the world. This evolution of American attitudes was prompted less by the destabilizing effects of the new Soviet delivery vehicles on the balance of power than by a succession of Soviet gains and U.S. setbacks in the nonnuclear area during the second half of the 1970s that appeared to signal a return to the confrontational spirit of the Cold War era.

The first of these was the projection of Soviet military influence into Africa, a development that occurred in the middle of the 1970s and which will be treated in detail below (see p. 385). Then, at the very beginning and the very end of 1979, the American geopolitical position was further weakened by important developments in southern Asia in states that had served to block Russian expansion toward the Persian Gulf and the Indian Ocean.

TURMOIL IN SOUTH ASIA

The first of these geopolitical transformations occurred in Iran. The regime of Shah Mohammed Reza Pahlevi, installed by the British and the Russians in 1941 and rescued from a Soviet-backed insurgency in its northernmost province in 1946 by Anglo-American pressure on Moscow, had become America's staunchest ally in the region after 1953, when the Central Intelligence Agency masterminded a coup that restored the shah to power after his ouster by the nationalist politician Mohammed Mossadegh. By the mid-1950s American firms had acquired equal control with the British-owned Anglo-Iranian Oil Company of the rich petroleum reserves of the country under an arrangement that supplied the government in Teheran with substantial oil royalties, which it used to finance a crash program of industrialization. In the early 1970s the Nixon administration began to equip the shah's military and naval forces with sophisticated weapons in order to enable Iran to replace Great Britain as the principal peacekeeping force of the anti-Communist bloc in the Persian Gulf. But throughout the year 1978 fierce opposition to the Pahlevi dynasty developed among a broad-based coalition of Shi'ite Muslim fundamentalists who detested the shah's secular policies and the Westernized life-style of his entourage, small merchants who resented the overwhelming and distorting influence of American multinational corporations on the Iranian economy, and the urban intelligentsia disenchanted with the repressive methods of the regime. In January 1979 massive street demonstrations forced the shah into exile and in the following month political power in Teheran was assumed by a fundamentalist Islamic movement loyal to the octogenarian Shi'ite clerical leader Ayatollah Ruhollah Khomeini.

Though neither the Soviet Union nor the small Iranian Communist, party, the Tudeh, had played a significant role in the Iranian revolution, its increasingly anti-American character dealt a devastating blow to Western interests in this strategically and economically important region. Pro-American elements in the Iranian political and military elite were executed, American economic assets in the country were seized, and American military installations (including the radar network deployed along the northern frontier to monitor Soviet military activity) were closed down. The abrupt cutback in Iranian oil production caused by the continuing domestic unrest in that country and the war with neighboring Iraq that broke out in December 1980, though of minimal concern to the United States (which received only 5 percent of its oil imports from Iran), produced serious economic difficulties for America's allies in Western Europe and Japan that were much more dependent on Persian Gulf oil. Moreover, the upsurge of Muslim fundamentalism in Iran threatened to spread throughout the Middle East, causing political instability and undermining pro-Western regimes in Saudi Arabia, Egypt, and elsewhere. The affair of the sixty-nine American embassy hostages in Teheran, seized by Iranian militants in November 1979 in an effort to pressure the United States government into extraditing the exiled shah (who had been admitted to a New York hospital for treatment of the cancer that finally killed him in July 1980), further embittered relations between Washington and Teheran.* In the meantime, fundamentalist Muslims attacked the United States consulate in Tripoli, Libya, and the U.S. embassy in Islamabad, Pakistan, raising the specter of a jihad, or holy war, against American interests throughout the Islamic world.

As the United States saw its longtime client state in Iran transformed throughout the year 1979 into a center of anti-American agitation, the Soviet Union embarked on its first overt military operation beyond the confines of its East European empire since the end of the Second World War by dispatching paratroops and armored columns to Afghanistan in December 1979. Like its neighbor Iran, Afghanistan had been the site of acute rivalry between tsarist Russia and Great Britain before the First World War and was formally recognized as a neutral buffer between Russia and British India in 1907. During the Cold War it continued to occupy this nonaligned status between the Soviet Union and the newly created state of Pakistan, the West's principal ally in South Asia. But unlike Iran, which as we have seen, was brought into the American-dominated security system after the evacuation of soviet forces from its northern provinces in 1946, Afghanistan gravitated toward the soviet orbit during the 1950s to become a kind of Finland of Asia, renewing an earlier nonaggression pact with Moscow and receiving substantial Russian economic aid. Then in April 1978 the Marxist Nur Mohammed Taraki led an insurrection that overthrew the leftist but nominally neutralist regime in Kabul and established an openly Marxist government, which in turn was toppled in the fall of 1979 by Taraki's second-in-command, Hafizullah Amin. In the meantime a fundamentalist Muslim insurgency against Amin's secular policies prompted concern in Moscow about the spread of Islamic fundamentalism to its own predominantly Muslim republics in Central Asia. So the Kremlin sent almost 100,000 Soviet troops into the country to replace Amin with the pro-Soviet Babrak Karmal and to restore order.

Though it had no vital interests in the country (which already had a pro-Soviet government for three years), Washington reacted to the Soviet action with such harshness as to cause observers to wonder whether detente had definitively come to an end. President Carter increased the 1981 defense budget by 5 percent in real terms, imposed an embargo on grain deliveries to the Soviet Union in excess of the minimum quantities specified in the 1975 agreement, restricted Soviet access to American fishing waters and high tech-

---

*In December 1979, the Iranian militants released sixteen female and black hostages, but the remaining fifty-three were not freed until Carter vacated the White House in January 1981.

Ayatollah Ruhollah Khomeini (1902–1989): A vigorous opponent of Shah Mohammed Reza Pahlevi of Iran because of the monarch's subservience to the United States and secular policies at home, this charismatic Shi'ite Muslim cleric returned from exile in 1979 to establish a theocratic state in his country. In doing so he helped to inspire a powerful movement of Islamic fundamentalism that spread across the globe. *(Getty Images)*

nology exports, and organized a boycott of the Olympic Games held in Moscow in July 1980. Carter also advised the United States Senate, which by then needed no prodding from the White House, to delay consideration of the SALT II treaty that had been signed in 1979 but was still unratified. Apparently fearing that the invasion of Afghanistan represented an attempt by the Soviets to profit from the American expulsion from Iran to position themselves for a future offensive toward the oil resources of the Persian Gulf and the Arabian peninsula as well as the warm waters of the Indian Ocean, President Carter announced in his January 1980 State of the Union Address that the United States considered the Gulf vital to its national interest and therefore would intervene directly to defend the region against Soviet aggression. Carter then took a number of steps to shore up the deteriorating American position in that part of the world. Relations with the military regime of General Zia ul-Haq of Pakistan, which had cooled because of his repressive internal security policies and his apparent interest in acquiring nuclear weapons, were improved. In the summer of 1980, Washington obtained base facilities for U.S. air and naval forces in Oman, Kenya, and Somalia. The American naval base on the British-owned island of Diego Garcia in the middle of the Indian Ocean was enlarged and upgraded to accommodate a more formidable American naval force to offset increased Soviet naval power there. Throughout the first half of the 1980s, the Reagan administration stepped up U.S. military aid to the Afghan resistance, enabling the insurgents to hold their own against the Soviet forces and their collaborators in Kabul.

PEACE AND WAR IN THE MIDDLE EAST

As the American position in the Red Sea, Persian Gulf, and Indian Ocean was challenged at the end of the 1970s, developments in the Middle East *enhanced* America's political influence in that volatile region. The Kremlin's unwillingness to deliver the requisite military assistance to its Arab clients to tip the balance against Israel, together with Kissinger's assiduous cultivation of Egyptian President Anwar Sadat, brought about a spectacular reversal of Egypt's policy toward the two superpowers. On March 15, 1976, Sadat renounced the 1971 Soviet-Egyptian Friendship Treaty and a month later cancelled Soviet naval privileges in Egyptian ports. President Carter resumed the Kissinger policy of elbowing the Soviets out of the peace negotiations between Israel and Egypt. The prospects for a successful resolution of the remaining differences between the two countries were greatly improved when Sadat made a spectacular trip to Jerusalem on November 19, 1977, in a bold, improvised attempt to break the deadlock in the stalled peace process. This symbolic gesture of goodwill by the charismatic Egyptian leader, together with the appreciative response of an Israeli public weary of the constant threat of war with neighboring Arab states, paved the way for a bilateral accord that the United States had been promoting since the midseventies. In September 1978 at Camp David, the American president successfully coaxed Sadat and Prime Minister Menachem Begin of Israel into signing an agreement that mandated the return of the Sinai peninsula to Egypt in two successive stages in 1980 and 1982 in exchange for Egypt's recognition of Israel's right to exist as a sovereign nation. While a vaguely worded understanding left the sensitive issue of Palestinian rights in the Gaza strip and on the West Bank for future negotiation, Egypt and Israel signed a peace treaty on March 26, 1979, exchanged formal diplomatic recognition in February 1980, and resumed their bilateral efforts to restore stability to the Middle East in the face of the unremitting hostility of the Palestinian political organizations and their supporters in the Arab world. Syria, Iraq, Libya, and Algeria took the lead in opposing the Camp David accords and received the strong support of the Soviet Union. But the Israeli-Egyptian rapprochement survived the assassination of President Sadat in October 1981 by Egyptian opponents of Camp David. It also continued in spite of a number of belligerent actions by the Begin government, including the destruction of the Iraqi nuclear reactor near Baghdad in June 1981, the bombardment of PLO offices in Beirut in July, the annexation of the Golan Heights in December, the removal of elected Arab mayors of several West Bank cities in March and April 1982, and the continued construction of permanent Israeli settlements on the West Bank in what many observers viewed as a prelude to de facto annexation. The final Israeli withdrawal from the Sinai took place on April 25, 1982, in accordance with the Camp David timetable, and Sadat's successor,

Egyptian President Anwar Sadat (1918–1981), U.S. President Jimmy Carter (1924–), and Israeli Prime Minister Menachem Begin (1913–1992) at Camp David, September, 1978: The resulting peace treaty was the first such agreement between Israel and an Arab state. The return of the Sinai Peninsula to Egypt in exchange for Egypt's recognition of Israel's right to exist set the precedent for the policy of "land for peace." The provision in the treaty for the election of a self-governing authority in the Israeli-occupied West Bank and Gaza proved to be a dead letter, postponing Palestinian hopes for an independent state to the indefinite future. *(National Archives)*

President Hosni Mubarak, reaffirmed his predecessor's policy of peaceful relations with Israel.

But the negotiations concerning the political status of the West Bank and Gaza showed no signs of progress amid an atmosphere of deteriorating relations between the Palestinian population of these areas and their Israeli occupiers. The Camp David accord had been based on President Carter's assumption that the removal of the Egyptian threat would make Israel more accommodating on the Palestinian issue. But Israeli Prime Minister Begin, who passionately believed in Israel's right to perpetual control of the West Bank, was emboldened to strengthen his country's military position and deal harshly with the Palestinians. In the meantime, the tense political and military situation in Lebanon set the stage for a Middle East explosion that almost derailed the peace process. As we have

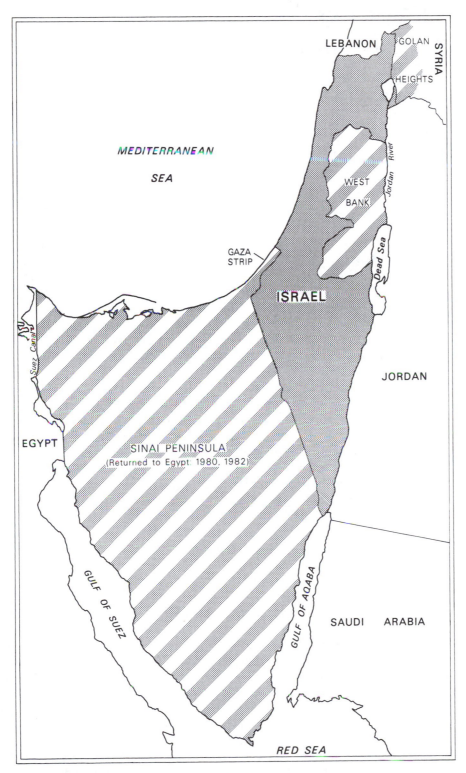

Israel and Its Occupied Territories After the Six-Day War

seen, the political leadership of the PLO and a large proportion of its military cadres had resettled in Lebanon after having been expelled from Jordan in 1970–71. Then, after a bloody clash between left- and right-wing Lebanese factions in the middle of the decade, a large contingent of Syrian troops was deployed in the Bekaa Valley of northeastern Lebanon as part of an Arab peacekeeping force. The Syrians promptly introduced jet fighters and ground-to-air missiles in Lebanon and lent support to the Palestinian units that were repeatedly shelling with Soviet-built artillery the Galilee area of northern Israel. In 1978 Israeli forces crossed into southern Lebanon and forced the PLO to fall back behind the Litani River, eighteen miles from the Israeli frontier, while a United Nations peacekeeping force was dispatched to southern Lebanon to separate the belligerents. But once the Palestinians established positions in southern Lebanon outside the UN buffer zone and resumed the shelling of Galilee, the Begin government decided to profit from the instability in Lebanon to establish once and for all a secure northern border.

Apparently believing that he had been given the "green light" by U.S. Secretary of State Alexander Haig, Begin sent about 60,000 Israeli infantry troops, accompanied by more than 500 tanks and 90 jet fighters, across the Lebanese frontier in early June 1982. The ground forces and tank columns overwhelmed the PLO strongholds in southern Lebanon; the American-built jet fighters used their American-built air-to-surface missiles to knock out all of the Soviet-built Syrian surface-to-air missile sites in the Bekaa Valley; the Israeli planes also used their American-built Sidewinder air-to-air missiles to destroy almost half of Syria's Soviet-built MiG jet fighters. In the meantime, Israeli infantry and tank columns closed in on Beirut as Israeli planes bombed the western part of the city where PLO headquarters were located. By the end of the summer a U.S.-sponsored agreement was worked out whereby the Palestinian political leadership and its military forces were evacuated from Lebanon under the protection of a multinational peacekeeping force consisting of American, French, and Italian marines.

The Israeli invasion of Lebanon in the summer of 1982 achieved its immediate objective: the elimination of the PLO as a military threat along Israel's northern frontier. The Israelis had also demonstrated that with their American-built weaponry they were capable of defeating the Syrians with their arsenal of Soviet-built missiles and fighter planes, thereby tarnishing Moscow's reputation as an effective military patron for the hard-line Arab states. But Israel's military triumph in Lebanon caused a deterioration of relations between the Begin government and the Reagan administration in the United States, which regarded the intervention as a threat to regional stability and expressed its displeasure by announcing an embargo on future sales of F-16 fighter planes to Israel.

In mid-September 1982, developments in Lebanon served to dampen U.S. enthusiasm for resuming an active pursuit of peace in that troubled country. Israeli military forces occupied the Muslim section of West Beirut after the assassination of Bashir Gemayel, the newly elected Christian president of Lebanon whom Israel had strongly supported on the expectation that he would agree to a separate peace with the Jewish state along the lines of Camp David. Two days later Gemayel's enraged followers burst into two Palestinian refugee camps in the Israeli-controlled area and massacred about eight hundred civilians while Israeli military authorities looked the other way. Since the United States had pledged to PLO leader Yassir Arafat that the Israelis would protect the Palestinian civilians remaining in Beirut after the evacuation of the PLO fighters, Reagan hastily arranged for the return of the multinational military contingent to provide some semblance of security. But the indefinite presence of American, French, and Italian peace-keeping forces in Lebanon angered the Shi'ite Muslims, who suspected the Westerners of favoring the Christians in the ongoing Lebanese civil war. A succession of terrorist attacks on American personnel in Lebanon culminated in the coup de gra$hkce of October 23, 1983, when a suicide mission blew up the headquarters of the marines outside Beirut, killing 241 American servicemen as they slept. After a face-saving interval, Reagan pulled all U.S. marines out of Lebanon and abandoned all hopes of mediating a settlement there.

The only sign of progress toward the reduction of tensions in the Middle East came in the fall of 1984, when the newly established coalition government in Israel headed by the Labor party leader, Shimon Peres, began the withdrawal of Israeli military units from the southern part of the country. In the meantime, Shi'ite Muslims, Druze, and Palestinians resumed their violent quarrels while the Lebanese government of Amin Gemayel, brother of the slain Christian leader, lapsed into total political impotence. But the Syrian army, lavishly reequipped by the Soviet Union, remained in northeastern Lebanon. Hafez al-Assad, who had come to power in Syria in 1970 just after the death of Egypt's Nasser, had built up his military forces with Soviet aid throughout the seventies as Sadat turned from Moscow to Washington. With Egypt isolated by Camp David and Iraq distracted by its war with Iran, Assad had become (in the eyes of many Arabs) the heir to Nasser as the leader of the Arab struggle against Israel in the eighties.

But the larger aspiration associated with Nasser's name, the quest for Arab unity, had proved as elusive as ever in the years since his death. Despite the common linguistic and religious heritage that linked most of the Arab peoples in the Middle East, the political fragmentation of the region continually prevented the realization of the Pan-Arab ideal. The sharp contrast between secular ideologies (such as that of the Baathist* ruling elites in Syria and Iraq) and Islamic fundamentalism was one cause of disunity. Another was the divergent positions taken by the various Arab states in the Cold War, with Egypt, Jordan, Saudi Arabia, and Oman maintaining close ties with the United States, while Syria, Iraq, and South Yemen sought and received military and diplomatic support from the Soviet Union. Opposition to the existence of the state of Israel and support for Palestinian nationalism appeared to be the major source of cohesion among the Arab states.

The Iraq-Iran War aggravated this disarray in the Arab world. From 1973 to 1979, Iraq's oil revenues had increased from $2 billion to $21 billion, enabling that country to build a formidable military establishment and equip it with weaponry obtainable on the international arms market. After becoming president of Iraq in 1979, Saddam Hussein apparently assumed that he could profit from the internal upheaval and international isolation of Iran by using his Soviet- and French-equipped army for a quick, decisive victory over the tattered remnants of the shah's military forces. But by 1982 the combination of a spirited Iranian counteroffensive and a sharp decline in Iraqi oil revenues due to oversupply on world markets transformed the conflict into a long war of attrition. If Saddam's ultimate objective was to establish himself as Nasser's heir by mobilizing the Arab world against the two non-Arab states in the Middle East—Israel and Iran—he failed

---

*The Baath party (otherwise known as the Arab Socialist Renaissance party), in power in Iraq (1963–2003) and Syria (1963–), advocates secularism, socialism, and Arab unity.

ignominiously. Syria's Assad, who presided over a secular Arab regime faced with an internal threat from Islamic fundamentalists, strongly supported the non-Arab Islamic regime of Khomeini against the secular Arab state of Iraq. The explanation of this apparent paradox was simple: Assad regarded his fellow Baathist head of state in Baghdad as his most likely rival in the Arab world. Libya, Algeria, and South Yemen also backed Iran against Iraq for their own reasons, while the rest of the Arab world closed ranks behind Saddam Hussein.

By the mid-1980s, the peace process in the Middle East had badly faltered, as the optimism engendered by the Camp David accords gave way to a bleak pessimism about the prospects of reaching a mutually acceptable resolution of the Israeli-Palestinian problem: Not a single other Arab state joined Egypt in acknowledging Israel's right to exist. On the contrary, Egypt was virtually drummed out of the Arab bloc at the Baghdad summit in 1978 and Sadat, as we have seen, paid with his life in 1981 for becoming the first Arab leader to recognize the Jewish state. Hard-line factions within the increasingly frustrated Palestinian movement resorted to terrorism to publicize its grievances against Israel, such as the murder of an elderly, disabled Jewish man after the highjacking of the Italian cruise ship *Achille Lauro* in 1985. On the other hand, the Israeli government thumbed its nose at the Camp David principle of Palestinian autonomy in the occupied territories by establishing ninety new Jewish settlements on the West Bank between 1977 and 1984 and granting generous tax subsidies and low-interest loans to entice Israeli citizens to relocate there. The negotiations on autonomy for the West Bank and Gaza mandated by the Camp David accords, which had advanced at a snail's pace since August 1979, were effectively killed by the Israeli invasion of Lebanon in 1982.

The goal of peace and stability was just as elusive outside the Israeli-Palestinian imbroglio. Lebanon had ceased to exist as a state in the proper sense of the term, with roving bands of Christian and Muslim gunmen, together with Syrian military forces in the north and Israeli soldiers in the south, providing what passed for law and order. The armed struggle between Iraq and Iran had taken on the appearance of a First World War-type stalemate, with no end in sight as the casualty lists lengthened. In the meantime, the two superpowers continued to arm and support their clients in the region, viewing the complex tangle of rivalries there through the lenses of the Cold War. Despite occasional outbursts of irritation at Israel (as, for example, in response to its invasion of Lebanon in 1982), the Reagan administration maintained intimate relations with the Jewish state. Israel had become, and remained, the world's largest recipient of U.S. foreign aid (about one-third of the total U.S. foreign aid budget) and cooperated actively with U.S. intelligence agencies in the Middle East and throughout the world. Egypt was number two on the list of U.S. aid recipients and, in return, accorded the United States a number of favors, including the use of Egyptian ports and air space in emergencies, the conducting of joint military maneuvers, and the sharing of intelligence. Washington also intensified its military ties to Saudi Arabia as part of a mutually advantageous relationship that included Riyadh's willingness to help stabilize world oil prices by increasing production as needed. The Soviet Union, though ejected from its Egyptian bases and frozen out of the Israeli-Palestinian peace process, resupplied the Syrian army after its defeat in Lebanon in 1982, furnished economic and military assistance to Iraq and South Yemen, and diplomatically supported the PLO in various world forums.

13

LATIN AMERICA'S QUEST FOR DEVELOPMENT AND INDEPENDENCE

The Cuban missile crisis had dramatically revealed the willingness of the Latin American states to endorse Washington's strategy of excluding Soviet influence from the hemisphere through the unilateral exercise of United States power. Once the option of removing the Castro regime was foreclosed by the Kennedy-Khrushchev agreement of 1962, the United States concentrated on isolating Cuba from its neighbors in order to prevent the spread of its noxious doctrines throughout the region. In response to evidence that Castro was furnishing arms to guerrilla movements in several Latin American countries, the OAS voted in July 1964 to impose economic sanctions on Cuba. All member governments of the inter-American organization except Mexico promptly severed diplomatic relations with Havana. Isolated in its region, Cuba became increasingly dependent on Moscow for economic and military assistance in exchange for strong support of Soviet foreign policy.

But the Marxist regime in Havana failed in its mission to export revolution to the rest of Latin America. Cuban-supported radical groups in half a dozen countries were crushed by U.S.-trained counterinsurgency forces. Even reformist groups with no apparent connection to Havana were suppressed by military or police forces supported directly or indirectly by Washington. The most dramatic instance of overt United States counterinsurgency activity in Latin America took place in the Dominican Republic, a small Caribbean country that, like Cuba, had submitted to various forms of United States domination since the early part of the century. On April 24, 1965, forces loyal to the reform-minded former president, Juan Bosch, who had been overthrown by a military coup two years earlier, took up arms against the junta in power. For the announced purpose of protecting U.S. citizens in the country, President Lyndon Johnson sent U.S. marines to the Dominican Republic without obtaining the consent of the OAS. Once there, they ensured that the Dominican Republic would not become another Cuba. For the first time since the advent of Franklin Roosevelt's Good Neighbor Policy in 1934, U.S. marines were on occupation duty in a sovereign state in Latin America. In national elections held in 1966 that were

The United States and Latin America

supervised by the Inter-American Peacekeeping Force, the conservative politician Joaquin Balaguer, a former ally of the dictator Raphael Trujillo who had been assassinated in 1961, assumed power.

The Dominican intervention in 1965 signified an important shift in priorities for the Latin American policy of the United States. The Johnson administration rapidly abandoned the commitment to the goals of social reform and economic development that had been encompassed in the original provisions of the Alliance for Progress. Indeed, the alliance fell far short of its founders' ambitious expectations: Latin American upper classes refused to submit to the tax and land reforms envisioned by the program, government officials pocketed American aid intended for economic development projects, and military regimes that had ousted civilian governments declined to restore democratic liberties. Far from exerting pressure on the social, political, and military elites of Latin America to uphold the progressive principles of the American aid program, the Johnson administration diverted alliance funds from economic development projects to counterinsurgency activities. Washington also accorded prompt diplomatic recognition to autocratic but reliably anti-Communist military regimes that had seized power from democratically elected governments, such as the junta that toppled the left-leaning President João Goulart of Brazil in April 1964.

The shift from the promotion of social reform and economic development to the suppression of Communist or Communist-related activity in Latin America continued under the Nixon administration. During the 1970 presidential election in Chile, the CIA spent lavishly to subsidize the opponents of a self-proclaimed Marxist named Salvadore Allende, who ran on a radical program of social and economic reform that included a pledge to nationalize the holdings of the large American copper companies that dominated the country's economy. When Allende became the first democratically elected Marxist president of a Latin American nation and promptly confiscated the property of the Anaconda and Kennecott copper interests, Washington proceeded to wage a major campaign to destabilize the new regime. This included subsidies for opposition newspapers and labor organizations, pressure on financial institutions to withhold credit, and covert encouragement to Chile's military establishment to rid the country of its Marxist government. With inflation raging, the balance-of-payment deficit widening, and social strife intensifying, the Chilean army moved to oust the Allende regime in 1973. The new military junta headed by General Augusto Pinochet thereupon instituted a pitiless campaign of repression against leftist groups in the country that dashed whatever hopes the supporters of Allende may have entertained of establishing the first Marxist state on the mainland of South America. Military governments in Argentina and Brazil also clamped down hard on domestic dissidents during the 1970s, striking out at communist, socialist, and liberal democratic elements alike.

Thus, in the decade after the Cuban missile crisis, Soviet influence in the western hemisphere was confined to Castro's embargoed, isolated outpost of Marxist-Leninism in the Caribbean. The United States took the lead in this strategy of containment, but most of the Latin American states proved to be loyal followers. The cause of anticommunism had always had an air of unreality about it during the fifties when communism itself seemed such a distant peril. It was only through the application of strong pressure, for example, that Dulles had been able to get the Latin American governments worked up about the supposed menace of communism in Central America during Washington's

Chile's 9/11: Armed guards protect Chilean President Salvadore Allende Gossens (1908–1973) during the military coup that overthrew him and led to his death, September 11, 1973: The coup followed three years of an intense campaign of covert operations waged by the Nixon administration to undermine the first democratically elected Marxist government in the world. It is unclear whether Allende died by his own hand or was killed in the crossfire as army troops stormed the Moneda Palace (the president's residence) in Santiago. *(Getty Images)*

campaign against the Arbenz regime in Guatemala in 1954. But as Cuba unmistakably gravitated toward the Soviet orbit during the early sixties and Castro raised the banner of revolution in Latin America, the entrenched oligarchies in the region had little difficulty perceiving the common interest that they shared with the United States in suppressing indigenous revolutionary activity in the hemisphere and forestalling the projection of Soviet influence there to exploit it.

But this notable increase in hemispheric solidarity as a consequence of the Cuban missile crisis concealed a contradictory trend that turned out to be the most significant feature of Latin America's international position since the early 1970s: This was the gradual, imperceptible loosening of the bonds of economic dependence and political subservience that had long tied that region to the United States. Latin America's gradual emancipation from United States domination was facilitated by two important developments. The first was the novel experience of sustained economic growth in the region, which prompted many of its countries to expand their export trade and diversify their foreign markets at the expense of their traditional customer and supplier to the north. The second was the advent of East-West detente, which eventually moderated Washington's traditional obsession with promoting hemispheric solidarity in anticipation of a Soviet security threat and therefore permitted the Latin American states greater latitude in the assertion of their sovereign rights and the pursuit of a more independent foreign policy.

From 1960 to 1973, the economies of Latin America grew at an average annual rate (after inflation) of almost 6 percent, far surpassing the real growth rates of the rest of the developing world. Several aspects of the economic takeoff of this traditionally backward region are worthy of note. First of all, it was "export driven": Foreign trade as a percentage of GNP more than doubled between 1970 and 1980 in Brazil, Mexico, Argentina, Chile, Ecuador, and Venezuela and substantially increased in other Latin American countries. Total Latin American exports increased by almost 11 percent a year from 1965 to 1973, compared to a 3.6 percent annual rate for the previous fifteen years. This expansion of Latin America's trade reflected a historic shift from its traditional reliance on commodity exports—primarily minerals and foodstuffs—to a newly acquired capability to market manufactured goods abroad. The proportion of manufactures in Latin America's total exports increased from 3.6 percent in 1960 to 17.2 percent in 1970. The region's exports of manufactured goods grew at an annual rate of 26.5 percent, compared to a 16.4 percent increase for the entire world during the same period. The export-led economic dynamism of Latin America in turn attracted foreign investment on an impressive scale. By the end of the seventies, many experts were predicting a glorious economic future for a region that had for so long languished in poverty and backwardness.

The expansion and intensification of Latin America's involvement in the international economic order inevitably detracted from its special commercial and financial relationship with the United States. By 1979, Latin America was exporting only 25 percent of its manufactured products to the United States, compared to 39 percent to countries within the region and 26 percent to the rest of the industrial world. From 1950 to 1980, Latin America's importance as a market for U.S. exports fell 37 percent, while the region's share of total U.S. imports declined by 66 percent. As the United States gradually disengaged from its dominant commercial position in Latin America, it also began to redirect its foreign investment to other parts of the world: The proportion of total United States foreign investment located in Latin America declined from roughly 25 percent in 1960 to about 12 percent in 1980, while European and Japanese investors increasingly moved in to take up the slack.

Latin America's increasing economic independence from the United States contributed to a new political assertiveness that challenged Washington's hegemonic position in the western hemisphere. At the height of the Cold War, the Latin American ruling elites tended to accept uncritically United States leadership in hemispheric affairs. We have seen how Washington had successfully mobilized the governments of that region to isolate Cuba after the missile crisis of 1962 and had not hesitated to intervene overtly (as in the case of the Dominican Republic in 1965) or covertly (as in the case of Chile in the early 1970s) to prevent the installation of unfriendly regimes that might be susceptible to Cuban (and therefore Soviet) influence. But by the middle of the 1970s, the emergence of global detente between the superpowers had greatly reduced U.S. anxieties about Soviet penetration of the western hemisphere. By that time, most of the Cuban-inspired insurgencies in Latin America had petered out. The capture and execution by Bolivian authorities of the legendary guerrilla leader Ernesto (Ché) Guevara in 1967 foreshadowed the fading of revolutionary hopes. Far from ushering in a period of revolutionary upheaval in Latin America, the Cuban revolution was followed by a succession of military coups (Brazil in 1964, Chile and Uruguay in 1973, and Argentina in 1976) that installed right-wing dictatorships dedicated to the suppression of the left. The decline of regional insurgency amid Soviet-American detente at the global level afforded Latin American countries much greater freedom to pursue their own national interests without reference to the traditional security concerns of the United States.

President Jimmy Carter attempted to resurrect the spirit of Roosevelt's Good Neighbor Policy and Kennedy's Alliance for Progress, cutting U.S. aid to dictatorships and promoting political liberalization, social reform, and better relations with the United States. Since 1965, talks between the United States and Panama concerning the future of the Panama Canal had dragged on inconclusively, as opponents in the United States vigorously denounced any proposal to relinquish U.S. control of the waterway and the five-mile-wide zone surrounding it as an intolerable threat to American security interests in the Caribbean. But in 1977 Carter obtained senatorial consent to a treaty that transferred to Panama immediate legal jurisdiction over the Canal Zone and the sole right to operate and defend the canal by the end of the century. The prospective disappearance of the most notorious symbol of "Yankee imperialism" in the western hemisphere reflected the increasing willingness of Washington to deal with the region on its own terms rather than as a theater of East-West rivalry.

Two years after the ratification of the Panama Canal Treaty, this new U.S. policy of military disengagement and support for political reform was again put to the test in two other countries in Central America. In a dramatic reversal of previous United States policy in the region, Carter tacitly approved the October 1979 coup against the right-wing Romero dictatorship in El Salvador that brought to power a progressive regime committed to social reform. In the same year the repressive, retrograde regime of Anastasio Somoza Debayle, whose family had ruled Nicaragua like a personal fief for over four decades with solid backing from Washington, was overthrown by a broad-based coalition dominated by an inner directorate of revolutionaries known as the Sandinistas.* Confronted with the first successful leftist insurrection in Latin America in many years, the Carter administration attempted in vain to promote a centrist, pro-American alternative to the Sandinistas. Washington also appealed to the OAS to dispatch a peacekeeping force to Nicaragua to preserve order, but was equally unsuccessful. While the Sandinistas enjoyed the rhetorical support of Fidel Castro, who had recently rekindled the spark of revolution in Latin America after a decade of dormancy, they had also received active encouragement from the neighboring non-Communist governments of Venezuela, Costa Rica, and Panama. Gone were the days, or so it seemed, when Washington could single-handedly determine the outcome of political rivalries in Latin America through the application of diplomatic pressure, economic sanctions, or in the extreme case, military force.

As it turned out, however, Latin America's newly acquired independence from the United States proved ephemeral and was sharply curtailed as a result of two important developments in the first half of the 1980s. The first of these was a severe and entirely unanticipated crisis in the international economic order that was to have particularly pow-

---

*Named after Cesar Augusto Sandino, the rebel leader who led the resistance to American marines stationed in Nicaragua before his assassination by the U.S.-trained national guard in 1934 (see page 193).

erful repercussions in the western hemisphere. During the previous decade, the petroleum-exporting countries that had amassed enormous profits from the dramatic increase in oil prices deposited these "petrodollars" in Western (and especially American) banks. As these financial institutions eagerly sought customers for their idle funds, they developed considerable respect for the creditworthiness of the governments of Latin America, whose record of economic growth and political stability stood in sharp contrast to other parts of the developing world. Consequently, while many of the most impoverished states of Africa found it impossible to attract foreign lending on a large scale, the international banking system recycled their huge petrodollar deposits to the treasuries of Latin America. The total foreign debt of the region increased astronomically: From $2.3 billion in 1970, it grew to $75 billion in 1975 and $229 billion in 1980. By 1983 the total foreign debt burden equaled roughly 47 percent of the region's total GNP, while annual interest payments exceeded a third of the value of its total exports for the year. By the beginning of the 1980s, Latin America accounted for over 60 percent of the entire foreign debt owed to commercial banks in the world. This underdeveloped region had paradoxically become a net exporter of capital as its huge annual debt repayments helped to finance the growing budget deficit in the United States.

Indebtedness is no cause for concern (the bankers tell us) so long as sufficient annual income is generated to service the debt. Unhappily for the countries (and banks) involved, the long period of postwar economic growth came to a screeching halt toward the end of the 1970s. The resulting global recession had the effect of reducing demand for Latin American goods at a time when exports were essential to earn the foreign exchange required to cover the mounting foreign debt. As a consequence, Latin America's combined GNP declined in 1982 for the first time since the end of the Second World War and dropped again in 1983.

Mexico furnishes the most dramatic case study of a Latin American country whose exaggerated aspirations for economic development were smothered by the economic downturn of the early 1980s. Between 1960 and 1972, Mexico's annual economic growth rate had average 6.8 percent. Already the most highly developed industrial economy in Latin America, Mexico profited handsomely from the discovery of vast new petroleum reserves in the midseventies just as the world price of oil was going through the roof. Mexican oil revenues quadrupled between 1977 and 1979, while the value of proven oil reserves in the country increased from $80 billion in 1976 to $898 billion in 1979. The intoxicating prospect of instant prosperity prompted the Mexican government to launch a massive program of public spending that was to be financed by a combination of expanded oil exports and heavy foreign borrowing against anticipated future oil revenues. Alas, in 1981 the unanticipated glut of petroleum supplies on the world market forced down the price of the product, sharply reducing the export earnings that were necessary to service Mexico's burgeoning foreign debt. In the summer of 1982, Latin America's largest oil exporter and most highly industrialized country ran out of foreign exchange and had to suspend payment to its foreign creditors. By the end of that year, most of the other Latin American governments were in arrears. The imprudent bankers who had abruptly plunged their surplus funds into Latin America during the 1970s just as abruptly withdrew them, thereby aggravating the financial crisis.

Approximately 38 percent of Latin America's foreign debt was held by United States banks. This circumstance, together with the fact that most of these obligations were

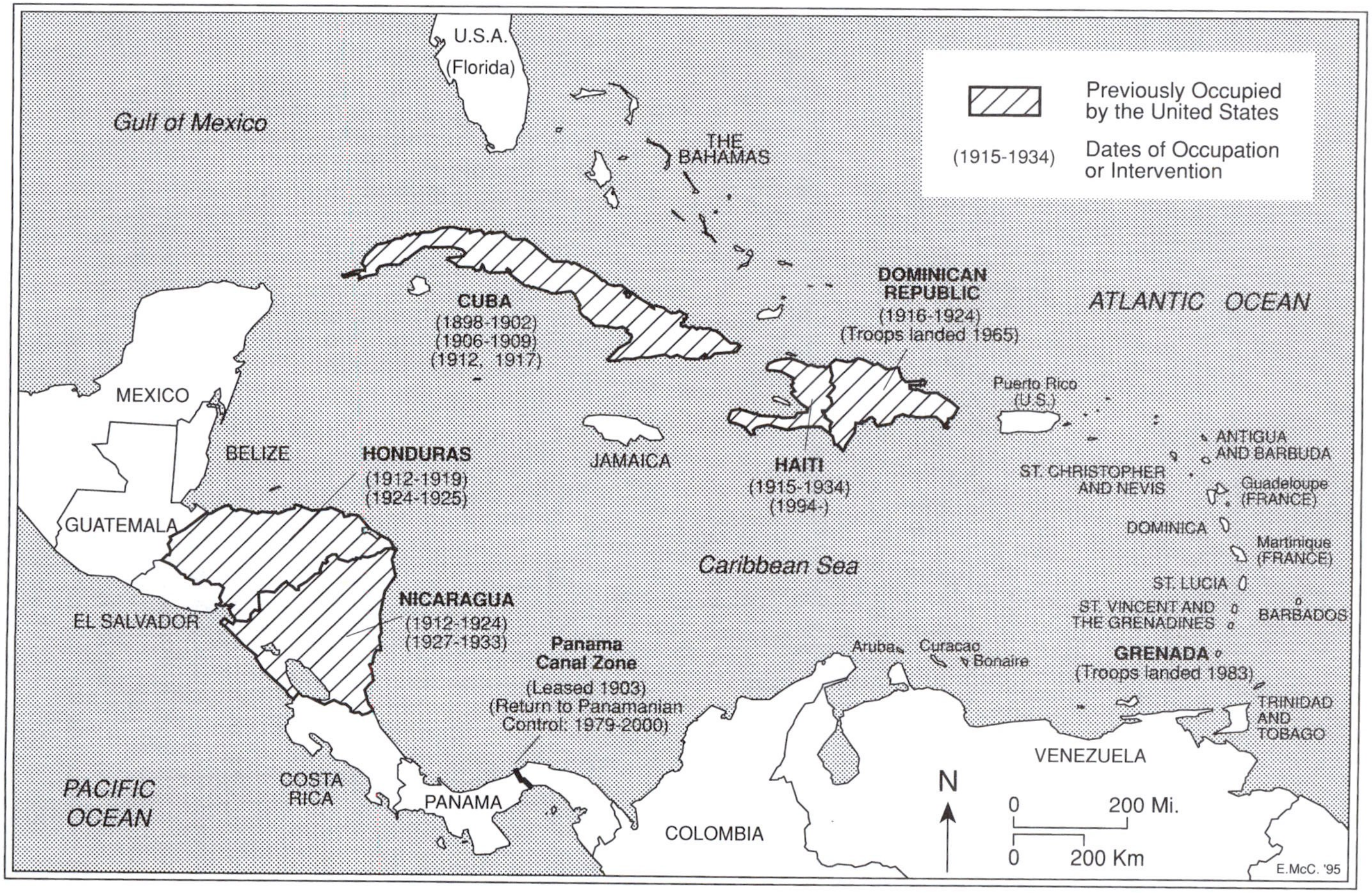
Previously Occupied by the United States
(1915-1934) Dates of Occupation or Intervention
U.S.A. (Florida)
Gulf of Mexico
THE BAHAMAS
CUBA
(1898-1902)
(1906-1909)
(1912, 1917)
DOMINICAN REPUBLIC
(1916-1924)
(Troops landed 1965)
ATLANTIC OCEAN
MEXICO
BELIZE
HONDURAS
(1912-1919)
(1924-1925)
JAMAICA
HAITI
(1915-1934)
(1994-)
Puerto Rico (U.S.)
ANTIGUA AND BARBUDA
ST. CHRISTOPHER AND NEVIS
Guadeloupe (FRANCE)
DOMINICA
Martinique (FRANCE)
GUATEMALA
Caribbean Sea
ST. LUCIA
ST. VINCENT AND THE GRENADINES
BARBADOS
NICARAGUA
(1912-1924)
(1927-1933)
EL SALVADOR
Panama Canal Zone
(Leased 1903)
(Return to Panamanian Control: 1979-2000)
Aruba
Curacao
Bonaire
GRENADA
(Troops landed 1983)
TRINIDAD AND TOBAGO
VENEZUELA
PACIFIC OCEAN
COSTA RICA
PANAMA
COLOMBIA
N
0 200 Mi.
0 200 Km
E.McC. '95

Central America and the Caribbean

denominated in dollars and set at variable interest rates, abruptly terminated the region's increasing economic independence from the United States. Latin America's economic development was revealed to be acutely vulnerable to the monetary and commercial policies of U.S. governmental and private institutions: The slightest increase in American interest rates by the Federal Reserve Board had an immediate and far-reaching effect on the economies of Latin America, as did the tough negotiating position taken by American banks holding the Latin American obligations. To make matters worse, the adoption of protectionist measures in the United States to preserve domestic jobs and profits—such as the Generalized System of Preferences scheme that had begun operation in January 1976—restricted Latin America's access to the American market and the desperately needed dollars to make the debt payments.

As the debt crisis of the first half of the 1980s rudely interrupted Latin America's progressive economic emancipation from the United States, the collapse of global detente and the revival of Cold War tensions during the same period reignited Washington's fears of Cuban/Soviet meddling in the Central American-Caribbean region and therefore revived the possibility of U.S. political and military intervention there. Signs of this renewed United States anxiety about political developments in Latin America first appeared during the last two years of the Carter administration. As relations between Washington and the increasingly pro-Cuban Sandinista regime in Nicaragua deteriorated throughout the year 1979, a pro-American government on the tiny Caribbean island of Grenada was overthrown by a revolutionary movement whose leader, Maurice Bishop, openly advertised his admiration for Fidel Castro and his disdain for the United States.

In the meantime, the mild attempts at social reform on the part of the new government of El Salvador had been blocked by the entrenched military and landowning oligarchy, which promptly gained control of the junta that had ousted the Romero dictatorship in 1979. In the following year a number of Salvadoran guerrilla organizations banded together to form a unified military command—the Farabundo Marti National Liberation Front (FMLN)—and a broad coalition of civilian supporters—the Democratic Revolutionary Front (FDR). When it was discovered in the winter of 1980–1981 that the Sandinistas in Nicaragua were supplying Cuban arms to the FMLN, Carter resumed deliveries of U.S. military aid—which had earlier been suspended in retaliation for human rights abuses—to the government in San Salvador. He also made plans for the termination of all economic assistance to Nicaragua before leaving the White House.

During his campaign for the presidency, Ronald Reagan had blamed Carter's preoccupation with promoting human rights for hastening the downfall of autocratic but friendly governments such as Somoza's in Nicaragua and Romero's in El Salvador, as well as for alienating the anti-Communist military regimes that governed Brazil and Argentina. Once in office, Reagan moved promptly to curb what he viewed as the spread of Cuban and Soviet influence in the region. He lifted all of the major restrictions on United States military assistance to those Latin American governments that had been found by his predecessor to be in violation of human rights and harshly condemned the influx of Cubans arms to the Sandinistas. In March 1981 Reagan authorized the CIA to organize and finance a destabilization campaign against Managua to be waged by a motley crew of former supporters of the deposed dictator Somoza and disenchanted rebels operating out of neighboring Honduras and Costa Rica as well as in remote regions within Nicaragua itself. In the spring of 1983 the CIA was found to have mined

Sandinista soldiers raising their rifles as they topple the government of Anastasio Somoza Debayle in Nicaragua, July 1979: Formed in 1961, the *Frente Sandinista de Liberación Nacional* (Sandinista National Liberation Front) was dominated by Marxists and received the active support of Fidel Castro, but its leaders, especially Daniel Ortega Saavadra, also appealed to a broad range of groups dissatisfied with the Somoza kleptocracy. Their close ties with Castro and radical socioeconomic reforms prompted the Reagan administration in Washington to pull out all the stops in a campaign to remove them from power. *(Getty Images)*

Nicaragua's harbors and conducted bombing raids on some of its oil storage depots. Faced with a congressional cutoff of military aid to the "Contras" seeking to topple the Sandinistas, the Reagan administration used the National Security Council (NSC) to raise funds from private and foreign donors to circumvent Congress. By 1985 the United States was enforcing a trade embargo and a credit boycott on Nicaragua to pressure the Sandinista regime.

On a number of occasions during the early 1980s, Reagan administration officials uttered ominous warnings about the resumption of an interventionist military policy in Central America if a Soviet- and Cuban-backed Nicaragua seriously threatened the stability of the region. Then developments in the Caribbean island of Grenada, ruled since 1979 by a pro-Castro government, provided the pretext for action. With the active encouragement of Moscow, the Cuban strongman reciprocated Grenadian President Maurice Bishop's expression of solidarity by delivering small arms for defensive purposes and providing skilled labor for the construction of an airport on the island, ostensibly to promote its tourism industry. These events evoked a predictably hostile response in

Washington, which suspended economic aid and attempted to organize opposition to Grenada among neighboring islands in the eastern Caribbean. When Bishop subsequently expressed a desire for reconciliation with the United States, he was overthrown and executed by radical elements within his own movement in October 1983.

The Reagan administration responded by launching an air, land, and sea invasion of Grenada to protect American medical students studying on the island and to prevent the airport under constructions from becoming a possible base for Soviet aircraft. After three days of combat with the Grenadian army and the Cuban construction crews, the 1,900 United States troops had toppled the radical government on the tiny island. A reliably pro-American regime was subsequently installed, which proceeded to complete the construction of the airport, but without the Cuban crews, to promote the country's tourism industry.

The invasion of Grenada was evidently intended as a warning to Nicaraguan President Daniel Ortega Saavedra that the Sandinistas' delivery of military aid to the rebels in El Salvador ran the risk of provoking a similar response from Washington. These developments symbolized the revival of the spirit of unilateralism in United States policy toward the Caribbean basin, a strategically vital region through which two-thirds of America's foreign trade passed. Ronald Reagan took up Teddy Roosevelt's Big Stick, which had been temporarily shelved by his predecessors, and did not hesitate to brandish it at potential adversaries, real or imagined. By the middle of the 1980s, Latin America's prospects for greater independence from the United States faded amid the revival of Cold War tensions in the Caribbean and Central America, just as the hopes for economic development were dashed by the twin curses of foreign indebtedness and industrial stagnation.

14

AFRICA: FROM INDEPENDENCE TO DEPENDENCY

The continent of Africa was the last region of the world to achieve liberation from European colonial domination in the twentieth century. During the late 1950s and the early 1960s—several years after the European powers had withdrawn from most of their imperial outposts in Asia and the Middle East—France, Great Britain, and Belgium relinquished control over their Africanpossessions. The immediate consequence was the abrupt proliferation of independent political units in an area that had been administered from London, Paris, and Brussels since the great age of imperial expansion before the Great War. In 1945 only four African states belonged to the newly established United Nations: Egypt, South Africa, Liberia, and Ethiopia. By the end of 1960, twenty-five new nations on the continent of Africa had joined the world organization, representing a quarter of its membership.

With the notable exceptions of Algeria and the Belgian Congo (subsequently renamed Zaire), the transition to national independence during this first phase of decolonization in Africa was relatively smooth and peaceful. The British and French had been compelled to acknowledge that their continued presence in Africa was untenable when both of the superpowers, not to speak of the newly liberated states throughout the rest of the Third World, opposed colonialism as an anachronism in the postwar era. On the other hand, the retrograde regimes of Salazar's Portugal and Franco's Spain would refuse to abandon the cause of colonial grandeur, clinging tenaciously to their African possessions until the disintegration of the Iberian dictatorships in the mid-1970s hastened the belated demise of these last two remnants of European imperial power on the continent. By 1984, the centenary of the Berlin Conference that had partitioned the continent into European spheres of influence, forty-five African countries operated as sovereign political units in the postcolonial world.

The achievement of national liberation by the former African subjects of France, Great Britain, and Belgium in the second half of the 1950s and early 1960s generated a euphoric sense of optimism. In May 1963, representatives of the new African countries assembled in

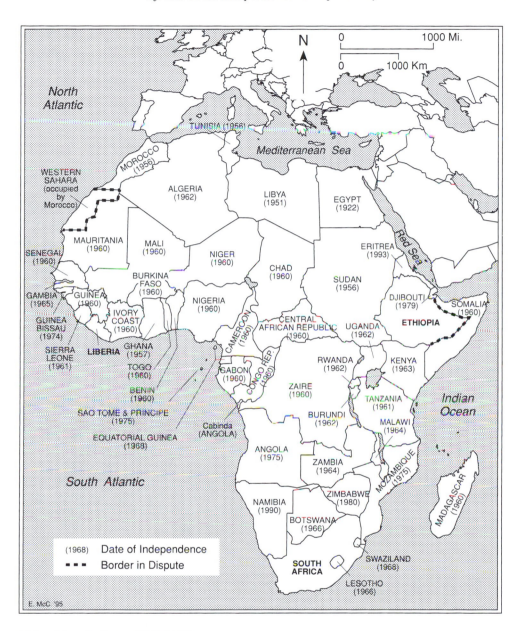

Africa After the Second World War

Addis Ababa, Ethiopia, to found the Organization of African Unity (OAU). Inspired by the ideology of Pan-Africanism that had been popularized by the defiant, charismatic leader of Ghana, Kwame Nkrumah, the OAU's charter enunciated a set of goals that were designed to strengthen the international position and protect the recently won independence of the fledgling member states so that their peoples could thrive and prosper amid their newly acquired freedom.

One of the cardinal principles enshrined in the OAU charter was the recognition of the overriding necessity to prevent territorial conflicts between rival African nations—such as Algeria's ongoing border dispute with Morocco—as well as civil strife between antagonistic groups within each nation—such as the bloody struggle in the former Belgian Congo between the central government and a secessionist movement in the mineral-rich province of Katanga (subsequently renamed Shaba). Such violence had to be averted above all because it threatened to unravel the fragile fabric of African independence by tempting extracontinental powers to exploit for their own benefit the resulting political instability and economic chaos. Accordingly, the member states of the new organization solemnly affirmed the absolute inviolability of the political frontiers that had been inherited from the colonial era, notwithstanding the fact that these borders had been drawn to suit the administrative convenience of the colonizers rather than the economic, strategic, and ethnographic conditions of the colonies.

The second goal of the OAU—as the very name behind that acronym implied—was the eventual political unification of the entire continent under the aegis of a single sovereign authority. How such an ambitious program was to be carried out amid the bewildering diversity of languages, ethnic groups, and religions was not specified. But some African leaders regarded *military* cooperation as the most effective means toward the ultimate end of continentwide political integration. Nkrumah himself had first proposed the establishment of a multinational African army in the early 1960s to restore order during the Congo crisis, and subsequent outbreaks of unrest prompted similar suggestions from various African heads of state. As with the principle of the inviolability of the territorial status quo, the prime motivation behind this enthusiasm for a multinational African military force was the need to remove any pretext for foreign interference in Africa's internal affairs.

The same was true for the third axiom of the OAU's Pan-African ideology: the necessity of neutrality in the Cold War. The founders of the new organization were intent on avoiding the fate of other third world peoples, whose independence had been compromised by the extension of superpower rivalry to their regions. Delegates of the new African states had taken an active role in the first international conference of the nonaligned movement at Belgrade in 1961, and the principle of nonalignment was recorded in the OAU charter two years later. Throughout the first decade of independence, the absence of significant Soviet and American interests in Africa spared that continent the trauma of East-West conflict that afflicted Asia during the same period.

But political independence from Europe and military disengagement from the Soviet-American confrontation were insufficient to guarantee postcolonial Africa a bright future. What Africa required above all else was a continentwide program of economic development on a massive scale. Of all the poverty-stricken regions of the non-Western world, Africa indisputably occupied the most precarious position: Though exceptionally well endowed with a variety of raw materials and agricultural products, the continent was sorely deficient in capital, technology, entrepreneurial skills, managerial expertise, and adequate markets for the commodities (mainly foodstuffs and minerals) that continued to represent a predominant proportion of its export trade. It also included the largest number of low-income, resource-poor, and landlocked countries on the face of the earth. A

President Kwame Nkrumah (1909–1972) of Ghana interviewed by American reporters in New York City, 1960: After leading the British colony of the Gold Coast to independence as Ghana in 1957, Nkrumah tirelessly promoted the cause of pan-Africanism and was instrumental in establishing the Organization of African Unity in 1963. His hopes of creating a "United States of Africa" proved unrealistic, and his autocratic tendencies led to his overthrow in 1966 by a military coup. *(Courtesy of the Library of Congress)*

mere recitation of the statistics tells the sad story: In the mid-1980s, only seven of the forty-five African societies had a per capita annual income of $1,000 or more. Although 10 percent of the world's population lived in Africa, its share of world industrial output was less than 1 percent. Unless this condition of extreme economic backwardness could be remedied, the noble aspirations for Africa's postcolonial future that had been generated in the optimistic era of independence and nonalignment would be dashed.

As they launched their ambitious campaign for economic development during the 1960s, the new states of Africa were confronted with two alternative paths: They could integrate their national economies into the flourishing international economic system dominated by the United States, Western Europe, and Japan. Or they could strive to disengage Africa from the world economic order and pursue a development strategy based on the principles of autarky and self-reliance. In light of Africa's desperate need for foreign investment, loans, aid, trade, technology and technical expertise, it is scarcely surprising that the ruling elites of the newly independent African states opted for membership in, rather than withdrawal from, the international economic order that alone could satisfy those requirements.

Consequently, postcolonial Africa promptly established strong links with the international monetary and trading system represented by such organizations as GATT, the IMF, and the World Bank. This involvement in the Western capitalist economic order yielded some notable benefits for the continent during the first decade of independence. The economic boom in the industrial world and the remarkable growth of international trade during the sixties generated ample capital for investment, loans, and development aid to the Third World while stimulating demand in the industrialized countries for the raw material and agricultural exports from Africa. Peace Corps volunteers from the United States arrived to provide much-needed technical and managerial expertise. The African countries became frequent customers at the soft loan windows of the IMF and the World Bank. They exported primary products to the industrial world in exchange for its manufactured goods.

But even amid the period of relative prosperity during the 1960s, some ominous trends had already begun to give rise to pessimism about Africa's future prospects for genuine independence and economic development. The first of these warning signs was the stubborn persistence of what has come to be known as "neoimperialism"—the retention by the former imperial powers of indirect control over their erstwhile colonies through the exercise of economic, political and military influence.

The phenomenon of British neoimperialism in Africa developed in a comparatively subtle, covert manner. Originally, London strove to retain a host of military privileges in many of the successor states of its African empire. The Anglo-Nigerian pact of 1960, for instance, reserved for the former colonial power the prerogatives of military intervention, of the retention of British military bases on Nigerian territory, and of the use of Nigerian airspace in times of emergency. But this heavy-handed approach to postcolonial security management represented such a blatant contradiction to the principle of national sovereignty that the Nigerian government summarily abrogated it within a year. Reading the handwriting on the wall, the British substantially reduced their overt security commitments in Africa (though London did not hesitate to send troops during the 1960s to bolster friendly regimes in Uganda, Kenya, and Tanzania). Instead, Great Britain concentrated on preserving its considerable economic influence in the region through the operations of British-based multinational corporations and financial institutions that had retained significant interests there. John Bull was still capable of exercising a residual cultural influence as well through the instrument of the Commonwealth,* a loosely affiliated association of former British dependencies that was dominated by the anglophone African states.

France exercised a much more direct, overt form of neoimperial power on the continent after its departure from the former territories of French West Africa and French Equatorial Africa in 1960. French security interests in tropical Africa were protected through a series of bilateral mutual defense pacts granting the former colonial power the right of military

---

*The adjective "British" was removed from the title in the postcolonial period to emphasize the multilateral nature of the organization.

intervention.† To bolster its position as Europe's "gendarme" in the region, Paris obtained the right to maintain garrisons in half-a-dozen West and Central African states. Since the mid-1960s, some 10,000 French military forces were stationed in Africa and its offshore islands, with six parachute infantry regiments and a parachute artillery regiment retained in the metropole for rapid deployment to the continent. A large French naval force regularly patrolled the western shores of the Indian Ocean. Paris utilized the territories of Senegal and Gabon as bases for covert intelligence operations in Africa, while French counterinsurgency experts trained the security forces of many of its client states there.

This extensive network of security agreements, combat units, and military installations enabled France to launch a number of military interventions in Africa in support of its own interests or those of its African protégés. In the 1960s French units left their barracks in Cameroon, Gabon, Niger, and Chad to defend client regimes under attack from dissident elements. On other occasions behind-the-scenes French influence was exercised to hasten the downfall of long-time antagonists—such as Modibo Keita of Mali in 1968—or former protégés who had fallen from grace—such as N'garta Tombalbaye of Chad (1975), Moktar Ould Daddah of Mauritania (1978), and Jean-Bedel Bokassa of the Central African Republic (1979). France also intervened in Zaire's Shaba (formerly Katanga) province in March 1977 and May–June 1978, ostensibly to rescue resident European nationals, but also to protect Zairian strongman Mobutu Sese Seko—the Western powers' most reliable client in Africa—against exiled security forces that had returned from their Angolan sanctuary to challenge his authority. Eventually the French contingents in Zaire were replaced by an all-African peacekeeping force, but one that was a far cry from Nkrumah's bold proposal in the early 1960s for the prevention of foreign intervention in African affairs: The brainchild of the Francophile president of Senegal, Léopold Senghor, the multinational army was dominated by contingents from the pro-French states of Morocco, Gabon, and Senegal and depended heavily on French technical and logistical support.

France's privileged security relationship with most of its former African colonies were reinforced by agreements in the economic field. At the time of the establishment of the European Economic Community in 1957, France had insisted on the inclusion in the Treaty of Rome of provisions preserving preferential trade terms for, and special financial relationships with, the overseas dependencies of member states. With Great Britain outside the EEC at the time, this meant that, with the advent of decolonization in the early 1960s, the vast majority of African countries involved were the successor states of French West Africa and French Equatorial Africa. The first Yaoundé convention of 1963 (which remained in force from 1964 to 1969) set up a European Development Fund (EDF) of $800 million, subsequently increased to $1 billion in the second Yaoundé accord of 1969 (which operated during the period 1970–75). The EDF was a foreign aid program (of which France and West Germany each bore roughly a third of the cost) that financed infrastructure and agricultural projects, with most of the appropriations going to sub-Saharan states

---

†At one time or another, France signed security agreements—some of which have since been abrogated—with Benin (formerly Dahomey), Burkina Faso (formerly Upper Volta), Cameroon, Central African Republic, Chad, Congo, Djibouti (formerly French Somaliland), Gabon, Ivory Coast, Madagascar, Mali, Mauritania, Niger, Togo, and Senegal.

with close ties to France such as the Ivory Coast, Senegal, and Cameroon. Language ties ensured the preponderance of French technicians and advisers on most EDF-financed projects, while French construction firms received a disproportionate share of the contracts based on EDF funds.

The preferential trade arrangements incorporated into the Yaoundé regime proved exceedingly advantageous to the EEC in general and France in particular. The vast bulk of EDF funds were earmarked for the purchase of manufactured products from Europe, while the Africans had to import grain from EEC countries at prices well above the going rate on world markets. In sum, the preferential commercial nexus codified in the two Yaoundé conventions ensured that France's membership in the EEC would not oblige her to sacrifice protected African markets and traditional sources of strategic raw materials (especially cobalt, uranium, phosphates, and bauxite) and tropical agricultural goods (mainly coffee and cocoa).

To complement this intimate trading relationship, a strong financial connection between France and her former African possessions was forged in the form of the "franc zone," a monetary association that tied the currencies of most sub-Saharan francophone African states (collectively designated as the African Financial Community [CFA] franc) to the French franc. The franc zone in effect established a common monetary system through the mechanism of free convertibility between the CFA and the French franc at fixed parity. This arrangement created an open channel through which French capital could flow in and out of the African countries within the franc zone without encountering the risks of exchange-rate instability or prohibitions against the repatriation of profits; this open invitation to French investors (at the expense of foreign competitors) yielded impressive results in French client states such as Senegal and the Ivory Coast, which became African havens for subsidiaries of multinational (but mainly French) corporations.

Just as France had insisted on the Yaoundé arrangement to preserve its preferential trade ties with francophone Africa after it joined the EEC, Great Britain demanded similar protection as it belatedly gained admission in 1972. A lengthy negotiation between the EEC and the OAU resulted in the first Lomé convention (Lomé I) of 1975, which established the concept of preferential trade between the community and a newly established bloc of former European colonies designated as the Association of African, Caribbean, and Pacific States (ACP).

The patent inequality of the Yaoundé conventions, which had granted the member states of the EEC (notably France) privileged access to African markets but excluded many African products from the European market, had been replaced in the Lomé system by much more favorable terms of trade for the Africans vis-à-vis the Europeans: Whereas all ACP manufactured products and 96 percent of ACP commodity exports were admitted duty-free in EEC Europe, the ACP states were permitted to retain their protectionist restrictions on imports from EEC countries. The agreement also established an aid program for the most impoverished of the African countries. The most advantageous feature of Lomé I from the African perspective was the creation of a commodity stabilization fund (STABEX), which provided financial compensation to African states when the price of their commodity exports dropped below a stipulated level. This latter innovation was hailed as a long-overdue solution to the problem of commodity price fluctuations that had plagued African countries that depended on the world market price of a single commodity for the major portion of their export earnings.

Though the Lomé regime conferred notable nonreciprocal advantages on the African countries, their representatives waged a spirited campaign to rectify some its defects during the renegotiation of the original agreement toward the end of the seventies. They complained bitterly about the inadequacy of the aid program, the rigorous conditions imposed, and the absence of African voices in the decision-making process concerning the disbursement of funds. Despite an increase in the amount of development assistance (which in any case was canceled out by inflation and population increases), the second Lomé convention of 1980 (Lomé II) encountered widespread opposition in Africa. The Lomé system was denounced by radical critics as an instrument of neoimperialism that perpetuated African dependency in the guise of "Eurafrican" economic cooperation and reinforced the continent's position of inferiority in an international division of labor dominated by high technology and automated manufacturing: By promoting the export of African commodities in exchange for European manufactures as the basis of Africa's foreign trade, the "Eurafrican nexus" discouraged the process of product and market diversification that had paved the way for the economic success of the newly industrializing countries (NICs) of East Asia (see p. 395). Instead of exploiting its comparative advantage of abundant, cheap labor to produce low-quality, low-price, manufactured goods and aggressively seek new markets abroad (à la Taiwan and South Korea), Africa remained hopelessly locked in the neocolonial embrace of Western Europe. The third renegotiation of the Lomé convention in 1985 (Lomé III) did not significantly alter this condition of increasing dependency and vulnerability.

Such advantages as Africa did obtain from its participation in the international economic system during the prosperity and expansion of the 1960s vanished as the world slid into deep recession in the 1970s. The two successive "oil shocks" of that decade devastated the economies of all the African nations save the handful with substantial petroleum reserves (such as Algeria, Nigeria, Libya, Gabon, Congo, and Cameroon) or diversified economies (such as Senegal and South Africa) that were able to export and attract foreign investment. On the other end of the developmental scale, those landlocked, resource-poor, or drought-ridden states such as Chad, Niger, Ethiopia, Uganda, and the Sudan were plunged into socioeconomic chaos. This striking contrast in economic performance between the fortunate few and the pitiful "basket cases" during the prolonged recession of the seventies and early eighties brought into bold relief the trend of uneven development that had afflicted the continent since independence and represented a formidable roadblock to African unity.

In the meantime, the problem of Africa's lopsided reliance on commodity exports returned to haunt it with a vengeance during the world recession: As prices of commodities other than petroleum sank to their lowest levels in three decades (reflecting the drop in demand in the recession-ridden industrial world), many African producers of primary products were driven to the wall. Unable to pay for essential imports of food and oil, most African nations had to rush hat in hand to the IMF and the commercial banks in the industrialized world. Africa's foreign debt soared, from $14.2 billion in 1973 to $42 billion in 1976 to over $150 billion by 1984. Unchecked population growth, drought, and decline in food production resulted in widespread famine and disease. The inevitable austerity measures imposed by the banks and the IMF as preconditions for future loans forced the African countries to slash domestic spending and curtail imports. The consequence was negative economic growth for most of the non-oil-exporting states and the transformation of the postindependence dream of Africa's glorious future into the nightmare of dependency and decline.

The first signs of Africa's economic stagnation during the early 1970s prompted a drastic suggestion for relief. At its tenth annual conference in Addis Ababa in 1973, the OAU formally called for the creation of a New International Economic Order (NIEO), an innocuous euphemism for a massive transfer of wealth from the developed countries of the northern hemisphere to the less developed countries (LDCs) of the south. The means to this end would include a drastic increase in development assistance from the industrial world, the cancellation of outstanding foreign debts, the establishment of commodity price stabilization schemes on a global basis, and the reduction of northern protectionism against LDC exports. This project for the reallocation of global economic resources based on need rather than the free-market criteria of supply and demand received the enthusiastic endorsement of the nonaligned movement later in the year, and of the UN General Assembly in 1974. But the proposal for an NIEO ran aground on the shoals of global recession by the end of the 1970s. The soaring rates of inflation and unemployment in the developed world were scarcely conducive to the spirit of altruism required for such a large-scale redistribution of global wealth. Instead, the industrial states responded to the economic downturn by adopting policies that merely aggravated Africa's economic crisis, such as the reduction of foreign aid commitments and the enactment of additional protectionist measures against imports from the Third World.

In December 1976 a proposal for the establishment of an African Economic Community, modeled on the EEC, obtained the support of a number of prominent African officials who regarded the political and economic balkanization of the African continent as a major obstacle to its economic development. But the failures of earlier Pan-African schemes furnished little hope to those who struggled to keep alive Nkrumah's ambitious project, and the movement petered out.

A middle ground between the bleak reality of balkanization and the utopian aspiration of continental unity was the prospect of regionalism. The emergence of regionalist aspirations in Africa reflected the failure of the economies of the individual African nations to fulfill postindependence expectations. In 1980 the African states endorsed the so-called Lagos Plan of Action (LPA) as an emergency response to the deteriorating economic conditions on the continent. While paying lip service to the ultimate objective of African economic unity by the end of the century, the LPA favored the strengthening of existing regional economic units and the formation of new ones as the most practical means of fostering economic growth in the short term and full continental integration in the long term. The principal regional associations were the Economic Community for West African States (ECOWAS), the Economic Community for Central African States (ECCAS), the Southern African Development Coordination Conference (SADCC), and the Preferential Trade Area (PTA) for East and Southern Africa. Together these organizations covered all of tropical Africa and represented the only existing mechanisms for economic cooperation that might reverse the trend toward economic decline.

The most promising of these regional associations was ECOWAS, founded in May 1975 in Lagos, Nigeria, by the representatives of fifteen West African nations. Based on the principle of collective self-reliance and regional cooperation, ECOWAS rapidly developed into a test case in Africa's campaign to loosen the neocolonial bonds with Europe that had been tightened in the Lomé system. In particular, Nigeria's dominant role in ECOWAS, together with its sponsorship of the LPA, signified a determined bid for regional leadership by that large, populous, resource-rich country as it celebrated the triumph of national unity over the Biafran secessionist challenge of the late sixties and enjoyed the financial windfall from skyrocketing oil prices in the seventies. Nigeria's hegemonic aspirations in West Africa conflicted with France's neoimperial relationship with its clients in the region. But anglophone Nigeria's cultural and linguistic isolation amid predominantly francophone neighbors who preferred Paris to Lagos as a source of guidance (and financial assistance) hampered Nigeria's ambition to become the dominant regional power in West Africa. The sharp decline in oil prices in the 1980s due to over-supply exposed the error of Nigeria's development strategy of relying on a single export commodity and resulted in a severe drop in that country's foreign exchange reserves. Nigeria's economic problems during the glut in world oil supplies damaged ECOWAS's emerging reputation as an indigenous alternative to the Eurafrican system in West Africa and as a model for regional integration for other parts of the continent.

The economic crisis that gripped Africa in the 1970s was accompanied by an epidemic of armed conflict, both within and between a number of African states, that aggravated the trend toward instability and insecurity on the continent. Two of these confrontations, the civil war in Chad and the rivalry between Morocco and Algeria over the former Span-ish Sahara, reduced to shambles the Pan-African ideal of the sanctity of frontiers and the sovereignty of postcolonial states. Worse, the new outbreak of violence in the seventies resulted in the very circumstance that the OAU had worked so hard (and so successfully) to prevent: the extension of the Cold War to Africa. Suddenly the Soviet Union appeared on the African scene, inevitably to be followed by the United States, and soon both super-powers were avidly courting clients and employing proxies as their global rivalry was extended to the continent.

The first of these developments occurred in July 1974 when the Kremlin concluded a pact with the East African state of Somalia, which committed the Soviets to train and equip the Somali army in exchange for access to naval facilities at the port of Berbera on the Gulf of Aden as well as the use of two Soviet-constructed airfields in the country. In the meantime the Russian navy had acquired access to the old British base at Aden on the opposite shore of the gulf through an agreement with the revolutionary regime in South Yemen that had been established in 1967 after the end of British colonial rule.

But the escalating Soviet involvement in the northwest littoral of the Indian Ocean was complicated by a regional rivalry between the new Soviet client state of Somalia and the self-styled "Marxist-Leninist" military regime in Ethiopia that had overthrown the pro-Western Emperor Haile Selassie in 1974 and terminated the country's long-standing rela-tionship with the United States in early 1977. When Somali President Mohammed Siad Barre launched a military invasion of Ethiopia with the intention of annexing the Ogaden region with its ethnic Somali inhabitants, he turned from Moscow to Washington for sup-port while the leftist regime in Addis Ababa predictably approached the Kremlin. In November 1977 Siad Barre abrogated the 1974 treaty of friendship, expelled all Soviet military personnel, and revoked Russian access to Somali naval and air facilities. In the meantime, Moscow began supplying Ethiopia with tanks, aircraft, and military advisers and air- and sea-lifted some 15,000 Cuban soldiers and their equipment to Ethiopia to relieve the beleaguered forces of the Ethiopian strongman, Mengistu Haile Mariam. By 1978 Ethiopia had defeated Somalia in the Ogaden and proceeded to reward its Soviet benefactor with naval facilities at the port of Massawa to compensate for its loss of the Somali port of Berbera.

Just as the collapse of Haile Selassie's forty-four-year-old monarchy in 1974 resulted in the establishment of a Soviet client state on the Horn of Africa, the breakup of the Portuguese colonial empire after the overthrow in the same year of the forty-two-year-old dictatorship in Lisbon afforded Moscow the opportunity to extend its influence to the southern tip of the continent. In 1975–76 the Soviet Union transported 17,000 Cuban troops together with tanks, armored personnel carriers, and small arms to the former Portuguese colony of Angola on the west coast of Africa to support the Marxist-oriented Popular Movement for the Liberation of Angola (MPLA) in its struggle with an American-backed rival organization, the UNITA movement. The triumph of the pro-Soviet faction in the Angolan civil war was assured in December 1975 when the United States Congress, as part of a post-Vietnam reaction against overseas military entanglements, voted to cut off American aid to UNITA. The victorious MPLA proceeded to form a Marxist government in Luanda; its president, Agostinho Neto, concluded a treaty of friendship and cooperation with the Soviet Union in October 1976; and Cuban troops remained in the country to combat rival guerrilla groups operating in the south. Moscow appeared at first glance to have gained a foothold in an African country with substantial oil reserves, vast untapped mineral resources, and a strategic location astride the sea route around the Cape of Good Hope. In fact, the Russians failed to obtain naval facilities on the Angolan coast; American multinational corporations such as Gulf Oil, General Tire, and Chase Manhattan Bank retained their large investments in the country; and Angolan President José Eduardo dos Santos (who assumed power after Neto's death in 1979) reduced his country's dependence on the Soviet Union and forged closer economic ties to the West.

Nevertheless, the Soviet Union had undeniably advanced its strategic interests in the Horn and southern Africa during the second half of the 1970s. Several hundred Russian military advisers and several thousand Cuban troops operated in countries on a continent that had previously been immune to Communist-bloc influence. In addition to the pro-Soviet regimes in Ethiopia and Angola, regimes that called themselves Marxist were established with Soviet-bloc assistance in Mozambique, the Congo Republic, and Benin (formerly Dahomey). In North Africa, the radical Arab regime of Colonel Muammar al-Qaddafi in Libya, which had toppled the pro-Western monarchy in 1969, nationalized American oil properties, closed down the American and British air bases in the country, received substantial Soviet economic and military assistance and generally supported Moscow's foreign policy goals. The ambitious Qaddafi also began to intervene in the internal affairs of the neighboring pro-Western regimes of Chad, the Sudan, Somalia, and Liberia in what appeared to be a campaign to establish Libya as the dominant power in its subregion.

As we have seen, Africa had been largely disengaged from the superpower rivalry that had drawn most other parts of the Third World into the Cold War. As Great Britain, France, and Belgium divested themselves of their African possessions, the newly independent states that were fashioned out of the former colonial empires refused to choose between Moscow and Washington in the East-West struggle. The few instances of superpower engagement in Africa before the mid-1970s—the establishment of American military bases in pre-Qaddafi Libya and Morocco, the unsuccessful Soviet intervention in the Congo—merely prove the rule. Africa played a minor role in United States foreign trade and investment and no role at all in American security concerns. Their former colonial masters in the European Community remained the most important economic partners of the newly independent African states, while France continued to exercise the principal foreign military function in its former domains on the continent. The Soviet Union lacked the capacity and apparently the will to sustain a major campaign to extend its influence to Africa. It was the belated collapse of the Portuguese and Ethiopian empires and the intensification of the struggle for black majority rule in Rhodesia (Zimbabwe) and South-West Africa (Namibia) that permitted Moscow to exploit this African turbulence for its own advantage at a time when the Kremlin had acquired the logistical capability to project its power to the African continent.

The response of the United States to the escalating Soviet involvement in Africa underwent a gradual transformation in the course of the second half of the 1970s. As noted earlier, the Ford-Kissinger administration was prevented from intervening in the Angolan civil war by a Congress traumatized by the Vietnam experience. The Carter administration originally displayed an uncharacteristic sensitivity to African concerns and deemphasized the global context of the regional conflicts that were sweeping the continent. The appointment of the prominent civil rights leader Andrew Young as America's first black ambassador to the United Nations; the repeal of the 1971 Byrd amendment (authorizing the importation of chrome from Rhodesia in violation of United Nations sanctions against that country's renegade white minority regime, which had declared its independence from Britain in 1965 rather than submit to black majority rule); the sustained effort to promote a negotiated settlement between South Africa and the South-West Africa People's Organization (SWAPO) with the goal of establishing black majority rule in South-West Africa—all of these actions signaled the determination of the new American president to identify his country with the liberationist aspirations of the African states rather than to see them as mere pawns in the East-West struggle.

But the Soviet-Cuban engagement in Africa gradually produced a shift of Carter administration policy in the direction of greater toughness, as indicated by its refusal to recognize the new Angolan regime unless Cuban troops were withdrawn from the country and its decision to assist French military forces that were dispatched to Zaire in the spring of 1978 to help the pro-Western Mobutu regime repel an invasion of Shaba province by exiles residing in the pro-Soviet state of Angola. From 1978 on, President Carter and his anti-Soviet national security adviser, Zbigniew Brzezinski, periodically warned Moscow that its activities in Africa were having an adverse effect on the fragile East-West detente that both Carter and Brezhnev wished to preserve.

The sharp reaction from Washington to the Soviet-Cuban activity in Africa reflected a concern that had been mounting ever since the oil embargo of 1973, namely, apprehension about a possible cutoff of a whole range of strategic minerals that the United States imported from Africa in large quantities: chrome, antimony, cobalt, vanadium, platinum, manganese, ferromanganese, and oil (of which Nigeria had become America's second-largest supplier). The destabilizing activities of the Soviet-backed regime of Qaddafi in Libya, as well as the Soviet-supported challenges to the autocratic American client state in Zaire, threatened to undermine the security of pro-Western regimes on the continent and jeopardize American access to their strategic resources. In a more general sense, the Soviet Union's intervention in Africa, either directly or through its Cuban ally, confirmed in the minds of American strategic thinkers that country's transformation from a Eurasian land power to a global power with worldwide air and naval capabilities. The rapid deployment of Cuban troops, tanks, and military equipment to Angola and Ethiopia seemed to demonstrate Moscow's ability to leapfrog the ring of containment states that had been forged by the United States during the Cold War era. The Soviet naval squadron that patrolled the Red Sea and the Indian Ocean from bases in Ethiopia and South Yemen was seen in Washington as a potential menace to the Western world's lifeline to the petroleum reserves of the Persian Gulf.

Thus, by the end of the 1970s, the OAU's hallowed maxims of African unity and nonalignment had been dealt a severe blow by the polarization of the continent along ideological lines: The francophone states of West and Central Africa, Zaire, Egypt, Morocco, the Sudan, Kenya, and Somalia had established or intensified security ties with the West. In the meantime Angola, Ethiopia, Guinea-Bissau (formerly Equatorial Guinea), Libya, and Mozambique openly identified with the Socialist bloc, while Algeria, Guinea, and Uganda received Soviet aid. This East-West rivalry in Africa opened deep fissures within the OAU: When the insurgents in Angola invited the covert intervention of South Africa and the government in Luanda welcomed Cuban troops in the mid-1970s, the organization split down the middle on the question of which side to support. Later, when the embattled regimes in Zaire and Chad looked to Paris for military assistance, they received encouragement from other pro-Western, conservative African leaders but aroused the ire of those African states that identified with the East bloc.

But the Soviet-American competition in Africa that had emerged so unexpectedly during the second half of the seventies proved to be short-lived because of Moscow's inability to supplement its military aid with much in the way of economic support (such as trade, loans, and investments). In particular, the inconvertibility of East bloc currencies precluded the expansion of African trade with Comecon countries beyond the customary bilateral barter schemes. By the time of Brezhnev's death in 1982, the Kremlin's bid for influence in Africa had failed ignominiously. In rapid succession, African countries that had once welcomed aid and advice from the East bloc—Egypt, Somalia, and Sudan—broke with their former benefactors and dislodged the Soviets from their privileged positions. Even those African states that retained some of the rhetoric of Marxist-Leninism, such as Angola, Mozambique, and Guinea, declined to seek admission to Comecon for the pragmatic economic reasons cited above. When they looked abroad for financial relief, it was not to Moscow, but to New York, London, Tokyo, Paris, or Washington (the IMF and the World Bank). Thus the Western bloc, due to its dominant position in the international economic system from which Africa could not, or would not, shake free, continued to exercise the dominant external influence on the continent throughout the 1980s.

The persistence of Africa's dependence on external powers in the Western world was graphically demonstrated in the civil war in Chad. For fifteen years this resource-poor, landlocked, ethnically divided country languished under the corrupt dictatorship of N'garta Tombalbaye, who displayed undisguised favoritism toward the settled Christian inhabitants of the south at the expense of the nomadic Islamic population in the north. In 1975 the overthrow and execution of Tombalbaye in a military coup plunged Chad into political chaos. In 1977 the northern Muslims, fortified by links with their coreligionists in the Arab world, called for the establishment of a separate Islamic republic. In the meantime, the adjacent Islamic state of Libya to the north exploited this civil conflict by invading and attempting to annex the northern portion of Chad known as the Aouzou strip. French military forces thereupon intervened and eventually backed the campaign led by Hissène Habré against Qaddafi's army and its indigenous allies in northern Chad. Efforts of the OAU to intervene in the dispute came to naught, and the intrusive French involvement in Habré's campaign to expel Libyan forces from Chad once again demonstrated Africa's dependence on foreign powers.*

Another blow to the cause of African unity and stability was the conflict that erupted during the same period in the territory known as the Spanish Sahara. In 1974 the government of Spain, weakened by the mortal illness of its longtime dictator, Francisco Franco, hastily unveiled plans for a plebiscite to enable the inhabitants of the country's last remaining colonial possession to determine their political future. The contiguous states of Morocco and Mauritania vigorously opposed this democratic method of decolonization, asserting their own historic claims to the territory (which possessed one of the world's largest deposits of phosphates). The Moroccan monarch, Hassan II, declared that the northern part of the territory belonged to "Greater Morocco," the twentieth-century reincarnation of an ancient Arab empire that once dominated the region. Faced with the prospect of conflict with African states over a territory it had already decided to evacuate, Madrid prudently shelved the idea of a plebiscite and concluded a secret agreement to hand over the northern two-thirds of the Spanish Sahara to Morocco and the southern one-third to Mauritania. When the last Spanish forces withdrew in February 1976, Moroccan and Mauritanian troops promptly occupied the zones alloted to them by their understanding with the departing colonial power.

But this territorial transfer had occurred without the assent of its inhabitants. In 1973 they had founded a national independence movement named Polisario (the Spanish acronym for the Popular Front for the Liberation of the Western Sahara) to hasten the departure of the colonial power. As Spain withdrew, Polisario promptly proclaimed a "Saharawi Republic," obtained diplomatic recognition from most member states of the OAU, and proceeded to wage guerrilla warfare against the occupation forces of Morocco and Mauritania. By 1979 the economically depressed, politically unstable Mauritania was compelled to withdraw its troops from, and renounce its territorial claims to, the southern third of the Western Sahara. Morocco thereupon moved its forces southward and proceeded to annex the area evacuated by the Mauritanians. In the meantime Algeria (which had quarreled with Morocco from 1962 to 1972 over their own postcolonial boundary) vigorously opposed Morocco's designs in the Western Sahara and furnished substantial diplomatic and economic support to Polisario. Throughout the 1980s, the Moroccan-Algerian rivalry in the Western Sahara remained another major impediment to the doomed cause of pan-African cooperation, splitting the OAU into pro-Rabat, pro-Algiers, and pro-Polisario factions.

Another casualty of the struggle over the Western Sahara was the hope for some type of regional cooperation among the peoples inhabiting the area of North Africa commonly known as the Maghreb,† which includes the countries of Algeria, Morocco, Tunisia, Mau-

---

*After the failure of the Libyan adventure in Chad, Habré was overthrown by a disgruntled former associate in 1990. France declined to intervene on behalf of its former protégé in what it viewed as a quarrel between rival Chadian leaders.

†The term "Maghreb" means "the Arab West" (literally "where the sun sets"), that is, the Arabic-speaking region of North Africa. It is contrasted with the "Mashreg" ("the Arab East"), which refers to the area known in the Western world as "the Middle East."

ritania, and Libya. Linked by a common language (Arabic) and religion (Islam) that set them apart from other African states, the countries of the Maghreb had groped for some type of regional identity and collective purpose ever since their liberation from European colonial control. But these linguistic and religious affinities proved to be inadequate sources of cohesion amid the national rivalries that plagued the region, such as the acrimonious border disputes between Algeria and Morocco and between Libya and Tunisia. These competing territorial ambitions were aggravated by the sharp ideological contrast among the Maghreb's constituent states: Morocco (a conservative, pro-Western monarchy), Algeria and Libya (radical republics with close ties to the East bloc), Tunisia (a conservative, pro-Western republic), and Mauritania (a military dictatorship). Thus, throughout the 1980s the Arabic-speaking states of North Africa were no more successful in forging a strong regional identity—as a less ambitious alternative to the elusive pan-African ideal—than were the francophone and anglophone countries south of the Sahara. The formation in 1991 of the Arab Maghreb Union by these five states seemed to some observers a promising step in that direction, to others little more than a desperate effort to coordinate regional economic activities in the face of Europe's move toward a single market in 1992.*

If postindependence Africa was being torn apart by the various disruptive tendencies—economic, ethnic, ideological—discussed above, there was one issue on which all of the African states agreed: the necessity of removing the last bastion of white supremacy on the continent, the system of racial separation, or apartheid, practiced in the Republic of South Africa† since 1948. As the white ruling elite in the British, French, and Belgian colonial possessions in Africa submitted to black majority rule at the beginning of the sixties, the white minority government of South Africa cracked down on the restive indigenous population that sought to emulate their brethren to the north. The massacre of sixty-seven unarmed black demonstrators by the South African police at Sharpeville in March 1960 was Pretoria's defiant response to the growing opposition to apartheid in this mineral-rich country. All attempts by the black majority to obtain the political rights that most other Africans had already acquired met with determined resistance from the ruling National party, mouthpiece of the Afrikkaner-speaking descendants of Dutch and French emigrants from seventeenth-century Europe. The African National Congress (ANC), originally a moderate organization founded in 1912 to defend South Africa's disenfranchised, exploited black majority, was brutally suppressed by South African security forces. One of its militants, an activist lawyer named Nelson Mandela, was arrested in 1962 and sentenced to life imprisonment, while the remainder of its leadership fled into exile. Precluded from engaging in legal political activity, the ANC endorsed the only alternative: armed struggle. The first major outbreak of violence came in 1976 when student riots in the black township of Soweto outside Johannesburg resulted in at least 575 deaths. In the meantime, organizations such as the OAU, the Commonwealth, and the UN continually denounced the South African regime while the ruling elites of the newly independent states insistently demanded the end of apartheid and the advent of black majority rule.

Throughout the sixties and well into the seventies, South Africa profited from the pres-

---

*See below, page 464.

†In 1961 the Union of South Africa, a member of the British Commonwealth since 1910, was transformed into an independent republic and severed its ties to the British crown.

ence of a protective shield across its northern border in the form of friendly, white-controlled states that had resisted the trend toward decolonization: the Portuguese possessions of Angola and Mozambique, the white minority regime in Rhodesia, and the former German colony of South-West Africa (which had been administered by South Africa since the end of World War I under a long-expired mandate from the long-defunct League of Nations).

But the emergence of the two self-professed Marxist-Leninist regimes in Angola and Mozambique in 1975, followed by the belated introduction of black majority rule in Rhodesia (renamed Zimbabwe) in 1980, confronted South Africa with antagonistic northern neighbors that were willing to lend aid and sanctuary to insurgents against the Pretoria regime. Throughout the eighties, South Africa clung tenaciously to South-West Africa (renamed Namibia) as its last remaining buffer against black Africa. But an insurrection launched by SWAPO, together with diplomatic pressure from the world community (including gentle prodding from Washington) forced South Africa to enter into negotiations for a transfer of sovereignty in Namibia and to soften the harshness of apartheid at home. As the talks on Namibia's political future bogged down, South African President P. W. Botha took some small steps to broaden the electoral base of his country's rigidly racist political system: A new constitution approved by referendum in November 1983 enfranchised the colored (mixed-race) and Asian minorities, establishing a tricameral parliament with a separate legislative chamber for the white (4.5 million), colored (2.6 million), and Asian (800,000) citizens (but continuing to exclude the 25 million members of the black majority).

The dangling of the carrot, represented by the talks on independence for Namibia and the granting of limited political reform within South Africa, was accompanied by the wielding of the stick against hostile states to the north: In 1980 South Africa began to apply strong pressure against neighboring regimes that had given sanctuary to ANC guerrillas. Economic and military assistance flowed from Pretoria to insurgent organizations such as the Mozambique National Resistance Movement (MNR) and UNITA in Angola. The unrelenting economic warfare and periodic search-and-destroy raids against Mozambique proved so successful in destabilizing the shaky regime of Samora Michel that it was obliged to sign the Nkomati Agreement with South Africa in March 1984, whereby South Africa agreed to terminate its support for the MNR in exchange for Mozambique's pledge to control the activities of the ANC guerillas on its territory.

But the internal challenge to the South African government continued, resulting in the declaration of a state of emergency in July 1985. With a handful of exceptions—including Hastings Banda of Malawi and Félix Houphouët-Boigny of the Ivory Coast—African leaders pursued a policy of economic sanctions, nonrecognition, and support for the ANC-led armed resistance within South Africa in order to bring down this last bastion of white privilege on the continent. In the meantime the Reagan administration in Washington pursued its policy of "constructive engagement," which was aimed at the conclusion of an agreement between South Africa and Angola that would lead to the simultaneous withdrawal of South African and Cuban forces from the latter country, as well as the eventual establishment of black majority rule in Namibia. But by the mid-1980s, the southern part of the African continent remained mired in violence and instability: insurgencies raged in Angola, Mozambique, Namibia, and South Africa while the two superpowers observed the chaotic situation with interest and concern.

15

THE FAR EAST: THE ROAD TO THE NEW CO-PROSPERITY SPHERE

THE MIRACLE OF JAPAN

At the end of the summer of 1945, the Japanese Empire lay in ruins. This once proud society had suffered a humiliating defeat in war, the loss of its colonial possessions, and the destruction of a quarter of its infrastructure by American strategic bombing (conventional as well as atomic). During its military occupation of the Japanese islands between 1945 and 1952, the United States had treated its former enemy with a combination of political firmness and economic leniency: By imposing on the defeated power a democratic political system and a constitution that renounced war and the development of the means to wage it, the occupying power banished the threat of Japanese militarism that had plagued East Asia for decades. But by acquiescing in, nay, actively encouraging, the *economic* recovery of Japan, the United States had set in motion the process whereby its former enemy was to become—within a generation of Hiroshima—its major commercial and financial competitor in the world.

We have already noted the important U.S. contribution to the economic recovery of Japan after the Second World War in the context of the emerging Cold War in Asia (see p. xxx): The provision of almost $2 billion of American aid—mostly in the form of food and raw materials, which were in dangerously short supply—rescued Japanese society from the immediate consequences of its wartime devastation. The abandonment of reparation requirements by the end of the 1940s removed a potentially damaging claim on Japanese production that might well have discouraged domestic savings, investment, and entrepreneurial activity. The revocation of plans to dissolve the industrial conglomerates that had collaborated with the imperial government before and during the war paved the way for the reemergence, in modified form, of old Zaibatsu powerhouses such as Mitsubishi, Mitsui, and Sumitomo. This American willingness to tolerate the cartelization of Japanese industry in the interest of efficiency and economy of scale also facilitated the formation of huge new firms on the Zaibatsu model, such as Hitachi, Toshiba, Toyota,

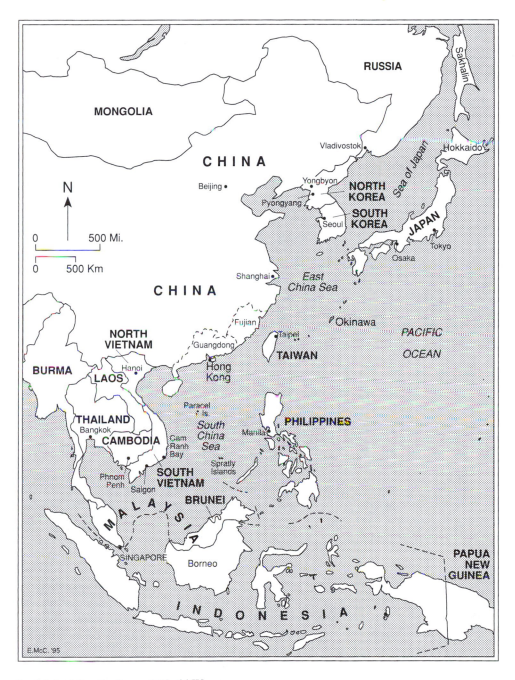

East Asia After the Second World War

and Nissan. By 1949 Japan had already attained its prewar level of productivity, owing in large part to the benevolent economic policy pursued by the U.S. military occupation authorities. In the following year, the Korean War added a powerful stimulus to Japanese industrial production in the form of American military purchases of war-related goods and equipment. Another notable American contribution to Japan's postwar economic revival was the provision of U.S. military protection under the mutual defense treaty of 1951: Postwar Japan never had to spend more than 1 percent of its GNP on defense, and the resulting financial savings were channeled into industrial reconstruction and development.

Though Japan got its head start in economic recovery because of these advantages provided by its privileged relationship with the United States, the Japanese state deserves considerable credit for pursuing policies that contributed to the extraordinary record of economic growth: Officials in charge of economic affairs, based in the Ministry of International Trade and Industry (MITI), the Ministry of Finance (MOF), and the Bank of Japan (BOJ), were empowered to grant tax breaks, import and export licenses, low-interest loans, and direct subsidies to targeted industries to enable them to compete in world markets. The state encouraged a small number of highly concentrated firms engaged in the export trade to focus on long-term growth at the expense of short-term profits, which led to the reinvestment of profits to spur technological innovation. Japanese firms retained the loyalty of a highly skilled labor force with guarantees of lifetime employment, wage and salary increases based on seniority, and corporate welfare benefits, which produced a veritable army of compliant workers willing to work longer hours at lower pay compared with their highly paid counterparts in Western industrial countries. The Japanese consumer's renowned frugality resulted in the highest savings rate in the world, which in some years approached 22 percent of disposable income.

This ethic of austerity emphasizing production over consumption, lifetime employment over labor militancy, and deferred over instant gratification resulted in the low labor costs and high capital formation that afforded the Japanese economy a comparative advantage on world markets. In short, the defeated country compensated for its comparative disadvantage of insufficient domestic supplies of food, fuel, and raw materials—which had been exacerbated by the lack of working capital caused by the wartime destruction of plant and equipment and the loss of the economic resources of its overseas empire—by generating trade surpluses with sales of finished manufactured goods abroad. With the funds earned from these overseas sales, this resource- and capital-poor country was able to pay for the essential commodity imports it required and to employ its accumulated capital to finance improvements of plant and equipment at home that increased its competitiveness abroad. Japan's extreme dependence on foreign trade for its economic prosperity required continuous access to foreign markets, which was facilitated by the steep tariff reductions throughout the world resulting from rounds of negotiations under the auspices of the General Agreement on Tariffs and Trade (GATT). It also profited from the low prices for food, raw materials, and energy compared with the prices of manufactured goods that constituted the major portion of its exports. From 1955 to 1973 Japan's gross national product had increased at an annual average rate of 9 percent, by far the highest of all industrial countries, making it the world's third-largest economy by 1968. That growth rate declined by half in the 1970s, when the collapse of the system of fixed exchange rates caused the value of the yen to rise and therefore Japanese exports to fall, when the increase in world oil prices caused a worldwide recession that reduced demand for Japan's products, and when protectionist sentiment in the United States and the European Community led to the erection of barriers to Japanese imports. But the rate of 4 to 5 percent it maintained thereafter enabled the country to reach second place behind the United States among the world's economic powers by the early 1980s.

During the 1960s Japanese workers began to demand and receive higher wages in labor-intensive industries such as textiles, iron, steel, and shipbuilding, while other low-wage East Asian countries began to compete with Japanese goods in this sector on world markets. This shift in Japan's comparative advantage cause a significant shift in the country's export strategy, as abundant capital replaced cheap labor as the country's comparative advantage over its competitors. Fortified with the accumulated profits from its foreign sales and its high domestic savings rate, Japan began to shift resources from the labor-intensive to the capital-intensive sector of the economy to promote exports of televisions, transistor radios, motorcycles, and automobiles (of which Japan became the world's largest producer by 1980). During the 1980s Japan began to draw on its well-educated, highly skilled workforce in science and technology to promote exports in the technology-intensive sector such as telecommunications equipment, office machines, precision instruments, and computers. As Japan followed this upward path of economic development, the bitter memories of the 1937–1945 period understandably prompted anxieties among its neighbors in East Asia that the former imperial power might use its economic might to attempt to dominate the region. Japan's failure to offer explicit apologies for its wartime conduct, together with incidents such as its refusal to modify school history textbooks that glossed over Tokyo's expansionist policies and visits by Japanese officials to nationalistic shrines, fed this distrust. But some East Asian countries recognized that Japan's stunning economic recovery offered a useful model of development that they themselves might follow. Following in the footsteps of Japan, these countries pursued strategies of export-oriented growth that enabled them to become major players in international trade by the mid-1980s.

THE RISE OF THE EAST ASIAN TIGERS

South Korea, Taiwan, Hong Kong, and Singapore—often referred to by international economists as the "Asian Tigers"—were the first countries in East Asia to emulate Japan's economic success by pursuing the strategy of export-oriented growth that catapulted them from third to first world status in a few decades, pulling far ahead of other developing countries in Latin America, Africa, and the Middle East. Like Japan at the end of World War II, these four countries were cursed with the disadvantage of overpopulation as well as an acute shortage of capital, food, raw materials, energy supplies, and arable land. Also like Japan, they compensated for these disadvantages by exploiting the presence of a large, docile, and mobile labor force by specializing in the production of cheap textile goods that did not require much capital investment or technological sophistication. As Japan moved out of the labor-intensive sector to export more advanced products, these four countries moved in to turn out low-cost textiles and apparel. In the 1970s they in turn moved up the product scale to export capital-intensive goods such as radios, televisions, sewing machines, and ships and within a decade were able to rely on an increasingly skilled, well-educated workforce to give the Japanese a run for their money in technology-intensive industries such as computers and biotechnology.

These four countries shared a few characteristics that help to explain their phenomenal success in rising from the morass of economic backwardness. First, all shared the common cultural heritage of Confucianism, whose celebration of the virtues of frugality, hard work, and self-discipline was conducive to the type of economic activity required for export-driven economic growth. Second, all had nondemocratic political systems, which enabled their governments to impose economic strategies on the population with little fear of the political consequences. Third, all had benefited from substantial financial aid from a foreign benefactor (Taiwan and South Korea from the United States, Singapore and Hong Kong from Great Britain). But amid these similarities there were some notable differences in the methods employed by the four countries to spur economic growth: At one extreme, the government of South Korea actively intervened in the economy by providing tax breaks and subsidies to certain chosen sectors and by retaining state control of certain basic industries. At the other extreme, the government of Hong Kong allowed firms in the British crown colony's businesses to operate without government interference or control. The policies of Taiwan and the city-state of Singapore fell somewhere in between these two extremes of what some economists have called South Korea's "state capitalism" on the one hand and Hong Kong's "laissez-faire capitalism" on the other. But whatever the similarities and differences among these four Asian countries, their phenomenal economic growth during the 1970s and 1980s enabled them to penetrate the markets not only of their own region but also of the United States and Europe.

The economic takeoff of Japan and then the four Asian Tigers soon had important repercussions for a group of neighboring countries—Indonesia, Malaysia, Thailand, and the Philippines—that in 1967 had established a regional organization known as the Association of Southeast Asian Nations (ASEAN). Unlike Japan and the Four Tigers, the ASEAN countries were blessed with abundant supplies of natural resources. They therefore developed a mutually advantageous trading relationship with the newly industrializing countries of Asia, shipping raw materials and fuel to Japan and the Tigers in exchange for manufactured goods and capital investment. But by the end of the 1970s the ASEAN countries became dissatisfied with this neocolonial role as commodity-producing suppliers of the industrializing countries to the north. Intent on emulating the success of their prosperous trading partners, these countries in turn adopted the export-oriented strategy of industrialization by exploiting their abundant supply of cheap labor to market low-cost textiles and other labor-intensive products. Soon the ASEAN countries were achieving impressive annual growth rates and beginning to capture markets abroad for their manufactured goods. But the path to industrialization was not a smooth one for these countries. Their continued dependence on commodity exports served as a drag on economic growth when world commodity prices declined in the seventies and eighties. They ran up huge foreign debts to finance their economic growth and found it increasingly difficult to service them. Their crash programs of economic modernization generated severe social problems as impoverished peasants poured into the overcrowded cities in search of work while those who stayed behind suffered from a severe maldistribution of land, resulting in insurgencies that were met with harsh repression by the governments. Soon the ASEAN countries' bid to follow in the path of Japan and the four Tigers to economic dominance in Asia ran into competition from another economic powerhouse in the region that boasted the world's largest population and Asia's most formidable military force.

THE DENG REVOLUTION IN CHINA

In an earlier chapter* we observed that the Sino-American rapprochement during the first half of the 1970s had been prompted primarily by their common concern about the expansion of Soviet military power, and secondarily by the prospect of mutually profitable economic relations between the two countries. But while the Sino-American entente may have served the purpose of counterbalancing Soviet military power during the second half of the decade, it proved to be a bitter disappointment for American business people eagerly eyeing the untapped China market of 800 million consumers, and even more so for the Chinese officials allied with Premier Zhou Enlai who had anticipated bounteous economic benefits in the form of trade, aid, loans, investments, and technology transfer from the capitalist countries.

China's first foray into the international economic system during the second half of the 1970s proved to be a false start that resulted in a colossal failure. After the death of Mao Zedong in 1976, his heir-apparent Hua Guofeng launched an ill-conceived campaign to modernize the Chinese economy by reverting to the old practice of promoting heavy industry through intrusive government planning while simultaneously soliciting foreign investment and loans from the industrialized world. A combination of excessive foreign borrowing, unsatisfactory contracts concluded with multinational firms, poor planning, and waste stopped the Chinese economy in its tracks. The lack of technical, managerial, and entrepreneurial expertise, together with the absence of a sufficient infrastructure, prevented the application of capital and technology that was flowing from Japan, the United States, and the European Community. In the years 1974–1977 the country's sluggish agricultural performance resulted in widespread famine that necessitated a substantial increase in food imports. China's inability to export manufactured products to pay for these essential food purchases abroad led to a fundamental reassessment of the first post-Mao development strategy and the cancellation or scaling back of most industrial projects in 1978.

The most important lesson learned from the experience of the 1970s was that China's best hope for economic modernization lay in discarding the remnants of the old Maoist plan of autarkic self-reliance and formulating a development strategy based on full integration in the international financial and trading system. The blueprints for such a scheme were readily at hand: The East Asian Tigers had overcome their own substantial handicaps to establish impressive records of economic growth while China remained mired in industrial backwardness. The Chinese leader who undertook to implement this new development strategy was Deng Xiaoping, a disciple of Mao's late second-in-command, Zhou Enlai. Between 1978 and 1981 Deng gradually purged those domestic opponents (including his rival for the succession, Hua Guofeng) who bitterly accused him of betray-

---

*See page 348.

Vice Premier Deng Xiaoping (1904–1997) of China and U.S. President Jimmy Carter (1924–) at the White House, January 29, 1979: The United States had just extended formal diplomatic recognition of the People's Republic of China, seven years after President Nixon's visit. The Chinese guest publicly expressed regret about "the period of unpleasantness between us for thirty years." By the end of the year the two countries began to cooperate even more closely in foreign policy with their joint opposition to the Soviet invasion and occupation of Afghanistan. *(National Archives)*

ing orthodox Maoist principles by exposing China's economy to the exploitative forces of the international capitalist order.

Deng's ambitious program for China's modernization required a fundamental restructuring of the country's economic system. From 1950 to 1980 China had constructed a gigantic industrial apparatus by dint of its own efforts. The only foreign assistance it had received was in the form of plant and equipment imports from the Soviet Union during the fifties. In line with the Soviet prototype, resources had been channeled into state-run heavy industries such as defense, metallurgy, chemicals, and petroleum. Goods were allocated by government planning rather than supply and demand, and production was earmarked for the domestic market rather than for export. Deng launched a bold campaign to shift priorities from heavy to light industry and from import-substitution to export-oriented production. He also introduced into this paragon of Marxist-Leninist orthodoxy a limited free market and private ownership of property. The result was the most spectacular transformation in China since the revolution of 1949.

The Chinese development strategy for the eighties was unabashedly based on the principle of the Open Door, once an epithet associated with Western imperial domination: Through *this* open door would pass loans, investment, trade, technology, and tourists from abroad, while Chinese college students headed in the other direction in search of educational opportunities in the industrialized world that were unavailable at home. But the door would be open to only a portion of China, which was divided for the purposes of foreign economic relations into two discrete geographical categories: The interior part of the country, backward, rural, and underdeveloped, would remain largely untouched by the outside world; it would be relegated to the subsidiary role of nurturing inland infant industries to produce goods for the domestic market. The coastal region, with about a quarter of the country's people, would be tightly integrated with the international commercial and financial system in the hope that foreign trade and capital would serve as the engines of economic development for the entire country.

The first step in this coastal development strategy was taken in 1979 with the creation of four "special economic zones" comprising the southern cities of Shenzhen, Zuhai, Shantou, and Xiamen. Foreign companies engaged in light manufacturing were encouraged through tax incentives to set up joint ventures with Chinese companies, or to create their own fully owned subsidiaries, for export-oriented production. By the end of 1983, 188 equity joint venture contracts had been concluded with multinational firms, mostly in the tourist, construction, textile, and oil exploration industries. In 1984 the Chinese government designated fourteen additional coastal cities and Hainan island as tax havens for foreign capital. It is ironic that many of the same treaty ports from which Western trading interests had dominated the economy of imperial and republican China became the principal sites of foreign investment and commercial development in the People's Republic. Throughout the 1980s the old imperialist bailiwick of Shanghai accounted for about 15 percent of China's total exports and 70 percent of its light industrial exports (such as clothing, textiles, bicycles, and sewing machines). Its inhabitants enjoyed a per capita income of $1,800, placing it on a par with Taiwan and South Korea (the two countries on whose free export zones the Chinese special economic zones on the southern coast had been modeled). Other success stories included Shenzhen next to Hong Kong and Zuhai opposite Macao. The glaring contrast between the booming coastal region and the backward hinterland left the impression of two separate countries, the one advancing into the industrialized world, the other languishing in the Third, or what some economists have begun to call the Fourth, World.

It is scarcely surprising, in light of the complementarity of their two economies, that the most important foreign promoter and beneficiary of China's entry into the world economic system was Japan. China possessed the oil, coal, and strategic raw materials that Japan required, while Japan had the capital, technology, and high-level manufactured goods that China needed. As Japan encountered protectionist pressures from its premier trading partner across the Pacific, the lure of the potentially vast market on the Asian mainland proved irresistible. By 1985, China had become Japan's second-leading trading partner behind the United States. These important commercial ties were matched by strong financial connections as well: Japan supplied about half the foreign credits that

China received from 1979 to 1983. Japanese direct investment in China soared from $100 million in 1985 to $2.2 billion in 1987.

After Japan, China's other great economic partner throughout the 1980s was the United States. Though the value of Sino-American trade remained half that of Sino-Japanese trade in that decade, the economic links between the two countries came to overshadow their common strategic interest as the Russian threat to both began to subside. Sino-American trade increased from a paltry $375 million in 1977—before the advent of the Deng export strategy—to $2.3 billion in 1979 and 5 billion in 1980. Exploiting its comparative advantage of abundant, cheap labor—Chinese wages averaged $.60 an hour, compared to $12 in Japan and $20 in the United States—China proceeded in the course of the 1980s to replace the East Asian Tigers as America's major supplier of low-cost clothing and textile products. The four most valuable commodities that the United States supplied to China during the 1980s were food from the American midwest, capital, technology, and managerial and technical skills. By 1988, U.S. firms had investment commitments totaling over $3 billion in nearly four-hundred joint ventures situated in the special economic zones on the southern coast. Unlike the first wave of quick-profit-seeking entrepreneurs of the 1970s, these U.S. businesses had invested for the long haul: A typical example is the set of contracts concluded with U.S. oil companies in the early 1980s to develop China's vast offshore oil reserves. By 1982 oil and oil products already accounted for 21 percent of China's exports. By 1988 China had become, with the help of U.S. and Japanese direct investment, the world's fifth-largest petroleum producer. In total, China attracted more than $7 billion of direct foreign investment from 1979 to 1987 at a time when the flow of private foreign capital to other developing countries had virtually dried up.

China's policy of acquiring foreign technology underwent a significant transformation after 1978. During the fifties, as we have seen, China had imported such technology as it received in the form of complete sets of equipment from the Soviet Union, largely in heavy industries such as metallurgy, electric power, and chemicals. The cutoff of Soviet technology deliveries after the Sino-Soviet split during the sixties thrust the country back on its own meager technological resources. Then the new opening to the capitalist world in the early seventies resulted in an expansion of foreign purchases, but the absence of a suitable infrastructure and inadequately trained managerial and technical personnel prevented China from adequately absorbing these technology imports. During the eighties China abandoned the old practice of importing complete plants in favor of a more discriminating strategy of acquiring key technologies and selected equipment through licensing agreements and joint ventures from the United States, Japan, and the European Community. The long-term goal was gradually to reduce dependence on foreign sources and establish a domestic technological base.

One of the principal impediments to the successful application of technology imports in China, in addition to the inadequate infrastructure, was the shortage of managerial and technical expertise. The decadence of the Chinese educational system, aggravated by the outburst of anti-intellectualism during the Cultural Revolution of the sixties, left China with a woefully insufficient supply of scientists, engineers, technicians, and managers to participate in the bold project of economic modernization that Deng had launched. Its only recourse was the acquisition of skills abroad. Between 1978 and 1988, almost 50,000 Chinese students were dispatched to foreign universities (two-thirds of them located in the United States) to learn subjects and techniques that were inadequately taught at home. The return of these educated young people proved to be a mixed blessing for the authorities in Beijing, however. While they had acquired the skills and training that were desperately needed by Chinese industry, they had been exposed to Western cultural influences and political ideas as well. The appearance on the streets of Chinese cities of women with makeup, young men in blue jeans, and teenagers of both genders with a taste for rock music, drugs, premarital sex, and other "Western" practices clashed with the puritanical ethic of Maoism that still prevailed in spite of the revolutionary economic innovations of the eighties. More seriously, the democratic principles that Chinese students had absorbed in the United States and Western Europe threatened to undermine the authoritarian, one-party system that continued to operate in China.

In addition to seeking bilateral loans and direct investments from the countries of the developed world, Dengist China also sought assistance from the various multinational organizations that ministered to the financial needs of the Third World. China joined the IMF in 1980 and promptly borrowed funds from that organization to finance its balance of payments deficits. In the same year it joined the World Bank and began to obtain loans for long-term development projects. In 1986 Beijing applied for formal membership in GATT, which would bring greater access to foreign markets, but also the obligation to disclose domestic economic practices to intrusive officials. China's increasing interest in cooperating with these three Western-dominated international organizations, which had long been denounced by the Maoist leadership as instruments of imperialist hegemony, signified its avid participation in the capitalist world order.

It also represented China's abandonment of the other developing nations in the Third World, whose interests it had championed against the superpowers in the Maoist years. By the end of the 1970s China had terminated its own economic assistance program to developing countries and was soon, as we have seen, competing with them for loans, aid, and direct investments from international agencies as well as Western banks and corporations. China's per capita GNP of $280 in the mid-1980s placed it 130th among the world's 169 countries. Yet the post-Mao leadership had decisively rejected the neo-Marxist dependency theory embraced by many intellectual defenders of Third World interests, which promoted national self-reliance and isolation from the world capitalist system. It had also repudiated the radical concept of the global transfer of wealth from north to south associated with the New International Economic Order. Instead, it had unconditionally embraced the familiar Western liberal model of national economic development through global interdependence, the international division of labor, and the pursuit of comparative advantage, which dictated fuller integration with (rather than isolation from or the radical restructuring of) the international trading and financial system.

The record of China's economic achievement during the 1980s was an impressive one: Its foreign trade grew from $38.6 billion in 1980 to almost $80 billion in 1987, with petroleum and petroleum products as well as textiles and clothing representing the major earners of foreign exchange. China's growth rates during the eighties surpassed those of the Asian Tigers. China also possessed a useful trump card that could be played in the future contest for economic primacy in Asia. This was its lavish endowment of raw materials and energy supplies, which represented a significant advantage over resource-poor competitors such as Japan and the Tigers. In any case, the long-slumbering giant of Asia had awakened, with incalculable consequences for its neighbors and the world.

As China began its radical *economic* reorientation in the late 1970s, it simultaneously pursued new *diplomatic* and *security* policies that also diverged sharply from past practices. In the diplomatic realm, Deng Xiaoping decisively abandoned Mao's doctrine equating both superpowers as China's adversaries in favor of a full-fledged rapprochement with the United States in the face of what he perceived as the greater threat from Moscow. The arrest in 1976 and the trial and imprisonment in 1980 of the so-called Gang of Four (which included Mao's widow Jiang Qing and three associates) signified Deng's triumph over the faction within the Chinese ruling elite that opposed the opening to the West. Evidence of Beijing's increasing diplomatic cooperation with Washington had already become evident in Africa, where it joined the United States and South Africa in support of an anti-Communist insurgency against the Soviet-backed government in Angola in 1975–76, backed the U.S. and French efforts to rescue the pro-Western Mobutu regime in Zaire in 1977–78 from a Soviet-supported insurrection, and denounced Cuba's military interventions in a number of African states.

At the end of 1978 Deng Xiaoping achieved a long-awaited political break-through that confirmed the new direction of Chinese foreign policy. This was the announcement on December 15, 1978, by President Carter that formal diplomatic relations between the United States and China would begin on January 1, 1979, and that the United States-Taiwan Defense Treaty of 1954 would expire a year beyond that date. Thereafter, the only security link between Washington and Taipei, those two old partners in the war against communism in Asia, would consist of the sale by the United States of defensive weaponry. While this agreement represented a major compromise on the part of the United States, it also signified a moderation of China's policy toward Taiwan. Though not explicitly renouncing the right to employ force to reacquire its way-ward province, Beijing increasingly appealed to Taipei for peaceful reconciliation on the basis of respect for the island's special economic practices.

The alignment of American and Chinese foreign policies in Africa and the establishment of diplomatic relations between Washington and Beijing set the stage for close U.S.-Chinese cooperation in Asia in the face of two developments that appeared to tip the balance of power in the region in favor of their common Soviet adversary. The first was the increasingly antagonistic activities of the recently reunified Communist state of Vietnam.* Throughout the year 1978, China's relations with its erstwhile ally against "American imperialism" in Asia had steadily deteriorated. The ostensible cause of this friction was the plight of the substantial Chinese minority in Vietnam, which was heavily concentrated in urban areas and predominated among the merchant classes. The combination of ethnic antagonism, socioeconomic resentment, and the suspicion that the Chinese nationals constituted a sort of fifth column to promote Beijing's interests in Vietnam prompted Hanoi to wage a harsh campaign to relocate many of the Chinese urban dwellers to the countryside after confiscating their property. This policy understandably elicited sharp protests from Deng on behalf of his maltreated compatriots.

But beneath the veneer of humanitarian concern for the plight of ethnic Chinese in Vietnam lay the more deeply felt fear of encirclement by the Soviet Union and what Bei-

---

*North and South Vietnam were reunified in April 1976, a year after the defeat of the U.S.-backed regime in Saigon (which was promptly renamed Ho Chi Minh City).

jing had increasingly come to regard as Moscow's client state in Hanoi. In spite of China's loyal support and military assistance during the war with the United States, Vietnam had taken several steps throughout 1978 to affirm its allegiance to the Soviet Union. In June, Hanoi obtained membership in the Soviet-controlled economic association Comecon, which prompted the retaliatory termination of all Chinese economic and technical assistance to Vietnam. In November it signed a treaty of friendship with Moscow, which provided for the stationing of Soviet air and naval units in the country. Reassured by these gestures of support from the Kremlin, Vietnam proceeded to launch a military invasion of its newly established Communist neighbor Cambodia (renamed Kampuchea) in December 1978. The purpose of the armed offensive, which succeeded in short order, was the overthrow of the Chinese-backed regime of the Khmer Rouge dictator Pol Pot and the installation of a Vietnamese puppet government in Phnom Penh. Hanoi's bid for regional hegemony on the Indochinese peninsula confronted Beijing with an aggressive, hostile neighbor to the south allied with adversary number one to the north, with its massive troop buildup and SS-20 missiles targeted on Chinese sites. China retaliated by dispatching its own military forces across the frontier into Vietnam in February 1979 to "teach the Vietnamese a lesson," before withdrawing them a couple of months later with the lesson still unlearned and Vietnamese units still occupying Cambodia.

The Vietnamese invasion of Cambodia reinforced the increasingly cooperative diplomatic relationship between Washington and Beijing. When Pol Pot and his Khmer Rouge followers retreated from Phnom Penh to harass the Vietnamese client government from guerrilla bases in the countryside, the United States and China jointly recognized him as the legitimate leader of Cambodia and sent him military supplies through Thailand, even in the face of mounting evidence that his regime had perpetrated grisly acts of genocide against its own population after its accession in 1975 that resulted in over a million deaths.

The second important source of cohesion in the budding partnership between Washington and Beijing was the Soviet invasion of Afghanistan at the end of 1979* which aggravated Chinese fears of Soviet encirclement as well as American anxieties about the security of oil reserves in the Persian Gulf. The two governments cooperated in supplying the anti-Soviet resistance within Afghanistan via Pakistan and coordinated a tough diplomatic campaign in various world forums—including a boycott of the 1980 Olympic Games in Moscow—to pressure Moscow to withdraw.

The advent of the Reagan administration in 1981 introduced a discordant note in the Sino-American relationship concerning the issue of Taiwan. During his presidential campaign candidate Reagan had denounced Carter for abandoning America's trusted anti-Communist ally, Taipei, and talked of restoring normal diplomatic relations with that government.† In June 1981 President Reagan appeared to reverse the Carter policy of disengagement from Taiwan by authorizing the sale of defensive military equipment to the island, prompting an angry rejoinder from Beijing. But Reagan's anti-Soviet geopolitical

---

*See page 357.

†The Taiwan Relations Act, passed by the U.S. Congress in 1979 as formal diplomatic relations were severed by President Carter, preserved an awkward kind of informal connection with the island by establishing an American Institute on Taiwan staffed by U.S. foreign service officers on temporary leave.

objectives eventually overshadowed his sentimental attachment to the old Nationalist Chinese stronghold on Formosa. A compromise arrangement was reached in August 1982 prescribing a gradual reduction of American military aid to Taiwan in exchange for Beijing's pledge to pursue its long-term goal of reunification through peaceful means. In 1986 President Chiang Ching-kuo, Chiang Kai-shek's son and heir, authorized unprecedented visits to the mainland for family reunions, and by the following year Chinese trade with Taiwan (mainly through Hong Kong) had surpassed $1 billion in value.

An intriguing precedent for the peaceful reunification of China and Taiwan was suggested by the agreement concluded between Beijing and London in September 1984 concerning the political future of Hong Kong. The pact specified that the old British crown colony would revert to Chinese sovereignty in 1997, but as a special administrative region enjoying a high degree of autonomy (including its own separate, fully convertible currency) as well as the prerogative of retaining its capitalist economic system for at least fifty years after its absorption.* The People's Republic stood to gain many advantages from a satisfactory resolution of the question of Hong Kong's future. By the end of the 1980s, the thriving little city-state had become China's largest trading partner, the entrepôt for over 10 percent of its exports, and a valuable source of foreign exchange in the form of remittances from Hong Kong Chinese to relatives in the People's Republic.

China's conciliatory effort to promote a peaceful annexation of the two Asian Tigers Hong Kong and Taiwan was paralleled by a marked improvement in its relations with the rest of non-Communist Asia. In an attempt to court the states of ASEAN, Beijing reduced its ties to Communist insurgent groups in Thailand, Malasia, and the Philippines, and cooperated with Thailand in supplying aid to the Cambodian resistance during the Vietnamese occupation. Most importantly, China's expanding trade relationship with Japan during the early eighties was reinforced by a diplomatic entente based on a shared concern about the Soviet military and naval buildup in the Far East and joint support for ASEAN's diplomatic initiative to persuade Vietnam to evacuate Cambodia. The Sino-Japanese rapprochement was not immune to the resurgence of ethnic animosity based on historical memories, however. In 1985 Japanese Prime Minister Yasuhiro Nakasone infuriated Chinese officials with a ceremonial visit to a cemetery for Second World War Japanese soldiers, and a year later Education Minister Fujio Masayuki was forced to resign after some ill-chosen remarks minimizing Japan's wartime atrocities in China.

But these atavistic outbursts did not disturb Sino-Japanese relations for very long. Likewise, though some friction between Washington and Beijing continued over such issues as the residual Cold War restrictions on technology transfer, U.S. textile protectionism, Chinese arms sales to various Middle Eastern regimes and staunch support for the Palestinian cause, and China's human rights abuses, the Sino-American rapprochement appeared firmly established by the mid-1980s on the basis of mutually beneficial economic ties as well as a modest amount of diplomatic coordination, military cooperation, and sharing of intelligence on Soviet military activities.

---

*In 1987 an agreement concerning the Portuguese territory of Macao prescribed its annexation by China at the end of 1999.

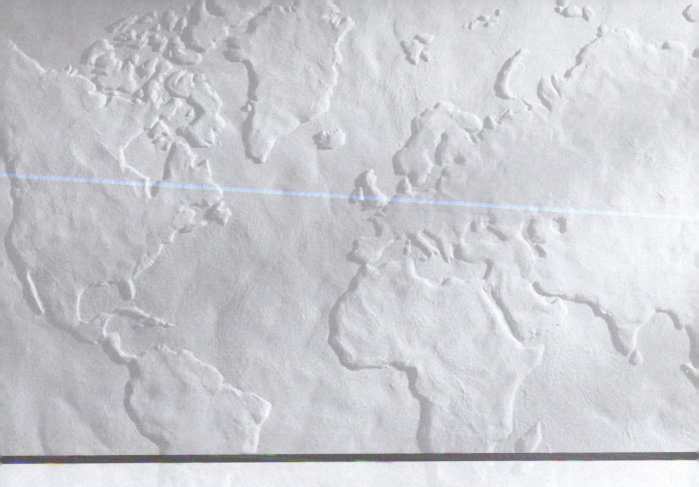

Part Three FROM COLD WAR TO NEW WORLD DISORDER (1985–2005)

16

MOSCOW, WASHINGTON, AND THE END OF THE SOVIET EMPIRE

The most significant development during the second half of the 1980s and the early 1990s was the definitive and entirely unanticipated end of the Cold War and the disappearance of the Soviet Union from the world scene. While it is fashionable in certain scholarly circles to deemphasize the significance of individuals as causal agents of historical change, it would be difficult to deny that these two events were both a direct consequence of the policies inaugurated by the man who became the general secretary of the Communist party of the Soviet Union in 1985. Unlike his predecessors, Mikhail Gorbachev had developed an appreciation of two uncomfortable realities about the Union of Soviet Socialist Republics. The first was that the deterioration of its economic system during the Brezhnev years had gravely imperiled that nation's capability of exercising power and influence in the world proportionate to its enormous size and population. The second was that the huge and ever-increasing technological advantage enjoyed by the United States vis-à-vis the Soviet Union ensured that the former country would prevail in the bilateral arms race—nuclear and conventional—that had been renewed after the brief period of detente in the 1970s.

Accordingly, the new Soviet leader resorted to the only policy that offered a possible solution to the twin problems of economic decline and military vulnerability: the quest for a settlement of all of his country's outstanding political disputes with its adversaries in the Western camp, particularly with the other superpower. The comparatively stable international environment resulting from such a settlement would permit the Soviet Union to redirect its limited internal resources to his pet project: a set of wide-ranging socioeconomic reforms including decentralization of decision making in industry and the introduction of free market practices to stimulate productivity in the consumer goods sector to improve the lives of the long-suffering Soviet population. In order to win popular support for this bold program of economic renovation Gorbachev simultaneously pressed for political reforms designed to permit greater public participation in the political life of the nation. This new political openness, or *glasnost,* accompanied economic restructur-

The first summit meeting between President Ronald Reagan (1911–2004) and General Secretary Mikhail Gorbachev (1931–), Geneva, November 19, 1985: Despite his antipathy for communism and the "Evil Empire," Reagan developed a good working relationship with the new Soviet leader. The result would be breathtaking breakthroughs in strategic arms control negotiations between the two superpowers during Reagan's second term. *(National Archives)*

ing, or *perestroika,* in a Soviet Union that had to be fundamentally reformed in order to assure its survival.

The first dramatic instance of Gorbachev's campaign to improve Soviet-American relations occurred in the most complex and dangerous area of superpower rivalry—the arms race. During the first half of the 1980s, the Reagan administration had undertaken a massive military buildup in virtually every category of weaponry: the deployment of intermediate-range nuclear weapons in Western Europe, the continued search for a suitable delivery system for the MX ICBM missile, the expansion of research and development on the space-based antimissile defense system designated as the Strategic Defense Initiative (SDI), the application of new technologies to the conventional defense capability of NATO, and the plan to create a six hundred-ship navy by the end of the eighties. Confronted with the impossible task of matching this stunning military buildup with his country's meager technological assets, Gorbachev desperately sought to negotiate an end to a military competition that could only exacerbate the internal economic crisis of his country. President Reagan, facing a huge budget deficit caused by the U.S. attempt to combine increased military spending with reduced taxation and squeezed by a congressional resolution requiring budgetary balance, proved receptive to Gorbachev's overtures. Consequently, the stalled arms control negotiations were resumed in 1985 at the behest of the two leaders.

At a summit conference in Reykyavik, Iceland, in October 1986, Reagan and Gorbachev—without any prior consultation with their respective allies—came to the verge of endorsing a remarkable proposal that would have abolished all ballistic missiles and possibly set the stage for total nuclear disarmament. But while this Utopian scheme came to naught, the two sides did make substantial progress on the more circumscribed issue of intermediate-range nuclear forces in Europe. In February 1987, Gorbachev agreed for the first time to consider the INF matter separately from the rest of the comprehensive arms control package that he had been promoting. Finally, after almost a year of intensive diplomacy, the two leaders signed a historic agreement in Washington on December 8, 1987, which eliminated all intermediate-range nuclear forces (that is, ground-based missiles with ranges from 500 to 5,500 kilometers) from the European theater. This agreement, which resembled Reagan's original proposal for a "zero option" in 1981, represented a significant compromise on the part of the Kremlin in a number of areas. First of all, it had abandoned its demand that the abolition of INF in Europe be accompanied by the termination of the SDI, which Moscow regarded as a potentially devastating threat to its strategy of nuclear deterrence. Second, Gorbachev agreed to the destruction of all of the 851 launchers and 1,836 missiles by the end of 1991 compared to the 283 launchers and 867 missiles that the United States had deployed in Western Europe. Third, he agreed to eliminate not only the Soviet SS-20 missiles located in the European part of the country, but also those deployed in Asia, thereby allaying the concerns of the country on which those missiles had been targeted: the People's Republic of China. Finally, the Kremlin broke with past practice by accepting an extremely intrusive verification procedure, which prescribed the exchange of extensive information about nuclear forces and on-site inspections to prevent violations of the pact.

The INF treaty was the first arms control agreement in a decade. While it removed only about one-fifth of the existing nuclear weapons in the world, it represented a significant departure from the cautious, incremental approach of arms control negotiations in the seventies. Unlike the two previous treaties dealing with strategic nuclear forces (SALT I and SALT II), the INF pact stipulated the elimination of an entire category of nuclear weapons instead of merely limiting the continued growth of existing forces. The Washington summit that produced the INF treaty also drew the broad outline of a strategic arms limitation agreement, which had eluded negotiators ever since the two superpowers resumed the stalled SALT process under the new designation START (Strategic Arms Reduction Talks) in 1982. After nine years of arduous negotiations, it fell to Reagan's successor in the White House, George H. W. Bush, to sign jointly with Gorbachev the historic agreement for strategic arms control in July 1991. The START treaty placed strict quantitative restrictions on ballistic missile warheads and launchers, required deep reductions in the highly accurate land-based ICBMs, and (like the INF treaty) provided for intrusive verification procedures. The practical effect of these various provisions was to reduce U.S. and Soviet strategic nuclear forces by about 30 percent. While the exclusion of certain strategic weapons systems from the START agreement—such as ICBMs equipped with Multiple Independently Targetable Reentry Vehicles (MIRV) and Sea-Launched Cruise Missiles (SLCM)—left lots of work for future negotiators, the arms race in strategic nuclear weapons had decelerated significantly by the beginning of the 1990s.

In the meantime both sides had announced a number of unilateral cuts in spending on conventional arms. The budget that President Reagan submitted to the Congress in early 1988 sacrificed the goal of a 600-ship navy that he had once enthusiastically endorsed. In a major speech at the United Nations in December 1988, Gorbachev announced a substantial cut in Soviet military forces to be completed by 1991. Much progress was also recorded in the reduction of conventional forces in Europe. The Mutual and Balanced Force Reduction (MBFR) talks between NATO and the Warsaw Pact had made no progress since 1973 because of Moscow's refusal to sacrifice its superiority in conventional military forces on the continent. In March 1989, these fruitless exchanges were replaced by a new negotiating forum known as the Conventional Armed Forces in Europe (CFE) talks. After only twenty months of negotiations, the twenty-two members of the two alliance systems signed the CFE Treaty on November 19, 1990. This agreement established a balance of conventional forces in Europe by requiring the Soviet Union to remove a large proportion of its tanks, armored vehicles, aircraft, helicopters, and artillery from the region west of the Ural Mountains.

But the achievements in the talks on mutual conventional arms reductions between the two military blocs in Europe were rendered moot by a spectacular series of political developments on the eastern half of the continent. As had been the case with Khrushchev's anti-Stalinist campaign in 1956, Gorbachev's denunciation of Brezhnev and his attempts to introduce economic and political reforms in the Soviet Union undermined the position of the hard-line, orthodox Communist bosses in Eastern Europe while inspiring reform-minded citizens to contest their authority. But the difference between 1956 and 1989 lay in the attitude of the Kremlin toward the satellites. Whereas Khrushchev had regarded them as indispensable allies against NATO, Gorbachev had come to view them as liabilities that received enormous economic benefits from the U.S.S.R. (in the form of trade subsidies, loans, cheap energy, and raw materials) while giving little in return. In light of the successful arms control negotiations with the West, their strategic value to Moscow became less apparent. Consequently, when the populations of Eastern Europe repudiated their Communist leaders in the course of the year 1989, they were able to do so without fear of a repetition of Hungary's experience in 1956 or Czechoslovakia's in 1968. On the contrary, Gorbachev actually appeared to look with favor on the revolutionary political changes that swept Eastern Europe as the 1980s came to a close.

The pace of change in the East bloc in 1989 was truly breathtaking, as the Soviet satellites cashiered their Communist leadership in rapid succession. Poland, with a popular and powerful labor movement (Solidarity) and an influential religious institution (the Catholic church) independent of government control, had the easiest time of it. In January 1989 the government of General Wojciech Jaruzelski, which had declared martial law in 1981 and outlawed the Solidarity movement, agreed to talks with the banned labor organization to resolve the country's serious economic and political problems. In the spring, Solidarity's status as an opposition party was legalized, and in the free elections held in June, its candidates won an overwhelming victory. In August, Tadeusz Mazowiecki, a staunch Catholic and Solidarity member, became prime minister of the first coalition government in the East bloc in forty-one years. He promptly introduced a number of free market economic reforms aimed at dismantling the Communist system of centralized government control.

In the meantime, the Hungarian parliament had authorized the formation of opposition parties in January 1989. Within a few months a special commission appointed by the Communist party had redefined the 1956 revolution as "a popular uprising against an oligarchic rule that had debased the nation"; Imre Nagy, the prime minister in 1956 who had been overthrown and executed by the Soviets, was publicly praised; and the closed frontier with Austria was thrown open. In January 1990, the Hungarian government requested the removal of all Soviet forces from the country, which Gorbachev agreed in March of the following year to complete by the summer of 1991. In Czechoslovakia the threat of a nationwide strike in the fall of 1989 forced the resignation of the hard-line president Gustav Husak in December 1989; he was replaced by the country's most renowned dissident, the playwright Vaclav Havel. In an act pregnant with historical symbolism, the Czechoslovak parliament elected as its speaker the elderly Alexander Dubček, whose political and economic reforms during the "Prague Spring" of 1968 had led to the Soviet military intervention in the summer. Like the Hungarians, the Czechoslovaks requested and received from Moscow the assurance that all Soviet troops would be withdrawn from their country by the summer of 1991.

The two Soviet satellites whose Communist ruling elites staunchly resisted change were Romania and the German Democratic Republic. The Romanian dictator, Nicolae Ceausescu, refused all compromise, even as his allies in the Warsaw Pact submitted to the sweeping domestic transformation mentioned above. But the revolutionary tide flowing through Eastern Europe could not be stopped, even in Ceausescu's retrograde police state. Facing hostile demonstrations on the streets of Bucharest in December 1989, the Romanian strongman tried to crush the insurrection but was caught and executed. As Ceausescu's counterpart in East Germany, Erich Honecker, attempted in vain to organize the forces of repression in that country, tumultuous street demonstrations demanding radical reform broke out in several East German cities. The opening of the Hungarian frontier with Austria in September 1989 enabled East German citizens to escape to the West, which they proceeded to do in large numbers. Within a month the ailing Honecker had resigned, and on November 9 his successor lifted all travel restrictions to the West and, in a historic act, opened the Berlin Wall that had been erected thirty-eight years earlier to dam the torrent of émigrés from the East German state. In free elections held on March 18, 1990, a center-right coalition won almost half of the votes, against 22 percent for a center-left group, and only 16 percent for the renamed remnant of the old Socialist Unity (Communist) party that had ruled the country for forty years. In April the parliament of the German Democratic Republic created a democratically elected government in the form of a coalition dominated by the center-right bloc aligned with the ruling Christian Democratic party in West Germany.

But the opening of the Berlin Wall, the collapse of the Communist regime, and the first free elections in East Germany unleashed a new political force that few observers had anticipated. Many of the East German refugees who streamed into the Federal Republic, as well as their compatriots who had remained behind to march in the streets against the Communist regime, openly expressed the long-deferred goal of many Germans on both sides of the Iron Curtain: the reunification of the two German states. By the time of the East German elections in March 1990, all of the major political groups in both German

President Reagan speaking at the Berlin Wall with East Berlin's Brandenburg Gate in the background, June 12, 1987: Appearing to mark the 750th anniversary of the divided city, the American president demanded: "Mr. Gorbachev, open this gate! Mr. Gorbachev, tear down this wall!" These words, which received hearty cheers from the audience of West Berliners, could be heard by some East Berliners as well. At the time, no one dreamed that the gate would be opened and the wall torn down less than three years later. *(National Archives)*

states had endorsed the cause. With the disintegration of the East German political apparatus and the decline of the Socialist Unity (Communist) party, the very raison d'être of the German Democratic Republic had vanished: The state had been created by the Soviet military occupation force and its ruling Communist elite had remained in power at the behest of the Kremlin. Once liberated from the fear of Soviet military intervention and political repression by the Communist apparatus, the populace of East Germany eagerly embraced the cause of reunification in the hope of reaping the economic and political benefits that would presumably flow from citizenship in a single Germany dominated by the capitalist, democratic institutions of the West. Conversely, the citizens of the Federal Republic had harbored the sentimental aspiration to be reunited with their compatriots in the east since 1949, when the goal of German unity had been enshrined in the constitution of the West German state.

The issue of German reunification introduced two complications in the otherwise smooth process of European detente that had unfolded at the end of the eighties. First of all, West German Chancellor Helmut Kohl's hesitation in formally recognizing the Oder-

Neisse Line as the eastern frontier of a reunited Germany prompted understandable concern in Poland that its newly acquired independence from the Soviet Union would be threatened by the revival of old territorial disputes with Germany. Second, Bonn's insistence (in concert with its partners in the Atlantic Alliance) that a reunified Germany be permitted to retain membership in NATO rather than (as demanded by the Soviet Union) reverting to neutrality generated serious misgivings in Moscow. But once Kohl accepted the permanence of the eastern frontiers and Gorbachev recognized that a united Germany within NATO would represent less of a menace to Soviet security than a united Germany cut loose from the constraints associated with alliance membership, the anxieties of Germany's neighbors dissipated. Consequently, after a round of negotiations among representatives of the two German states and the four foreign powers that enjoyed residual occupation rights (the United States, Great Britain, the Soviet Union, and France), the legal basis for German reunification was laid. On October 3, 1990, the frontier markers that had separated the two German states since 1949 were removed, and the most visible symbol of the Cold War had passed into history. With the disappearance of East Germany and the repudiation of communism and Moscow's authority by the remaining East European states, the dissolution of the Soviet-led trading system Comecon in June 1991 and of the Warsaw Pact in July came as no surprise.

Even before the collapse of the Soviet Union's satellite system in Eastern Europe, Gorbachev had begun to scale back Soviet military and political commitments abroad. He moved first to cut his country's losses in the costly war in Afghanistan, which had dragged on since 1979 with victory nowhere in sight, owing to the tenacious resistance of the Muslim mujahideen armed by the United States and China via Pakistan. In early 1988 the Kremlin announced that all Soviet troops would be withdrawn within ten months, regardless of the fate of the Soviet-installed puppet regime in Kabul, and in February 1989 the last retreating Soviet soldier crossed the frontier.

Gorbachev's abandonment of Afghanistan was soon followed by a settlement of the other conflict in Asia that had poisoned relations between Moscow on the one hand and Washington and Beijing on the other since the late 1970s. In December 1988 the new ruling elite in Hanoi, under persistent prodding from its Soviet patron, announced a major troop withdrawal from Cambodia. By the summer of 1989 most of the Vietnamese units had returned home, leaving the Hanoi-installed government in Phnom Penh to its own devices in its civil war with the rebel coalition, which included the Khmer Rouge organization. In the meantime the U.S.S.R. began to withdraw its naval and air forces from Cam Ranh Bay in Vietnam and in 1990 announced a major withdrawal of ground troops and a sharp reduction in economic assistance to its old ally. The leaders in Hanoi followed in Gorbachev's footsteps by renouncing the centralized economic planning learned from the Soviet Union in favor of a market-based economy and began to solicit Western investment.

As East-West rivalries in Asia dissipated, long-standing disputes between U.S. and Soviet surrogates in Africa were terminated by skillful diplomacy. In December 1988 South Africa agreed to a cease-fire with the SWAPO rebel organization in Namibia and consented to a UN-supervised election there in exchange for the phased withdrawal of the 53,000 Cuban troops stationed in neighboring Angola by July 1991. After winning the Namibia elections in November 1989, SWAPO leader Sam Nujoma was installed in March 1990 as its first president after having encouraged white businessmen and farmers to remain in the country. Meanwhile, the withdrawal of all South African military forces from Angola in late November 1989, together with the evacuation of Cuban troops that had been protecting the Marxist MPLA government in that country, set the stage for negotiations to terminate the civil war in the former Portuguese colony. In the meantime, the Soviet-American proxy war on the Horn of Africa petered out as Washington and Moscow left their clients in the region, Somalia and Ethiopia, respectively, to fend for themselves. In 1991 Ethiopia's strongman, Mengistu Haile Mariam, and Somalia's dictator, Mohammed Siad Barre, succumbed to internal insurrections. Both left their countries in economic chaos and political anarchy.*

As the Soviet Union lost control of its satellite system in Eastern Europe and abandoned its clients in the Third World at the end of the 1980s, the internal political structure of the country itself began to unravel. Paradoxically, the severe crisis that Gorbachev confronted was exacerbated by the very political reforms that he had initiated: In June 1988 the Nineteenth Party Congress established a new Congress of People's Deputies, two-thirds of whose members would be selected by democratic means. The Supreme Soviet chosen from the freely elected Congress of People's Deputies in May 1989 provided the Soviet population with their first taste of genuine democracy. Grievances that had been ignored or suppressed in the pre-Gorbachev years became the subject of intense nationwide debate. The high expectations that had been stimulated by the new spirit of *glasnost* and *perestroika* were disappointed as the deteriorating political and economic conditions in the U.S.S.R. became apparent.

Signs of the economic decline of the Soviet Union were ubiquitous. Agricultural production had fallen far below government targets, oil and coal production declined, GNP dropped 2 percent in 1990 (the worst record since the Second World War), the foreign debt swelled, and trade deficits increased. In the summer of 1989, widespread strikes broke out in a number of cities in protest against severe shortages of basic consumer goods. Despite the government's efforts at fundamental economic reform, the fruits of *perestroika* scarcely represented an improvement over the "period of stagnation" under Brezhnev. In the meantime, long-suppressed nationalist discontent bubbled to the surface throughout 1990 in many of the non-Russian republics: ethnic strife between Christian Armenians and the Muslims of Azerbaijan in the Caucasus; rioting by Muslims in the Central Asian republics of Uzbekistan, Kazakhstan, and Tajikistan; declarations of independence or claims of political sovereignty by parliaments in Ukraine, Georgia, Armenia, and Moldavia. But the most vociferous resistance to Soviet authority came in the three Baltic states that had been annexed by the U.S.S.R. in 1940. The anti-Soviet government in Lithuania that came to power in March 1990 promptly declared its independence from the Soviet Union and instructing its young men to refuse to submit to Soviet military conscription. Within a few months, Latvia and Estonia had followed suit.

Reacting to these events, Gorbachev determined that the political disintegration of the Soviet system had gone far enough. In early 1991 Soviet military units intervened in the Baltic states, as Gorbachev, who had assumed the presidency in the previous year, appeared to align himself with those forces hostile to further reform (such as the army, the KGB, and the Communist party) that had formed the backbone of the old order he had

---

*See page 454.

overthrown. With the resignation of liberal Foreign Minister Eduard Shevardnadze in December 1990, the advocates of reform began to pin their hopes on another one of Gorbachev's disillusioned collaborators, Boris Yeltsin. After his selection by the Supreme Soviet of the Russian Republic as its chairman in May 1990, Yeltsin insistently pressed for increased democratization, the introduction of a market economy, and greater autonomy for the Soviet republics,including his own. His election as president of Russia by popular vote in June 1991 gave Yeltsin the mandate to push forward with his ambitious program of reform. He promptly announced plans to liberalize the Russian economy and took the ultimate step of banning the Communist Party. It was evident that what Yeltsin had in mind for the Russian Republic went far beyond the cautious proposals that had been emanating from Gorbachev in the Kremlin.

In the meantime the Soviet president's nimble balancing act between the entrenched ruling elite and the impatient advocates of structural reform had run its course. He had allied with the hard-liners by dispatching troops to the Baltics to smother the forces of ethnic nationalism that threatened the very existence of the Soviet Union. But Gorbachev's ploy to consolidate his authority by securing public endorsement of a reformed union backfired in March 1991, when only nine of the fifteen constituent republics participated in a nationwide referendum on the subject. Referenda in the three Baltic republics recorded huge majorities in favor of total independence, while Ukraine, Georgia, the Caucasus, the republics of Central Asia, and Russia itself seethed with secessionist discontent. By the summer of 1991 the three pillars of the Soviet system constructed by Lenin and Stalin in the early 1920s—the Communist Party, the command economy, and the multinational union—faced a formidable challenge from the emerging forces of democracy, free market capitalism, and ethnic nationalism. The man who had opened this Pandora's box by attempting to reform the Communist system from within without challenging its legitimacy was overtaken by events.

The embattled defenders of the old order struck back on August 19, 1991, in a desperate bid to reverse the course of recent Soviet history. A conspiracy involving the KGB, the army, and hard-liners within Gorbachev's own entourage detained the vacationing president in his Crimean villa, declared a six-month state of emergency, and formed an interim government under his conservative vice president, Gennady Yanaev. Within a few days the coup collapsed as a result of resolute action by Yeltsin, whose public opposition to the plot inspired massive public support and won over the rank and file of the military. Though Gorbachev returned to Moscow and attempted to reassume his presidential duties, the creaky system he had sought to prop up through internal reform was beyond repair. The new president of the Russian Republic became the man of the hour as the political institutions of Gorbachev's refurbished union rapidly disintegrated in the autumn of 1991. One by one, each of the constituent republics declared its independence, obtained foreign recognition, and applied for membership in the United Nations as a sovereign state. On December 21 eleven of the fifteen new nations formed a loose-knit association called the Commonwealth of Independent States to replace the Union of Soviet Socialist Republics. On December 25 Mikhail Gorbachev resigned the presidency of a political entity that had vanished from the world scene and retired to a life of lucrative leisure.

The collapse of the Soviet Union at the end of 1991 confronted the international community with a complex set of legal, political, and security dilemmas. Some were promptly and effortlessly resolved, as with the designation of Russia as the heir to the permanent Soviet seat on the United Nations Security Council. Two in particular proved to be far more challenging: The first was the question of the future disposition of the formidable stockpile of nuclear weapons that had accumulated in the Soviet Union during the Cold War. The second was the political status of the numerous ethnic minorities that resided within the frontiers of the newly independent states. For the next several years Yeltsin and his counterparts in a number of the non-Russian republics grappled with these two controversies as the outside world observed with intense interest.

The international community was understandably anxious about the fate of the nuclear warheads that remained in four of the former Soviet Republics—Russia, Belarus, Ukraine, and Kazakhstan—after the U.S.S.R. had ceased to exist at the end of 1991. This topic will be addressed in the section of the last chapter dealing with arms control and will not be reviewed here.* Suffice it to say that the sudden and unanticipated appearance of these new nuclear states, together with the initial uncertainty concerning the custody and control of the weapons of mass destruction that they had inherited from the Soviet Union, became a matter of utmost concern to the rest of the world during the first half of the 1990s. During the same period many of the fifteen Soviet successor states wrestled with internal threats to their stability caused by the explosive force of ethnic nationalism that had been released by the demise of the old multinational union. Adopting the same "divide and rule" strategy employed by the European powers in Africa in the age of imperial expansion, Stalin had drawn the internal administrative borders of the Soviet Union to ensure the presence of at least one large minority group within each republic. This patchwork of ethnically diverse subnational political units enabled the Kremlin to play one group off against another and prevented the emergence of a unified national consciousness within each region. The removal of Moscow's heavy hand resulted in an upsurge of acute ethnic antagonism between former subject peoples as they struggled to define and defend their national identity.

This was particularly evident in the Caucasus, which along with the Balkan peninsula was the historic intersection of Christianity and Islam at the southeastern gateway to Europe. The Christian Armenians inhabiting the enclave of Nagorno-Karabakh within Muslim Azerbaijan declined to recognize Azeri sovereignty and received diplomatic support and military aid from Armenia in their bid for secession. Georgia faced separatist challenges from the inhabitants of Abkhazia and South Ossetia, who sought unification with their northern brethren inside the Russian Federation. In the autumn of 1993 the new Georgian head of state, Gorbachev's former foreign minister Eduard Shevardnadze, had to request Russian military assistance to restore order amid spreading economic chaos and political unrest.

The Russian Federation itself, which had been formed in March 1992, was buffeted by ethnic tensions all along its Caucasian frontier. The Ingush and North Ossetes violently disputed the border between them. The Muslim inhabitants of Chechnya, a mountainous region that had been annexed by the tsars in the 1870s after a long and bloody guerrilla war, declared its independence as the Soviet Union disintegrated at the end of 1991. Yeltsin promptly dispatched military forces to reassert Moscow's authority, but the combination of stiff resistance from Chechen partisans and vocal opposition to the interven-

---

*See page 497.

tion within Russia compelled him to withdraw. After tolerating the de facto secession of the rebellious province for three years, the Russian president finally yielded to his advisers in the military and security services who warned that the loss of Chechnya's important oil reserves would seriously jeopardize Russian security interests in the northern Caucasus and embolden other non-Slavic minorities within the multiethnic Russian Federation to break away.

In December 1994 some forty thousand Russian infantrymen and hundreds of tanks poured into Chechnya in an effort to suppress the separatist rebellion led by President Dzhokar Dudayev. It took the disorganized, undisciplined Russian army two months to capture the Chechen capital of Grozny, which it later lost to returning Chechen forces. After a cease fire was negotiated in the summer of 1996, Russia lost de facto control of Chechnya. But the breakaway regime in Grozny failed to obtain international recognition as foreign powers, led by the United States, dismissed the conflict as an internal Russian affair. In 1999 Islamic militants in Chechnya crossed over into the neighboring Russian province of Dagestan to incite rebellion there and were accused by Russian authorities of organizing terrorist bombings in Moscow that killed several civilians. At the end of the year Russian military units again poured into the breakaway province to suppress the defiant Chechen resistance in Grozny. After Yeltsin was replaced by his protégé Vladimir Putin at the beginning of 2000, Moscow tightened the screws on Chechnya with the full support of Russian public opinion.

Beyond the combustible Caucasus, territorial disputes flared up all across the territory of the former Soviet Union. West of the Urals, Ukraine and Russia wrangled over control of the Crimean peninsula (including its strategically located Black Sea ports),* which had been transferred from Russian to Ukrainian sovereignty in the mid-fifties despite its Russian-speaking majority. Twelve million Russians residing in eastern Ukraine became restive under Kiev's rule. The Russians in Estonia and Latvia, who constitute 30 percent and 34 percent of the population, respectively, suffered discriminatory political treatment at the hands of their new Baltic masters and their vigorous protests evoked a sympathetic response in Moscow. In the former Soviet Republic of Moldavia (renamed Moldova after achieving independence in 1991), the Russian-speaking minority established a breakaway republic on a strip of territory east of the Dniester River in reaction to indications that the Romanian-speaking Moldovans were contemplating unification with Romania. Unable to reassert its authority east of the Dniester, the Moldovan government had to acquiesce in the presence of a "peacekeeping" force in the form of the Russian Fourteenth Army, whose soldiers openly sided with their rebellious ethnic brethren. Though an agreement was reached in 1994 for a phased Russian withdrawal over three years, the circumstances surrounding the establishment and preservation of the "Dniester Republic" reflected Moscow's apparent willingness to protect the interests of the Russian diaspora in the Soviet successor states.

Ethnic tensions also boiled over in the five newly independent republics of Central Asia: Kazakhstan, Kyrgyzstan (formerly Kirghizia), Tajikistan, Turkmenistan (formerly

---

*Russia claimed title to the Black Sea fleet based in the Crimean (hence Ukrainian) ports of Sevastapol and Odessa. An agreement was finally signed in the spring of 1997 which divided the fleet between the two countries.

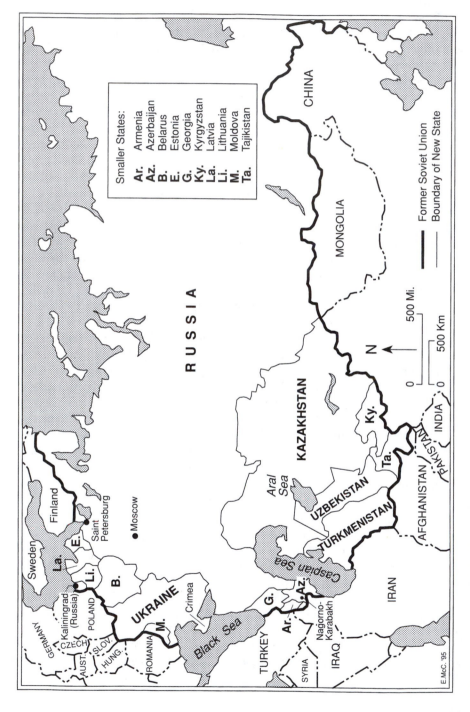

The Successor States of the Former Soviet Union

Turkmenia), and Uzbekistan. The disappearance of Soviet military power and Marxist-Leninist ideology from this region in the early 1990s had unleashed linguistic and religious forces that attracted the attention of ambitious regional powers intent on filling the vacuum. Turkey avidly courted the Turkic-speaking Kyrgyz, Turkmen, and Uzbeks, while Iran forged ties with the Persian-speaking Tajiks. The power of religion also exercised a potent influence on the post-Soviet destiny of Central Asia as a result of the final victory of the Muslim mujahideen over the Soviet-backed regime in nearby Afghanistan. After the departure of Soviet troops in February 1989 the Afghan government of Mohammed Najibullah clung to power for the next three years, profiting from the revival of ethnic and tribal rivalries that shattered the cohesion of the resistance movement. But the collapse of the Soviet Union at the end of 1991 sealed the fate of its puppet state in Kabul. In April 1992 the mujahideen seized control of the capital city and established an Islamic state in place of the defunct Marxist regime. The fall of Kabul gave inspiration to the Islamic movements that had sprouted in all five Central Asian republics to challenge the ex-Communist, secular ruling elites that retained political power after independence. Pakistan, the longtime patron of the Islamic resistance in Afghanistan, cultivated close links with the Islamic opposition in the Central Asian republics in the hope of replacing Russia as the dominant foreign influence in the region on the basis of a common devotion to the teachings of the Koran.

Incapable of coping with the growing domestic threat of Islamic fundamentalism (whose advocates often allied with pro-democracy opposition forces), the governments of the Central Asian republics appealed to Moscow for assistance in the autumn of 1992. Russian military units, operating under the aegis of the Commonwealth of Independent States in conjunction with troops dispatched by the secular government of Uzbekistan, intervened in Tajikistan at the request of that country's embattled regime. After ruthlessly crushing the opposition coalition in the winter of 1992–93, some twenty-five thousand Russian soldiers together with token forces from the other Central Asian republics remained on "peacekeeping" duty in Tajikistan to protect Moscow's traditional clients among the clans that ruled the country.

In the meantime, Afghanistan had begun a headlong slide into anarchy following the mujahideen's liberation of Kabul on April 25, 1992. The coalition of guerrilla organizations that had ousted the Soviet client regime rapidly degenerated into a bewildering array of ethnic and linguistic factions struggling for supremacy. The most important squabble pitted the Pashto-speaking Pashtuns of the southeast against a perpetually shifting alliance of rival linguistic and tribal groups to the north and west, including Persian-speaking Tajiks and Turkic-speaking Uzbeks. The mountainous country that had been long considered a convenient buffer between Russian Central Asia and whatever power dominated the Indian subcontinent appeared on the verge of disintegration along ethnic lines. The ongoing civil war in Afghanistan, which devastated its capital city from 1992 to 1995, predictably piqued the interest of aspiring regional powers once Moscow and Washington had washed their hands of the affair. Pakistan, Iran, and Uzbekistan sought to expand their influence by patronizing rival factions in the Afghan imbroglio.*

---

*See page 451.

The Central Asian Republics of the Former Soviet Union

Russia, concerned that the ethnic, linguistic, and religious turmoil in Afghanistan might infect the republics of Central Asia and even spill over its own southern frontier, prudently retained its peacekeeping forces in Tajikistan with the full support of its Central Asian clients. While Tajikistan was becoming a de facto Russian protectorate, Kazakhstan (the largest and most economically advanced of the five republics in the region) remained on exceedingly cordial terms with Moscow. The large number of Russian-speaking Slavs that had migrated there from European Russia actually outnumbered the indigenous Kazakhs and proudly clung to their linguistic and cultural identity. The Kazakh government felt obliged to accommodate its Russian-speaking economic elite lest it develop into a source of internal subversion. Compared to neighboring Afghanistan and the Caucasian countries across the Caspian Sea, the five Central Asian republics have collectively enjoyed a period of relative peace and stability since achieving independence from Moscow in 1991. This advantageous condition reflects Russia's interest in promoting pacification in the region without attempting to reassert its former authority.

The upsurge in nationalist agitation within and beyond the frontiers of Russia during the 1990s coincided with a severe economic crisis that gripped that newly sovereign country during its rapid and painful transition to a free market economy. Yeltsin and his team relentlessly pursued policies of economic liberalization such as the privatization of over half of the state enterprises, the legalization of land ownership, the reduction of government subsidies to inefficient firms, and the abolition of price controls that caused severe short-term dislocations in Russian society. The combination of raging inflation, declining production, speculation, corruption, and shortages of consumer goods eroded much of the goodwill that Yeltsin had accumulated in the aftermath of the 1991 coup and spawned a vociferous political opposition. This comprised an unlikely alliance between hard-line Communists opposed to his economic and political reforms and a new breed of Russian nationalists who deplored the decline of Russian power and prestige in the world. Throughout 1993 Yeltsin and his opponents waged an acrimonious political battle in the Russian parliament until September of that year, when the Russian president dissolved the legislative body, assumed emergency powers to defend his program of democratic political reform and economic liberalization, and announced new parliamentary elections to determine public sentiment. Later that month Yeltsin ordered a military assault on the parliament building where his political enemies, including his former vice president, General Alexander Rutskoi, and the speaker of the parliament, Ruslan Khasbulatov, had congregated to plot his political demise. The site of the parliament in flames and his opponents being led off to prison seemed to herald the definitive triumph of Yeltsin and his reformist program.

We have already seen that Russia had assumed a greater assertiveness in its relations with the non-Russian successor states. Many of the new republics welcomed the restoration of closer ties with Moscow. After the initial wave of postindependence euphoria it became evident that the dissolution of the Soviet Union had proved a mixed blessing for the non-Russian republics. Most suffered severe economic hardships as Moscow terminated the system of credits and subsidies to which they had become accustomed in the Soviet era. Others faced ethnic and religious threats to their stability and territorial integrity that they could not handle by themselves. Apart from the fiercely independent Baltics and Ukraine, the non-Russian successor states sought to strengthen their economic and security ties with Russia in order to cope more effectively with their daunting domestic difficulties and organize their national defense. The Russian military presence in Belarus, Georgia, Moldova, Tajikistan, and Turkmenistan with the approval of those governments, together with a military basing agreement with Armenia, served as reminders of Moscow's continuing influence beyond the frontiers of the Russian Federation. The initial response of the United States to the economic and political turbulence in its former Cold War adversary was generally supportive and sympathetic. American economists flocked to Moscow to advise the Kremlin on how to transform a command economy to the type of free market economic system that Yeltsin and his closest associates believed was the key to the country's future. The United States backed large loans from the International Monetary Fund to Russia in the aftermath of two severe crises that threatened the stability of the country, the first in 1994 following the failed coup against Yeltsin the previous year, the second in 1998 after a sharp decline in the value of the ruble amid widespread fears of a total economic collapse. For the remainder of his term Yeltsin pursued tough economic policies designed to stabilize the currency, combat inflation, reduce tax evasion, and continue the privatization of Russian industry. This behavior earned the Russian president high marks in Washington and guaranteed continuing U.S. support.

There were some sources of irritation in the Russian-American relationship in the decade after the collapse of the Soviet Union: Washington's decision to abrogate the Anti-Ballistic Missile Treaty and to pursue the National Missile Defense System, to expand NATO to include former members of the old Warsaw Pact, and to wage war against Russia's Slavic protégé Serbia over the conflict in Kosovo all generated resentment in Moscow. But these resentments did not lead to the reemergence of a powerful anti-American sentiment in Russia that would derail the rapprochement between the two countries. Conversely, U.S. public opinion was disapproving of the violations of human rights abuses in Chechnya and violent measures that Yeltsin employed at home to remain in power. But just as Washington had turned a blind eye to China's massacre of the demonstrators in Beijing's Tiananmen Square and its subsequent repression of dissent, the Clinton administration refrained from criticizing the Russian army's rough behavior in Chechnya and Yeltsin's decision to order artillery attacks against the Russian parliament during a dispute with his political adversaries in 1993. After Yeltsin abruptly resigned at the end of 1999 and turned over power to his hand-picked successor, the former KGB officer Vladimir Putin, Russian-American relations continued on an even keel. Neither the Russian army's continuing human rights abuses in Chechnya after the second conflict in that province began in 1999 nor Putin's repressive measures against the Russian press and his domestic political enemies in the early years of the twenty-first century elicited more than pro forma protests from Washington. As flawed as the Russian economic and political system appeared to Western observers, it was far preferable to the alternative of a resurrected communism or the type of aggressive Russian nationalism advocated by some figures on the extreme right. Washington's tolerance of Russia's repressive policies became even more pronounced under the George W. Bush administration after September 11, 2001. Putin shrewdly linked the Islamic rebels in Chechnya to the Islamic militants who had organized the attacks on New York and Washington and was welcomed by the White House as a loyal ally in the war against terrorism.

17

EUROPE: INTEGRATION AND DISINTEGRATION

THE RESURRECTION OF THE EUROPEAN IDEA

The unanticipated *disintegration* of the East European Communist bloc at the end of the 1980s coincided with the less sensational but equally significant progress toward *integration* on the part of the countries of Western Europe. The impulse toward West European economic cooperation that had originated with the Treaty of Rome in 1957 enjoyed a revival in the mid-1980s after many years of false starts and unfulfilled expectations. The Single European Act of 1986 stipulated that by the beginning of 1993 all barriers to the free movement of goods, services, capital, and labor among the twelve member states of the European Community* would be removed, enabling firms within the EC to reduce costs by expanding production to meet the demands of this enormous market of more than 380 million consumers. This revitalized campaign for European economic integration retained its momentum for the rest of the decade under the resolute leadership of the new president of the European Commission, Jacques Delors.† In the spring of 1989 he unveiled an ambitious plan for a European Monetary Union (EMU), which in the short term would coordinate exchange rates more effectively and in the long term was expected to serve as the nucleus of a European central bank that would issue a common currency.

---

*The original six signatories of the Treaty of Rome (France, Germany, Italy, Belgium, the Netherlands, and Luxembourg) plus Great Britain, Ireland, Denmark, Greece, Spain, and Portugal. The term European Community refers to the association of countries formed in 1967 from the European Economic Community, the European Coal and Steel Community, and the European Atomic Energy Community (Euratom).

†The European Commission, with its headquarters in Brussels, exercises the executive power of the European Community (later renamed the European Union). The European Parliament in Strasbourg constitutes the embryonic legislative body of the Community (Union).

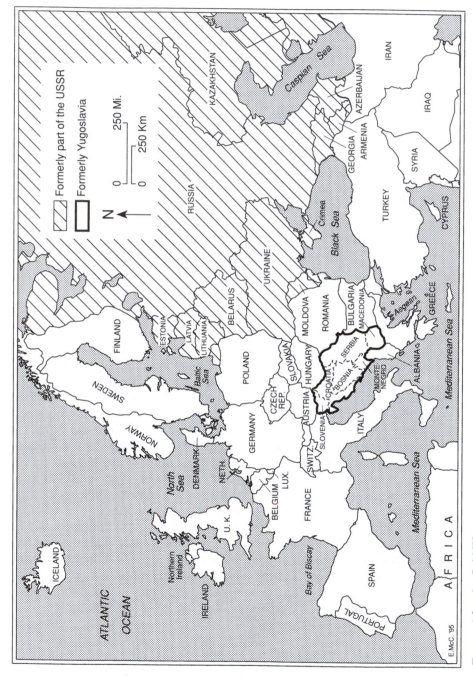

Europe After the Cold War

But the sudden and unexpected collapse of the Soviet empire in Eastern Europe, the end of the Cold War, and the unification of Germany in 1989–90 confronted the proponents of European unity with a novel set of challenges. Foremost among these was the question of the future relationship between the European Community and the former Soviet satellites. When the members of the recently defunct Comecon eagerly applied for membership in the EC, the governments of Western Europe were placed in an exceedingly embarrassing position. Did not the recently emancipated citizens of Budapest, Prague, and Warsaw, who avidly embraced the principles of political democracy and free market capitalism and proudly reaffirmed their historic links to the common cultural heritage of the West, deserve to participate in the emerging supranational European entity as much as their counterparts in London, Paris, and Berlin?

The recurrent question of enlarging the Community's membership had always provoked intense controversy, and the candidacy of the former Soviet satellites was no exception. Some member states feared that the precipitate admission of the untested, underdeveloped countries to the east would overburden the Community's institutions and sap its economic base. Others worried that their own products would encounter stiff competition from the exports from the low-wage East European states, which were eagerly redirecting their foreign trade from Russia to Western Europe. Though the EC promptly established the European Reconstruction Development Bank in December 1989 to provide emergency financial assistance to the fledgling democracies to the east, it hesitated to welcome them into the fold for the reasons summarized above. Instead, the West Europeans sought to placate them with a series of "association agreements" that prescribed the gradual removal of trade barriers over a ten-year period and vaguely alluded to the possibility of eventual membership,. But after turning the cold shoulder to the indigent refugees from Comecon, the European Community readily agreed to consider applications from the affluent members of the European Free Trade Association (Austria, Finland, Norway, and Sweden), which had emerged in 1960 as a rival to the old European Economic Community. Negotiations with those four countries began in 1993, and on January 1, 1995, all of them but Norway (whose voters rejected membership in a November 1994 referendum) formally joined the organization.

In the meantime the lengthy and laborious discussions among existing members to accelerate the progress of economic and political integration finally produced a landmark agreement in December 1991. The Treaty on European Union (or the Maastricht Treaty, as it came to be known after the Dutch city where its final provisions were worked out) formally endorsed the objective of a common European currency by 1999. The provision for monetary union, which concluded a decade-long behind-the-scenes skirmish among technocrats over the arcane details of managing exchange rates, interest rates, money supply, and the like, was indisputably the most far-reaching of all the policies adopted at Maastricht. The ultimate objective was to achieve a rough convergence of monetary and fiscal policies among the signatory countries by empowering a Community institution free from political interference from the member governments to manage such matters as interest rates and the money supply. This implied nothing less than the eventual transfer of monetary authority—one of the traditional hallmarks of national sovereignty—from the finance ministries of the individual EC countries to an organ of the emerging supranational entity.

Though the Single European Market went into effect on schedule at the beginning of 1993, the Maastricht pact ran into rough sledding as the governments of the member states prepared to submit it for popular or parliamentary approval. The deepening recession in the EC countries inspired second thoughts in many of them about the wisdom of sacrificing national control of domestic economic policy to that elusive abstraction called "Europe." Public resentment against anonymous, meddling Eurocrats from Brussels mounted in Great Britain as the full extent of Maastricht's intrusiveness became apparent to the general public. Shrill critics in France blamed that country's high unemployment rate on the influx of cheap goods and labor permitted under the single market arrangement. Germans, already suffering from inflationary pressures caused by the emergency expenditures required to absorb the inhabitants of the former GDR, fretted that the deutsche mark would continually be called on to bail out the weaker currencies under the European Monetary Union's exchange rate mechanism.

These manifold anxieties about the impending quantum leap into supranationalism reached a fever pitch in June 1992, when Denmark unexpectedly rejected the Maastricht Treaty in a nationwide referendum. The British government jumped at the opportunity afforded by the Danish rejection to postpone its own acceptance of the pact, while German opponents challenged its compatibility with the federal constitution. But public appreciation of the long-term advantages of economic integration remained a potent countervailing force that eventually ensured a satisfactory compromise. One by one the principal obstacles to acceptance vanished in the course of intense bargaining, as a number of escape clauses were prudently added to those already embedded in Maastricht in order to allay the concerns of various member states. In May 1993 Denmark approved the Treaty on European Union in a second referendum and the British parliament tendered its approbation. As the treaty became operational the following November, the "European Community" was transformed into the more integrationist-sounding "European Union."

At a conference in Madrid in December 1995, the fifteen finance ministers of the newly expanded European Union took a number of bold steps toward the elusive goal of full economic integration. They reaffirmed the Maastricht commitment to the creation of a common European currency by 1999; they established a precise timetable for the achievement of full monetary union; and they finally gave the successor of the mark, franc, lira, etc. a name: the "euro". Since Maastricht had established stringent conditions for membership in the proposed European Monetary Union (EMU)—including the reduction of annual public deficits below 3% and a total public debt below 60% of gross domestic product—it became clear that not all fifteen members of the EU would be willing or able to join the EMU by the target date. But the momentum toward monetary union was maintained in spite of serious economic difficulties that several aspirants to membership experienced as a result of the economic downturn that gripped Europe in the closing years of the century. On March 26, 1998, the European Commission issued a recommendation, approved by the European Council the following May, that eleven of the fifteen EU members be admitted to the EMU in 1999. The exceptions were Great Britain, Denmark, and Sweden (which had opted for various reasons to remain outside for the time being) and Greece (the only one of the fifteen that failed to meet the Maastricht criteria for entry, though it was finally admitted in 2001).

To the surprise of many Euroskeptics, the other eleven members of the EU adopted the single currency at the prescribed deadline of January 1, 1999, when all bank and credit card transactions were henceforth conducted in euros. In 2002 the newly minted coins and newly printed banknotes replaced the national currencies with a minimum of disruption. In the meantime the European Central Bank had assumed control over the money supply, interest rates, and other functions traditionally exercised by the individual central banks of the member states. The adoption of the euro did not result in the total integration of the eleven economic systems. One of the remaining obstacles to be overcome was the discrepancy in tax rates and social welfare costs among the member states, which gave the firms of some a competitive advantage over others. Another was the de facto immobility of labor due to linguistic, ethnic, and cultural considerations that inhibited workers in countries of high unemployment from exercising their right of unrestricted migration to seek jobs in EU countries with better opportunities. Despite these residual roadblocks to full integration, however, the establishment by the European Union of a common currency under the jurisdiction of a Europe-wide central bank by the end of the twentieth century was a monumental achievement. It vindicated the intrepid vision of the small band of reformers after the Second World War who saw economic cooperation as the most effective means of assuring prosperity and security for the old continent.

While the sections of the Maastricht Treaty dealing with social and economic policy received the most public attention, a provision of the pact also endorsed the objective of a Common Foreign and Security Policy (CFSP) and the creation of a multinational military instrument to implement it. This important innovation represented a kind of insurance policy against the day when the United States would withdraw militarily from Europe in response to the recent disappearance of the Soviet menace that forty years ago had brought American troops to the continent in the first place.

Earlier European (and particularly French) proposals for defense autonomy—from de Gaulle's strident critique of Washington's dominance of NATO in the sixties to Mitterrand's more discreet bid to revive the moribund Western European Union (WEU) during the eighties—had engendered opposition in the United States on the grounds that an exclusively European defense entity would (at best) duplicate tasks already performed by NATO and (at worst) undermine the cohesion of the alliance. But the coincidence of the end of the Cold War and the advent of a severe recession in 1989 prompted a public clamor in the United States for military retrenchment in order to address domestic economic problems. Consequently, traditional U.S. concerns about an exclusively European security system rapidly dissipated. President Bush's unilateral proposal in 1991 to remove all short-range, ground-based nuclear weapons from Europe, Canada's announcement in the following year that it would withdraw all of its troops from the continent by 1994, and President Clinton's decision in 1993 to reduce the U.S. contingent in NATO to 100,000 by the end of 1996, seemed to convey the same message: The Europeans would be expected to bear a much greater share of the defense burden.

Reading the handwriting on the wall, French President François Mitterrand and German Chancellor Helmut Kohl dusted off their old scheme for a Franco-German military force as the nucleus of a European army under the aegis of the WEU. In May 1992 France and Germany concluded an agreement to fashion from their respective military forces a thirty-five thousand-person European Army Corps (Eurocorps). After Belgium agreed to contribute a mechanized division, the three nations established an organizational head-quarters in Strasbourg in November 1993, and Spain and Luxembourg subsequently joined. But despite all the rhetoric about European defense cooperation, the renovated European Union failed the first test of its capacity to manage regional security in the post-Cold War environment. Faced with the first outbreak of large-scale violence on the continent since 1945 in the former Yugoslavia, Europe proved capable of devising neither a diplomatic nor a military solution to the conflagration in its own backyard.*

The efforts to forge a framework for European security cooperation in the first half of the 1990s coincided with a profound identity crisis within NATO itself as the United States and its European partners pondered the future role of the Atlantic alliance in a world without the Warsaw Pact and the Soviet Union. One of many items on the agenda of the Atlantic alliance was the question of NATO's relationship to the rudimentary military structure of the WEU. The first combined meeting of the two organizations in June 1993 attempted to resolve logistical problems related to their combined enforcement of the UN economic sanctions against Serbia in the Adriatic and established ground rules for future collaboration.

But plans for European defense cooperation, which had received a high priority after the end of the Cold War and the reduction of American military manpower in NATO, remained inchoate and vague. The highly touted Eurocorps conducted its first official exercises in November 1995 with French, German, Spanish, Belgian and Luxembourger units. But the WEU, once thought to be the nucleus for the common European defense identity, labored in vain to define a special role for itself within the EU. When Germany and France formally proposed the gradual merger of the two organizations in 1997 in the hopes that the WEU would eventually become the military arm of the EU, Great Britain and the neutral states (Austria, Finland, Sweden, and Ireland) blocked the proposal. When push came to shove in the Balkans during the Bosnian crisis (see below, page 432), it was neither the Eurocorps nor the WEU but NATO that employed its air power to force an end to the fighting and then supervise the peace settlement in that troubled country. The EU's inability to stop the killing in Bosnia confirmed the Union's failure to forge a common security policy to match its common monetary policy.

Ever since President François Mitterrand and Chancellor Helmut Kohl revived the long-moribund WEU in the early 1980s, the initiative for the development of a separate European defense identity had come from France and Germany. But at an EU summit in Austria in October 1998, the recently elected British prime minister Tony Blair, dismayed by the Union's embarrassing military unpreparedness during the Balkan crisis, withdrew the traditional British objection to military cooperation within the EU. Blair and French President Jacques Chirac then issued a joint declaration in Saint Malo on December 4, 1998, which challenged the EU to adopt an autonomous military capability separate from NATO under the title European Security and Defense Policy (ESDP). This goal was endorsed at the June 1999 EU summit in Cologne after the embarrassingly deficient performance of European forces during the U.S.-led air campaign in Kosovo (see page 436). At the end of the year a comprehensive plan for ESDP was elaborated at the Helsinki meeting of the European Council. The first very small operations of an EU mil-

---

*See page xxx.

itary force took place in 2003 in the former Yugoslavia, where EU contingents replaced UN and NATO missions in Bosnia and Macedonia, respectively. A half-century after France had first broached the plan for a European Defense Community, Europe finally seemed prepared to make a serious effort to create a multinational army of its own. But the question remained whether the member states of the EU would be willing to appropriate the funds necessary to finance the "autonomous military capability" specified. The European members of NATO collectively spent about half as much on defense as did the United States, and their defense expenditures fell by 22 percent in real terms from the time of the collapse of the Soviet Union to the end of the twentieth century.

Amid the success of monetary integration and the sluggish progress of military integration during the last half of the 1990s, the EU confronted the controversial issue of the expansion of its membership. The European Commission issued an "Agenda 2000" in the summer of 1997 which put the states that had applied for membership on notice that they would have to meet a set of stringent criteria adopted in 1993, including democratic political institutions, a market economy, and a willingness to accept the EU's regulations. On reviewing the various applications the Commission designated six countries—Cyprus, the Czech Republic, Estonia, Hungary, Slovenia, and Poland—as suitable candidates to enter into preliminary negotiations for admission. After the European Council endorsed the Commission's recommendation in December 1997, enlargement talks with the six approved candidates opened in March 1998. Soon thereafter, Latvia, Lithuania, Malta, and Slovakia were added to the list. Turkey, a loyal NATO ally which had formerly applied for EU membership in 1987, deeply resented its exclusion as the EC opened accession negotiations with Cyprus and the former Communist countries. The Turkish government was also outraged at the EU's handling of the candidacy of Cyprus, which in 1974 had been partitioned into Greek and Turkish sectors. The EU announced that if the Turkish portion of the divided island refused to participate—which it did until it received the international recognition that no foreign power was prepared to give—the accession negotiations would be conducted with the Greek Cypriot delegation alone. The prospect of the Greek sector of Cyprus entering the EU while the Turkish sector (and Turkey proper) remained outside the Union generated acute bitterness in Ankara. Many Turks perceived the ulterior motive of religious and cultural prejudice behind the EU's refusal to admit what would be Europe's first predominantly Muslim member state. After intensive and prolonged accession talks, the ten candidate countries were admitted to the Union on May 1, 2004, instantly increasing its membership from fifteen to twenty-five.

As the accession negotiations proceeded, many European leaders came to the conclusion that the achievement of genuine political integration for the European Union would require the creation of a written constitution. During the early years of the twenty-first century, legal experts met with the political representatives of the member states to undertake the arduous task of drafting a document that would be acceptable to all members. Strong differences of opinion over the size and powers of the European Commission, the precise definition of "qualified majority voting" (which would eventually replace the old system requiring unanimity), and the allocation of votes among member states slowed the process. But the enlargement of the EU from fifteen to twenty-five states in May 2004 gave a new impetus to these constitutional deliberations. A compromise was finally agreed to on June 18, 2004, a date that some devout integrationists compared with the Fourth of July for the United States. When the heads of state of the member countries put their signatures to a draft treaty establishing the new constitution four months later, the new European constitution was ready to be presented to the twenty-five member states for ratification. After so many false starts and reversals, the old dream of Jean Monnet and his associates of a United States of Europe seemed on the verge of becoming a reality at last. Then the failure of the French and Dutch electorates to approve the constitution in the spring of 2005 derailed once again the movement toward full European political integration.

In addition to launching the new wave of expansion, the EU Commission's Agenda 2000 had proposed fundamental reforms of two controversial programs that had long consumed most of the Union's annual budget. The first was the Common Agricultural Policy (CAP), an elaborate set of subsidies that guaranteed farmers fixed prices for their goods. The CAP had been a long-standing source of friction within the EU that pitted members with large agricultural sectors (such as France) that benefited from the price supports against those with small farming populations (such as Great Britain) that had to finance the subsidies as well as pay higher prices for food products. The second was the provision for "sectoral funds" earmarked to promote economic growth in less developed member states (such as Portugal and Greece). The projected addition of predominantly agricultural, underdeveloped countries from Central and Eastern Europe in the new century threatened to overwhelm both the CAP and sectoral funds budgets unless both programs were radically recast. But France blocked all attempts to reform the CAP at the expense of its politically powerful farmers, while the poorer member states in southern Europe pressed for an increase in the sectoral fund portion of the budget to protect their share of the money when the Central and East European states began to assert their claims to development assistance. In sum, the prospects for genuine reform of the EU's complex budget continued to be a major challenge for Brussels officials.

While the EU contemplated the admission of the former Communist states of Eastern Europe, the question of those countries' relationship with NATO became a topic of intense controversy. Though the Soviet Union, and then the Russian Federation, scrupulously honored Gorbachev's pledges to remove all Red Army units from the former Soviet satellites, these fledgling democracies felt exposed, unprotected, and in need of reliable allies during periods of regional instability. This sense of insecurity among the countries of Eastern Europe intensified at each sign of political turmoil or outburst of nationalistic rhetoric in Russia. As former members of Comecon, Czechoslovakia (and later the Czech Republic and Slovakia), Hungary, and Poland had sought admission to the EC to solve their economic problems. As former signatories of the Warsaw Pact the same three countries applied for membership in NATO in order to obtain protection against a possible security threat from Russia in the future.

When Moscow expressed displeasure at the prospect of its former clients joining a U.S.-dominated military alliance that might well be construed as an anti-Russian coalition, NATO planners devised various innocuous alternatives to allay East European apprehensions without offending the Russians. After rebuffing the Czech, Hungarian, and Polish bids for prompt admission, NATO established in late 1991 a new entity called the North Atlantic Cooperation Council (NACC), which comprised all members of NATO, all former members of the Warsaw Pact, and all of the Soviet successor states. President Clinton subsequently unveiled a Partnership for Peace plan in January 1994 that envisaged various modes of military cooperation between NATO and the armies of the former Communist bloc in Europe as well as any former Soviet republics or neutral countries that would wish to join. At every hint by NATO that the former Warsaw Pact satellites' applications for admission would be considered, Yeltsin issued dire warnings and proposed instead that the exclusive Atlantic Alliance be replaced by the all-inclusive Conference on (later renamed Organization for) Security and Cooperation in Europe as the guardian of continental peace and stability. But the governments of Poland, Hungary, and the Czech Republic persevered, and in March 1999 finally gained admission to the Atlantic Alliance. Mired in economic crisis and dependent on the American-dominated IMF for financial assistance, Russia could do nothing to prevent the extension of the NATO area into its traditional sphere of influence. By the end of the twentieth century the Russian leadership had resigned itself to the inevitability of NATO's expansion even farther to the east. Yeltsin's successor, Vladimir Putin, issued only pro forma protests as the Western alliance welcomed seven more former Communist members in April 2004: Bulgaria, Romania, Slovakia, and Slovenia, as well as three countries that had once been part of the Soviet Union itself—the Baltic states of Estonia, Latvia, and Lithuania.

In the meantime the historic curses of economic backwardness and ethnic antagonism remained the two potential sources of instability in Central and Eastern Europe. The rapid transition from command to market economies, which included the privatization of nationalized enterprises, the reduction of government subsidies, and the removal of price controls, caused painful adjustments in these societies. The tepid response of Western Europe to Eastern Europe's urgent appeals for financial assistance and trade advantages aggravated the socioeconomic tensions that had been unleashed by these unfulfilled hopes. West European lending and investment in the east fell far short of expectations, a circumstance that was due in part to the severe recession that gripped the industrialized world during the early 1990s. Though the European Union replaced the Soviet Union as Eastern Europe's largest trading partner between 1989 and 1994, the benefits for the former Communist countries were not immediately apparent: They collectively ran a huge trade deficit with the West due to the high tariffs and stringent quotas imposed by the protectionist EC.

The ancient nationalist antagonisms that had been submerged during the four decades of enforced Communist solidarity resurfaced in the newly liberated states of Eastern Europe at the end of the Cold War. The country that managed to cope most effectively with this problem was the multiethnic state of Czechoslovakia. As the Red Army withdrew in 1991, it became evident that a substantial proportion of the Slovaks in the eastern half of the country preferred self-rule to subordinate status within the Czech-dominated state. Intent on terminating the endless ethnic bickering that had plagued the country since its liberation from Soviet domination, President Vaclav Havel chose the path of least resistance. After a remarkably cordial series of negotiations concerning the appropriate division of the country's economic and military assets, the country split into the Czech Republic and Slovakia on January 1, 1993. This amicable separation left the new state of Slovakia with a potentially disruptive separatist problem of its own in the form of half a million discontented Hungarians. Nor were the Czechoslovak successor states the only countries in Eastern Europe to face this predicament. Two million Hungarians in the Transylvanian region of Romania, an indeterminate number of Belorussians and Ukrainians in eastern Poland, and other discontented minorities represented latent threats to stability in the region.

THE BALKAN TRAGEDY

The most poignant casualty of this resurgence of ethnic nationalism in Europe was the population of the multinational, multireligious, multilingual state of Yugoslavia. The death in 1980 of Josip Broz Tito, whose thirty-five-year rule had successfully kept the lid on the multiethnic cauldron in this renegade Communist country on the Balkan peninsula, had ushered in a decade of rising tension among the inhabitants of its six federated republics and two autonomous regions.* In the summer of 1991 Slovenia and Croatia, the two most Westernized, anti-Communist, and economically advanced republics in the federation, declared their independence amid sporadic clashes between the partisans of secession and the Yugoslav federal army. That military organization remained under the effective control of Serbia, the largest and most populous of the Yugoslav republics, whose citizens were widely scattered throughout the disintegrating state. The Serb minority in Croatia and Slovenia, in collusion with the remnants of the Serb-dominated Yugoslav federal army, took up arms against the new states whose claim to sovereignty signified the demise of the federation in which the Serbs had long enjoyed a privileged status.

Peace was mercifully restored to Croatia and Slovenia by early 1992 through a cease-fire agreement brokered by UN mediators and monitored by a UN peacekeeping force. But the pacification of Croatia and Slovenia set the stage for the bloodiest conflict in Europe since the end of the Second World War. After the European Community formally recognized the independence of the two secessionist republics in January 1992, a request for recognition arrived from the neighboring republic of Bosnia-Herzegovina (an ethnically diverse region composed of roughly 44 percent Muslim Slavs, 33 percent Serbs, and 17 percent Croats). The Serbs of Bosnia, unwilling to be submerged in a state certain to be controlled by its Muslim majority, defiantly declared the independence of their own ethnic enclave and boycotted a referendum that resulted in the declaration of Bosnia-Herzegovina's independence in March. Though the federal Yugoslav army evacuated Bosnia in the spring of 1992, many of its Serbian members stayed behind to assist their ethnic brethren in the breakaway republic as they took up arms against its Muslim-dominated government with the covert support of the Serbian regime in Belgrade. In the months to come the Bosnian Serb forces placed the capital city of Sarajevo under siege, subjected its starving population to continuous mortar fire, and inaugurated a pitiless campaign to expel Muslim civilians from Serb-controlled areas that contributed a new term to the vocabulary of international politics: ethnic cleansing. The Red Cross eventually found all three factions guilty of violating the Geneva conventions on the rules of warfare, as television screens throughout the world carried graphic reports of wholesale looting, gang rape, and slaughter of innocent civilians.

The international community responded to the carnage in Bosnia through a variety of channels. As noted above, the European Community failed to reach consensus on an appropriate policy toward the crisis apart from according prompt recognition to the Yugoslav successor states as the federal republic disintegrated in 1992, cooperating in the enforcement of economic sanctions against Serbia, and dispatching envoys to conduct

---

*The six federated republics included Bosnia-Herzegovina, Croatia, Macedonia, Montenegro, Serbia, and Slovenia. The two autonomous regions (within Serbia) were Kosovo and Vojvodina.

The Balkan Peninsula After the Breakup of Yugoslavia

fruitless negotiations with the warring factions. NATO exerted a modicum of direct influence on the tragic situation after its decision in the spring of 1993 to enforce a UN-authorized "no-fly" zone over Bosnia in order to prevent the Serbs from supplementing their artillery barrages against Muslim positions with air strikes. In February 1994 U.S. aircraft shot down a few Serb planes that had bombed Muslim targets in violation of the no-fly zone. The threat of NATO air strikes against Serb forces besieging Sarajevo brought a suspension of the random mortar attacks on that city's defenseless population. The Clinton administration in Washington, preoccupied with domestic issues and wary of foreign entanglements after its chastening experience in Somalia,* resorted to air power as a means of avoiding the commitment of ground troops to the Balkan quagmire.

---

*See page 456.

Secretary of State Warren Christopher had attempted in vain to persuade the European powers in the spring of 1993 to join the United States in launching air strikes against Bosnian Serb artillery positions and supply lines. The European members of NATO rebuffed this U.S. initiative because of fears that such actions would endanger their own troops that were actively participating in the only peacekeeping forces stationed on former Yugoslav territory. These were the two United Nations Protection Forces (UNPROFOR I and II) established in 1992 to shield humanitarian aid missions dispatched from abroad and to police designated "protected areas" in Croatia and Bosnia-Herzegovina. The UN had no more success than the Atlanticist and European organizations in promoting the reestablishment of peace and stability in the former Yugoslavia. None of the belligerents displayed much willingness to cooperate with the blue-helmeted peace-keeping forces from the world organization. The peace plan jointly proposed at the beginning of 1993 by Cyrus Vance on behalf of the UN and Lord Owen representing the EC, which would have set up ten autonomous provinces within Bosnia-Herzegovina, was overwhelmingly rejected by the Bosnia Serbs because it would have deprived them of the 70 percent of Serbian territory they had won on the battlefield. A second plan in July 1994 by the so-called Contact Group, comprising the United States, Russia, Britain, France, and Germany, which proposed assigning the Bosnian Serbs half of a partitioned country, failed to win their support for the same reason. This recalcitrance eventually even antagonized the Serbian government itself. In the following month Belgrade ended its political and economic support for the Bosnian Serbs because of their refusal to accept the latest peace plan and closed the Serbian border with Bosnia-Herzegovina in order to cut off the flow of supplies to the Serb forces still fighting there. The failure of all efforts at mediation and the inability of either side to achieve a decisive military breakthrough condemned the populace of Bosnia-Herzegovina, combatants and civilians alike, to a seemingly endless cycle of stalemate and slaughter.

The Bosnian nightmare also generated acute strains within NATO, revealing a wide divergence of strategic interests between the United States and its major European allies. It appeared ironic that the longest lasting military alliance in modern history never had to engage in combat with its designated adversary, only to launch its first military operation after the end of the Cold War in a region far removed from the historic flash point along the old inter-German frontier. In the fall of 1994 a string of Bosnian Serb military successes prompted the United States to stop enforcing the arms embargo against the Muslim forces and to renew its pressure on the British and French to endorse NATO air strikes against Serbian positions threatening UN-designated protected territory inhabited mainly by Muslin civilians. But by that time London and Paris vigorously opposed Washington's attempt to shore up the faltering Muslims as a recipe for prolonging a conflict that they desperately wanted to end and in which their own ground forces operated for impartial humanitarian purposes.

In the spring of 1995, intensive Bosnian Serb shelling of Sarajevo finally spurred NATO into action. When the Bosnian Serb leadership ignored an ultimatum to halt the artillery attacks, NATO aircraft bombed the Bosnian Serb stronghold of Pale. The Bosnian Serb leader Radovan Karadzik and his military commander General Ratko Mladic responded to the NATO raids by ordering their troops to take hundreds of UNPROFOR personnel hostage and hold them near potential bombing targets to dissuade NATO from resuming its air campaign. Though Serbian president Slobodan Milosevic pressured the

Bosnian Serbs into releasing the United Nations hostages within a few weeks, the hostage-taking had demonstrated the impotence of the UN in the region and prompted the Clinton administration to press for an extensive NATO air campaign to counter Bosnian Serb assaults against the designated "safe areas."

In the meantime the Bosnian Muslim regime in Sarajevo and the government of Croatia had joined forces in March 1994 to forge a Bosnian-Croat Federation to cope with the increasingly bellicose Serbian populations within their respective territories. The Croatian regime of Franjo Tudjman, which had received substantial military assistance and advice from the United States, launched a military operation in the Krajina region adjacent to Bosnia which had been occupied by Croatian Serb forces since the end of the brief Serb-Croat war in 1991. The immediate result of the offensive was a brutal operation of "ethnic cleansing" as Croatian military units massacred Croatian Serbs, destroyed their villages, and expelled some 150,000 of them to Serb-controlled territory in Bosnia as well as to Serbia itself.

During the Croatian Serb retreat from the Krajina, a Bosnian Serb mortar attack on a market place in Sarajevo on August 28, 1995, killed thirty-seven shoppers. This brutal act against civilians in a "safe area" prompted a massive NATO air assault against ethnic Serb positions throughout Bosnia that had two important consequences. First, the Bosnian Serb leadership finally consented to move its artillery out of range of the Bosnian Muslim capital. Secondly, the Bosnian Serbs agreed to join a negotiating team headed by Serbian President Milosevic to seek a diplomatic settlement to the bloody conflict. American envoy Richard Holbrooke brokered a sixty-day cease-fire beginning on October 12, 1995, during which peace talks were conducted in Dayton, Ohio, based on an informal understanding reached earlier in Geneva. The Dayton Agreement was initialed on November 21 by Serbian President Milosevic, Croatian President Tudjman, and Bosnian President Alija Izetbegovic, and was formally signed by the three leaders at the Elysée Palace in Paris on December 14. The agreement preserved the sovereignty of Bosnia but formally recognized two distinct "entities" within its borders: the Bosnian-Croat Federation and a Bosnian Serb Republic. A federal government representing the three principal ethnic groups wielded supreme political authority. A NATO-controlled multinational peace implementation force (IFOR) of 60,000 troops (which was subsequently reduced to about 20,000 by the end of the century) replaced the departing United Nations operation (UNPROFOR) as the country's supreme security organization.

The Dayton accord thus established a de facto NATO protectorate in a war-ravaged country which, though ostensibly held together by a superficial federal structure under a weak central government, had in effect been partitioned into three ethnic-based regions. Of the 2.3 million people who had been displaced by the war, less than a fifth returned to their country of origin, and most of those settled in territory protected by the military forces of their own ethnic group. The rest were accorded temporary asylum in foreign countries, with Germany taking in the largest number. An International Criminal Tribunal for Former Yugoslavia that had been established in the Hague indicted several alleged war criminals for their participation in the Balkan blood bath. Though a number of mid-level culprits from all three major ethnic groups were arrested, those at the top (including the Bosnian Serb leaders Karadzic and Mladic) remained at large.

The United States trained and equipped the army of the Muslim-Croat Federation in order to build it up to twice the armed strength of the Bosnian Serb Republic on the assumption that Serbia would fight alongside its ethnic brethren in any future conflict between the two Bosnian political entities. The original objective was to create a rough balance of power in the country that would stabilize the political situation there. In the meantime the de facto partition of Bosnia became a fait accompli, as neither the Bosnian Croats nor the Bosnian Serbs were willing to cooperate with the Muslim-dominated government in Sarajevo. The only possible alternative to the partition of the country into ethnically homogenous sectors was the return and resettlement of refugees throughout the country. But such an ambitious operation would require the indefinite presence of a NATO ground force that was large enough to protect the returning refugees, a costly and risky commitment that no member country of the alliance was prepared to make.

As the political situation in the devastated, ethnically-cleansed country of Bosnia stabilized under the watchful eyes of the NATO-led peace implementation force, another long-simmering ethnic conflict boiled over within Serbia itself. Its autonomous southern province of Kosovo contained a 90 percent ethnic Albanian majority that had become increasingly resentful of its discriminatory treatment by the Serb-dominated government in Belgrade. When the financial collapse of Albania proper in 1997 (caused by a fraudulent investment scheme) led to the disintegration of that country's national army, large quantities of its weapons were acquired by the radical wing of the ethnic Albanians in Kosovo known as the Kosovo Liberation Army (KLA). As the KLA openly called for secession, Serbian President Milosevic sought to crush the rebellion by encouraging Serb paramilitary forces in Kosovo to terrorize Kosovar Albanians into leaving the country. The peripatetic U.S. negotiator Richard Holbrooke patched together a temporary arrangement with Milosevic on October 13, 1998, which led to the withdrawal of Serbian regular army units from Kosovo but left the ethnic Serb paramilitary forces behind to resume their work of intimidation. The Holbrooke-Milosevic deal temporarily ended the violence in Kosovo while Serbian officials and Kosovar Albanian leaders negotiated a formal agreement at a conference jointly sponsored by France and Great Britain in Rambouillet, France, in February 1999. The two antagonists had been forced to the conference table by the joint pressure of the United States and Russia, which at that stage were cooperating in the so-called Contact Group of foreign powers to promote a peaceful settlement of the latest eruption of communal violence in the Balkans.

At Rambouillet Milosevic acceded to Albanian demands for a referendum in Kosovo to determine its political future at the end of three years, a concession which would doubtless have resulted in a vote for independence in light of the huge Albanian majority in the province and its growing resentment at Serbian domination. But the Serbian president rejected the military provisions of the accord, which provided for the deployment of Western ground forces to monitor the agreement. He then dispatched Serbian infantry and armor to the northern part of Kosovo. The Serb forces began evicting ethnic Albanians from their homes, burning their villages, and forcing many of them to flee across the Albanian frontier.

After Holbrooke and representatives of the European Union failed to persuade Milosevic to affix his signature to the Rambouillet agreement containing the military protocol, which the Kosovar Albanians had signed, NATO mounted a retaliatory air assault against Serbia (still formally known as the Federal Republic of Yugoslavia) on March 24, 1999. While the NATO planes carried out almost 10,000 bombing missions against military targets and civilian infrastructure thoughout the country for seventy-nine straight days, the Serb paramilitaries in Kosovo accelerated their ruthless campaign of ethnic cleansing against the Kosovar Albanians. The air campaign was terminated on June 10, after Milosevic's government agreed to withdraw all Yugoslav forces from Kosovo and to permit the deployment of a NATO-led multinational ground force (KFOR) to oversee the return of Albanian refugees and provide security for the province. Once the multinational force replaced the departed Yugoslav forces, over 70 percent of the one million Albanian refugees returned to Kosovo. Some of them took revenge against the Serb minority for the death of about ten thousand of their countrymen during Milosevic's campaign of ethnic cleansing, destroying the homes of Kosovar Serbs and forcing many of them to seek refuge in Serbia proper.

The European Union assumed the major financial burden of reconstructing the devastated region in partnership with over four hundred NGOs that provided private aid and personnel to dispense it. By the early years of the twenty-first century, the EU was effectively administering and policing Bosnia and Kosovo, belatedly taking responsibility for preserving security in two European hot spots after the United States had dominated the diplomatic and military decision making in the region throughout the 1990s. The Europeans also took charge of the juridical issue of the alleged war crimes committed by the Serbian leader. When Milosevic refused to abide by the election results in 2000 that brought the opposition leader Vojislav Kostunica to power, he was abandoned by his army and security forces and resigned. In June 2001 the disgraced Serbian leader was imprisoned in the Hague and in February 2002 was put on trial at the International War Crimes Tribunal. After so many years, Europe had finally taken steps to put its own house in order.

18

ASIA AT THE CROSSROADS

ECONOMIC GROWTH AND SECURITY DILEMMAS IN EAST ASIA

By the mid-1990s East Asia enjoyed the dual advantage of sustained economic growth and regional stability. With the notable exception of Japan (whose long and spectacular advancement had slowed), the export-oriented economies of the region continued to flourish due to their comparative advantages in labor and production costs. During the same period the region basked in an unprecedented period of peace. For the first time since the 1930s, East Asia was spared the trauma of war of civil conflict. Within this increasingly favorable regional environment the great national success story was the spectacular economic performance of China. While the rest of the world languished in recession, the People's Republic of China (PRC) recorded annual GNP increases of 7, 12, and 13 percent during 1991–93. This impressive performance vindicated the reformers allied with the octogenarian *eminence grise* Deng Xiaoping, who had abandoned the economic principles of Marxist-Leninism in the face of bitter opposition from orthodox defenders of the Communist faith.

The ruling elite in Beijing responded to the collapse of communism in the Soviet Union by accelerating the economic transformation of China in the hope of avoiding the fate of their counterparts in Moscow. In so doing they outmaneuvered their orthodox critics who denounced Deng as a Chinese Gorbachev whose radical economic reforms threatened to stimulate the same kind of political opposition to the Communist dictatorship. Unlike Gorbachev, however, Deng and his prime minister, Li Peng, steadfastly refused to permit the kind of political liberalization that would threaten the party's monopoly on power. The first dramatic demonstration of this hard-line policy was the government's response to the million protesting students who had converged on Beijing's Tiananmen Square in the spring of 1989 to dramatize their demands for greater political freedom with hunger strikes and noisy public demonstrations before the ubiquitous Western television cameras. The Chinese government, observing with apprehension the declining fortunes of the Communist parties in Eastern Europe, called in the People's Liberation Army to suppress the peaceful protest in early June. The resulting massacre of about 1,300 unarmed civilians brought an end to internal political dissent within the People's Republic. The imprisonment of domestic dissidents, even as foreign trade representatives and investment bankers came calling, signified that Beijing's policy of opening the Chinese economy to the outside world would not be accompanied by a liberalization of China's internal political system.

Though the Tiananmen Square massacre prompted indignant public outcries in many countries, foreign governments and business interests reacted with considerable caution. Indeed, China enjoyed a virtual immunity from international criticism of its refusal to reform its repressive political system because of its potential value as a trading partner and investment market for the industrial powers of the world. Therein lies one of the keys to the divergent political paths taken by the two Communist powers after the widespread popular unrest that buffeted both societies at the end of the 1980s. The disintegrating Soviet economy condemned the reforming regime in Moscow to a position of abject dependence on foreign assistance, and therefore rendered it vulnerable to foreign pressure for political reform. The booming economy of China, on the other hand, dissuaded those Western nations that eagerly eyed its markets for their exports and capital investment from jeopardizing those prospects with offensive criticism of its political practices.

Thus, after a brief interval following the Tiananmen massacre, Japan and the Western industrial nations unobtrusively restored normal economic relations with the PRC. In response to China's annual applications for most-favored nation (MFN) trade status in the early 1990s, the Bush administration concluded that the advantages to the United States of preserving profitable economic links with China outweighed concerns about that country's blatant violation of its own citizens' human rights. Washington therefore recoiled from brandishing the threat of revoking the preferential trade status as a means of promoting democratization in China. The Clinton administration resumed the policy of its predecessor by granting Beijing annual renewals of MFN status in the absence of evidence that repressive policies had been curtailed. Neighboring capitalist countries such as Taiwan and South Korea relocated labor-intensive manufacturing operations to the China coast in order to take advantage of China's comparatively low labor costs, while Japan and the ASEAN countries expanded their trade with coastal China.

As that economically booming region tightened its links to the world economy, signs of religious and ethnic discontent appeared in certain areas along China's landlocked western periphery: The long-festering wound of Tibetan separatism was accompanied by other sources of regional dissidence. Islamic militants in the western province of Xinjiang drew inspiration from their coreligionists in the Central Asian republics who had recently achieved independence from the U.S.S.R. These faint rumblings of opposition to central authority along the Chinese periphery represented reminders of that country's anomalous status as one of the world's last great multinational states after the disintegration of the Soviet Union into its constituent ethnic components.

China's spectacular economic growth in the early 1990s coincided with its acquisition of absolute military security in East Asia for the first time since the establishment of the People's Republic in 1949. The collapse of the Soviet Union and the contraction of American naval power in the western Pacific eliminated the only impediments to China's strategic superiority in its region. This unprecedented condition of invulnerability emboldened Beijing to conduct a relatively aggressive diplomacy on behalf of traditional as well as more recently acquired foreign policy goals. Concerned that the democratic reforms introduced in 1992 by the new British governor general of Hong Kong might contaminate the already increasingly independent-minded coastal provinces on the mainland, Beijing condemned those measures and preemptively pronounced them null and void on the expiration of British sovereignty over the crown colony. When the bustling little hotbed of entrepreneurial capitalism in Asia was formally absorbed by China on July 1, 1997, it retained a considerable degree of autonomy from the Communist government in Beijing. But it was clear that China was firmly in control of Hong Kong and could tighten the screws whenever it wished to do so.

As the date for China's recovery of Hong Kong approached, the indigenous inhabitants of the island of Taiwan had begun to discuss the taboo topic of a declaration of independence from the mainland in order to preclude a similar fate. In March 1995, China reacted to this political rhetoric by test-firing several missiles off the Taiwan coast. Provocative Chinese military exercises in the Taiwan Strait the following year prompted the dispatch of two U.S. aircraft carrier battle groups to the region as a signal of Washington's determination to prevent Taiwan's forcible reunification with the mainland.

Before he died of a long and debilitating illness in February 1997, Deng Xiaoping, the architect of China's economic reform in the post-Mao era, mounted an assault on the principal roadblock to full-scale modernization in China: the inefficient, money-losing, state-owned industries inherited from the Maoist era. Deng's hand-picked successor, Jiang Zemin, promptly signaled his intention to resume the reformist campaign of his mentor by removing from the regime's ruling circles the last of the old-guard defenders of Communist orthodoxy. The new president thereupon attempted to restructure the unproductive nationalized firms and the financially troubled state-run banks, which had squandered a fortune in unproductive loans and investments. This restructuring of the old state-run industrial and financial enterprises resulted in the dismissal of millions of workers who had grown accustomed not only to the guarantee of lifetime employment but also to the provision of a wide range of employer-sponsored social services. By the summer of 1998, the Communist regime in China faced the unfamiliar challenge of worker protest, as many of those dismissed from their jobs in the interests of greater efficiency and productivity took to the streets to publicize their opposition to the new policies. This socio-economic unrest coincided with mounting demands from religious groups for greater freedom to practice their faith and hints of separatist agitation in Tibet, Xinjiang, and other regions with non-Chinese majorities. Though a crackdown by the authorities kept the lid on this simmering discontent, Jiang's new government was confronted with the possibility that its bold campaign of economic modernization could generate tensions within Chinese society that would be difficult to contain.

In the meantime the Clinton administration sought to expand Sino-American trade and to forge an acceptable arrangement to liberalize China's trading practices in order to enable it to enter the new World Trade Organization (WTO) that replaced GATT in 1995. China's bid to join the WTO had been thwarted by its inordinately high tariff rates as well as its egregious violation of intellectual property rights through pirated computer software and compact disk sales. An agreement between Beijing and Washington was finally reached in the fall of 1999, paving the way for China's entry into the world body in 2001. This economic entente contrasted with a set of political disagreements between the two countries. Beijing was alarmed by American plans to develop a theater missile defense system in Asia which, though ostensibly intended to protect Japan from nuclear attack, threatened to impair the political effectiveness of China's nuclear sword of Damocles hanging over Taiwan.* Evidence of alleged Chinese espionage at American nuclear research facilities uncovered in 1999 contributed to anti-Chinese sentiment in the United States, as did Beijing's harsh treatment of political and religious dissidents and its continual crackdown in Tibet. Conversely, the accidental bombing of the Chinese embassy in Belgrade during the NATO air campaign against Serbia in the spring of 1999 unleashed anti-American sentiment in China.

Throughout the 1990s Beijing advanced new territorial claims to the Spratly and Paracel island groups in the South China Sea, which are believed to possess substantial oil and natural gas reserves. This claim pitted the PRC against its old adversary Vietnam, as well as the ASEAN states Indonesia, Malaysia, and the Philippines, which had hired oil companies to prospect on their behalf within the territorial limits of some of the islands. China's increasing assertiveness in the Taiwan Strait and the South China Sea occasioned considerable anxiety among her neighbors in the new East Asian power vacuum caused by the disappearance of the Soviet Union and the reduced American military and naval presence. But none of these political and territorial disputes degenerated into the type of confrontation that spells regional instability.

The only part of East Asia that counted as a genuine trouble spot in the 1990s and the early years of the twenty-first century was the Korean peninsula. The immediate source of the trouble there was the apparent bid by North Korea to acquire a nuclear capability as compensation for its diminished political and economic position caused by the collapse of the Communist bloc and the disappearance of its Soviet patron. Though a reluctant signatory of the Nuclear Non-Proliferation Treaty (NPT) in 1985, North Korea refused to sign the requisite agreement with the International Atomic Energy Agency (IAEA) to permit on-site inspections to verify compliance with the treaty provisions. By the end of the 1980s the Communist regime of Kim Il Sung was widely suspected of having extracted enough weapons-grade plutonium from the waste products of its commercial nuclear reactors in Yongbyon, a city about sixty miles north of the capital of Pyongyang, to produce several atomic bombs. Responding to diplomatic pressure from its traditional allies Russia and China as well as to economic incentives from its longtime antagonists, Japan and the United States, Pyongyang finally agreed in 1991 to open its nuclear facilities to international inspection. But for the next three years the wily North Korean dictator placed every conceivable obstacle in the path of the frustrated inspectors from the IAEA. After numerous instances of stalling and reneging on agreements, Kim's refusal to permit inspection of specified sites in the spring of 1994 finally triggered a declaration of noncompliance from the agency, and Washington pressed for United Nations trade sanctions.

That threat was enough to prompt yet another volte-face as North Korea hastily agreed to seek a solution to the problem through direct exchanges with the United States. After the death in July 1994 of the eighty-two-year-old North Korean leader, who had ruled his country since its creation in 1948, his son and hand-picked successor Kim Jong Il promptly consented to freeze its nuclear weapons development program, gradually dismantle its existing nuclear facilities, and permit international inspection of the two sus-

---

*See page 403.

pect sites. In exchange the Clinton administration agreed to supply North Korea with oil for factories and homes as compensation for the energy production it agreed to forgo by closing its nuclear plants. An international consortium led by Japan and South Korea was formed to finance the construction of two light-water reactors—which produce far less plutonium than the graphite-core reactors at Yongbyon—to meet North Korea's long-term energy requirements.

The orthodox Stalinist regime in Pyongyang represented a curious historical relic after the breakup of the Soviet Union and the decision by the Chinese Communist leadership to follow the "capitalist road" to economic development. In the early nineties North Korea's traditional economic benefactors in Moscow and Beijing terminated the lavish subsidies they had provided during the Cold War, demanding hard currency payments for their exports at world market prices. China's diplomatic recognition of, and expanding trade contacts with, North Korea's bitter rival on the peninsula must have generated intense anxiety in Pyongyang. The only trump left in Kim Il Sung's (and then Kim Jong Il's) hand was the nuclear card, which could be played at the appropriate moment to show that it was still a force to be reckoned with in the region. Since the mid-1990s, North Korea's growth rate declined precipitously, while a virtual breakdown in food production led to acute malnutrition and starvation. South Korea sent food shipments northward as a gesture of goodwill and intensified its efforts to reach a final settlement with its old rival. At the urging of the United States and South Korea, North Korea finally agreed to attend so-called Four Party Talks (including the two Korean states, the U.S., and China) to discuss means of reaching a peace settlement on the peninsula. Two rounds of negotiations were held in Geneva throughout 1998, but they were deadlocked when North Korea insisted on the withdrawal of all United States military forces from South Korea and the conclusion of a separate bilateral treaty between North Korea and the United States. A breakthrough of sorts occurred in November 1998 when South Korean tourists were permitted to visit the North for the first time since the two governments were established fifty years earlier. South Korean corporations eagerly developed plans for joint ventures that would accord them access to North Korea's cheap labor and abundant raw materials. South Korean President Kim Dae Jung's "sunshine policy" of detente with the North reached its apogee in June 2000, when he became the first South Korean chief of state to visit North Korea. At the end of the summit, the two sides pledged to work for national unification and agreed to further cooperation.

For all the euphoria of North-South detente, North Korea's descent into economic chaos and starvation lent an air of urgency to the existing concerns about its capacity to become a nuclear state. The international consortium created to implement the 1994 agreement began construction of the two light-water reactors in North Korea in the summer of 1997, and the financing of the project was arranged the following year. But when IAEA inspection teams uncovered evidence that underground sites might contain reactors capable of producing weapons-grade plutonium in violation of the 1994 agreement, the North Korean government rejected all requests for unrestricted inspection of the suspected sites. Amid the growing concerns about a possible clandestine nuclear weapons program in North Korea, Pyongyang made significant progress in the development of a delivery system for such nuclear weapons as it may produce. Without warning it test-fired a ballistic missile over Japanese territory on August 31, 1998. Evidence continued to accumulate that North Korea had not abandoned its ambitions to develop a nuclear capability. When confronted by the new Bush administration with this evidence in 2002, Pyongyang expelled the IAEA inspectors at the end of the year and then formally withdrew from the Non-Proliferation Treaty in January 2003. During the next few years China took the lead in sponsoring a series of multilateral negotiations to resolve the issue that eventually included representatives from the two Koreas, China, Russia, and the United States. During these long, drawn-out talks, the enigmatic North Korean leader Kim Jong Il seemed to be playing the nuclear card to extract concessions from his negotiating partners to shore up his isolated regime. From South Korea, Russia, and China he sought financial assistance for the North's collapsing economy; from the United States he sought a nonaggression pact to ensure against a U.S. military attack, particularly after President Bush included North Korea as part of the "Axis of Evil" in his January 2002 State of the Union Address and later demonstrated his willingness to use military force to topple unfriendly regimes in Afghanistan and Iraq.

Amid the remarkable economic growth of China and the ominous nuclear ambitions of North Korea, those two Communist countries' historic regional adversary had fallen on uncharacteristically hard times. Japan, whose economic expansion had provoked the envy of the world and spawned slavish imitators throughout East Asia, suffered its worst economic slowdown since the end of the Second World War. The social tensions that inevitably resulted from a long and severe recession were exacerbated by two contentious controversies in Japan's relations with the United States. The first was the incessant transpacific conflict with the United States over trade policy, which erupted into strongly worded American complaints about Japanese protectionism, particularly concerning exports of automobiles and automobile parts, semiconductors, and rice. The second source of Japanese—American tension was the dispute over military burden sharing. Many Americans began to express reservations about continuing to provide security protection to Japan while that country flooded the U.S. market with its products and shielded its domestic farms and factories from American competition. Though Tokyo reluctantly bowed to American pressure and consented to increase its share of the costs of maintaining U.S. military forces on its territory to 70 percent by 1995, the issue left bitter tastes in mouths on both sides of the Pacific.

The debate over sharing the cost of Japan's defense in East Asia coincided with a wide-ranging reassessment of Japan's future international role in the post-Cold War era. The principal question was whether Tokyo should revoke its longstanding prohibition against participation in overseas operations by the Japanese military forces. Japan had contributed financially to the military campaign against Iraq in 1991, but parliamentary opposition prevented the government of Toshiki Kaifu from dispatching units of the Japanese army (or Self-Defense Force, as it is euphemistically named) to join the multinational contingent in the Persian Gulf. But in the spring of 1991 Kaifu dispatched Japanese naval minesweepers to the Gulf as part of a postwar operation to secure the sea-lanes for oil tankers, the first time since World War II that Japanese naval forces had been sent overseas. In October 1992 Kaifu's successor, Kiichi Miyazawa, furnished a small contingent of Japanese military engineers to the United Nations peacekeeping operation in Cambodia to assist in construction projects, the first foreign assignment of Japanese ground troops since the war. The bitter memories of earlier Japanese transgressions abroad were periodically rekindled by public relations gaffes such as the Japanese Diet's refusal to issue a formal apology on the fiftieth anniversary of the attack on Pearl Harbor and its refusal to provide financial compensation to surviving Korean women who had been forced into prostitution by Japanese military units during the war. But the past half-century of Japan's military passivity and diplomatic prudence seemed to have attenuated those atavistic anxieties. In light of the expanding military and economic might of China, many of Japan's neighbors began to appreciate her potential role as a counterveiling force in the evolving balance of power in East Asia.

After reaffirming the Japanese-American Security Treaty in 1996, Tokyo and Washington redefined the nature of that bilateral security relationship the following year. Among other things, the new agreement obliged Japan to provide logistical support to U.S. military forces in the event of conflict in the Far East, though the precise geographical area covered by the agreement was left ambiguous. It was evident that this enhanced security cooperation between Japan and the United States was directed at North Korea, whose apparent determination to acquire nuclear weapons caused considerable alarm in Tokyo. The North Korean ballistic missile test across Japanese territory in August 1998 was the last straw. It led directly to Japan's endorsement of an American proposal to begin joint research on a theater missile defense system in East Asia that would employ satellites, radar, and sea-based missiles to identify and intercept incoming ballistic missiles. The most notable source of dissension in the Japanese-American alliance was the presence of U.S. servicepeople on the island of Okinawa, whose citizens exerted intense political pressure on the government in Tokyo to reduce the conspicuous and overbearing American military presence there. Though a compromise of sorts was reached in 1996, when the two countries agreed to convert the large U.S. Marine base on the small island into a heliport, resentment against the intrusive presence of foreign military units continued to brew.

The relationship between the United States and Asia in general underwent a fundamental evolution after the end of the Cold War. While the U.S. retained important trade and investment stakes across the Pacific, the recession of Soviet power in the Far East and the economic difficulties of the early 1990s prompted a reassessment of American security interests in the region. As domestic issues increasingly dominated the political agenda in the United States, American public opinion began to question the wisdom of maintaining a massive and costly U.S. military presence in a part of the world where the enemy had vanished and the allies were running up huge trade surpluses with their transpacific protector. The most conspicuous consequence of this reappraisal of America's future security role in Asia was the closure of the American naval base at Subic Bay in the Philippines, the principal supply and repair center for the Seventh Fleet. But compensatory arrangements for emergency access to base facilities in Malaysia, Indonesia, Singapore, and Brunei were promptly negotiated, while the Seventh Fleet retained its home port at Yokosuka in Japan, and a contingent of thirty-seven thousand U.S. Army and Air Force personnel remained to bolster the defensive capability of South Korea. Nevertheless, the withdrawal from the Philippines seemed to some observers the symbol of a subtle shift in American priorities in East Asia. Economic interests would thereafter take precedence over security concerns in a comparatively stable and secure area.

Yet the preservation of this blessed state of regional stability could hardly be taken for granted in a part of the world that had been torn by international and civil strife from the early 1930s to the end of the Cold War. This was all the more evident in light of the sharp increase in arms purchases by the rapidly industrializing countries in the region during the early 1990s. The organization of a multilateral mechanism to ensure Asian regional security in the post-Cold War era therefore became a matter of considerable urgency for the nations concerned, lest an individual power such as China (with its nuclear arsenal, expanding naval power, and booming economy) be tempted unilaterally to fill the strategic vacuum left by the disintegration of the Soviet Union and the recession of American power. In contrast to Europe and the western hemisphere, however, Asia lacked an existing security mechanism such as NATO, the WEU, or the OAS that could be adapted to the new strategic circumstances. Dulles's old brainchild, SEATO, had never amounted to much more than a figleaf for America's military engagement in Indochina and had disappeared in 1977 without fanfare after the Vietnamese triumph in the midseventies.

In the early 1990s two alternative but potentially complementary initiatives materialized to address the dilemma of organizing East Asian security in the post-Cold War era. The first of these emanated from the Association of South-East Asian Nations (ASEAN), an initially loose-knit organization that sought to expand its role as a multilateral force for stability in the region. In May 1993 ASEAN officials proposed that the diplomatic machinery specified in the organization's Treaty of Amity and Cooperation serve as a means of settling regional disputes. In July of the same year the organization's foreign ministers hosted a meeting in Singapore to which representatives of all powers with interests in Asia and the Pacific were invited. This unprecedented official gathering decided to convene an ASEAN Regional Forum the following year to review the entire question of Asian security in light of the new geopolitical realities of the 1990s. The eighteen-nation ASEAN Regional Forum held its inaugural meeting at Bangkok in July 1994 amid high hopes for future cooperation to ensure East Asian peace and stability, but nothing of any significance resulted from the meeting.

In the meantime, the ASEAN security initiative had run into competition from an unexpected overture from Washington. In July 1993 President Clinton invited Asian leaders to assemble in Seattle after the annual meeting of the Asia-Pacific Economic Cooperation Conference (APEC), an informal organization established in 1989 at Australia's suggestion to discuss economic issues of interest to nations on the Pacific rim. Though the Seattle meeting produced nothing more than innocuous declarations, the question became whether ASEAN and its new Regional Forum or the U.S.-dominated APEC would serve as the nucleus for a post-Cold War security arrangement in Asia.

At the November 1994 APEC summit in Jakarta, Indonesia, Clinton persuaded the leaders of the eighteen Pacific rim nations to endorse a vaguely worded, nonbinding declaration establishing the concept of a Pacific economic community in which the United States would play a leading role. APEC set up a working group under Japanese leadership that was instructed to draft a blueprint for implementing the goal of a Pacific free trade zone. In the meantime, ASEAN's attempts to forge a regional security system in Southeast Asia continued. In 1995 the organization admitted Vietnam into the fold and formally resolved to incorporate all other countries in the region by the end of the decade. Myanmar (formerly Burma) and Laos joined in 1997, followed by Cambodia in 1999. At its 1995 Bangkok summit the ASEAN states had also concluded a treaty which designated South East Asia as a nuclear weapons-free zone, obliging each signatory to refrain from producing or testing nuclear weapons. The expansion of its membership and the commitment to regional nuclear disarmament seemed to suggest that ASEAN was poised to become a regional collective security system worthy of the name. But the organization's Regional Forum, which had been set up in 1993 as an embryonic collective security system for Southeast Asia, had proved totally ineffectual amid the escalating tension in the region's two trouble spots in the Taiwan Strait and the South China Sea.

The longtime Prime Minister of Malaysia, Mahathir Mohamad, became the leading exponent of a coherent political, social, and cultural ideology that was designed to unite the diverse population groups within ASEAN. Borrowing heavily from the policies and pronouncements of former Prime Minister Lee Kuan Yew of Singapore, Mahathir and his followers preached a return to "Asian values" as the basis of a successful program of development for the countries of the region: authoritarian government, hierarchical social order, and state control of economic life were preferable to the "Western values" of political democracy, civic culture, and market capitalism. But in 1997 the miraculous economic growth of East Asia that had impressed the world for more than three decades suffered a sharp setback when the currencies and financial markets of Thailand, South Korea, Indonesia, and Malaysia collapsed.

None of the renowned Asian "Tigers" were exempt from the spreading economic crisis. Two of South Korea's largest steel companies and its third-largest automobile firm went bankrupt. When the South Korean won plunged to record lows, the government rushed to the IMF in November and secured a loan of $57 billion, the largest amount ever provided to a single country by the international lending organization. The IMF attached its customary stiff conditions to the bailout, including demands that the highly protected South Korean economy be opened to foreign imports and the country's notoriously restrictive financial markets be made more accessible to foreign investors. The new government of the reforming President Kim Dae Jung that took power in 1998 undertook a radical restructuring of the South Korean economy, closing money-losing banks, investment firms, and industrial conglomerates while streamlining those that survived and forcing them to adapt to foreign competition. These measures led to bankruptcies of inefficient firms and increasing unemployment, which generated widespread protests thoughout the century.

The regional financial crisis of 1997–98 severely tested the concept of "Asian values" that Malaysia's Mahathir had advertised as the recipe for future progress. While most of the battered economies of the region were forced to adopt "Western" policies of economic liberalization to ensure the flow of IMF funds, the Malaysian Prime Minister defiantly refused to capitulate. Mahathir blamed the Asian financial debacle on foreign exchange speculators from the developed world and imposed exchange controls to shield Malaysia from the iniquitous effects of globalization. But as the other countries in the region dutifully bowed to the requirements of the IMF and other multinational financial institutions in order to shore up their battered treasuries, Malaysia was left as an isolated champion of "Asian values" amid a global economic order dominated by the developed countries of the West.

When the Asian financial crisis hit Indonesia, it aggravated the long-simmering domestic political crisis in that country and led to the forced resignation in May 1998 of President Suharto, who had ruled that country with an iron fist for thirty-two years. A sprawling nation of over seventeen thousand islands with a population of 200 million, Indonesia casts a long shadow over Southeast Asia. Under Suharto's predecessor, President Sukarno, the country had pursued an aggressive policy of regional expansion. One of the major reasons for the establishment of ASEAN in August 1967 had been to enmesh

Indonesia in a multilateral system of regional cooperation that would curb its hegemonic ambitions, just as the European Economic Community had been set up in part to harness West Germany's energies for the greater good of the region. Apart from its occupation and annexation of the former Portuguese territory of East Timor in 1975, Suharto's regime maintained a relatively low profile in Southeast Asia, compared to Sukarno's expansionist policies, as it turned inward to concentrate on a crash program of economic development. By the beginning of the 1990s Indonesia had recorded impressive growth rates and seemed poised to become the next "Asian Tiger." But the onset of the financial crisis in 1998 sent the economy into a tailspin. The rupiah lost almost three-quarters of its value, serious shortages of food developed, and poverty and unemployment spread. The economic crisis led to a revival of xenophobic violence against the ethnic Chinese minority that dominated the commercial life of the country.

Suharto's successor faced not only the continued economic crisis but also a revival of separatist agitation in East Timor. In January 1999 the Indonesian government pledged to conduct a referendum permitting the East Timorese to choose between autonomy within Indonesia and independence. The remainder of the year was marked by an escalation of violence between the pro-independence faction and pro-Indonesian groups backed by the Indonesian military, which had opposed the government's decision to consult the citizens of the island. The referendum, which was finally held under United Nations auspices in 1999, recorded a majority for independence. After an explosion of violence by anti-independence militias and Indonesian army contingents that terrorized the population, order was finally restored by Australian troops acting on behalf of the UN Security Council. Under the auspices of a UN peacekeeping force, East Timor finally obtained its independence in the spring of 2002.

The one example of a successful bid to end armed conflict in Southeast Asia during the 1900s was the termination of the fourteen-year civil war in Cambodia. This remnant of the cold war was disposed of by the intervention of the United Nations together with some old-fashioned great-power diplomacy by Beijing and Washington. Pressure from the Kremlin had induced Vietnam to withdraw troops from Cambodia in 1989, while the United States was urging the coalition of resistance groups to seek a negotiated settlement. The regime in Phnom Penh opened peace talks in Paris with the three rebel factions that had recently coalesced under the titular authority of Prince Norodom Sihanouk. In 1990 the United Nations Security Council began to assume an active role in promoting a resolution of the Cambodian conflict. In the meantime the political crisis in the Soviet Union left Moscow's protégés in Hanoi vulnerable to the intense pressure exerted by China and the United States—the two principal foreign supporters of the Cambodian rebels—to persuade the puppet state in Phnom Penh to accept a compromise settlement. Finally, after two years of intensive negotiations and several abortive cease-fires, the four parties to the dispute signed a peace accord in Paris on October 23, 1991. It established a United Nations Transitional Authority in Cambodia (UNTAC) to operate in partnership with a supreme national council chaired by Sihanouk and comprising representatives of the three insurgent groups and the Vietnamese-backed government. By the end of the year Sihanouk and the Khmer Rouge officials had returned to Phnom Penh from their havens in China and Thailand, respectively. UNTAC, whose twenty-two thousand military and civilian personnel represented the most formidable peacekeeping force ever deployed by the United Nations, began to arrive in the spring of 1992 to enforce the cease-fire, supervise the disarmament of the contending military forces, and prepare for nationwide elections scheduled for the following May.

Though abandoned by their longtime sponsors in Beijing, the Khmer Rouge refused to disarm, prevented UNTAC personnel from registering voters in the areas under their control, and announced in November 1992 their intention to boycott the forthcoming elections in protest against the favoritism allegedly shown by UNTAC toward the government. The May 1993 elections, which were certified as free and fair by the UN observers, resulted in a plurality for the party headed by Sihanouk's eldest son, Prince Norodom Ranariddh. In the following month he formed a provisional government in coalition with the former head of the Vietnamese puppet regime, Hun Sen. Sihanouk mounted his former throne as head of a constitutional monarchy in September, the remaining UNTAC troops departed in November, and by early 1994 the two former rebel factions had joined forces with military units of the former government against the Khmer Rouge. In June 1994, after renewing their campaign of intimidation and violence, the Khmer Rouge representatives in Phnom Penh were expelled from the capital. A traumatized society that had suffered one of the most grisly outbreaks of genocide in this century embarked on a period of relative peace and stability for the first time in fourteen years. This benign outcome was facilitated by the fundamental shift in the Asian balance of power occasioned by the decline of the Soviet Union. Vietnam, relegated to a position of political isolation and military vulnerability by the loss of its traditional protector, was driven to seek an accommodation with its old adversaries in Washington and Beijing at the expense of its grandiose dreams of dominion over all of Indochina. With the end of the Cold War, the United Nations was able to devise a settlement that proved satisfactory to all but the recalcitrant partisans of Pol Pot.

TENSIONS IN SOUTH ASIA

While most of Asia enjoyed a period of relative peace, stability, and economic growth since the end of the Cold War, the two powers on the Indian subcontinent—India and Pakistan—resumed the rancorous rivalry that has persisted since their emergence as independent states after the Second World War. The partition of the "crown jewel" of the British Empire into a predominantly Hindu (though ostensibly secular) India and a devoutly Muslim Pakistan, together with the exchange of almost two million refugees in the summer of 1947, had been undertaken for the purpose of forming as ethnically homogeneous new states as possible in order to minimize friction between members of these historically antipathetic religious groups. But the massive population transfers had left better memories of atrocities committed by both sides. The Muslims who predominated in India's northernmost state of Kashmir agitated for independence from the Hindu-dominated government in Delhi, for which they received strong encouragement and considerable financial support from the Islamic government of Pakistan. India's experimental schemes of autonomy for Kashmir, undertaken periodically in order to assuage the secessionist ardor of the state's Muslim citizens and therefore deprive Pakistan of any pretext for interfering in India's internal affairs, came to naught. Two major wars, perennial border skirmishes, and fiery political rhetoric in Delhi and Islamabad poisoned relations between the two successor states of British India for decades to come. The most

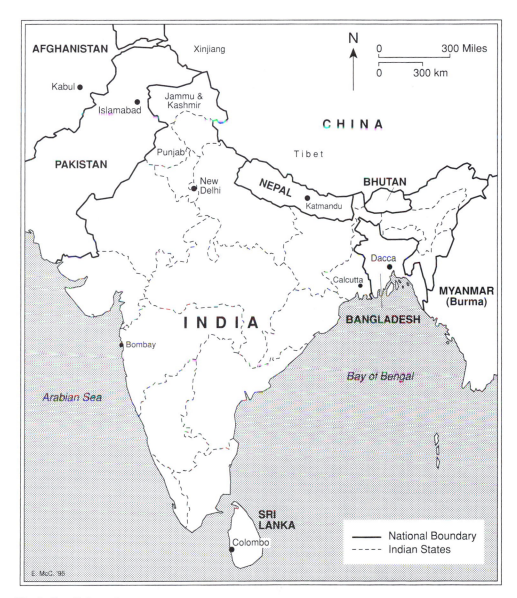

The Indian Subcontinent

recent upsurge of Muslim secessionist insurgency in Kashmir, covertly supported by
Pakistan, began in 1989 and continued into the twenty-first century.

India's relentless quarrel with Pakistan over Kashmir was rivaled in intensity by two
long-standing controversies with the People's Republic of China. The first was a border
dispute between Delhi and Beijing that had flared up sporadically since the autumn of
1962, when Indian and Chinese forces came to blows over the contested territory. The

second concerned Tibet, an isolated, mountainous kingdom to India's north, which had been invaded and annexed by China in the autumn of 1950 while the world's attention was distracted by the Korean War. Though the Communist regime in Beijing initially granted the Tibetans a modicum of autonomy and permitted them to retain their spiritual and political leader, the Dalai Lama, clashes between the Buddhist population and the Communist police recurred throughout the fifties. In 1959 Chinese Prime Minister Zhou Enlai dissolved the Tibetan regional government headed by the Dalai Lama, who promptly crossed the border into India where he was granted political asylum. Thereafter, as China strove to eradicate the Buddhist religion in its rebellious province, India took the lead in mobilizing world opinion against Beijing's repressive policy there. The combination of the Sino-Indian border dispute and the controversy over Tibet kept the two neighbors at sword's point.

While continuing to affirm its commitment to the nonaligned movement, India became increasingly apprehensive about the practical consequences of its isolated position in the Cold War world and recognized the need for allies. After Nehru's death in 1964, India accelerated its orientation toward the Soviet Union, which had already begun to furnish it with diplomatic support and economic assistance in Nehru's final years. The rapprochement between Delhi and Moscow was directly related to the Sino-Soviet split, as each country came to regard China as its principal antagonist. In the meantime the United States cultivated increasingly warm relations with India's regional rival, Pakistan. The Nixon administration openly sided with that country in its brief, ill-fated war with India in 1971, which led to the secession of East Pakistan and its birth as the independent state of Bangladesh. In the aftermath of India's military victory Washington undertook to restore the military capability of Pakistan to counter that of what it increasingly regarded as the Kremlin's client state on the subcontinent. Islamabad reciprocated this solicitude by using its good offices to promote the emerging reconciliation between Washington and Beijing (with which Pakistan maintained cordial relations on the basis of their common hostility to India). This intimate Sino-Pakistani-American collaboration reached its height after the Soviet invasion of Afghanistan in 1979. These three powers jointly supported the Islamic resistance to the Russian military occupation forces and their Afghan allies in Kabul.*

The end of the Cold War and the withdrawal of Soviet military forces from Afghanistan at the end of the eighties set the stage for a major geopolitical realignment in South Asia. No longer obsessed with the putative menace of Soviet expansion toward the warm waters of the Indian Ocean, policy makers in Washington began to focus on two other threats to the stability of South Asia that paradoxically emanated from America's longtime ally in the region. The first of these was the looming phenomenon of Islamic fundamentalism that will be discussed at greater length in subsequent chapters on the Middle East and North Africa.† The Islamic Republic of Pakistan, whose citizens were subjected to the legal provisions of the *Sharia*,‡ began in the early 1990s to culti-

---

*See page 390.

†See pages 463, 472.

‡The Islamic code of religious law based on the teachings of the Koran and the traditional sayings of Mohammed.

vate close relations with other Muslim states including Iran, Afghanistan, and the newly independent republics of Soviet Central Asia.* Pakistan's shift from an anti-Soviet to a pro-Islamic foreign policy coincided with another development that caused strains in the U.S.-Pakistani partnership. Ever since India tested an atomic weapon in 1974, Pakistan had been suspected of undertaking a clandestine nuclear program of its own to match its regional rival. Alarmed at the prospect of nuclear proliferation on the Indian subcontinent, the U.S. Senate passed a resolution in 1986 requiring the termination of Washington's generous economic and military assistance program to Pakistan unless the State Department could certify that the recipient of that largess was not engaged in the development of nuclear weapons. When the State Department acknowledged in 1990 that it could no longer give such assurances, Washington terminated its military assistance program to Pakistan.

Another source of tension between the United States and its former ally Pakistan was the latter power's intervention in the internal affairs of the neighboring state of Afghanistan. After the Soviet military withdrawal in 1989, the Kremlin's puppet regime clung to power in Kabul for three more years before a coalition of Islamic resistance groups seized the capital city on April 25, 1992, and proceeded to liquidate all vestiges of the Communist administration. But bitter ethnic conflict among the Pashto-speaking Pashtuns, Persian-speaking Tajiks and Hazaras, and Turkic-speaking Uzbeks plunged Afghanistan into a lethal and destructive civil war as regional military commanders assumed de facto control of most of the country. By the mid-1990s a devout sect of Sunni Muslim Pashtuns named the Taliban had mounted an armed insurrection with the goal of ending corruption, breaking the authority of the regional warlords, restoring social order, and establishing a regime based on Islamic principles. The Islamic republic of neighboring Pakistan promptly lent its support to the Taliban in a bid to extend its influence in the war-torn country. With Pakistan's support the Taliban forces swept into Kabul in 1996 as the Tajik, Uzbek, and Hazara fighters retreated to a mountainous enclave in the northwestern part of the country to conduct a rear-guard campaign against the new government. The Taliban proceeded to establish a puritanical Islamic regime with rigid codes of dress and behavior based a strict interpretation of the Koran. It also provided training camps for young fundamentalist Islamic volunteers from Arab countries who had come to Afghanistan to defend the Taliban regime against the fighters in the northeastern mountains who had coalesced as the Northern Alliance. When one of these radical Islamic groups, al-Qaeda, began to stage terrorist attacks against American targets, the Clinton administration in Washington began an unsuccessful attempt to pressure Pakistan into suspending its support for the haven for terrorist groups that Afghanistan had become (see page 510).

The loosening of U.S. ties with Pakistan was accompanied by an improvement of Washington's relations with India, whose traditional foreign policy had been thrown into disarray by the demise of its patron and benefactor in Moscow. Pleased by the suspension of U.S. aid to Pakistan and sharing America's concern about the prospect of Pakistan's "Islamic bomb," India proved receptive to U.S. initiatives in 1991–92 for closer military and naval cooperation between the two countries. This Indo-American rap-

---

*See page 419.

prochement coincided with an ideological evolution within India in the form of Prime Minister Rajiv Gandhi's campaign to liberalize the state-controlled economic system at the end of the 1980s. By terminating government subsidies, reducing protective tariffs, and abolishing restrictions on foreign investment, India joined the international economic system from which it had long sought to insulate itself.

The stakes in the Indo-Pakistani conflict were raised by the progress of nuclear weapons programs in both countries. India exploded a nuclear device in 1974 but since that time continually denied possessing atomic bombs, insisting on the peaceful commercial intent of its research and development efforts. But India steadfastly refused to sign the Nuclear Non-Proliferation Treaty (NPT) unless it became universal (that is, all countries signed) and nondiscriminatory (that is, the five powers with nuclear weapons agreed to dispose of them). Pakistan also declined to sign the NPT in light of the policy of its regional rival. Both countries began to develop delivery systems in the form of short- and medium-range missiles, raising the specter of a competitive nuclear arms race on the subcontinent.

The covert Indo-Pakistani nuclear competition suddenly became overt in May 1998, when India announced that it had conducted five underground nuclear tests. The purpose of the tests was twofold: first, to counter the formidable nuclear arsenal of its other archrival, China; second, to match the embryonic nuclear capability that Pakistan had been developing (with Chinese assistance) for more than two decades. Jolted into action by the Indian tests, Pakistan withstood intense pressure from the United States and defiantly conducted two underground tests of its own toward the end of the month. The United States, Japan, and other powers promptly imposed sanctions on the two countries, but when financially strapped Pakistan was about to default on its foreign debt the Clinton administration rescinded most of the sanctions as the IMF rushed in with a rescue package. The nuclearization of the Indian subcontinent therefore became an accomplished fact. It dealt a serious blow to the cause of nonproliferation, prompting other nonnuclear states to reconsider their willingness to forego membership in a club of states possessing weapons of mass destruction that had been expanded from five to seven. Continual conflict over Kashmir brought India and Pakistan into the most dangerous confrontation between two nuclear powers since the Cuban Missile Crisis, though both sides backed away from the brink. But the presence of nuclear weapons and the means of delivering them on the volatile Indian subcontinent remained a powerful reminder that the end of the Cold War did not end the threat of nuclear annihilation in the world.

19

AFRICA ON ITS OWN: ETHNIC CONFLICT, AUTOCRACY, AND UNDERDEVELOPMENT

As in all other parts of the world, the end of the Cold War influenced political developments in Africa in a number of important ways. The termination of the East-West rivalry on that continent facilitated settlements in its various civil conflicts, in which the two superpowers had been indirectly involved since the mid-1970s. The disappearance of the Soviet threat enabled Western nations to apply greater pressure on friendly regimes in Africa to reform autocratic political systems previously tolerated in the interests of combating communism. But the end of the ideological antagonism between Moscow and Washington and their regional clients did not bring peace, prosperity, and stability to Africa. Instead, an eruption of ethnic, tribal, clan, and religious violence since the early 1990s threatened the territorial integrity of states, shattered truces in civil wars, and impeded the progress of democratization by enabling politicians to exploit separatist tensions in order to seize or maintain dictatorial power.

The hopes for democratization in Africa that had flourished during the 1980s were also undermined by a set of deep-seated economic problems that continued to grip the continent. The heavy burden of international indebtedness, the desperate need for foreign investment, disadvantageous terms of trade, and agricultural backwardness continued to inhibit Africa's economic growth. The prosperous nations of the industrialized West lost interest in courting African regimes with aid programs when the collapse of the Communist bloc removed the need for foreign allies in the East-West struggle. The end of the Cold War deprived Africa of the attention she had received from nervous NATO leaders when Cuban troops patrolled the streets of Angolan cities and Soviet naval vessels docked at Somali ports.

The disengagement of the two superpowers from Africa at the end of the 1980s set the stage for the engagement of the international community on an unprecedented scale. The appearance of multinational peacekeeping missions under the auspices of the United

Nations and its designated representatives were intended not to promote the national interest of the participating countries (as had always been the case in the past), but rather to promote the stability, protect the civilian populations, and ensure the relief of the subject country. Never before had foreign intervention in Africa been inspired by such seemingly altruistic motives, and never before had the United Nations played such an activist role on the continent. But these operations represented belated, piecemeal efforts to limit the immediate consequences of anarchy, poverty, and civil war. What was desperately needed, and entirely lacking, were comprehensive solutions to Africa's long-term problems.

The Horn of Africa had become one of the most hotly contested sites of superpower rivalry in the latter stages of the Cold War, when Washington and Moscow lavished economic and military aid on their respective client states in the region in order to advance their own interests. With the breakup of the Soviet Union and the consequent decline in the strategic value of the Horn to the United States, the former beneficiaries of this superpower patronage were abruptly left to their own devices. The first two casualties of this precipitous disengagement were the corrupt, repressive regimes in Somalia and Ethiopia that had been avidly courted by Washington and Moscow in the period of East-West global rivalry. The collapse of the dictatorships in Mogadishu and Addis Ababa resulted not in stable governments based on popular consent, but rather anarchical conditions in which tribe and clan replaced the nation as the repository of public loyalty. In the Sudan, one repressive regime gave way to another, which promptly raised the banner of Islamic fundamentalism to bolster its claim to absolute power.

The fourteen-year-old despotism of Mengistu Haile Mariam in Ethiopia was cashiered on May 21, 1991, by an insurgent group, dominated by inhabitants of the northern province of Tigre, known as the Ethiopian People's Revolutionary Democratic Front. The front's leader, Meles Senawi, inherited a country that was splintered into sixty-four different ethnic groups that shared in common nothing but a determination to resist the authority of the central government in Addis Ababa. In order to placate these dissident factions, Meles granted each a high degree of autonomy within its region, including the all-important prerogative of speaking the local language or dialect.

But autonomy proved insufficient for the militants in two of the most powerful ethnic groups in the polyglot country. The Oromos, who constituted approximately 40 percent of the population, grew increasingly dissatisfied with the new Tigrayan-dominated government and began to consider the alternative of secession. The inhabitants of the former Italian colony of Eritrea on the Red Sea, which had been federated with Ethiopia in 1952, had been fighting for their own separate state since 1971. After the demise of the Mengistu dictatorship, the Eritreans demanded and obtained a referendum on full independence. In May 1993 they voted overwhelmingly to sever their ties with Ethiopia, and a new African state was born. Though the secession of Ethiopia's northern province transpired without bloodshed, it set an ominous precedent not only for the other restive ethnic groups in that truncated country but also for dissident minorities elsewhere in Africa. It was the first violation of the Organization of African Unity's solemn dictum that the territorial integrity of the postcolonial states be preserved at all costs lest the principle of self-determination become an agent of political disintegration throughout the continent. Though successful in obtaining prompt recognition from foreign powers, Africa's newest nation was plagued from its inception by a potentially disruptive religious schism that perfectly illustrated the problem that prompted the OAU's original admonition: The country is equally divided between Christians and Muslims, a malignant combination that (as we shall see) gravely impaired the stability of neighboring Sudan. Eritrea also experienced continual conflicts with Ethiopia, which had lost its ports on the Red Sea when Eritrea seceded in 1993. The resulting friction over the payments Ethiopia was obliged to make for access to these ports, aggravated by a border dispute between the two countries, erupted in an armed conflict in May 1998 which continued into the next century.

Somalia, Ethiopia's perennial antagonist on the Horn of Africa, faced an even more tragic fate after the deposition of *its* strongman, Mohammed Siad Barre, on January 27, 1991. As in Ethiopia, the concept of national identity vanished amid the resurgence of particularist sentiments. Although the Somalis (unlike the Ethiopians) constitute a relatively homogeneous ethnic and religious population, clans and subclans exert the strongest claim on popular loyalty. Ali Mahdi Mohammed, Siad Barre's successor from a branch of the Hawiye clan, failed to establish his authority over rival clans and subclans as the central administrative structure of the Somali state disintegrated and the fragile economy collapsed throughout 1991. General Mohammed Farah Aideed from a rival Hawiye subclan forcefully contested the authority of the central government in Mogadishu, while other local warlords also took up arms to defend their turf. In May the Issaq clan declared an independent "Somaliland Republic" in the northern portion of the country that had been a British protectorate before uniting with the former Italian Somaliland to form the postcolonial state in 1960. Unlike the Eritreans the Isaaqs failed to secure foreign recognition of their statehood. But they faced little interference from what passed for the central government in Mogadishu, which after the overthrow of "interim president" Ali Mahdi Mohammed in the fall of 1992, proved incapable of exercising even a modicum of authority anywhere in the country. Throughout the year 1992 Somalia degenerated into a nightmare of starvation, disease, and violence. Over 400,000 Somalis starved to death as fourteen different private armies jockeyed for power, killing innocent civilians and plundering food shipments from international humanitarian agencies and foreign governments.

In response to the heartrending news reports and pictures of the widespread suffering caused by this man-made famine, the United Nations decided to take action. The Security Council declared an arms embargo on Somalia in order to stem the flow of weapons to the bickering warlords and established an international peacekeeping force called the United Nations Operation in Somalia (UNOSOM). For the remainder of the year UNOSOM failed in its mission to protect relief conveys delivering food and medicine to Somalia's starving, disease-ridden population because of bureaucratic roadblocks and legal constraints that prevented it from employing force against the warlords and their armed gangs. At the end of 1992 the Security Council authorized the United States to assume control of a much larger international force empowered to use "all necessary means" to facilitate relief operations. This forty thousand-person task force (UNITAF) of soldiers from more than twenty countries—the first genuinely humanitarian military operation in the history of the United Nations—succeeded in opening up most of the supply routes and reducing the incidence of looting throughout the winter and spring of 1993. In May of that year UNITAF turned over its peacekeeping responsibilities in Somalia to a revamped United Nations force (UNOSOM II) that was armed with the authority to enforce its will that had been denied UNOSOM I. A four thousand-person U.S. unit remained with the UN mission until American casualties prompted President Clinton to begin withdrawing it in early 1994. Sporadic clashes between UN troops and local militias continued as Somalia remained mired in anarchy and unrest. When the UN mandate expired in March 1995 and the last blue helmeted units withdrew, Somalia was left to its own devices.

Acute ethnic violence plagued Somalia's other neighbor on the Horn of Africa as well. In Sudan, Africa's largest nation, the military regime of General Omar Hassan al-Bashir that had seized power in the summer of 1989 came under the domination of a fundamentalist Muslim movement called the National Islamic Front. The Muslim ruling elite from the northern part of the country intensified a long-standing campaign to apply the Islamic legal system (*Sharia*) to the predominantly Christian south. Southern rebels in the Sudan People's Liberation Army (SPLA), which had been resisting the application of Islamic law to their region since the early 1980s, stepped up their attacks against government forces. The civil war between rebel contingents from the Christian south (supported by predominantly Christian Ethiopia) and government forces from the Muslim north (backed by the fundamentalist regime in Iran as well as the secular Arab states of Iraq and Libya) raged throughout the 1990s. The continuing tension in Sudan demonstrated that religion must be added to ethnicity, clan loyalty, and regional identity as potential threats to national unity and state sovereignty in Africa. This internal struggle acquired an international significance when the Sudanese government allegedly began to sponsor terrorist acts on behalf of Islamic fundamentalism abroad, including an assassination attempt against Egyptian President Hosni Mubarak (who had cracked down on radical Islamists in his own country) in 1995. Egypt accused Sudan of establishing training camps for radical Islamic militants, including thousands of battle-seasoned veterans of the struggle in Afghanistan against the Russian occupation forces. The United States later took the lead in denouncing the Sudanese government's alleged support for international terrorism, imposing economic sanctions against Khartoum in 1997.

Concerned about the maltreatment of Christians by the Sudanese government and attracted by the prospect of tapping the country's potentially valuable oil reserves, the Bush administration in Washington exerted strong pressure on the two sides in the Sudanese civil war to reach a settlement that would end the fighting that had taken more than two million lives since 1983. By the end of 2003 President Bashir and the southern rebel leader John Gareng had reached a tentative agreement whereby the government, in exchange for an end to the insurgency, would share oil revenues with the south, offer the region greater autonomy, and exempt its Christian population from punishments dictated by the *Sharia.* But in the meantime the western region of Darfur had mounted an insurrection to demand greater economic aid from the central government. Just as the regime in Khartoum was winding down its counterinsurgency operations in the south, it launched a massive bombing campaign coordinated with murderous raids by local "Arab" militias in the west to snuff out the incipient rebellion there. Darfur's population is almost entirely Muslim, so the new conflict lacked the religious overtones of the civil war between north and south. But it assumed a racial and social dimension, pitting a government-sponsored militia composed of seminomadic livestock herders who claim "Arab" descent against the segment of the population who claims black "African" descent and practices sedentary agriculture. The massive campaign of ethnic violence, including killings, rape, and ethnic cleansing mounted by the Arab militias, prompted international condemnation and accusations of genocide by governments and non-governmental organizations.

The difficulty in terminating the civil war in Angola revealed that the end of outside intervention by the superpowers and their partners did not guarantee a return to regional stability in Africa. Foreign involvement in the bitter conflict in the former Portuguese colony had come to a close at the end of the 1980s with the simultaneous withdrawal of the South African forces backing the anti-Communist rebel faction and Cuban troops assisting the self-proclaimed Marxist government.* Intensive negotiations had finally resulted in a peace agreement signed on May 31, 1991, in Bicesse, Portugal, by Jonas Savimbi of UNITA, the Ovimbundu-dominated rebel movement, and Angolan President José Eduardo dos Santos of the ruling MPLA representing the non-Ovimbundu majority. The Bicesse Accord provided for a cease-fire preparatory to the country's first free elections scheduled for the autumn of 1992 under the supervision of United Nations personnel. After the two factions agreed to form a coalition government and combine their military forces in a joint national army, legislative elections were held on schedule at the end of September with massive voter participation. The ruling MPLA, which had jettisoned its Marxist program and cultivated cordial relations with the West after the departure of its Cuban mercenaries and Soviet advisers, won 54 percent of the vote compared to UNITA's 34 percent. Refusing to accept the electoral results, Savimbi withdrew his troops from the integrated national army and resumed his guerrilla warfare against the MPLA which brought more than two-thirds of the country under his control within a few months. After Washington cut off all subsidies to UNITA and recognized the new legally elected Angolan government, Savimbi had to finance his military effort with illegal diamond-mining operations in the northern regions of Angola under UNITA control. In the autumn of 1994 a new UN-brokered power-sharing agreement known as the Lusaka Accords was finally reached for a cease-fire, the disarmament of the UNITA rebels, and the creation of a national army composed of soldiers from both sides. But Savimbi ignored the agreement and resumed his insurgency until Angolan government forces captured and killed the legendary guerrilla leader in February 2002.

The most lethal manifestation of interethnic tension in Africa was the resumption of the perpetual strife between the Tutsi and Hutu in Rwanda, the diminutive former Belgian colony sandwiched between Zaire and Tanzania in the Great Lakes region of East Africa. Ever since its independence in 1962, periodic insurrections against the Tutsi ruling elite by the disenfranchised Hutu majority in the small country resulted in the systematic annihilation of hundreds of thousands of innocent civilians in both groups. In the latest of these tragic incidents the military forces of the Rwandan Hutu, who had finally managed to acquire control of the government in 1973, massacred at least half a million members of the Tutsi minority in an orgy of genocide during the spring and summer of 1994. When the Tutsi-controlled Rwandan Patriotic Front led by Paul Kagame gained the upper hand, some 1.7 million diseased and destitute Hutu fled to refugee camps in neighboring Zaire and several thousand more to Tanzania. Vigorous efforts by the United Nations High Commission for Refugees to repatriate the Rwandan Hutu were hampered

---

*See page 414.

by their fear of revenge at the hands of the surviving Tutsi population, despite the Rwandan government's solemn assurances of protection for the innocent and fair judicial proceedings for those accused of genocide.

The tense political situation in Rwanda eventually became entangled in a complex web of civil and interstate conflicts that spread throughout Central Africa during the second half of the 1990s. The first of these struggles was prompted by the disintegration of Mobutu Sese Seko's corrupt autocracy in Zaire. Mobutu was induced by the United States, France, Belgium, and other foreign donors, creditors, and trade partners in 1991 to convoke a national conference to draft a democratic constitution and to form a coalition government with the opposition leader Etienne Tshisekedi. Amid inflation raging at an annual rate of 1,000 percent, widespread rioting and looting by soldiers unwilling to receive monthly salaries in the worthless national currency, and interventions by French and Belgian paratroop units to protect their countries' nationals, Mobutu (who was ill with cancer) gradually lost his iron grip. In May 1997 Laurent Kabila's Alliance of the Democratic Forces for the Liberation of Congo-Zaire finally ousted the thirty-two-year-old dictatorship in Zaire (which was promptly renamed the Democratic Republic of Congo).

Once in power, Kabila's army, which had received contributions of troops and military advice from neighboring Rwanda during its successful offensive against Mobutu's security forces, repaid its Rwandan Tutsi supporters by attacking the Rwandan Hutu who had sought refuge in eastern Zaire/Congo rather than risk retribution for the 1994 genocide by returning to their homeland. The United States had supported Kabila's insurrection against Mobutu once the Congolese strongman had lost his usefulness as a bastion of anti-Communism in Central Africa after the end of the Cold War. Though expressing stern disapproval of the violence against the Hutu, Washington attempted to maintain cordial relations with the new regime in Kinshasa that controlled an abundant supply of copper, cobalt, gold, and diamonds.

Then an abrupt policy change executed by Kabila plunged the Democratic Republic of Congo into a war in the summer of 1998 that eventually drew in seven of its neighbors, reflecting the increasing willingness of African states to violate national borders in the defense of their vital interests. First, the new Congolese president suspended his campaign against the Hutu refugees in the eastern part of the country, whom his Rwandan allies regarded as a potential threat to the security of their Tutsi-dominated state. He thereupon dismissed most of the Rwandan Tutsi military advisers who had come to Kinshasa to help reorganize the Congolese army. Taking advantage of a mutiny among Congolese military units and the emergence of an insurgent movement in the eastern region, Rwanda and Uganda (which also feared incursions from the Hutu refugee camps) sent military forces into the Congo in an all-out bid to topple Kabila's government. Angola, Namibia, and Zimbabwe rallied to Kabila's support from the south while Chad and Sudan lent assistance to the embattled Congolese government from the north. A cease-fire initiated by the United States, France, and Belgium finally took hold in the summer of 1999. But as soldiers from six armies roamed the war-ravaged country, and their officers looted its mineral wealth, Kabila alienated his supporters with his autocratic methods and was assassinated at the beginning of 2001. Though the armed forces were eventually withdrawn, Africa's wealthiest country, the size of Western Europe, was in shambles after decades of corruption, repression, and war.

The ferocious tribal conflict between Hutu and Tutsi in Rwanda in 1994 was reenacted in the small neighboring country of Burundi, where (as in Rwanda) the Hutu constituted the majority while the Tutsi controlled the military and the government. In 1993 Melchior Ndadaye had become Burundi's first Hutu president after a free and fair election, but a few months later was overthrown and executed by a dissident faction of the Tutsi-dominated army. Though the coup failed, it unleashed a wave of Hutu attacks against Tutsis that forced thousands of refugees to seek refuge in Rwanda, Zaire, and Tanzania and plunged the little country into political and economic chaos. In the summer of 1996 a group of Tutsi officers finally succeeded in toppling the Hutu president and later organized a campaign to destroy the political power of the Hutu by forcibly resettling them in rural areas. As in Rwanda, this African variant of genocide and ethnic cleansing transpired amid an attitude of relative indifference on the part of the international community.

With the spread of intra- and inter-state conflict in Africa since the early 1990s many looked to Nigeria, West Africa's wealthiest and most powerful country with a quarter of the continent's population, as a potential promoter of regional stability. After nine years of military rule Nigeria took what seemed to be a major step toward democratization by conducting free presidential elections in June 1993. But when the popular opposition leader Chief Moshood K. O. Abiola from western Nigeria appeared to have won at the polls, President Ibrahim Babangida, the army general representing the northern military elite that had long dominated the country's political system, declared the election null and void on the grounds of voting irregularities. A nationwide protest movement, reinforced by American and British pressure, forced General Babangida to step down. But after a brief transitional period he was replaced by his former defense minister and protégé General Sani Abacha. This development followed the pattern of Nigerian political behavior since 1965, when the military had seized power five years after independence and continued to rule either directly or through civilian surrogates for the next three decades. Though Nigeria's vast oil reserves afforded it the potential for substantial economic development, it suffered from a host of disabilities that prevented it from fulfilling its great promise: the hodgepodge of some 250 ethnic groups that inhibits the development of national loyalties; the endemic political corruption flowing from the hope of instant wealth from oil sales; and the decline in oil revenues (which account for over 90% of Nigeria's export earnings) caused by the low world price for crude after the dramatic increases of the 1970s. By the mid-1990s this oil-rich country had defaulted on most of its foreign debt and was obliged to adopt the usual stringent measures of economic liberalization in exchange for emergency loans from the IMF and the World Bank. In June 1998 General Abacha died and was replaced by General Abdusalam Abubakar, who immediately took steps to dismantle the edifice of authoritarian military rule by allowing political parties to operate and freeing hundreds of political prisoners. The presidential election of February 1999 was won by General Olusegun Obasanjo, a former president who held the distinction of being the only Nigerian military leader who had voluntarily relinquished power to a civilian successor. But the military continued to exercise strong influence on the government, raising questions about the future of democracy in this important African country.

In spite of its political and economic difficulties, Nigeria possessed the largest, best equipped army in West Africa, which enabled it to serve as the principal force for regional stability in the 1990s through the threat and, occasionally, the use of military force. Nigerian units dominated the peacekeeping force known as the West African Cease-fire Monitoring Group (ECOMOG) that had been dispatched to Liberia in 1990 by the Economic Community of West African States (ECOWAS). ECOMOG had originally intervened in Liberia to prevent the insurgent leader Charles Taylor (who represented the Gao and Mano ethnic groups) from seizing power after the murder in 1990 of President Samuel Doe (whose government was dominated by the Krahns). For the next seven years a bloody civil war destroyed the economy and caused more than 150,000 deaths as the contending factions fought to a stalemate before finally agreeing to a cease fire. Elections conducted under ECOMOG's supervision in July 1997 brought to power through democratic means none other than the Patriotic National Front of Liberia of Charles Taylor, the man whose insurgency had caused the civil war and precipitated the ECOMOG intervention in the first place. Nigerian-dominated ECOMOG units remained in Liberia to supervise the disarmament and demobilization of the various armed factions operating throughout the devastated country, but also (many observers suspected) to look after Nigeria's strategic and economic interests in Liberia as well.

The next opportunity for Nigeria to expand its regional influence occurred in Sierra Leone, where a dissident military faction called the Armed Forces Revolutionary Council joined with Revolutionary United Front rebels to overthrew the government of President Ahmed Tejan Kabbah in May 1997. In February 1998 Nigerian military units were dispatched to the small West African country, where they promptly expelled the rebel forces from the capital and reinstalled the civilian government. A month later the sixteen member states of ECOWAS endorsed the unilateral Nigerian operation in Sierra Leone and voted to transform its Nigerian-dominated military wing ECOMOG into a permanent West African security organization. The Nigerian military government's intervention in Liberia and Sierra Leone on behalf of democratic rule smacked of hypocrisy in light of its own refusal to tolerate democracy at home, which had prompted harsh criticism from Western countries and its expulsion from the Commonwealth in 1995. But its willingness to employ military force to cope with instability in neighboring countries, together with its dominant position in ECOWAS and ECOMOG, enhanced Nigeria's position as the regional hegemon in West Africa.

Since the end of the Cold War, Africa, was marked by the persistence of entrenched autocracies and the suppression of opposition parties or blatant manipulation of the electoral process in countries such as Cameroon, the Central African Republic, Congo, Guinea, and Togo. A military junta took power in Gambia in 1994 and in Niger in 1996. But progress toward multiparty democracy was evident in a few African states. Zambia's Kenneth Kaunda and Benin's Mathieu Kerekou yielded to pressure from external aid donors and domestic public opinion to allow free elections, and both willingly handed over power to the leaders of victorious opposition parties. Hastings Banda, the longtime autocrat in Malawi, was peacefully driven into opposition. In the Ivory Coast the death in December 1993 of President Félix Houphouëet-Boigny, who had ruled the former French colony as a benevolent despot since independence in 1960, resulted in multiparty elections.

The most dramatic instance of democratization and political power sharing on the continent during the first half of the 1990s occurred in the Republic of South Africa. The new white-only government of F.W. de Klerk that took office in 1989 began to initiate a number of domestic political reforms designed to promote racial reconciliation in the land of apartheid. De Klerk surprised world observers by abolishing the racial segregation of beaches, parks, and libraries; permitting mass demonstrations by dissidents; and in February 1990, legalizing the African National Congress (ANC) and releasing one of its militants, Nelson Mandela, after twenty-six years in prison. The ANC, deprived of its sanctuaries in Angola and its military aid from the Soviet Union (following Gorbachev's decision to terminate support for resistance movements in the developing world), was prepared to deemphasize its commitment to revolutionary violence in favor of negotiations with the more enlightened government in Pretoria. Throughout the year 1991 de Klerk took several bold steps toward the pursuit of a dialogue with the ANC (represented by Mandela, who was elected president in July of that year) concerning political power sharing with the black majority.

In December 1991 delegations representing all the major black and white political factions met in Johannesburg as the Convention for a Democratic South Africa (CODESA) to discuss means of implementing the general goals of multiracial adult suffrage and multiparty democracy that had already been embraced by most of the parties. Faced with bitter opposition from the Conservative party on his right, the intrepid de Klerk submitted his policy to the white citizens of South Africa in the form of a referendum accompanied by his threat to resign if it were rejected. On March 17, 1992, two-thirds of the white voters endorsed the prime minister's policy of resuming negotiations with the ANC, thereby sealing the fate of the white minority's political monopoly. In the meantime, the abolition of the last vestiges of apartheid, such as the racially determined residency requirement and the obligation of birth registry by race, led to the removal of most of the international sanctions that had been imposed on South Africa in the mid-1980s.

Representatives of twenty-one political groups participating in the CODESA deliberations bargained intensively until November 18, 1993, when they formally adopted an interim constitution for the country pending the drafting of a permanent one by the end of the century. The interim constitution abolished the pseudoindependent black homelands and established the democratically elected National Assembly, which would choose the president and function both as a legislature and a constituent assembly empowered to draft a permanent constitution. In the meantime, the first multiracial national elections under universal adult suffrage were scheduled for April 1994. To no one's surprise, the ANC won a solid majority. Control of the state was transferred by scrupulously legal means from the white ruling elite that had reigned unchecked for almost three and a half centuries to the representatives of the formerly disenfranchised black majority. The erstwhile revolutionary Mandela assumed the presidency of the new multiracial, democratic state, with de Klerk serving as deputy president and Chief Mangosuthu Buthelezi, leader of the Zulu territory on the east coast and a rival of Mandela, as minister of home affairs. Mandela and de Klerk subsequently shared the Nobel Peace Prize for their successful resolution of independent Africa's longest and most intractable conflict.

The prospects for peace, prosperity, and security in South Africa seemed brighter in the mid-1990s than ever before as whites, blacks, and people of mixed heritage looked to the future with relative optimism. The 1994 agreement that terminated white rule was designed to encourage the white minority, especially businesspeople and farmers, to remain in South Africa rather than to follow the precedent of white minorities in the rest of the continent that fled to Europe with their valuable skills and portable financial assets.

South African Prime Min-
ister F. W. de Klerk
(1936–) and African
National Congress leader
Nelson Mandela (1918–)
display their Nobel Peace
Prizes to journalists,
December 10, 1993: De
Klerk abolished apartheid,
freed Mandela from prison
after twenty-six years at
hard labor, and set in
motion the movement of
democratic reform in South
Africa that would bring
Mandela to the presidency
of the country in the following year. *(Getty Images)*

There was some white emigration and capital flight, caused in part by an increase in violent crime and a steep slump in the economy during the second half of the decade. But
Mandela's conciliatory policies engendered a remarkable degree of racial harmony in the
former bastion of apartheid. After the June 1999 presidential elections he bequeathed to
his hand-picked successor, Thabo Mbeki, a bold experiment in multiracial harmony.

Since the early 1990s, the Arab societies along the Mediterranean shore of Africa
experienced an explosive upsurge of Islamic fundamentalism with potentially significant
consequences for the future stability of that region. All across North Africa unemployed
or underpaid young people who faced bleak economic futures proved susceptible to the
allure of Islamic protest movements that denounced the corruption and culturally decadent practices of the secular regimes that had held power for the entire postcolonial
period. If there is any truth to Marx's definition of religion as the opiate of the people, the
Maghreb in the first half of the 1990s represented a perfect case study of a messianic reli-

gious movement furnishing comfort to destitute populations without hope of improvement and resentful of the political authorities held responsible for their plight.

The phenomenon began in Algeria, the former French possession in North Africa that had been ruled by a one-party, secular socialist regime since independence in 1962.* In 1989 President Chadli Bendjedid had launched a bold reform program designed to loosen up the autocratic structure of the Algerian state in the hope of promoting solutions to the country's acute economic difficulties. One of the early results of this project of internal liberalization was the emergence of political opposition groups that challenged the political authority of the National Liberation Front (widely known by its French acronym FLN), which had engineered the successful rebellion against the French colonial system and controlled the state apparatus after independence. The most popular of those dissident organizations was the Islamic Salvation Front (FIS), which denounced the secular policies of the government in Algiers and demanded the establishment of a state based on orthodox Islamic principles as a means to social as well as spiritual salvation. After recording impressive political gains in the municipal elections of June 1990, the FIS routed the FLN in the first round of national legislative elections in December 1991 and appeared poised to assume power as antigovernment demonstrations swept the country at the turn of the year. But in January 1992 Bendjedid abruptly resigned in favor of a government dominated by high-ranking military officers, who proceeded to declare martial law, cancel the second round of elections, ban the FIS, and arrest its leaders. Succeeding years were marked by violent clashes between the army, which took direct control of the Algerian state in January 1994, and the increasingly vociferous advocates of the potent new political force of "Islamism." In 1995 former General Lamine Zeroual was elected president in ostensibly free elections, but he proceeded to rule in close consultation with the officer corps and its civilian allies. A group of armed Islamist zealots, responded to the electoral chicanery by inaugurating a campaign of terror, which included kidnapping, bombing, murder, and mutilation. By the end of the century, over sixty thousand people had died in this bitter conflict. In the meantime Algeria's severe economic crisis, caused by its overdependence on oil as a source of export earnings during a decade of declining world petroleum prices, plunged the country into a financial crisis during the second half of the 1990s that required the rescheduling of its foreign debt and a massive influx of loans from the International Monetary Fund and the World Bank.

Elsewhere in North Africa secular regimes applauded the Algerian government's crackdown on the FIS and took steps to curb their own Islamist opposition. Egyptian President Hosni Mubarek waged a relentless campaign against the Muslim Brotherhood, which had survived earlier attempts by Nasser and Sadat to eradicate it as a political force. The governments of Tunisia (a secular one-party state like Algeria) and Morocco (a conservative monarchy) both severely restricted the activities of fundamentalist groups in their midst in the hope of inoculating these societies against "the Algerian disease." Western Europe faced something of a dilemma as it observed this mounting tension between secular Arab governments and their Islamist opposition. It was difficult for Western countries promoting the spread of democratic principles and practices throughout the world to countenance the repressive methods employed by the embattled regimes

---

*See pages 274–275.

in the Maghreb to stifle Islamic dissent. But European leaders worried about a massive trans-Mediterranean exodus of refugees from an Islamicized North Africa that would severely strain their social welfare systems and fan the already smoldering fires of domestic racism.

The Islamist challenge to Africa north of the Sahara did not prevent the countries situated there from achieving notable progress toward greater regional stability and cooperation after a tumultuous decade. One of the two sources of conflict in North Africa during the 1980s was the civil war in Chad between a strong Muslim secessionist movement in the north (supported by neighboring Libya) and the central government (backed by France, the former colonial power).* But at the end of the decade, Libyan strongman Muammar al-Qaddafi, who at one point had asserted territorial claims to northern part of Chad, withdrew his military forces from the territory. At the same time, France reduced its support for the central government that was battling the northern Muslims and their Libyan patrons. The civil war thereafter dwindled to a low-intensity conflict punctuated by sporadic clashes between the two factions.

The other regional cause célèbre in North Africa was Morocco's peremptory annexation of the former Spanish (renamed Western) Sahara, which had been abandoned by Spain in the mid-1970s.† In the face of bitter opposition led by Algeria, Morocco's King Hassan finally agreed to consult the indigenous population of the phosphate-rich territory to determine their wishes. The United Nations dispatched a task force to the Western Sahara in 1991 to lay the groundwork for an eventual referendum. But Morocco refused to deal with the indigious national liberation movement Polisario, which resumed its low-intensity guerrilla war against the Moroccan forces, so plans for the proposed referendum were continually postponed.

While Rabat and Algiers sought a peaceful solution to their dispute in the Western Sahara, all of the countries in the Maghreb explored ways of coordinating their economic activities in the face of Europe's rapid progress toward a single market in 1993. As we have seen, the postcolonial African states had failed to make any headway toward the ambitious goal of Pan-African economic integration, and even more modest proposals for economic cooperation at the subregional level had proved elusive.‡ The five states of North Africa finally took a significant step in that direction in 1991 by establishing a subregional organization called the Arab Maghreb Union. Two years later they worked out the rudiments of an institutional apparatus, including a permanent secretariat and a development bank, and engaged in far-reaching discussions about the possibility of creating a customs union. The bitter, long-standing rivalry between Morocco and Algeria continued to represent a serious obstacle to closer integration in the Maghreb.

The political events in Europe as the Cold War came to an end had a critical impact on Africa. As Gorbachev's Soviet Union sharply curtailed its foreign aid programs to the Third World at the end of the 1980s, the United States and Western Europe began to receive urgent requests from the newly liberated states of Eastern Europe for credits,

---

*See page 388.

†See page 389.

‡See page 384.

investment, and aid for their struggling economies. This preoccupation with promoting democracy and market-based economies in the former Soviet satellites and then in the former Soviet republics inevitably diverted Western attention from Africa's desperate economic plight: Already burdened with an enormous foreign debt, African countries were able to attract very little new commercial lending. Since banks in the developed world tended to shun the impoverished countries of the continent as poor credit risks, over 90 percent of Africa's foreign loans derived from foreign governments or multinational lending agencies such as the IMF and the World Bank. International investors also hesitated to sink their funds into African projects. Since the mid-1980s direct private investment declined in Africa while tripling in Latin America and increasing fivefold in East Asia. One of the consequences of this drying up of foreign lending and investment has been the continent's virtual absence from the emerging global trading system: By the mid-1990s, as many of the formerly underdeveloped countries in Asia and Latin America became active participants in the international trading system, Africa accounted for a paltry 2 percent of total world trade.

In sum, the end of the Cold War proved to be a mixed blessing for Africa. On the one hand, it reduced the likelihood of external interference in the affairs of the continent. On the other hand, the resulting decline in Africa's strategic importance to the Western bloc revived the traditional attitude of relative indifference that had characterized the policies of the United States and most European countries before the advent of East-West rivalry there in the mid-1970s. The human tragedies in Somalia and Rwanda in the 1990s inspired an outpouring of humanitarian assistance from the developed world and a flurry of activity in the United Nations. But the absence of significant economic or strategic interests in the region on the part of the world's major powers limited the scope of that involvement, particularly in a period of budget-cutting austerity and preoccupation with domestic problems. The United States, France, and Great Britain all developed programs to train and equip African military forces to serve in peacekeeping operations in order to avoid being drawn into African conflicts (in which their own vital interests were not at stake). These external powers applauded the peacekeeping operations of Nigeria and ECOMOG in West Africa, but they stopped short of providing financial support to back up their rhetoric.

The developed country that had taken the most active role in African affairs since independence was France, the major foreign aid donor to the continent that did not hesitate to wield economic influence and military power on behalf of its interests and those of its African clients.* But even the traditional banker and gendarme of Africa began to loosen its historically intimate ties to the continent during the 1990s. France's military involvement in Africa became less intense after the civil war in Chad wound down in 1990. The humanitarian interventions in the civil conflicts in Somalia (under UN auspices) and Rwanda (with UN approval) involved small numbers of troops and were of limited duration. While garrisons of the Foreign Legion remained in half-a-dozen African countries as tangible symbols of Paris's commitment to its Francophone clients on the continent, the end of the Cold War together with the mounting preoccupation with Euro-

---

*See page 381.

pean economic integration pushed African security concerns into the background. In December 1997 France announced that it would cut by almost 40% the size of its armed forces stationed in its former African colonies and close several French military bases by the end of the century.

France also took steps to loosen somewhat the privileged economic links that the former colonial power had continued to enjoy with its former possessions in West Africa after granting them independence in the early sixties. The cornerstone of this special relationship was the complex set of monetary arrangements governing the so-called African Financial Community (CFA).* By guaranteeing a fixed parity of one French franc to fifty CFA francs, Paris ensured that the fourteen African countries in the franc zone† would enjoy the privilege of possessing Africa's only readily convertible currencies. While this commitment to maintain the fixed parity of the CFA franc cost the French treasury several billion dollars a year, it served to cement France's ties to her former African empire and yielded substantial economic advantages to the former colonial power. French industry enjoyed preferential access to African commodities, especially oil and minerals. French export firms enjoyed guaranteed markets for their manufactured products, and French investors found lucrative outlets for their savings. The major benefit for the African countries was that the monetary discipline imposed on them by having their currencies tied to the French franc resulted in lower inflation and more sustained growth than the rest of Africa during the first two decades after independence.

But the cozy relationship between France and its former colonies in sub-Saharan Africa had begun to fray in the mid-1980s as the economies of the CFA countries started to decline and the French government began to focus its attention on Europe. In the meantime other Western nations and international financial institutions criticized France's de facto subsidy to the franc zone countries as a vehicle for French financial hegemony that discriminated against foreign competitors and inhibited West African economic growth by encouraging waste and inefficiency. France finally bowed to this foreign pressure in January 1994 by abruptly cutting the African franc's value from 50 to 1 to 100 to 1. Though the IMF and the World Bank confidently predicted that the long-overdue devaluation would encourage new foreign investment and stimulate exports in Francophone Africa, the short-term consequences were exceedingly painful for many of the CFA countries. The instantaneous doubling of domestic prices combined with government-imposed wage freezes led to widespread labor unrest and acute popular discontent as peoples' ability to purchase food, medicine, and other essential goods was reduced. What seemed to some observers to be moderation of France's regional ambitions in Africa following the disengagement of the two superpowers left that continent (for better or for worse) more isolated and alone in the early twenty-first century than it had ever been.

Amid the economic crises, financial difficulties, and military conflicts that have afflicted Africa since the end of the Cold War, by far the most serious threat to the people of that continent has been the scourge of acquired immune deficiency syndrome

---

*See page 382.

†Benin, Burkina Faso, Cameroon, Central African Republic, Chad, Congo, the Comoros, Gabon, Ivory Coast, Mali, Niger, Senegal, and Togo are the former French colonies in the franc zone. Equatorial Guinea, a former Spanish colony, joined in 1985.

(AIDS) that began in the 1980s and reached pandemic proportions by the end of the twentieth century. The principal carriers of this debilitating and eventually fatal disease were the military forces who intervened in the numerous domestic conflicts and civil wars mentioned above. Soldiers recruited from sexually active age groups who spend long periods of time away from their families with money to spend attract prostitutes and drug dealers, the two main sources of AIDs infection. The civil wars in Liberia and Sierra Leone resulted in the influx of thousands of peacekeepers, a large proportion of whom returned to their country of origin infected with the deadly virus as they resumed sexual activity in their communities. The presence of half a dozen foreign armies in the Democratic Republic of Congo in the late 1990s resulted in enormous infection rates. Health officials have estimated that 30 percent of soldiers in African national armies or peacekeeping forces have been infected and that AIDS has become the principal cause of death of men in uniform in many countries on the continent. By the year 2000 25 million Africans had been infected with the disease, three-quarters of the world's total; twenty-four of the twenty-five countries with the highest infection rate were in Africa. One important result of this pandemic has been a sharp drop in life expectancy in many African countries, reversing the promising trend of recent decades caused by improvements in sanitation and health care.

In addition to its catastrophic consequences for public health, AIDS has had a profound impact on the economic development of Africa. Death or disability caused by AIDS has contributed to a severe shortage of skilled workers in many African countries, reducing those countries' chances of breaking out of the extreme poverty that has represented the continent's curse for so many years. The costs of caring for those afflicted with the disease strained national budgets, siphoning off resources that would otherwise be available for education, housing, or the promotion of economic growth. The spread of AIDs across the continent also discouraged foreign investment and tourism, aggravating existing difficulties in obtaining scarce capital and foreign exchange. It has been estimated that AIDS will be responsible for a reduction in many African countries' gross domestic product by as much as one-fifth in the first decade of the twenty-first century. Reacting to the expanding crisis in Africa, U.S. President Bill Clinton declared in 2000 that HIV/AIDS represented a "national security threat" that could provoke acute political instability and economic chaos across the globe and create failed states that would be breeding grounds for terrorism. By the beginning of the twenty-first century, infection rates were on the rise in Asia, Latin America, and the successor states of the former Soviet Union as well. The African experience with this modern version of the Black Death threatened to become the harbinger of a global trend that could dash the hopes for economic development and global stability in the twenty-first century.

20

THE MIDDLE EAST: THE ELUSIVE QUEST FOR PEACE, PROSPERITY, AND STABILITY

As the Cold War wound down in the second half of the 1980s, Moscow and Washington also cooperated to dampen regional rivalries between their clients in the Middle East. The Soviet Union pressured Syria and the Palestine Liberation Organization to abandon the cause of armed victory and to seek a negotiated settlement with Israel, while the United States urged the Jewish state to forswear annexation of the occupied territories and halt all settlement activity there. A complicating factor was the unanticipated Palestinian uprising (or *Intifada*) on the West Bank and Gaza in December 1987, which represented a spontaneous popular reaction to the failure of the autonomy talks concerning the occupied territories. It also revealed that the Palestinians there had lost faith in the PLO and the Arab states to bring about an end to the Israeli occupation and were driven to take matters into their own hands. The cease-fire in the Iran-Iraq War in August 1988 refocused Arab and world attention on the Palestinian problem. Facing the threat of a civilian insurrection consisting of rock throwing and arson, Israel responded with harsh countermeasures that provoked international condemnation, including strong words and renewed pressure for a negotiated settlement from its American patrons.

With Moscow curtailing its support for Syria and the PLO while permitting Soviet Jews to emigrate to Israel in record numbers, the Bush administration grew impatient with the recalcitrance of the government of Yitzhak Shamir in Jerusalem, which refused to negotiate with the PLO or to envision any kind of Palestinian political entity on the West Bank. After the PLO formally endorsed UN resolution 242, recognized Israel's right to exist in peace and security, and renounced terrorism, the United States ended its boycott of the Palestinian organization and opened talks with PLO representatives in Tunis. Egypt was officially readmitted to the Arab League at its Casablanca summit in 1989 without being obliged to renounce its 1979 peace treaty with Israel, an implicit acceptance by the other Arab states of the legitimacy of negotiation with the Jewish state.

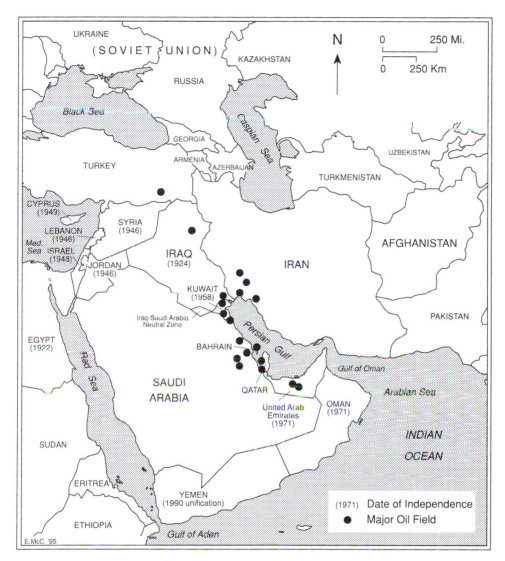

The Middle East at the Turn of the Century

Syria, isolated in the Arab world and abandoned by its Soviet benefactor, was driven to seek a rapprochement with Egypt and tone down its anti-Israel rhetoric. By the opening of the new decade, the end of the Iran-Iraq War, the reentry of Egypt into the Arab camp, and the isolation of hard-line Syria made the prospects for peace and stability in the Middle East seem better than they had been since the Lebanese debacle of 1982–83.

The signal event that prompted a fundamental transformation of the geopolitical landscape of the Middle East in the last decade of the twentieth century was the invasion and annexation by Iraq of the adjacent, oil-rich emirate of Kuwait in the summer of 1990. The Iraqi seizure of Kuwait had originally been justified by the government in Baghdad not only on the basis of territorial claims dating from the era of the Ottoman Empire, but also by a recent set of grievances: The Iraqi dictator, Saddam Hussein, charged that the emirate's royal family had jeopardized Iraq's economic situation by expanding oil production to depress the world price, illegally diverting oil from Iraqi wells, and refusing to write off Iraq's huge debt incurred during its eight-year war with Iran. But when the Bush administration promptly persuaded the United Nations Security Council to approve extensive economic sanctions against Iraq and later to authorize the use of military force to expel Iraqi forces from Kuwait if they did not withdraw before January 15, 1991, Saddam Hussein tried to redefine the impending confrontation as an Arab-Muslim "Holy War" against the West and its ally in the region, Israel. After securing the diplomatic backing of its former adversary (and Iraq's former patron and supplier) in Moscow, the United States assembled a military force in Saudi Arabia consisting of NATO allies, such as Great Britain and France, together with those Arab states, such as Egypt, Saudi Arabia, and Syria, that feared the consequences of Iraq's hegemony in the region. After the expiration of the UN deadline for the evacuation of Kuwait, the U.S.-led coalition launched a devastating air campaign against Iraqi military targets and then a ground offensive into Kuwait and southern Iraq. The result was a swift military triumph that ejected Iraqi forces from Kuwait and thwarted Saddam Hussein's aspirations for territorial expansion in the Persian Gulf and political leadership in the Arab world.

The outcome of the Gulf War vastly enhanced Washington's credibility as patron and protector in the Middle East. Though Saudi Arabia, Kuwait, and the other Gulf states paid about two-thirds of the $71 billion cost of the war compared to $7.4 billion from the United States,* it was American diplomacy that assembled the victorious coalition and U.S. military power that routed the Iraqi army. The disintegration of the Soviet Union at the end of the year left the United States in an unrivaled position of supremacy in this oil-rich, strategically significant part of the world. In the meantime Iraq had suffered an ignominious defeat on the battlefield and faced total diplomatic isolation in the United Nations. Saddam Hussein's regime was subjected by the international community to a set of costly financial penalties and humiliating infringements on Iraqi sovereignty: The Security Council extracted from Iraq a pledge to pay billions of dollars in war reparations to Kuwait for the damage caused during its recent occupation. An international embargo on Iraqi oil denied Saddam funds to finance essential imports for his shattered economy. In May 1991 United Nations inspection teams entered Iraq to begin the process of identifying and supervising the dismantling of the arsenal of nuclear, chemical, and biological weapons programs that Saddam had launched in the past decade.

Yet defeated Iraq had not been definitively displaced as a regional power on the Persian Gulf. The cease-fire in the land war after only one hundred hours of combat had enabled Saddam's elite personal army, the Republican Guard, to escape virtually unscathed. This formidable military force enabled him to preserve his country's territorial integrity and retain his own political authority by ruthlessly quelling insurrections of Kurdish separatists in the north, Shi'ite rebels in the south, and dissident elements within his own military.

---

*Japan and Germany, two great powers that were precluded by the lingering legacy of World War II from participating militarily in the military operation, contributed to the UN effort by footing the rest of the bill.

Operation Desert Shield: Members of the first battalion, 325st Airborne Infantry Regiment explain the operation of a mortar to Saudi Arabian national guardsmen, 1990: The largest U.S. deployment since the Vietnam War was undertaken at the request of Saudi Arabia's King Fahd to prevent Iraqi troops who had recently invaded Kuwait from seizing his kingdom's oil fields. The Americans remained in Saudi Arabia after their participation in Operation Desert Storm, which expelled the Iraqi forces from Kuwait the following year. This prompted the Saudi dissident Osama bin Laden to organize a campaign of terror against the United States, whose "infidel" soldiers, he complained, desecrated by their very presence the Islamic holy sites of Mecca and Medina located in the desert kingdom. *(Getty Images)*

For the remainder of the decade Hussein played a game of cat and mouse with the United Nations inspection team (UNSCOM) as it attempted to ferret out evidence of Iraq's arsenal of the proscribed weapons of mass destruction. Baghdad's continual foot-dragging coincided with the emergence of sharp differences among the five permanent members of the Security Council on how to handle Iraq. When UNSCOM reported the Iraqi obstructionism in 1997 and requested UN action to compel compliance, Russia, China, and France raised objections to the Anglo-American proposal for an extension of the economic sanctions that prevented all imports except food and medicine from reaching Iraq. President Hussein exploited this split by expelling from his country all American members of UNSCOM, whom he accused of conducting espionage for their own nation, a move that brought the inspection team's operation to a halt.

As the U.S. and Great Britain beefed up their military and naval presence in the Gulf and threatened military action if the inspections were not permitted to resume, the Iraqi leader defiantly denied UNSCOM access to certain "presidential sites" where UN technicians believed biological and chemical materials were located. In December 1998 the United States and Great Britain finally lost patience and unleashed a four-day attack against Iraq with bombers and cruise missiles directed not only suspected sites of weapons development but also the political and military infrastructure of the regime, reflecting Washington's and London's determination to topple the Iraqi government. They also provided military aid to Iraqi opposition movements and the two main Kurdish political parties. Saddam Hussein responded to the Anglo-American air campaign and political warfare by terminating all cooperation with the weapons inspection regime and evicting UNSCOM from the country. American and British warplanes continued to patrol the "no-fly" zones in the north and south that had been established after the Gulf War while the economic sanctions on Iraq remained in force. But the weapons inspection operation had come to an end without dispelling the strong suspicion that Iraq still possessed weapons of mass destruction.*

As the postwar economic and military sanctions tamed—at least temporarily—the Baathist regime in Baghdad, the immediate threat to regional stability from the fundamentalist Islamic regime in Teheran dissipated as well. The death of Ayatollah Ruhollah Khomeini in 1989 left an immense power vacuum in the Islamic Republic, which the octogenarian cleric had ruled with a unique combination of spiritual and political authority. President Ayatollah Ali Khamenei succeeded Khomeini as Supreme Leader, but effective control of the state apparatus devolved on the former parliamentary speaker, Hojatoleslam Hashemi Rafsanjani, who succeeded Khamenei as president. The pragmatic Rafsanjani and his new cabinet of technocrats jettisoned many of the orthodox Islamic principles of Khomeini in order to pursue policies appropriate to a modernizing state intent on expanding its regional influence and achieving economic growth. When precepts in the Koran or the *Sharia* clashed with the practical requirements of modern life—as with the prohibition against interest charges in money lending—theological doctrine increasingly succumbed to the demands of modernity.

This shift in priorities by Khomeini's successors, which antagonized dogmatic devotees of the late Ayatollah's rigid Shi'ite theocracy, modulated the militancy that had characterized Iran's relations with foreign states since the revolution of 1978–79. Rafsanjani maintained a policy of scrupulous neutrality during the Gulf War instead of exploiting the distress of his country's former enemy in Baghdad to expand Iran's power in the region and complicate the U.S.-led coalition's postwar plans. In the hope of attracting foreign investment and lending to rebuild Iran's war-ravaged economy, he sought to improve relations with the West by inducing the Iranian-backed Hizbollah movement in Lebanon to release several American and British hostages. The reformist forces in Iran won a stunning victory over the guardians of the old orthodoxy in 1997, when the progressive cleric Mohammed Khatami was unexpectedly elected president with almost 70% of the vote. The new Iranian head of state boldly proposed reconciliation with the West, advocating the rule of law, respect for individual liberties, and an opening to foreign cultural influences. The president's progressive rhetoric placed him in opposition to

---

*This suspicion was proved unfounded after the U.S. invasion of Iraq in 2003, when it was discovered, to the surprise of the intelligence agencies, that the regime's arsenal of chemical and biological weapons had been destroyed in the previous decade and it nuclear program remained in a rudimentary stage.

the conservative, anti-Western Supreme Leader Ayatollah Khamenei and his fellow defenders of the Khomeini legacy. But by the beginning of the new century, the clerical hard-liners had reasserted their dominance in Iran, blocking Khatami's efforts at political reform and reaffirming the Khomeini policy of hostility to the West.

One of the unforeseen consequences of the multinational military operation against Iraq in January 1991 was its beneficial effect on the peace negotiations between Israel and its Arab neighbors that had stagnated since the Israeli invasion of Lebanon in 1982. This was so for a number of reasons. First of all, Arab unity had been shattered by the war, with the Palestine Liberation Organization joining Jordan and Libya in support of Baghdad while Syria, Egypt, Saudi Arabia, and the smaller Gulf states enlisted in the Western-led coalition against Iraq. In retaliation for Arafat's endorsement of Saddam Hussein's aggression, Saudi Arabia and Kuwait abruptly terminated the lavish financial subsidies that they had been furnishing to the PLO. The rift in the Arab ranks, the financial weakness of the PLO deprived of its Gulf oil money, and the cutoff of military and economic support for Syria and Iraq from the disintegrating Communist bloc afforded the state of Israel an unprecedented margin of security. While this more congenial geopolitical environment did not alter the inflexible attitudes of the hard-line Likud government of Prime Minister Yitzhak Shamir, Israeli public opinion quickly perceived the opportunities afforded by the disarray in an Arab world that had seemed monolithically menacing for so long. The PLO, enfeebled by the simultaneous loss of its benefactors in the Gulf and its sponsors in the Kremlin, became more amenable to compromise that it had ever been. Assad of Syria, also chastened by the loss the Soviet economic aid and political patronage, became increasingly susceptible to American pressure as he turned to the only remaining superpower for compensatory support.

One of the reasons that President Bush and his secretary of state, James Baker, were able to assemble and sustain the improbable coalition that humbled Iraq in 1991 was their implicit pledge to press for a mutually satisfactory resolution of the Arab-Israeli conflict after the Gulf War. Israel had long eschewed contact with the PLO leadership in Tunis, considering it irredeemably committed to violence as the means of achieving its political objectives and suspecting it of harboring the ultimate hope of removing the Jewish state from the map of the Middle East. Arafat's reckless support for Saddam Hussein's position during the Gulf War as Iraqi Scud missiles fell on Israeli cities appeared to confirm that assessment. In the meantime, the PLO's political weakness in the aftermath of the Gulf War enhanced the prestige of the local Palestinian leadership in the Israeli-occupied territories. Accordingly, the Bush administration succeeded in enticing a group of relatively moderate Palestinians unaffiliated with the PLO to meet face-to-face with Israeli negotiators as part of the official Jordanian delegation to Middle East peace talks in Madrid at the end of October 1991. Throughout the winter and spring of 1992 Baker coordinated a complex set of bilateral encounters between Arab and Israeli representatives in Washington in a bold attempt to broker the type of comprehensive settlement that had eluded American administrations since Jimmy Carter's preliminary and partial breakthrough at Camp David in 1978.

In spite of this strenuous American diplomatic effort, the sessions in Madrid and Washington were impeded by two irksome problems, one substantive and the other procedural. The substantive obstacle to a Palestinian-Israeli agreement was the familiar question of the political status of the West Bank and the Gaza Strip: Ever since the withdrawal of the Labor party from the Israeli governing coalition in March 1990, the Likud government had sponsored a housing construction program for Jewish settlers in those two occupied territories that was bound to complicate all autonomy proposals for their predominantly Arab populations. Shamir obstinately forbade serious discussion of territorial compromises since he had no intention of sacrificing a square inch of land that he considered an integral part of historic Israel. The procedural stumbling block to progress in these peace negotiations was the absence of the PLO. Despite its temporary eclipse after the Gulf War, Arafat's organization still remained the most popular advocate of the Palestinian national cause in the eyes of the people it presumed to represent. However much Shamir and his associates might have abhorred the movement and its flamboyant chief, a lasting peace settlement between Israel and the Palestinians was unimaginable without the PLO's seal of approval.

Throughout the year 1992 the political situation in the Middle East shifted dramatically in such a way as to put the derailed peace talks back on track. The first significant breakthrough occurred as a result of the unprecedented participation of Syria in serious peace talks with Israel. This development seemed to signify Assad's heightened interest in a land-for-peace deal that would return the Golan Heights to Syria (as Sadat had regained the Sinai peninsula for Egypt fifteen years earlier) in exchange for recognition of and security guarantees for the Jewish state. It also may have reflected his expectation that a conciliatory policy toward Israel would enhance the prospects for the American economic assistance that Syria avidly coveted. The second breakthrough was the triumph of the Labor party in the Israeli parliamentary elections in June, which ended fifteen years of rule by the right-wing Likud coalition in Jerusalem. The new Labor prime minister, Yitzhak Rabin, abruptly reversed Shamir's policy toward the occupied territories by imposing a partial freeze on Jewish settlements there. This gesture of goodwill paved the way for more productive exchanges with the Arab delegates at the U.S.-sponsored peace talks that had resumed in Washington at the end of August. It also had the effect of unblocking $10 billion worth U.S. government loan guarantees to resettle recent Russian Jewish emigrés to Israel, which had been withheld by the Bush administration as punishment for Likud's provocative house-building program in the West Bank and Gaza.

The electoral defeat of President Bush and his energetic secretary of state temporarily interrupted the momentum of the multifaceted Middle East parleys that Baker had coordinated like a master juggler. In the meantime, vigorous opposition to a land-for-peace exchange emanated from the 115,000 Israeli pioneers in the occupied territories, who feared for the future of the settlements that they had been encouraged to establish by Likud officials in the past decade and a half. From the other extreme, radical Islamic groups operating in the West Bank and Gaza, such as Hamas and Islamic Jihad, vociferously denounced the Arab meetings with representatives of the Jewish state currently underway in Washington as an ignominious betrayal of the Palestinian cause.

The expanding influence of these Islamic extremists in the occupied territories occurred at the expense of the PLO leadership in Tunis, whose status in the Arab world had already been undermined by the events described above. Syria's decision to join the Middle East negotiations sent shock waves through the PLO high command. What Arafat feared most of all from Assad was a Sadat-like, bilateral bargain with Israel that would restore Syrian sovereignty on the Golan at the expense of Palestinian claims in the West Bank and Gaza. The Israeli insistence on negotiating with the various Arab delegations separately and sequentially rather than in a vast multilateral forum increased the risk that the PLO would be sacrificed by Arab states more intent on pursuing their particular national interests than in altruistically supporting the campaign to secure for the stateless Palestinians a homeland of their own.

This fear of abandonment prompted Arafat to launch a preemptive campaign to reach his own accommodation with the Jewish state. The evolving political situation in Israel coincidently proved conducive to such an accommodation with the perennial enemy: The Labor party had long favored the type of territorial compromise with the Palestinians that Shamir and the Likud had steadfastly opposed, and Rabin periodically reiterated his new government's interest in a land-for-peace arrangement after assuming power in June 1992. Israelis of various ideological persuasions had grown weary of the political as well as financial burdens of the occupation in the West Bank and Gaza. While the *Intifada* had failed to undermine Israeli military authority in the territories, it revealed the perpetual menace of domestic unrest that could only intensify amid the unmistakable demographic trend of dramatic population increases among Palestinians under Israeli rule. Finally, the emergence in the territories of radical Islamic groups that denounced the PLO for its caution and moderation transformed Arafat's reputation in Israel from enemy number one to a preferable alternative to the zealots of Hamas and Islamic Jihad.

While the unwieldy Middle East peace negotiations in Washington got nowhere, Israeli Prime Minister Rabin decided to respond to Arafat's overtures by switching from the Syrian to the Palestinian priority. Top secret talks between small, tight-knit delegations from Israel and the PLO were organized in Oslo by Norwegian Foreign Minister Johan Jørgen Holst. On August 20, 1993, Israeli and PLO representatives initialed the so-called Oslo Declaration of Principles, and on September 13 Arafat and Rabin signed the historic agreement in Washington under the benevolent gaze of President Bill Clinton. U.S. officials had known about the secret exchanges in Norway, but learned of the actual terms only after the negotiations were completed. The poignant spectacle of the chairman of the Palestine Liberation Organization and the prime minister of Israel shaking hands on the White House lawn marked a dramatic turning point in the history of the Israeli Palestinian conflict. Five days before the signing ceremony, Rabin and Arafat had exchanged letters confirming Israel's recognition of the PLO as the official representative of the Palestinian people and the PLO's affirmation of Israel's right to exist and its rejection of violence as a means of achieving its political goals.

The crux of the 1993 pact between Israel and the PLO was to be found in the section covering the political future of the two occupied territories and their Palestinian majorities. The agreement established a five-year transitional procedure for the transfer to Palestinian sovereignty of the entire Gaza strip and of the city of Jericho and its environs in the West Bank. During this interim period, the so-called Palestinian Authority created in May 1994 would gradually acquire control of all internal affairs in the two specific regions, while Israel would retain authority over their foreign relations as well as over all matters affecting the security of any remaining Jewish settlements there. In spite of bureaucratic foot-dragging and isolated outbursts of violent opposition from hard-liners on both sides—such as the massacre of twenty-nine Arabs during prayers in a Hebron mosque by a fanatical Jewish settler and sporadic assaults on Israeli soldiers and suicide bombings by radical Islamic opponents of the pact—the two sides proceeded to implement the agreement throughout 1994. The departing Israeli military units and civil ser-

Fond but premature hopes for peace in the Middle East: Israeli Prime Minister Yitzhak Rabin and Palestine Liberation Organization leader Yasser Arafat shake hands on the White House lawn with President Bill Clinton looking on, September 13, 1993. The ceremony marked the signing of a declaration of principles for peace between Israelis and Palestinians negotiated earlier in Oslo, Norway, which foresaw the gradual withdrawal of Israeli forces from the Gaza Strip and the West Bank and the achievement of a final settlement by February 1999. The "peace process" bogged down amid mutual recrimination and collapsed altogether by the end of Clinton's presidency. *(Getty Images)*

vants turned over their functions to newly reestablished Palestinian police forces and administrative agencies. Arafat later paid a historic visit to the squalid refugee camps in Gaza where he received the ardent acclamation of his people. International donors led by the World Bank supplied funds to balance the Palestinian Authority's budget until sufficient tax revenues could be raised. As this first phase of the transfer of power came to an end, Arafat, Rabin, and Israeli Foreign Minister Shimon Peres shared the 1994 Nobel Peace Prize for their path-breaking efforts at reaching a durable Middle East peace.

The issues left unresolved by the PLO-Israeli peace accord were predictably the most intractable of all: One was the question of the future status of Jerusalem, the holy city of both Jewish and Muslim faiths that had been partitioned between Israel and Jordan in 1948 and then unified under Israeli control after the Six-Day War in 1967. Another was the long-standing grievance of the Palestinian refugees and their offspring who had fled during the first Arab-Israeli war in 1948 and resettled—temporarily, as many of them believed—in half a dozen countries throughout the Middle East. Would they obtain the right to return to their homeland and, if so, under what conditions? What political future lay in store for the West Bank beyond the confines of the Palestinian enclave in Jericho: How far could the principle of autonomy be extended without depriving the citizens of Israel of a credible assurance of safety and security? Future negotiators would also have to determine the fate of the numerous Jewish settlements scattered throughout the predominantly Arab populations of the West Bank, which were hailed by many Israelis as the vanguard of the campaign to restore the Greater Israel of biblical times but denounced by many Arabs as impediments to Palestinian self-determination.

In addition to these pending matters between Israel and the PLO, the question of the Jewish state's relationship with Jordan and Syria also remained unresolved. A major breakthrough occurred in August 1994 when King Hussein hastily followed in Arafat's footsteps to Washington for a handshaking ceremony with Rabin, during which the two leaders signed a nonbelligerency pact. The following October they joined President Clinton at the Jordanian-Israeli border to proclaim the end of the forty-six-year state of war between the two neighboring countries. Jordan thus became the second Arab country in the region, after Egypt in 1979, to agree to full diplomatic and economic ties with the Jewish state. Having earlier relinquished Jordan's claim to the West Bank that it had lost in the 1967 war, Hussein had issued no territorial demands and was therefore able to reach a quick understanding with Rabin.

In spite of the dramatic breakthrough represented by Israel's agreements with the PLO and Jordan, it was clear that a comprehensive and durable peace in the Middle East was inconceivable without the participation of Syria. Assad had been trumped by Arafat (who had entreated the Syrian president not to sign a separate agreement with Israel while secretly preparing his own bilateral deal with the Jewish state) and upstaged by Hussein. Syria's participation in the unfolding Middle East settlement continued to hinge on a satisfactory arrangement for the Golan Heights. Israel's claim to that barren buffer zone lacked the sentimental fervor that fueled its historic claims to the West Bank, with its more than 100,000 settlers in towns with recognizable biblical names. But practical considerations precluded a simple solution even there: The Golan's strategic importance to Israel derived from its pre-1967 status as a glacis from which Syria could shell with impunity Israeli settlements in the valleys below. As the site of the headwaters of the Jordan River, the source of 40 percent of Israel's water supply, it assumed an economic significance as well. These knotty problems, together with the multitude of matters in dispute between Israel and Jordan and Israel and the PLO, were enough to keep negotiators from both sides busy for years to come.

Under persistent prodding by the United States, Israel and the Palestine Liberation Organization signed an Interim Agreement in 1995 to implement the crucial provisions of the 1993 Oslo Agreement within four years. While Israeli and Palestinian negotiators haggled over the details, extremist opponents of reconciliation in both camps did their best to sabotage the effort to reach a mutually acceptable compromise. Amid the harsh rhetorical campaign in Israel mounted by the Likud opposition against the ruling Labor party's concessions to the PLO, Israeli Prime Minister Yitzhak Rabin was assassinated on November 4, 1995, by a Jewish opponent of the peace settlement. Thus was the architect of Israel's military victory in 1967, who had spent more than a quarter of a century in defending the Jewish state, cut down when he opted for a diplomatic settlement of the Arab-Israeli conflict. In the early spring of 1996 Hamas did its part to undermine Arafat's new conciliatory policy and derail the peace process by unleashing a number of terrorist attacks that killed almost sixty civilians in several Israeli cities. Despite this upsurge in violence Rabin's successor Shimon Peres honored an important provision of the agreement reached with Arafat in September 1995, which provided for the transfer of military authority in six West Bank towns (including Ramallah and Bethlehem) from the Israeli army to the Palestinian Authority by the end of the year. After this first stage of the Israeli withdrawal from the West Bank, Arafat's supporters won an overwhelming victory in the first ever Palestinian elections for a Legislative Council on January 20, 1996. Arafat's electorial triumph over his rejectionist critics appeared to reveal strong Palestinian support for a negotiated settlement.

While Syria consolidated its hegemonic position in Lebanon and permitted the terrorist group Hizbollah to launch raids from Southern Lebanon against Israel, Assad faced a new threat from Syria's old antagonist to the north. In the summer and fall of 1998 Turkey exerted strong (and eventually successful) pressure on Syria to terminate its support for the Kurdish separatist movement PKK, which had used havens in Syria and in Syrian-controlled territory in Lebanon since the mid-1980s to conduct a guerrilla campaign on behalf of a separate Kurdish state in western Turkey. Turkey's position in the region was bolstered by the establishment of a close security partnership with Israel in 1996, which was strongly supported by the two countries' American ally. The new alliance between Ankara and Jerusalem confronted Assad with the nightmare of a two-front war in the event of conflict with either of the two countries with which Syria had territorial disputes.

With Egypt, Jordan, and the PLO engaged in peace negotiations with Israel and Syria weakened by the Turkish-Israeli security partnership, some optimists in Israel entertained visions of an ultimate peace accord based on shared economic self-interest that would ultimately consign the old military conflicts and political rivalries to the dustbin of history. If France and Germany could overcome their ancient tribal hatreds and jointly spearhead a successful movement of supranational cooperation in Europe, the argument went, why should Israel and its Arab neighbors not be able to find common ground based in a mutually beneficial commitment to economic development and regional integration? Such optimism was dealt a severe setback with the election of a Likud government in Israel in May 1996. Though governing with a razor-thin political majority, the new Prime Minister, Binyamin Netanyahu, had ousted the Labor government of Shimon Peres on a campaign pledge to revise the 1993 Oslo Agreement in Israel's favor. Netanyahu's dependence on religious and right-wing nationalist parties in his ruling coalition led the new government to permit and provide financial incentives for a major expansion of Jewish settlements in the West Bank, where the Jewish population swelled to more than 150,000 by the end of 1996. This aggressive settlement policy predictably antagonized the Palestinians, damaged Arafat's credibility among his constituency, and strengthened the position of Hamas and other opponents of the peace settlement.

The head of the Palestinian Authority also proved unable to curb violent acts committed by these rejectionist groups, both in PA-controlled parts of the West Bank and in Israel itself. Netanyahu responded to each suicide bombing by closing Israel's borders to Palestinian workers (causing economic hardship for the people concerned) and accelerating the construction of new Jewish settlements (further undermining Arafat's claim that the peace process would yield tangible benefits for the Palestinian residents of the West Bank). Both Arafat and Netanyahu seemed constrained by their political constituencies from taking the necessary risks to achieve a lasting peace. The Palestinian Authority Chairman did not dare to suppress Hamas for fear of sparking an internecine struggle within the Palestinian movement that might threaten the dominant position of his own organization, which had already come under intense criticism for its rampant corruption and authoritarian practices. The Israeli prime minister was continually required by the thinness of his majority to cater to the groups within his governing coalition that favored the expansion of West Bank settlements.

In exasperation with the snail's pace of peace negotiations, Arafat attempted to jump start the process in 1998 by threatening a unilateral declaration of Palestinian statehood when the interim period of the peace agreement expired on May 4, 1999. This threat, together with strong pressure from the Clinton administration, brought the Likud government of Israel back to the conference table at talks near Washington, D.C. Arafat and Netanyahu both signed the Wye River Memorandum which stipulated a series of Israeli withdrawals from the West Bank in exchange for Arafat's pledge to implement a number of security measures and to remove the anti-Israeli language from the Palestinian National Charter. But after carrying out the first stage of the withdrawal from West Bank areas in November 1998, Israel accused the Palestinian Authority of violating the Wye Agreement and abruptly suspended further implementation of its provisions. Within a month Netanyahu's enemies patched together a majority to dissolve the Knesset and hold new elections in May 1999. Labor won the elections, bringing its new head, former General Ehud Barak, to power on a pledge to breathe new life into the dormant peace process. Barak promptly attempted to jump start the stalled talks with the Palestinian Authority over the West Bank and the moribund negotiations with Syria over the Golan Heights.

After reaching agreement with Arafat to revive the "final status talks" on all outstanding issues, Barak resumed the Israel troop withdrawals from the West Bank that Netanyahu had suspended. Then President Bill Clinton summoned the Israeli and Palestinian leaders to Camp David for what turned out to be a two-week marathon negotiating session in July 2000. Neither side was willing to put an offer in writing, but Barak (with Clinton's endorsement) presented orally as the "bases for negotiations" what seemed to be a very bold and generous set of suggestions, including Palestinian sovereignty over more than 90 percent of the West Bank and over the Muslim and Christian quarters of the Old City of Jerusalem. Instead of responding with a counteroffer, Arafat continued to insist on full sovereignty over all sections of Jerusalem that had been conquered by Israel in the 1967 war, a concession that Barak could never agree to because it would mean the loss of the Jewish quarter including the "Wailing Wall." The Palestinian leader also reiterated the "right of return" of the Palestinian refugees from the 1948 war to pre-1967 Israel, a dealbreaker for the Israelis because it would threaten the Jewish numerical majority in the Jewish state. The summit meeting ended in failure, as did subsequent meetings between Israeli and Palestinian negotiators in the remainder of Clinton's presidency.

In the meantime the last flickering hopes for a negotiated settlement and the creation of a Palestinian state were extinguished following the visit in September 2000 by the Israeli right-wing opposition leader Ariel Sharon to the Jewish holy site in Jerusalem known as the Temple Mount, which also contained the al-Aqsa Mosque and the site where Mohammed reportedly ascended into heaven. The provocative appearance at Islam's third-holiest site by the Israeli leader reviled by Palestinians for his indirect role in the massacre of Palestinian refugees in Beirut in 1982 set off a wave of Palestinian rioting in the West Bank and Gaza that ushered in a cycle of bloodshed that eventually came to be known as the "second intifada." Reacting to the violence and leaked information about Barak's concessions to Arafat at Camp David, the Israeli public voted the Labor Party out of office in the elections of February 2001, and Sharon took power intent on crushing the Palestinian uprising. A wave of Palestinian suicide bombings in the West Bank and Israel proper, followed by harsh Israeli reprisals, brought the Oslo peace process to a screeching halt. Accusing Arafat of authorizing suicide bombings and armed attacks against Israeli civilians, Sharon condemned the Palestinian leader to virtual house arrest in his bombed-out headquarters in Ramallah. The new Bush administration in Washington also shunned Arafat, seeking alternative Palestinian interlocutors to restart negotiations for the creation of a Palestinian state based on a "road map" unveiled in the spring of 2003. But sporadic outbreaks of suicide bombing and attacks against Israeli citizens, followed by the inevitable Israeli reprisals causing substantial Palestinian casualties, prevented any progress.

In the absence of bilateral talks with the Palestinians, Sharon launched a unilateral strategy of his own: In 2002 he began construction of a high security fence along the border with the West Bank to protect Israel against infiltration by potential suicide bombers. But the barrier snaked several miles into the West Bank to enclose many Israeli settlements in territory claimed by Palestinians for a future Palestinian state, prompting sharp protests from Arafat and company. Two years later the Israeli prime minister announced his intention to remove all Jewish settlements from the Gaza Strip and a few from the West Bank as a gesture of good faith to Palestinian moderates. This unprecedented offer to remove Jewish settlements by Israel's most ardent champion of the settlement policy in the occupied territories did not mollify the Palestinian leadership, which complained that unilateral dictates were an unacceptable substitute for bilateral negotiations to create and establish the borders of a Palestinian state. The tenth anniversary of the 1993 Oslo I accord passed almost without notice as the dream of peace between Israelis and Palestinians became a distant memory. Then Yasser Arafat's death in November 2004 eventually prompted a flurry of hope that the Israeli government might be able to reach a compromise with Arafat's successor, Mahmoud Abbas (Abu Mazen), leading to a durable settlement of the long and deadly dispute.

21

LATIN AMERICA: DEMOCRACY, FREE MARKETS, AND REGIONAL SECURITY

As in most other regions of the world, the two watchwords for Latin America since the early 1990s were political democracy and economic liberalism. But progress toward democratization and a market economy was threatened by the persistent problems of foreign debt, inflation, gross inequalities of income distribution, political corruption, and violence that had been inherited from the past. Narcotics production in Colombia, Bolivia, and Peru continued to flourish, while Chile and Venezuela became and Mexico remained notorious transit points for distribution to North American consumers. Neither a program jointly administered by the United States and Latin American governments to eliminate the cultivation of coca nor highly publicized campaigns against the Colombian and Mexican drug cartels had any appreciable effect on the problem.

Amid these intractable difficulties, the ruling elites of most Latin American countries were converted to the belief that economic salvation lay in adopting the market-oriented strategy for growth that had been successfully employed by the newly industrializing countries of East Asia. This approach had been pioneered in the 1980s by the military regime of General Augusto Pinochet in Chile in an effort to curb that country's rampant inflation and promote industrialization. The civilian government of Patricio Aylwin, who succeeded Pinochet in 1990 after winning the first free election held in that country since the army overthrew Marxist President Salvadore Allende Gossens in 1973, retained the general's free market policies that had reversed Chile's economic decline. During the same period President Carlos Salinas de Gortari of Mexico, whose country had approached the brink of economic catastrophe by the mid-1980s as export earnings plummeted with the drop in world oil prices, foreign debt soared, budgetary deficits, widened, and inflation spiraled out of control, turned in desperation to the same free market techniques that were being successfully employed in Chile. By the mid-1990s most of the

South America at the Turn of the Twenty-First Century

other states of Latin America had jumped on the free-market bandwagon, slashing government subsidies, reducing tariffs, and promoting export-oriented growth.

An increasingly popular remedy for these governments' financial distress was the sale of state-owned firms to private investors. Though only Castro's Cuba and Sandinistan Nicaragua had pursued the nationalization of industry for reasons of socialist ideology, many Latin American countries had long practiced a form of state capitalism in which a substantial proportion of their industrial sectors was owned and operated by the government. In the early 1990s Mexico, Brazil, Argentina, Venezuela, and Peru followed the Chilean example by auctioning off many of these public enterprises to the highest bidders. The ostensible purpose of this massive transfer of ownership and control was to eradicate the notoriously wasteful, inefficient practices, of protected, subsidized state firms by subjecting them to the competitive conditions of the free market. But an additional bonus from the sale of the nation's assets was the influx of revenue to the hard-pressed state treasuries, which enabled them to service their burdensome domestic debt.

This newly acquired propensity for free market principles, in Latin America predictably evoked an appreciative response in Washington, which in turn engendered hopes of developing closer trade and investment ties with the United States. In 1990 the Bush administration had encouraged such expectations by floating the concept of a free trade zone for the western hemisphere—an initiative dubbed "Enterprise for the Americas"—in what some observers interpreted as an insurance policy taken out by the United States in anticipation of formidable economic blocs forming in Europe and East Asia. But Latin American hopes of joining a gigantic hemispheric trading system suffered a temporary setback when Washington retreated to the more circumscribed objective of intensifying commercial links among the three countries of North America alone.

The origins of what was to become known as the North American Free Trade Agreement (NAFTA) lay in the bilateral treaty signed by the United States and its most important trading partner, Canada, in 1987, which eliminated all tariffs and other trade barriers between the two countries within two years. President Salinas of Mexico (who had recently secured an advantageous debt settlement with his country's foreign creditors and begun to implement the free market economic program mentioned above) thereupon pressed Washington for a bilateral free trade arrangement modeled on the U.S.-Canadian pact. Both governments appreciated the growing importance of the economic ties between the two countries and their implications for the future. Mexico had already become the third largest trading partner of the United States. Its 90 million citizens represented a huge potential market for American exports as well as an abundant source of comparatively cheap labor for American manufacturing industries willing to transfer their production facilities south of the Rio Grande. From Mexico's point of view, the United States accounted for almost 85 percent of its total foreign trade and offered the opportunity for both an expanded market for its emerging export industries and a massive infusion of investment capital for its economic development.

Persuaded of the reciprocal advantages that both countries stood to reap from the removal of the remaining barriers to each other's exports, the administrations of presidents Salinas and Bush initiated in March 1990 bilateral talks that were later expanded to include America's new free trade partner, Canada. The leaders of the three North American countries signed a complex trilateral treaty in 1992 to phase out all impediments to free trade among the three parties within twenty years. NAFTA was ratified by the legislatures of the signatory states in the following year and went into effect on January 1, 1994.

The political and business elites of the other states in the hemisphere worried that the anticipated diversion of American foreign trade and investment to Mexico would leave them at a distinct disadvantage. The Latin America nations scrambled to patch together subregional trading arrangements among themselves to compensate for their exclusion from the NAFTA behemoth, with its 370 million consumers and $6 trillion in annual production. Many officials and businesspersons also harbored the hope that by phasing out protectionism among themselves they would be preparing their economies for the day when the North American trade zone expanded southward. In 1991 the four countries situated on the so-called southern cone of South America—Argentina, Brazil, Paraguay, and Uruguay—established a regional common market (Mercado Comun del Sur, or Mercosur) with the ultimate goal of removing all intraregional tariffs. The advantages of the new duty-free customs union had already become apparent in 1993, when trade within the region had increased by two-thirds in three years. In 1992 the already existing Andean Group—Bolivia, Colombia, Ecuador, Peru, and Venezuela—cut almost all regional tariffs to zero and saw Andean trade surge 30 percent the following year. After islands in the Caribbean developed plans for a regional common market (Caricom) in 1992, the six member nations of the Central American Common Market that had been stillborn since 1964 signed an agreement in 1993 to work toward the elimination of trade barriers among themselves.

The phenomenal growth of free trade within Latin America during the 1990s was accompanied by a new openness to the outside world as well. The average tariff imposed by Latin American nations on foreign goods declined from 56 percent in 1985 to 15 percent in 1993. The principal beneficiary of this decline of protectionism was the United States, with which Latin America was conducting half of its foreign trade by the mid-1990s. This orgy of Latin-American tariff cutting, together with the region's expanding trade connections with North America that had made Latin America the world's fastest growing market for U.S. exports, gave new life to President Bush's original concept of a free trade zone from Alaska to Argentina. Throughout the first year of NAFTA's operation, the Latin American states lobbied intensively in Washington, Ottawa, and Mexico City to obtain entrée to the fledgling regional trading system. At a summit meeting of the thirty-four nations of the western hemisphere in Miami in December 1994, President Clinton responded to the insistent entreaties of the Latin American free marketeers by unveiling a modified version of the Bush scheme for a free trade zone for the entire western hemisphere.

The enthusiastic adoption of free market domestic principles and liberal foreign economic policies in Latin America did not transpire without painful political consequences. By abandoning the traditional strategies of protectionism, import substitution, and government subsidies in favor of free trade and export-driven growth, Latin American governments had deliberately exposed the less productive sectors of their domestic economies to potentially destructive foreign competition. In so doing they ran the risk of increasing the disparity in income and wealth that was already the worst in the world, as the influx of cheap foreign goods and the reduction of government subsidies forced marginal enterprises into bankruptcy and their workers into unemployment. The unfettered opportunity for entrepreneurial success, which classical liberal economic theory hailed as the engine of national economic growth, threatened (at least in the short run) to exacerbate social tensions and generate political conflict between the haves and have-nots of the region.

The evolution toward a market economy in Latin America during the early 1990s was accompanied by a distinctive turn toward political democracy in a region long accustomed to various types of authoritarianism. The transition from military to civilian rule in major countries such as Argentina, Brazil, and Chile had already begun in the 1980s. The aging symbols of the earlier authoritarian era, such as Augusto Pinochet of Chile, Alfredo Stroessner of Paraguay, and the military officers of the juntas that had ruled Argentina and Brazil, were succeeded by civilian politicians who obtained power by peaceful, legal means and wielded it with proper respect for human rights and parliamentary procedures.

In Mexico, the Institutional Revolutionary Party (PRI), which had controlled the government since 1929 through a combination of political patronage, manipulation of the mass media, and electoral fraud, gradually lost its iron grip on power in the course of the 1990s. An Indian insurrection in the impoverished province of Chiapas at the beginning of 1994, while reflecting the socioeconomic grievances of an oppressed minority, also called attention to the endemic corruption in Mexico's political system. The steep and sudden decline of the peso on foreign exchange markets later in the year left Mexico on the brink of insolvency until the U.S. Treasury Department came to the rescue in February 1995 with an emergency loan package. But the austerity measures imposed by the Mexican government caused a sharp increase in unemployment, interest rates, and sales taxes that rekindled fears of social unrest and generated growing opposition to the PRI. The monopoly on power exercised by the world's longest-ruling political party was finally ended in 1997, when the PRI lost control of the lower house of the parliament for the first time in sixty-eight years. Then in 2000 the party lost the presidency to the leader of a center-right electoral coalition, Vicente Fox. This peaceful transfer of power heralded the emergence of a vibrant political culture in Mexico after many decades of one-party rule.

The few exceptions to this general trend toward democratization in Latin America during the 1990s are worth pondering because each represents a significant theme in contemporary Latin American political culture. The first is Castro's Cuba, the western hemisphere's principal casualty of the collapse of the Soviet Union because of its economic dependence on the Kremlin. The cutoff of subsidies and low-interest loans from Moscow in the early 1990s, combined with the continuation of the U.S. trade embargo, contributed to severe shortages of food, fuel, and other essential commodities. Though defiantly reaffirming the Marxist-Leninist ideology that he had appropriated as a youthful revolutionary leader thirty years earlier, Castro did make one notable concession to the capitalist ideology he so despised. In 1995 Cuba passed legislation designed to attract foreign investment by permitting full ownership of domestic firms and the repatriation of profits. This policy led to some European and Canadian business deals, which ran afoul of U.S. legislation imposing sanctions on foreign companies that invest in Cuban properties that had been confiscated from American owners after the revolution. Cuba's condition of extreme political and economic isolation in a region increasingly enamored of democratic institutions and the free-market path to economic development, the unwavering enmity of the million-odd émigrés concentrated in the nearby state of Florida, and the growing discontent among those who had remained behind to endure acute economic deprivation continued to pose a serious challenge to Castro's authority. But the aging revolutionary had weathered many political storms, economic crises, military invasions, and assassination attempts in the course of his long and eventful career and showed no signs of contemplating retirement.

Less than a hundred miles east of Cuba lay another exception to the general trend toward democratization in Latin America. François "Papa Doc" Duvalier had ruled impoverished Haiti with a toxic combination of corruption and brutality from 1957 to 1971, when he transferred power to his son Jean-Claude "Baby Doc" shortly before his own death. Though inheriting his father's ability to intimidate his opponents and lavishly reward his loyal supporters among the Haitian elite, the younger Duvalier succumbed to an insurgency in 1986. After three decades of the Duvalier dictatorship, Haiti was the poorest country in the western hemisphere. Three out of four adults were illiterate, one out of five children died before the age of five, and wealth was concentrated in the hands of an oligarchy residing in a few of the small country's major cities. In February 1991 a charismatic Catholic priest, Father Jean-Bertrand Aristide, assumed the presidency after winning the first free elections in decades on a platform of sweeping social and political reform. The following September the upper echelon of the Haitian military, closely linked to the socioeconomic elite whose privileged position was threatened by the distributive program of the popular new chief executive, deposed Aristide and forced him into exile in the United States.

Intense diplomatic and economic pressure from the Clinton administration, the OAS, and the UN forced the Haitian junta in 1993 to restore Aristide to power. But the military leaders dragged their feet on procedural matters related to Aristide's reinstatement as the United States was forcibly repatriating thousands of Haitian refugees who had fled oppression on the island. When it became evident that the economic sanctions were punishing the Haitian masses without having any appreciable effect on the brazen generals in Port-au-Prince, U.S. troops occupied the country and forcibly reinstated Aristide in the autumn of 1994. Just as five years earlier, when the U.S. military overthrew, captured, and returned Panamanian dictator Manuel Noriega to the United States to face drug-smuggling charges, democracy had to be imposed externally by force of arms. But the reinstatement of Aristide did not usher in a period of peace, stability, and democracy in Haiti. Barred from running for reelection in 1996, Aristide returned to the presidential palace after a highly contested election in 2000. Four years later growing opposition to the country's first democratically elected chief executive's increasingly dictatorial rule led to nationwide riots and violence that forced Aristide leave the country. Ironically, it was the United States, which had restored him to power ten years earlier, that pressured him to step down after it became evident that he had lost the support of the majority of Haitian citizens.

The third exception to the democratic trend in Latin America was Peru. Its democratically elected president, Alberto Fujimori, suspended the constitution, dissolved the parliament, and placed opposition politicians under house arrest in 1992 on the pretext of coping more effectively with the scourges of hyper-inflation, drug trafficking, and terrorism. After rewriting the Peruvian constitution to permit himself to run for office again, Fujimori was reelected in 1995 with over 65 percent of the vote. While Fujimori's undemocratic methods provoked criticism at home and abroad, the achievements of his government won widespread domestic and international support: inflation was cut in half; the country recorded impressive rates of economic growth; the leader of Sendero Luminoso (Shining Path), a terrorist organization financed by narcotics profits, was captured and jailed; both the Shining Path and the Tupac Amaru revolutionary movement declined in influence; and incidents of political and drug-related violence declined sharply. Though Fujimori won reelection in 2000, widespread allegations of electoral fraud and bribery of legislators forced him to resign while visiting Japan, where he remained and eventually obtained citizenship to avoid criminal charges that had been brought against him in Peru. But despite Fujimori's ignominious fall from power, Peru's apparent success in curing its ruinous domestic ills by what might be called mildly authoritarian means represented an alluring alternative to parliamentary democracy in a region long vulnerable to the appeal of the strongman.

Latin America's great success story during the 1990s was the termination of the bloody civil wars in Nicaragua and El Salvador that had wracked Central America throughout the previous decade. The Nicaraguan peace plan drafted by Costa Rican President Oscar Arias Sanchez and endorsed by five Central American heads of state in August 1987 offered a solution in the form of a cease-fire, the end of all external military aid to the belligerents, and the holding of free democratic elections. The government of Sandinista President Daniel Ortega Saavedra, weakened by the reduction of Soviet aid and pressured by Gorbachev to compromise, proceeded to institute a unilateral cease-fire in March 1988. In February 1989 it announced its decision to conduct the free elections called for in the Arias Plan within a year. Similarly chastened by a cutoff of U.S. aid, the Contras lay down their arms and agreed to seek power with ballots rather than bullets. Despite the horrible economic conditions in Nicaragua after a decade of civil war and a U.S. trade embargo, the Sandinistas expected to win the elections held in February 1990. Instead, they were defeated by a broad-based coalition of opposition parties headed by a disillusioned former official in the Sandinista government, Violeta Barrios de Chamorro. In April she replaced Ortega in a peaceful transfer of power.

The fall of the Sandinistas and the crisis of the Soviet Union undermined the position of the rebel army in El Salvador, the Democratic Revolutionary Front and its military wing, the Farabundo Marti National Liberation Front (FMLN), which had been fighting the right-wing government for a decade. U.S. pressure on the government to seek a negotiated settlement led to the beginning of peace talks under the auspices of the United Nations in April 1990. By January 1992 they had produced a cease-fire supervised by a UN observer force (ONUSAL). The fourteen-year civil war, which had caused more than seventy five thousand deaths and terrible destruction, came to an end as the FMLN agreed to participate in national elections scheduled for 1997. When the FMLN and the ruling National Democratic Alliance each won a third of the seats in the parliament, political bargaining replaced gunfire as the preferred means of settling doctrinal differences. With the end of the bloody civil wars in Nicaragua and El Salvador, Central America enjoyed peace and stability for the first time in a decade and a half.

The shift in U.S. policy toward Latin America during the last decade of the twentieth century was most graphically revealed in Washington's relations with Panama. The treaty signed by President Jimmy Carter and Panamanian President Omar Torrijos Herrera in 1977 had transferred to Panama full control of the Panama Canal by the end of the century (see page 370). In a second and often overlooked treaty signed by the two heads of state at the same time, the United States retained the perpetual right to intervene militarily to defend the canal against any threat that might prevent the free passage of ships of all nations. General Torrijos, the Panamanian leader who had won the prize that had eluded all of his predecessors, was killed in a suspicious airplane crash in 1981. Two years later General Manuel Noriega, who was later accused of having sabotaged Torrijos's plane, became head of the Panama Defense Force (PDF) and proceeded to run the country behind the scenes with an iron fist. Though officials in the Reagan administration were uneasy about the repressive tactics and the growing corruption in Panama, they refused to pressure Noriega into respecting democratic procedures for two reasons: First, as a longtime paid informant of the U.S. Central Intelligence Agency, he had supplied Washington with information about left-wing groups throughout Central America. Second, he had provided strong support for the U.S.-backed Contras in their military campaign against the leftist Sandinista government in Nicaragua. In short, as had so often been the case during the Cold War, anticommunism took precedence over support for democracy.

But during the second half of the 1990s, two developments prompted the U.S. government to turn against its former protégé in Panama. The first was the winding-down of the Cold War confrontation between Washington and Moscow in Central America, which was reflected in Gorbachev's increasing pressure on the Sandinistas to seek an accommodation with their adversaries and Reagan's suspension of aid to the Nicaraguan Contras. As the decline of the perceived threat of communism in Latin America reduced the value of Noriega's services to Washington, his dictatorial, corrupt record became an acute embarrassment to a government that was touting the virtues of democracy throughout the world. In the meantime a new threat had emerged to replace the receding menace of communism: During the 1980s Peru and Bolivia had become the principal source of the massive quantities of illegal drugs, particularly cocaine, that flowed into the United States and led to skyrocketing rates of addiction, particularly in the inner cities. Impoverished farmers in those countries sold their crop of coca leaves to middlemen who reduced the leaves to a paste and then flew them to factories set up by drug cartels in Colombia, where the drug was refined and smuggled into the United States. In February 1988 the Reagan administration formally declared that illegal drugs had become the major threat to American society and launched a "war on drugs" to replace the vanishing Cold War. In the same month, two federal grand juries in Florida indicted General Noriega for drug trafficking, accusing him of allowing the Colombian Medellin cartel to transport cocaine to the United States through Panama in exchange for millions of dollars in bribes. The Reagan administration attempted to oust this ally-turned-enemy in the war on drugs by economic pressure and covert operations, but to no avail. Noriega brazenly annulled the presidential elections that had been won by a political opponent and declared himself head of state. Finally, when a U.S. marine was murdered by members of the Panama Defense Force in December 1989 amid a torrent of anti-American rhetoric emanating from the Panamanian government, President George H. W. Bush ordered a military invasion of the country to topple the dictator. After the first military operation that Washington had undertaken since the end of the Second World War that was not related to the perceived threat of communism, Noriega was captured, tried, and convicted of drug trafficking and was sentenced to forty years in prison.

With the overthrow of Noriega and the establishment of a democratic government in Panama, plans for the implementation of the Panama Canal Treaty signed by Carter and Torrijos in 1977 proceeded without incident. On December 31, 1999, a historic event took place when the American flag was lowered for the last time in the Panama Canal Zone and the famous waterway reverted to full Panamanian control. In the meantime the

United States Southern Command, the agent of U.S. military hegemony in the Central America-Caribbean region, had been relocated from the zone to Miami. The withdrawal from the Panama Canal at the end of the twentieth century marked, at least symbolically, the end of the era of U.S. dominance in Latin America that had begun with the military victory over Spain at the end of the last century.

22

FROM THE OLD TO THE NEW CENTURY

THE QUEST FOR INTERNATIONAL COOPERATION AFTER THE COLD WAR

The power and resilience of nationalism have been demonstrated across the globe since the end of the Cold War. Not only within the defunct Soviet Union and the former Communist half of Europe, but also throughout the non-Western world, long-dormant sentiments of ethnic identity resurfaced to challenge the legitimacy of existing territorial arrangements. In its benign, neo-Wilsonian version, the principle of national self-determination led to a peaceful realignment of old frontiers or the delineation of new ones (as in the former Czechoslovakia and former Soviet republics such as Ukraine). In its malignant version (as in the former Yugoslavia and the region of Chechnya in the Russian Federation), the consciousness of ethnic particularity incited animosities that resulted in horrific acts of violence against innocent people. Amid this renaissance of nationalism in the post-Cold War era, however, the opposite trend of internationalism and the quest for international cooperation also emerged as an important force in the world.

The search for international cooperation as a substitute for international conflict and competition as the most rational means of preserving peace and stability in the world has a long pedigree. The earliest important attempt to bring that noble dream down to earth was the Hague Conference of 1899, an intergovernmental gathering attended by delegates of all the major world powers that drew up the world's first set of regulations governing the behavior of states toward one another. The first part of this international code of conduct sought to reduce the likelihood of armed conflict by establishing procedures for the peaceful settlement of international disputes through mediation and arbitration. The second sought to establish rules for "civilized" conduct in war by prohibiting certain practices deemed inhumane, such as the dropping of explosives from balloons—the airplane had not yet been invented—and "the diffusion of asphyxiating or deleterious gases" in combat. These laudable efforts failed to prevent both the outbreak of the most lethal and destructive war in history and such proscribed acts as aerial bombardment and the use of poison gas by all sides in that war. We have also seen how the valiant attempts of the founders of the League of Nations after the First World War were unable to establish a durable and effective mechanism of collective security, as the old system of bilateral alliances and arms races was resurrected by the great powers of the day.

Similarly, the original expectation that the United Nations organization would play a prominent role in enforcing international security after the end of World War II was cut short by the Cold War. The global rivalry between the Communist and anti-Communist blocs during the first forty years after the Second World War precluded the kind of cooperative spirit that would have been required for the UN to function as anything more than a forum for the international exchange of opinion. Its only significant operation on behalf of collective security during that period, the military intervention in Korea in 1950, had depended on an exceptional circumstance that would never recur: the Soviet boycott of the Security Council, which permitted a unique display of unanimity in support of the use of force to repel an armed attack. The few other instances of UN intervention in military conflicts were of limited scope and minimal consequence: Most were related to the monitoring of the periodic cease-fires that punctuated the continuous war in the Middle East. As the Cold War wound down at the beginning of the 1990s and Soviet-American acrimony faded, however, the world body was afforded its first opportunity to rediscover the global security role that its architects had originally envisioned for it. The role of the Security Council in imposing economic sanctions on Iraq after its invasion of Kuwait in 1990 and then in approving the use of military force in expelling the Iraqi army from Kuwait in 1991 greatly enhanced the prestige of the world body as a mechanism for preventing or punishing aggression. But the UN's initial foray into post-Cold War peacekeeping proved to be its most successful undertaking and therefore became a model for such activities in the future. As world attention was riveted on the dramatic events unfolding in Eastern Europe and the Soviet Union in 1990–91, the decade-long civil war in El Salvador came to an end through the good offices of the United Nations.* The Security Council thereupon dispatched an observer mission (ONUSAL) to the country to monitor the cease-fire and collect the weapons that the rebel movement had consented to turn in. In this way the world body helped to defuse a long and bitter civil dispute that had become swept up in the East-West struggle during the previous decade.

During the first half of the 1990s, the task of facilitating demobilization and reconciliation after civil wars had became a leitmotif of United Nations' policymaking in the aftermath of the Cold War. In addition to the operation in El Salvador, UN peacekeeping forces intervened in civil conflicts in Angola, Bosnia, Cambodia, Croatia, El Salvador, Macedonia, Mozambique, Rwanda, Somalia, and the Western Sahara. The multifarious objectives of these operations included protecting civilian populations, assuring the delivery of relief supplies, supervising cease-fires, disarming combatants, and preparing and monitoring elections or referenda. The balance sheet for these United Nations activities includes the notable successes in El Salvador and Cambodia as well as the disappointing failures in Angola, Somalia, and Rwanda. The salient fact about this sudden upsurge of UN activity in hotspots across the globe was what seemed at the time to be the resuscitation of the world organization as an influential actor on the world stage in the post-Cold War world.

---

*See page 487.

But the numerous UN peacekeeping operations in the 1990s were conducted in poor countries for universally recognized humanitarian purposes amid conflicts that did not directly engage the vital interests of the great powers of the world. When those interests *were* engaged, as in the case of the Kosovo conflict at the end of the decade when the threat of a Russian veto prevented Security Council action against Serbia, the UN was pushed aside in favor of military action by a regional alliance, the North Atlantic Treaty Organization. The Kosovo operation set a precedent for the invasion of Iraq by the U.S.-led coalition in 2003 without Security Council approval, which severely undermined the reputation of the world body as the proper forum for handling international disputes.

THE MANAGEMENT OF THE GLOBAL ECONOMY

The earliest and most successful example of international cooperation in the post-World War II era was the series of multilateral negotiations to promote the expansion of world trade. As we have seen, GATT had been established in 1947 as a forum for negotiating the reduction of tariffs and other barriers to the free exchange of goods across national boundaries.* In the course of eight international meetings (or "rounds"† as they were called) since its founding year, GATT coordinated a substantial reduction of world tariff levels among the major trading nations of the non-Communist world. As an active participant in the new multinational mechanism for the promotion of free trade, the United States had seen its average tariff drop from 25 percent at the end of World War II to 5 percent by the mid-1980s. The first seven GATT negotiations had focused primarily on reducing tariffs on manufactured goods. The Uruguay Round, a complex multilateral set of negotiations involving 123 nations between 1986 and 1994, delved into a number of other areas including the politically sensitive problem of trade barriers in the agricultural sector.

The Uruguay Round proved to be much more acrimonious than any of the participants had anticipated. GATT's prior success in lowering tariffs had not produced the free trade nirvana envisioned by classical liberal economic theory. On the contrary, the earlier tariff reductions and the growing interdependence of the world economies had generated a new clamor for protectionism once inefficient industries and farms felt the sting of foreign competition. Governments responded to these pressures by adopting informal measures to exclude foreign products without violating GATT guidelines. Japan, which unabashedly insulated its domestic agriculture from foreign competition with high tariffs and stringent quotas because of the formidable political power of its farmers' lobby, reduced its tariffs on manufactured goods below the level of most advanced industrial countries while relying on a set of covert barriers to manufactured imports. These included a tight-knit internal distribution system that effectively discriminated against

---

*See page 246.

†The first Geneva Round (1947), the Annecy Round (1949), the Torquay Round (1950–51), the Second Geneva Round (1955–56), the Third Geneva (Dillon) Round (1959–62), the Fourth Geneva (Kennedy) Round (1963–67), the Tokyo round (1973–79), and the Uruguay Round (1986–94).

foreign companies, preferential government purchasing arrangements with domestic firms, and legal roadblocks to the purchase of Japanese firms by foreign interests.

The European Community wielded an exceedingly effective nontariff barrier to food imports known as the Common Agricultural Policy (CAP). Originally a bilateral bargain between France and Germany to insulate their comparatively inefficient but politically powerful farmers from foreign competition, the CAP developed into a formidable bureaucratic mechanism to provide price supports for European food products when domestic prices fell below world levels and subsidize the export of foodstuffs when surpluses accumulate. European farmers were thus able to sell their food domestically at artificially high prices and export it at artificially low prices, at the expense of both European consumers and foreign competitors.

United States trade negotiators, responding to complaints from American farmers and exporters, insistently pressed Japan and the European Community to open up their markets or risk retaliation as the Uruguay Round dragged on into the 1990s. Just as the Cold War was winding down, many observers worried that it would be replaced by a trade war among the former members of the anti-Communist coalition. The bitter disputes that erupted during the Uruguay Round between the United States and its European and Japanese trading partners revealed that the once-dominant economic power in the world had lost the ability to impose its will by the end of the 1980s. U.S. motivations for entering into the North American Free Trade Agreement with Canada and Mexico and then launching the bolder scheme for a trading system for the entire western hemisphere in part represented a defensive reaction against what some American policymakers saw as the ominous emergence of protectionist commercial blocs across the Atlantic and the Pacific. The approval at the GATT treaty by the U.S. Congress at the end of 1994 finally paved the way for the gradual implementation of the multilateral agreement that would cut global tariffs by an average of one-third. Other sweeping features of the GATT agreement included the total elimination of a number of notorious import quotas (such as Japan's rice quota and the U.S. sugar and textile quota) and the extension for the first time of protection to "intellectual property" such as patents, copyrights, and trademarks in order to curb the rampant piracy of movies, compact disks, computer software, and prescription drugs. Since American tariffs were already relatively low compared to those of most of its principal competitors, and since most of the newly protected "intellectual property" was produced by American firms, the United States derived the greatest benefit as other foreign countries adopted the new trading rules.

Opposition to the agreement in the United States centered on the creation of the World Trade Organization (WTO), which formally replaced the forty-seven-year-old GATT as the governing body of world trade rules on January 1, 1995. Sufficient congressional concern was expressed about the prospective loss of sovereignty to a panel of WTO judges empowered to assess penalties against nations violating the new trade rules that a number of escape clauses to protect American national interests were added. Notwithstanding the various conditions and caveats that some signatory countries insisted on, the successful completion of the Uruguay Round and the creation of the WTO in the mid-1990s appeared to reduce the possibility of global commercial warfare and the international political tensions that it would inevitably generate. As the Uruguay Round's provisions were phased in, world trade faced fewer politically imposed obstacles than at any time since the Second World War. The parallel development of the EU, NAFTA, and other regional (and potentially discriminatory) trading systems that might appear on the world scene represented the only significant potential threat to the multilateral, nondiscriminatory recipe for trade expansion represented by the GATT/WTO philosophy.

The Uruguay Round of multilateral trade negotiations was largely an affair of the advanced industrial nations in North America, Europe, and East Asia. The less developed countries of Africa and Latin America found it difficult to participate effectively in the international trading system until they could overcome the major obstacle to their economic development, namely, an acute shortage of working capital. The only readily available sources of such capital were the savings that had accumulated in the wealthy countries of the industrialized north. During the first two decades after the Second World War, a small proportion of those savings reached the developing countries in the form of government aid programs and direct foreign investment. Though meager in comparison to the these countries' desperate needs, these two types of capital transfer proved relatively advantageous to the recipients: Government foreign aid was provided either as an outright gift or at low or no interest. Direct investment in Third World countries by private firms, though often resulting in the repatriation of profits, at least left the host country with the physical assets, technology, and skills that the capital had helped to develop.

During the 1970s and 1980s the volume of both government foreign aid to and private direct investment in the developing world declined significantly. To bridge the gap these capital-starved countries increasingly sought loans from commercial banks (most of which were based in Europe, North America, and Japan) as well as from the two major international lending institutions, the International Monetary Fund and the World Bank. While the commercial banks and the international lending agencies had committed funds to the Third World before, they increased the scale of their lending dramatically in these two decades to replace the shrinking government aid and direct investment.

The principal cause of this expansion of commercial bank lending to the Third World was the sudden quadrupling of world oil prices in 1973, which left the OPEC countries awash in dollar-denominated oil profits that they promptly deposited in American and European banks to ensure their safety and earn the highest rate of interest. The only way that these banks could in turn make money on this money was by lending it out at a higher interest rate than that paid to their depositors. To the banks' dismay, however, the deep economic slump caused by the oil price increases had dampened demand for loans in the industrialized world, as businesses and private individuals cut back spending. Unable to find sufficient business in Europe and the United States, the commercial banks hastened to strike deals with treasury officials of developing countries, particularly from Africa and Latin America. The IMF and the World Bank complemented the commercial banks' quest for profitable lending opportunities in the Third World by sharply increasing their own lending operations for the broader purpose of promoting economic growth in the recipient countries. Underlying the strategy of both the commercial banks and the official lending organizations was the optimistic assumption that this massive flow of capital would generate a spurt in exports from developing countries that would earn sufficient foreign exchange to service their burgeoning foreign debt. In this way loans to Third World countries would pay for themselves, while the export earnings in excess of the debt service requirements would be available to finance further domestic economic growth. The expanding economies of the Third World would in turn generate demand for products from the industrialized countries, forging a mutually advantageous financial nexus between north and south. It was a multibillion dollar bet that none of the players could lose. The results of this new wave of lending were astonishing: The total medium- and long-term debt of developing countries skyrocketed from $70 billion in 1970, to $400 billion in 1979, to $1.3 trillion in 1989.

On a superficial level this massive southward flow of capital seemed a godsend to those on the receiving end of the transactions: It supplied countries blessed with abundant natural resources, land, and labor with the one essential factor of production— investment capital—that they were incapable of generating on their own because of their low rate of domestic savings. But, as the recipient countries were to learn very quickly, the money from the commercial banks carried a high price tag. Unlike government aid programs, the commercial bank loans were tendered at market rates; worse, instead of running for a fixed term, most of them carried variable interest rates, which tied them to the changing cost of funds in the industrialized world. Unlike direct investments, repayment of principal and interest was required at regular intervals regardless of whether the loan was producing sufficient income for its recipients. During the early 1980s, as global interest rates rose to historic levels and a deep recession in the industrialized world reduced demand for (and therefore depressed the prices of) Third World commodities, many of the developing countries that had borrowed so heavily from the commercial banks and international financial institutions found that they were unable to generate sufficient export earnings to service their foreign debt. The world faced the prospect of a massive default that would severely undermine the international financial system and cause economic chaos in many countries.

Mexico's debt crisis of 1982, which has been discussed in an earlier chapter on Latin America,* was merely the most dramatic instance of the financial malaise that afflicted dozens of developing countries that had borrowed heavily abroad in the previous decade. The task of devising a solution to the Third World debt crisis of the 1980s devolved principally on the international agency that had been established to assist countries experiencing financial difficulties: the IMF. The first response was based on the assumption that the developing countries had caused their own misfortune by profligate spending, budget deficits, and over-valued currencies that inhibited exports. The debtor countries would be forced to swallow a bitter pill to cure the disease and enable them to resume payments on their foreign debts and begin their economic recovery. Accordingly, the IMF loan packages for debtor countries in arrears on their commercial loans required currency devaluation, the reduction of subsidies on basic commodities, and cuts in government spending to balance their budgets. While this belt-tightening produced the desired result of reducing the debtor countries' trade deficits, the domestic price increases and cuts in government spending provoked widespread social unrest that brought with it the threat of political instability. Worse, the cure did not seem to be working, as many Latin American and African countries continued to fall behind on their debt payments while some teetered on the brink of financial collapse.

But many debtors in the developing world rejected the proposition that their own mismanagement and profligacy was solely responsible for the debt crisis. They demanded

---

*See page 371.

that the creditor countries bear part of the burden of remedying the deteriorating situation by agreeing to forgive a significant portion of their debt. Some of them even considered banding together in "debtors' cartels" to threaten their creditors with a joint repudiation of their financial obligations that would undermine the already shaky foundations of the international banking system. In response, the Bush administration issued a new proposal in March 1989 known as the Brady Plan (after Treasury Secretary Nicholas Brady). It acknowledged for the first time that debt reduction represented a necessary part of any successful strategy for managing the debt crisis and contained a set of incentives as well as sacrifices for both parties to the dispute. The banks were allowed to exchange their bonds for new ones with either a reduced principal or lower interest rate. Repayment of the new bonds would be guaranteed by special earmarked funds to be raised through a new round of borrowing by the IMF, the World Bank, and the governments of several advanced industrial states. The commercial banks thus avoided the risk of default by sacrificing a portion of their anticipated foreign loan profits. In exchange for obtaining this reduction of existing debt and the possibility of future loans, the developing countries were required to implement a series of austerity measures devised by the IMF to restore their financial stability.

Throughout the 1990s many Latin American governments reduced their annual debt payments through these "Brady bonds," which gave them a much-needed breathing space as they concentrated on promoting economic development. This process led to the replacement of an increasing proportion of commercial bank debt by debt held by multilateral lending institutions (especially the IMF and the World Bank). The increasing global influence of these two vestiges of the Bretton Woods system, together with the aforementioned progress in trade liberalization under the auspices of GATT and its successors, the WTO, represented an intriguing paradox: In an era of privatization in the economic sphere and heightened national consciousness in the political sphere, these publicly financed multilateral agencies expanded their role in managing the trading and monetary systems of the world.

THE MIXED RECORD OF ARMS CONTROL

The most spectacular instance of multilateral cooperation in the post-Cold War era occurred in the realm of arms control. For four decades the massive buildup of weaponry in all categories—conventional, biological, chemical, and nuclear—had drained funds from domestic programs and increased international insecurity. The few successful efforts to restrain the arms race required years of laborious negotiation and produced limited results. By the middle of the 1980s both of the two superpowers possessed the capability of destroying each other and most of the world's population. On the continent of Europe two enormous armies equipped with a formidable array of military hardware faced each other along the "central front" of the Cold War. Many countries in the world were stockpiling chemical and biological weapons in anticipation of an exotic new type of warfare whose devastating consequences for humankind and its natural environment could scarcely be imagined. Yet as the Cold War came to an end and the Communist bloc disintegrated at the end of the decade, the major military powers of the world achieved breathtaking progress in arms control agreements that had eluded them for so many years.

The continent of Europe had become the most highly militarized region of the world in the course of the Cold War. As we have seen, while NATO was in the midst of preparing to deploy a new generation of conventional weapons of stunning technological sophistication, the two alliance systems signed the Treaty on Conventional Armed Forces in Europe (CFE) in November 1990,* The CFE pact, which rectified the imbalance in conventional forces on the continent by requiring deep cuts on the Soviet side, was rendered moot as the Warsaw Pact disbanded in 1990 and the Soviet Union disintegrated into fifteen independent republics at the end of 1991. The eight Soviet successor states located in the treaty zone divided up the military equipment of the defunct U.S.S.R. and promptly consented to abide by the agreed-upon limits on conventional arms. After the CFE treaty officially entered into effect on July 17, 1992, the eight European republics of the former Soviet Union scrupulously complied with its provisions as revealed by inspections carried out by multinational verification teams.

Amid this notable progress in conventional arms control in Europe, the abortive Soviet coup in the summer of 1991 sparked a series of sweeping reductions in U.S. and Soviet nuclear forces and the cancellation of nuclear modernization programs initiated in the last years of the Cold War. This rapid succession of nuclear arms reductions began on September 27, 1991, when President Bush proposed that both sides dismantle all of their ground-launched tactical nuclear weapons (TNWs). When Gorbachev reciprocated a week later, all such short-range nuclear weapons in Europe were earmarked for oblivion. After the collapse of the Soviet Union in December 1991, the new republics readily agreed to transfer all of the roughly seventeen thousand TNWs to Russian territory for eventual destruction.

The remarkable progress in strategic arms control recorded during the Gorbachev years (1985–91) had already substantially reduced the long-range nuclear forces of the United States and the Soviet Union. The pinnacle of this achievement was reached in July 1991, when Gorbachev and President Bush signed the Strategic Arms Reduction Treaty (START I) that had been under consideration since 1982. Within a few months, however, the legality of this landmark agreement was brought into question by the disintegration of the Soviet Union into fifteen sovereign political units. The approximately twelve thousand warheads constituting the former Soviet Union's land-based strategic nuclear forces—the ICBMs capable of reaching foreign targets anywhere in the world—were dispersed among the four successor states—Russia, Ukraine, Belarus (formerly Belorussia), and Kazakhstan—where they had been located. The latter three non-Russian republics possessed almost a third of the former U.S.S.R.'s strategic nuclear arsenal. In the spring of 1992 the four former Soviet nuclear states, under pressure from Washington, resolved the legal predicament of the warheads' status by joining the United States in signing the Lisbon Protocol to START I. Through this arrangement they formally assumed all of the former Soviet Union's obligations under the arms control agreement. Recognizing Russia as the rightful heir to the defunct superpower's nuclear arsenal, Ukraine, Belarus, and Kazakhstan also pledged to sign the Nuclear Non-Proliferation Treaty as nonnuclear states and to transfer all of their nuclear warheads to the Russian Federation within seven years.

*See page 410.

In the meantime Bush had renewed his campaign for steep reductions in strategic arms, unilaterally cancelling virtually the entire U.S. nuclear modernization program (including the MX, Midgetman, and advanced cruise missiles) and proposing drastic reductions in the number of warheads on existing ground- and sea-launched weapons systems. Russian President Boris Yeltsin quickly responded to these American initiatives by confirming the earlier reductions agreed to by Gorbachev and expressing strong interest in maintaining the momentum of reciprocal strategic arms cuts. At their first summit meeting in the summer of 1992, Bush and Yeltsin reached agreement on a successor to START I. On January 3, 1993, in Moscow the two presidents affixed their signatures to the second Strategic Arms Reduction Treaty (START II), which provided for a 25 percent reduction of each country's strategic forces to 3,000–3,500 warheads over ten years and stipulated the total elimination of the notorious multiwarhead (MIR Ved) ICBMs that had served as the focus of the strategic arms negotiations from their beginning in November 1969.

But the implementation of START II had to await the entry into force of the START I agreement that had been signed in July 1991 and confirmed by the four nuclear successor states to the Soviet Union in the Lisbon Protocol of May 1992. After some foot-dragging by Ukraine, which extracted security guarantees and pledges of financial aid to compensate for its resignation from the nuclear club, an agreement was reached to transfer all of the former Soviet Union's nuclear material to Russian custody at the January 1994 Moscow summit meeting of Presidents Clinton and Yeltsin. The two heads of state issued the dramatic announcement that their long-range missiles would no longer be targeted at each other's territory. Though a purely symbolic gesture, because retargeting can be achieved in a few minutes, the joint declaration symbolized how far the world had progressed toward strategic arms limitation since the heyday of the Cold War.

As the START I treaty entered into effect in 1994 and inspections of the two nuclear arsenals began a year later, the START II treaty sparked intense opposition in the Russian parliament that delayed its ratification. One of the motivating factors was Russian resentment at the expansion of NATO to include the former Warsaw Pact states of Poland, Hungary, and the Czech Republic. Another was anger at the Clinton administration's refusal to rule out the construction of a national missile defense (NMD) system in violation of the Anti-Ballistic Missile Treaty. Another was the NATO bombing campaign against Serbia in 1999, which further inflamed Russian public opinion against the United States. In April 2000 the Russian Duma finally ratified the Strategic Arms Reduction Treaty seven years after it was signed, paving the way for the reduction by the United States and Russia of the number of their nuclear warheads from roughly 6,000 to no more than 3,500 by the year 2007. Two years later, in May 2002, Presidents George W. Bush and Vladimir Putin moved this strategic arms reduction process to an even higher level by signing an agreement that promised to bring the number of warheads deployed by each country down to the range of 1,700–2,220 within ten years. Though this pact was full of escape clauses and qualifications, it represented the culmination of the long, tortured process of strategic arms control initiated by Richard Nixon and Leonid Brezhnev thirty years earlier.

Significant strides were also made in the decades-long campaign to limit nuclear testing, as the United States, Russia, and France each unilaterally declared moratoria in 1992 and their leaders publicly endorsed a comprehensive nuclear test ban. After Great Britain joined the moratorium on testing, the Geneva Conference on Disarmament decided in August 1993 to open formal negotiations on a Comprehensive Test Ban Treaty (CTBT) (which would extend the old Limited Test Ban Treaty banning tests in the atmosphere and in the sea to include underground tests). China alone refused to fall in step with the other nuclear powers, breaking its self-imposed moratorium in 1993 and again in 1994 with underground tests at its Lop Nor testing site in Xinjiang. China justified the tests on the grounds that it lagged far behind the other nuclear powers in the sophistication of its nuclear weaponry and needed to bridge the gap before the anticipated Comprehensive Test Ban Treaty became effective in order to establish the credibility of its nuclear deterrent. France also resumed its nuclear testing program after a three and a half year moratorium with six tests at its site on Mururoa Atoll in the South Pacific in 1995–96. But it was American rather than Chinese or French recalcitrance that shattered the hopes for ending all nuclear testing in the world. Dissatisfied with existing inspection procedures to verify compliance, the U.S. Senate rejected the CTBT in November 1999.

As the world's nuclear states sought to reduce their nuclear arsenals and to curb nuclear testing during the 1990s, the issue of nuclear proliferation became an important item on the arms control agenda. The international mechanism for preventing the spread of nuclear weapons is the Nuclear Non-Proliferation Treaty (NPT), which entered into force in March 1970 and eventually was signed by most countries of the world. The NPT forbade the signatories that did not already possess nuclear weapons from ever acquiring them and obligated those that did—the United States, the Soviet Union, and Great Britain—to pledge never to assist other countries to join the nuclear club. The other two nuclear powers that had long declined to sign the NPT, France and China, finally agreed to do so in 1992.

It had been evident for some time, however, that many other countries of the world were fully capable of manufacturing nuclear weapons if they chose to do so. This was true not only of industrial societies blessed with an advanced technological base and an abundant supply of scientists and engineers. It was also true of developing countries with substantial financial assets (such as some of the oil-producing nations in the Middle East and North Africa) that could purchase the requisite technology and expertise from foreign sources. The countries thought to possess or be capable of producing nuclear weapons that had refused to sign the NPT included South Africa, India, Pakistan, and Israel.* It was no coincidence that all four had been engaged in recurrent conflicts with regional antagonists—white-ruled South Africa with virtually all of the other countries on its continent, Israel with its Arab neighbors, and India and Pakistan with each other. All of these embattled states may have regarded their putative ability to produce nuclear weapons at a moment's notice—or, in Israel's case, its alleged possession of warheads and a delivery system—as an effective deterrent to aggression by hostile neighbors. The threat of nuclear proliferation posed by this handful of nonsignatories was compounded

---

*As we have seen, India tested an atomic device in 1974 but denied possessing nuclear weapons until carrying out a series of nuclear tests in May 1998, which prompted Pakistan to follow suit (see page 452). Israel was widely believed to possess several hundred nuclear warheads as well as an effective delivery system. South Africa acknowledged in 1993 that it had produced six nuclear warheads in the course of the 1980s before destroying them in 1990 and signing the NPT a year later.

by the problem of those signatories that were suspected of violating the treaty and concealing their clandestine nuclear programs from the agency charged with its enforcement, the International Atomic Energy Administration (IAEA) based in Vienna. The list of suspects included Iran, Iraq, Libya, and North Korea. While little was known of the nuclear ambitions and capabilities of Iran and Libya, a great deal of such information came to light in early 1990s about North Korea and Iraq.

North Korea became the first signatory to renounce the NPT and overtly challenge the IAEA's investigatory authority to verify compliance with the treaty in 1993. Though a temporarily satisfactory resolution of that controversy was achieved in 1994, it became apparent that Pyongyang was intent on circumventing the restrictions of the agreement in order to acquire a nuclear capability (see page 442). The precedent of North Korea's defiance of the treaty and its enforcement agency remained for other aspiring nuclear powers to ponder. The full extent of Iraq's nuclear aspirations became known to the world in the aftermath of the Gulf War in 1991. The UN inspection team that was dispatched to the defeated country discovered a clandestine nuclear weapons program more advanced than anticipated together with a rudimentary delivery system comprising hundreds of ballistic missiles. As a consequence, Iraq became the first state to undergo compulsory denuclearization under the supervision of inspectors from the UN and the IAEA, until the inspection regime was suspended indefinitely in December 1998 and then resumed during the Bush administration's preparation for a military invasion of the country in 2002.*

At the fifth NPT review conference that convened in New York City in the spring of 1995 to discuss terms for the renewal of the treaty, the 5 nuclear and 160 nonnuclear powers in attendance approved for the first time an indefinite extension of the treaty, with the nonbinding provision that the existing nuclear states agree to a Comprehensive Test Ban Treaty (CTBT) and that progress be made toward total nuclear disarmament. The U.S. Senate's rejection of the CTBT in the fall of 1999, together with the absence of progress in the reduction of existing nuclear arsenals, strengthened the position of nonnuclear states that criticized the hypocrisy of the five nuclear states in preaching nonproliferation while preserving their nuclear stockpiles. Two such critics were India and Pakistan, which had declined to sign the NPT and joined the nuclear club in 1998.

This question of nuclear proliferation paradoxically assumed greater urgency after the decline of the Soviet nuclear weapons industry and the disintegration of the country itself. The frightful prospect of impecunious laboratory technicians smuggling stolen supplies of weapons-grade uranium or plutonium out of one the four nuclear republics and selling them abroad to the highest bidder became a major source of concern to the international community. Pressure from Washington and other foreign powers induced these states to tighten up their procedures for ensuring the security of the nuclear waste materials stored on their territory. Another source of concern was the widespread unemployment in Russia's nuclear weapons industry caused by the country's general economic decline and the massive cuts in its defense budget after the various arms control agreements began to be implemented. This situation prompted anxious speculation in the West that highly skilled

---

*See page 471.

but unemployed nuclear scientists and engineers would be tempted to sell their valuable services to the governments of aspiring nuclear powers, just as expatriate German scientists had helped to develop the nuclear programs of both superpowers during and after World War II. As a partial solution to this problem the U.S. government offered to provide financial subsidies to research centers in Russia to employ scientists laid off by the nuclear weapons industry. But the clandestine spread of fissile material and of nuclear expertise remained a sobering possibility as long as the Russian economy continued to deteriorate.

The progress in limiting the development, testing, and proliferation of nuclear weapons since the end of the Cold War was accompanied by an energetic campaign to eliminate two other categories of military hardware. Whereas the five nuclear powers stopped short of surrendering their nuclear warheads and dismantling their delivery systems, most of the countries of the world eagerly embraced the campaign to banish for all time the frightful scourge of biological and chemical warfare. Though the Biological Weapons Convention of 1972 that entered into force in 1975 prohibited the production and possession of biological weapons, efforts to enforce it were continually hampered by the impossibility of devising foolproof verification procedures. In 1992 Russia, after conceding that it had violated the provisions of the treaty from the very beginning by secretly stockpiling bacteriological weapons, joined the United States and Great Britain in agreeing to permit unrestricted access to biological facilities for international inspection teams. Beginning in 1994, the convention signatories conducted negotiations to establish credible inspection procedures to verify compliance. But in July 2001 the United States refused to support the convention on the grounds that the procedures under consideration were ineffective and might reveal trade secrets of American pharmaceutical companies.

The prospects for the abolition of chemical weaponry proved considerably brighter. The Geneva Protocol of 1925, reflecting the widespread revulsion against the poison gas attacks of World War I, prohibited the use but not the possession of chemical weapons. The two superpowers as well as many other countries that had accumulated enormous stockpiles of chemical weapons during the Cold War were therefore technically in compliance with that old international agreement. The disappearance of the Soviet threat prompted President George H. W. Bush to attempt to close this gaping loophole in international law. In the spring of 1991 he offered to destroy all American stocks of chemical weapons within ten years after an agreement banning their possession entered into force. The Chemical Weapons Convention, which had been under discussion in the United Nations for two decades, was finally completed and opened for signature at the beginning of 1993 and entered into force in 1997. This landmark agreement replaced the Geneva Protocol (1925) by prohibiting the production, acquisition, and exportation of chemical weapons and requiring the destruction of all stocks of such weapons within ten years of the agreement's entry into force. Since a civilian chemical industry can shift to weapons production on very short notice, stringent verification procedures (including challenge inspections and immediate access to all chemical production facilities) were specified and accepted by all the signatories. But several of the countries suspected of possessing chemical weapons declined to sign the convention. Those that did and admitted to having chemical weapons programs, including India, China, and South Korea, accepted intrusive inspections of their facilities. One of the conspicuous holdouts was Iraq, whose use of chemicals during the war with Iran in the 1980s had helped to stimulate public support for the ban in the first place.

THE EXPANDING ROLE OF INTERNATIONAL NONGOVERNMENTAL ORGANIZATIONS

One of the most notable developments as the Cold War came to an end was the growing power and importance of international nongovernmental organizations (INGOs) that transcended national frontiers and escaped the supervision of the world's sovereign states. Despite the wide divergence of goals sought by these INGOs, they shared a commitment to establish what Akira Iriye has called an "international civil society": an alternative network of relations among the world's people dedicated to pursuing the common good apart from the particular national interests of governments. The two most important forerunners of these organizations began operation in the 1920s under the auspices of the League of Nations. The World Health Organization (which promoted the eradication of infectious diseases) and the International Labor Organization (which campaigned for improved conditions for workers) set the precedent for international cooperation to address world problems that could not be solved by national action alone. After the Second World War, the new United Nations inspired the formation of a wide range of intergovernmental and nongovernmental international organizations dedicated to combating various social ills throughout the world. The United Nations Educational, Scientific and Cultural Organization (UNESCO) was founded as a specialized agency of the new world body toward the end of 1945 to improve the educational facilities in economically underdeveloped countries and encourage the dissemination of scientific and cultural information to enrich the lives of their people. The United Nations International Children's Emergency Fund was initially set up at the end of 1946 to supply malnourished children with dried milk in areas recovering from the war. After its name was changed to the United Nations Children's Fund (UNICEF) in 1953, it began to finance relief projects to assist children caught up in war, civil conflict, or natural disasters.

In addition to these and other UN agencies, a number of private organizations unconnected to national governments appeared on the world scene to perform humanitarian services. The Oxford Committee for Famine Relief (OXFAM), established in Great Britain in 1942, became a model for dozens of similar organizations in many countries that provided food to starving people throughout the world. At the end of 1945 the Cooperative for American Remittances to Europe (CARE) was established to distribute donated packages of food, clothing, medicines, and other necessities to needy citizens in postwar Europe. After the populations of Europe got back on their feet, CARE and other humanitarian organizations refocused their energies to provide aid to the newly independent countries of the developing world. The Association Mondiale de La Lutte Contre la Faim (the International Association for the Struggle Against Hunger), founded in France in 1956, was followed in the English-speaking world by Africare and Food for the Hungry International, both formed in 1971. In the meantime, American philanthropic organizations such as the Ford and Rockefeller Foundations specialized in providing grants to promote economic growth in developing countries.

Another set of international nongovernmental organizations launched a worldwide campaign to protect the natural environment from degradation caused by human activity. Environmentalist INGOs such as Greenpeace, the Sierra Club, and Friends of the Earth derived their inspiration from the influential book by Rachel Carson, *Silent Spring* (1962), which exposed the calamitous environmental consequences of the increasing use of chemical fertilizers and pesticides to expand agricultural productivity. These groups pressured national governments to enact laws to protect the environment and penalize individuals or private corporations that damage it. This flurry of activity by environmentalist INGOs prompted the United Nations to convene the first International Conference on the Human Environment in Stockholm in 1972. The Stockholm Conference cited scientific studies recording the extent of environmental degradation in the world and brought the issue to public attention. At the second UN conference on the environment held in Rio de Janeiro in 1992, which came to be known as the "Earth Summit," representatives of INGOs played a prominent role in several national delegations. At a privately organized "Global Forum" held in Rio during the Earth Summit, INGOs took the industrialized nations of the world to task for permitting their multinational corporations to commit a wide range of environmental sins in the developing world, notably the destruction of the rain forests, the pollution of rivers, lakes, and the oceans, and the threat to endangered species of animals.

An additional environmental issue raised for the first time at the Rio Earth Summit of 1992 was the concern about "global warming." Since the 1940s scientists had noticed that the world's temperature was increasing at an unusually fast rate. While investigations revealed the natural occurrence of heat-trapping properties of gases in the earth's atmosphere, a committee of UN scientists determined that energy use by humans in industry, agriculture, and transportation may be adding to the natural concentration of "greenhouse gases" such as carbon dioxide, methane, and nitrous oxide. Impressed by this growing body of scientific data, the representatives of the 154 nations at the Rio conference approved a "Framework Convention on Climate Change" that had recently been drafted by the UN General Assembly, which advocated international action to address the problem of the human causes of global warming. Because the industrial nations produced the bulk of emissions of the gases suspected of contributing to climate change, the conference called upon them to take the lead in solving the problem. A follow-up meeting in Berlin in 1995 clarified the critical issues involved, setting the stage for a major international conference on global warming that was convened at Kyoto two years later.

Attended by representatives of 161 countries and 236 INGOs, the Kyoto Conference of 1997 approved an amendment, or protocol, to the UN Framework Convention on Climate Change approved at the Rio Earth Summit. Under the protocol, thirty-seven industrialized nations agreed to reduce greenhouse gas emissions, caused mainly from burning coal and oil, by an average of 5.2 percent below 1990 levels by the year 2012. But after the European Union, Japan, Canada, and other industrialized nations ratified the pact, the world's major producer of greenhouse gases repudiated it in 2001. U.S. President George W. Bush criticized the agreement for imposing burdensome and unnecessary environmental restrictions on businesses that would hamper economic growth and endanger the jobs of American workers. Washington also complained about the unfairness of the loopholes in the protocol that exempted less-developed countries, including such emerging

The "Earth Summit" at Rio de Janeiro, June 14, 1992: Brazilian President Fernando Collor de Mello (right) acknowledges applause after his closing speech to the unprecedented international gathering. To the left of Collor is UN Secretary General Boutros Boutros-Galli, who put the international organization's prestige behind the meeting. Owing to the intense pressure from the 2,400 representatives of nongovernmental organizations who attended the conference, national governments were forced for the first time to devote attention to the growing threats to the environment posed by the economic policies of the member states. *(Getty Images)*

economic powerhouses as China and India, from its restrictions. The advocates of the campaign to combat global warming howled in protest. But they were relieved when the Russian Federation, after dragging its heels for several years, finally approved the Kyoto Protocol in November 2004, enabling it to enter into force in February 2005. Though many environmentalist groups considered the Kyoto Protocol little more than a "baby step" toward the goal of reversing global warming, it represented an impressive example of the effectiveness of nongovernmental organizations in publicizing their concerns and inducing governments to take remedial action.

The battle over the Kyoto Protocol highlighted a dilemma that the environmentalist INGOs had to confront in many of the worldwide campaigns that they waged: the conflict between the desirable goal of protecting the natural environment and the equally desirable goal of promoting economic growth to alleviate poverty and improve the living conditions of the world's population. Another example of this dilemma was the conflict noted earlier between the objective of increasing food production to reduce malnutrition in poor countries through the use of chemical fertilizers and pesticides, a project popularly known as the "Green Revolution," and concerns about protecting the environment. Still another example of this dilemma was the promotion of gigantic public works projects, such as the controversial Gorges dam on the Yangtze River of China, which produced much-needed hydroelectric power, irrigation, and drinking water but also destroyed the ecological system at the construction site and violated the property rights of the thousands of inhabitants who had to be relocated. In response to this apparent conflict between economic well-being and environmental protection, the environmentalist groups developed and sought public support for the new concept of "sustainable growth," which attempted to strike a balance between the two goals.

Although the advent of the Cold War had reinforced the power of the state at the expense of private groups interested in foreign affairs, it did not prevent the emergence of a number of nongovernmental organizations dedicated to the promotion of world peace, international understanding, and an end to the nuclear arms race. One of the earliest of these groups was the United World Federalists, established in 1947 at the beginning of the Cold War to agitate for the creation of a world government. An international conference of nongovernmental organizations held in Hiroshima, Japan, in 1955 issued a ringing call for a worldwide ban on the production of nuclear weapons. The Pugwash Conference on Science and World Affairs in 1957 assembled scientists from both sides of the Iron Curtain who appealed for world nuclear disarmament and established a permanent organization to promote that goal. In the same year the formation in the United States of the National Committee for a Sane Nuclear Policy (SANE), followed by the creation of the Women Strike for Peace organization in 1961, kept alive the cause of the opposition to nuclear weapons and support for peaceful coexistence with the Soviet Union. The organization Greenpeace, established in 1970 in Vancouver, Canada, by Canadians and American expatriates to protest planned U.S. nuclear tests off the coast of Alaska, mounted an international campaign against nuclear testing. In 1985 the organization dispatched four ships to the island of Mururoa in French Polynesia to protest French nuclear testing there. While the small fleet was at anchor in the harbor of Auckland, New Zealand, French intelligence agents blew up one of the ships, killing a crew member and setting off a worldwide protest that brought attention to the anti-testing cause.

Another cause that engaged the interest of several influential INGOs after the Second World War was the promotion of human rights. In response to the murderous activities undertaken by the defeated Axis powers, the United Nations General Assembly adopted the Universal Declaration of Human Rights on December 10, 1948, and urged all member states to abide by its provisions. The declaration began with the sweeping assertion that "All human beings are born free and equal in dignity and rights" and declared that all are entitled to those rights without distinction of "race, color, sex, language, religion, political or other opinion, national or social origin, property, birth or other status." It proceeded to enumerate a number of fundamental rights enjoyed by all members of the human race, including the right to life, liberty, security, freedom of speech, freedom of religion, equality before the law, the presumption of innocence until proved guilty in a fair trial, and protection against arbitrary arrest, detention, or exile. For the first three decades after the Second World War, the Universal Declaration remained a dead letter because of another guiding principle of the United Nations: the freedom of individual member states from external interference in their internal affairs. Some of the UN's most prominent members, including two with permanent seats on the Security Council—the Soviet Union and China (both Nationalist and Communist)—were notorious violators of human rights. If the world's great powers could not be held to account for their actions, then how could the rest of the member states be?

In the absence of effective UN action to protect human rights, the cause was kept alive by several international nongovernmental organizations that sprang up during the Cold War. The first of these was Amnesty International, founded in 1961 to send observers to prisons in many countries to ensure their proper treatment. Amnesty International later expanded its activities to publicize all violations of the Universal Declaration of Human Rights and pressure the accused governments to suspend the activities in question. A group of volunteer European physicians working in Nigeria to care for civilians during the Biafran Civil War of the 1960s was outraged by the diversion of food aid by the warring factions (which caused a catastrophic famine) as well as by the abuse of human rights on both sides. The group promptly founded a humanitarian organization called Médecins sans Frontières (Doctors Without Borders) to provide medical care to people afflicted by famine and diseases and to publicize the suffering of civilians caught up in wars.

As we have seen, the famous "basket three" provisions of the Helsinki Declaration of 1975 signed by the United States, Canada, the Soviet Union, and the Communist and non-Communist countries of Europe led to the establishment of an agency that monitored compliance with the human rights provisions of the Declaration and received numerous complaints from dissident groups behind the Iron Curtain that embarrassed the Communist regimes of Eastern Europe (see page 314). Originally named Helsinki Watch with the charge to monitor human rights abuses in Europe, the organization later extended its investigatory activities to other regions—Americas Watch (1981), Asia Watch (1985), etc.—until the various regional "Watch Committees" were merged into the organization Human Rights Watch in 1988. Since then Human Rights Watch has conducted extensive investigations into allegations of human rights abuses, issued annual reports exposing the abuses, and demanded that governments terminate the unacceptable practices. Though the absence of enforcement mechanisms prevented any remedial action, the proliferation of such international nongovernmental "watchdog" groups challenged the nation state's hitherto unquestioned right to treat its citizens as it pleased.

GLOBALIZATION AND ITS DISCONTENTS

The most powerful groups of international entities that increasingly operated independently of the nation state's control were the hundreds of multinational corporations that produce and distribute most of the goods consumed by the world's population. The decline of communism as a political ideology coincided with the triumph of the classical liberal doctrine that championed unregulated trade, capital flows, and labor migration as prerequisites for sustained economic growth. It claimed that the unfettered operation of the free market based on the law of supply and demand would promote maximum efficiency of production and distribution by providing unlimited access to goods, capital, technology, and labor. In the course of the last decade of the twentieth century, as many barriers to the free movement of products and money were swept away, markets for international trade, lending, and investment achieved such a high level of integration that economists coined a new term for the new phenomenon. "Globalization" became the watchword for this new international economic order of the post-Cold War era: Multinational corporations produced and sold their goods, and financial institutions lent and invested their capital throughout the world, with fewer and fewer political restrictions and with less and less regard for the particular interests of these companies' host countries.

This integration of world markets was facilitated by revolutionary innovations in communications technology such as the Internet and satellite television, which connected producers and consumers in a global network of commercial transactions beyond the reach of national governments. Industrial firms based in the developed world relocated their production facilities to countries in the developing world in order to escape the comparatively high labor costs and stringent environmental regulations imposed by the governments of their country of origin. The efficient new communications technologies and the integration of financial markets enabled banks, mutual funds, insurance companies, and other financial institutions to shift their loans and investments from country to country at a moment's notice in search of the highest return, affecting interest rates, currency exchange rates, and employment rates in individual countries. Some critics of this aspect of globalization began to complain that the governments of the world were in danger of losing their traditional ability to look after the welfare of their own citizens.

The integration of commercial and capital markets led to conflicts between the two types of organizations that epitomized the phenomenon of globalization. The multinational corporations that profited handsomely from the expansion of world trade and the opening-up of capital markets increasingly came under fire from several international nongovernmental organizations, whose dedication to such issues as the preservation of workers' rights and the protection of the natural environment caused them to have second thoughts about the very process of globalization they had originally supported. At the third ministerial meeting of the World Trade Organization (WTO) in Seattle in 1999, several INGOs sponsored boisterous demonstrations against the recently established international body charged with the enforcement of global trading rules. A motley collection of farmers, environmentalists, labor union officials, and consumer advocates loudly denounced the WTO's campaign to dismantle national barriers to the free flow of goods and capital for favoring the economic interests of multinational corporations at the expense of workers' wages and the protection of the environment. The Seattle protest, followed by a more disruptive and violent one at the 2001 annual meeting in Genoa of the G-8 advanced industrial nations, signified the disintegration of the consensus in support of globalization that had emerged in the last decade of the twentieth century. An increasing number of nongovernmental advocacy groups came to regard the liberalization of trade and capital flows, together with such institutional agents of globalization as the WTO, the G-8, the International Monetary Fund, and the World Bank, as the cause rather than the cure of the world's economic difficulties.

The negative reaction to the *economic* effects of globalization on the part of protest groups based in the developed world was complemented by a contemporaneous reaction to the *cultural* effects of globalization. Some observers had celebrated the advent of a "global culture" as a result of the revolution in communications technology that brought all the world's people in direct contact with one another. But critics of this development complained that globalization had in reality become a vehicle for "Americanization," the spread of the only remaining superpower's cultural influence across the globe. The

Militants from environmentalist and human rights organizations protest at a ministerial meeting of the World Trade Organization in Seattle, December 3, 1999: Demonstrators took to the streets to criticize what they saw as the organization's dedication to the goals of free trade at the expense of workers' rights, the environment, and other issues. This protest represented the first notable public display of dissatisfaction with certain features of globalization. *(Getty Images)*

increasing popularity of American films, television programs, music, and styles of dress among young people in many parts of the world provoked resistance to this growing American cultural dominance by those intent on defending their local traditions against the encroachments of what they disdained as an alien culture.

The most vociferous resistance to America's cultural influence emanated from groups in the Middle East and Asia that espoused and sought to defend a radical brand of Islam. The ostensible motivations for this growing anti-Americanism in the Muslim world were (1) Washington's unswerving support of Israel and (2) the stationing (at the request of Saudi Arabia) of U.S. military forces near the Muslim holy cities of Mecca and Medina after the Gulf War of 1991. But radical Islam's declaration of *jihad,* or holy war, against the United States and its European allies also represented a defensive reaction by devotees of a traditionalist, hierarchical, theocratic social order with puritanical rules of dress, speech, behavior, and relations between the sexes to the threat posed by the seductive images broadcast across the globe by the mass media showing the secular, liberal, flamboyant lifestyle of the West. This counteroffensive against the "decadent" cultural values

Osama bin Laden (1957–): Born to a wealthy Saudi family, bin Laden organized an underground movement dedicated to a radical brand of Islam and declared a "holy" war against the United States in the mid-1990s. His principal objective was the liberation of the three holiest Muslim sites in Mecca, Medina, and Jerusalem from the control of "infidels" and their allies, but he also called more generally for a defense of Islamic values against Western cultural influences. The attacks that he masterminded against the symbols of American economic and military power in New York City and Washington, D.C., respectively, on September 11, 2001, prompted the U.S.-led global war on terror. *(Getty Images)*

of the "infidels" was mounted not by the governments of the Islamic world, whose rulers were economically linked to and militarily dependent on the West, but rather by transnational militant groups that operated underground and outside the law. Lacking the conventional armed forces of a sovereign state, these groups recruited fighters among the alienated, underemployed young men of North Africa, the Middle East, and South Asia, whose societies had failed to benefit from the export-driven economic growth that had raised the living standards of many other developing countries in the last two decades of the twentieth century. Fired by religious fanaticism and visions of martyrdom for the faith, these young men became the foot soldiers of the clandestine army that resorted to the tactics of terrorism to achieve its goals.

Most acts of radical Islamic terrorism were directed at American targets in an effort to disrupt the dynamics of daily life and spread fear and anxiety among the general population. The first such act occurred in 1993, when a car bomb left in New York City's World Trade Center by a small band of Islamic terrorists killed six people and injured more than a thousand. Soon a much larger, better-trained, and better-financed Islamic terrorist movement got into the act. Al-Qaeda ("military base" in Arabic) was established in Afghanistan at the end of the Soviet occupation in 1989 by a fugitive Saudi millionaire named Osama bin Laden, who had been supplying funds to the anti-Soviet Islamic insurgency. The original goal of the new organization was to convert the thousands of Arab volunteers who had remained in Afghanistan after their successful *jihad* against the Soviets into a clandestine armed movement to defend Islamic communities under attack in places such as Bosnia, Chechnya, Kashmir, and Palestine. After several years of self-imposed exile, Bin Laden returned to Afghanistan in 1996 as a guest of the Taliban, the fundamentalist Islamic government that had seized power in Kabul (see page 451). He set up training camps for Arab volunteers who were pouring into the country to defend the Taliban regime against an insurgency in the northern part of the country. Bin Laden and his associates soon began to view the United States as the principal enemy of Islam, for the reasons indicated above, and began planning a series of attacks on American targets.

Al-Qaeda scored its first success in 1998 with a truck bomb attack against the American embassies in Nairobi, Kenya, and Dar-es-Salaam, Tanzania, leaving 220 dead. Two years later the movement organized an attack by a small boat laden with explosives against the American warship U.S.S. *Cole* docked at the port of Aden in Yemen, killing seventeen sailors. The most spectacular achievement of al-Qaeda came on September 11, 2001, when its militants hijacked commercial airliners and flew them into the World Trade Center in New York and the Pentagon building in Washington, killing some three thousand people and causing tens of billions of dollars in damage and economic dislocation.

WASHINGTON'S WAR ON TERRORISM

The Bush administration's response to the attacks against the American homeland on September 11, 2001, was a declaration of a worldwide war against terrorist groups and governments that shelter them. With the full support of the UN Security Council and the European members of NATO, the United States mounted a military offensive in the autumn of 2001 that, in alliance with various Afghan warlords and their fighters, succeeded in overthrowing the Taliban regime. To facilitate this military operation, Washington obtained base facilities and overflight rights from neighboring states such as Uzbekistan and Tajikistan. It also persuaded the military ruler of Pakistan, General Pervez Musharraf, to reverse his country's support for the Taliban and cooperate with the campaign against al-Qaeda in exchange for substantial economic assistance and the tacit acceptance of Pakistan's nuclear status. Though bin Laden and Taliban leader Mullah Mohammed Omar escaped and vanished, American forces captured or killed many of the top al-Qaeda officials and dismantled much of the terrorist group's infrastructure. In the following year a *loya jirga* (or conference of Afghan notables) approved an interim government under the chairmanship of Hamid Karzai, a moderate Pashtun leader acceptable to the Tajik, Uzbek, and Hazara ethnic groups that had fought alongside American forces against the Taliban. In December 2004 Karzai was elected president after the country's first free elections, though the authority of the central government in Kabul was contested by regional military commanders who continued to rule their own domains.

The military operation that toppled the Taliban regime in Afghanistan in the autumn of 2002 was the first battle in Washington's declared war on terrorism. It put the world on notice that any government that harbored terrorist groups with a global reach such as al-Qaeda would suffer a similar fate. A year after the September 11 attacks, the Bush administration unveiled a new national security doctrine based on the principle of preemption. According to this new doctrine, the United States reserved the right to mount a preemptive military attack against states that harbored terrorists or possessed or sought to acquire chemical, biological, or nuclear weapons (collectively referred to as "weapons of mass destruction") that could threaten the security of the United States and its allies.

The first application of this doctrine of preemption was the U.S. invasion of Iraq and the overthrow of the Saddam Hussein regime in the spring of 2003. The government in Washington justified this military operation, which was undertaken without the approval of the United Nations Security Council and in the face of stiff opposition from Russia, China, and U.S. NATO allies such as Germany and France, on the grounds that the government in Baghdad had violated UN resolutions by accumulating stockpiles of chemical and biological weapons and mounting a massive effort to acquire a nuclear capability. Washington also claimed that the Iraqi regime had developed close ties with al-Qaeda and other radical Islamic terrorist groups, raising the horrific prospect that they would gain access to weapons much more lethal than the hijacked airplanes of September 11, 2001. After the beginning of the U.S. occupation of Iraq, the justification for the American invasion was undercut when no weapons of mass destruction and no evidence of collusion between Saddam Hussein's secular Arab government and al-Qaeda were found. But by that time the rationale for the U.S. military action had shifted. The forcible replacement of Saddam Hussein's despotic regime with an Iraqi government chosen by the country's first free elections in 2005, it was argued, would set a precedent that would lead to the spread of democracy throughout the Arab world. The proliferation of democratic political institutions in a region long subjected to the oppressive rule of secular and theocratic dictatorships would remove the sources of Islamic terrorism that had replaced Soviet communism as enemy number one for the United States.

The continuation of a deadly and destructive insurgency against U.S. occupation forces and their supporters in Iraq after the overthrow and capture of Saddam Hussein posed a major threat to the implementation of the democratic project that the Bush administration doggedly pursued as the best hope for peace and stability in the Middle East. In the meantime evidence began to mount that North Korea and Iran were attempting to acquire nuclear weapons. Fully absorbed by its costly counterinsurgency operation in Iraq, the United States appeared reluctant to apply the new doctrine of preemption to two "rogue states" that seemed to fit all the criteria that had been invoked to justify the overthrow of Saddam Hussein: Both Iran and North Korea were virulently anti-American dictatorships that had supported terrorist groups and seemed bent on acquiring weapons of mass destruction.

The American military operation that overthrew the government of Saddam Hussein in Iraq, justified by the new national strategic doctrine of preemptive war, signified that the world's only remaining superpower intended to act unilaterally, without the approval of its allies or the United Nations, when it considered its vital interests to be at stake. This unilateralist approach to foreign policy was confirmed by a number of actions taken by the U.S. government in the early years of the twenty-first century. The most dramatic of these actions came in June 2002, when the Bush administration ignored strong protests from Russia and withdrew from the Anti-Ballistic Missile Treaty that the two superpowers had signed thirty years earlier, a move that enabled the United States to proceed with its program to deploy a national missile defense system to protect the country from the threat of nuclear attack. Washington had also refused to become a party to a number of international agreements approved by most other nations in the world because the agreements were thought to unduly constrain America's ability to protect its vital security or economic interests: the Comprehensive Test Ban Treaty, the Land Mines Convention, the Biological Weapons Convention, the International Criminal Court, and the Kyoto Protocol to the United Nations Convention on Climate Change.

In normal times, a country with overwhelming military and economic dominance in the world could be expected to resist restrictions on its freedom of action imposed by international agreements. The terrorist attacks on the American homeland on September 11, 2001, strengthened the determination of the U.S. government to pursue its go-it-alone policy and to refuse to allow the security of its citizens to be based on international agreements that lack mechanisms of enforcement or international agencies that lack accountability. At the end of the Cold War, there had been much talk of a "new world order" based on the principle of international cooperation. Some foresaw the emergence of a "global community," a "world without borders" in recognition of the reality that the major challenges confronting the nations of the world in the twenty-first century—such as arms control, the threat to the environment, the HIV-AIDS epidemic, and narcotics trafficking—have global consequences and therefore require global solutions. But the fear and anxiety caused by the new threat of international terrorism at the beginning of the new century reinforced the power of the state as the ultimate guarantor of the safety and well-being of its people.

GLOSSARY OF INTERNATIONAL ECONOMICS TERMINOLOGY

Autarky: Total national economic self-sufficiency, that is, the ability to obtain all essential goods and services from domestic sources.

Balance of Payments: A summary statement of all economic transactions between private citizens or government agencies of one country with all other countries of the world during a particular year. The balance-of-payments statement includes not only exports and imports of merchandise (the balance of trade) but also such activities as foreign tourist expenditures, transportation costs, insurance premiums and indemnities, and investment income.

Balance of Trade: The difference in value between a nation's total merchandise imports and exports during a particular year. The balance of trade is only one part of the balance of total earnings and expenditures of a nation in its transactions with the rest of the world (the balance of payments).

Barter: The exchange of specified quantities of products at a specified ratio without any monetary transactions taking place. Barter arrangements between countries are usually undertaken to circumvent obstacles to foreign exchange.

Capital Intensive Industry: An industry in which the cost of capital represents a relatively large percentage of the total production costs.

Central Bank: A bank (such as the Federal Reserve Board in the United States, the Bank of England, etc.) that holds the exclusive right to print and distribute the national currency of a nation and coordinates its banking and monetary activities.

Comparative Advantage: The particular ability of a country to produce a product or service relatively more cheaply than other products or services because of the factors of production (land, labor, capital, or technology) with which it is endowed. In international trade theory, the principle of comparative advantage explains why a particular country should concentrate on producing and exporting a product or service for which its cost advantage is greatest while importing from other countries those products or services for which it has a lesser cost advantage.

Debt Service: The payment of interest and principal due on a debt.

Devaluation: A government-engineered reduction in the value of a national currency in relation to other national currencies or gold, usually undertaken to promote exports and reduce imports.

Direct Investment: The purchase by citizens of one country of the material assets or the stock of corporations located in another country that establishes ownership and control of the assets or the enterprise by the foreign investor.

Exchange Control: Government regulation of the purchase and sale of foreign currencies, usually undertaken to prevent the flight of capital abroad.

Factor of Production (or Productive Factor):   An economic resource that goes into the production of a good. The four major productive factors are land (including natural resources located on or under it), capital, labor, and technology.

Foreign Exchange: The purchase and sale of national currencies; often used to designate the total value of foreign currencies held by citizens of a particular country, as in "Poland's shortage of foreign exchange."

Gross Domestic Product: The total value of goods produced and services provided by a particular nation's economy during a particular year excluding transactions with other countries.

Gross National Product: The total value of all goods produced and services provided by a particular nation's economy during a particular year.

Import Quota: A government-established restriction on the importation of items into a country. The quota may be specified in terms of either the monetary value or the physical amount of the imported item, and it may apply to all imports of a specific item or to all imports from a specific country.

Labor Intensive Industry: An industry in which the cost of labor represents a relatively large percentage of the total costs of production.

Land Intensive Industry: An industry in which the cost of land represents a relatively large percentage of the total costs of production.

Most Favored Nation Principle: The requirement that all parties to a trade agreement must be granted any tariff reduction that is negotiated between or among any signatories of the agreement.

Portfolio Investment: The purchase by citizens of one country of the financial instruments or securities issued by a foreign government or corporation without the acquisition of ownership or control.

Tariff (or Customs Duty):   A tax on the importation of particular goods, levied by a national government and payable to it when the item crosses the nation's customs boundary. Originally a device to raise revenue, tariffs were subsequently employed to discourage imports that might undersell the products of domestic industries that the government wished to protect.

Technology Intensive Industry: An industry in which the cost of technology represents a relatively large percentage of the total costs of production.

GLOSSARY OF NUCLEAR WEAPONS TERMINOLOGY

Anti Ballistic Missile System (ABM):   A defensive system designed to intercept and destroy an incoming ballistic missile before it reaches its target. After the end of the Cold War it was widely referred to by the new term National Missile Defense (NMD).

Atomic Bomb: A bomb whose destructive power results from the immense amount of energy suddenly released when a chain reaction of nuclear fission is set off by neutron bombardment in the atoms of a charge of plutonium or uranium 235. Used by the United States against the Japanese cities of Hiroshima and Nagasaki in August 1945 and first tested by the Soviet Union in August 1949.

B-52 Bomber: The long-range manned bomber employed by the United States Air Force from the mid-1950s through the 1980s.

Cruise Missile: An unmanned aircraft with a nuclear warhead and a self-contained guidance system that can be launched from the ground, from ships at or under the sea, and from manned aircraft. The cruise missile is very difficult to detect by radar. The earliest non-nuclear version of the cruise missile was the German V-1 used against Great Britain toward the end of the Second World War.

Delivery System: The means by which a nuclear weapon is transported to its target. During the Cold War, the two superpowers developed three main types of delivery systems for their strategic arsenals: long-range bombers, intercontinental ballistic missiles (ICBMs), and submarine-launched ballistic missiles (SLBMs).

Hydrogen (or Thermonuclear) Bomb: A bomb based on nuclear fusion with an explosive force many times stronger than the atomic bombs employed against Japan. The H-bomb was first tested by the United States in November 1952 and by the Soviet Union in August 1953.

Intercontinental Ballistic Missile (ICBM):   During the Cold War, a missile launched from the United States that was capable of reaching targets in the Soviet Union, and vice versa.

Multiple Reentry Vehicles (MRV):   Several warheads attached to a missile; they are aimed at a single target.

Multiple Independently Targetable Reentry Vehicles (MIRV):   Several warheads attached to a single missile; they can be aimed at separate targets.

Mutual Assured Destruction (MAD):   The condition of approximate strategic parity attained by the U.S. and the U.S.S.R. by the end of the 1960s whereby each superpower possessed sufficient strategic forces to withstand a first strike and inflict unacceptable damage on the other in retaliation. The resulting inability to "win" a nuclear war was thought to enhance deterrence and therefore minimize the likelihood of either superpower's risking a nuclear exchange.

Missile Experimental (MX):   An American ICBM with ten warheads that was proposed during the Carter administration as a replacement for the vulnerable Minuteman ICBM. It was abandoned by President George H. W. Bush in 1992.

Neutron Bomb: A short-range nuclear missile authorized and then canceled by the Carter administration. Its combination of high radiation and low heat and blast characteristics maximized its lethal effects on humans while minimizing destruction of the territory attacked. Soviet propagandists thus denounced it as "the ultimate capitalist weapon," which kills people but spares property.

Pershing II Ballistic Missile: An intermediate-range ballistic missile deployed in Western Europe by NATO after 1983 in response to the deployment of the SS-20 intermediate-range missile by the Soviet Union. Both systems were scrapped as a consequence of the INF Treaty of 1987.

Strategic Nuclear Forces: During the Cold War, nuclear weapons that could hit the Soviet Union from the United States or from American submarines at sea, and vice versa.

Submarine-Launched Ballistic Missile (SLBM):   A ballistic missile launched from submarines, which is less accurate than the land-based missile but much less vulnerable to a disarming first strike because a submerged submarine is difficult to locate.

Surface-to-Air Missile (SAM):   A short-range missile used to shoot down manned aircraft.

Surface-to-Surface-20 (SS-20) Missile: An intermediate-range, land-based ballistic missile with independently targetable warheads that was deployed by the Soviet Union after 1977 and targeted on America's allies in Western Europe. The SS-20 missiles were dismantled as a result of the INF agreement of 1987.

Tactical Nuclear Weapons (TNW):   Short-range nuclear weapons in the form of artillery shells, short-range missiles, bombs, or mines. Also known as battlefield nuclear weapons.

Warhead: The forward section of a missile; it contains the explosive charge.

BIBLIOGRAPHY

Because this book is addressed principally to undergraduates, graduate students, and laypersons rather than scholarly specialists, the following bibliography contains no references to collections of primary sources, articles in professional journals, highly specialized monographs, or foreign-language studies.

PROLOGUE: THE GLOBAL CONTEXT OF INTERNATIONAL RELATIONS AT THE BEGINNING OF THE TWENTIETH CENTURY

The Europeanization of the World

Cain, Peter, and Tony Hopkins, *British Imperialism, 1688–2000* (2001)

Conklin, Alice L., *A Mission to Civilize: The Republican Idea in France and West Africa, 1895–1930* (1997)

Conklin, Alice, and Ian Christopher Fletcher, *European Imperialism 1830–1930: Climax and Contraction* (1998)

Curtin, Philip D., *The World and the West: The European Challenge and the Overseas Response in the Age of Empire* (2002)

Dewey, Clive, and A. G. Hopkins, eds., *The Imperial Impact: Studies in the Economic History of Africa and India* (1978)

Hodgart, Alan, *The Economics of European Imperialism* (1977)

James, Lawrence, *The Rise and Fall of the British Empire* (1977)

Robinson, Ronald, and John Gallagher, with Alice Denny, *Africa and the Victorians* (1970)

Singer, Barnet, *Cultured Force: Makers and Defenders of the French Colonial Empire* (2004)

Thornton, A. P., *Doctrines of Imperialism* (1965)

The Rise of Japanese Power in East Asia

Auslin, Michael R., *Negotiating with Imperialism: The Unequal Treaties and the Culture of Japanese Diplomacy* (2004)

Beasley, W. G., *Japanese Imperialism 1894–1945* (1996)

Daniels, Roger, *The Politics of Prejudice: The Anti-Japanese Movement in California and the Struggle for Japanese Exclusion* (1962)

Duus, Peter, *The Abacus and the Sword: The Japanese Penetration of Korea, 1895–1910* (1998)

Iriye, Akira, *Pacific Estrangement: Japanese and American Expansion, 1897–1911* (1972)

Karnow, Stanley, *In Our Image: America's Empire in the Philippines* (1989)

Klein, Lawrence, and Kazushi Ohkawa, eds., *Economic Growth: The Japanese Experience since the Meiji Era* (1968)

Narangoa, Li, and Robert Cribb, eds., *Imperial Japan and National Identities in Asia, 1895–1945* (2003)

Neu, Charles E., *The Troubled Encounter: The United States and Japan* (1975)

Okamoto, Shumpei, *The Japanese Oligarchy and Russo-Japanese War* (1970)

The Rise of American Power in the Western Hemisphere

Bernstein, Marvin, ed., *Foreign Investment in Latin America* (1966)

Connell-Smith, Gordon, *The United States and Latin America* (1974)

Gilderhus, Mark, *The Second Century: U.S.-Latin American Relations since 1989* (2000)

Haley, P. Edward, *Revolution and Intervention: The Diplomacy of Taft and Wilson with Mexico, 1910–1917* (1970)

Healy, David F., *The United States in Cuba, 1898–1902* (1963)

LaFeber, Walter, *The Panama Canal: The Crisis in Historical Perspective* (1978)

Langley, Lester D., *The Cuban Policy of the United States: A Brief History* (1968)

Langley, Lester D., *Struggle for the American Mediterranean: United States-European Rivalry in the Gulf-Caribbean, 1776–1904* (1976)

LaRosa, Michael, and Frank O. Mora, eds., *Neighborly Adversaries: Readings in U.S.-Latin American Relations* (1999)

Liss, Sheldon B., *Diplomacy and Dependency: Venezuela, the United States, and the Americas* (1978)

Millit, Allan R., *The Politics of Intervention: The Military Occupation of Cuba, 1906–1909* (1968)

Munro, Dana G., *Intervention and Dollar Diplomacy in the Caribbean, 1900–1921* (1964)

Pearce, Jenny, *Under the Eagle: U.S. Intervention in Central America and the Caribbean* (1982)

Pérez, Louis A., Jr., *Cuba under the Platt Amendment, 1902–1934* (1986)

Peterson, Harold F., *Argentina and the United States, 1810–1960* (1964)

Pike, Frederick B., *Chile and the United States* (1963)

Platt, Desmond, *Latin America and British Trade, 1806–1914* (1972)

Rosenberg, Emily S., *Financial Missionaries of the World: The Politics and Culture of Dollar Diplomacy, 1900–1930* (1999)

Rotberg, Robert I., *Haiti* (1971)

Schmitt, Karl, *Mexico and the United States, 1821–1973* (1973)

Schoonover, Thomas, *The United States and Central America, 1960–1911* (1991)

Schoultz, Lars, *Beneath the United States: A History of U.S. Policy toward Latin America* (1998)

Smith, Peter H., *Talons of the Eagle: Dynamics of U.S.-Latin American Relations* (2000)

A Shrinking Earth and the Geopolitical Worldview

Aron, Raymond, *Peace and War: A Theory of International Relations* (1966)

Challener, Richard D., *Admirals, Generals, and American Foreign Policy, 1898–1914* (1973)

Livezy, William E., *Mahan on Sea Power* (1981)

Mackinder, Halford J., *Democratic Ideals and Reality* (1962)

Morgenthau, Hans J., *Politics among Nations: The Struggle for Power and Peace* (1973)

Paret, Peter, Gordon A. Craig, and Felix Gilbert, eds., *Makers of Modern Strategy* (1986)

Prescott, J. R. V., *Boundaries and Frontiers* (1978)

Weigert, Hans W., et al., *Principles of Political Geography* (1960)

Zimmermann, Warren, *First Great Triumph: How Five Americans Made Their Country a World Power* (2002)

The Development of an International Economy

Adler, J. H., ed., *Capital Movements and International Development* (1967)

Allen, G. C., *A Short Economic History of Modern Japan* (1972)

Ashworth, William, *A Short History of the International Economy since 1850* (1975)

Davis, L. E., et al., *American Economic History: The Development of a National Economy* (1965)

Dunning, J. H., *Studies in International Investment* (1970)

Feis, Herbert, *Europe: The World's Banker, 1870–1914* (1965)

Kindleberger, Charles, *Economic Growth in France and Britain, 1851–1950* (1964)

Landes, David, *The Unbound Prometheus* (1969)

Latham, A. J. H., *The International Economy and the Undeveloped World, 1865–1914* (1978)

O'Rourke, Kevin H., and Jeffrey G. Williamson, *Globalization and History: The Evolution of a Nineteenth-Century Atlantic Economy* (2001)

Pomeranz, Kenneth, *The Great Divergence: China, Europe, and the Making of the Modern World Economy* (2000)

Pomeranz, Kenneth, and Steven Topik, *The World that Trade Created: Culture, Society, and the World Economy, 1400 to the Present* (2000)

Rostow, W. W., *The World Economy: History and Prospect* (1978)

Saul, S. B., *Studies in British Overseas Trade, 1870–1914* (1960)

Scammell, W. M., *The London Discount Market* (1968)

Seavoy, Ronald E., *Origins and Growth of the Global Economy: From the Fifteenth Century Onward* (2003)

Thomas, B., *Migration and Economic Growth* (1973)

Woodruff, William, *The Emergence of an International Economy* (1970)

PART ONE: THE THIRTY YEARS' WAR (1914–1945)

1. Germany's Bid for European Dominance

Calleo, David, *The German Problem Reconsidered: Germany and World Order, 1870 to the Present* (1978)

Collier, Basil, *The Lion and the Eagle: British and Anglo-American Strategy, 1900–1950* (1972)

Devlin, Patrick, *Too Proud to Fight: Woodrow Wilson's Neutrality* (1975)

Fischer, Fritz, *Germany's Aims in the First World War* (1967)

Ferguson, Niall, *The Pity of War: Explaining World War I* (2000)

Fromkin, David, *Europe's Last Summer: Who Started the Great War in 1914?* (2004)

Gregory, Ross, *The Origins of American Intervention in the First World War* (1971)

Hamilton, Richard F., and Holger H. Herwig, eds., *The Origins of World War I* (2003)

Martel, Gordon, The *Origins of the First World War* (1996)

McDougall, Walter, *France's Rhineland Diplomacy, 1914–1924* (1978)

Mombauer, Annika, et al., eds., *Helmuth von Moltke and the Origins of the First World War* (2001)

Moses, John A., *The Politics of Illusion: The Fischer Controversy in German Historiography* (1975)

Steiner, Zara S., and Keith Neilson, *Britain and the Origins of the First World War: Second Edition* (2003)

Stevenson, David, *Cataclysm: The First World War as Political Tragedy* (2004)

Stevenson, David, *The First World War and International Politics* (1988)

Stevenson, David, *French War Aims against Germany, 1914–1918* (1982)

Strachan, Hew, *The First World War* (2004)

Trachtenberg, Marc, *Reparation and World Politics* (1980)

Unterberger, Betty Miller, *The United States, Revolutionary Russia, and the Rise of Czechoslovakia* (1989)

Wheeler-Bennett, John W., *Brest-Litovsk: The Forgotten Peace* (1971)

2. The Peace of Paris and the New International Order

Ambrosius, Lloyd, *Wilsonian Statecraft: Theory and Practice of Liberal Internationalism during World War I* (1991)

Ambrosius, Lloyd, *Woodrow Wilson and the American Diplomatic Tradition: The Treaty Fight in Perspective* (1987)

Boemeke, Manfred F., Gerald D. Feldman, and Elizabeth Glazer, eds., *The Treaty of Versailles: A Reassessment after 75 Years* (1998)

Elcock, Howard, *Portrait of a Decision: The Council of Four and the Treaty of Versailles* (1972)

Fromkin, David, *A Peace to End All Peace: The Fall of the Ottoman Empire and the Creation of the Modern Middle East* (2001)

Fry, Michael G., *Illusions of Security: North Atlantic Diplomacy, 1918–22* (1972)

Goldstein, Erik, *The First World War Peace Settlements, 1919–1925* (2002)

Goldstein, Erik, *Winning the Peace: British Diplomatic Strategy, Peace Planning, and the Paris Peace Conference, 1916–1920* (1991)

Henig, Ruth B., *Versailles and After, 1919–1933* (1995)

Keylor, William R., ed., *The Legacy of the Great War: Peacemaking in Paris, 1919* (1997)

Marks, Sally, *The Ebbing of European Ascendency: An International History of the World, 1914–1945* (2002)

Marks, Sally, *The Illusion of Peace: International Relations in Europe, 1918–1933* (2003)

MacMillan, Margaret, *Paris 1919: Six Months that Changed the World* (2003)

Mayer, Arno J., *Politics and Diplomacy of Peacemaking: Containment and Counterrevolution at Versailles, 1918–1919* (1967)

Sharp, Alan, *The Versailles Settlement* (1991)

Silverman, Dan P., *Reconstructing Europe after the Great War* (1982)

Walworth, Arthur, *Wilson and His Peacemakers: American Diplomacy and the Paris Peace Conference, 1919* (1986)

3. The Western World in the Twenties

The Illusion of Economic Restoration

Aldcroft, Derek H., *From Versailles to Wall Street: 1918–1929* (1977)

Alford, B. W. E., *Depression and Recovery: British Economic Growth, 1918–1939* (1972)

Balderston, Theo, ed., *The World Economy and National Economies in the Interwar Slump* (2003)

Dow, J. C. R., and Christopher Dow, *Major Recessions: Britain and the World 1920–1995* (1999)

Drummond, Ian, *British Economic Policy and the Empire, 1919–1932* (1972)

Felix, David, *Walther Rathenau and the Weimar Republic: The Politics of Reparations* (1971)

Hoff, Joan, *American Business and Foreign Policy, 1920–1933* (1971)

Hogan, Michael J., *Informal Entente: The Private Structure of Cooperation in Anglo-American Economic Diplomacy, 1918–1928* (1977)

Koistinen, Paul A. C., *Planning War, Pursuing Peace: The Political Economy of American Warfare, 1920–1939* (1998)

Leffler, Melvyn P., *The Elusive Quest: America's Pursuit of European Stability and French Security, 1919–1933* (1979)

Maier, Charles S., *Recasting Bourgeois Europe: Stabilization in France, Germany, and Italy in the Decade after World War I* (1975)

Rowland, Benjamin M., ed., *Balance of Power or Hegemony: The Interwar Monetary System* (1976)

Rupieper, Herman J., *The Cuno Government and Reparations, 1921–1923* (1979)

Schuker, Stephen A., *American Reparations to Germany, 1919–1933* (1988)

Schuker, Stephen A., *The End of French Predominance in Europe: The Financial Crisis of 1924 and the Adoption of the Dawes Plan* (1976)

Wilkins, Mira, *The Maturing of Multinational Enterprise: American Business Interests Abroad from 1914 to 1970* (1974)

The Illusion of Continental Security

Adamthwaite, Anthony, *Grandeur and Misery: France's Bid for Power in Europe, 1914–1940* (1995)

Fink, Carole, *The Genoa Conference: European Diplomacy, 1921–1922* (1984)

Henig, Ruth B., ed., *The League of Nations* (1973)

Hoff, Joan, *Ideology and Economics: U.S. Relations with the Soviet Union, 1918–1933* (1974)

Howard, Michael, *The Continental Commitment: The Dilemma of British Defense Policy in the Era of the Two World Wars* (1972)

Jacobson, Jon, *Locarno Diplomacy: Germany and the West, 1925–1929* (1972)

Keiger, John, *France and the World since 1870* (2001)

Lynch, Cecelia, *Beyond Appeasement: Interpreting Interwar Peace Movements in World Politics* (1999)

Marks, Sally, *The Ebbing of European Ascendency: An International History of the World, 1914–1945* (2002)

Marks, Sally, *The Illusion of Peace: Europe's International Relations, 1918–1933* (2003)

Nelson, Keith L., *Victors Divided: America and the Allies in Germany, 1918–1923* (1975)

Offner, Arnold A., *The Origins of the Second World War: American Foreign Policy and World Politics, 1917–1941* (1975)

Orde, Anne, *Great Britain and International Security, 1920–1926* (1978)

Ostrower, Gary B., *Collective Insecurity: The United States and the League of Nations during the Early Thirties* (1979)

Price, Christopher, *Britain, America and Rearmament in the 1930s: The Cost of Failure* (2001)

Raffo, P., *The League of Nations* (1974)

Rhodes, Benjamin D., *United States Foreign Policy in the Interwar Period, 1918–1941: The Golden Age of American Diplomatic and Military Complacency* (2001)

Ulam, Adam, *Expansion and Coexistence: The History of Soviet Foreign Policy, 1917–1973* (1974)

Wilt, Alan F., *Food for War: Agriculture and Rearmament in Britain before the Second World War* (2001)

4. The Western World in the Thirties

The Collapse of the World Economic Order

Adams, Frederick C., *Economic Diplomacy: The Export-Import Bank and American Foreign Policy, 1934–1939* (1976)

Carroll, Bernice A., *Design for Total War: Arms and Economics in the Third Reich* (1968)

Gardner, Lloyd C., *Economic Aspects of New Deal Diplomacy* (1964)

Hall, Thomas E., and J. David Ferguson, *The Great Depression: An International Disaster of Perverse Economic Policies* (1998)

Hehn, Paul N., *A Low Dishonest Decade: The Great Powers, Eastern Europe, and the Economic Origins of World War II, 1930–1941* (2002)

Kaiser, David, *Economic Diplomacy and the Origins of the Second World War: Germany, Britain, France, and Eastern Europe, 1930–1939* (1980)

Kemp, Tom, *The French Economy, 1913–1939* (1972)

Kindleberger, Charles, *The World in Depression, 1929–1939* (1973)

Maddison, Angus, *The World Economy in the 20th Century* (1989)

McIlvaine, Robert, *The Great Depression: America, 1929–1941* (1993)

Richardson, H. W., *Economic Recovery in Britain, 1932–1939* (1967)

Rothermund, Dietmar, *The Global Impact of the Great Depression 1929–1939* (1996)

The Collapse of the European Security System

Adamthwaite, Anthony, *France and the Coming of the Second World War* (1977)

Adamthwaite, Anthony, *The Making of the Second World War* (1979)

Baer, George W., *Test Case: Italy, Ethiopia, and the League of Nations* (1976)

Brooke-Shepard, Gordon, *Anschluss: The Rape of Austria* (1976)

Carley, Michael Jabara, *1939: The Alliance that Never Was and the Coming of World War II* (1999)

Cienciala, Anna M., *Poland and the Western Powers, 1938–39* (1968)

Cloverdale, John F., *Italian Intervention in the Spanish Civil War* (1975)

Cowling, Maurice, *The Impact of Hitler: British Politics and British Policy, 1933–1940* (1975)

Divine, Robert A., *The Illusion of Neutrality* (1962)

Douglas, Roy, *In the Year of Munich* (1977)

Eilard, Murray L., *Woodrow Wilson: Architect of World War II* (1992)

Goldstein, Erik, and Igor Lukes, et al., eds., *The Munich Crisis, 1938: Prelude to World War II* (2000)

Hardie, Frank, *The Abyssinian Crisis* (1974)

Jordan, Nicole, *The Popular Front and Central Europe: The Dilemma of French Impotence, 1918–1940* (1992)

Komjathy, Anthony T., *The Crises of France's East Central European Diplomacy, 1933–1938* (1977)

McDonough, Frank, Richard Brown, and David Smith, eds., *The Origins of the First and Second World Wars* (1997)

Middlemas, Keith, *Diplomacy of Illusion: The British Government and Germany, 1937–1939* (1971)

Offner, Arnold A., *American Appeasement: United States Foreign Policy and Germany, 1933–1938* (1969)

Ragsdale, Hugh, *The Soviets, the Munich Crisis, and the Coming of World War II* (2004)

Rich, Norman, *Hitler's War Aims* (2 vols., 1973–74)

Remak, Joachim, *The Origins of the Second World War* (1976)

Rock, William R., *British Appeasement in the 1930s* (1977)

Shay, Robert Paul, *British Rearmament in the Thirties* (1977)

Smelser, Ronald M., *The Sudeten Problem, 1933–1938* (1975)

Smith, Denis Mack, *Mussolini's Roman Empire* (1976)

Taylor, A. J. P., *Origins of the Second World War* (1961)

Thomas, Hugh, *The Spanish Civil War* (1961)

Traina, Richard P., *American Diplomacy and the Spanish Civil War* (1968)

Weinberg, Gerhard, *The Foreign Policy of Hitler's Germany* (2 vols., 1970, 1979)

Young, Robert, *In Command of France: French Foreign Policy and Military Planning, 1933–1940* (1978)

5. Germany's Second Bid for European Dominance

Ambrose, Stephen A., *D-Day: June 6, 1944: The Climactic Battle of World War II* (1995)

Armitage, Michael, et al., *World War II Day by Day* (2004)

Beitzell, Robert, *The Uneasy Alliance: America, Britain, and Russia, 1941–1943* (1972)

Blatt, Joel, ed., *The French Defeat of 1940: Reassessments* (2000)

Buhite, Russell H., *Decisions at Yalta: An Appraisal of Summit Diplomacy* (1986)

Calber, Basil, *The Battle of Britain* (1962)

Calvocoressi, Peter, and Guy Wint, *Total War: Causes and Courses of the Second World War* (1979)

Carill, Paul, *Hitler's War in Russia* (1964)

Clemens, Diane Shaver, *Yalta* (1970)

Dawidowicz, Lucy S., *The War against the Jews* (1975)

D'Este, Carlo, *Decision in Normandy* (2000)

Divine, Robert A., *Roosevelt and World War II* (1969)

Fehrenbach, T. R., *FDR's Undeclared War, 1939–1941* (1967)

Feis, Herbert, *Between War and Peace: The Potsdam Conference* (1960)

Goodhart, Philip, *Fifty Ships that Saved the World: The Foundations of Anglo-American Alliance* (1965)

Hart, B. H. Liddell, *History of the Second World War* (1970)

Hastings, Max, *Armageddon: The Battle for Germany, 1944–1945* (2004)

Heering, George C., Jr., *Aid to Russia, 1941–1946* (1973)

Jackson, G. F., *The Battle for Italy* (1967)

Kimball, Warren R., *Forged in War: Roosevelt, Churchill, and the Second World War* (1997)

Kimball, Warren R., *The Most Unsordid Act: Lend-Lease, 1939–1941* (1969)

Lukacs, John, *The Last European War: September 1939–December 1941* (1976)

Marrus, Michael R., *The Holocaust in History* (1987)

Mastny, Vojtech, *Russia's Road to the Cold War: Diplomacy, Warfare, and the Politics of Communism, 1941–45* (1979)

May, Ernest, *Strange Victory: Hitler's Conquest of France* (2001)

Mee, Charles A., Jr., *Meeting at Potsdam* (1995)

Milward, Alan S., *The German Economy at War* (1965)

Milward, Alan S., *War, Economy, and Society: 1939–1945* (1977)

Weinberg, Gerhard, *A World at Arms: A Global History of World War II* (1994)

Willmott, H. P., Robin Cross, Charles Messenger, and Richard Overy, *World War II* (2004)

Wilson, Theodore A., *The First Summit: Roosevelt and Churchill at Placentia Bay, 1941* (1969)

Winterbotham, F. W., *The Ultra Secret* (1974)

Wright, Gordon, *The Ordeal of Total War, 1939–45* (1968)

Wyman, David S., *The Abandonment of the Jews: America and the Holocaust, 1941–1945* (1984)

6. The Confirmation of United States Supremacy in Latin-America

The Era of Direct Domination

Brandes, Joseph, *Herbert Hoover and Economic Diplomacy: Department of Commerce Policy, 1921–1928* (1962)

Geiger, Theodore, and Liesel Goode, *The General Electric Company in Brazil* (1961)

Green, David, *The Containment of Latin America* (1971)

Greib, Kenneth J., *The Latin American Policy of Warren G. Harding* (1976)

Kamman, William, *A Search for Stability: United States Diplomacy toward Nicaragua, 1925–1933* (1968)

Karnes, Thomas L., *Tropical Enterprise: The Standard Fruit and Steamship Company in Latin America* (1978)

Krenn, Michael L., *U.S. Policy toward Economic Nationalism in Latin America, 1917–1929* (1990)

Lowenthal, Abraham F., *Exporting Democracy: The United States and Latin America: Case Studies* (1991)

Macaulay, Neill, *The Sandino Affair* (1967)

Munro, Dana M., *The United States and the Caribbean Republics, 1921–1933* (1974)

O'Brien, Thomas F., *The Century of U.S. Capitalism in Latin America* (1991)

Ronning, C. Neal, *Intervention in Latin America* (1971)

Schmidt, Hans, *The United States Occupation of Haiti, 1915–1934* (1971)

Sheinin, David, *Searching for Authority: Pan Americanism, Diplomacy, and Politics in US-Argentine Relations, 1910–1930* (1998)

Smith, Robert F., *The United States and Cuba: Business and Diplomacy, 1917–1960* (1960)

Smith, Robert F., *The United States and Revolutionary Nationalism in Mexico, 1916–1932* (1972)

Steward, Dick, *Trade and Hemisphere* (1975)

Thorp, Rosemary, *Progress, Poverty, and Exclusion: An Economic History of Latin America in the 20th Century* (1998)

Tulchin, Joseph, *Aftermath of War: World War I and United States Policy toward Latin America* (1971)

Wilkins, Mira, *The Maturing of Multinational Enterprise: American Business Abroad from 1914–1970* (1974)

The Era of Indirect Hegemony

Adams, Frederick C., *Economic Diplomacy: The Export-Import Bank and American Foreign Policy, 1934–1939* (1976)

Bethell, Leslie, and Ian Roxborough, eds., *Latin America between the Second World War and the Cold War: Crisis and Containment, 1944–1948* (1997)

Caballero, Manuel, and Alan Knight, eds., *Latin America and the Comintern, 1919–1943* (2002)

Callcott, Wilfred H., *The Western Hemisphere: Its Influence on United States Foreign Policies to the End of World War II* (1968)

Farer, Tom J., ed., *The Future of the Inter-American System* (1979)

Friedman, Max Paul, *Nazis and Good Neighbors: The United States Campaign against the Germans of Latin America in World War II* (2003)

Frye, Alton B., *Nazi Germany and the Western Hemisphere, 1933–1941* (1967)

Gardner, Lloyd, *Economic Aspects of New Deal Diplomacy* (1964)

Hilton, Stanley, *Brazil and the Great Powers, 1930–1939* (1975)

Hilton, Stanley, *Hitler's Secret War in South America, 1939–1945* (1981)

Inman, Samuel G., *Inter-American Conferences, 1926–1954* (1965)

McCann, Frank D., Jr., *The Brazilian-American Alliance, 1937–1945* (1973)

Mecham, J. Lloyd, *The United States and Inter-American Security, 1889–1960* (1961)

Paz, Alberto Conil, and Gustavo Ferrari, *Argentina's Foreign Policy, 1930–1962* (1962)

Roorda, Eric Paul, *The Dictator Next Door: The Good Neighbor Policy and the Trujillo Regime in the Dominican Republic, 1930–1945* (1998)

Schmitz, David, *Thank God They're on Our Side: The United States and Rightwing Dictatorships* (1999)

Wood, Bryce, *The Making of the Good Neighbor Policy* (1961)

Wood, Bryce, *The United States and the Latin American Wars, 1932–1942* (1966)

7. The Confirmation of Japan's Supremacy in East Asia

The Period of Peaceful Penetration

Barnhart, Michael A., *Japan Prepares for Total War: The Search for Economic Security, 1919–1941* (1987)

Cohen, Warren I., *America's Response to China: An Interpretive History of Sino-American Relations* (1971)

Coox, Alvin D., and Hilroy Conroy, eds., *China and Japan: Search for Balance since World War I* (1978)

Dayer, Roberta A., *Bankers and Diplomats in China, 1917–1925* (1980)

Dingman, Roger, *Power in the Pacific: The Origins of Naval Arms Limitation, 1914–1922* (1970)

Goldstein, Erik, et al., *The Washington Conference, 1921–22: Naval Rivalry, East Asian Stability, and the Road to Pearl Harbor* (1994)

Humphreys, Leonard A., *The Way of the Heavenly Sword: The Japanese Army in the 1920's* (1995)

Iriye, Akira, *After Imperialism: The Search for Order in the Far East, 1921–1931* (1965)

Kawamura, Noriko, *Turbulence in the Pacific: Japanese-U.S. Relations during World War I* (2000)

Larence, James L., *Organized Business and the Myth of the China Market* (1981)

Linn, Brian McAllister, *Guardians of Empire: The U.S. Army and the Pacific, 1902–1940* (1999)

Livingston, William S., and William Roger Louis, eds., *Australia, New Zealand, and the Pacific Islands since the First World War* (1979)

Louis, William Roger, *British Strategy in the Far East, 1919–1939* (1971)

Nish, Ian, *Alliance in Decline: A Study of Anglo-Japanese Relations* (1972)

Nish, Ian, *Japanese Foreign Policy in the Interwar Period* (2002)

O'Connor, Raymond G., *Perilous Equilibrium: The United States and the London Naval Conference of 1930* (1962)

Tuchman, Barbara, *Stilwell and the American Experience in China, 1911–1945* (1971)

Wheeler, Gerald E., *Prelude to Pearl Harbor: The United States Navy and the Far East, 1921–1931* (1963)

The Period of Military Expansion and the War in Asia

Best, Anthony, *Britain, Japan, and Pearl Harbor: Avoiding War in East Asia, 1936–41* (1995)

Borg, Dorothy, and Shumpei Okomoto, eds., *Pearl Harbor as History: Japanese-American Relations, 1931–1941* (1973)

Chang, Iris, *The Rape of Nanking: The Forgotten Holocaust of World War II* (1998)

Crowley, James B., *Japan's Quest for Autonomy: National Security and Foreign Policy, 1930–1938* (1966)

Collier, Basil, *The War in the Far East* (1970)

Daniels, Roger, *Concentration Camps USA: Japanese-Americans and World War II* (1971)

Dower, John, *War without Mercy: Race and Power in the Pacific War* (1986)

Endicott, Stephen L., *Diplomacy and Enterprise: British China Policy 1933–1937* (1975)

Frank, Richard B., *Downfall: The End of the Imperial Japanese Empire* (1999)

Girdner, Audrie, and Annie Loftis, *The Great Betrayal: The Evacuation of the Japanese-Americans during World War II* (1969)

Hasegawa, Tsuyoshi, *Racing the Enemy: Stalin, Truman, and the Surrender of Japan* (2005)

Iriye, Akira, *Power and Culture: The Japanese-American War, 1941–1945* (1981)

Lamb, Margaret, and Nicholas Tarling, *From Versailles to Pearl Harbor: The Origins of the Second World War in Europe and Asia* (2001)

Lebra, Joyce C., *Japan's Greater East Asia Co-Prosperity Sphere in World War II* (1975)

Lee, Bradford A., *Britain and the Sino-Japanese War, 1937–1939* (1973)

Lowe, Peter, *Great Britain and the Origins of the Pacific War* (1977)

Lu, David J., *From the Marco Polo Bridge to Pearl Harbor: Japan's Entry into World War II* (1961)

Mestill, J. M., *The Hollow Alliance: Germany and Japan* (1966)

Morley, James W., ed., *Deterrent Diplomacy: Japan, Germany, and the USSR, 1935–1940* (1976)

Ogata, Sadaka, *Defiance in Manchuria: The Making of Japanese Foreign Policy, 1931–1932* (1964)

Prang, Gordon, *At Dawn We Slept* (1981)

Presseisen, E. L., *Germany and Japan: A Study in Totalitarian Diplomacy* (1969)

Schom, Alan M., *The Eagle and the Rising Sun: The Japanese-American War 1941–1943: Pearl Harbor through Guadalcanal* (2003)

Sherwin, Martin J., *A World Destroyed: Hiroshima and the Origins of the Arms Race* (2001)

Sun, Youli, *China and the Origins of the Pacific War, 1931–41* (1996)

Tarling, Nicholas, *Britain, Southeast Asia, and the Onset of the Pacific War* (1996)

Tarling, Nicholas, *A Sudden Rampage: The Japanese Occupation of Southeast Asia 1941–1945* (2001)

Thorne, Christopher, *Allies of a Kind: The United States, Britain, and War against Japan, 1941–1945* (1978)

Thorne, Christopher, *The Limits of Foreign Policy: The West, the League, and the Far Eastern Crisis of 1931–1933* (1972)

Toland, John, *Infamy: Pearl Harbor and Its Aftermath* (1982)

Trotter, Ann, *Britain and East Asia, 1933–1937* (1975)

Yoshihashi, Takehiko, *Conspiracy at Mukden: The Rise of the Japanese Military* (1963)

Young, Louise, *Japan's Total Empire: Manchuria and the Culture of Wartime Imperialism* (1999)

PART TWO: THE COLD WAR BETWEEN THE SUPERPOWERS (1945–1985)

8. The Formation of the Bipolar World in the Truman-Stalin Era

Alperowitz, Gar, *Atomic Diplomacy* (1965)

Ambrose, Stephen, *1945 Eisenhower and Berlin* (1971)

Backer, John H., *Priming the Germany Economy: American Occupation Policies, 1945–48* (1971)

Beitzell, Robert, *The Uneasy Alliance: America, Britain, and Russia, 1941–1943* (1973)

Bernstein, Barton J., ed., *The Atomic Bomb* (1975)

Brown, Colin, and Peter J. Mooney, *Cold War to Détente, 1945–1980* (1981)

Cleveland, Harlan, *NATO: The Transatlantic Bargain* (1970)

Davis, Lynn E., *The Cold War Begins: Soviet-American Conflict over Eastern Europe* (1974)

DePorte, A. W., *Europe between the Superpowers* (1979)

Eisenberg, Carolyn, *Drawing the Line: The American Decision to Divide Germany, 1944–1949* (1998)

Freeland, Richard, *The Truman Doctrine and the Origins of McCarthyism* (1971)

Gaddis, John Lewis, *The United States and the Origins of the Cold War, 1941–47* (1972)

Gimbel, John, *The Origins of the Marshall Plan* (1976)

Grosser, Alfred, *The Western Alliance* (1980)

Hahn, Peter, L., *United States, Great Britain, and Egypt, 1945–1956: Strategy and Diplomacy in the Early Cold War* (2004)

Hogan, Michael J., *The Marshall Plan: America, Britain, and the Reconstruction of Western Europe, 1947–1952* (1987)

Iatrides, John O., *Revolt in Athens* (1972)

Kimball, Warren F., *Swords into Plowshares? The Morgenthau Plan for Defeated Nazi Germany, 1943–46* (1976)

Kuklick, Bruce, *American Policy and the Division of Germany* (1972)

Kuniholm, Bruce R., *The Origins of the Cold War in the Near East: Great Power Conflict and Diplomacy in Iran, Turkey, and Greece* (1980)

LaFeber, Walter, *America, Russia, and the Cold War: 1945–2002* (2002)

Leffler, Melvyn P., *A Preponderance of Power: National Security, the Truman Administration, and the Cold War* (1992)

Mastny, Vojtech, *The Cold War and Soviet Insecurity: The Stalin Years* (1998)

McCauley, Martin, ed., *Communist Power in Europe, 1944–1949* (1977)

Mooney, Peter J., *The Soviet Superpower* (1982)

Offner, Arnold A., *Another Such Victory: President Truman and the Cold War* (2002)

Paterson, Thomas, *Soviet-American Confrontation, Postwar Reconstruction, and the Origins of the Cold War* (1973)

Pollard, Robert A., *Economic Security and the Origins of the Cold War* (1985)

Powaski, Ronald E., *The Cold War* (1998)

Ramazani, Rouhollah K., *Iran's Foreign Policy, 1941–1973* (1975)

Rubenstein, Alvin Z., *Soviet Foreign Policy since World War II* (1981)

Smyser, W. R., *From Yalta to Berlin: The Cold War Struggle over Germany* (1999)

Wolfe, Thomas, *Soviet Power and Europe, 1945–1970* (1970)

Xydis, Stephen G., *Greece and the Great Powers, 1944–47* (1963)

Yergin, Daniel, *Shattered Shatered Peace: The Origins of the Cold War and the National Security State* (1977)

Zubok, Vladislav, and Constantine Pleshakov, *Inside the Kremlin's Cold War: From Stalin to Khrushchev* (1996)

9. Coexistence and Confrontation

Alexander, Charles, *Holding the Line* (1975)

Allison, Graham, and Philip Zelikow, *Essence of Decision: Explaining the Cuban Missile Crisis* (1999)

Bain, Kenneth Ray, *The March to Zion: United States Policy and the Founding of Israel* (1979)

Deschloss, Michael, *The Crisis Years: Kennedy and Khrushchev, 1960–1963* (1991)

Bloomfield, Lincoln, Walter C. Clemens, Jr., and Franklyn Griffiths, *Khrushchev and the Arms Race: Soviet Interests in Arms Control and Disarmament, 1954–1964* (1966)

Brands, H. W., Jr., *Cold Warriors: Eisenhower's Generation and American Foreign Policy* (1988)

Catudal, Honore M., Jr., *The Diplomacy of the Quadripartite Agreement on Berlin* (1977)

Cohn, Helen Desfosses, *Soviet Policy toward Black Africa* (1972)

Cooper, Chester, *The Lion's Last Roar: Suez, 1956* (1978)

Crankshaw, Edward, *Khrushchev* (1966)

Detzer, David, *The Brink* (1979)

Dinerstein, Herbert S., *The Making of a Missile Crisis: October 1962* (1976)

Divine, Robert A., *Blowing on the Wind: The Nuclear Test Ban Debate, 1954–1960* (1978)

Divine, Robert A., *Eisenhower and the Cold War* (1980)

Donaldson, Robert H., *Soviet Policy toward India* (1976)

Frankel, Max, *High Noon in the Cold War: Kennedy, Khrushchev, and the Cuban Missile Crisis* (2004)

Gambone, Michael D., *Eisenhower, Somoza, and the Cold War in Nicaragua: 1953–1961* (1997)

Ginsburgs, George B., and Alvin Z. Rubenstein, eds., *Soviet Foreign Policy toward Western Europe* (1978)

Guhin, Michael, *John Foster Dulles: A Statesman and His Times* (1972)

Hargreaves, John D., *The End of Colonial Rule in West Africa: Essays in Contemporary History* (1979)

Higgins, Trumbull, *The Perfect Failure: Kennedy, Eisenhower, and the Bay of Pigs* (1987)

Hixson, Walter L., *Parting the Curtain: Propaganda, Culture, and the Cold War, 1945–1961* (1997)

Hoopes, Townsend, *The Devil and John Foster Dulles* (1973)

Horne, Alistair, *Savage War of Peace* (1978)

Immermann, Richard H., *The CIA in Guatemala* (1983)

Immermann, Richard H., *John Foster Dulles: Pragmatism and Power in U.S. Foreign Policy* (1992)

Joshua, Wynfred, and Stephen P. Gilbert, *Arms for the Third World: Soviet Military Aid Diplomacy* (1969)

Jukes, Geoffrey, *The Soviet Union in Asia* (1973)

Kanet, Roger, ed., *The Soviet Union and the Developing Nations* (1974)

Kleiman, Aaron S., *Soviet Russia and the Middle East* (1970)

Krammer, Arnold, *The Forgotten Friendship: Israel and the Soviet Bloc, 1947–1953* (1974)

Kunz, Diane, *The Economic Diplomacy of the Suez Crisis* (1991)

McGeehan, Robert, *The German Rearmament Question: American Diplomacy and European Defense after World War II* (1971)

Morgan, Roger, *The United States and West Germany* (1974)

Noer, Thomas J., *Cold War and Black Liberation: The United States and White Rule in Africa, 1948–1968* (1985)

Polk, W. R., *The United States and the Arab World* (1965)

Rabe, Stephen G., *Eisenhower and Latin America: The Foreign Policy of Anticommunism* (1988)

Rabe, Stephen G., *The Most Dangerous Area in the World: John F. Kennedy Confronts Communist Revolution in Latin America* (1999)

Remington, Robin A., *The Warsaw Pact* (1971)

Sachar, Howard M., *Europe Leaves the Middle East, 1936–1954* (1972)

Safran, Nadav, *From War to War: The Arab-Israeli Confrontation, 1948–1967* (1969)

Schick, Jack, *The Berlin Crises, 1958–62* (1974)

Schlesinger, Stephen, and Stephen Kinser, *Bitter Fruit: The Untold Story of the American Coup in Guatemala* (1983)

Skilling, H. G., *Communism National and International: Eastern Europe after Stalin* (1964)

Slusser, Robert M., *The Berlin Crisis of 1961* (1973)

Smolansky, Oles, *The Soviet Union and the Arab World under Khrushchev* (1974)

Stookey, Robert W., *America and the Arab States* (1975)

Talbott, John, *The War without a Name: The French in Algeria, 1954–1962* (1980)

Thomas, Hugh, *The Suez Affair* (1966)

Walton, Richard J., *Cold War and Counterrevolution: The Foreign Policy of John F. Kennedy* (1972)

Welch, Richard E., *Response to Revolution: The United States and the Cuban Revolution, 1959–1961* (1985)

Williams, Ann, *Britain and France in the Middle East and North Africa, 1914–1967* (1969)

Willis, F. Roy, *France, Germany, and the New Europe, 1945–1967* (1968)

Zauberman, Alfred, *Industrial Progress in Poland, Czechoslovakia, and East Germany, 1937–1962* (1964)

Zinner, Paul E., *Revolution in Hungary* (1964)

10. Detente and Multipolarity

Baily, Samuel, *The United States and the Development of Latin America, 1945–1975* (1977)

Barnet, Richard J., *The Giants: Russia and America* (1977)

Battah, Abdalla M., and Yehuda Lukacs, eds., *The Arab-Israeli Conflict: Two Decades of Change* (1988)

Bell, Coral, *The Diplomacy of Detente: The Kissinger Era* (1977)

Bell, G., *The Euro-Dollar Market and the International Financial System* (1973)

Bromke, Adam, and Derry Novak, eds., *The Communist States in the Era of Détente, 1971–1977* (1979)

Camps, Miriam, *European Unification in the Sixties* (1966)

Cass, Ilana, *Soviet Involvement in the Middle East: Policy Formulation, 1966–1973* (1978)

Confino, M., and S. Shamir, eds., *The USSR and the Middle East* (1973)

Davis, Walter M., ed., *Latin America and the Cold War* (1978)

Emadi, Hafizullah, *Politics of the Dispossessed: Superpowers and Developments in the Middle East* (2001)

Feste, Karen A., *Expanding the Frontiers: Superpower Intervention in the Cold War* (1992)

Floyd, David, *Rumania: Russia's Dissident Ally* (1965)

Freedman, Robert O., *Soviet Policy toward the Middle East since 1970* (1978)

Garthoff, Raymond L., *Detente and Confrontation: American-Soviet Relations from Nixon to Reagan* (1994)

Garthoff, Raymond L., *A Journey through the Cold War: A Memoir of Containment and Coexistence* (2001)

George, Alexander L., and Richard Smoke, *Deterrence in American Foreign Policy* (1975)

Ginsburgs, George B., and Alvin Z. Rubenstein, eds., *Soviet Foreign Policy toward Western Europe* (1978)

Goldhamer, Herbert, *The Foreign Powers in Latin America* (1972)

Griffith, William E., *The Ostpolitik of the Federal Republic of Germany* (1978)

Grogin, R. C., *Natural Enemies: The United States and the Soviet Union in the Cold War, 1917–1991* (2001)

Harrison, Michael, *Reluctant Ally: France and Atlantic Security* (1981)

Hartmann, Frederick H., *Germany between East and West: The Reunification Problem* (1965)

Hurewitz, J. C., *Soviet-American Rivalry in the Middle East* (1969)

Jacobsen, C. G., *Soviet Strategic Initiatives: Challenge and Response* (1979)

Jonsson, Christer, *Soviet Bargaining Behavior: The Nuclear Test Ban Case* (1979)

Kaiser, Karl, *German Foreign Policy in Transition* (1968)

Kintner, William R., and Harriet F. Scott, eds., *The Nuclear Revolution in Soviet Military Affairs* (1968)

Kohl, Wilfred L., *French Nuclear Diplomacy* (1971)

Kolkowicz, Roman, et al., *The Soviet Union and Arms Control* (1973)

Kolodziej, Edward, *French International Policy under De Gaulle and Pompidou* (1974)

Kraft, Joseph, *The Grand Design: From Common Market to Atlantic Partnership* (1962)

LaFeber, Walter, *America, Russia, and the Cold War, 1945–2002* (2002)

Langley, Lester, *The United States and the Caribbean in the Twentieth Century* (1985)

Larson, Thomas B., *Disarmament and Soviet Policy, 1964–1968* (1969)

Larson, Thomas B., *Soviet-American Rivalry* (1978)

Mason, E. S., and R. E. Asher, *The World Bank since Bretton Woods* (1973)

Mayne, Richard, *The Recovery of Europe, 1945–1973* (1973)

McGwire, Michael, and John Donnell, eds., *Soviet Naval Influence: Domestic and Foreign Dimensions* (1977)

Miller, Nicola, *Soviet Relations with Latin America, 1959–1987* (1989)

Mishal, Shaul, *West Bank/East Bank: The Palestinians in Jordan, 1949–1967* (1978)

Newhouse, John, *Cold Dawn: The Story of SALT* (1973)

Nitze, Paul, et al., *Securing the Seas: The Soviet Naval Challenge and Western Alliance Options* (1979)

Pfaltzgraff, Robert L., Jr., *Britain Faces Europe* (1969)

Pierre, Andrew, *Nuclear Politics: The British Experience with an Independent Strategic Force, 1939–1970* (1972)

Quant, William B., *Decade of Decision: American Policy toward the Arab-Israeli Conflict, 1967–1976* (1977)

Safran, Nadav, *Israel: The Embattled Ally* (1978)

Salibi, Kamal S., *Crossroads to Civil War: Lebanon, 1958–1976* (1976)

Sarotte, Mary A., *Dealing with the Devil: East Germany, Détente, and Ostpolitik, 1969–1973* (2001)

Schaefer, Henry W., *COMECON and the Politics of Integration* (1972)

Schmidt, Dana A., *Armageddon in the Middle East: Arab vs. Israeli through the October War* (1974)

Schulzinger, Robert D., *Henry Kissinger: Doctor of Diplomacy* (1989)

Scott, Harriet F., and William F. Scott, *The Armed Forces of the USSR* (1979)

Sheehan, Edward F., *The Arabs, Israelis, and Kissinger* (1976)

Smith, Gerard C., *Doubletalk: The Story of the First Strategic Arms Limitation Talks* (1980)

Solomon, Robert, *The International Monetary System, 1945–1976* (1977)

Spiegel, Steven L., et al., eds., *The Soviet-American Competition in the Middle East* (1988)

Sugar, Peter F., and Ivo J. Lederer, eds., *Nationalism in Eastern Europe* (1969)

Szaz, Zoltan M., *Germany's Eastern Frontiers: The Problem of the Oder-Niesse Line* (1960)

Talbott, Strobe, *Endgame: The Inside Story of SALT II* (1980)

Tew, B., *International Monetary Cooperation, 1945–1970* (1970)

Tigrid, Pavel, *Why Dubček Fell* (1971)

Trachtenberg, Marc, ed., *Between Empire and Alliance: America and Europe during the Cold War* (2003)

Valenta, Jiri, *Soviet Intervention in Czechoslovakia, 1968* (1979)

Van der Beugel, Ernst H., *From Marshall Aid to Atlantic Partnership: European Integration as a Concern of American Foreign Policy* (1966)

Walsh, A. E., and J. Paxton, *Into Europe: The Structure and Development of the Common Market* (1972)

Wettig, Gerhard, *Community and Conflict in the Socialist Camp: The Soviet Union, East Germany, and the German Problem, 1965–1972* (1975)

Willrich, Mason, and John Rhinelander, eds., *SALT: The Moscow Agreements and Beyond* (1974)

Zeman, Z. A. B., *Prague Spring* (1969)

11. The Rise of China and the Cold War in Asia

An, Tai Sung, *The Sino-Soviet Territorial Dispute* (1973)

Buckley, Roger, *U.S.-Japan Alliance Diplomacy, 1945–1990* (1992)

Chang, Gordon H., *Friends and Enemies: The United States, China, and the Soviet Union, 1948–1972* (1990)

Chen Jian, *China's Road to the Korean War: The Making of the Sino-American Confrontation* (1994)

Chen, Jian, *Mao's China and the Cold War* (2001)

Chiang, Hsiang-tse, *The United States and China* (1988)

Chu-yuan, Chêng, *Economic Relations between Peking and Moscow, 1949–1963* (1964)

Cohen, Warren I., and Akira Iriye, eds., *The Great Powers and Asia, 1953–1960* (1990)

Cumings, Bruce, *The Origins of the Korean War* (1981)

Dickson, Bruce, and Harry Harding, eds., *Economic Relations in the Asian-Pacific Region* (1987)

Dower, John, *Embracing Defeat: Japan in the Wake of World War II* (2000)

Ellison, Herbert, *Japan and the Pacific Quadrille: The Major Powers in East Asia* (1987)

Foot, Rosemary, *The Wrong War: American Policy and the Dimensions of the Korean Conflict, 1950–1953* (1990)

Forsberg, Aaron, *America and the Japanese Miracle: The Cold War Context of Japan's Postwar Economic Revival, 1950–1960* (1999)

Gardner, Lloyd, ed., *The Great Nixon Turnaround* (1973)

Ginsburgs, George, and Carl F. Pinkele, *The Sino-Soviet Territorial Dispute, 1949–64* (1978)

Goncharov, John Lewis, and Xue Litai, *Uncertain Partners: Stalin, Mao, and the Korean War* (1993)

Griffith, William E., *The Sino-Soviet Rift* (1964)

Griffith, William E., ed., *Communism in Europe: Continuity, Change, and the Sino-Soviet Dispute* (1966)

Hart, Robert A., *The Eccentric Tradition: American Diplomacy in the Far East* (1976)

Hastings, Max, *The Korean War* (1987)

Heering, George C., *America's Longest War: The United States and Vietnam, 1950–1975* (1986)

Hershberg, James G., *The Cold War in Asia* (1996)

Hsiao, Gene T., ed., *The Sino-American Detente and Its Policy Implications* (1974)

Hunt, Michael H., *Lyndon Johnson's War: America's Cold War Crusade in Vietnam, 1945–1968* (1997)

Irving, F. E. M., *The First Indochina War: French and American Policy, 1945–1954* (1975)

Karnow, Stanley, *Vietnam: A History* (1983)

Kim, Young C., *Japanese-Soviet Relations* (1974)

Klein, Christina, *Cold War Orientalism: Asia in the Middlebrow Imagination, 1945–1961* (2003)

Lach, Donald F., and Edmund S. Wehrle, *International Politics in East Asia since World War II* (1975)

LaFeber, Walter, *U.S.-Japanese Relations throughout History* (1998)

Lee, William, *The Korean War Was Stalin's Show* (1999)

Low, Alfred D., *The Sino-Soviet Dispute* (1978)

Nagai, Yonasuke, and Akira Iriye, eds., *The Origins of the Cold War in Asia* (1977)

Nelsen, Harvey W., *Power and Insecurity: Beijing, Moscow, and Washington, 1949–1988* (1989)

Pepper, Suzanne, *Civil War in China: The Political Struggle, 1945–1949* (1978)

Poole, Peter, *The United States and Indochina from FDR to Nixon* (1973)

Ross, Robert S., Jiang Changbin, and Changbin Jiang, *Re-Examining the Cold War: U.S.-China Diplomacy, 1954–1973* (2001)

Schaller, Michael, *Altered States: The United States and Japan since the Occupation* (1997)

Schaller, Michael, *The American Occupation of Japan* (1985)

Schaller, Michael, *The United States and China in the Twentieth Century* (1990)

Searingen, Robert, *The Soviet Union and Postwar Japan: Escalating Challenge and Response* (1978)

Shewmaker, Kenneth E., *Americans and the Chinese Communists, 1927–1945* (1971)

Simmons, Robert R., *The Strained Alliance: Peking, Pyongyang, Moscow, and the Politics of the Korean Civil War* (1975)

Stevenson, Charles A., *The End of Nowhere: American Policy toward Laos since 1954* (1972)

Stueck, William, *The Korean War: An International History* (1995)

Thornton, Richard C., *Odd Man Out: Truman, Stalin, Mao, and the Origins of Korean War* (2001)

Vishwanathan, Savitri, *Normalization of Japanese-Soviet Relations, 1945–1970* (1973)

Weathersby, Kathryn, *Soviet Aims in Korea and the Origins of the Korean War, 1945–1950: Evidence from the Russian Archives* (1993)

Young, Marilyn, *Vietnam Wars, 1945–1990* (1991)

Zhang, Shu Guang, *Economic Cold War: America's Embargo against China and the Sino-Soviet Alliance 1949–1963* (2001)

12. The Resurgence of East-West Tension

Ahrari, Mohammed E., *OPEC: The Failing Giant* (1986)

Aronson, Geoffrey, *Creating Facts: Israel, Palestinians, and the West Bank* (1987)

Belassa, Bela, *Change and Challenge in the World Economy* (1985)

Bickerton, Ian J., and Carla L. Klausner, *A Concise History of the Arab-Israeli Conflict* (1998)

Blacker, Coit D., *Reluctant Warriors: The United States, the Soviet Union, and Arms Control* (1987)

Chubin, Shahram, *Iran and Iraq at War* (1988)

Douglass, Joseph D., Jr., *Soviet Military Strategy in Europe* (1980)

Friedman, Thomas, *From Beirut to Jerusalem* (1989)

Gartoff, Raymond L., *Detente and Confrontation* (1985)

Geiger, Theodore, *The Future of the International System: The United States and the World Political Economy* (1988)

Gieling, Saskia, *Religion and War in Revolutionary Iran* (1999)

Gilmour, David, *Lebanon: The Fractured Country* (1983)

Hiro, Dilip, *Holy Wars: The Rise of Islamic Fundamentalism* (1989)

Holm, Hans-Henrich, and Nikolaj Peterson, *The European Missiles Crisis* (1984)

Homouda, Omar F., et al., eds., *The Future of the International Monetary System* (1989)

Karsh, Efraim, *The Iran-Iraq War 1980–1988* (2002)

Kennedy, Paul, *The Rise and Fall of the Great Powers* (1987)

King, Ralph, *The Iran-Iraq War: The Political Implications* (1987)

Klass, Rosanne, ed., *Afghanistan: The Great Game Revisited* (1988)

Mastny, Vojtech, *Helsinki, Human Rights, and European Security* (1986)

Meyer, Karl E., and Shareen Blair Brysac, *Tournament of Shadows: The Great Game and the Race for Empire in Central Asia* (1999)

Munson, Henry, Jr., *Islam and Revolution in the Middle East* (1988)

Nitze, Paul H., et al., *Securing the Seas: The Soviet Naval Challenge and Western Alliance Options* (1979)

Quandt, William B., *Camp David: Peacemaking and Politics* (1986)

Quandt, William B., ed., *The Middle East: Ten Years after Camp David* (1988)

Rubin, Barry, *Paved with Good Intentions: The American Experience in Iran* (1980)

Saikal, Amin, *Islam and the West: Conflict or Cooperation?* (2003)

Schoenbaum, David, *The United States and the State of Israel* (1993)

Simonian, Haig, *The Privileged Partnership: Franco-German Relations in the European Community, 1969–1984* (1985)

Stevenson, W., *The Rise and Fall of Detente* (1985)

Urban, Mark L., *War in Afghanistan* (1988)

Wells, Samuel F., and Mark Bruzonsky, *Security in the Middle East: Regional Change and Great Power Strategies* (1987)

Wolpert, Stanley, *Roots of Confrontation in South Asia: Afghanistan, Pakistan, India, and the Superpowers* (1982)

13. Latin America's Quest for Development and Independence

Biles, Robert E., *Inter-American Relations: The Latin American Perspective* (1988)

Brock, Philip, M. B. Connoly, and C. Gonzalez-Vega, eds., *Latin American Debt and Readjustment* (1991)

Carothers, Tom H., *In the Name of Democracy: U.S. Policy toward Latin America in the Reagan Years* (1991)

Child, Jack, *Geopolitics and Conflict in South America: Quarrels among Neighbors* (1985)

Coatsworth, John H., *Central America and the United States: The Clients and the Colossus* (1994)

Dietz, James L., and J. L. Street, *Latin America's Economic Development* (1987)

Duran, Esperanza, *European Interests in Latin America* (1985)

Farer, Tom J., *The Grand Strategy of the United States in Latin America* (1988)

Findling, John E., *Close Neighbors, Distant Friends: United States-Central American Relations* (1987)

Grandin, Greg, *The Last Colonial Massacre: Latin America in the Cold War* (2004)

LeFeber, Walter, *Inevitable Revolutions: The United States in Central America* (1983)

McDonald, Scott B., *The Caribbean after Grenada* (1988)

Middlebrook, Kevin, and Carlos Rico, eds., *The United States and Latin America* (1986)

Miller, Nicola, *Soviet Relations with Latin America, 1959–1987* (1989)

Morley, Morris, *Imperial State and Revolution: The United States and Cuba, 1952–1986* (1988)

Pastor, Robert, *Condemned to Repetition: The United States and Nicaragua* (1987)

Pastor, Robert, *Whirlpool: U.S. Foreign Policy toward Latin America and the Caribbean* (1992)

Ramirez, Miguel D., Antonio Jorge, and Jorge Salazar-Carillo, eds., *The Latin American Debt* (1992)

Tussie, Diana, ed., *Latin America in the World Economy* (1983)

14. Africa: From Independence to Dependency

Albright, David E., *The USSR and Sub-Sahara Africa in the 1980s* (1983)

Aluko, Olajide, *Africa and the Great Powers in the 1980s* (1987)

Bala, Mohammed, *Africa and Non-Alignment: A Study in the Foreign Relations of New Nations* (1982)

Barber, James, and John Barratt, *South Africa's Foreign Policy: The Search for Status and Security, 1945–1988* (1990)

Calvocoressi, Peter, *Independent Africa and the World* (1985)

Chamberlain, M. E., *Decolonization: The Fall of European Empires* (1985)

Davidson, Basil, *The Black Man's Burden: Africa and the Curse of the Nation-State* (1992)

Dickson, David, *United States Foreign Policy towards Sub-Sahara Africa* (1985)

Farer, Tom J., *Clouds on the Horn of Africa: The Widening Storm* (1979)

Fieldhouse, D. K., *Black Africa, 1945–1980: Economic Decolonization and Arrested Development* (1986)

Gavshon, Arthur, *Crisis in Africa: Battleground of East and West* (1984)

Hargreaves, John D., *The End of Colonial Rule in West Africa: Essays in Contemporary History* (1979)

Havnevik, Kjell, ed., *The IMF and the World Bank in Africa* (1987)

Holland, R. F., *European Decolonization, 1918–1981: An Introductory Survey* (1985)

Lapping, Brian, *The End of Empire* (1989)

Marte, L. F., *Political Cycles in International Relations: The Cold War and Africa* (1994)

Mohammed, Bala, *Africa and Non-Alignment: A Study in the Foreign Relations of New Nations* (1982)

Noer, Thomas, *Cold War and Black Liberation: The United States and White Rule in Africa, 1948–1968* (1985)

Okbazghi, Yohannes, *The United States and the Horn of Africa: An Analytical Study of Pattern and Process* (1997)

Onimode, Bade, ed., *The IMF, the World Bank, and African Debt* (1989)

Onwuka, Ralph I., and Timothy M. Shaw, *Africa and World Politics* (1989)

Parfitt, Trevor, *The African Debt Crisis* (1989)

Percox, David, *Britain, Kenya, and the Cold War: Imperial Defence, Colonial Security and Decolonisation* (2004)

Riley, Stephen A., *African Debt and Western Interests* (1989)

Sandbrook, Richard, *The Politics of Africa's Economic Recovery* (1993)

Shaw, Timothy, *Reformism and Revisionism in Africa's Political Economy in the 1990s* (1993)

Somerville, Keith, *Foreign Military Intervention in Africa* (1990)

Wright, Stephen, and Janice N. Brownfoot, *Africa and World Politics* (1987)

15. The Far East: The Road to the New Co-Prosperity Sphere

Austin, Greg, and Stuart Harris, *Japan and Greater China: Political Economy and Military Power in the Asian Century* (2001)

Chang, Gordon H., *Friends and Enemies: The United States, China, and the Soviet Union, 1948–1972* (1991)

Chiang, Hsiang-tse, *The United States and China* (1988)

Dickson, Bruce, and Harry Harding, eds., *Economic Relations in the Asian-Pacific Region* (1987)

Ellison, Herbert J., *Japan and the Pacific Quadrille: The Major Powers in East Asia* (1987)

Huang, Xiaoming, *The Rise and Fall of the East Asian Growth System, 1951–2000: Institutional Competitiveness and Rapid Economic Growth* (2004)

Johnston, Alistair, and Robert S. Ross, *Engaging China: The Management of an Emerging Power* (1999)

Kim, Ilpyong J., *The Strategic Triangle: China, the United States, and the Soviet Union* (1987)

Kim, Samuel S., *China and the World* (1989)

Kleinberg, Robert, *China's "Opening" to the Outside World: The Experiment with Foreign Capitalism* (1990)

Klenner, Wolfgang, ed., *Trends of Economic Development in East Asia* (1989)

Leifer, Michael, *ASEAN and the Security of South East Asia* (1989)

Linder, Steffan B., *The Pacific Century: Economic and Political Consequences of Asian-Pacific Dynamism* (1986)

Matray, James I., *Japan's Emergence as a Global Power* (2000)

Ozaki, Robert S., and Walter Arnold, eds., *Japan's Foreign Relations: A Global Search for Economic Security* (1985)

Prestowitz, Clyde V., Jr., *Trading Places: How We Allowed Japan to Take the Lead* (1988)

Rostow, W. W., *The United States and the Regional Organization of Asia and the Pacific, 1965–1985* (1986)

Sutter, Robert G., *Chinese Foreign Policy: Developments after Mao* (1986)

Thompson, Roger C., *The Pacific Basin since 1945* (1994)

Wolferen, Karel G. von, *The Enigma of Japanese Power* (1989)

Wong, John, *The Political Economy of China's Changing Relations with Southeast Asia* (1984)

Woronoff, Jon, *Asia's "Miracle Economies"* (1991)

Yahuda, Michael, *The International Politics of the Asia-Pacific, 1945–1995* (1996)

PART THREE: FROM COLD WAR TO NEW WORLD DISORDER

16. Moscow, Washington, and the End of the Soviet Empire

Allison, Roy, *Military Forces in the Soviet Successor States* (1993)

Beschloss, Michael, and Strobe Talbot, *At the Highest Levels: The Inside Story of the End of the Cold War* (1993)

Bisley, Nick, *The End of the Cold War and the Causes of Soviet Collapse* (2004)

Blacker, Coit D., *Reluctant Warriors: The United States, the Soviet Union, and Arms Control* (1987)

Bowker, Mike, *Russian Foreign Policy and the End of the Cold War* (1997)

Dannreuther, Roland, *Creating New States in Central Asia* (1994)

De Nevers, Renée, *Russia's Strategic Renovation* (1994)

Gaddis, John Lewis, *The United States and the End of the Cold War* (1992)

Garthoff, Raymond L., *The Great Transition: American-Soviet Relations and the End of the Cold War* (1994)

Garton Ash, Timothy, *The Magic Lantern: The Revolution of '89 Witnessed in Warsaw, Budapest, Berlin, and Prague* (1990)

Goldman, Marshall I., *Lost Opportunity: Why Economic Reforms in Russia Have Not Worked* (1994)

Hogan, Michael J., ed., *The End of the Cold War: Its Meaning and Implications* (1992)

Hutchings, Robert L., *American Diplomacy and the End of the Cold War: An Insider's Account of U.S. Policy in Europe, 1982–1992* (1997)

Jarausch, Konrad H., *The Rush to German Unity* (1994)

Kennedy, Paul, *Preparing for the Next Century* (1993)

Lieby, Richard, *The Unification of Germany, 1989–90* (1999)

Stokes, Gail, *The Walls Came Tumbling Down: The Collapse of Communism in Eastern Europe* (1993)

Zelikow, Philip, and Condoleeza Rice, *Germany United and Europe Transformed* (1997)

17. Europe: Integration and Disintegration

Anderson, Jeffrey, *German Unification and the Union of Europe: The Domestic Politics of Integration Policy* (1999)

Ash, Timothy Gorton, *In Europe's Name: Germany and the Divided Continent* (1993)

Calleo, David P., and Richard C. Leone, *Rethinking Europe's Future* (2001)

Dinan, Desmond, *Ever Closer Union: An Introduction to European Integration* (1999)

Fromkin, David, *Kosovo Crossing* (1999)

Garton Ash, Timothy, *In Europe's Name: Germany and the Divided Continent* (1993)

Glenny, Misha, *The Fall of Yugoslavia* (1992)

Jarausch, Konrad H., *The Rush to German Unity* (1994)

Jopp, Mathias, *The Strategic Implications of European Integration* (1994)

Marsh, David, *The Bundesbank: The Bank that Rules Europe* (1994)

Mortimer, Edward, *European Security after the Cold War* (1992)

Nelson, Brent F., and Alexander Stubb, *The European Union: Readings on the Theory and Practice of European Integration* (2003)

Rosamond, Ben, *Theories of European Integration* (2000)

Urwin, D. W., *The Community of Europe: A History of European Integration since 1945* (1995)

Wallace, William, *The Transformation of Western Europe* (1990)

Wood, David M., and Birol A. Yesilada, *The Emerging European Union* (1996)

Zametica, John, *The Yugoslav Conflict* (1992)

Zielonka, Jan, *Security in Central Europe* (1992)

18. Asia at the Crossroads

Acharya, Amitav, A *New Regional Order in South-East Asia: ASEAN in the Post-Cold War Era* (1991)

Bajpai, Kanti, *South Asia after the Cold War: International Perspectives* (1993)

Bose, Sugata, and Ayesha Jalal, *Modern South Asia: History, Culture, Political Economy* (2004)

Boyd, Gavin, *Pacific Trade, Investment, and Politics* (1989)

Bresnan, John, *From Dominoes to Dynamos: The Transformation of Southeast Asia* (1997)

Drysdale, Peter, and David Vines, *Europe, East Asia, and APEC: A Shared Global Agenda* (1998)

Garten, Jeffrey E., *A Cold Peace: America, Japan, Germany, and the Struggle for Supremacy* (1992)

Gunder Frank, André, *Reorient: Global Economy in the Asian Age* (1998)

Hardt, John P., and Young C. Kim, eds., *Economic Cooperation in the Asia-Pacific Region* (1990)

Harris, Stuart, and James Cotton, eds., *The End of the Cold War in Northeast Asia* (1991)

Hook, Glenn D., Christopher W. Hughes, Hugo Dobson, and Julie Gilson, *Japan's International Relations: Politics, Economics, and Security* (2001)

Howell, Jude, *China Opens Its Doors: The Politics of Economic Transition* (1993)

Kim, Eun Mee, *The Four Asian Tigers: Economic Development & the Global Political Economy* (1999)

Kleinberg, Robert, *China's "Opening" to the Outside World: The Experiment with Foreign Capitalism* (1990)

Lukauskas, Arvid John, and Francisco L. Rivera-Batiz, *The Political Economy of the East Asian Crisis and Its Aftermath: Tigers in Distress* (2001)

Oppenheim, Philip, *Trade Wars: Japan versus the West* (1992)

Rozman, Gilbert, *Japan's Response to the Gorbachev Era* (1991)

Simon, Sheldon W., *East Asian Security in the Post-Cold War Era* (1997)

Thomas, Raju G. C., *South Asian Security in the 1990s* (1993)

Woronoff, Jon, *Asia's "Miracle" Economies* (1991)

Wurfel, David, and Bruce Burton, eds., *The Political Economy of Foreign Policy in Southeast Asia* (1990)

Yahuda, Michael, *The International Politics of Asia-Pacific, 1945–1995* (1996)

19. Africa on Its Own: Ethnic Conflict, Autocracy, and Underdevelopment

Aryeetey, Ernest, Julius Court, Machiko Nissanke, and Beatrice Weder, *Asia and Africa in the Global Economy* (2003)

Ayittey, George B. N., *Africa in Chaos* (1998)

Clapham, Christopher, *Africa and the International System: The Politics of State Survival* (1996)

Davidson, Basil, *The Black Man's Burden: Africa and the Curse of the Nation-State* (1992)

Makinda, Samuel M., *Security in the Horn of Africa* (1992)

Parfitt, Trevor, *The African Debt Crisis* (1989)

Phillips, Lucie Colvin, and Diery Seck, *Fixing African Economies: Policy Research for Development* (2003)

Sandbrook, Richard, *The Politics of Africa's Economic Recovery* (1993)

Shaw, Timothy, *Reformism and Revisionism in Africa's Political Economy in the 1990s* (1993)

Somerville, Keith, *Foreign Military Intervention in Africa* (1990)

Spencer, Claire, *The Maghreb in the 1990s* (1993)

Zack-Williams, Tunde, Diane Frost, and Alex Thomson, eds., *Africa in Crisis: New Challenges and Possibilities* (2002)

20. The Middle East: The Illusive Quest for Peace, Prosperity, and Stability

Freedman, Laurence, and Efraim Karsh, *The Gulf Conflict, 1990–91* (1993)

Garfinkle, Adam, *Israel and Jordan in the Shadow of War* (1992)

Hinnebusch, Raymond, *Syria* (2002)

Karsh, Efraim, *Soviet Policy towards Syria since 1970* (1991)

Khalidi, Rashid, *Resurrecting Empire: Western Footprints and America's Perilous Path in the Middle East* (2004)

Lustik, Ian S., ed., *Arab-Israeli Relations in World Politics* (1994)

McCausland, Jeffrey, *The Gulf Conflict: A Military Analysis* (1993)

Melman, Yossi, and Dan Raviv, *Behind the Uprising: Israelis, Jordanians, and Palestinians* (1989)

Morris, Benny, Charles Tripp, Julia A. Clancy-Smith, Israel Gershoni, Roger Owen, Yezid Sayigh, and Judith E. Tucker, eds., *The Birth of the Palestinian Refugee Problem Revisited* (2003)

Organsky, A. F. K., *The $36 Billion Bargain: Strategy and Politics in U.S. Assistance to Israel* (1990)

Quandt, William B., *Peace Process: American Diplomacy and the Arab-Israeli Conflict since 1967* (1993)

Ross, Dennis, *The Missing Peace: The Inside Story of the Fight for Middle East Peace* (2004)

Schoenbaum, David, *The United States and the State of Israel* (1993)

Smolansky, David, *The USSR and Iraq: The Soviet Quest for Influence* (1991)

21. Latin America: Democracy, Free Markets, and Regional Security

Atkins, G. Pope, *Latin America in the International System* (1995)

Brock, Philip, et al., eds., *Latin American Debt and Readjustment* (1989)

Carothers, Tom H., *In the Name of Democracy: U.S. Policy toward Latin America in the Reagan Years* (1991)

Dent, David W., *U.S.-Latin American Policymaking* (1995)

Desch, Michael C., *When the Third World Matters: Latin America and United States Grand Strategy* (1993)

Gutman, Roy, *Banana Diplomacy: The Making of American Foreign Policy in Nicaragua* (1988)

Kjonnerod, L. Erik, ed., *Evolving U.S. Strategy for Latin America and the Caribbean* (1992)

Mora, Frank O., and Jeanne A. K. Hey, *Latin American and Caribbean Foreign Policy* (2003)

Pastor, Robert A., *Whirlpool: U.S. Foreign Policy toward Latin America and the Caribbean* (1992)

Ramirez, Miguel D., Antonio Jorge, and Jorge Salazar-Carrillo, eds., *The Latin American Debt* (1992)

Ramirez, Miguel D., Antonio Jorge, and Jorge Salazar-Carrillo, eds., *Mexico's Economic Crisis: Its Origins and Consequences* (1989)

Randall, Laura, *The Political Economy of Latin America in the Postwar Period* (1997)

Robinson, William I., *A Faustian Bargain: U.S. Intervention in the Nicaraguan Election and American Foreign Policy in the Post-Cold War Era* (1992)

Skidmore, Thomas E., and Peter H. Smith, *Modern Latin America* (2000)

Wiarda, Howard J., *The Democratic Revolution in Latin America* (1990)

22. From the Old to the New Century

Allison, Roy, *Military Forces in the Soviet Successor States* (1993)

Appadurai, Arjun, *Modernity at Large: Cultural Dimensions of Globalization* (1998)

Bacevich, Andrew, *The American Empire: The Realities and Consequences of U.S. Diplomacy* (1992)

Baehr, Peter R., and Leon Gordenker, *The United Nations in the 1990s* (1992)

Bailey, Kathleen C., *Doomsday Weapons in the Hands of Many* (1991)

Berdal, Mats R., *Whither UN Peacekeeping?* (1993)

Bhagwati, Jagdish, *The World Trading System at Risk* (1991)

Boli, John, and George M. Thomas, eds., *Constructing World Culture: International Nongovernmental Organizations since 1875* (1999)

Carter, April, *Success and Failure in Arms Control Negotiations* (1989)

Cohen, Stephen, *Failed Crusade: America and the Tragedy of Post-Communist Russia* (2000)

De Nevers, Renée, *Russia's Strategic Renovation* (1994)

Diehl, Paul F., ed., *The Politics of Global Governance: International Organizations in an Interdependent World* (1997)

Ferguson, Niall, *Colossus: The Price of America's Empire* (2004)

Foerster, Schuyler, et al., *Defining Stability: Conventional Arms Control in a Changing Europe* (1989)

Fukuyama, Francis, *The End of History and the Last Man* (1993)

Goldman, Marshall I., *Lost Opportunity: Why Economic Reforms in Russia Have Not Worked* (1994)

Held, David, et al., *Global Transformations: Politics, Economics, and Culture* (1999)

Huntington, Samuel, *The Clash of Civilizations and the Remaking of World Order* (1998)

Hutton, Will, and Anthony Giddens, eds., *On the Edge: Living with Global Capitalism* (2000)

Iriye, Akira, *Cultural Internationalism and World Order* (1997)

Iriye, Akira, *Global Community: The Role of International Organizations in the Making of the Contemporary World* (2002)

Kagan, Robert, *Of Paradise and Power: America and Europe in the New World Order* (2003)

Kaplan, Robert, *The Coming Anarchy: Shattering the Dreams of the Post-Cold War* (2003)

Keck, Margaret E., and Kathryn Sikkink, eds., *Activists beyond Borders: Advocacy Networks in International Politics* (1998)

Lairson, Thomas D., and David Skidmore, *International Political Economy: The Struggle for Power and Wealth* (1993)

Leebaert, Derek, *The Fifty-Year Wound: How America's Cold War Victory Has Shaped Our World* (2003)

Mingst, Karen A., and Margaret P. Karns, *The United Nations in the Post-Cold War Era* (1999)

Muller, Harald, et al., *Nuclear Non-Proliferation and Global Order* (1994)

Nye, Joseph, *The Paradox of American Power* (2002)

Patrick, Stewart, and Shepard Forman, *Multilateralism and U.S. Foreign Policy: Ambivalent Engagement* (2001)

Roberts, Adam, and Benedict Kingsburg, eds., *United Nations, Divided World: The U.N.'s Role in International Relations* (1993)

Roberts, Brad, *Chemical Disarmament and International Security* (1992)

Rueckert, George L., *Global Double Zero: The INF Treaty from Its Origins to Implementation* (1993)

Rupp, Leila J., *Worlds of Women: The Making of an International Women's Movement* (1997)

Sampson, Anthony, *The Arms Bazaar in the Nineties: From Krupp to Saddam* (1991)

Schechter, Michael G., ed., *Innovation in Multilateralism* (1999)

Smolansky, Bettie M., and Oles M. Smolansky, *The Lost Equilibrium: International Relations in the Post-Soviet Era* (2001)

Spero, Joan E., and Jeffrey Hart, *The Politics of International Economic Relations* (2002)

Stalker, Peter, *Workers without Frontiers: The Impact of Globalization on International Migration* (2000)

Taylor, Trevor, *The Collapse of the Soviet Empire: Managing the Regional Fallout* (1992)

Todd, Emmanuel, *After the Empire: The Breakdown of the American Order* (2003)

Weber, Steve, *Cooperation and Discord in U.S.-Soviet Arms Control* (1991)

The most useful English-language sources for analyses of contemporary international developments are the following periodicals: *Foreign Affairs, Foreign Policy, World Politics, International Security, Human Development Report, Survival,* the occasional papers of the International Institute for Strategic Studies published under the rubric "Adelphi Papers," and the two indispensable annual publications of the latter organization, entitled *Strategic Survey* and *The Military Balance.*

INDEX